SERVICES MARKETING

CONCEPTS, STRATEGIES AND CASES

D1471962

SERVICES MARKETING

CONCEPTS, STRATEGIES AND CASES

K. Douglas Hoffman
John E. G. Bateson
Emma H. Wood
Alexandra K. Kenyon

CENGAGE
Learning·

Australia • Brazil • Japan • Korea • Mexico • Singapore • Spain • United Kingdom • United States

CENGAGE
Learning·

Services Marketing - Concepts, Strategies and Cases, First Edition
K. Douglas Hoffman, John E. G. Bateson, Emma H. Wood and Alexandra K. Kenyon

For product information and technology assistance, contact **emea.info@cengage.com**.

For permission to use material from this text or product, and for permission queries, email **emea.permissions@cengage.com**.

British Library Cataloguing-in-Publication Data
A catalogue record for this book is available from the British Library.

ISBN: 9781473709126

Cengage Learning EMEA
Cheriton House, North Way, Andover, Hampshire, SP10 5BE
United Kingdom

Cengage Learning products are represented in Canada by Nelson Education Ltd.

For your lifelong learning solutions, visit
www.cengage.co.uk

Purchase your next print book, e-book or e-chapter at
www.cengagebrain.com

Printed in the UK by Lightning Source
1 2 3 4 5 6 7 8 9 10 – 13

Brief **contents**

Contents

About the authors

K. Douglas Hoffman is a Professor of Marketing at Colorado State University. He received his B.S. from the Ohio State University, and his M.B.A. and D.B.A. from the University of Kentucky. Over the past twenty years, Doug has taught courses such as Principles of Marketing, Services Marketing, E-Marketing, Retail Management and Marketing Management. His primary teaching and research passion is in the Services Marketing area where he started the first Services Marketing classes at Mississippi State University, the University of North Carolina at Wilmington and Colorado State University. He has also taught courses as a visiting professor at the Helsinki School of Economics and Business Administration in Helsinki, Finland; the Institute of Industrial Policy Studies in Seoul, South Korea; and Thammasat University in Bangkok, Thailand.

Doug has been formally recognized for teaching excellence at Colorado State University and the University of North Carolina at Wilmington. In addition, he has served as the Education Coordinator for the Services Marketing Special Interest Group of the American Marketing Association. Doug has published a variety of articles in academic and practitioner journals and is the co-author of three textbooks:

> *Services Marketing: Concepts, Strategies, and Cases,* Third Edition, Thomson South-Western
>
> *Managing Services Marketing,* Fourth Edition, Thomson South-Western
>
> *Marketing Principles and Best Practices,* Third Edition, Thomson South-Western

Doug's current research and consulting activities are primarily in the areas of customer service/satisfaction, service failure and recovery, and services marketing education.

John E. G. Bateson is the Group Chief Executive Officer, SHL Group, plc. He was Associate Professor of Marketing at the London Business School, England, and a visiting associate professor at the Stanford Business School. Prior to teaching, he was a brand manager with Lever Brothers and marketing manager with Philips.

Dr Bateson holds an undergraduate degree from Imperial College, London, a master's degree from London Business School, and a Ph.D. in marketing from the Harvard Business School. He has published extensively in the services marketing literature, including the *Journal of Marketing Research, Journal of Retailing, Marketing Science* and *Journal of Consumer Research.*

He is also the author of *Managing Services Marketing: Text and Readings* (South-Western) and *Marketing Public Transit: A Strategic Approach* (Praeger).

Dr Bateson was actively involved with the formation of the services division of the American Marketing Association. He served on the Services Council for four years and has chaired sessions of the AMA Services Marketing Conference. He also serves on the steering committee of the Marketing Science Institute. Dr Bateson consults extensively in the services sector.

Emma H. Wood is Reader in Events and Festivals Marketing at Leeds Metroploitan University. Dr Wood is based within the UK Centre for Events Management, and her research and teaching are within the areas of marketing research, marketing communications, strategy and consumer behaviour. Emma has considerable marketing experience within a range of industries and has worked in the UK, South East Asia and Australia. She has been involved in numerous major research projects and her consultancy work is specialized in the area of experiential marketing evaluation and public sector marketing. Her academic and consultancy research work is regularly disseminated at national and international conferences, and through academic journals including the *Journal of Marketing Communications, International Journal of Non-Profit and Voluntary Sector Marketing* and the *Journal of Public Sector Management*. She is editor of the *Journal of Policy Research in Tourism, Leisure and Events* and also sits on the editorial board of two services marketing related periodicals. Emma's co-authored book *Innovative Marketing Communications* was published in 2006 by Elsevier. Emma is also the founding member and Chair of the Event Marketing special interest group within the Academy of Marketing.

Alexandra J. Kenyon is a Senior Lecturer in research, marketing and consumer behaviour at Leeds Metropolitan University. Dr Kenyon has completed a number of papers regarding alcohol and advertising and is working with the alcohol industry regarding alcohol awareness with young people. Dr Kenyon has professional experience of marketing and promotional activity in the entertainment and finance industry. Her work has been published in the *Journal of Advertising Research, International Journal of Marketing Research, EuroMed Journal of Business* and *British Food Journal*. Dr Kenyon has also presented at international conferences on marketing, advertising and corporate responsibilities. She has also contributed to academic books *Strategic Marketing & Retail Thought, Fundamentals of Marketing Research* and *Consumer Behaviour Research* and is currently researching material to co-author a book titled *Alcohol and Ethics*.

Acknowledgements

With all Emma's love to Guy, Alice, Katy and Edith, and with Alexandra's love to her dearest husband Steve.

We would like thank the editorial team at Cengage especially Leandra Paoli, Charlotte Loveridge and Leonora Dawson-Bowling.

We would also like to thank the following colleagues for providing additional case study material:

- Dr. Stephen Henderson, Leeds Metropolitan University
- Dr. Steve Oakes, University of Liverpool
- Prof. Poul Housman Andersen, Aarhus Business School
- Ann Torres, National University of Ireland
- Ronan de Kervenoael, Aston Business School & D. Selcen O. Aykac, Ozyegin University
- De Witts Business School

We are very appreciative of the insightful comments made on the adaptation proposal and through ongoing chapter reviews by the following colleagues:

- Christo Boshoff, Nelson Mandela Metropolitan University
- Tracy Harwood, De Montfort University
- Erwin Losekoot, University of Strathclyde
- Allard van Riel, University of Liège
- Åsa Wallström, Luleå University of Technology

Preface

The primary objective of *Services Marketing: Concepts, Strategies and Cases* is to provide materials that not only introduce you to the field of services marketing but also acquaint you with specific customer service issues. The business world now demands, in addition to traditional business knowledge, increasing employee competence in customer satisfaction, service quality and customer service, skills that are essential in growing and sustaining the existing customer base.

Approach of services marketing: Concepts, strategies and cases

The European edition of *Services Marketing: Concepts, Strategies and Cases* purposely examines the use of services marketing as a competitive weapon from a broader perspective. Consequently, we view services marketing not only as a marketing tool for service firms, but also as a means of gaining competitive advantage for those companies that market products on the tangible dominant side of the continuum. As a result, business examples used throughout the text reflect a wide array of firms representing a variety of service economy sectors including education and health services, financial activities, government, information, leisure and hospitality, professional and business services, transportation and utilities, wholesale and retail trade, and other services.

Ultimately, the *service sector* is one of the three main categories of a developed economy – the other two being *industrial* and *agricultural*. Traditionally, economies throughout the world tend to transition themselves from an *agricultural economy* to an *industrial economy* (e.g, manufacturing and mining) to a *service economy*. The United Kingdom was the first economy in the modern world to make this transition. Several other countries including the US, Japan, Germany and France have made this transition and many more are expected to do so at an accelerated rate.

We live in interesting times! The increased rate of transformation from an agricultural to a manufacturing to a service-based economy has generally been caused by a highly competitive international marketplace. Simply stated, goods are more amenable to international trade than services, making them more vulnerable to competitive actions. In other words, countries that industrialized their economies first eventually come under competitive attack by other countries that are newly making the transition from an agricultural to an industrial economy. These newcomer countries offer lower production costs (especially labour), which is attractive to industry. Consequently, as industrial sectors flow from one country to the next, the countries they abandon begin to more heavily rely on the growth of their service sectors as the mainstay of their economies. This whole process repeats itself over and over again as other less developed countries enter the fray, consequently, facilitating the transformation from agriculture to industrial to service-based economies.

Structure of the Book

Services Marketing: Concepts, Strategies and Cases is divided into four main parts. The first part, 'An Overview of Services Marketing', concentrates on defining services marketing and discusses in detail the fundamental concepts and strategies that differentiate the marketing of services from the marketing of tangible goods. The primary objective of Part 1 is to establish a core knowledge base that will be built upon throughout the remainder of the text.

Chapter 1 provides an introduction to the field of services marketing. It establishes the importance of the service sector in the world economy and the need for services marketing education. Chapter 2 focuses more deeply on the fundamental differences between goods and services and their corresponding managerial implications. Chapter 3 provides an overview of the service sector and focuses on the service industry subsectors and the most substantial changes taking place within the service sector. New concepts such as the 'aging consumer' and the growth in international outservicing are presented, and predicted keys to success within the service encounter are also discussed. Chapter 4 focuses on consumer and business purchase decision issues as they relate to the services field. Consumers often approach service purchases differently from the way they approach the purchase of goods. The first part of the book concludes with Chapter 5, which takes an in-depth look at the information and marketing research needed in order to successfully plan and manage the marketing of services.

The second part of the book, 'Service Strategy: Managing the Service Experience', is dedicated to topics that concern the management of the service encounter. Due to the consumer's involvement in the production of services, many new challenges are presented that do not frequently occur within the manufacturing sector. The primary topics in Part 2 are strategic issues related to the marketing mix as well as the Servuction Model including process, pricing, promotion, physical evidence, and people (employee and customer) issues.

Chapter 6 considers the importance of service innovation and development in an increasingly competitive environment. Chapter 7 provides an overview of service operations, pinpointing the areas where special managerial attention is needed in the construction of the service process. In addition, the importance of balancing operations and marketing functions in service operations is discussed. Chapters 8 and 9 focus on pricing and communication issues as they relate specifically to service firms. Chapter 10 examines the development and management of the service firm's physical environment. Chapter 11 discusses the many challenges associated with managing employees within the service experience. The service business, by its very definition, is a people business and requires talented managers who can navigate the thin line between the needs of the organization, its employees and its customers. Chapter 12 explores the art of managing service consumers. Due to the impact of inseparability, the consumer's role in service production can both facilitate and hinder the exchange process. Hence, developing a strategic understanding of how the consumer can be effectively managed within the service encounter is critical. Part 2 concludes with Chapter 13 which introduces the fundamental components as well as the advantages and disadvantages associated with customer relationship management (CRM) systems.

Part 3, 'Assessing and Improving Service Delivery', focuses on customer satisfaction and service quality issues. Methods are presented for tracking service failures and employee recovery efforts, as well as customer retention strategies. Ideally, assessing and improving the service delivery system will lead to 'seamless service' – provided without interruption, confusion, or hassle to the customer.

Chapter 14 presents an overview of the importance and benefits of customer satisfaction and the special factors to consider regarding measurement issues. Chapter 15 builds from the materials presented in Chapter 14 and discusses conceptual and measurement issues pertaining to service quality and service quality information systems. Chapter 16 presents methods for tracking service failures and employee service recovery efforts, and includes an example of a questionnaire used in such studies (see Chapter 16 appendix). It also focuses on the often forgotten benefits of customer retention and discusses strategies that maximize a firm's customer retention efforts. Chapter 17 pulls the ideas in the book together in a manner that demonstrates the delivery of flawless customer service and considers the overall strategy and planing of services. The text part of the book concludes with a look to the future. Chapter 18 considers these current and future issues and trends that are likely to impact upon services marketing.

Part 4 of the book consists of cases that are specifically relevant to each of the chapters and also integrates other topics discussed throughout the text. The cases are to be used at the instructor's discretion to give students realistic practice in using the concepts presented in the book. Many of these cases have been purposely written to include an international and/or e-business flavour to reflect the changing business climate and the wide variety of issues that face service marketers today. You can find tasters for Cases 16, 17 and 18 with the full cases available on the website.

What's new in the international edition?

This edition maintains the basic structure of the book but strengthens its European applicability through the inclusion of wide-ranging European-based material whilst retaining some of the internationally known US and global examples and case studies. The coverage of the examples and cases has been expanded to incorporate a greater spread of service industry sectors and the inclusion of small and medium-sized enterprises and public and not-for-profit organizations.

Throughout the text the discussion of the concepts and issues relating to business-to-business markets has been strengthened. The B2B sector of services marketing is often overlooked but is one of the main employers and revenue generators in the European and US markets.

A major addition to the text is an additional chapter covering marketing research for services. This chapter makes services marketing students more aware of the importance of understanding forces that operate in the external environment and of basing decisions on information gathered from a range of both internal and external sources.

A further chapter addition focuses on service innovation and new service development. This vital aspect of service organization competitiveness and success is covered as part of the service strategy section and ensures that the text reflects current trends in both academic research and service industry practice.

A revised chapter on customer relationship management ensures that this vital aspect of services marketing is covered and again reflects current practitioner and academic trends.

Chapter 17 has been extended to include covereage of strategy and planning and the service firm and an additional final chapter has been added to cover future trends and issues reflecting both changes in industry practice and academic research focus.

Finally, the references and source material have been adapted and expanded to ensure that they reflect a range of international authors and publications and fit with the requirement for students to read material from a variety of sources. A reference list and details of 'further reading' is provided at the end of each chapter.

In closing, we hope that you enjoy the book and your services marketing course. Education is itself a service experience. As a participant in this service experience, you are expected to participate in class discussions. Take advantage of the opportunities provided you during this course, and become an integral component of the education production process. Regardless of your area of study, the services marketing course has much to offer.

We would sincerely appreciate any comments or suggestions you would care to share with us. We believe that this text will heighten your sensitivity to services, and because of that belief, we leave you with this promise: We guarantee that after completing this book and your services marketing course, you will never look at a service experience in the same way again. This new view will become increasingly frustrating for most of you, as you will encounter many experiences that are less than satisfactory. Learn from these negative experiences, relish the positive encounters, and use this information to make a difference when it is your turn to set the standards for others to follow. As evangelists of services marketing, we could ask for no greater reward.

Walk through tour

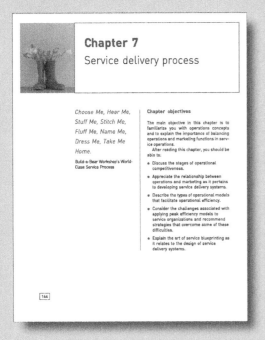

Chapter objectives appear at the start of each chapter to help you monitor your understanding and progress through each chapter.

Services in context opening vignettes represent a variety of companies and relevant services marketing issues.

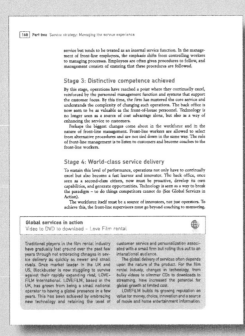

Global services in action feature in every chapter and provide international examples of services marketing concepts and strategies.

B2B services in action feature in every chapter and provide B2B examples of services marketing strategies and concepts.

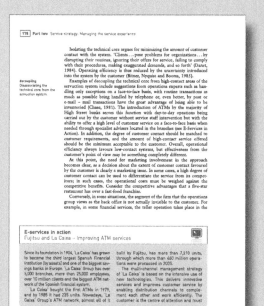

E-Services in action feature in every chapter and provide e-business examples of services marketing strategies and concepts.

Discussion questions help reinforce and test your knowledge and understanding.

Case links guide you to relevant case studies in Part four allowing you to explore key themes.

Summary – each chapter ends with a comprehensive summary that provides a thorough recap of the issues in each chapter, helping you to assess your understanding and revise key content.

About the website

Visit the *Services Marketing: Concepts, Strategies and Cases* website at **www.cengage.co.uk/ hoffman** to find further valuable teaching and learning material, including:

FOR LECTURERS

- Instructor's Manual including teaching material built around the content of the chapters
- PowerPoint slides available for each chapter to serve as a teaching aid for lecture presentations
- Cases 16, 17 and 18 continued in full
- New cases and questions exclusive to the website
- Additional notes on cases from the textbook
- Answers to end of chapter questions.

FOR STUDENTS

- Multiple choice questions for each chapter to test your learning
- Links to useful websites and other resources
- Cases 16, 17 and 18 continued in full
- Glossary explaining key terms.

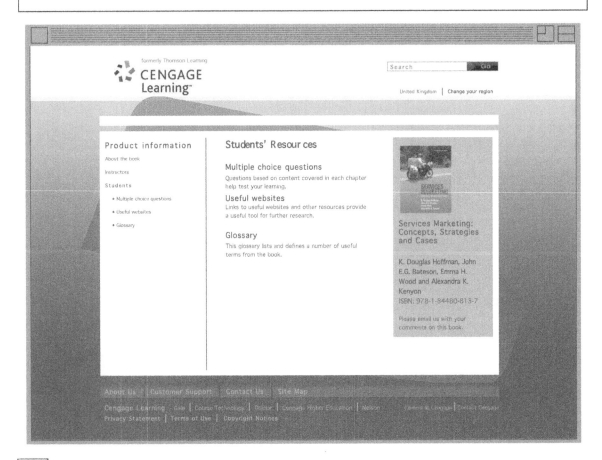

Part one
An overview of services marketing

Services Marketing: Concepts, Strategies and Cases is divided into three main parts. Part 1, An overview of services marketing, concentrates on defining services marketing and discusses in detail the fundamental concepts and strategies that differentiate the marketing of services from the marketing of tangible goods. The primary objective for Part 1 is to establish a core knowledge base that will be built upon throughout the remainder of the text. Part 1 concludes by highlighting the fact that through research, organizations can anticipate and accommodate the ever changing needs of their target market.

1

Chapter 1
An introduction to services

Economic value, like the coffee bean, progresses from commodities to goods to services to experiences.

(Pine & Gilmore, 1999, *The Experience Economy*)

Chapter objectives

This chapter provides an introduction to the field of services marketing. This chapter discusses the basic differences between goods and services and the factors necessary for the creation of the service experience. In addition, the chapter establishes the importance of the service sector in the world economy and the need for services marketing education.

After reading this chapter, you should be able to:

- Understand the basic differences between goods and services.

- Appreciate the factors that create the customer's service experience.

- Comprehend the driving forces behind the increasing demand for services marketing knowledge.

- Understand the two organization models used in service firms: the industrial management model and the market-focused management model.

Services in context
Enhance the experience

The service sector consists of a number of industries but perhaps none more compelling than the hospitality industry. The hospitality industry comprises a variety of segments including accommodation, travel, and tourism. Within this industry, today's success stories include those firms that are truly creative in the manner in which they enhance the customer experience.

When guests check into their hotel rooms in any major city tonight, they're likely to find a plush bed with extra pillows and a personal alarm clock on the night stand. When they stroll into the bathroom, they'll probably see a hair dryer, extra-thick towels and maybe even an electric towel-warmer. At one time, perhaps, a hotel chain might have called these things perks or amenities. But no longer. In fact, today, such accoutrements are merely the cost of entry for a hotel chain's category, not the brand differentiators they once were. And guests know it. They've come to expect the frills as standard fare.

So how's a travel or hospitality brand supposed to stand out? In a word, experience. Today, closing the sale (or the reservation) is all about allowing customers to take charge of their own experience. That, in turn, means showering them with every conceivable option and amenity that a competitor forgot to think of.

This new competitive reality has driven Westin and Sheraton to waft signature scents into hotel lobbies while parent company, Starwood Hotels & Resorts, has launched loft accommodations dubbed Aloft and an upscale, yet-to-be named extended stay hotel brand. Another hotel chain is delving into sensory branding with an in-room Sensation Bar sporting pomegranate lip balm and lavender pillow spray. Offering a choice of pillow and mattress options for the individual has become an expected service rather than an extra benefit in the upper-end of the accommodation market.

Similar moves to enhance customer experience are happening in other areas. Hertz Car Rental has met the leisure traveller's yearning for an exciting driving experience through the Fun Collection, a reservable choice of sporty models, convertibles, coupes and utility vehicles. Avis have recently unveiled a pilot programme to provide customers with battery-operated mobility scooters in the trunk.

This ever increasing drive to create a better and better experience has also extended to the high seas. Royal Caribbean International® has installed a cantilevered whirlpool, jutting out high above the ocean on its ship, *Liberty of the Seas*®.

Source: Adapted from Beirne (2006)

SOURCE © ROYAL CARIBBEAN INTERNATIONAL®

Royal Caribbean International® provides guests with breath-taking views from their cantilevered whirlpools, 112 feet above the water's surface.

Introduction

The idea that consumption (whether of goods or services) is an experience is not new and has been written about in the economic literature since the 1950s and has more recently (1980s) entered the realm of marketing (Holbrook, 2006). The key element for services marketing is that the 'experience' is often protracted and complex and, whenever possible, should be made enjoyable.

Services are everywhere we turn, whether it be travel to an exotic tourism destination, a visit to the doctor, a church service, a meal at our favourite restaurant, or a day at college. More and more countries, particularly the so-called industrialized countries, are finding that the majority of employment is being generated by their service sectors, as shown in Table 1.1. Indeed, in 2006 world employment in services overtook employment in agriculture for the first time in human history (International Labour Office, 2007) and it is predicted that over 67 per cent of the European workforce will be employed in the service industries by 2015 (Tarantino, 2006). However, the growth of the service sector does not lie just within traditional service industries such as leisure and hospitality, education and health, financial and insurance services, and professional and business services. Traditional goods producers such as automotive, computer and numerous other manufacturers are now turning to the service aspects of their operations to establish a differential advantage in the marketplace as well as to generate additional sources of revenue for their firms. In essence, these companies, which used to compete by marketing 'boxes' (tangible goods), have now switched their competitive focus to the provision of unmatched, unparalleled customer services.

Ample evidence exists that documents this transition from selling 'boxes' to service competition (see B2B Services in Action). Traditional goods-producing industries such as the car industry are now emphasizing the service aspects of their businesses such as low interest financing, extended warranties, free insurance and breakdown cover. Simultaneously, less is being heard about the tangible aspects of vehicles such as engine features and acceleration. Similarly, the personal computer industry promotes in-home repairs, 24-hour customer service and software upgrades; and the satellite television industry is now boasting the benefits of live TV pause and record, pay-per-view alternatives and security options to prevent children from viewing certain programming.

Table 1.1		Agriculture		Industry		Services	
		1996	2006	1996	2006	1996	2006
Sectoral shares in employment (%)	World	43.1	41.6	21.4	32.1	35.5	42.2
Source Adapted from International Labour Office (2007).	Developed economies (including EU)	5.2	3.2	28.5	24.2	66.4	72.7
	Europe	9.1	7.2	29.1	27.2	61.8	65.6

Overall, this new 'global services era' is characterized by:

- economies and labour force figures that are dominated by the service sector;
- more customer involvement in strategic business decisions;
- products that are increasingly market-focused and much more responsive to the changing needs of the marketplace;
- the development of technologies that assist customers and employees in the provision of services;
- empowered employees who have more discretionary freedom to develop customized solutions to special customer requests and solve customer complaints on-the-spot with minimal inconvenience;
- and the emergence of new service industries and the 'service imperative' where the intangible aspects of the product are increasingly the key features that differentiate products in the marketplace.

service imperative
Reflects the view that the intangible aspects of products are becoming the key features that differentiate the product in the marketplace.

It is clear that the service sectors in many countries are no longer manufacturing's poor cousin. Services provide the bulk of the wealth and are an important source of employment and exports for many countries. In addition, there are countless examples of firms using the service imperative to drive their businesses forward to profit and growth. Many of these are highlighted in the Services in Action boxes located throughout the remainder of the text. This service boom is expected to continue.

What is a service?

Admittedly, the distinction between goods and services is not always perfectly clear. In fact, providing an example of a pure good or a pure service is very difficult, if not impossible. A pure good would imply that the benefits received by the consumer contained no elements supplied by service. Similarly, a pure service would contain no elements of goods.

In reality, many services contain at least some goods elements, such as the menu selections at a café, the bank statement from the local bank, or the written policy from an insurance company. Also, most goods offer at least a delivery service. For example, simple table salt is delivered to the grocery store, and the company that sells it may offer innovative invoicing methods that further differentiate it from its competitors.

The distinction between goods and services is further obscured by firms that conduct business on both sides of the fence. For example, consider the music industry which now offers hard copy (tangible) products in the form of CDs alongside digital downloads with 40 per cent of worldwide music industry revenue now coming from sales to mobile phone users (Keynote, 2006). What was once a good is rapidly becoming a service. General Motors, the 'goods' manufacturing giant, generates a significant percentage of its revenue from its financial and insurance businesses, and IBM, generally thought of as major goods producer, now generates more than half of their revenue from services. The transition from goods producer to service provider can be found to varying degrees throughout much of the industrial sector. One of the world's largest steel producers now considers its service-related activities to be the dominant force within its overall business strategy (OECD, 2000).

Despite the confusion, the following definitions should provide a sound starting point in developing an understanding of the differences between goods and services. In general, goods can be defined as objects, devices, or things, whereas services can be defined as deeds, efforts, or performances (Berry, 1980). Moreover, we would like to note that when the term product is mentioned, it refers to both goods and services and is used in such a manner throughout the remainder of this text. Ultimately, the primary difference between goods and services is the property of *intangibility*. By definition, intangible products lack physical substance. As a result, intangible products face a host of services marketing problems that are not always adequately solved by traditional goods-related marketing solutions. These differences are discussed in detail in Chapter 2, Fundamental Differences Between Goods and Services.

goods Objects, devices, or things.

services Deeds, efforts, or performances.

product Either a good or a service.

The scale of market entities

An interesting perspective regarding the differences between goods and services is provided by the scale of market entities (Shostack, 1977). The scale of market entities suggests a continuum of products based on their tangibility where goods are tangible dominant and services are intangible dominant. The core benefit of a tangible dominant product typically involves a physical possession that contains service elements to a lesser degree. For example, a car is a tangible dominant product that provides transportation. As the product becomes more and more tangible dominant, fewer service aspects are apparent, for example table salt. In contrast, intangible dominant products do not involve the physical possession of a product and can only be experienced. Like the car, an airline provides transportation, but the customer does not physically possess the plane. The airline customer experiences the flight; consequently, service aspects dominate the product's core benefit and tangible elements are present to a lesser degree. In comparison, fast food businesses, which contain both a goods and a service component, fall in the middle of the continuum.

scale of market entities The scale that displays a range of products along a continuum based on their tangibility.

tangible dominant Goods that possess physical properties that can be felt, tasted and seen prior to the consumer's purchase decision.

intangible dominant Services that lack the physical properties that can be sensed by consumers prior to the purchase decision.

This scale of market entities reveals two important lessons. Firstly, there really may be no such thing as a pure product or pure service. Products are seemingly a bundle of tangible and intangible elements that combine to varying degrees. Secondly, the tangible aspects of an intangible dominant product and the intangible aspects of a tangible dominant product are an important source of product differentiation and new revenue streams. For example, businesses that produce tangible dominant products and ignore, or at least forget about, the service (intangible) aspects of their product offering are overlooking a vital component of their businesses. By defining their businesses too narrowly, these firms have developed classic cases of marketing myopia (Levitt, 1960). For example, the typical family pizza restaurant may myopically view itself as being in the pizza business and primarily focus on the pizza product itself.

marketing myopia Condition of firms that define their businesses too narrowly.

However, a broader view of the business recognizes that it is providing the consumer with a reasonably priced food product in a convenient format surrounded by an experience that has been deliberately created for the targeted consumer. Interestingly, adding service aspects to a product often transforms the product from a commodity into an experience, and by doing so, dramatically increases the revenue-producing opportunities of the product.

For example, when priced as a raw *commodity,* coffee beans are worth little more than $1.60 per pound, roasters sell the coffee on as a *good* at $20–26 per pound and a coffee retailer such as Starbucks, who creates a *service experience,* makes 52 espressos from a pound of coffee, pushing the value to $160 per pound (Seager, 2007). In this instance, the whole process of ordering, creation and consumption becomes 'a pleasurable, even theatrical' experience. Hence, economic value, like the coffee bean, progresses from *commodities* to *goods* to *services* to *experiences* (Pine and Gilmore, 1999). In the previous example, coffee was transformed from a raw commodity valued at approximately $1.00 per pound to $4–$5 per cup – a markup as much as 5,000 per cent!

The molecular model

Molecular models further expand our understanding of the basic differences between goods and services. A molecular model is a pictorial representation of the relationship between the tangible and intangible elements of a firm's operation (Shostack, 1977). One of the primary benefits obtained from developing a molecular model is that it is a management tool that offers the opportunity to visualize the firm's entire bundle of benefits that its product offers customers. Figure 1.1 applies the molecular model to the purchase of a DVD film (tangible dominant) and a visit to the cinema (intangible dominant). The cinema differs from a DVD in that, typically, consumers do not physically possess the cinema or the film shown at it. Consumers in this case purchase the core benefit of entertainment and all of the corresponding tangible (denoted by solid-lined circles) and intangible benefits (denoted by dashed-lined circles) that are associated with a cinema visit. In contrast, a consumer who purchases a DVD is primarily benefited by the ownership of a physical possession that renders a service – entertainment.

molecular model A conceptual model of the relationship between tangible and intangible components of a firm's operations.

The diagrams provided in Figure 1.1 are oversimplifications of the bundle of benefits that ultimately comprise the cinema experience and DVD ownership. From a managerial perspective, an elaboration of these models would identify the tangible and intangible product components that need to be effectively managed. For example, the successful cinema experience is determined not just by the viewing of an entertaining film and the molecular model could easily be expanded to include:

- cinema accessibility/parking (intangible element)
- other people in the audience (tangible element)
- service from ushers (intangible element)
- seat comfort and position (tangible elements)
- toilet facilities (tangible).

Similarly, the DVD model could be expanded to include:

- retail outlet accessibility (intangible element)
- retail outlet layout (tangible element)
- sales service (intangible element)
- payment options (intangible element)
- other complementary products on offer (tangible elements).

The overriding benefit obtained by developing molecular models is an appreciation for the intangible and tangible elements that comprise most products. Once managers understand this broadened view of their products, they can do a much better job of understanding customer needs, servicing those needs more effectively and differentiating their product-offering from competitors. The molecular model also demonstrates that consumers' service 'knowledge' and goods 'knowledge' are not obtained in the same manner. With tangible dominant products, goods 'knowledge' is obtained by focusing on the physical aspects of the product itself. In contrast, consumers evaluate

Figure 1.1

Molecular models for cinema visit and DVD purchase

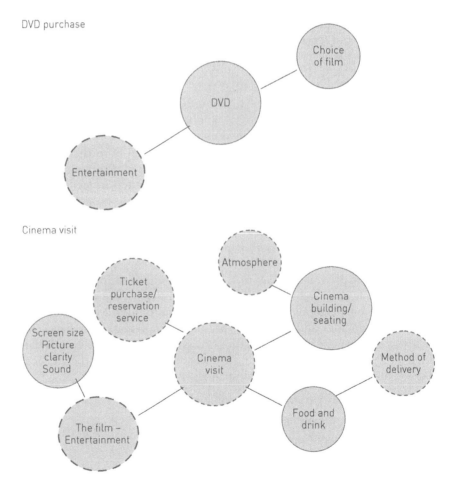

intangible dominant products based on the experience that surrounds the core benefit of the product. Hence, understanding the importance and components of the service experience is critical.

Framing the service experience: The servuction model

Because of the intangible nature of service products, service knowledge is acquired differently from knowledge pertaining to goods. For example, consumers can sample tangible dominant products such as soft drinks and biscuits prior to purchase. In contrast, a consumer cannot sample an intangible dominant product such as a haircut, a theatre performance, or a consultant's advice prior to purchase. Hence, service knowledge is gained through the experience of receiving the actual service itself. Ultimately, when a consumer purchases a service, he or she is actually purchasing an experience!

All products, be they goods or services, deliver a bundle of benefits to the consumer (Bateson, 1992). The benefit concept is the encapsulation of these tangible and intangible benefits in the consumer's mind. For a tangible dominant good such as Daz laundry detergent, for example, the core benefit concept might simply be cleaning. However for other individuals, it might also include attributes built into the product that go beyond the mere powder or liquid, such as cleanliness, whiteness, and/or motherhood (it's a widely held belief in some cultures that the cleanliness of children's clothes is a reflection upon their mother). The determination of what the bundle of benefits comprises – the benefit concept purchased by consumers – is the heart of marketing, and it transcends all goods and services.

In contrast to goods, services deliver a bundle of benefits through the experience that is created for the consumer. For example, most consumers of Daz will never see the inside of the manufacturing plant where it is produced; they will most likely never interact with the factory workers who produce the detergent nor with the management staff that directs the workers; and they will also generally not use Daz in the company of other consumers. In contrast, restaurant customers are physically present in the 'factory' where the food is produced; these customers do interact with the workers who prepare and serve the food as well as with the management staff that runs the restaurant. Moreover, restaurant customers consume the service in the presence of other customers where they may influence one another's service experience. One particularly simple but powerful model that illustrates factors that influence the service experience is the servuction model depicted in Figure 1.2. The servuction model consists of four factors that directly influence customers' service experiences:

1 servicescape (visible)
2 contact personnel/service providers (visible)
3 other customers (visible)
4 organizations and systems (invisible)

benefit concept The encapsulation of the benefits of a product in the consumer's mind.

servuction model A model used to illustrate the factors that influence the service experience, including those that are visible to the consumer and those that are not.

The first three factors are plainly visible to customers. In contrast, organization and systems, although profoundly impacting the customer's experience, are typically invisible to the customer.

The servicescape

servicescape All the non-living features that comprise the service environment.

The term servicescape refers to the use of physical evidence to design service environments. Due to the intangibility of services, customers often have trouble evaluating the quality of service objectively. As a result, consumers rely on the physical evidence that surrounds the service to help them form their evaluations. Hence, the servicescape consists of *ambient conditions* such as room temperature and music; *inanimate objects* that assist the firm in completing its tasks, such as furnishings and business equipment; and *other physical evidence*, for example, signs, symbols, and personal artefacts such as family pictures and personal collections. The use of physical evidence varies by the type of service firm. Service firms such as hospitals, resorts and child-care centres often use physical evidence extensively as they design facilities and other tangibles associated with the service. In contrast, service firms such as insurance agencies and printers use limited physical evidence. Regardless of the variation in usage, all service firms need to recognize the importance of managing the servicescape, because of its role in:

- packaging the service
- facilitating the service delivery process
- socializing customers and employees
- differentiating the firm from its competitors.

Contact personnel/Service providers

contact personnel Employees other than the primary service provider who briefly interact with the customer.

Contact personnel are employees other than the primary service provider who briefly interact with the customer. Typical examples of contact personnel are parking attendants, receptionists and security personnel. In

Figure 1.2

The servuction model

Source Adapted from E. Langeard, J. Bateson, C. Lovelock, and P. Eiglier, *Marketing of Services: New Insights from Consumers and Managers*, Report No 81–104, Cambridge, MA: Marketing Sciences Institute, 1981.

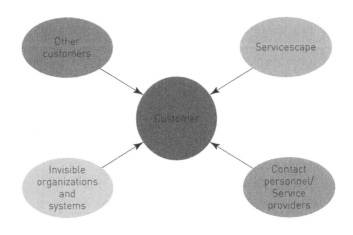

contrast, service providers are the primary providers of the core service, such as a waiter or waitress, dentist, bank clerk, or college lecturer.

Unlike the consumption of goods, the consumption of services often takes place where the service is produced (e.g., dentist's office, restaurant, and hair salon) or where the service is provided at the consumer's residence or workplace (e.g., gardener, decorator, cleaning service). Regardless of the service delivery location, interactions between consumers and contact personnel/service providers are commonplace. As a result, service providers have a dramatic impact on the service experience. Zemke and Anderson (1990) categorize what irritates customers most about service providers as:

- *Apathy:* What comedian George Carlin refers to as DILLIGAD – Do I look like I give a damn?
- *Brush-off:* Attempts to get rid of the customer by dismissing the customer completely . . . the 'I want you to go away' syndrome.
- *Coldness:* Indifferent service providers who could not care less what the customer really wants.
- *Condescension:* The 'you are the client/patient, so you must be stupid' approach.
- *Robotism:* When the customers are treated simply as inputs into a system that must be processed.
- *Rulebook:* Providers who live by the rules of the organization even when those rules do not make good sense.
- *Runaround:* Passing the customer off to another provider, who will simply pass them off to yet another provider.

Service personnel perform the dual functions of interacting with customers and reporting back to the internal organization. Strategically, service personnel are an important source of product differentiation. It is often challenging for a service organization to differentiate itself from other similar organizations in terms of the benefit bundle it offers or its delivery system. For example, many airlines offer similar bundles of benefits and fly the same types of aircraft from the same airports to the same destinations. Therefore, their only hope of a competitive advantage is from the service level – the way things are done. Hence, the factor that often distinguishes one airline from another is the poise and attitude of its service providers. Singapore Airlines, for example, enjoys an excellent reputation due in large part to the beauty and grace of its flight attendants. Virgin airline also gains competitive advantage through distinctive cabin staff, but focuses this through their friendliness and ability to provide fun and entertainment on a long journey. Other firms that hold a differential advantage over competitors based on personnel include the Hard Rock Café, Ritz Carlton and Disney Enterprises. This is not just the realm of large multinationals, however; many of the winners of the UK Service Excellence Awards come from smaller enterprises such as Wrapit (2005 Small Business Winner), an online wedding list service discussed in the E-Services in Action box. Given the importance of service providers and other contact personnel, Chapter 10 is devoted to a discussion of the recruiting, training, and empowering of personnel.

service providers The primary providers of a core service, such as a waiter or waitress, dentist, physician, or college instructor.

E-services in action
Mixing self-service and personal service: Wrapit Plc

Over the years, consumers have been increasingly exposed to a vast variety of self-service technologies (SSTs). SSTs include websites, kiosks, automated telephone systems and ATMs, just to name a few. These marvels of technological development allow customers to book their own flights, manage their own finances, prepurchase movie tickets and track shipped packages without ever talking to a real live human being.

In theory, self-service technologies are a win-win proposition. The customer is the recipient of faster, reliable and more convenient service at a lower price. Similarly, the company benefits from lower operating costs and a greater supply of labour that is now able to conduct tasks other than servicing customers face-to-face. Self-service is to the service sector what mass production is to manufacturing – a process used to develop products more cheaply and on a massive scale.

Despite the apparent advantages associated with self-service technologies, not everyone is thrilled. Many are beginning to question the true motivations of companies that utilize self-service technologies. Is the primary goal to provide improved customer service or simply to lower operating costs and distance the company from its high-maintenance consumers? If you ever waited an inordinate amount of time in an automated telephone queue or found that the telephone menu selections are not organized in a manner that addresses your particular question, you are not alone.

One company that is successfully combining personal service with self-service to provide real customer service is Wrapit Plc, an innovative service company offering something unique to its customers. Anyone who has ever compiled a wedding list knows what a daunting task it can be. You'll find yourself trudging around floor after floor of the department store, notebook in hand, trying to find out what's available in what colour and whether they will go with items from a completely different department. Then, as the big day nears, finding out what's been bought or changing your list can be a nightmare too.

Which is why Pepita Diamand came up with the idea for Wrapit, an innovative online wedding-list service. Says Diamand, a Canadian: 'I discovered that wedding lists weren't doing what they should be doing. They often left guests disappointed, and they didn't manage couples correctly.' Moreover, nobody was using the internet to operate what is essentially a fulfilment application naturally suited to the web.

How does it work? Couples have a consultation, typically at Wrapit's smart central London showroom, where the consultant helps them assemble their list from items in-store and those in a web-based catalogue. The list is then made available to guests via the Wrapit website as a mini-catalogue; they can order their chosen gift with a few clicks. The couple receive e-mail updates advising them every time an item is bought, and they can modify the list, deleting or adding items when they want to.

To deliver this service, Wrapit built a proprietary system that presents the catalogue, manages the fulfilment and offers a variety of additional services of benefit to couples. For example, it can generate a tailor-made thank-you card to each guest. Wrapit gives its customers a clear timetable of when gifts will be delivered, and its own drivers deliver everything to ensure the best possible service.

SOURCE PETER ALVEY/ALAMY

Wrapit's staff are mostly smart, highly moti-vated young women who have an instant rapport with their target customers. Some are actresses between jobs, others are parents, but the com-pany has devised a flexible rostering system to fit in with their lifestyles. The firm sets great store on recruiting people of the right calibre. 'If the right person comes along, then we'll find a job for them', says Diamand.

In 2007 Wrapit managed the wedding lists of 2,000 couples. It had already expanded into franchises and set itself the ambitious target of capturing some 6 per cent of the market, worth around £24 million, by 2008. The market for wedding lists is growing as they achieve wider social acceptance. Wrapit's high-tech, customer-friendly formula looks set to win a growing slice of it, even if the firm can't count on getting much in the way of repeat business.

Sources: 'Do it yourself', *The Economist* (18 Septem-ber 2004), 372 (8393), p. 16.
Customer Service Award Winner: Small business cat-egory: Management Today 2007 www. wrapit.co.uk

Other customers

Ultimately, the success of many service encounters depends on how effec-tively the service firm manages its clientele. A wide range of service establish-ments such as restaurants, hotels, airlines and dentist surgeries serve multiple customers simultaneously. Hence, other customers can have a profound impact on an individual's service experience. Research has shown that the presence of other customers can enhance or detract from an individual's service experience (Grove and Fisk, 1997; Martin, 1996). The influence of other customers can be *active* or *passive*. For instance, examples of other customers actively detracting from one's service experience include unruly customers in a restaurant or a night club, children crying during a flight, or theatregoers carrying on a conversation during a play. Some passive examples include customers who show up late for appointments, thereby delaying each subsequent appointment; an exceptionally tall individual who sits directly in front of another customer at the cinema; or the impact of being part of a crowd, which increases the waiting time for everyone in the group.

Though many customer actions that enhance or detract from the service experience are difficult to predict, service organizations can attempt to manage the behaviour of customers so that they coexist peacefully. For example, firms can manage waiting times so that customers who arrive earlier than others get first priority, clearly target specific age segments to minimize potential conflicts between younger and older customers, and provide separate dining facilities for smokers and customers with children. Many train companies now have 'quiet'-carriages where mobile phone use is not allowed and low-cost airlines that do not have seat allocations allow customers who check in first to board first.

Invisible organization and systems

Thus far, the servuction model suggests that the benefits derived by Customer A are influenced by the interaction with (1) the servicescape, (2) contact personnel and/or service providers, and (3) other customers. The benefits are therefore derived from an interactive process that takes place throughout the service experience. Of course, the visible components of service firms cannot exist in isolation, and indeed, they have to be supported by invisible components. For example, any high street bank will have computer systems behind-the-scenes processing customer information and electronically transferring money around the world. Most parcel delivery firms have complex logistical computer software controlling and tracking shipments and even the smallest of restaurants will have a kitchen, food preparation and storage area not usually on view to the customer.

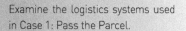

Case link

Examine the logistics systems used in Case 1: Pass the Parcel.

invisible organization and systems That part of a firm that reflects the rules, regulations and processes upon which the organization is based.

The invisible organization and systems reflect the rules, regulations and processes upon which the organization is based. As a result, although they are invisible to the customer, they have a very profound effect on the consumer's service experience. The invisible organization and systems determine factors such as information forms to be completed by customers, the number of employees working in the firm at any given time and the policies of the organization regarding countless decisions that may range from the substitution of menu items to whether the firm accepts student cards for price discounts.

The four components of the servuction model combine to create the experience for the consumer, and it is the experience that creates the bundle of benefits for the consumer. Creating 'experiences' for customers is not a new idea. The entertainment industry and venues such as Disney have been doing it for years. Others, particularly in the hospitality sector, have recently picked up on the idea and have introduced 'experience' product concepts such as the Hard Rock Café and Planet Hollywood. The question facing many other types of service providers is how to transform their own operations into memorable experiences for the customer. One unique example is provided by the domestic drain maintenance company, Drain Doctor. This otherwise unpleasant business is transformed through the use of smartly uniformed, customer service trained engineers, fun logos and a free 'Drain Doctor' figure with every call out. In this instance, a mundane and often distasteful service has been transformed into a memorable, possibly pleasant event for the customer.

Perhaps the most profound implication of the servuction model is that it demonstrates that consumers are an integral part of the service process. Their participation may be active or passive, but they are always involved in the service delivery process. This has a significant effect on the nature of the services marketing task and provides a number of challenges that are not typically faced by goods manufacturers. These challenges increase when marketing services cross international boundaries (see Global Services in Action).

Why study services?

Over the past 35 years, substantial changes have taken place in the global business environment. Emerging service sectors (profit and nonprofit) are

---

Global services in action
Obstacles to service exports

Given the dominance of services in most economies, the share of total world exports attributed to services is relatively low – approximately 22 per cent in 2004. Motivations for engaging in service exporting are plentiful, including profit motivations, escaping saturated domestic markets, tax advantages and discovering new ideas and new sources of supply. However, service growth in international trade has been hindered by several factors, many of which can be attributed to the unique properties of service products (e.g. intangibility, inseparability, heterogeneity and perishability). Obstacles to exporting services include the following:

- Many services are difficult to inventory and transport (e.g., legal advice or surgery).

- Service delivery is often a face-to-face encounter and requires the customer and the provider to be in the same physical location (e.g., hairstylist or dentist).

- Service providers are often small firms and lack the resources and expertise needed to conduct business at an international level (e.g., landscaper or accountant).

- Services are often customized. Cultural differences and product variations may limit demand in international marketplaces.

- Trade barriers such as ownership, control issues and limitations on physical establishments may also hinder service exports.

- Restrictions on local establishments and operations; for example, most countries restrict the cross-border provision of one or more professional services. Doctors, lawyers and accountants who are qualified in one country will most likely have to be recertified in order to provide services in another country.

Reducing barriers to service trade is a complex matter. Services cross a wide spectrum of business activities (e.g., surgery vs. lawncare); therefore, it is difficult to address service trade in terms of generalizations. Removing service trade barriers must be approached one service sector at a time. The good news is that service exports are increasing and currently outpacing the annual growth rate of their tangible goods counterparts. The fastest growing service exports between 1999 and 2004 were computer and information services, insurance services and financial services. The slowest were construction, government and travel services.

Sources: Organization for Economic Co-Operation and Development (OECD) (2000), *The Service Economy, STI: Business and Industry Policy Forum Series*, pp. 24–27
OECD (2006) Structure and trends in international trade in services. www.oecd.org (accessed 20 February 2007)

now dominating economies that were once known for their industrial manufacturing strength. Coinciding with the tremendous growth in the global service economy, the demand for individuals who command services marketing expertise is also greatly expanding. Practitioners in the services field have quickly learned that traditional marketing strategies and managerial models, with roots based in the goods-producing manufacturing sector, do not always apply to their unique service industries. More specifically, the demand for services marketing knowledge has been fuelled by the following:

- the tremendous growth in service-sector employment;
- increasing service-sector contributions to the world economy; and
- a revolutionary change of managerial philosophy in how service firms should organize their companies.

Service sector in the global economy

Throughout the industrialized world, the growth and shifting of employment from manufacturing to services is evident (see Table 1.1). The service industries have not only grown in size, but along the way they have absorbed all the jobs shed by traditional industries, such as agriculture, mining and manufacturing. In 1990, services accounted for 58 per cent of GDP in Japan and 60 per cent of total GDP in the European Community. In 2006, services had grown to 73.1 per cent of GDP in Japan and 70.5 per cent of GDP in the European Community (CIA, 2007). The service sector employs 144 million persons, or over 65 per cent of the workforce, in the European Community, whereas industrial employment has declined steadily to approximately 27 per cent.

In the United States in 1984 service industries employed 74 per cent of the workforce and by 2006, that figure had risen to just over 82 per cent with the service sector accounting for 78.6 per cent of GDP. The change in China has been even more marked with 31 per cent of employment now recorded as being in the service industries and 40 per cent of GDP contributed by the service sector (ibid.).

Even these numbers conceal the true contribution of services to economic growth, because service employees on the direct payroll of goods companies are counted as industrial employees. The service division of IBM, one of the largest worldwide service organizations, is counted as being in the goods, not the service sector because their core business is viewed as computers and electronics. In contrast, IBM views itself as a major service provider in the 'business solutions' industry (see B2B Services in Action). A truer picture can be obtained by looking at the combination of persons formally employed in the services sector – such as independent architectural or accounting firms – and the persons employed in those same jobs but working for firms based in the goods sector (Ginzberg and Vojta, 1981).

One of the consequences of this change has been a change in the shape of the workforce itself. For example, the bulk of new jobs created in the industrialized world over the past 30 years have been white-collar jobs, in higher-level professional, technical, administrative and sales positions. Experts monitoring the economy note that as services have replaced goods as the most dominant force in the economy, 'human capital' has replaced physical capital as the important source of investment.

Worldwide economic growth has fuelled the growth of the service sector, as increasing prosperity means that companies, institutions and individuals have become more willing to trade money for time and to buy services rather

---

B2B services in action
IBM: From boxes to services

Traditional manufacturing firms are increasingly reorienting themselves around services. In these cases, the manufacturing firm is basing its marketing strategy on the philosophy that by serving customers well through supplementary services, the value of the tangible core product ('the box') is enhanced. IBM is an example of such a firm.

When most people think about IBM, they think about its celebrated history as the manufacturer of tangible products such as the typewriter, personal computers, workstations, notebooks, desktops, servers, printing systems and other assorted accessories. However, in recent years IBM has transitioned itself from a manufacturer to a provider of business solutions. For example, IBM and its corporate partners offer a number of services to both small and large business customers that are designed to:

- boost workplace efficiency
- build a flexible infrastructure
- enhance financial management
- enhance security, privacy and compliance
- improve the customer experience
- increase business innovation
- manage human capital
- optimize IT investments
- optimize supply chains and operations
- streamline business processes.

These services now come under the remit of a new strategic business unit, Integrated Communications Services (ICS). In 2006 ICS launched thirty new service products and the employees at IBM have been encouraged to become more customer focused through specializing in services rather than goods.

Essentially, IBM has spent over 100 years in the business of information handling, as nearly all of its products were designed and developed to record, process, communicate, store and retrieve information. By focusing on customer-oriented service solutions in combination with the innovation and development of new products, IBM differentiates itself from the competition, enhances the value of its core products and establishes new revenue streams for the company.

Sources: http://www-03.ibm.com/ibm/history/history/history_intro.html; http://www1.ibm.com/services/us/index.wss/gen_bt accessed 31 January 2005; John R. Delaney, 'IBM Corp.', *PC Magazine* (9 April 2002), 21 (7). A. Bednarz (2006) 'Customers applaud IBM services' facelift', *Network World*, 23 (38), p. 25.

SOURCE ISTOCK.COM/LAJOS RÉPÁSI

IBM differentiates itself from its competition by focusing more on customer-oriented service solutions.

than spend time doing things for themselves. New technology has led to considerable changes in the nature of many services and in the development of new services. Higher disposable incomes have led to a proliferation of personal services, particularly in the entertainment sector. Growth has meant an increase not only in the overall volume of services, but in the variety and diversity of services offered.

The result has been phenomenal growth in service industries. All developed economies now have large service sectors, and this is a continuing trend in the rapidly developing economies of countries such as China and India. In addition, many service firms now operate internationally, and exports of services are also increasing (see Global Services in Action).

Despite the growth of the service sector, the idea that an economy cannot survive without relying on manufacturing to create wealth continues to dominate business and political thinking in the West. *The Economist* magazine noted in 1992: 'That services cannot thrive without a strong manufacturing "base" is a claim rarely challenged. The opposite argument – that manufacturing needs services – is hardly ever put.' Today, it is hard to avoid the conclusion that it is services, not manufacturing, that are the real creators of wealth in many countries. Indeed, without demand for transportation services there would be little need for aeroplanes, lorries, buses and ships. Moreover, without demand for information and entertainment services, the need for theatre complexes, printing presses, televisions and computers would collapse.

The services revolution: A change in perspective

Without a doubt, the world economy is experiencing the most substantial period of change in its economic history since the industrial revolution. Accompanying this change has been a shift in the philosophy of how service firms should organize their businesses. Many feel that the management model currently in place, the *industrial management model,* needs to be replaced by a *market-focused management model* if service companies are to survive and thrive (Schelsinger and Heskett, 1991). Service marketing professionals who understand the pros and cons of both models will be needed to make the necessary changes.

The industrial management model

industrial management model An approach to organizing a firm that focuses on revenues and operating costs and ignores the role personnel play in generating customer satisfaction and sustainable profits.

The industrial management model, which has its roots in the manufacturing sector, is still employed today by many service organizations. Organizations that follow the industrial management model believe that (1) location strategies, sales promotions and advertising drive sales revenue; and that (2) labour and other operating costs should be kept as low as possible. In sum, the industrial model focuses on revenues and operating costs and ignores (or at least forgets) the role personnel play in generating customer satisfaction and sustainable profits. Given the role that people play throughout the service encounter, it is sadly ironic that the industrial model continues to be embraced by many of today's companies.

Followers of the industrial model believe that good employees are difficult to find and support the view that 'all things being equal, it is better to rely on technology, machines, and systems than on human beings' (The Economist, 2004). Followers of this approach believe that most employees are indifferent, unskilled and incapable of fulfilling any duties beyond performing simple tasks. Consequently, jobs under the industrial model are narrowly defined to leave little room for employees to exercise judgement. Moreover, employees are held to low job performance expectations, their wages are kept as low as possible, and few opportunities for advancement are available.

As opposed to valuing front-line employees, the industrial model places a higher value on upper and middle managers while viewing the people who deliver service to the customer as the 'bottom of the barrel'. The industrial approach assumes that only managers can solve problems; consequently, resolving customer problems quickly becomes almost impossible as additional steps are built into the service delivery process.

The industrial model, therefore, by definition guarantees a cycle of failure as service failures are designed directly into the system. Due to its lack of support for front-line personnel, the industrial approach, albeit unintentionally, actually encourages front-line employees to be indifferent to customer problems. In essence, the system prohibits the front-line employee from taking any action even if the employee wants to assist in correcting the problem. Customer reactions to this type of treatment are not surprising. Two-thirds of customers who now defect from their former suppliers do so not because of the product, but because of the indifference and unhelpfulness of the person providing the service (Schlesinger and Heskett, 1991).

In further attempts to reduce operating costs, many firms that embrace the industrial model have replaced their full-time personnel with less experienced and less committed part-time personnel. These individuals are paid less than full-time personnel and receive fewer, if any, company benefits. In some instances, companies routinely release workers before mandatory raises and other benefits begin, in an attempt to keep operating costs down.

The consequences associated with the industrial model in regard to service organizations have been self-destructive. The industrial model has produced dead-end front-line jobs, poor pay, superficial training, no opportunity for advancement, and little, if any, access to company benefits. Moreover, the industrial approach has led to customer dissatisfaction, flat or declining sales revenues, high employee turnover and little or no growth in overall service productivity. In summary, many believe that the industrial approach is bad for customers, employees, shareholders and the countries in which this philosophy continues to be embraced.

The market-focused management model

In contrast to the industrial management model, proponents of the market-focused management model believe that the purpose of the firm is to serve the customer (Schlesinger and Heskett, 1991). Consequently, logic suggests that the firm should be *organized in a manner that supports the people who*

market-focused management model A new organizational model that focuses on the components of the firm that facilitate the firm's service delivery system.

serve the customer. By following this approach, service delivery becomes the focus of the system and the overall differential advantage in terms of competitive strategy.

The framework that supports this change in philosophy is based on the services triangle presented in Figure 1.3 The services triangle depicts six key relationships. Firstly, the firm's service strategy must be communicated to its customers. If superior service is the focus of the organization and the key point of differentiation by which it distinguishes itself from competitors, the customer needs to be made aware of the firm's commitment to excellence. Secondly, the service strategy also needs to be communicated to the firm's employees. Good service starts at the top, and management must lead by example. If top management is not committed to the process, front-line employees who interact with the firm's customers will be ineffective at best.

The third relationship depicted within the triangle focuses on the consistency of the service strategy and the systems that are developed to run the day-to-day operations. The systems, like those discussed as the invisible components of the servuction model, should flow logically from the service strategy and enhance the service encounter for employees and customers alike. The fourth relationship involves the impact of organizational systems upon customers. Interactions with the firm's systems should facilitate the customer's service experience. Too often, systems are designed for the sole purpose of keeping a small minority of customers from taking advantage of the company. Meanwhile, the majority of honest customers are forced to suffer through systems and policies that treat them as suspects instead of valued assets.

The fifth relationship within the services triangle pinpoints the importance of organizational systems and employee efforts. Organizational systems and policies should not be obstacles in the way of employees wishing to provide good service. For example, in the interests of standardization, in one well known fast-food chain employees are forbidden from selling the product without the standard pickle regardless of whether the customer wants it.

Figure 1.3

The services triangle

Source Adapted from Karl Albrecht and Ron Zemke, *Service America* (Homewood, IL: Dow Jones-Irwin, 1985), pp. 31–47.

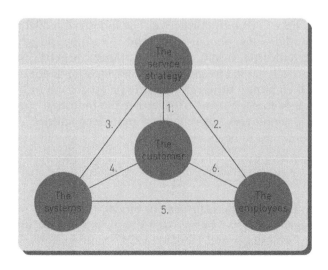

Finally, the last relationship is perhaps the most important of them all – the customer/service provider interaction. These interactions represent critical incidents or 'moments of truth'. The quality of this interaction is often the driving force in customer satisfaction evaluations.

The market-focused management model, supported by the services triangle, is based on the belief that employees, in general, want to do good work. Hence, proponents of this model are more optimistic regarding their faith in human nature. As such, the market-focused management approach encourages investing in people as much as it does investing in machines. For example, the primary purpose of technology is viewed as a means to assist front-line personnel, not to replace them or monitor and control their activities. In addition, data once collected and controlled by middle managers are now made readily available to front-line personnel.

A comparison of the two approaches

In contrast to the industrial management model, the market-focused management model recognizes that employee turnover and customer satisfaction are clearly related. Consequently, the market-focused management model emphasizes the recruitment and training of front-line personnel and ties pay to performance at every level throughout the organization. The benefits of superior training and compensation programmes are clear. For example, a survey by the Chartered Institute of Personnel and Development found that 95 per cent of employers see training as a way to improve retention, but also as a way to avoid recruitment costs and reduce sick leave (Vowler, 2005). Better-trained and better-paid employees provide better service, need less supervision, and are more likely to stay on the job. In turn, their customers are more satisfied, return to make purchases more often and purchase more when they do return.

Understandably there is also a correlation between customer satisfaction and the proportion of full-time to part-time employees. As you might expect, the higher the proportion of full-time to part-time employees, the more satisfied the customers. Full-time employees tend to be more knowledgeable, more available and more motivated to satisfy customers.

In further contrast to the industrial management model philosophy, proponents of the market-focused management model refuse to sacrifice competent and motivated full-time personnel in the name of lower operating costs. The benefits of maintaining a highly motivated full-time staff are clear. As evidence, companies that pay their employees more than competitors pay often find that as a percentage of sales, their labour costs are actually lower than industry averages.

One final difference between the industrial management model and the market-focused management model is that the latter attempts to utilize innovative data to examine the firm's performance by looking beyond generally accepted accounting principles. Traditional accounting principles reflect the sales orientation of the old industrial management model. New accounting measures that reflect the focus on customer orientation need to be developed and refined. The new measures of interest include the value of customer retention as opposed to obtaining new customers, the costs of employee turnover, the value of employee training and the monetary benefits associated with service recovery – making amends with the customer when the service delivery system fails. What is therefore required is a reversal of the traditional top-down, management-first approach, the need to turn the service firm upside-down and recognize the importance of the large number of personnel who are in close contact with the customer.

Given what has been presented thus far, it should be clear that the field of services marketing is much broader than what is discussed in a traditional marketing class. As such, many of the concepts and strategies presented in this text have their origins in management science, human resources and psychology as well as marketing. Ultimately, services marketing is about managing the compromising relationships that must exist among marketing, operations and human resources.

Summary

Services permeate every aspect of our lives; consequently, the need for services marketing knowledge is greater today than ever before. When defining services, the distinction between goods and services is often not perfectly clear. In general, goods are defined as objects, devices, or things, whereas services are defined as deeds, efforts, or performances. Very few, if any, products can be classified as pure services or pure goods. The scale of market entities and the molecular model illustrate how various goods and services vary according to their tangibility.

When a consumer purchases a service, he or she purchases an experience. The four components of the servuction model create the experience for the consumer – the servicescape, service providers/contact personnel, other customers, and the invisible organization and systems. In turn, the service experience that is created delivers a bundle of benefits to the consumer. In contrast to the production of goods, the servuction model demonstrates that service consumers are an integral part of the service production process.

Recent developments have fuelled the demand for services marketing knowledge. First, tremendous growth has occurred in service-sector employment and in the service sector's contribution to many countries' gross domestic product. The demand for services marketing knowledge has also been driven by a change in perspective in how service firms should manage their companies. Organizations that follow the traditional industrial management model believe that (1) location strategies sales promotions and advertising drive sales revenue; and (2) labour and other operating costs should be kept as low as possible. The industrial management model focuses on revenues and operating costs and ignores, or at least forgets, the role personnel play in generating customer satisfaction and sustainable profits.

In contrast, proponents of the market-focused management model believe that the purpose of the firm is to serve the customer. Consequently, logic suggests that the firm should organize itself in a manner that supports the people who serve the customer. By following this approach, service delivery becomes the focus of the system and the overall differential advantage in terms of competitive strategy. The basic concepts and outcomes associated with the market-focused management model are illustrated in the services triangle depicted in Figure 1.3.

Discussion questions

1 Define and provide examples of the following terms: goods, services and products.

2 Evaluate the use of the scale of market entities and the molecular model in distinguishing between good and services.

3 Discuss the relevance of the scale of market entities to marketing myopia.

4 Apply the molecular model to Wrapit Plc (E-Services in Action) and to a department store gift service. Compare and discuss.

5 Utilizing the servuction model, describe your classroom experience. How would your servuction model change as you describe the experience at a local restaurant?

6 Critically evaluate the suitability of the industrial management model in modern service industries.

7 Evaluate the benefits and drawbacks of the market-focused management model.

8 Discuss the relevance of the services triangle to the market-focused management model.

References and further reading

Bateson, J. E. G. (1992) *Managing Services Marketing: Text and Readings*, Fort Worth, TX: Dryden Press.

Beirne, M. (2006) 'Beds of beauty, flights of fancy', *Brandweek* 47 (25).

Berry, L. L. (1980) 'Services marketing is different', *Business Magazine* (May–June): 24–29.

CIA (2007) 'The World Factbook', www.cia.gov/cia/publications/factbook, accessed 18 February 2007.

The Economist (1994) 'The manufacturing myth', *The Economist* (March): 91.

The Economist (2004) 'Do it yourself', *The Economist* 372 (8393)(18 September): 16.

Ginzberg, E. and Vojta, G. J. (1981) 'The service sector of the U.S. Economy', *Scientific American* 244 (3): 31–39.

Grove, S. J. and Fisk, R. P. (1997) 'The impact of other customers on service experiences: a critical incident examination of getting along', *Journal of Retailing* 73 (1): 63–85.

Holbrook, M. B. (2006) 'The consumption experience – Something new, something old, something borrowed, something sold', *Journal of Macromarketing* 26: 259–266.

International Labour Office (2007) *Global Employment Trends Brief*, January, www.ilo.org.

Keynote (2006) *The Music Industry Report*, www.keynote.co.uk.

Levitt, T. (1960) 'Marketing myopia', *Harvard Business Review* 38 (July–August): 24–47.

Martin, Charles L. (1996) 'Consumer-to-consumer relationships: satisfaction with other consumers' public behavior', *Journal of Consumer Affairs* 30 (1): 146–148.

Mattoo, A., Rathindran, R. and Subramanian, A. (2006) 'Measuring services trade liberalization and its impact on economic growth: an illustration', *Journal of Economic Integration* 21 (1): 64–98.

Mizuno, M. (2005) 'Development of the service sector in Japan and its implications for the economy', *Pacific Economic Review* 10 (4): 485–492.

OECD (2006) 'Enhancing the performance of the services sector: the service economy in OECD countries', *OECD Industry, Services and Trade* 2005 (8): 28–63.

Organization for Economic Co-Operation and Development (OECD) (2000) *The Service Economy, STI: Business and Industry Policy Forum Series*.

Pine, J. B. II and Gilmore, J. H. (1999) *The Experience Economy*, Boston, MA: Harvard Business School Press.

Schlesinger, Leonard A. and Heskett, James L. (1991) 'The service-driven service company', *Harvard Business Review* (September–October): 71–75.

Schreider, B. (1994) 'A service perspective towards a customer-focused HRM', *International Journal of Service Industry Management* 5 (1): 64–76.

Seager, A. (2007) 'Starbucks stirred by fair trade film', *The Guardian*, 29 January.

Shostack, L. G. (1977) 'Breaking free from product marketing', *Journal of Marketing* 41 (April): 73–80.

Tarantino, G. C. (2006) *Imputation, Estimation and Prediction using the Key Indicators of theLabour Market (KILM) Data Set*, Employment Strategy Department, International Labour Office.

Van Dierdonck, R. and Brandt, G. (1988) 'Focused factory in service industries', in Johnston, R. (ed.), *The Management of Service Operations*, IFS: Springer-Verlag.

Vowler, J. (2005) 'How effective training aids staff retention', *Computer Weekly*, 15 November, p. 40.

Wakefield, K. L. and Blodgett, G. (1994) 'The importance of servicescapes in leisure service settings', *Journal of Services Marketing* 8 (3): 66–76.

Zemke, R. and Anderson, K. (1990) 'Customers from Hell', *Training*, February, pp 25–29.

Chapter 2

Fundamental differences between goods and services

It is wrong to imply that services are just like goods 'except' for intangibility. By such logic, apples are just like oranges, except for their 'appleness'.

(Shostack, 1977: 73)

Chapter objectives

This chapter discusses the basic differences between goods and services, the marketing problems that arise due to these differences and possible solutions to the problems created by these differences.

After reading this chapter, you should be able to:

- Understand the characteristics of intangibility, inseparability, heterogeneity and perishability.

- Discuss the marketing problems associated with intangibility and their possible solutions.

- Describe the marketing problems associated with inseparability and their possible solutions.

- Explain the marketing problems associated with heterogeneity and their possible solutions.

- Identify the marketing problems associated with perishability and their possible solutions.

- Consider the impact of intangibility, inseparability, heterogeneity and perishability on marketing's relationship to other functions within the service organization.

Services in context
The AOL avatar

Service companies are unique from manufacturers in that they do not produce anything tangible from scratch. Consequently, service firms often face challenges such as how do you market a product that no one can see; price a product that has no cost of goods sold; inventory a product that cannot be stored; or distribute a product that seems inextricably linked to its provider? One company that has excelled at all of these challenges is the internet provider AOL.

AOL's earlier UK campaign made use of a 'virtual reality' female character to add tangibility and personality to the product. The character appeared in the ads to explain the product's use and benefits in 'slice of life' type situations allowing the potential AOL user to visualize their own use of this highly intangible product. Since then their communication campaigns have increased in terms of maturity, audience engagement and expenditure. One of their most recent multimedia campaign encourages debate on the pros and cons of the internet via TV, radio and poster ads and related web-based discussions.

Introduction

Approximately 25 years ago the marketing discipline changed, with services breaking free from product marketing through the work of services marketing pioneers Shostack (1977), Grönroos (1978), Zeithaml (1981) and Lovelock (1983). This change was born out of recognition that the classical product marketing literature did not do justice to the unique qualities of services. Services had distinctive characteristics which made them fundamentally different from products. Thus, the services marketing discipline emerged. Since then a great deal of work has been undertaken to manage the implications of these distinctive characteristics of services (Van der Zwan and Bhamra, 2003)

In the beginning the work towards accumulating services marketing knowledge was slow. In fact, not until 1970 was services marketing even considered to be an academic field. One of the reasons that the field of services marketing was slow to grow within the academic community was that many marketing educators felt that the marketing of services was not significantly different from the marketing of goods. Markets still needed to be segmented, target markets still needed to be sought, and marketing mixes that catered to the needs of the firm's

intangibility A distinguishing characteristic of services that makes them unable to be touched or sensed in the same manner as physical goods.

inseparability A distinguishing characteristic of services that reflects the interconnection among the service provider, the customer involved in receiving the service, and other customers sharing the service experience.

heterogeneity A distinguishing characteristic of services that reflects the variation in consistency from one service transaction to the next.

perishability A distinguishing characteristic of services in that they cannot be saved, their unused capacity cannot be reserved and they cannot be inventoried.

intended target market still needed to be developed. However, since those early days, a great deal has been written regarding specific differences between goods and services and their corresponding marketing implications. The majority of these differences are primarily attributed to four unique characteristics – intangibility, inseparability, heterogeneity and perishability (Bateson, 1995).

Services are said to be intangible because they are performances rather than objects. They cannot be touched or seen in the same manner as goods. Instead, they are experienced, and consumers' judgements about them tend to be more subjective than objective. Inseparability of production and consumption refers to the fact that whereas goods are first produced, then sold, and then consumed, services are sold first and then produced and consumed simultaneously. For example, an airline passenger first purchases a ticket and then flies, consuming the in-flight service as it is produced.

Heterogeneity refers to the potential for service performance to vary from one service transaction to the next. Services are produced by people; consequently, variability is inherent in the production process. This lack of consistency cannot be eliminated as it frequently can be with goods. Finally, perishability means that services cannot be saved; unused capacity in services cannot be reserved, and services themselves cannot be inventoried. Consequently, perishability leads to formidable challenges relating to the balancing of supply and demand.

This chapter focuses on each of these four unique characteristics that differentiate the marketing of services from the marketing of goods. Because services fall in many places along the continuum that ranges from tangible dominant to intangible dominant, as described by the scale of market entities in Chapter 1, the magnitude and subsequent impact that each of these four characteristics has on the marketing of individual services will vary.

Intangibility

Of the four unique characteristics that distinguish goods from services, intangibility is the primary source from which the other three characteristics emerge. As discussed in Chapter 1, services are defined as performances, deeds and efforts; whereas goods are defined as objects, devices and things. As a result of their intangibility, services cannot be seen, felt, tasted, or touched in the same manner as physical goods can be sensed.

For example, compare the differences between purchasing a cinema ticket and purchasing a pair of shoes. The shoes are tangible goods, so the shoes can be objectively evaluated before the actual purchase. You can pick up the shoes, feel the quality of materials from which they are constructed, view their specific style and colour and actually put them on your feet and sample the fit. After the purchase, you can take the shoes home, and you now have ownership and the physical possession of a tangible object.

In comparison, consider the purchase of a service such as a film to be enjoyed at a local cinema. In this instance, the customer purchases a cinema ticket, which entitles the consumer to an experience. Because the cinema experience is intangible, it is subjectively evaluated; that is, consumers of services must rely on the judgements of others who have previously experienced the service for prepurchase information. As the information provided by others is based on their own sets of expectations and perceptions, opinions will differ regarding the value of the experience. For example, if you ask five movie-goers what they thought about the film *Harry Potter and the Goblet of Fire*, they are likely to express five different opinions ranging from 'I loved it!' to 'I hated it!' After viewing the film the customer returns home with a memory of the experience and retains the physical ownership of only a ticket stub.

Marketing problems caused by intangibility

As a result of the intangibility of services, a number of marketing challenges arise that are not normally faced when marketing tangible goods. More specifically, these challenges include the lack of service inventories, the lack of patent protection or copyright, the difficulties involved in displaying and communicating the attributes of the service to its intended target market, and the special challenges involved in the pricing of services. The following sections address these challenges and offer possible solutions to minimize their effects.

Lack of service inventories. Because of their intangibility, services cannot be inventoried. As a result, supplies of services cannot be stored as buffers against periods of high demand. For example, doctors cannot produce and store physical check-ups to be used at a later date; theatre seats that are not sold for the afternoon matinee cannot be added to the theatre for the evening show; and the Automobile Association cannot inventory roadside assistance to be distributed during peak periods. Consequently, customers are commonly forced to wait for desired services, and service providers are limited in how much they can sell by how much they can produce. The crux of the matter is that the inability to maintain an inventory translates into constant supply and demand problems. In fact, the lack of service inventories presents so many challenges to marketers that it has earned its own name – perishability. Specific problems associated with perishability and the strategies associated with minimizing its effects are discussed in much greater detail later in the chapter.

Lack of patent protection. Because of the property of intangibility, services are not easily patentable. What is there to patent? Human labour and effort are not protected. Firms sometimes advertise that their processes are patented; however, the reality is that the tangible machinery involved in the process is protected, not the process itself. One challenge faced by the lack of patent protection is that new or existing services may be easily copied. Consequently, it is difficult to maintain a firm's differential service advantage over attentive competitors for long periods.

The various types of intellectual property protection are: copyright (protects material, such as literature, art, music, sound recordings, films and broadcasts); designs (protect the visual appearance or eye appeal of products); patents (protect the technical and functional aspects of products and processes); and trade marks (protect signs that can distinguish the goods and services of one trader from those of another). Innovative and unique services need to obtain as much protection as possible through these although this is harder to prove for physical products. For more information visit www. patent.gov.uk and www.european-patent-office.org.

Difficulty in displaying or communicating services. The promotion of services presents yet another set of special challenges to the service marketer and is discussed in greater detail in Chapter 9, Developing the Service Communications Mix. The root of the challenge is this: How do you get customers to take notice of your product when they cannot see it? For example, consider the insurance industry. Insurance is a complicated product for many people. As customers, we cannot see it, we are unable to sample it prior to purchase and many of us do not understand it. Insurance seems to cost an awful lot of money, and the benefits of its purchase are not realized until some future time, if at all. In fact, if we do not use it, we are supposed to consider ourselves lucky. Why should spending thousands a year on something the customer never uses make them feel lucky? As can be seen, intangibility makes the task of explaining your product's merits to consumers highly challenging.

Difficulty in pricing services. Typically products' prices are based on cost-plus pricing. This means that the producing firm calculates the cost of producing the product and adds a predetermined markup to that figure. The challenge involved in the pricing of services is that there is no easily calculable cost of goods sold, as the primary cost of producing a service is labour and the value of the service is often not directly related to this cost.

For example, let's say you are very competent in the field of mathematics. Taking notice of your expertise in the field, a student who is struggling with his maths assignments wants to hire you as a tutor. What would you charge per hour? What are the costs involved?

Based on feedback from other services marketing classes faced with this example, students usually begin laughing and indicate that they would engage in premium pricing and charge the student €100 per hour. After reality sets in, students quickly realize that it is very difficult to place a value on their time. Specific considerations usually emerge, such as how much money the tutor could make doing something else and the opportunity costs associated with not being able to enjoy as much free time or not spending time with friends and family. Typically the consensus is that the tutor should charge something comparable to the fees charged by other tutors. The problem with this response is that it still does not answer the original question, that is, how was this competitive-based price originally calculated?

Possible solutions to intangibility problems

Marketing practitioners have implemented a number of strategies in the attempt to offset or minimize the marketing challenges posed by intangibility. These strategies include the use of tangible clues to help 'tangibilize' the service, the use of personal sources of information to help spread the word about service alternatives, and the creation of strong organizational images to reduce the amount of perceived risk associated with service purchases. Although marketers may not be totally capable of eliminating the effects of intangibility, strategies such as these have provided innovative solutions for many service industries.

The use of tangible clues. Given the absence of tangible properties, services are evaluated differently from goods. In many instances, consumers look at the physical evidence **or** tangible clues that surround the service to assist them in making service evaluations. Tangible clues may include such evidence as the quality of furniture in a lawyer's office, the appearance of the personnel in a bank and the quality of paper used for an insurance policy.

Tangible clues are also often used in services advertising. As previously discussed, because of intangibility, firms often find it difficult to effectively communicate their service offerings to consumers. Returning to the insurance example, the major challenge of an insurance firm is to communicate to consumers in a 30-second television advertisement what the specific firm has to offer and how the firm is different from every other insurance firm. One strategy embraced by many service firms is to use some form of tangible clues in advertising. Churchill Insurance uses 'the nodding dog' and promises to say 'Oh, yes', Norwich Union uses a likeable TV personality and the phrase 'Let us quote you happy' and Sheila's Wheels insurance for female drivers uses a pink handbag symbol and distinctive singing Aussie girls in the TV ads. The lesson that all these companies have learned over time is that the services they sell are abstract to the consumer and therefore difficult for the average consumer to understand. The answer to this challenge was to provide tangible clues that were easily understood by the public and directly related to the bundle of benefits the services provided. For example, AA 'We go the extra mile' stresses their commitment to finding the cheapest quote, Legal and General's umbrella 'Protect your home and family with a name you know' emphasizes safety and security and Privilege's 'You don't have to be posh to be privileged' denotes a quality service for a reasonable price.

physical evidence/ tangible clues The physical characteristics that surround a service to assist consumers in making service evaluations, such as the quality of furnishings, the appearance of personnel, or the quality of paper stock used to produce the firm's brochure.

The use of personal sources of information. As consumers of services lack any objective means of evaluating services, they often rely on the subjective evaluations relayed by friends, family and a variety of other opinion leaders. For example, when moving to a new town and seeking a family dentist, consumers will often ask co-workers and neighbours for referrals. Hence, in purchasing services, personal sources of information become more important to consumers than nonpersonal sources such as the mass media (e.g., television, radio and the Yellow Pages). The same is true for business services where past client lists, testimonials and references are important sources of information.

Personal sources of information such as friends, family and other opinion leaders are types of word-of-mouth or referral communications that consumers use to gather information about services. One strategy often used to stimulate word-of-mouth is to offer incentives to existing customers to tell their friends about a firm's offerings. This technique is used to a great extent by internet firms where a referral can be sent easily and cheaply by e-mail or

personal sources Sources such as friends, family, and other opinion leaders that consumers use to gather information about a service.

nonpersonal sources Sources such as mass advertising that consumers use to gather information about a service.

entered on a web forum. For example, many of the e-banking companies offer incentives such as a free case of wine or €100 credit to your account if a recommended friend opens an account. Sky TV offers a month's free service to existing subscribers if their friends take out a subscription and Virgin Fitness Clubs reward members with a free personal trainer session if they persuade a friend to join. Mass advertising that features customer testimonials (real or acted) can also be used effectively in a similar way to word-of-mouth. Examples include legal firms' advertisements featuring former clients who have had successful compensation claims, and travel company advertisements depicting customers describing the quality of service they received. This use of 'real life' customers can add credibility to the promotional message and tangibility to the service.

Creation of a strong organizational image. Another strategy utilized to minimize the effects of intangibility is to create a strong organizational image. Due to intangibility and the lack of objective sources of information to evaluate services, the amount of perceived risk associated with service purchases is generally greater than their goods counterparts. In an attempt to combat the higher levels of perceived risk, some service firms have spent a great deal of effort, time and money in developing a nationally and often internationally known organizational image. Sometimes, however, a strong image in one area of the business can have a negative effect on others (see B2B Services in Action). Usually though, a well known and respected corporate image lowers the level of perceived risk experienced by potential customers and, in some instances, lowers the reliance on personal sources of information when making service provider choices. For example, the consumer who is moving to a new town may bypass personal referrals and automatically seek out the nearest KwikFit garage for their car repairs based on the firm's organizational image. In this case, the national firm, through image development and subsequent brand awareness, has developed a differential advantage over small, local firms of which the consumer is unaware. Table 2.1 summarizes the marketing problems and possible solutions for minimizing the challenges of intangibility.

organizational image
The perception an organization presents to the public; if well known and respected, lowers the perceived risk of potential customers making service provider choices.

Table 2.1	Characteristic	Marketing problems	Possible solutions
Intangibility: Marketing problems and possible solutions	Intangibility	Lack of service inventories	Use of tangible clues
		Lack of patent protection	Use of personal sources of information
		Difficulty in displaying or communicating services	Creation of a strong organizational image
		Difficulty in pricing services	

Inseparability

One of the most intriguing characteristics of the service experience involves the concept of inseparability. Inseparability reflects the interconnection between the service provider, the customer involved in receiving the service and other customers sharing the same experience. Unlike the goods

---

B2B services in action
Helping Royal Mail mean business

Royal Mail is one of the unsung successes of British business. More efficient than many of its global counterparts, it delivers a staggering 75 million mail items a night, 86 per cent of which is business mail (by business mail we mean anything from bills and orders to direct mail or magazine subscriptions). Despite providing UK plc's business oxygen, Royal Mail is rarely considered a 'business' provider.

Despite Royal Mail's enormous contribution to UK plc, its customers' perception was different. It appeared that most businesses viewed mail as a utility 'in the walls, like the plumbing' visible only when something went wrong. With the exception of the marketing specialist, most did not consider mail a useful business tool in the way that IT and telephony had become, with enough status these days to merit representation on the board.

Like its product, Royal Mail the organization also lacked a real business profile. It was seen to have little understanding of the issues that business faced and little interest in tackling them. Whereas other business suppliers like BT or IBM had used advertising to build a strong business profile, Royal Mail was comparatively invisible. Over 300 years of delivering the nation's hopes and fears, social icons such as post boxes and the successful Royal Mail consumer advertising campaign 'I saw this and thought of you' had further masked Royal Mail's business voice.

The response required a thorough understanding of today's business world and the need to radically change Royal Mail's brand attitude among a key group of individuals, and to put this across through a credible, differentiating business tone of voice.

Source: Adapted from Account Planning Group, 1999, Available from www.warc.com

manufacturer, who may seldom see an actual customer while producing the good in a secluded factory, service providers are often in constant contact with their customers and must construct their service operations with the customer's physical presence in mind. In this way production and consumption of the service happen simultaneously. For example, a musical performance is created (produced) as it is experienced (consumed) by the audience. This interaction between customer and service provider defines a critical incident. Critical incidents represent the greatest opportunity for both gains and losses in regard to customer satisfaction and retention.

critical incident
A specific interaction between a customer and a service provider.

Marketing problems caused by inseparability

The inseparable nature of services poses a number of unique challenges for marketing practitioners. Firstly, in many instances, the execution of the service often requires the physical presence of the service provider. As a result, service providers require different skill sets from a manufacturer who may never actually interact with a customer. Secondly, customer involvement in the service delivery process presents a number of other challenges. Customers often dictate the type of service to be delivered, the length of the service delivery process and the cycle of service demand. Quite frankly, customer involvement often jeopardizes the efficiency of the service operation. Thirdly, services are often a shared experience among a number of customers. Consequently, problems may arise as customers adversely influence one another's service experience or, alternatively, the presence of other customers can enhance the experience. For example, a noisy adjacent table in a restaurant may detract from the enjoyment of a romantic meal, but a busy restaurant often has a more attractive atmosphere than an empty restaurant. Finally, inseparability presents a number of challenges pertaining to the mass production of services. A single service provider can produce only a finite amount of service. In addition, only so many customers can travel to one physical location to consume a service.

Physical connection of the service provider to the service. For the production of many services to occur, the service provider must be physically present to deliver the service. For example, dental services require the physical presence of a dentist or hygienist, construction services require builders, and in-home services such as carpet cleaning require a service provider to complete the work. Because of the intangibility of services, the service provider becomes a tangible clue on which at least part of the customer's evaluation of the service experience becomes based.

As tangible clues, service providers are particularly evaluated according to their use of language, clothing, personal hygiene and interpersonal communication skills. Many service firms have long appreciated the impact that public contact personnel have on the firm's overall evaluation. For example, wearing uniforms or conforming to dress codes is often required of service employees to reflect professionalism. Other service firms, such as restaurants, often place their most articulate and attractive personnel in public contact positions such as waiter, host/hostess and bartender. Personnel who do not have these skills and traits are often employed in areas that are invisible to the consumer, such as the kitchen and dish room areas.

Face-to-face interactions with customers make employee satisfaction crucial. Without a doubt, employee satisfaction and customer satisfaction are directly related. Dissatisfied employees who are visible to customers will translate into lower consumer perceptions of the firm's performance. The importance of employee satisfaction within service firms cannot be overemphasized. Customers will never be the number one priority in a company where employees are treated poorly. Employees should be viewed and treated as internal customers of the firm. This issue is discussed in much greater detail in Chapter 11, People Issues: Managing Service Employees.

Involvement of the customer in the production process. The second defining characteristic of inseparability is that the customer is involved in the production process. The customer's involvement in the production process may vary from (1) a requirement that the customer be physically present to receive the service, as in dental services, a haircut, or IT training; (2) a need for the customer to be present only to start and stop the service, as in dry cleaning and auto repair; and (3) a need for the customer to be only mentally present, as in participation in college courses that are transmitted via the internet. The level of customer contact also varies greatly in business-to-business (B2B) service delivery such as consultancy and design services, staff training, or machinery maintenance. Each scenario reflects different levels of customer contact, and as a result each service delivery system should be designed differently.

Unlike goods, which are produced, sold and then consumed, services are first sold and then produced and consumed simultaneously because of inseparability. For example, a box of breakfast cereal is produced in a factory, shipped to a store where it is sold, and then consumed by customers at a place and time of the customer's choosing. In contrast, services are produced and consumed simultaneously, so consumption takes place inside the service factory. As a result, service firms must design their operations to accommodate the customer's presence.

European banking has learnt a hard lesson relating to the unique service characteristic of inseparability and its effect on everyday operations. The drive to reduce costs and increase profit margins coupled with improvements in technology in the 1990s led many High Street banks to shut local branches, to outsource to non-national call centres and to automate many of their services. The backlash from customers has been fierce and has grown in momentum, leading several banks to rethink their policies. These banks have reintroduced the 'personal' factor into personal banking by increasing the amount of service provider and customer contact and thus offering the customer a better service experience. Some of the improvements that have been implemented in these financial institutions include the following:

- reopening of local branches
- dedicated advisers giving continuity of contact
- phone services all nationally based
- more convenient opening hours.

The bottom line for many of these institutions is that 'technical excellence' is not enough to succeed in a competitive consumer banking market.

Listening and responding to customer feedback and recognizing the front-line employees as an integral part of the service delivery process often points to improvements in the overall service experience.

Overall, as customer contact increases, the efficiency of the operation decreases. The customer's involvement in the production process creates uncertainties in the scheduling of production. More specifically, the customer has a direct impact on the type of service desired, the length of the service delivery process and the cycle of service demand. Attempting to balance consumer needs with efficient operating procedures is a delicate art.

Regarding the cycle of demand, restaurants would be more efficient if consumers would smooth their demands for food throughout the day as opposed to eating primarily during breakfast, lunch and dinner hours. As one frustrated, senior-citizen McDonald's employee told a customer, 'These people would get better service if they all didn't show up at the same time!' Further complications arise as consumers also dictate the nature or type of service needed. This is particularly frustrating for healthcare workers who provide services to waiting emergency-room patients. Every patient has a different need, some needs are more immediate than others, and you never know what the next ambulance will deliver. Obviously, this scenario is frustrating for waiting patients as well as for the healthcare providers. Finally, even when consumer needs are the same, some consumers ask more questions and/or need more attention than others, thereby affecting the length of demand. As a result, fixed schedules are difficult to adhere to without delays.

During the customer's interaction with the service provider, the customer provides inputs into the service production process. As such, the customer often plays a key role in the successful completion of the service encounter. For example, a patient who feels ill must be able to accurately describe his or her symptoms to a doctor to receive proper treatment. Not only must the symptoms be described accurately, but the patient must also take the recommended dosage of medicines prescribed. In this case, the customer (the patient) becomes a key player in the service production process and can directly influence the outcome of the process itself. Failure of the patient to follow recommended instructions will likely lead to a dissatisfactory service experience. The customer will probably blame the service provider, even though the service provider fulfilled his or her part of the transaction. For example, a hairdresser who cuts, colours and styles just as directed by the customer will not provide as satisfactory a service as the stylist who works with the customer to advise on and moderate their requirements based on their professional experience. In this way the service is created, adapted and customized through the interaction of the provider and the customer.

Another issue directly related to the consumer's presence in the service factory concerns the appearance of the service factory itself. Service factories must be built with consumers' presence in mind. Consequently, the service factory not only provides the service, but in and of itself becomes a key tangible clue in the formation of consumer perceptions regarding service quality. The design and management of the service factory is discussed in much greater detail in Chapter 10, Managing the Firm's Physical Evidence.

Involvement of other customers in the production process. The presence of other customers during the service encounter is the third defining characteristic of inseparability. Because production and consumption occur simultaneously, several customers often share a common service experience. This 'shared experience' can be negative or positive.

The marketing challenges presented by having other customers involved in the production process generally reflect the negative aspects of their involvement. Restaurants once again provide an ideal setting for examples of negative events, including smokers violating the space of non-smokers and vice versa, families with young children sharing the same space with adult couples seeking a quiet dining experience, drunk customers interacting with sober patrons, and the occasional lovers' quarrel that spills over into the aisles. Overall, the primary challenge concerns effectively managing different market segments with different needs within a single service environment. Such will be the case if mobile phone use is approved on airlines. Some passengers will see the addition of this service as overwhelmingly positive while others will view it as noise pollution.

The impact of 'other customers' is not always negative. On the positive side, audience reaction in the form of laughter or screams of terror often enhances the show at a theatre. Similarly, a crowded pub or bar may facilitate the opportunity for social interaction, and a happy crowd may make a concert an even more pleasurable event. As social creatures, humans tend to frequent places of business and feel more comfortable in places that have other customers in them. In fact, the lack of other customers may act as a tangible clue that the impending experience may be less than satisfactory. For example, if given the choice of dining at one of two new restaurants, would you select a restaurant that had no cars in the car park, or would you choose a restaurant down the street with a full car park? In the absence of other information, which restaurant would most potential customers believe would be the better dining experience? Similarly the theatre manager knows that empty seats adversely affect an audience and those with foresight have a pool of 'audience volunteers' they can call on to fill the seats at short notice and lessen the empty auditorium atmosphere.

Special challenges in mass production of services. One final obstacle presented by inseparability is how to successfully mass produce services. The problems pertaining to mass production are twofold. Firstly, because the service provider is directly linked to the service being produced, an individual service provider can produce only a limited supply. Consequently, the question arises: How does one provide enough service product to meet the demand of the mass market? The second problem directly relates to the consumer's involvement in the production process. Consumers interested in a particular provider's services would have to travel to the provider's location. Hence, one of the problems associated with inseparability is how to sell intangible products to a geographically widespread target market.

Possible solutions to inseparability problems

Similar to the solutions proposed for intangibility, marketing practitioners have developed a number of strategies in the attempt to offset or minimize the marketing challenges posed by inseparability. These strategies include

(1) an increased emphasis placed on the selection and training of public contact personnel to ensure that the right types of employees are in the right jobs; (2) the implementation of consumer management strategies that facilitate a positive service encounter for all consumers sharing the same service experience; and (3) the use of multi-site locations to offset the mass production challenges posed by inseparability.

Selecting and training public contact personnel. Contact personnel, unlike goods, are not inanimate objects, and being human, they exhibit variations in behaviour that cannot be controlled by the service process. Moreover, the attitudes and emotions of contact personnel are visible to the customer and can affect the service experience for better or worse. Surly or unhappy employees can affect both customers with whom they come into direct contact and other employees. On the other hand, a bright, highly motivated employee can create a more pleasant service experience for everyone who comes into contact with that person.

As a result of the frequency and depth of interactions between service providers and consumers, selection of service personnel with superior communication and interpersonal skills is a must. In addition, training personnel once they are on the job is also necessary. A case in point is Birmingham City Council. Birmingham City Council has a comprehensive Customer Service Strategy which is changing the way services are delivered, 'to put customers at the heart of everything that we do'. This has been achieved through developing a realistic and flexible customer service strategy founded in delivery. It uses an approach that breaks down traditional barriers between departmental silos, making life simpler for the customer. The new approach has achieved performance improvements of 19 per cent in both efficiency and call handling.

Similarly Maidstone Borough Council has successfully implemented a number of new policies and processes to improve customer service. These include training for all staff, Customer Action Teams, mystery shopping and a new complaints system. The whole process is now performance driven using a mixture of technology (CRM, queuing systems and telephony) and cultural change.

Too often, newly hired employees are often left to fend for themselves. A large percentage of consumer complaints about service focus on the action or inaction of employees. Critics of service quality have focused on 'robotic' responses by staff who have been trained in using the technology associated with the business but not in dealing with different types of customers, a complaint often levelled at those service companies that use call centres. Experts in service quality believe that employees must also be trained in 'soft' management skills such as reliability, responsiveness, empathy, assurance and managing the intangibles that surround the service.

selection and training A strategy that minimizes the impact of inseparability by hiring and educating employees in such a way that the customer's service experience is positive and the employees are properly equipped to handle customers and their needs.

consumer management A strategy service personnel can implement that minimizes the impact of inseparability, such as separating smokers from nonsmokers in a restaurant.

Consumer management. The problems created by inseparability can also be minimized through effective consumer management. Separating smokers from non-smokers is an example of one way to minimize the impact on other customers. Sending directions and check-in procedures to travellers before they arrive at the airport can help control the length of the service encounter. Restaurant reservation systems may help smooth out demand created by traditional cycles. Providing delivery services may eliminate the need for many consumers to be physically present within a service factory, thereby increasing the firm's operating efficiencies. Finally, isolating the technical core of the business from the consumer allows for consumer involvement but limits the customer's direct impact on the firm's operations. For example, the typical neighbourhood dry cleaning business is designed so that customers are attended to at the front counter; meanwhile, the core operation is located in an area of the building where customer contact is not permitted. The management of service consumers is discussed in much greater detail in Chapter 12, People Issues: Managing Service Customers.

Use of multi-site locations. To offset the effects of inseparability on centralized mass production, service firms that mass produce do so by setting up multiple locations. Typical examples include Showcase cinemas, Specsavers opticians, Toni and Guy hair salons and McDonald's restuarants. Multi-site locations serve at least two purposes. Firstly, because the consumer is involved in the production process, multi-site locations limit the distance the consumer must travel to purchase the service. Secondly, each multi-site location is staffed by different service providers, each of whom can produce their own supply of services to serve their local market. Multi-site locations act as factories in the field. Without them, every consumer who desired legal services would have to travel to a single location that housed all the lawyers in the country plus all their clients for that day. Obviously, this is not practical or realistic. Multi-sites can also be one way to achieve a global presence for services which are often intrinsically difficult to export. The football industry is one successful example of this (see Global Services in Action)

The use of multi-site locations is not without its own set of special challenges. Each site is staffed by different service providers who have their own personalities and their own sets of skills. For example, every Specsaver optician does not have the same personality and the same set of skills. The differences in personnel are particularly troublesome for service firms attempting to establish a consistent image by providing a standardized product. The variability in performance from one multi-site location to another and even from one provider to another within a single location leads us to the next special characteristic of services – heterogeneity. Table 2.2 identifies the marketing problems and strategies for overcoming the challenges of inseparability.

multi-site locations A way service firms that mass produce combat inseparability, involving multiple locations to limit the distance the consumers have to travel and staffing each location differently to serve a local market.

factories in the field Another name for multi-site locations.

Characteristic	Marketing problems	Possible solutions
Inseparability	Physical connection of the service provider to the service	Selecting and training public contact personnel
	Involvement of the customer in the production process	Consumer management
	Special challenges in mass production of services	Use of multi-site locations

Table 2.2

Inseparability: Marketing problems and possible solutions

Heterogeneity

One of the most frequently stressed differences between goods and services is heterogeneity – the variation in consistency from one service transaction to the next. Service encounters occur in real time, and consumers are already involved in the factory, so if something goes wrong during the service

---

Global services in action
Football industry's global marketplace

'Hundreds of clubs and firms involved in the football business gathered at the picturesque Jumeriah Beach Resort in Dubai to hear what the global future holds for the industry, and to try and pick up contracts and advice to help them run their operations more profitably.'

A variety of companies were represented, trying to cash in on the sport that's become a multi-billion dollar business. Delegates included perimeter advertising agencies, web developers, customer relations managers, stadium designers, playing pitch manufacturers and sports academies all exhibiting at the Madinat Jumeriah hotel. Also in attendance were film-makers, politicians, bankers and executives from clubs across Europe, Asia and Africa, plus representatives from big-name sponsors and brands such as Nike, Adidas, Sony, Vodafone, 3, and Mastercard.

Many of the biggest clubs in the world, such as Manchester United and Real Madrid were represented here, as were other English clubs such as Aston Villa, Arsenal and Chelsea, all hoping to exchange commercial expertise in a bid to drive up their profits. One delegation attracting a lot of attention was the one from Iraq, looking to rebuild its footballing future and secure continuing help in relaunching the game, as far as it possible, in their country.

A gauge of the importance of the football economy can be seen in the fact that £300m of soccer-related business was done in Dubai in two days in 2003 and much the same has been achieved each year since. A sign of the football industry's importance to Britain can be seen in the fact that the government sent a delegation from UK Trade and Investment. In its sales pitch to drum up business for UK plc it asserted: 'We know the people you need to know... if you are looking for partners, goods or services from the UK in the sports infrastructure arena (we) can help to take your business further, faster.'

A major outcome of this type of exposure is illustrated by the London team, Arsenal's recent business success in signing a deal worth as much as £100m over 15 years, by having its new stadium sponsored by Dubai-based Emirates airline.

Football is no longer a Saturday afternoon's entertainment or as purists would have it 'the beautiful game' but an increasingly valuable service commodity being bought and sold in the global market place.

Sources: Adapted from B. Wilson (2004) http://news.bbc.co.uk/go/pr/fr/-/2/hi/business/4045673.stm.www.fa.org.

Arsenal Football Club's new stadium sponsored by Dubai-based Emirates airline.

process, it is too late to institute quality-control measures before the service reaches the customer. Indeed, the customer (or other customers who share the service experience with the primary customer) may be part of the quality problem. If, in a hotel, something goes wrong during the night's stay, the lodging experience for a customer is bound to be affected; the manager cannot logically ask the customer to leave the hotel, re-enter, and start the experience from the beginning.

Heterogeneity, almost by definition, makes it impossible for a service operation to achieve perfect quality on an ongoing basis. Manufacturing operations may also have problems achieving this sort of target, but they can isolate mistakes and correct them over time, since mistakes tend to reoccur at the same points in the process. In contrast, many errors in service operations are one-time events; the waiter who drops a plate of food in a customer's lap creates a service failure that can be neither foreseen nor corrected ahead of time.

Another challenge heterogeneity presents is that not only does the consistency of service vary from firm to firm and among personnel within a single firm, but it also varies when interacting with the same service provider on a daily basis. For example, some McDonald's franchises have helpful and smiling employees, whereas other McDonald's franchises employ individuals who act like robots. Not only can this be said for different franchises, but the same is true within a single franchise on a daily basis because of the mood swings of individuals.

Marketing problems caused by heterogeneity

The major obstacles presented by heterogeneity translate into the fact that service standardization and quality control are difficult to achieve. Why is this so? Because of the inseparability characteristic previously discussed, you now know that in many instances the service provider must be present to provide the service. Firms such as financial institutions employ a multitude of front-line service providers. As an individual, each employee has a different personality and interacts with customers differently. In addition, each employee may act differently from one day to the next as a result of mood changes as well as numerous other factors. For example, many students who work in bars or restaurants frequently acknowledge that the quality of interaction between themselves and customers will vary from night to night and even from table to table. Hotel desk clerks, airline reservationists and business-to-business service personnel would respond similarly.

The marketing problems created by heterogeneity are particularly frustrating. A firm could produce the best product in the world, but if an employee is having a 'bad day', a customer's perceptions may be adversely affected. The firm may never have another opportunity to serve that customer. Returning to our McDonald's example, the franchisee may pay €400,000 for the franchise and the right to sell a 'proven product'. However, the real secret to each individual franchise's success is the 16-year-old behind the counter who is interacting with customers and operating the cash register. Can you imagine the franchisee who has just spent €400,000 for the franchise trying to sleep at night while thinking that his or her livelihood depends on the 'teenager' behind the counter? It does!

Possible solutions to heterogeneity problems

Solutions proposed to offset the challenges posed by heterogeneity could be considered complete opposites of one another. On one hand, some service firms use the heterogeneous nature of services to provide customized services. In this case, the service offering is tailored to the individual needs of the consumer. The second possible solution is to develop a service delivery system that standardizes the service offering – every consumer receives essentially the same type and level of service. Each of these opposing strategies encompasses a different set of advantages and disadvantages.

customization Taking advantage of the variation inherent in each service encounter by developing services that meet each customer's exact specifications.

Customization. One possible solution to the problems created by heterogeneity is to take advantage of the variation inherent in each service encounter and customize the service. Customization develops services that meet each customer's individual needs. Producers of goods typically manufacture the good in an environment that is isolated from the customer. As such, mass-produced goods do not meet individual customer needs. However, because both the customer and the service provider are involved in the service delivery process, it is easier to customize the service based on the customer's specific instructions.

Note that there are tradeoffs associated with a customized service. On one hand, if everything is provided exactly to the customer's specifications, the customer ends up with a service that meets his or her specific needs; however, the service will take longer to produce. Consequently, the provider can obtain higher prices, which lead to higher profit margins for the provider. Providers pursuing a customization strategy focus on profit margins on a per-customer basis as opposed to achieving profits through a mass volume or turnover strategy.

The downside of providing customized services is threefold. First, customers may not be willing to pay the higher prices associated with customized services. Second, the speed of service delivery may be an issue. customized services take extra time to provide and deliver, and the customer may not have the luxury of waiting for the final product. Finally, customers may not be willing to face the uncertainty associated with customized services. Each customized service is different, so the customer is never sure exactly what the final product will be until it is delivered. So, do customers prefer customized services over standardized services? Intuitively, most believe that customers would prefer customized products; however, the answer is, 'it depends'. If price, speed of delivery and consistency of performance are issues, the customer will probably be happier with a standardized service.

standardization To produce a consistent service product from one transaction to the next.

Standardization. Standardizing the service is a second possible solution to the problems created by heterogeneity. The goal of standardization is to produce a consistent service product from one transaction to the next. Service firms can attempt to standardize their service through intensive training of their service providers, through self-service, or through automation. Training certainly helps reduce extreme variations in performance. However, despite all the training in the world, employees ultimately will continue to vary somewhat from one transaction to the next. One way to eliminate this variance is to replace human labour with machines.

A financial institution's automatic teller machine (ATM) and an automated car wash are prime examples of standardized services that appeal to consumers' convenience-oriented needs. In both instances, consumers key in their service request by answering a series of predetermined automated prompts and the service is then provided accordingly. This type of system minimizes the amount of customer contact and variations in quality during the order and delivery processes. E-Services in Action provides a discussion of the possibilities for 'automation' within public sector services.

E-services in action
Government online

On the face of it, the internet offers an increasingly cost-effective means of connecting policy makers and citizens: a wire runs from the offices of the policy makers into virtually every school, every hospital, every workplace, and into increasingly more homes. The possibilities for two-way communication over the internet are considerable. It is therefore not surprising that governments are trying to persuade their citizens to communicate with them electronically.

The benefits of government online for policy makers are numerous and include quicker and easier dissemination of information, more opportunities to inform and consult with citizens, as well as opportunities to market and deliver some services electronically. Potentially the impact of this could be to reduce operating costs as well as to drive up service quality.

The benefits for government online users are also substantial: a greater choice of ways to communicate with government; improved access to information; increased availability of access (in some cases 24 hours a day and seven days a week); and in some cases improved responsiveness from government.

However implementing e-government raises a number of issues. According to the Commission of the European Communities, 'these include safeguarding trust and confidence in online interaction with governments, widespread access to online services so that no digital divide is created, interoperability for information exchange across organizational and national boundaries and advancing pan-European services that support mobility in the Internal Market and European Citizenship'.

Types of use

Thousands of citizens around the world were asked about the different types of interaction they had with government online. TNS developed a typology of government online use, as follows:

- *Information Seekers* – Have used the internet to get information from a government website.
- *Downloaders* – Used the internet to print off government forms that were then sent by post or fax (e.g. tax form, form to claim government rebates).
- *Consulters* – Used the internet to express a point of view or participate in community consultations with government. This category was introduced from the 2002 study onwards.
- *Providers* – Used the internet to provide personal/household information to government.
- *Transactors* – Used the internet to pay for government services or products through

the use of a credit card or bank account number (e.g. rates, driving licences, recycle bins, traffic fines).

- *Non-users* – Have not used the internet to get or provide information or transact with government.

Some countries could make the argument that their citizens prefer to access government information and services using traditional routes (such as through literature, face-to-face meetings or via telephone). Where good traditional services exist this may well be the case. However, there may be a financial argument for more strenuously promoting the choice of online alternatives. Increasingly commercial organizations find they can offer financial discounts for customers choosing to transact with them online.

The research supports the view that providing citizens with choice of access is not enough. The public need to be aware that the service exists and have the technology and skills to access it, and the services themselves must be those that they need and want.

Source: Adapted from D. Dalziel (2004) TNS Social Research, United Kingdom.

On the positive side, standardization leads to lower consumer prices, consistency of performance and faster service delivery. However, some consumer groups believe that standardization sends the message that the firm does not really care about individual consumer needs and is attempting to distance itself from the customer. Perceived distancing is particularly an issue as organizations are increasingly replacing human labour with machines such as automated phone services. In many instances, customers are becoming increasingly frustrated when forced to select from a menu of phone messages. Of course, standardization and customization do not have to be all-or-nothing propositions. Numerous companies, particularly in the travel and tourism arena, provide a standardized core product and allow consumers to select options to semi-customize their final outcome. Table 2.3 lists the special marketing challenges posed by heterogeneity and possible solutions to those challenges.

Perishability

The fourth and final unique characteristic that distinguishes goods from services is perishability. Perishability refers to the fact that services cannot be saved, their unused capacity cannot be reserved and they cannot be

Table 2.3	Characteristic	Marketing problems	Possible solutions
Heterogeneity: Marketing problems and possible solutions	Heterogeneity	Difficult to standardize service and quality control	Customization Standardization – consistent service

inventoried. Unlike goods that can be stored and sold at a later date, services that are not sold when they become available cease to exist. For example, hotel rooms that go unoccupied for the evening cannot be stored and used at a later date; airline seats that are not sold cannot be inventoried and added on to aircraft during the holiday season, when airline seats are scarce; and service providers such as dentists, lawyers and hairstylists cannot regain the time lost from an empty client appointment book.

Some service firms find it possible to inventory part of their service process. Mechanics can, for example, inventory spare parts for a fairly lengthy period; however, garages cannot inventory the entire service experience. Spare capacity in the system cannot be saved for times of peak demand.

The inability to inventory creates profound difficulties for marketing services. When dealing with tangible goods, the ability to create an inventory means that production and consumption of the goods can be separated in time and space. In other words, a good can be produced in one locality in Europe and transported for sale in another. Similarly, a good can be produced in January and not released into the channels of distribution until June. In contrast, most services are consumed at the point of production. From a goods-marketing manager's point of view, concerns about when and where the customer consumes the product are important in understanding consumer behaviour and motivation but are largely irrelevant in day-to-day operations.

The existence of inventory also greatly facilitates quality control in goods-producing organizations. Statistical sampling techniques can be used on warehouse stock to select individual items for testing, to the point of destruction if necessary (e.g., car crash tests). The sampling process can be set up to ensure minimum variability in the quality of product released for distribution. Quality-control systems also provide numerical targets against which managers can work. It is thus possible for Procter & Gamble to produce tens of millions of packages of Tide laundry detergent that are essentially identical. In contrast, when you purchase a room at a hotel, you are likely to experience a wide range of factors that may influence your good night's sleep. Issues such as air conditioning, plumbing and noisy neighbours factor into the hotel guest's experience.

Finally, in goods-producing businesses, inventory performs the function of separating the marketing and the production departments. In many organizations, stock is actually sold at a transfer price from one department to another. The two parts of the firm have what amounts to a contract for quality and volumes. Once this contract has been negotiated, each department is able to work relatively independently of the other. In service firms, however, marketing and operations constantly interact with each other – because of the inability to inventory the product (Bateson, 1997).

Marketing problems caused by perishability

Without the benefit of carrying an inventory, matching demand and supply within most services firms is a major challenge. In fact, because of the unpredictable nature of consumer demand for services, the only way that supply matches demand is by accident! For example, as a manager, try to imagine scheduling checkout staff at a supermarket. Although we can estimate the times of the day that the shop will experience increased demand, that demand may fluctuate widely within any 15-minute interval. Now try to imagine forecasting demand for a hospital's emergency ward, an entertainment theme park, or a ski resort. Demand can be 'guesstimated' but will rarely be exact. Simply stated, consumer demand for many services at any given time is unpredictable. The lack of inventories and the need for the service provider to provide the service leads to several possible demand and supply scenarios. In contrast to their service-producing counterparts, manufacturers of goods could more easily adapt to these scenarios through selling or creating inventories.

Higher demand than maximum available supply. Within this scenario, consumer demand simply outpaces what the firm can supply, which results in long waiting periods and, in many cases, unhappy customers. Business may be lost to competitors as waiting times become too excessive for consumers to endure. Ironically, in cases of consistent excess consumer demand, consumers may continue to attempt to patronize a firm out of curiosity and/or the social status obtained by telling others of their experience: 'We finally got in to see the show!' This has certainly been true of the Glastonbury music festival where demand consistently outstrips supply and thousands of unlucky would-be attendees wait for the next year. The organizers have encouraged the participation and loyalty of those unable to gain a ticket through web-based communities and TV, radio, web and pod casts of the event.

Higher demand than optimal supply level. In many instances, the consequences associated with demand exceeding optimal supply may be worse than when demand exceeds maximum available capacity. By accepting the customer's business, the firm implicitly promises to provide the same level of service that it always provides, regardless of the quantity demanded. For example, it seems that airlines typically staff flights with the same number of flight attendants regardless of the number of tickets actually sold. However, when demand exceeds optimal levels, the service provided is generally at inferior levels. As a result, customer expectations are not met, and customer dissatisfaction and negative word-of-mouth publicity results.

When demand exceeds optimal supply levels, the temptation is to accept the additional business. However, in many instances the firm's personnel and operations are not up to the task of delivering service effectively beyond optimal demand levels. For example, suppose that a landscaper became very successful in a short time by providing high-quality services to upscale customers. As the word spread to other potential clients, demand for the landscaper's time dramatically increased. As the firm expanded to serve new clients via the purchase of new equipment and the hiring of new personnel, the landscaper quickly found that he was losing control over the quality of service delivered by his firm. His new personnel simply did not provide the same level of service that his original customer base had grown accustomed to receiving. Over time the landscaper lost his new clients as well as his old clients, and he eventually filed for bankruptcy. In this case the service traits of perishability, inseparability and heterogeneity all took their toll on the business.

Lower demand than optimal supply level. As we discussed earlier, providing the exact number of supermarket checkouts needed at any given time is a challenge for most shop managers. One solution would be to staff each line with a full-time cashier; however, this strategy would result in an inefficient deployment of the firm's resources. During times when demand is below optimal capacity, resources are underutilized (e.g., cashiers are standing around), and operating costs are needlessly increased.

Demand and supply at optimal levels. The optimal scenario is to have demand match supply. This scenario describes the situation in which customers do not wait in long queues and in which employees are utilized to their optimal capacity. Because services cannot be stored, a buffer to ease excess demand cannot be developed. Moreover, service providers are not machines and cannot produce a limitless supply. Consequently, service demand and supply rarely balance. Customers do at times experience lengthy waits, and service providers are sometimes faced with no one to serve.

Possible solutions to perishability problems

Because service demand and supply balance only by accident, service firms have developed strategies that attempt to adjust supply and demand to achieve a balance. The strategies presented here are possible solutions to overcome the difficulties associated with the perishability of services (Sasser, 1976). The first group of strategies concerns the management of the firm's demand. This discussion is followed by a second group of strategies that focuses on managing supply.

Demand strategy: Creative pricing. Creative pricing strategies are often used by service firms to help smooth demand fluctuations. For example, offering price reductions in the form of 'earlybird specials' and 'matinees' have worked well for restaurants and cinemas, respectively. Price-conscious target markets, such as families with children, are willing to alter their demand patterns for the cost savings. At the same time, service firms are willing to offer price reductions to attract customers during non-peak hours, thereby making their operations more efficient. By shifting demand to other periods, the firm can accommodate more customers and provide better service during periods in which demand in the past has been (1) turned away because of limited supply, and (2) not served as well as usual because demand surpasses optimal supply levels.

Creative pricing has also been used to target specific groups such as senior citizens, children and their parents (families), and students. This type of pricing strategy has not only helped smooth fluctuating demand but has also aided in separating diverse target markets from sharing the same consumption experience at the same time. For example, by providing family-type specials during late afternoon and early evening hours, a restaurant significantly reduces the amount of potential conflict between its 'family customers' and its 'adult-only customers', who generally dine later in the evening.

creative pricing Pricing strategie often used by service firms to help smooth demand fluctuations, such as offering 'matinee' prices or 'earlybird specials' to shift demand from peak to non-peak periods.

Price incentives have also been used recently to persuade customers to use the company's website. Customers who are willing to place their orders on the internet may do so 24 hours a day, 7 days a week. Increasing website usage reduces demand for personal service during regular business hours.

Demand strategy: Reservation systems. Another common strategy used to reduce fluctuations in demand is to implement a reservation system by which consumers ultimately reserve a portion of the firm's services for a particular time slot. Typical service firms that use reservation systems include restaurants, doctors of all varieties, golf courses (tee times), and day spas. On the plus side, reservations reduce the customer's risk of not receiving the service and minimize the time spent waiting in line for the service to be available. Reservation systems also allow service firms to prepare in advance for a known quantity of demand. Consequently, the customer and the firm benefit from improved service.

Despite the advantages of a reservation system, a host of disadvantages also accompanies this strategy. First, someone must maintain the reservation system, which adds additional cost to the operation. Next, customers do not always show up on time or sometimes fail to show up at all. As a result, the operation ends up with unused services and lost revenues. For example, a common strategy for some golfers (particularly young and single) is to reserve a tee time at two or three different golf courses at two or three different times on the same day. Depending on their whims and which golf course they decide to play that particular day, the golfers choose which tee time to use, leaving the other two golf courses holding the tee for a foursome that is not going to show up. Given that the greens fee for an 18-hole round with buggy averages at least €75, the golf course has just lost €300 that it could have otherwise collected by filling the spot with another foursome.

Another drawback of reservation systems is that they offer to the customer an implied guarantee that the service will be available at a specified time, thereby increasing the customer's expectation. All too often, this implied guarantee is not met. For example, customers with early appointments may show up late, causing a chain reaction of delayed appointments for the rest of the day. Similarly, the rate at which restaurant tables turn over is difficult to determine and is further compounded by the size of the party sitting at a table compared with the size of the party waiting for a table. In addition, GPs often schedule as many as four patients at the same appointment time in an attempt to serve patient demand. Despite the use of reservation systems, customers may still end up waiting and become even more unhappy (compared with a 'first come, first serve' system) because of the implied promise made by the reservation system.

Demand strategy: Development of complementary services. The trials and tribulations associated with perishability can also be buffered by developing complementary services that directly relate to the core service offering. A lounge in a restaurant is a typical example of a complementary service that not only provides the space to store customers while they wait but also provides the restaurant with an additional source of revenue. Similarly, golf courses often provide putting greens for their customers as a form of complementary service. Although free of charge to customers, the putting green occupies the customers' time, thereby minimizing their perceived waiting time. The result is more satisfied customers. Other complementary services that have been developed to help manage demand include tea and coffee at the hairdressers, bars and restaurants at cinemas, reading materials in doctors' offices and televisions in the waiting areas of hospital emergency rooms.

Demand strategy: Development of non-peak demand. The effects of perishability can also be modified by developing non-peak demand. Non-peak demand development utilizes service downtime to prepare in advance for peak periods, and/or to market to different market segments with different demand patterns. Consequently, non-peak demand development can reduce the effects of perishability in two ways. Firstly, employees can be cross-trained during non-peak demand periods to perform a variety of other duties to assist fellow personnel (e.g., dishwashers may be trained to set up and clear tables) during peak demand periods. In addition, although services cannot be stored, the tangibles associated with the service (such as salads at a restaurant) can be pre-prepared and ready prior to the service encounter. Advance preparation activities such as these free personnel to perform other types of service when needed.

> **Non-peak demand development** A strategy in which service providers use their downtime to prepare in advance for peak periods or by marketing to a different segment that has a different demand pattern from the firm's traditional market segment.

Secondly, non-peak demand can also be developed to generate additional revenues by marketing to a different market segment that has a different demand pattern from the firm's traditional segment. For example, fitness centres have filled non-peak demand by marketing to housewives, senior citizens and shift workers (e.g., factory workers, nurses, students and teachers) who use gym during the morning and afternoon hours, which are traditionally slow periods during weekdays. These groups exhibit different demand patterns from traditional gym users, who work from 8:00 am to 5:00 pm and demand services in the late afternoons, early evenings and at weekends.

Supply strategy: Part-time employee utilization. In addition to managing consumer demand, the effects of perishability can also be minimized through strategies that make additional supply available in times of need. One such supply strategy is the use of part-time employees to assist during peak demand periods. For many years, retailers have successfully used part-time employees to increase their supply of service during the holidays.

> **part-time employees** Employees who typically assist during peak demand periods and who generally work fewer than 40 hours per week.

The advantages of employing part-time workers as opposed to adding additional full-time staff include lower labour costs and a flexible labour force that can be employed when needed and released during non-peak periods. On the negative side, using part-time employees sometimes causes consumers to associate the firm with lower job skills and lack of motivation and organizational commitment. Such traits subsequently lead to dissatisfied customers. However, these disadvantages appear most commonly in organizations that staff their operations with part-time workers on a full-time basis as opposed to employing part-time employees only during peak demand periods.

capacity sharing
Strategy to increase the supply of service by forming a type of co-op among service providers that permits co-op members to expand their supply of service as a whole.

Supply strategy: Capacity sharing. Another method of increasing the supply of service is capacity sharing, forming a type of service co-op with other service providers, which permits the co-op to expand its supply of service as a whole. For example, many professional service providers are combining their efforts by sharing the cost and storage of expensive diagnostic equipment. By sharing the cost, each service firm is able to supply forms of service it may not otherwise be able to provide because of the prohibitive costs associated with such equipment. In addition, the funds saved through cost sharing are freed to be spent on additional resources such as equipment, supplies and additional personnel, thereby expanding the supply of service to consumers even further. Dental surgeries and other private medical group practices offer typical examples of capacity sharing in application, as do hairdressers operating out of a shared salon.

expansion preparation
Planning for future expansion in advance and taking a long-term orientation to physical facilities and growth.

Supply strategy: Advance preparation for expansion. Although the strategy of expansion preparation does not provide a 'quick fix' to the supply problems associated with perishability, it may save months in reacting to demand pressures, not to mention thousands of euros in expansion costs. In an effort to prepare in advance for expansion, many service firms are taking a long-term orientation with regard to constructing their physical facilities.

For example, one local airport was built with future expansion in mind. This facility was built on an isolated portion of the airport property, where no adjoining structure would interfere with future growth. All plumbing and electrical lines were extended to the ends on both sides of the building and capped, making 'hook-ups' easier when expansion becomes a reality. Even the road leading to the terminal was curved in the expectation that new terminal additions will follow along this predetermined pattern.

third parties A supply strategy in which a service firm uses an outside party to service customers and thereby save on costs and personnel.

Supply strategy: Utilization of third parties. A service firm can also expand its supply of a service through use of third parties. Service organizations frequently use third parties to service customers and thereby save on costs and personnel. Travel agencies are a typical example. Travel agents provide the same information to customers as an airline's own representatives. This third-party arrangement, however, enables the airline to reduce the number of personnel it employs to make flight reservations and lets it redirect the efforts of existing personnel to other service areas. The cost savings associated with using third parties is evidenced by the airlines' willingness to pay commissions to travel agencies for booking flights.

Note that although the use of third parties increases the supply of service, this type of arrangement may expose customers to competitive offerings as well. As a result, a trade-off does exist. Many third parties, such as travel agents, represent a variety of suppliers. A customer who intended to book a flight on British Airways may end up taking a Lufthansa flight because of a more compatible flight schedule and/or a less expensive fare. This type of competitive information would not have been available if the customer had called British Airways directly to make the flight reservation.

Supply strategy: Increase in customer participation. Another method for increasing the supply of service available is to have the customer perform part of the service. For example, in many fast-food restaurants, customer participation means giving customers a cup and expecting them to fill their own drink orders. In other restaurants, customers make their own salads at a 'salad bar', and make their own chocolate sundaes at the 'dessert bar'. Sainsbury's now have self-service checkouts where customers scan their own purchases and pay by credit or debit card. A more extreme example is the Formule1 hotel chain which operates almost without personnel using automated entry and payment systems, self-service breakfasts from machines and even self-cleaning toilets.

customer participation
A supply strategy that increases the supply of service by having the customer perform part of the service, such as providing a salad bar or dessert bar in a restaurant.

Without a doubt we are performing more and more of our own services every day. We pump our own petrol, complete our own bank transactions at cash points (ATMs), pack our own shopping at supermarkets and even assemble our own furniture. In fact, one of the major advantages of a website is that it enables customers to help themselves, or at least be more prepared when they request help from service personnel. However, although self-service does free employees to provide other services, a number of advantages and disadvantages are associated with customer participation. The willingness of customers to provide their own service is generally a function of convenience, price and customization. For example, ATMs offer the customer the convenience of 24-hour banking, and Dell Computers provides customers the opportunity to configure their own personal computer order to their individual specifications.

In contrast, customer participation may also be associated with a number of disadvantages that predominantly concern loss of control. In many instances, the more the customer becomes a major player in the production of the service, the less control the service firm is able to maintain over the quality of the service provided. For example, the doctor who instructs a patient to administer his own medicine relinquishes control over the outcome of the prescribed care. Quality control may also suffer as a result of confused customers who decrease the efficiency of the operating system. Customer confusion in a self-service environment is likely to affect not only the outcome of the confused customer's service, but also the delivery process of other customers who are sharing that customer's experience. For example, customers who are standing in line behind a customer who is using an automatic check-in for the first time experience the effects of the new customer's learning curve.

The loss of quality control may also be accompanied by the loss of control over operating costs. Self-service, particularly in the food industry, is associated with waste as a result of abuse of the system. Customers may take more food than they would normally order and then consume or share food with non-paying friends.

Finally, increasing customer participation may be interpreted by some customers as the service firm's attempt to distance itself from the customer. As a result, the image of an uncaring, unresponsive and out-of-touch firm may develop, driving many customers away to full-service competitors. Hence, the trade-off is apparent. While increasing customer participation frees service providers to provide additional services and may provide the customer with increased convenience, opportunities for customization, and reduced prices, this strategy may also create unhappy customers who are forced to fend for themselves. Table 2.4 provides a list of possible solutions to the various marketing problems posed by perishability.

The role of marketing in the service firm

This chapter has outlined some of the factors that characterize services marketing in general, and some of the problems that service marketers face. Due to the effects of intangibility, inseparability, heterogeneity and perishability, marketing plays a very different role in service-oriented organizations than it does in pure goods organizations. As a result of the effects of intangibility, inseparability, heterogeneity and perishability, this chapter has shown how closely the different components of the service organization are interwoven. The invisible and visible parts of the organization, the contact personnel and the physical environment, the organization and its customers, and indeed the customers themselves, are all bound together by a complex series of relationships. Consequently the marketing staff must maintain a much closer relationship with the rest of the service organization than is customary in many goods businesses. The concept of the operations department being responsible for producing the product and the marketing department being responsible for selling it cannot work in a service firm. This is

Table 2.4	Characteristic	Marketing problems	Possible solutions
Perishability: Marketing problems and possible solutions	Perishability	Higher demand than maximum available supply	*Demand strategy*: Creative pricing
			Demand strategy: Reservation systems
		Higher demand than optimal supply level	*Demand strategy*: Development of complementary services
		Lower demand than optimal supply level	*Demand strategy*: Development of non-peak demand
			Supply strategy: Part-time employee utilization
			Supply strategy: Capacity sharing
			Supply strategy: Advance preparation for expansion
			Supply strategy: Utilization of third parties
			Supply strategy: Increase in customer participation

clearly demonstrated in the Global Services in Action box where the marketing of the service (football) is far wider than the core operational aspects of 'football' as entertainment.

Summary

The major differences between the marketing of goods and the marketing of services are most commonly attributed to four distinguishing characteristics – intangibility, inseparability, heterogeneity and perishability. This chapter has discussed the marketing challenges presented by these four characteristics and possible solutions that minimize their impact on service firms.

Intangibility means that services lack physical substance and therefore cannot be touched or evaluated like goods. The marketing challenges associated with intangibility include difficulties in communicating services to consumers, pricing decisions, patent protection, and storage of services for future use. Strategies developed to offset the challenges posed by intangibility include the use of tangible clues, organizational image development and the development of personal sources of information that consumers access when selecting service providers.

Inseparability reflects the interconnection between service providers and their customers. Unlike the producers of goods, service providers engage in face-to-face interactions with their customers, who are directly involved in the service production process. Strategies developed to minimize the challenges of inseparability include the selective screening and thorough training of customer contact personnel, the implementation of strategies that attempt to manage customers throughout the service experience and the use of multi-site facilities to overcome the inseparability difficulties associated with centralized mass production.

Heterogeneity pertains to the variability inherent in the service delivery process. The primary marketing problem associated with heterogeneity is that standardization and quality control are difficult for a service firm to provide on a regular basis. Service firms typically react to heterogeneity in two diverse directions. Some firms try to standardize performance by replacing human labour with machines. In contrast, other firms take advantage of the variability by offering customized services that meet individual customer needs. Neither strategy is universally superior, because customer preference for customization versus standardization is dependent on price, speed of delivery and consistency of performance.

Perishability refers to the service provider's inability to store or inventory services. Services that are not used at their appointed time cease to exist. Moreover, because services cannot be inventoried, the few times that supply matches demand often occur by accident. A variety of strategies have been developed to try to offset the potential problems created by perishability. Some strategies attack the problems by attempting to manage demand, while others attempt to manage supply. Demand management strategies include creative pricing strategies, reservation systems, staging demand through complementary services and developing non-peak demand periods. Supply management strategies include using part-time employees, capacity sharing, third-party utilization, increasing customer participation in the production process and preparing in advance for future expansion to reduce the response time in reaction to demand increases.

Because of the challenges posed by intangibility, inseparability, heterogeneity and perishability, marketing plays a very different role in service-oriented organizations than it does in pure goods organizations. Traditional management practices, which work under the premises that the operations department is solely responsible for producing the product and the marketing department is solely responsible for selling it, cannot work in a service firm. The four characteristics presented in this chapter that distinguish the marketing of goods from the marketing of services provide ample evidence that the invisible and visible parts of the organization, the contact personnel, the physical environment, and the organization and its customers are bound together by a complex set of relationships. As a result, marketing must maintain a much closer relationship with the rest of the service organization than is customary in a traditional goods manufacturing plant.

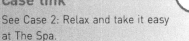

Case link

See Case 2: Relax and take it easy at The Spa.

Notes

1 The framework for this chapter was adapted from Figures 2 and 3 in Valerie A. Zeithaml, A. Parasuraman and Leonard L. Berry, 'Problems and Strategies in Services Marketing', *Journal of Marketing* 49 (Spring 1985): 33–46. For a more in-depth discussion of each of the problems and strategies associated with services marketing, consult Figures 2 and 3 in this article for the appropriate list of references.

Discussion questions

1 Discuss how the unique service characteristics of intangibility, inseparability, heterogeneity and perishability apply to the case 'Relax and take it easy at The Spa'.

2 Explain why the pricing of services is particularly difficult in comparison with the pricing of goods.

3 Evaluate the strategies used by the insurance industry to minimize the effects of intangibility. Illustrate your answer with examples of companies who have done this successfully and those that have not.

4 Discuss the implications of having the customer involved in the production process.

5 Provide examples of the difficulties in standardization and quality control throughout the service delivery process.

6 Evaluate the benefits and drawbacks to the customer of (1) a customized service or (2) a standardized service.

7 Discuss the limitations associated with a service firm's inability to maintain inventories.

References and further reading

Bateson, J. E. G. (1995) *Managing Services Marketing*, 3rd ed., Fort Worth, TX: Dryden Press.

Berry, L. L. and Parasuraman, A. (1993) 'Building a new academic field – the case of services marketing', *Journal of Retailing* 69 (1).

Gabbott, M. and Hogg, G. (1997) *Contemporary Services Marketing: A Reader*, London: Dryden Press.

Grönroos, C. (1978) 'A service-oriented approach to marketing of services', *European Journal of Marketing* 12 (8): 588–601.

Gummesson, E. (1987) 'Lip service – a neglected area in services marketing', *Journal of Services Marketing* 1: 22.

Lovelock, C. H. (1983) 'Classifying services to gain strategic marketing insights', *Journal of Marketing* 47 (Summer): 9–20.

Price, J. (2005) 'Making a difference where it counts: Birmingham's delivery experience', *Strategic Director of Adults & Communities, Birmingham City Council*, www.publicsectorforums.co.uk/.

Sasser, W. E. (1976) 'Match supply and demand in service industries', *Harvard Business Review* (November/December): 133–140.

Shostack, G. L. (1977) 'Breaking away from product marketing', *Journal of Marketing* 41 (April): 73–80.

Taylor, P. (2005) 'CRM and customer care – Batman & Robin or Basil and Sibil', *Assistant Director for Customer Services, Maidstone Borough Council*, http://www.publicsectorforums.co.uk.

Van der Zwan, F. and Bhamra, T. (2003) 'Services marketing: taking up the sustainable development challenge', *Journal of Services Marketing* 17 (4): 341–356.

Zeithaml, V. A. (1981) 'How consumer evaluation processes differ between goods and services', in J. H. Donnelly and W. R. George, eds, *Marketing of Service*, Chicago, IL: AMA.

Zeithaml, V. A. and Bitner, M. J. (1996) *Services Marketing*, Singapore: McGraw-Hill.

Chapter 3
An overview of the services sector

The scientist who pauses to examine every anomaly he notes will seldom get significant work done

(Kuhn, 1970)

Chapter objectives

This chapter provides an overview of the service economy by introducing the main service sectors. Although on the surface many of these sectors seem quite diverse, service classification schemes are discussed that assist in our understanding of the commonalities among service industries. Trends and concerns pertaining to the growth of service industries are presented, which further our understanding of the service economy. Finally, this chapter explores the predicted keys to success within the service sector.

After reading this chapter, you should be able to:

- Describe the main sectors that comprise the service economy.

- Discuss how classification schemes that identify commonalities among service industries can be used as learning tools.

- Identify the trends and concerns pertaining to the growth of the service economy.

- Address the keys to operating a successful service firm.

Services in context
Giants rule

The international lodging industry is a vital part of the travel and tourism trade and is one of the largest economic forces in the world. Accounting for 11 per cent of the world's economic output and more than 250 million jobs, the hotel industry is the third-largest foreign currency earner. The World Travel and Tourism Council estimated that total worldwide travel and tourism revenues would reach US$7.9 trillion in 2005. The industry is dominated by hotel chains, especially in the United States and Europe, although Asia saw a supply increase of 10 per cent in 2003, the largest rise worldwide. Most of the world's largest hotel chains are based in the United States. Attempting to expand their customer base, hotel chains, led by Holiday Inn, have turned to segmentation, offering various types of lodging facilities based on size, service, and space.

According to a 2004 MKG Consulting survey, the world's top ten hotel groups handle three-quarters of the global hotel market, which totalled approximately 4.6 million rooms. About 70 per cent of these hotels are located in Europe and North America, according to the International Hotel Association.

Operating in nearly 100 countries, Accor is one of Europe's leading hotel franchises.

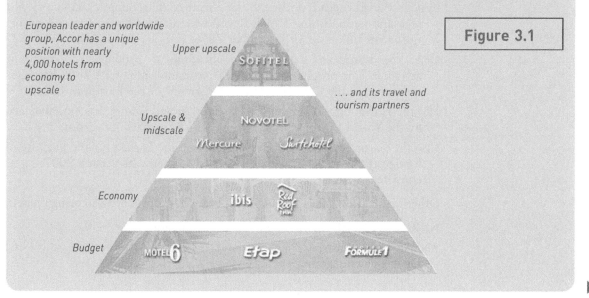

European leader and worldwide group, Accor has a unique position with nearly 4,000 hotels from economy to upscale

Upper upscale — SOFITEL

... and its travel and tourism partners

Upscale & midscale — NOVOTEL, Mercure, Suitehotel

Economy — ibis, Red Roof Inn

Budget — MOTEL 6, Etap, FORMULE1

Figure 3.1

A major European player in the hotel industry is French industry giant Accor who own and manage a wide portfolio of brands operating across the world. However, in France and the United Kingdom small, independent hotels still account for about 50 per cent of the market's value.

In thirty-five years Accor has built a unique network of more than 4,100 hotels. It sees its balanced hotel portfolio as a major asset through growth phases and hard times alike with a range of brands targeting each market segment, international coverage to match worldwide demand, and a preference for direct management.

Sources: Accor (2007), Gale Group (2006).

Introduction

Thus far, we have discussed the basic differences between goods and services in Chapters 1 and 2. The focus of this chapter is the service economy. We take an in-depth look into the service economy by providing an overview of the main service economy sectors including education, health and government services, financial activities, communication and media, leisure and hospitality, professional and business services, transportation and utilities, and wholesale and retail trade. These service sectors relate to the European classification system (NACE) of economic activities and products, which is currently being revised. The revision of the NACE codes and other international and national classification systems comes under the remit of 'Operation 2007', and was being finalized in 2007. The revision concerns:

Case link

For a study of how to expand sales through services, see Case 16: Kenny's Bookshop.

ISIC and CPC: the UN statistical classifications of activities and products, respectively, adopted by the UN Statistical Commission in March 2006.

NACE: the European statistical classification of economic activities. The regulation establishing NACE Rev. 2 was adopted by the Council of the European Union on 19 December 2006.

CPA: the European statistical classification of products by economic activities. The proposal for a regulation establishing CPA 2008 has been submitted to the Council and the Parliament of the European Union.

HS: the Harmonized Commodity Description and Coding System, managed by the World Custom Organization, which finalized its version 2007.

CN: the European statistical classification of goods used for the purpose of foreign trade statistics, which is revised annually. Its version 2007 is consistent with HS 2007.

Other regional classifications of products and industries are also being revised:

NAICS: the North American Industry Classification

ANZSIC: the Australia-New Zealand system of classification and JSIC: Japan's classification.

These revisions are motivated by the need to adapt the classifications to changes in the world economy. The revised classifications reflect the growing importance of service activities in the economy over the past 15 years, mainly due to developments in information and communication technologies (ICT). Table 3.1 details the main classifications within the revised system and highlights those which refer to service sectors.

A prime use of ISIC is for internationally comparable reporting of economic statistics by activity or industry in many statistical domains: for this reason, the new ISIC also reflects the outcome of a convergence exercise between NACE and NAICS (Eurostat, 2007).

A	Agriculture, Forestry and Fishing	
B	Mining and quarrying	
C	Manufacturing	
D	Electricity, gas, steam and air conditioning supply	
E	Water supply, sewerage, waste management and remediation activities	
F	Construction	
G	Wholesale and retail trade; repair of motor vehicles and motorcycles	S*
I	Accommodation and food service activities	S*
H	Transportation and storage	S*
J	Information and communication	S*
K	Financial and insurance activities	S*
L	Real estate activities	S*
M	Professional, scientific and technical activities	S*
N	Administrative and support service activities	S*
O	Public administration and defence; compulsory social security	S*
P	Education	S*

Table 3.1

2007 revised industry classifications (ISIC Rev. 4 – NACE Rev. 2)

▶

Q	Human health and social work activities	S*
R	Arts, entertainment and recreation	S*
S	Other service activities	S*
T	Activities of households as employers; undifferentiated goods- and services-producing activities of households for own use	
U	Activities of extraterritorial organizations and bodies	

S* = service sector

Other service classification schemes are also presented, which highlight the commonalities among these service industries. For example, you might wonder what a bank clerk and an airline ticket agent have in common. The answer is quite a lot! This chapter also discusses the major influences and concerns pertaining to the growth of the service economy. Clearly, technological, socio-cultural and competitive forces impact the economy's direction and rate of growth. Concerns about the economy's reliance on its service sector and the continued decline of its industrial sector are also discussed. Finally, we conclude with a summary of the predicted key factors that many believe lead to success within the service sector.

What is the service economy?

service economy
Includes the 'soft parts' of the economy consisting of several sectors.

It is generally accepted that the service economy includes the 'soft parts' of the economy consisting of several industry sectors – education and health services, financial activities, government, information, leisure and hospitality, professional and business services, transportation and utilities, wholesale and retail trade, and other services. The *service sector* is one of the three main categories of a developed economy – the other two being *industrial* and *agricultural*. Traditionally, economies throughout the world tend towards a transition from an *agricultural economy* to an *industrial economy* (e.g, manufacturing and mining) to a *service economy*. Viewing the service sector as a third stage in economic development has led to it being termed the 'tertiary' sector of the economy. The United Kingdom was the first economy in the modern world to make this transition. Several other countries including the US, Japan, Germany and France have made this transition and many more are expected to do so at an accelerated rate. The increased rate of transformation has generally been caused by a competitive marketplace. Simply stated, goods are more amenable to international trade than services, thereby making them more vulnerable to competitive actions. Countries that industrialize their economies first eventually come under attack by other countries that are newly making the transition from an agricultural to an industrial economy. These 'newcomer' countries offer lower production costs (especially labour), which is attractive to industry. Consequently, as industrial sectors flow from one country to the next, the countries they abandon begin to rely more heavily on the growth of their service sectors as the mainstay of their economies. This whole process repeats itself over and over again as other less developed countries enter the fray, consequently facilitating the transformation from agriculture to industrial to service-based economies.

The European Commission sees services as important for the developed as well as for developing country economies. The rapidly expanding services sector is contributing more to economic growth and job creation worldwide than any other sector. The services sector is accounting for some three-quarters of the gross domestic product (GDP) for the EU and on average for 50 per cent for the developing countries. Additionally, over three-quarters of EU jobs are in the services sector. No country can prosper today without an efficient service infrastructure as:

- It is the prerequisite for economic performance. Producers and exporters of textiles, cars or computers will not be competitive without access to efficient banking, insurance, accountancy, telecom or transport systems.
- It is a prerequisite for development: access to world-class services helps exporters and producers in developing countries to capitalize on their economic strength.
- It leads to consumer savings, faster innovation and technology transfer.
- It contributes to long-term investment.

(European Commission, 2007)

An overview of the main service industry sectors driving the world economy is provided below, with much of the material provided by Eurostat, the statistical data service for the European Commission.

SOURCE © ELENATHEWISE/DREAMSTIME.COM

Education and health services and the public sector

The education and health services sector consists of two parts: (1) the educational services subsector and (2) the healthcare and social assistance subsector. The educational services sector includes schools, colleges, universities and training centres. One in four Europeans are currently enrolled in educational institutions, rising to almost one in three in some countries (Iceland has the highest participation rate). Accordingly, educational services, including both public and private institutions, are one of the largest employers and public expenditure on education accounts for an average of 6 per cent of European GDP (European Commission, 2005). The healthcare and social assistance sector comprises health services such as hospitals, nursing care facilities, doctors (general practitioners), health centres and home healthcare services. In turn, social assistance includes individual and family services, vocational rehabilitation services, community food and housing, and emergency and other relief services. Healthcare expenditure in the European union represented 7.7 per cent of GDP in 2003 and is set to rise due largely to ageing populations (Eurostat, 2007b).

The government or public sector consists of publicly owned establishments of national, regional and local agencies that administer, oversee and manage public programmes. Examples of such agencies include those that set policies, create laws, adjudicate civil and criminal legal cases, provide public safety and national defence. Public schools and public hospitals are also included in the government sector. Government sector employment is projected to have the lowest rate of increase of any other service sector.

Financial services

Financial services provide instruments to both businesses and consumers in the form of products that are essentially savings or loans, or products to transfer and pool risk. Changes in financing techniques have increased the possibilities open to business to fund investment, while consumers have a wider array of choices for credit, savings and payment methods.

The finance and insurance industries experienced growing deregulation, globalization and consolidation into the mid-2000s. As countries throughout the world – including industrial leaders such as Japan, the United States, Germany and France – liberalized their finance systems, banks and insurance brokers pursued foreign markets and began to integrate their services. In addition, banks and insurers continued consolidating in order to achieve cost-effective economies of scale and scope, as well as to increase their product offerings to customers. Rankings of the world's largest financial service firms were repeatedly reshuffled as mergers created new industry giants; many companies ended 2004 with total assets valued over US$1 trillion. In total, the banking industry's top 1000 banks had total assets of US$52.39 trillion in 2004 (Gale Group, 2006b). According to national accounts, in Europe, financial services (NACE Section J) generated EUR 489.4 billion of value added in 2004. According to results from the Labour Force Survey 6.1 million persons were employed in financial services in 2005 in Euro-25. Of these just over three-fifths (62.1%) were employed in financial intermediation activities other than insurance and pension funding, one-fifth (20.8%) in insurance and pension funding activities, while the remainder (17.0%) were occupied in activities auxiliary to financial intermediation.

Communications and media

The information sector consists of establishments that produce and distribute information and cultural products, provide the means to distribute or transmit these products, and/or process data. Major players in this sector include publishing industries (both traditional and internet publishing), the film and sound recording industries, the broadcasting industries, the telecommunication industries, internet service providers and web search portals, data processing industries, and information services industries. A distinction has to be made between traditional activities (for example, postal services) for which growth is rather stable and other more modern activities (such as mobile telephony and electronic publishing), for which growth developments are more marked (Eurostat, 2006).

The information technology services market realized exceptional growth in the late 1990s. IT services represented US$350 billion worldwide in programming, systems integration, consulting, outsourcing, education and training, and maintenance services revenues in 1998 alone. By 2004, this value had increased to US$607.8 billion. The world leader in the IT service sector continued to be IBM, accounting for 7.6 per cent of the total sales worldwide.

Following the economic downturn of the early 2000s, which lasted into 2003, the IT services industry suffered through declining revenues and mass job insecurity. By 2004, industry consolidation was the norm; *InternetWeek* reported 57 mergers and acquisitions in the first half of the year alone. The overall outlook for outsourcing was positive, with more growth expected in management services. As of the mid-2000s, 59 per cent of the market remained with US companies (Gale Group, 2006c).

Communications, publishing and printing together generated EUR 321.0 billion of value added in the EU-25 in 2003 and employed 4.8 million persons. Telecommunications generated the largest part of the sectoral value added in 2003, accounting for over half (54.2%) of the total, while publishing, printing and the reproduction of recorded media was the second largest subsector with a 28.0 per cent share of value added; the smallest part of this sector was post and courier activities which generated less than one-fifth (17.9%) of sectoral value added. The composition of the sector in employment terms was very different, as less than one-quarter (23.8%) of the sectoral workforce was employed in telecommunications. Despite having the lowest value added share, post and courier activities had the largest workforce of the three subsectors covered, with 38.3 per cent of the communications, publishing and printing total, marginally higher than the share recorded for publishing, printing and the reproduction of recorded media (37.9%).

This is one sector that is becoming harder to delineate with the increasing convergence of telecommunications, computing and media broadcasting technologies (see E-Services in Action later in this chapter).

Leisure and hospitality

The leisure and hospitality sector comprises two sectors – the arts, entertainment and recreation sector; and the accommodation and food services sector. The arts, entertainment and recreation sector includes establishments that (1) produce, promote, or participate in live performances, events, or exhibits intended for public viewing; (2) preserve and exhibit objects and sites of historical, cultural, or educational interest; and (3) operate facilities that provide amusement, hobby and leisure-time interests. The number of people needed in arts and entertainment occupations is set to increase up to 2010. The fastest-growing occupations are expected to be in artistic and literary categories. The sector is also heavily dependent on self-employed freelancers, short-contract workers and volunteers. The majority of arts and entertainment companies are small and medium-sized enterprises (SMEs) (fewer than 10 employees) (National Guidance Research Forum, 2007).

The accommodation and food services subsector (hospitality industries) includes establishments providing lodging and/or meal, snack, or beverage preparation for immediate consumption. This sector accounts for 12 per cent of European Union GDP (IHRA, 2002) and emerged as one of the largest employers accounting for 11.9 per cent of the total workforce, with 8.2 million persons employed in the EU-25 (Eurostat, 2007).

Hotels, food services and drinking places provide many young people with their first job, with the highest proportion of young people being employed in this sector. There is also a larger proportion of female and part-time workers in this sector than in other service industries. A growing subsector that combines travel, accommodation and entertainment and provides a business service is discussed in B2B Services in Action.

B2B services in action
MICE tourism

MICE tourism is fundamentally different from general business tourism as it has everything to do with tourism industry infrastructure, marketing and perception. MICE tourism is the new buzzword in international tourism markets and relates to various forms of business tourism involving groups of business travellers rather than individual business travellers. MICE stands for: meetings, incentives, conferences and exhibitions.

A meeting is defined as an event designed to bring people together for the purpose of exchanging information, either from within one company or organization or from a broader spectrum of people: cocktail functions, product launches, lunch, dinner and breakfast meetings, as well as special occasions such as weddings would constitute a meeting as defined by the WTO.

Incentives are the second category of this market segment and include travel to a foreign country or domestically as part of a motivational incentive scheme to increase or reward employee effort.

The definition of conferences is highly contentious but is generally accepted as being a multi-day event having at least 100 delegates attending the event for the purpose of exchanging information. Such a conference is termed to be an international conference if 40 per cent of the delegates originate from outside the host country. Conferences are thus differentiated from meetings by both the duration of the event and the number of people attending.

Finally exhibitions involve the bringing together of people for the purposes of viewing products and services.

The attraction of the MICE industry is based predominantly on the fact that it is the fastest-growing segment of the tourism market. Internationally MICE tourism accounted for $90 billion in 1997 and the industry is growing at between 8 and 10 per cent per annum.

Europe is home to the world's top city in terms of organized meetings – Vienna (although Berlin hosts more meetings). Stockholm, Helsinki and Prague have been the fastest-growing destinations in recent years, whilst Copenhagen currently holds the strongest position worldwide in terms of the number of meetings scheduled to be held between now and 2015.

Vienna became Europe's new number-one meetings city in 2003, taking over from Barcelona, which had led the field the previous year. Stockholm held position, whilst Berlin rose from ninth to fourth place, and Lisbon to fifth.

After a difficult few years, the US looks set to return to form, with 60 per cent more meetings scheduled for the next decade than its closest competitor, Australia. This points to a re-emergence of the North American market, and a possible loss of market share for Europe. However, the healthy number of meetings posted for the recently ailing Italian, British and French markets bodes well for their turnaround. The changing fortunes of MICE host nations is partly due to the fact that 53 per cent of world meetings and conferences rotate world-wide, with the remaining 47 per cent being rotated around specific regions such as Europe (27%) and Asia (4%), with $47.7 billion spent on internationally rotating MICE activities.

Sources: Cope (2005) MICE Tourism – Europe – May 2005, Mintel.
Johannesburg Tourism (2007), Tourism Strategy, available from www.joburg.org.za/unicity/tourism.

Professional and business services

Growth in this sector has been rapid due to the outsourcing phenomenon that has seen many enterprises use service providers for non-core professional activities (such as the development of software, accounting, or legal services) or operational activities (such as industrial cleaning and security services). Value added generated in 2003 by the EU-25's business services (NACE Divisions 72 and 74) sector was EUR 703 billion and 18.1 million persons were employed in this sector (Eurostat, 2007). Professional, scientific, and technical services is one of the highest paying industries across all supersectors. The professional and business services supersector includes a multitude of activities such as legal advice and representation, accounting, bookkeeping, payroll services, engineering, research services, advertising services, veterinary services, office administration, hiring and placement of personnel, clerical services, security and surveillance services, cleaning, and waste disposal services.

Transport services

Transport services include: land transport, which includes railways, urban transport systems, road and other land transport, as well as transport by pipelines; water transport; air transport; auxiliary transport activities and travel agencies. The transport services sector (NACE Divisions 60 to 63) in the EU-25 generated EUR 334 billion of value added in 2003. Some 8 million persons were employed and the strongest growth was for supporting and auxiliary transport activities and activities of travel agencies (NACE Division 63), for which annual growth averaged 2.1 per cent per annum over the five-year period 2000 to 2005. Environmental issues remain of great importance to this sector, as transport is a major source of emissions and noise, as well as land use (see Global Services in Action).

Wholesale and retail trade

Wholesaling activity consists of selling to retailers or to industrial, commercial, institutional and professional users. Wholesalers can act on a fee or contract basis as agents or for their own account. In the supply chain, wholesalers are located between producers and users, providing know-how and knowledge in markets for which they have expertise. Competition

---

Global services in action
EU transport policies failing on climate

Introduction

The surge in transport demand means that greenhouse-gas emissions from the sector are still steadily increasing, threatening the EU's Kyoto goals, according to the European Environment Agency. In the context of the Kyoto Protocol, the EU has committed itself to reducing greenhouse-gas emissions (GHG) by 8 per cent, compared with 1990 levels, before 2012. Transport is responsible for around one-fifth of all GHG emissions in the EU.

In 2001, the EU set out a ten-year strategy to make its transport sector more sustainable, mainly by breaking the link between growth in transport and economic growth and by shifting towards more sustainable transport modes (intermodality), such as railways, water transport and public transport. However, the Commission's mid-term review of the White Paper, adopted in June 2006, makes no reference to curbing overall transport growth, instead advocating the 'decoupling of transport growth from its negative effects'.

Recent proposals aimed at introducing cleaner fuels such as biofuels and imposing caps on CO2 emissions from cars also appear to go in this direction.

Issues

While emissions from most sectors, such as energy supply, industry and agriculture, dropped between 1990 and 2004 in the EU-15, greenhouse-gas emissions from transport rose by 26 per cent, as the intro-duction of green technologies failed to keep up with the spiralling demand for transport, says a report by the European Environment Agency (EEA), published on 26 February 2007.

Air transport volumes increased the most in that period (by 86%), but road transport is the biggest problem, as it accounts for 93 per cent of greenhouse gas from transport.

The study says that failure to internalize transport's external costs through pricing mechanisms and massive government transport subsidies, amounting to between €270 and €290 billion annually – of which at least half go towards roads – are largely to blame for the rapid growth in transport volumes. Furthermore, such policies also serve to direct transport choices towards less environmentally friendly modes.

The report also highlights the effect that transport is having on our health. With nearly one-quarter of the EU population living less than 500 meters from a road carrying more than three million vehicles per year, the EEA estimates that almost four million 'life-years' are lost annually because of high pollution levels.

Industry responses

The International Road Transport Union (IRU) believes that investing in new road infrastructure is part of the solution: 'Limited infrastructure causes traffic jams with growing aggravation... Clearing bottlenecks, building new infrastructure and making existing road systems work more efficiently helps reduce the environmental impact of city roads.'

The European Road Federation (ERF) said: 'There is no reason to expect CO2 emissions to decrease at the same rate in all sectors.' It underlined that, according to the Stern Report, the economic cost of CO2 reduction would be minimized with a tax of about €20–25 per tonne of CO2 and adds: 'The specific taxes already paid by the road transportation sector in most European countries represent about ten times the amount. Road transport, therefore, is spearheading the battle for CO2 reduction and if its lead were followed by all other sectors of the economy then CO2 emissions would be under control.'

International Association of Public Transport (UITP) states that: 'We need to reduce the volume of traffic. Technology alone cannot provide a solution, we have to change people's behaviour too', suggesting that the EU should set non-binding targets for all member states, to reduce car traffic by 1 per cent annually over the next five years.

Source: Published: Monday 26 February 2007, Updated: Thursday 1 March 2007, Euractiv.com.

within the wholesale trade activity is often centred on providing more efficient or more sophisticated value added services. Wholesalers can provide a range of services from basic storage and break of bulk, sorting, grading and logistics to pre- and post-production operations. Value added in the EU-25's wholesale trade sector (NACE Division 51) was EUR 423.8 billion in 2003, and 8.8 million persons were employed in it. The largest wholesale trade subsector in value added and employment terms was the wholesale trade of consumer goods.

Retail trade provides an interface between producers and consumers. Typically, one or several distributors intervene before a product which leaves the factory gate reaches the final consumer, the last of which is a retailer. Most retail trade jobs (83 per cent) consist of sales and administrative support positions. In 2003, the retail trade and repair sector (NACE Division 52) employed some 16.0 million persons in the EU-25, while value added was EUR 366.9 billion.

E-commerce in recent years has played an increasing role in the shopping patterns of consumers, who may prefer to order goods from their home for convenience, or alternatively purchase items from afar that are not on offer locally. According to Eurostat's information society statistics, some

SOURCE CHRIS HEWES/MILD PLACES PHOTOGRAPHY/ALAMY

Retailers such as B&Q provide an interface between producers and consumers.

8 per cent of the turnover of distributive trades (including motor trades and wholesale trades as well as retail trade and repair) enterprises with ten or more persons employed was derived from e-commerce in 2005.

Real estate, renting, leasing

Real estate, renting and R&D enterprises enable their clients to focus on their own activities and reduce the need to occupy their own personnel on ancillary or supporting tasks or, in the case of real estate, renting and leasing services, to commit their own capital. It is widely believed that outsourcing of these activities has increased within the EU and will continue to do so. While research and development enterprises essentially provide business services, a large part of real estate, renting and leasing services are provided to households. Value added generated in 2003 by the EU-25 real estate, renting and R&D sector was EUR 290 billion, with 3.3 million persons employed in this sector.

Service classification schemes: What can service industries learn from one another?

The service sectors discussed earlier illustrate the diversity of activities within the service economy. Our next objective is to determine what service firms in different sectors can learn from one another. Clearly, there will be exceptions. However, as the opening quotation in this chapter states, 'The scientist who pauses to examine every anomaly he notes will seldom get significant work done.' Consequently, one of the major themes of this text is to convey the message that service sectors should not be studied as separate entities (such as banking, transportation, business services, healthcare, and food service firms). Seemingly too often, companies diminish their own chances to develop truly innovative ideas by examining only the practices of competitors within their own industries. Many service industries share common service delivery challenges and therefore would benefit from sharing their knowledge with each other. Unfortunately, many service firms look only to firms within their own industry for guidance. For example, banks look to other banks, insurance companies look to other insurance companies, and so on. This myopic approach slows the progress of truly unique service innovations within each of the respective industries. One needs only to consider the advances that hospitals could make if they borrowed concepts from restaurants and hotels instead of relying only on other hospitals for innovative service ideas.

Marketing has traditionally developed classification schemes to facilitate our managerial understanding of how different products share similar characteristics. For example, the consumer products classification scheme of *convenience*, *shopping*, and *specialty* products taught in introductory marketing classes aids our understanding of how consumers spend their time shopping and their information requirements for various products. Similarly, the industrial products classification scheme of *raw materials*, *supplies*, *accessories*, *component parts and materials,* and *installations* has led to numerous implications concerning promotional mix strategies, types of goods purchased, evaluation processes, usage behaviour, and purchasing procedures, to name a few.

Classification schemes applied solely to services have also been developed to facilitate our understanding of what different types of service operations have in common. Early attempts at developing classification categories are presented in Table 3.2 and include the following:

- degree of tangibility
- skill level of the service provider
- labour intensiveness
- degree of customer contact
- goal of the service provider.

Although somewhat helpful in developing our understanding of what different services have in common, early service classification schemes failed to provide meaningful managerial implications to marketers. Subsequent classification schemes have been developed, which have proven to be more useful (Lovelock, 1983). Presented in Tables 3.3 through 3.7, these classification categories include the following:

- Understanding the nature of the service.
- Is the nature of the service a tangible action or intangible action?
- Is the direct recipient of the service a person or a thing?
- Relationships with the customer.
- Is the nature of the service delivery continuous or discrete?
- Does the service firm have a membership relationship with its customers or no formal relationship?
- Customization and judgement in service delivery.
- Is the extent to which customer contact personnel exercise judgement in meeting customer needs high or low?
- Is the extent to which service characteristics are customized high or low?

Degree of tangibility	Labor intensiveness	Goal of the service provider
Owned goods	People-based	Profit
Rented goods	Equipment-based	Nonprofit
Nongoods		

Skill level of the service provider		Degree of customer contact
Professional		High
Nonprofessional		Low

Table 3.2

Traditional service classifications

- The nature of demand relative to supply.
- Can peak demand usually be met without a major delay or does peak demand regularly exceed capacity?
- Is the extent to which demand fluctuates over time wide or narrow?
- Method of service delivery.
- What is the nature of the interaction between the customer and the organization? Does the customer go to the service organization? Does the service organization come to the customer? Do customer and service organization transact business at arm's length?
- Is service available at a single site or multiple sites?

Table 3.3	What is the nature of the service act?	Who or what is the direct recipient of the service?	
Understanding the nature of the service act		**People**	**Things**
Source Christopher H. Lovelock, 'Classifying Services to Gain Strategic Marketing Insights', *Journal of Marketing* 47 (Summer 1983), pp. 9–20. Reprinted by permission of the American Marketing Association.	**Tangible actions**	Services directed at people's bodies	Services directed at goods and other physical possessions
		Health care	Freight transportation
		Passenger transportation	Industrial equipment repair and maintenance
		Beauty salons	Janitorial services
		Exercise clinics	Laundry and dry cleaning
		Restaurants	Landscaping/lawn care
		Haircutting	Veterinary care
	Intangible actions	Services directed at people's minds	Services directed at intangible assets
		Education	Banking
		Broadcasting	Legal services
		Information services	Accounting
		Theatres	Securities
		Museums	Insurance

Nature of service delivery	Type of relationship between the service organization and its customers	
	'Membership' relationship	No formal relationship
Continuous delivery of service	Insurance Telephone subscription College enrollment Banking Automobile association	Radio station Police protection Lighthouse Public highway
Discrete transactions	Long-distance phone calls Theatre series subscriptions Commuter ticket or transit pass	Car rental Mail service Toll highway Pay phone Movie theatre Public transportation Restaurant

Table 3.4

Relationships with customers

Source Christopher H. Lovelock, 'Classifying Services to Gain Strategic Marketing Insights', *Journal of Marketing* 47 (Summer 1983), pp. 9–20. Reprinted by permission of the American Marketing Association.

Extent to which customer contact personnel exercise judgement in meeting individual customer needs	Extent to which service characteristics are customized	
	High	Low
High	Legal services Health care/surgery Architectural design Executive search firm Real-estate agency Taxi service Beautician Plumber Education (tutorials)	Education (large classes) Preventive health programmes
Low	Telephone service Hotel services Retail banking (excluding major loans) Good restaurant	Public transportation Routine appliance repair Fast-food restaurant Movie theatre Spectator sports

Table 3.5

Customization and judgement in service delivery

Source Christopher H. Lovelock, 'Classifying Services to Gain Strategic Marketing Insight', *Journal of Marketing* 47 (Summer 1983), pp. 9–20. Reprinted by permission of the American Marketing Association.

Services marketing classes may want to discuss each of these classification schemes and their marketing implications. For example, many service jobs such as a bank clerk and an airline gate agent, who on the surface seem quite different, actually perform similar tasks and experience many of the same

Table 3.6

The nature of demand for the service relative to supply

Source Christopher H. Lovelock, 'Classifying Services to Gain Strategic Marketing Insight', *Journal of Marketing* 47 (Summer 1983), pp. 9–20. Reprinted by permission of the American Marketing Association.

Extent to which supply is constrained	Extent of demand fluctuations over time	
	Wide	**Narrow**
Peak demand can usually be met without a major delay	Electricity Natural gas Telephone Hospital maternity unit Police and fire emergencies	Insurance Legal services Banking Laundry and dry cleaning
Peak demand regularly exceeds capacity	Accounting and tax preparation Passenger transportation Hotels and motels Restaurants Theatres	Services similar to those above but that have insufficient capacity for their base level of business

Table 3.7

Method of service delivery

Source Christopher H. Lovelock, 'Classifying Services to Gain Strategic Marketing Insight', *Journal of Marketing* 47 (Summer 1983), pp. 9–20. Reprinted by permission of the American Marketing Association.

Nature of interaction between customer and service organization	Availability of service outlets	
	Single site	**Multiple site**
Customer goes to service organization	Theatre Barbershop	Bus service Fast-food chain
Service organization comes to customer	Lawn care service Pest control service Taxi	Mail delivery Automobile emergency repairs
Customer and service organization transact at arm's length (mail or electronic communications)	Credit card company Local TV station	Broadcast network Telephone company

customer-related challenges throughout a typical day. Consequently, lessons that have been learned in the front lines of banking operations may be of value to those who work on the front lines of the airline industry.

Service economy growth: Key influences and concerns

Several key forces continue to influence the growth of the service sector. These forces include the emergence of technologically based e-services, socio-cultural forces derived from an aging population, and the competitive force of 'out-servicing', which involves the *offshoring, outsourcing,* and *industrialization* of many services. The continued growth and dominance of the service sector has been met with some criticism. As the manufacturing base in many countries declines there is an increased fear amongst some individuals (and governments) that without manufacturing, there will be little for people to service.

Technological influences: The emergence of e-services

One of the most profound changes driving the growth of the service economy and the way service firms conduct business has been the phenomenal advance in technology, in particular the internet. Sometime around 1996, the obsession with the internet began. Thousands of businesses, customers, employees and partners got wired to one another and began conducting business processes online ('e-business'). Eventually, more and more customers (B2B and B2C) became wired and formed a critical mass. Through repeated usage, customer trust dramatically increased, and the Net became a viable means for revenue production and economic growth ('e-commerce').

E-service defined. What exactly is an e-service? According to Hewlett-Packard (www.e-service.hp.com), 'an e-service is an electronic service available via the Net that completes tasks, solves problems, or conducts transactions. E-services can be used by people, businesses and other e-services and can be accessed via a wide range of 'information appliances'. E-services that are available today include your local bank's online account services, mail package tracking services, online tax return completion, and SMS updates on football team performances. In essence, an e-service is any asset that is made available via the Net or other electronic medium that creates new efficiencies and new revenue streams (see E-Services in Action). In an internet context, the term *asset* can include any software application that is placed on the net and made available as an *ap-on-tap*. Applications-on-tap refer to e-services that are available for rent on the internet. Those who provide aps-on-tap are known as ASPs (application service providers). One of the many intriguing aspects of e-services is that they apparently overcome many of the traditional challenges faced by service marketers – namely, intangibility, inseparability, heterogeneity

e-service An electronic service available via the Net and other IT tools that completes tasks, solves problems, or conducts transactions.

applications-on-tap Computer programs, such as word processing or web design, that can be rented via e-service providers.

ASPs Application Service Providers: e-service organizations that rent computer programs such as word processing or web design applications.

and perishability. This is particularly true of information-based services (Lovelock and Gummesson, 2004; Pitt et al., 1999).

Managing intangibility. Perhaps the main problem associated with intangibility is that service marketers have nothing to show the customer. E-services can overcome some of the challenges provided by intangibility by using the web to provide evidence of service. For example, an innovative Ford Motor Company dealership is planning to install video cameras in its service bays to provide a live feed to the dealership's website. This strategy will enable customers to visit the service bay (without actually being there) and check on

---

E-services in action
Digital convergence is coming of age

Europe's economy is beginning to reap the benefits of ever-more interlinked and interoperable online technologies, but many obstacles remain to be overcome.

The convergence of different information-society technologies, such as cable television and radio, fixed-line and mobile telephony and the internet became a reality only quite recently, as a result of technological progress that made high-bandwidth connections available to most citizens in the developed world, using different mobile- and fixed-connection methods. Convergence is expected to completely change the way people access digital content. Consequently, it will result in many new business models and have important job-creation effects.

Europe is second behind Japan and Korea (but before North America) for mobile content distribution and mobile TV, and second behind the US for broadband content distribution.

- *Textual content* generated, in 2005, the most important revenues on the internet (around €850 million per year). This was, however, equivalent to no more than 2 per cent of the publishing industry's total annual revenues. By 2010, this percentage is predicted to raise to 5.4 per cent or €2 billion, coming in second after games.

- Online and mobile *games* generated almost €700 million in revenues in 2005;

they are predicted to become the single biggest source of revenue on the internet, generating €2.3 billion in 2010.

- *Videos and movies:* This market is deemed to become the fastest-growing in the near future, with an expected growth of revenues from €30 million in 2005 to €1.2 billion in 2010. The lion's share of revenues, researchers say, will come from membership-based video-on-demand services.

- *Music:* The foremost market for online distribution in Europe, with Apple's iTunes still in the lead. In 2005, €120 million in turnover and €67 million in profit were generated. Until 2010, these figures are expected to increase by a factor of ten.

- *Radio:* 15 million Europeans listen to streaming radio broadcasts every week. By 2010, that figure is expected to more than double, and 11 million Europeans are expected to listen to podcasts regularly. Radio will, however, remain to be first and foremost an on-the-air medium, with €250 million or 5 per cent of all radio advertising revenues coming from the online market.

Source: EurActiv.com, Published: Friday 26 January 2007, Updated: Tuesday 6 February 2007.

their vehicle's progress throughout the day. Other websites such as the Royal Automobile Club (RAC) in Europe provide tangible evidence by e-mailing new members who join online almost instantaneously with the new member's membership number and policy document. Green Flag roadside rescue sends an automated yet very reassuring text message to stranded motorists to confirm that help is on its way and give an estimated time of arrival. E-services also make tangible the intangible by providing additional evidence such as the appearance of the site, the frequency of information updates, the accuracy of information, the speed of the server and ease of navigation. The use of tools such as virtual exhibitions, web- and podcasts can also be used to increase tangibility online. Through these, customers are able to sample information-based e-services prior to purchase, which is not true of traditional physical-based services such as hairstyling, surgical procedures and dental services.

Managing inseparability. Inseparability reflects the simultaneity of service production and consumption. Inseparability also describes services as a shared experience in which, in many cases, the producer and the consumer both have to be present in order for the transaction to be completed. In addition, other customers are often involved in the service delivery process and the mass production of services is difficult if not impossible. E-services minimize the impact of inseparability in numerous ways. Firstly, the service provider and the customer no longer need to occupy the same physical space to complete the transaction. Customers submit their requests from one location and the order is received and processed by the provider at another location. Secondly, customers can initiate and consume the transaction in their own home or office; consequently, consumption is no longer a shared experience with other customers. In addition, e-services enable the mass production of information-based services. For example, customers wishing to download music are able to do so 24 hours a day 7 days a week.

Managing heterogeneity. The characteristic of heterogeneity reflects the variability in quality of service provided from one transaction to the next. When services are provided by people, variations are going to occur and mistakes will happen in real time. Service providers are human and they have good days and bad days. In contrast, e-services are electronically based; variations in quality provided from one customer to the next should be minimal. The airline's website, the bank's automated teller machine, and the credit card company's automated telephone system provide the same level of service consistently day-in and day-out. In addition, other e-services that perhaps monitor customer service conversations may assist future customer service training sessions as typical problems are identified and resolved, and appropriate responses to customer complaints are formalized.

As discussed in Chapter 2, one of the possible solutions to minimize the challenges presented by heterogeneity is to provide customized solutions. Because of the modularity of e-services, solutions to individual customer requests can be more easily customized. For example, an airline passenger can easily book departure and return flights online that best meet his or her individual schedules. E-services help customers help themselves, thereby transferring the service production process into the hands of consumers. Information that is requested on websites requires that consumers become active participants in the process to the point where the customers themselves are actually becoming 'partial employees'. For example, if a customer places an order over the phone, the service firm has a paid employee who answers that phone, records the order, and requests billing and shipping information. By providing an access portal on the web, that same company can reduce its labour costs by having customers input that same information on the company's website. In essence, the customer is now working for the service provider.

Another suggested method to reduce the negative effects of heterogeneity is to standardize (or industrialize) the service. Once again, e-services can be very effective. Because e-services are accessed at a distance (e.g., web, mobile phone, and PDA), customer involvement in the actual production process is minimized. Customers are often purposely led step by step to control the flow of the process. Because one-third of customer complaints are related to problems caused by the customers, a number of companies are instituting fail-safe procedures into their online operations. Examples include informing customers what information they are going to need prior to the encounter, providing online map services so that customers will not get lost driving to physical locations, requesting that customers enter e-mail addresses twice to cut down on data entry errors, and having customers 'click' as opposed to type in choices and information whenever possible.

Managing perishability. Perishability reflects the challenges faced by service marketers as a result of the inability to inventory services. Supply and demand problems are rampant. Services that are not consumed at their appointed time cease to exist. Hotel rooms that are not sold on Thursday night cannot be added to the supply of rooms available for occupancy on Friday night. E-services are not faced with these same problems. E-services are available 24 hours a day, 7 days a week. Applications not purchased one day are available for sale the next. E-services such as online auctions can help airlines fill unused capacity. On the demand side of the equation, if ten customers want to rent the same e-service application on the same day, this is not a problem. Although not perfect, information-based e-services can handle supply and demand fluctuations with much greater ease than most other types of physical-based services, such as restaurants, hospitals and hotels.

E-services are able to overcome many of the traditional challenges faced by service marketers as a result of three main properties – *quantization*, the ability to *search*, and the ability to *automate*. Traditional service firms often bundle their offerings to the customer. For example, a hotel may bundle the room, breakfast and dinner, and a show for one price. Quantization (the breaking down of services [modularity] into component parts) allows opportunities for unparalleled mass customization. In addition, search – the ability and ease at which information can be sought, facilitates ultra-efficient information markets. As such, supply and demand can be more carefully monitored and matched. Finally, by offering consumers choices on a 24/7 basis,

quantization The breaking down of monolithic services into modular components.

search The ability and ease at which information can be sought.

automation – replacing tasks that require human labour with machines, overcomes the traditional limitations of time and space. The objectivity of online transactions can also be used to create greater trust in the service process. For example, ticket allocation for oversubscribed events (eg. The Football World Cup, Glastonbury Festival) has been successfully automated to reassure customers of the fairness of the process and also to prevent ticket touting (the selling on of tickets at a higher price). In 2007, Michael Eavis, the organizer of Glastonbury Festival, used an online application and allocation system requiring a digital photo of the applicant to ensure that the person buying the ticket was the person attending. This move was instigated in order to prevent the ticket fraud and ticket auctioning that had marred the festival's reputation in previous years.

automation Replacing tasks that required human labour with machines.

Socio-cultural influences: Ageing

A second key trend influencing the growth of the service economy involves the many demographic changes that are taking place throughout the world. In essence, a type of chain reaction is occurring that facilitates the growth of the service sector. Consumers have less time than ever to accomplish their various roles. The growth in the number of time-pressured consumers has led to an increase in time-saving services such as restaurants, housekeeping services, laundry services, hairstyling shops and tax preparation services. The time saved through the use of these services is now being spent on entertainment, travel and recreation services.

The continued growth of the service sector throughout the world will be influenced by each area's demographic make-up.

In 1950 all European countries had an elderly population age 65 and above of some 45 million; in 1995 the population age 65+ had already more than doubled to 101 million; by 2050 Europe will have 173 million people aged 65 and above. Ageing is most serious in Southern Europe. According to UN projections, almost one-third of the population (32.5%) will be aged 65 or older in 2050. In Northern Europe, by contrast, 'only' 25 per cent of the population will be aged 65 or older in 2050 (ERD, 2007). In addition, advances in healthcare and more health-conscious consumers have led to a dramatic growth in 'older' market segments who are living longer but are also healthier and more active than before. Although the immediate implication is an increase in demand for healthcare-related services, other service sectors stand to benefit from an ageing population. The over-50 age group also controls a large proportion of wealth and has a higher level of discretionary income and leisure time than the younger population. In fact, the term woofs, which stands for 'well-off older folks', has been coined to represent this group's purchasing power. It has also been noted that this particular group is engaged in 'down ageing' – acting younger than one's years. As a result, amusement and recreation services are one of the fastest employment growth industries within the service sector. In addition, personal services that assist older age groups in accomplishing everyday activities are also experiencing increases in demand.

woofs 'Well-off older folks,' that segment of the population that controls 77 per cent of the nation's assets and 50 per cent of its discretionary income.

Consider the fact that since 2006 the Baby Boomers have been turning 60. This large market grew up with the frugality of the post-war years but have changed along the way. They expect to live longer and healthier lives and generally feel and act younger than those before them. However, the wealthier Baby Boomers are also less well equipped than their forbears to deal with the financial frustrations of older age, as they experience a long period of economic inactivity. On a more tactical level, it is to be assumed that digital media will become increasingly relevant to targeting this audience, as the Baby Boomers age and take their different patterns of media consumption with them (Wood and Armstrong, 2006).

Competitive influences: Outservicing

offshoring The migration of domestic jobs to foreign host countries.

outsourcing The purchase and use of labor from a source outside the company.

industrialization Mechanized or automated services that replaced human labour with machines.

Service sector growth is undoubtedly also being impacted by 'outservicing', which involves the *offshoring (international outsourcing)*, *outsourcing*, and *industrialization* of many services. In developed countries, there is a tremendous amount of anxiety over international outsourcing of services and a belief that one-way outsourcing from developed countries to developing countries will lead to massive job losses in countries such as the United States and United Kingdom. However, Amiti and Wei (2005) provide evidence that most developed countries tend to run surpluses (the rest of the world outsources more to them than the reverse) in, for example, business services and computer and information services. In fact, the United States and the United Kingdom have run the largest and second largest surpluses in services trade in the world in recent years (Amiti and Wei, 2005).

The migration pattern of service jobs should be somewhat predictable. In many cases it is based on economic diversity and a common language. For example, the English-speaking world consists of some of the most developed economies (US, UK and Australia) and some of the poorest (India and Pakistan). Consequently, India and Pakistan offer a competitive advantage (wage structure) to host service jobs that serve the more developed English-speaking economies. An example of this is the location of UK and US based firm call centres in India. In contrast, much of the worldwide Spanish-speaking population has roughly the same income distribution. As a result, one would expect less offshoring of service jobs within Spanish-speaking economies. Similarly, isolated languages such as Italian should spare Italy from the offshoring phenomenon.

The loss of corporate service jobs is fuelled by other sources as well – *domestic outsourcing* and the industrialization of services. Because of outsourcing, many middle-class corporate jobs are now undertaken by independent contractors. Although this phenomenon has fuelled the growth of the professional business services sector, wages and benefits for these jobs are often lower. Technological advances have industrialized (automated) many services, further taking its toll on the service sector workforce. Information-based services are most at risk for automation. We have already experienced the transition of automated simple services (e.g., data entry and credit card processing) to more complex services (e.g., market research, tax returns, billing and customer service). Experts predict that the automation of engineering, management, publishing, financial services and education are not far behind. Interestingly, not all service sectors are necessarily vulnerable. The physical services such as nursing, construction workers, hairstyling, restaurant and hotel workers, which require the physical presence of the service worker and customer, seem to be the most protected, although there is an increase in 'health tourism' from and within several European countries. This phenomenon occurs when medical treatment can be obtained more quickly and easily in other countries and, as an extra bonus, can be combined with a holiday.

Service sector growth concerns: To make or to serve?

Although the service economy is growing in leaps and bounds, not everyone is rejoicing. Materialismo snobbery (Raynor, 1993) reflects the attitude that only manufacturing can create real wealth and that all other sectors of the economy are parasitic and/or inconsequential. Materialismic individuals believe that without manufacturing, there will be little for people to service. As a result, more people will be available to do less work, driving wages down and subsequently decreasing the standard of living. This view is sometimes expressed by even mainstream economists. According to them, real wealth in a society is created only by visible products that are generated by agriculture or industry. The services sector which produces invisibles does not lead to any improvement of wealth on a long-term basis. This skepticism about the services sector derives from the inability to store the products of the sector for future use which could be considered as a symbol of the wealth of a nation. Hence, its growth over and above the growth of storable product sectors would make a country dependent on the rest of the world (Wijewardena, 2006).

materialismo snobbery Belief that without manufacturing there will be less for people to service and so more people available to do less work.

The service sector produces 'intangible' goods, some well known – government, health, education – and some quite new – modern communications, information, and business services. Producing services tends to require relatively less *natural capital* and more *human capital* than producing agricultural or industrial goods. As a result, demand has grown for more educated workers, prompting countries to invest more in education – an overall benefit to their people. Another benefit of the growing service sector is that by using fewer natural resources than agriculture or industry, it puts less pressure on the local, regional and global environment. Conserving natural capital and building up human capital may help global development become more environmentally and socially sustainable. Growth of the service sector will not, however, be a miracle solution to the problem of sustainability, because agricultural and industrial growth are also necessary to meet the needs of the growing world population (World Bank, 2007).

Table 3.8 shows the rise in GDP accountable to the service sector in countries around the world. It has been suggested that countries which generate a share of 60 per cent and above from the services sector have been able to record a sustainable GDP expansion over the years. The larger share of services has not, as claimed by critics, retarded growth. In fact, growth in the services sector has helped them to improve both agriculture and the industry sectors on efficiency grounds, infusing sustainability to those two sectors as well. It can be argued that a share of about 65 to 70 per cent in the service sector provides a country with immense prospects for wealth creation, provided it gains competitive advantage in the production of such services. In this context, the future growth prospects available to China are enormous, since its service sector still accounts for only 35 per cent of its GDP (Wijewardena, 2006). Manufacturing is not, therefore, superior to services or vice versa. The two are interdependent. In fact, half of all manufacturing workers perform service-type jobs (Economist, 1993).

Although some experts disagree, some believe that because of the poor wages paid by some service industries, the shift of the economy away from manufacturing will lead to a further dichotomization of wealth – the rich will get richer and the poor will get poorer. Without a doubt, the service sector has many low-paying jobs. For individuals under the age of 30, service jobs pay 25 per cent less than manufacturing jobs. Some experts believe that as the manufacturing sector continues to decline, the supply of labour available for service jobs will increase, driving wages even lower.

However, not everyone in services is poorly paid. For example, in the finance and wholesale trade, salaries are much closer to manufacturing wages. Moreover, an increasing number of service personnel are highly skilled and employed in knowledge-based industries. Overall, service wages seem to be catching up with wages obtained via manufacturing employment. The concern over wages associated with service employment is real, and continued acceptance of the industrial management model (presented

dichotomization of wealth The rich get richer and the poor get poorer.

Table 3.8	The share of the services sector	Per cent of GDP			
		1960	1980	1995	2004
	UK	53	54	66	72
	Australia	51	58	70	71
	France	52	62	71	73
	Japan	42	54	60	68
	USA	58	64	72	75
	Singapore	78	61	64	65
	Hong Kong	62	67	83	88
	China	20	21	31	35
	India	30	36	41	52
	Sri Lanka	48	43	52	58

Service sector percentage contribution to GDP 1960–2004

Source Wijewardena, 2006: 4.

in Chapter 1) within service industries will do nothing but perpetuate the problem. 'Most service enterprises consist of a well-paid brain trust and poorly paid support staff – $500-an-hour lawyers and $5-an-hour secretaries' (Raynor, 1993).

Pay is not the only issue being raised in service sector employment. A comprehensive study (NESY Project) conducted in Europe in 2001 concludes that 'the organization of many service activities in EU countries is not socially sustainable. Symptoms of this predicament are people withdrawing from employment early because of excessive workloads, labour shortages in times of unemployment and short-termist attitudes to training.' The researchers call for an open debate on the so-called 'service paradox'; the more that person-related services are demanded, the greater the likelihood that people will be forced to work at times when other people do not. Individuals will struggle to manage unpredictable working-time patterns to coordinate family and leisure time. If there is a broad social consensus that the service offer should be expanded in terms of time it must be clear that this will require new flexibility compromises, the cost of which will be reflected in the costs of services (Gerhardt, 2001).

Predicted keys to success within the service sector

Several common themes to success become clear when examining the growth of the service sector. First, many of the successful firms excel at niche marketing. Niche marketing strategies include focusing on particular consumer groups and/or filling voids in specific locations. This has been seen in the hotel sector with the rise in 'boutique' hotels and with greater and greater fragmentation and specialization in many business services particularly within the areas of information, communication and the media.

The second key to success seems to be directly related to the firm's ability to master technological change. The impact of technology on the worldwide service sector is undeniable. Firms that view technology as a source of innovation as opposed to a 'necessary evil' are particularly successful. Improvements in technology have enabled successful service firms to open new avenues of communication between themselves and their customers. Other technological innovations have led to improved services that permit more customer involvement in the service delivery process, offering the dual advantages of decreasing customer-handling costs while providing customers with convenient services. Automatic teller machines (ATMs) and a variety of online services are prime examples.

Other keys to success are the service firms' abilities to excel at customer service and develop compelling service experiences. Because of the absence of a tangible product, successful service firms must look to their customer service delivery systems to differentiate themselves from competitors. In 1898, Caesar Ritz, the founder of Ritz Hotels, became the manager of the struggling Savoy Hotel in London. Ritz understood men and women and their desire for beautiful things, and he went to great lengths to achieve the atmosphere he desired. Firstly, he turned the Savoy into a centre of cultural activity by introducing an orchestra to the dining room and extending the dining period. Proper evening attire was made compulsory, and unescorted women were prohibited from the premises. Ritz also understood his guests' need for romance. For a time, the lower dining room of the Savoy was converted into a Venetian waterway, complete with gondolas and gondoliers who sang Italian love songs. So it seems that regardless of the industry involved, one common thread connects all service firms that are successful – service excellence, the ability to continuously provide courteous, professional and caring service to customers (Brush and Schultz, 1995).

customer retention
Focusing the firm's marketing efforts toward the existing customer base.

The final key to success, which differentiates successful service firms from mediocre ones, is an understanding of the value of customer retention – focusing the firm's marketing efforts towards the existing customer base. Successful service firms understand the multiple benefits of retaining existing customers: (1) the marketing costs associated with retaining customers are much lower than the costs associated with acquiring new customers; (2) existing customers tend to purchase more services more frequently; (3) current customers are more familiar with the firm's personnel and procedures and are therefore more efficient in their service transactions; and (4) reducing customer defections by 5 per cent in some industries can increase profits by as much as 50 per cent. Businesses commonly lose 50 per cent of their customers every five years (Reicheld, 1996). However, most companies have no idea how many customers are lost or the reasons for their defections (Gonzalez, Hoffman and Ingram, 2005). Consequently, companies that do not excel at customer retention are destined to make the same mistakes over and over. The lack of attention paid to customer retention can be explained by the time-honoured tradition of conquest marketing – the pursuit of new customers as opposed to the retention of existing ones.

conquest marketing The pursuit of new customers as opposed to the retention of existing ones.

Summary

This chapter has provided an overview of the service sector by discussing the following:

- the main sectors that comprise the service economy
- service classification schemes that identify commonalities among diverse service industries
- the trends and concerns that pertain to the growth of the service economy
- the predicted keys to success within the service sector.

It is generally accepted that the service economy includes the 'soft parts' of the economy consisting of several industry sectors – education, health and public sector services, financial activities, communication, media and information, leisure and hospitality, professional and business services, transport, wholesale and retail trade, and real estate, renting and leasing services. The *service sector* is one of the three main categories of a developed economy – the other two being *industrial* and *agricultural*. Traditionally, economies throughout the world tend to go through a transition from an *agricultural economy* to an *industrial economy* (e.g., manufacturing and mining) to a *service economy*.

The many service sectors illustrate the diversity of activities within the service economy. Many service industries share common service delivery challenges and therefore would benefit from sharing their knowledge with each other. Classification schemes applied solely to services have also been developed to facilitate our understanding of what different types of service operations have in common. Services marketing classes may want to discuss each of these classification schemes and their marketing implications.

Several key forces continue to influence the growth of the service sector. These forces include the emergence of technologically based e-services, socio-cultural forces derived from an ageing population, and the competitive force of 'outservicing', which involves the *offshoring*, *outsourcing*, and *automation* of many services. The continued growth and dominance of the service sector has been met with some criticism. *Materialismic* individuals believe that without manufacturing, there will be little for people to service.

Several guidelines to success become clear when examining the growth and dominance of the service sector across industries. These strategies include excelling at niche marketing; providing customer service and developing compelling service experiences far superior to that offered by competitors; mastering technological change; and excelling at customer retention.

Discussion questions

1 Investigate the growth rates of three of the main service sectors. Discuss the main growth drivers and any inhibitors/threats to growth within these sectors.

2 Define the term 'e-service'. Identify and evaluate some of the more recent developments in e-services.

3 The hospitality industry has a reputation for long hours and poor pay. Use a variety of sources to find evidence for and against this suggestion.

4 Service firms can learn a great deal from other firms in other industries. Discuss the strategies that appear to be linked with success across the service spectrum.

5 Discuss the marketing implications of Table 3.3, 'Understanding the Nature of the Service Act'.

6 Define and discuss the term *materialismo snobbery*.

7 Discuss the changing economy of either China or India in terms of transition from agriculture to industry to service dominant. What are the future implications for European service providers?

8 Evaluate the practice of international outsourcing. What are the advantages and disadvantages to a) the outsourcing organization, b) the economy, c) the consumer?

9 Using examples, explain how an e-service can minimize the problems caused by inseparability that traditionally impact other types of traditional service firms.

References and further reading

Accor (2007) www.accor.com, accessed February 2007.

Amiti, M. and Wei, S.-J. (2005) 'Fear of service outsourcing: is it justified?', *Economic Policy* 20 (42) 308–347.

Brush, R. L. and Schulz, T. (1995) 'Pioneers and leaders in the hospitality industry', in *Hospitality Management*, 7th ed., Robert A. Brymer, ed., Dubuque, Iowa: Kendall/ Hunt Publishing, pp. 24–34.

The Economist (1993) 'Wealth in services', *The Economist*, 20 February, p. 16.

The Economist (1994) 'The manufacturing myth', *The Economist*, 19 March, p. 92.

ERD (European Rural Development) (2007) *Demography*, available from www.iiasa.ac.at/Research/ERD/DB/data/ hum/dem/dem_2.htm.

European Commission (2005) *Key data on education in Europe 2005*, Belgium: Eurydice.

European Commission (2007), ec.europa.eu/trade/issues/ sectoral/services/, accessed February 2007.

Eurostat (2007a) 'Operation 2007', www.eurostat.ec. europa.eu, accessed February 2007.

Eurostat (2007b) *Europe in figures – Eurostat yearbook 2006–07 – Health*.

Gale Group (2006a) 'Global Industry Overview: Hotels and Other Lodging Places', *Encyclopedia of Global Industries*, Thomson Publishing, www.galegroup.com.

Gale Group (2006b) 'Global Industry Overview: Banking and Insurance', *Encyclopedia of Global Industries*, Thomson Publishing, www.gale group.com.

Gerhardt, B. (2001) *New Forms of Employment and Working Time in the Service Economy*, Brussels: European Commission, available from http:// ec.europa.eu/research/social-sciences/knowledge/ projects/article_3519_en.htm.

Gonzalez, G. R., Hoffman, K.D. and Ingram, T. N. (2005) 'Improving relationship selling through failure analysis and recovery efforts: a framework and call to action', *Journal of Personal Selling and Sales Management* 25 (1): 57–65.

Greenhalgh, C. and Gregory, M. (2001) 'Structural change and the emergence of the new service economy', *Oxford Bulletin of Economics and Statistics* 63 (s1): 629–646.

IH&RA (2002) 'Europe's Huge Growth Potential', Hospitality Leaders' Summit Highlights, www. hospitalitynet.org/news.

Karmarkar, U. (2004) 'Will you survive the services revolution?', *Harvard Business Review* 82 (6): pp. 100–108.

Kuhn T. S. (1970) *The Structure of Scientific Revolutions*, 2nd ed., Chicago: University of Chicago Press.

Lovelock, C. H. (1983) 'Classifying services to gain strategic marketing insights', *Journal of Marketing* 47 (Summer) 9–20.

Lovelock, Christopher and Gummesson, Evert (2004) 'Whither services marketing? In search of a new paradigm and fresh perspectives', *Journal of Service Research* 7 (1) 20–41.

National Guidance Research Forum (2007) www. guidance-research.org/future-trends/arts/summary, accessed March 2007.

Pitt, Leyland F., Berthon, Pierre and Watson, Richard T. (1999) 'Cyberservice: taming service marketing problems with the World Wide Web', *Business Horizons* 42 (1) 11–18.

Raynor, M. E. (1992) 'After materialismo', *Across the Board* 29: 28–41.

Reichheld, F. F. (1996) 'Learning from customer defections', *Harvard Business Review* (March–April): 56–69.

Wood, F. and Armstrong, J. (2006) 'From cohort to communications: connecting with the over 50's', Annual Conference of the Market Research Society, 2006.

Wijewardena, W.A. (2006) 'Services sector growth – an unstable growth component or a sustainable wealth creator? The case of Sri Lanka', Text of the Professor Sirisena Tilakaratna Memorial Lecture, Deputy Governor of the Central Bank of Sri Lanka, at the Center for Banking Studies, Rajagiriya, 15 December 2006.

WorldBank (2007) www.worldbank.org/depweb/beyond/ beyondco/beg_09.pdf.

Chapter 4

The consumer decision process in services marketing

The consumer's mind is still closed to us; it is a 'black box' that remains sealed. We can observe inputs to the box and the decisions made as a result, but we can never know how the act of processing inputs (information) truly happens.

John E. G. Bateson

Chapter objectives

In this chapter we discuss consumer decision process issues as they relate to the purchase of services.

After reading this chapter, you should be able to:

- Appreciate the six steps that comprise the consumer decision process model.

- Comprehend the special considerations of service purchases as they pertain to the pre-purchase, consumption, and post-purchase stages of the consumer decision process model.

- Describe models that attempt to explain the consumer's post-purchase evaluation.

- Describe models that are specific for purchases made by organizations

Services in context
Online services retailing on the increase

The internet revolution has made a tremendous impact on consumer decision-making processes. The web has acted as a new source of stimuli that has opened consumer eyes to sets of unforeseen needs and wants. Consumer behaviour, when shopping for services online, also provides specialist, unbiased information not available to shoppers on the High Street. Information search is now available at a click of a button via search engines such as Google, Yahoo, AskJeeves (UK), Libertysurf (France), Freenet (Italy) and so on. However, most consumers tend to use only one search engine as they begin their search for information, but sophisticated Netizens will use three or four (White, 2007). Whilst searching for information, the consumers can view offerings from their service provider that they did not know even existed! Additionally, consumers can visit social shopping sites and blogs where consumers, just like them, review products and services and supply 'expert' information about what they have tried and tested (www.customerreview.com, www.e-opinions.com and www.productopia.com). For the millions of UK grocery shoppers there is an information website called MySupermarket.co.uk which compares prices of all the major supermarkets and compiles a 'virtual shopping basket' to compare prices of the total basket at each of the different supermarkets. This is great if a consumer has a limited budget, a large family or both!

The age profile of internet users is at the younger end. In the UK, Germany and France the dominant age profile is 25–34 years old with approximately 25 per cent of users in that age group (TGI Europa, 2000). However, Spain and Italy have a younger profile with 30 per cent of users aged 15–24 years old. The reasons why consumers use the internet vary from country to country. Britain has the highest number of Internet users who actually purchase services online. Germans find banking online their most popular use. Spanish Netizens visit more chat-rooms than the British, who in turn use the e-mail feature more often than their Spanish counterparts (Wicken, 2001).

Despite its hype and 24-hour availability, consumers feel there are risks involved when shopping online. Therefore, as consumers evaluate the alternatives available to them, they search for organizations where they can reduce the perceived risks associated with buying from a faceless retailer. The perceived risks include 1) Performance Risk – will the service consumers expect to receive be the service that they actually receive?; 2) Financial Risk – there is a fear that consumers will lose their money; and 3) Time Risk – time may be wasted seeking recompence for poor-quality service, or repair or return of goods may be difficult (Ko et al., 2004). See details about Perceived Risks later in this Chapter. Once a choice has been selected, the web provides a plethora of purchase avenues and allows us to share our own insights pertaining to the product after purchase and use. Clearly, the web has revolutionized consumer decision making.

In addition to transforming consumer decision making, web traffic is growing for services usually supplied by 'bricks and mortar' organizations. Indeed by 2010 online grocery shopping in the UK is predicted to grow by 20 per cent year-on-year (Business Wire, 2007). The leaders in the UK are Tesco, Sainsbury, Asda WalMart and Waitrose. Each month 10 per cent of the UK population are logging on to the supermarket websites for their groceries, CDs, DVDs and houseware. The market leader, Tesco, currently enjoys £1 billion in online sales (Yorkshire Post, 2006), but generally, for every £100 spent on groceries only £2 is spent online.

Consumers who would prefer to sit in the comfort of their own home, rather than the noisy, busy supermarket aisles, first search the supermarket websites and choose the supplier based on cost of delivery – varying between £3.75 and £5.00 – or delivery dates and times that are convenient to them. Consumers can then search at leisure the products available by moving around the website, clicking on pictures of their favourite foods, information about recipes or checking out the 'special offers'.

Some online grocery shoppers like the idea that they are helping to save the environment from congestion and pollution by encouraging consumers to leave their cars at home and let the supermarkets deliver groceries to multiple homes in one trip. Consumers who wish for the convenience of online grocery shopping to help the environment can also decide to buy from smaller local retailers who provide fresh local produce that are low in 'food miles'. Some smaller grocery retailers are competing against the supermarket giants; these include Wild Star Food Company and The Whitby Catch. Helen Rogers, the Managing Director of Wild Star Food Company, says 'There are numerous economic, environmental and social reasons why we always prefer to stock local products.' Clearly Wild Star Food Company will attract shoppers who also prefer to buy local produce.

Grocery shopping online, therefore, is easy and time-efficient for the consumer. Similarly, the number and frequency of consumers using the internet for their groceries is growing. However, one final thought, internet grocery shopping is stress free and convenient for our busy lifestyles, but human interaction is part of our nature. Therefore, would we only want the impersonality of shopping online? Or is grocery shopping with your partner or house-mate a social event that is worth the effort?

Sources: Business Wire Between 2006 and 2010, 'The UK Internet Grocery Market is Expected to Rise by More than 20% Year on Year', 8 May 2007 Tuesday 8:00 AM GMT.
H. Ko, J. Jung, J. Y. Kim, and S. W. Shim (2004) 'Cross-Cultural Differences in Perceived Risk of Online Shopping', *Journal of Interactive Advertising*, 4(2), Spring.
H. Wallop (2007) Fridge 'will stock up online as it empties', *Daily Telegraph* (London), 11 June 2007.
R. White (2007) 'Search Marketing', *WARC Best Practice*, June 2007.
G. Wicken (2001) 'A deeper understanding of European Internet Users', *Admap Magazine*, September, Issue 420.
Yorkshire Post (2006) 'Small stores go online to take on the supermarkets', 19 October 2006.
www.wildstarfood.com.

Introduction

Consumer orientation lies at the heart of the marketing concept (Bateson, 1992). As marketers, we are required to understand our consumers and to build our organizations around them. This requirement is particularly important for services because consumers like choices and their choice determines whether organizations thrive or fail. Indeed it is more important than ever to understand consumers, how they choose amongst the vast array of alternative services offered to them, and how they evaluate these services once they have received them. Additionally, organizations are consumers too. Businesses also require services in order to function. The first section, therefore, will begin by considering the consumer as an individual, purchasing services for themselves or their household. Organizational buying behaviour, however, has unique characteristics and will, therefore, be discussed separately towards the end of this chapter.

The consumer decision process has three stages: *pre-purchase, consumption, and post-purchase evaluation*. The consumer uses this process model to make his or her decision. Although varieties of models have been developed and are discussed in this chapter, it is important to point out that no model is perfect. As the quotation at the beginning of the chapter says, 'The consumer's mind is still closed to us; it is a "black box" that remains sealed. However, we can observe inputs to the box and the decisions made as a result, but we can never know how the act of processing inputs (information) truly happens.'

If the models are not perfect, why bother with such models? Whether marketing managers like it or not, every time consumers make marketing decisions, they are basing their decisions on some form of buying model and these consumer buying models help marketing managers understand buyer behaviour. Quite often these models are implicit and seldom shared with others, representing, in effect, the marketing manager's own experience. However, every time a price is changed, a new service is offered, or an advertising campaign begins, some assumptions have to be made about how the consumer will react.

The purpose of this chapter is to discuss the consumer decision process as it relates to the purchase of services. Due to the unique characteristics of services, there are differences that exist between the ways consumers make decisions regarding services as opposed to the ways they make decisions regarding goods. This chapter, therefore, has been constructed in three sections. The first section is a broad overview of the consumer decision-making process. It provides a summary of the process and its applications to marketing decisions. The second section of the chapter is dedicated to specific considerations about the consumer decision-making process as it relates to services. The final section will provide a summary of the buying behaviour of organizations.

The consumer decision process: An overview

consumer decision process The three-step process consumers use to make purchase decisions; includes the pre-purchase stage, the consumption stage, and the post-purchase evaluation stage.

To market services effectively, marketing managers need to understand the thought processes used by consumers during each of the stages of the consumer decision process: the pre-purchase choice among alternatives, the consumer's reaction during consumption, and the post-purchase evaluation of satisfaction (see Figure 4.1). Although we can never truly know the

Figure 4.1

Consumer decision process

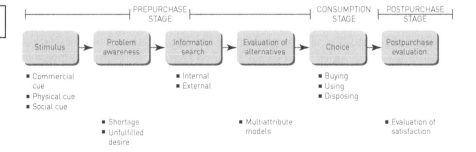

thought process used by the individual when making that choice, the consumer decision process helps to structure our thinking and to guide our marketing research regarding consumer behaviour. Let's begin this discussion by focusing on the pre-purchase stage of the model, which includes the stimulus, problem awareness, information search and evaluation of alternatives.

Case link

For family holiday services, see Case 3: Center Parcs.

The pre-purchase stage: The stimulus

Consumers do not spontaneously buy or consume services. Consumers are in fact driven by *internal* motivations and *external* factors which constitute a stimulus. The internal motivational drives incite the need for a service, product or experience (Reid and Bojanic, 2006; Arnould, Price and Zinkhan, 2002; MacInnis, Moorman, and Jaworski, 1991). There are many different types of physiological or psychological needs and organizations must understand the needs of their consumers so that they can provide additional services and products to their existing portfolio.

stimulus The thought, action, or motivation that incites a person to consider a purchase.

For example, travellers would expect hotels to satisfy their physiological needs such as hunger and rest. However, they would also expect their psychological needs to be satisfied. These psychological needs vary depending on the type of traveller. For instance, female business travellers need to feel safe and secure, whilst rich, young, fashionable travellers may wish to satisfy their status needs.

So far we have discussed motivational needs. It is important, at this stage, to distinguish between needs and wants. Needs are the physiological or psychological requirements that drive behaviour, such as hunger, rest, safety and status discussed earlier. Wants, however, are the different forms of consumption that satisfy the need. Returning to the female business traveller, who needs to feel safe and secure, in order to satisfy that *need* she may *want* spy holes so that she can see who has knocked on her room door and CCTV cameras in well lit corridors and car parks. The rich young, fashionable travellers, satisfying their status *needs*, may *want* exceptional, discrete service, a Michelin-starred restaurant and luxurious décor throughout. Therefore, the hotel must understand the different needs of their consumers and supply the appropriate forms of consumption.

There are many theories concerning motivation and needs. During the mid-1900s an eminent psychologist Abraham Maslow developed a model (Figure 4.2) which depicts the needs of consumers in a pyramid. The needs at the bottom of the pyramid are the basic *physiological* needs such as the need for food, water or sleep. Many service industries can satisfy these basic needs, for example a café's offering 'grab and go' food and drinks. Once the basic physiological needs are satisfied, an individual can progress to the next level in the pyramid. The *safety* needs, referred to by Maslow, have been identified with the female traveller. Hilton and Grange City in London have 'women-only' floors or suites in their hotels to accommodate the need to satisfy the personal security of their female guests. Our safety needs are also satisfied by knowing there is a dedicated police force or the UK's National Health Service will provide for us when we are ill.

Individuals have a strong desire to belong and feel accepted, hence Maslow's *social* needs section deals with the inner motivation to gain friendship and love from family and social circles. Many service industries help cater for this need; from Center Parcs family breaks, to music festivals such as Sziget Music Festival in Budapest, and retailers such as Mango all help consumers belong to a socially accepted group of like-minded individuals.

Consumers who feel that they belong and are accepted may now seek to satisfy their *esteem* needs. Individuals need to satisfy their ego needs through things such as visiting a car sales room that has the latest Audi S4 to having a pair of hand-crafted shoes made by James Taylor and Sons, London. Organizations help individuals feel respected by others through the service they have chosen; and at the same time individuals gain self-respect through the experience they have received by the service organization.

Self-actualization is the highest level of need and relates to the achievement of an ultimate goal, or realizing potential. Services such as universities help students reach their ultimate goals through education and qualifications. Holiday tour operators may also satisfy this need by taking their customers to places such as the Colosseum in Rome.

The stimulus that also leads to need recognition and motivation may be derived from commercial (promotional) cue or a social cue. Commercial cues are the result of promotional efforts. For example, a consumer may be exposed to an advertisement about learning a new language at a local college. As a result, the individual may begin to assess his or her current situation and the possibility of enrolling at the college to learn Spanish and meet new people. Similarly, social cues are obtained from the individual's peer group or from the family. For example, using a friend's broadband service may motivate an individual to upgrade their own internet connection so that they can keep their Facebook Profile up to date.

commercial cue An event or motivation that provides a stimulus to the consumer and is a promotional effort on the part of the company.

social cue An event or motivation that provides a stimulus to the consumer, obtained from the individual's peer group or from significant others.

Figure 4.2

Maslow's Hierarchy of Needs

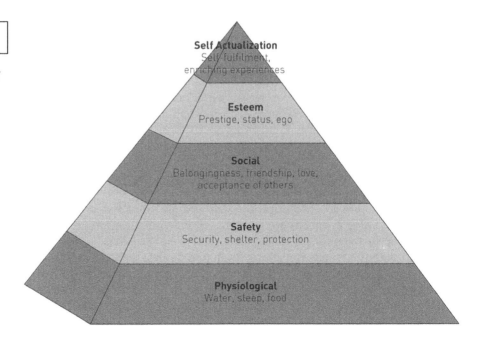

The pre-purchase stage: Problem awareness

Once the consumer has received the stimulus, the next phase of the process is problem awareness. During the problem awareness phase, the consumer examines whether a need truly exists and whether consumption of a product or service can satisfy the need. This stage produces a state of tension between the *actual* state – the state the consumer is in now and the *ideal* state. As can be seen from Figure 4.3 (problem awareness state), if an individual's ideal state and their actual state is the same, there is no tension. However, if there is a difference between the actual state and the ideal state, a tension is created and the void between the ideal and actual state must be filled. A purchase relieves the tension and equilibrium is restored. There is an opportunity here for the marketer to suggest ideas and solutions as 'new ideal states'. For example, Interrail.net may promote their Global Pass as an opportunity to see Europe by train. A student may see this promotion and a tension will occur between their actual state and their 'new ideal state' of visiting towns and cities in Europe. If the tension is strong the student may purchase an Interrail ticket.

In contrast, if the student does not feel the tension between their actual state and the ideal state, the decision process stops at this point. If tension is created, the decision process continues on to the information search stage.

> **problem awareness**
> The second phase of the pre-purchase stage, in which the consumer determines whether a need exists for the product.

The pre-purchase stage: Information search

The recognition of a problem demands a solution from the individual, which usually implies that a potential purchase will ensue. The individual searches for alternatives during the information search phase of the pre-purchase stage (see E-Services in Action). As the name implies, during the information search phase, the consumer collects information regarding possible alternatives. It is clear that in all consumer decision making, consumers seldom consider all feasible alternatives. Instead, they have a limited list of options chosen on the basis of past experience, convenience and knowledge. This list is often referred to by theorists as the evoked set – the set of 'brands' that comes to the consumer's mind when thinking about a particular product category and from which the choice will be made.

For example, Grant needs to socialize to celebrate his 21st birthday. He wants to visit a restaurant with his friends. When he considers the alternatives, he engages in an internal search. An internal search accesses the consumer's own memories about possible alternative restaurants. In this example, the

> **information search**
> The phase in the pre-purchase stage in which the consumer collects information on possible alternatives.

> **evoked set** The limited set of 'brands' that comes to the consumer's mind when thinking about a particular product category from which the purchase choice will be made.

> **internal search**
> A passive approach to gathering information in which the consumer's own memory is the main source of information about a product.

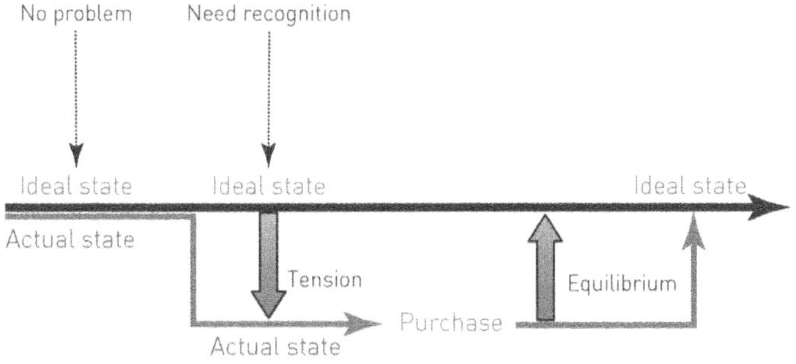

Figure 4.3

Problem awareness state

previous knowledge may be based on his previous visits to restaurants and knowledge he has from listening to his friends and family discussing their own visits to restaurants. An internal search is a passive approach to gathering information.

external search A proactive approach to gathering information in which the consumer collects new information from sources outside the consumer's own experience.

The internal search may be followed by an external search, which would involve the collection of new information obtained via the local newspapers that review local restaurants, asking the opinions of friends and family, and/ or looking on the internet for blogs and customer reviews of restaurants in the consumer's local town or city.

evaluation of alternatives The phase of the pre-purchase stage in which the consumer places a value or 'rank' on each alternative.

The pre-purchase stage: Evaluation of alternatives

Once relevant information has been collected from both internal and external sources, the consumer arrives at a set of alternative solutions to the recognized problem. The possible solutions are considered in the evaluation of alternatives

---

E-services in action
The consumer decision process as it relates to e-commerce

The internet revolution has made a tremendous impact on consumer decision making. Information search, evaluation of alternatives, and purchase processes have been particularly impacted. The following checklist maximizes the effectiveness of e-marketers in each of these areas.

Information Search:

1 Ease of navigation – is it easy to move throughout the website?

2 Speed of page downloads – does each page load quickly enough?

3 Effectiveness of search features – are search features returning the information users are looking for?

4 Frequency of product updates – is product information updated often enough to meet user needs?

Evaluation of Alternatives:

1 Ease of product comparisons – is it easy to compare the different products the website offers?

2 Product descriptions – are product descriptions accurate, clear and

comprehensive enough to allow customers to make informed decisions?

3 Contacting customer service representatives – are customer service phone numbers easy to locate?

4 In-stock status – are out-of-stock products flagged before the customer proceeds to the checkout process?

Purchase:

1 Security and privacy issues – do users feel comfortable transmitting personal information?

2 Checkout process – are users able to move through the checkout process in a reasonable amount of time?

3 Payment options – are payment options offered that non-buyers desire?

4 Delivery options – are delivery options offered that non-buyers desire?

5 Ordering instructions – are ordering instructions easy to understand?

Source: Adapted from Jody Dodson, 'What's Wrong with Your Website', *Target Marketing*, 23 [2] [February 2000], pp. 135–139.

phase of the consumer decision process. This phase may consist of a non-systematic evaluation of alternatives, such as the use of intuition – simply choosing an alternative by relying on a 'gut-level feeling' – or it may involve a systematic evaluation technique, such as a multi-attribute model. Such systematic models utilize a set of formalized steps to arrive at a decision.

Marketing theorists have made extensive use of multi-attribute models to simulate the process of evaluating products (Reid and Bojanic, 2006) According to these models, consumers employ a number of attributes or criteria as basic references when evaluating a service. For example, Grant may compare alternative restaurant attributes based on fun atmosphere, quality of food, price, location. Consumers compute their preference for the service by combining the scores of the service on each individual attribute.

Within the evaluation of alternatives phase of the decision process, consumers are assumed to create a matrix similar to the one shown in Table 4.1 to compare alternatives. The example in the table is the choice of a restaurant for Grant's 21st birthday. Across the top of the table are two types of variables. The first is the evoked set of brands to be evaluated. As previously mentioned, this evoked set will, for various reasons, be less than an exhaustive list of all possible choices; in this example it includes Teppan-Yaki Japanese Restaurant; Casa Mia; Bonviveur Restaurant; TGI Fridays. The second type of variable is the importance rating with which the consumer ranks the various attributes that constitute the vertical axis of the table. For example, in Table 4.1, the consumer rates fun atmosphere as the most important attribute, followed by price, and so on. To complete the table, the consumer rates each brand on each attribute based on his or her

non-systematic evaluation Choosing among alternatives in a random fashion or by a 'gut-level feeling' approach.

systematic evaluation Choosing among alternatives by using a set of formalized steps to arrive at a decision.

Attributes	Evoked sets of brands				Importance weights
	TGI Fridays	Bonviveur	Casa Mia	Teppan-Yaki Japanese Restaurant	
Fun atmosphere	10	4	8	7	10
Price	9	5	7	3	9
Service Delivery	9	6	8	9	8
Quality of food	6	10	6	8	7
Location	7	8	8	7	6

Table 4.1

A typical multi-attribute choice matrix

expectations of each attribute. For example, this particular consumer gives Bonviveur Restaurant good marks for quality of food, location and price but perceives the restaurant to be not as strong on 'fun atmosphere'.

Given such a table, various choice processes have been suggested with which the consumer can use the table to make a decision. The linear compensatory approach proposes that the consumer creates a global score for each brand by multiplying the rating of the brand on each attribute by the importance attached to the attribute and adding the scores together. TGI Fridays would score 10×10 (fun atmosphere) plus 10×9 (price) plus 10×7 (location), and so on. The restaurant with the highest score, in this example TGI Fridays, is then chosen.

linear compensatory approach A systematic model that proposes that the consumer creates a global score for each brand by multiplying the rating of the brand on each attribute by the importance attached to the attribute and adding the scores together.

lexicographic approach A systematic model that proposes that the consumer makes a decision by examining each attribute, starting with the most important, to rule out alternatives.

Another type of multi-attribute approach that has been suggested is the lexicographic approach. This approach describes so-called 'lazy decision makers' who try to minimize the effort involved. They look at each attribute in turn, starting with the most important, and try to make a decision. The individual whose preferences are shown in Table 4.1 would look first at fun atmosphere and rule out Bonviveur Restaurant. Next, price would rule out Teppan-Yaki Japanese Restaurant. At this stage, the choice is reduced to Casa Mia and TGI Fridays, but quality of food produces a tie in the scoring. Finally, the choice would be made in favour of Casa Mia based on the next attribute, location. Thus, a different decision rule results in a different choice: Casa Mia under the lexicographic model and TGI Fridays under the linear compensatory model.

Given the popularity of multi-attribute models, it is no surprise that they have been used to describe and explain the consumer's service decision processes. The merit of these models lies in their simplicity and explicitness. The attributes identified cover a wide range of concerns related to the service experience, and they are easily understood by service managers. For example, analysing consumer multi-attribute models provides the following:

- a list of alternatives that are included in the evoked set
- the list of criteria that consumers consider when making purchase decisions
- the importance weights attached to each criteria
- performance beliefs associated with a particular firm
- performance beliefs associated with the competition.

The tasks for management when using these models are relatively straightforward. For example, advertising can be used to stress a particular attribute on which the firm's service appears to be weak in the mind of consumers. A restaurant may have a highly priced menu but advertising may encourage consumers who are looking for excellent food quality to 'ignore' the cost over the expectations of quality food. If necessary, competitive advertising can also be used to try to reduce the attribute scores obtained by competitors. For example, many restaurants attract consumers by promoting their awards and media reviews and challenging the consumer to find a better restaurant.

The consumption stage: Choice

Thus far, we have discussed the pre-purchase stage of the consumer decision process, which described the stimulus, problem awareness, information search, and evaluation of alternatives phases. An important outcome of the pre-purchase stage is a decision to choose a certain brand from the service category. During this consumption stage, the consumer may make a *store choice* – deciding to purchase from a particular outlet, or a *non-store choice* – deciding to purchase from the internet, or a variety of mail-order possibilities. This decision is accompanied by a set of expectations about the performance of the service or products provided. In the case of a service such as a haircut, the consumer takes part in the service offered and pays for that service. Alternatively, in the case of a service where a product is also bought, such as purchasing a mobile phone from Phones4u, the consumer takes part in the service offered through the advice given by the phone retailer. The consumer then uses the product and disposes of any solid waste remaining. The activities of buying, using and disposing are grouped together and labelled the consumption process (Nicosia and Mayer, 1976).

consumption process
The activities of buying, using and disposing of a product.

The post-purchase stage: Post-purchase evaluation

Once a choice has been made and as the service or product is being consumed, post-purchase evaluation takes place. During this stage, consumers may experience varying levels of cognitive dissonance – doubt that the correct purchase decision has been made. Marketers often attempt to minimize the consumer's cognitive dissonance by reassuring the customer that the correct decision has been made. Strategies to minimize cognitive dissonance include after-sale contact with the customer, providing a reassuring e-mail after a consumer has booked their Interrail ticket on-line, providing warranties and guarantees where appropriate and reinforcing the consumer's decision through the firm's advertising. For example, learning through the universities advertising that they have been nationally recognized by the *Times Higher Education* would positively reinforce the consumer's enrolment decision. Simply stated, post-purchase evaluation is all about customer satisfaction, and customer satisfaction is the key outcome of the marketing process. Customer

cognitive dissonance
Doubt in the consumer's mind regarding the correctness of the purchase decision.

Attributes	Expected score from Table 4.1	Perceived score	Importance weights
Fun atmosphere	10	6	10
Price	9	3.5	9
Service delivery	9	7	8
Quality of food	6	6	7
Location	7	7	6

Table 4.2

Restaurant selection: A post-purchase evaluation for TGI Fridays

satisfaction is achieved when consumers' perceptions meet or exceed their expectations (see Table 4.2). Customer satisfaction is an end in itself, but is also the source of word-of-mouth recommendations and can thus stimulate further purchases.

During the evaluation process of the post-purchase stage, multi-attribute models can once again be utilized. For this process, the choice of restaurants is replaced by two columns. The first is the score expected by the consumer on each attribute. The second is the perceived score on each attribute obtained by the consumer after they have visited the restaurant. The satisfaction score is then derived by creating a global score of the comparisons between perceptions and expectations weighted by the importance of each attribute. This is shown in Table 4.2.

In this example, Grant chose TGI Fridays by using the multi-attribute choice matrix shown in Table 4.1 and based on the linear compensatory approach. The expected levels on each attribute are, therefore, taken from that matrix. In reality, the prices had increased significantly and the fun atmosphere did not live up to expectations. Grant, therefore, downgraded his evaluation on those attributes. The smaller the gap between expectations and perceptions, the more positive the post-purchase evaluation.

Special considerations pertaining to services

Although the consumer decision process model applies to both goods and services, unique considerations arise with respect to service purchases. Many of these special considerations can be directly attributed to the unique service characteristics of intangibility, inseparability, heterogeneity and perishability. The considerations addressed in this part of the chapter help in developing a deeper understanding of the challenges faced when marketing services.

Global services in action
Managing visitor expectations: Finland – What it is not

Customer satisfaction is commonly measured as a comparison between customer perceptions ('what customers think they received') and customer expectations ('what customers thought they were going to receive'). As such, service marketers can increase customer satisfaction by lowering expectations or by enhancing perceptions. In an attempt to manage tourist expectations about the country and people of Finland, the *Helsinki Guide* publishes the following list in its visitor publications:

1 Finland is not a small country nor is it close to the North Pole.

2 Finland is not awfully cold all the time, and polar bears do not roam the streets of Helsinki.

3 Finnish is not a Slavic language, and only very few Finns speak Russian which, of course, is a pity.

4 Finland did not suffer too badly from any war-time occupation.

5 Finns and Lapps are not the same thing.

6 Finland is not, and has never been a member of the Eastern Block – if there is one anymore.

7 Finns don't drink as much as the rumours say.

8 Finns don't eat just fish.

9 Finland is not the country of limitless sex that it is made out to be.

10 Finland is not in a very uncomfortable position between East and West.

Visitors flying to Finland on Finnair receive an extra dose of 'expectation management'. During the last hour of flight, a 30-minute film titled 'The Finnish Way' is shown to passengers.

Source: virtual.finland.fi/People/way_of_life.asp, accessed 15 April 2005; *Helsinki Guide (2000)*, Karprint Publishers (Jan.–Feb.), p. 16.

'Finland is not awfully cold all the time...'

SOURCE COURTESY OF MATTI KOLHO

Pre-purchase stage considerations: Perceived risk

In comparison with goods consumers, consumers of services tend to perceive a higher level of risk during the pre-purchase decision stage. The concept of perceived risk as an explanation for customer purchasing behaviour was first suggested in the 1960s (Guseman, 1981; Bauer, 1960). The central theory is that consumer behaviour involves risk in the sense that any action taken by a consumer will produce consequences that he or she cannot anticipate with any certainty, and some of which are likely to be unpleasant. Perceived risk is proposed to consist of two dimensions:

- *Consequence* – the degree of importance and/or danger of the outcomes derived from any consumer decision.
- *Uncertainty* – the subjective possibility of the occurrence of these outcomes.

For example, Penelope deciding to have cosmetic surgery to reshape her nose provides an excellent example of how consequence and uncertainty play a major role in service purchases. With respect to uncertainty, Penelope may have never undergone surgery before. Moreover, even though the surgeon has performed the operation successfully in the past, the patient is not guaranteed that this particular surgery will end with the same successful outcome. In addition, uncertainty is likely to increase as Penelope has chosen a 'new nose' prior to the operation and may not like the image she and the plastic surgeon created. Similarly, the after-effects and care are essential following surgery and the patient may not know how to deal with the pain, bruising and swelling. The consequences of a poor decision regarding Penelope's cosmetic surgery could be life-threatening or her self-esteem may plummet if she is not happy with her new image.

financial risk The possibility of a monetary loss if the purchase goes wrong or fails to operate correctly.

performance risk The possibility that the item or service purchased will not perform the task for which it was purchased.

physical risk The possibility that if something does go wrong, injury could be inflicted on the purchaser.

social risk The possibility of a loss in personal social status associated with a particular purchase.

psychological risk The possibility that a purchase will affect an individual's self-esteem.

Types of risk. As the idea of consumer-perceived risk developed, five types of perceived risk were identified, based on five different kinds of outcomes: financial, performance, physical, social and psychological (Kaplan et al., 1974). Financial risk assumes that financial loss could occur if the purchase goes wrong or fails to operate correctly. Performance risk relates to the idea that the item or service purchased will not perform the task for which it was purchased. The physical risk of a purchase can emerge if something does go wrong and injury is inflicted on the purchaser. Social risk suggests that there might be a loss of personal social status associated with a particular purchase (e.g., a fear that one's peer group will react negatively – 'You went where?'). Psychological risk pertains to the influence of the purchase upon the individual's self-esteem. For example, you will not consider being seen in certain clothes or you will refuse to visit certain nightclubs because they are not consistent with your self-image.

Risk and standardization. Much of the heightened level of perceived risk can be attributed to the difficulty in producing a standardized service product. In Chapter 2, we introduced the concept of heterogeneity. Because a service is an experience involving highly complex interactions, it is, not surprisingly, very difficult to replicate the experience from customer to customer or from day to day. As a result, the customer may find it difficult to predict precisely the quality of service he or she will be buying. The fact that Sven, the golfing instructor, provided a good golf lesson for your friend does not mean that he will provide the same lesson for you. Perceived risk, therefore, tends to be higher for purchasing services in contrast to the purchase of goods.

Consequence and uncertainty play a key role in service purchase.

Co-producer risk. The involvement of the consumer in the 'production process of services' is another source of increased perceived risk. Co-producer risk is directly related to the concept of inseparability. Once again, surgery is a good example of the consumer's involvement in the production process. Unlike goods, which can be purchased and taken away, services cannot be taken home and used in private, where the buyer's mistakes will not be visible. Instead, the consumer must take part in the ritual of the service itself. To be part of such a process and not to know exactly what is going on clearly increases the uncertainty about the consequences, particularly the physical consequences of being involved in a service encounter such as surgery, or the social consequences of doing the 'wrong' thing, such as wearing the wrong type of clothing to an important dinner party.

Case link
See Case 3: Center Parcs.

Risk and information. Others have argued that the higher levels of risk associated with service purchases are due to the limited information that is readily available before the purchase decision is made. For example, the economics literature suggests that goods and services possess three different types of attribute (Bateman, 1967):

- *Search attributes* – attributes that can be determined prior to purchase.
- *Experience attributes* – attributes that can be evaluated only during and after the production process.
- *Credence attributes* – attributes that cannot be evaluated confidently even immediately after receipt of the good or service.

Because of the intangible nature of services, it is often extremely difficult for consumers to objectively evaluate a service before it is bought. Services thus have very few search attributes. In contrast, goods can be touched, seen, smelled, heard and, in some instances, tasted prior to purchase and are therefore predominantly characterized by search attributes.

A large proportion of the properties possessed by services (e.g., the friendliness of the flight attendants of a particular airline or the skill level of a hairstylist) can be discovered by consumers only during and after the consumption of the service; these are thus experience attributes. Moreover, some of the properties of many services (e.g., how good a golf lesson you have had or how well your cosmetic surgeon performs services) cannot be assessed even after the service is completed; these are called credence attributes. All in all, due to the properties of intangibility (which limits search attributes), inseparability (which increases credence attributes), and the variation in quality provided by service personnel, services tend to be characterized by experience and credence attributes.

Risk and brand loyalty. Most consumers do not like taking risks; therefore, it would seem obvious that they will try, whenever possible, to reduce risk during the purchase process. One strategy is to be brand- or store-loyal (Hong-Youl Ha, 2006; Odekerken-Schroder et al., 2001). Brand loyalty is based on the degree to which the consumer has obtained satisfaction in the past. If consumers have been satisfied in the past with their supplier of service, they have little incentive to risk trying someone or something new. For example, satisfied users of Skype may see little reason to switch their loyalty to another free internet telephony service.

Having been satisfied in a high-risk purchase, a consumer is less likely to experiment with a different purchase. Maintaining a long-term relationship with the same service provider, in and of itself helps to reduce the perceived risk associated with the purchase. This is why it is common to observe consumers acquiring services from the same garage, dentist, or hairstylist over long periods of time.

Brand loyalty may also be higher in purchasing services due to the limited number of alternative choices available. This is particularly true of professional services, where acceptable substitutes may not be available. In contrast, consumers of goods generally have more substitutes available in a given area. Moreover, purchasing alternative goods does not represent the same level of increased risk as purchasing alternative services.

switching costs Costs that accrue when changing vendors.

Finally, brand loyalty may also be higher for services due to the switching costs that can accrue when changing from one service provider to another. A wide array of switching costs can be accrued, depending on the product involved. Consider, for example, the switching costs involved in changing from one brand of petrol station to another compared with the costs involved in changing a broadband service provider. Typical switching costs include the following:

- *Search costs* – the time it takes to seek out new alternatives that offer the same or better download speed.
- *Transaction costs* – the costs associated with new equipment such as a modem.
- *Learning costs* – costs such as time and money that are associated with learning new systems, such as new versions of browsers or music- and work-related software packages.
- *Loyal customer discounts* – discounts that are given for maintaining the same service over time, such as low-cost up-grade to higher band-width and free telephone number and 24-hour technical support team. Such discounts are sacrificed when switching from one supplier to the next.
- *Customer habit* – costs associated with changing established behaviour patterns.
- *Emotional costs* – emotional turmoil that one may experience when severing a long-term relationship with a provider. Emotional costs are

particularly high when a personal relationship has developed between the client and the provider.

- *Cognitive costs* – costs in terms of the time it takes simply thinking about making a change in service providers.

Pre-purchase stage considerations: The importance of personal sources of information

Another special consideration during the pre-purchase stage is the importance of personal sources of information. Research has shown that in the area of communications, personal forms such as word-of-mouth references and information from opinion leaders are often given more importance than company-controlled communications. A reference from a friend becomes more important when the purchase to be made has a

---

B2B services in action
Hotels outsourcing services – business to business

Hotels, traditionally, have provided all services for the benefit of their guests. Outsourcing many of the hotels' internally managed peripheral services, such as laundry, maintenance and security is becoming the norm. However, following changes in hotel guest behaviour – guests preferred to eat out in familiar restaurants – and also financial underachievement in many hotel restaurants, some hotel groups are now outsourcing or co-branding their food and beverage offer. Current times are beneficial for business-to-business service providers to sieze the opportunity to expand their operations into the hotel sector.

With regard to peripheral services, many hotels do not provide a laundry service for guests, nor do they clean and prepare their own laundry. Business-to-business organizations such as Capital Linen provide high-quality laundry services. Capital Linen are a family-run business, but they provide laundry services for many large and small organizations, from hospitals and care homes, to hotels, restaurants and clubs. Capital Linen provides a bespoke linen service to hotels and restaurants who demand crisp, fresh white linen every day. They also provide schedules to suit organizations that require a quick and speedy service. Outsourcing laundry services, therefore, is an efficient way to keep asset and staff costs low. Other business-to-business outsourcing services include maintenance of indoor plants, shop management, in-house movie and entertainment services and installation and servicing of safes in the hotel rooms.

SOURCE ISTOCK

▶

Several hotels also desire to outsource their food and beverage provision. This is due to high fixed and variable (staff and materials) costs, high perishability and high turnover of casual staff. Additionally hotel restaurants lack a fun, romantic or exciting atmosphere as the restaurant has to be all things to all people. Hotel groups, therefore, have either eliminated the restaurant business entirely or at least reduced the offer to a caféstyle self-service. Travelodge have looked carefully at their portfolio and considered the needs of their consumers. For example, Travelodge Hotels in busy cities provide a vending service for drinks and snacks. Other Travelodge Hotels share space with Burger King, Harry Ramsdens or Little Chef so that their consumers can visit alternative restaurants that they are familiar with. There is a third alternative of visiting Travelodge where there is a Bar Café restaurant serving breakfast and evening meals which enable consumers to take their time and enjoy the facilities available. Therefore, outsourcing gives a platform for different business-to-business relationships from the vending services to full service restaurants.

Sources: N. Hemmington and C. King (2000) 'Key Dimensions of Outsourcing Hotel Food and Beverage Services', *International Journal of Contemporary Hospitality* 12 (4): 256–261. D. Lamminmaki (2005) 'Why Do Hotels Outsource? An Investigation Using Asset Specificity', *International Journal of Contemporary Hospitality* 17 (6): 516–528. www.catiallinen. co.uk. www.travelodge.co.uk.

greater risk. For example, Jean needs to choose a kennel for the family dog. This can be a stressful choice as Jean hopes the kennel staff will give their dog a happy and caring service for two weeks. That stress can be reduced by a recommendation from someone whose judgement Jean trusts and can lead to her feeling more confident about the choice of service.

Similarly, evidence suggests that opinion leaders play an important role in the purchase of services. An opinion leader in a community is an individual who is looked to for advice. Within the perceived-risk framework, an opinion leader can be viewed as a source of reduced social risk. Choosing a kennel for the first time may lead to uncertainty about the quality of the outcome. However, the consumer might be reassured by the fact that the friend who recommended the service is widely known to have good judgement in such matters and will convey this to others in their mutual social group. In this way, the opinion leader's judgement partially substitutes for the consumer's own.

In addition to reducing perceived risk, the importance of personal sources of information to service consumers is relevant for a number of other reasons. Due to the intangibility of services, mass media are not as effective in communicating the qualities of the service compared with personal sources of information. For example, would Penelope have felt comfortable purchasing services for her nose re-alignment only from a 30-second television advertisement by a surgeon whom she had never heard of before? Moreover, would it be feasible to adequately describe the surgical procedure during a 30-second television spot? Overall, personal sources of information become more important as objective standards for evaluation decrease and as the complexity of the product being marketed increases.

Other reasons that consumers rely to such a great extent on personal sources of information is that non-personal sources may simply not be available because of professional restrictions or negative attitudes regarding the use of advertising. Alternatively, many service providers are small and may lack the resources or knowledge to advertise. For example, dentists, dog-grooming services and tennis coaches may not have the financial resources to advertise on television or radio. Similarly, they have the expertise in their chosen field but may never have had to take marketing or communications classes at university or college; therefore, they lack the knowledge in how to put together a promotional campaign. Indeed, most have no idea what a target market is, what a marketing mix is for, or what a marketing plan entails. Regardless of their training and subsequent status, professional service providers are operating businesses and must effectively compete in order to maintain their livelihoods. The bottom line is that many professional service providers either lack the knowledge or feel uncomfortable marketing their services.

Pre-purchase stage considerations: Fewer alternatives to consider

In comparison with goods, consumers of services tend to evaluate a smaller number of alternative sources of supply during the pre-purchase stage for a variety of reasons. First, each service provider tends to offer only one brand. For example, Bedale Building Contractors sell only one brand of building work. Similarly, your dentist provides only one brand of dental care. In contrast, consumers shopping for a television generally have many brands to consider at each of the many different retail locations that they could visit.

The second reason the evoked set tends to be smaller pertains to the number of establishments providing the same service. The tendency in services is to have a smaller number of outlets providing the same service. For example, a market can support only so many physiotherapists, IT consultants or window cleaners. In comparison, retailers selling similar goods such as clothes or shoes tend to be available in many locations within the shopping centre. The difference between the distribution of goods and services relates directly to the diversification of the product mix. Retailers of goods sell many products under many brand names, thereby earning their revenues through many different sources. Due to the diversified product mix, the same goods are available at many locations. In contrast, the survival of the service firm is dependent upon selling only one brand of service.

A third reason consumers consider fewer service alternatives relates to the lack of available pre-purchase information. Consumers of services simply are not aware of as many service substitutes and/or choose not to undertake the time-consuming task of obtaining information from competing service providers. In contrast, consumers of goods often simply look at what is on the store's shelves and are able to compare prices as well as a number of other factors such as ingredients, construction quality, feel and scent.

Pre-purchase stage considerations: Self-service as a viable alternative

Another difference between goods and services in the pre-purchase choice stage of the consumer decision process is that self-provision or 'Do It Yourself' often becomes a viable alternative for such services as garden maintenance, fence installation, housekeeping, painting and a number of other services. In comparison, consumers rarely consider building a microwave instead of purchasing one from a local retailer. For obvious reasons, many professional service providers are not generally competing against the self-service alternative. However, some self-service solutions such as homeopathic medicines do exist.

Consumption stage considerations

The consumption of goods can be divided into three activities: buying, using and disposing. The three activities occur in a definite buy–use–dispose order and have clear boundaries between them. The customer buys a box of detergent at a supermarket, uses it at home in the washing machine and disposes of the empty box after the detergent is used up.

This scenario does not apply to the consumption of services, however. First of all, no clear-cut boundary or definite sequence exists between the acquisition and the use of services because there is no transfer of ownership. Because of the prolonged interactions between the customer and the service provider, the production, acquisition and use of services become entangled and appear to be a single process (Walker, 1995). Furthermore, the concept of disposal is irrelevant because of the intangibility and experiential nature of services.

Without a doubt, the consumption stage is more complex for services in comparison with that of goods. The servuction system concept introduced in Chapter 1 suggests that the benefits bought by a customer consist of the experience that is delivered through an interactive process. Even when a service is rendered to something that the consumer owns, such as a car, rather than to the individual's person, such as health care, the service production/consumption process often involves a sequence of personal interactions (face-to-face or by telephone) between the customer and the service provider (Hogg et al., 2003). Interactions between the customer and the company's facilities and personnel are inevitable. The service experience is acquired through the interactive interface between the service providers and their consumers and how they both react to the many intangible elements received during and after the experience (Svensson, 2006).

Perhaps the most important outcome of these interactions is the contradiction of the idea that post-choice evaluation occurs only at a certain point in time after use. The use of goods is essentially free from any kind of direct marketer influence. For example, the manufacturer of the coffee you drank this morning had no interaction with you whatsoever. Consumers of goods, therefore, can choose when, where and how they will use a good. On the other hand, service organizations play an active role in customer consumption activities because services are produced and consumed simultaneously.

For example, there is interaction between the staff in a coffee shop and the consumer as soon as the transaction begins. The member of staff has a direct influence over the enjoyment of the service received, from their initial warm and friendly greeting to the taste and temperature of the coffee and the physical environment of the coffee shop itself.

No service can be produced or used with either the consumer or the service firm absent. Due to the extended service delivery process, many believe that the consumer's post-choice evaluation occurs both during and after the use of services, rather than only afterward. In other words, consumers evaluate the service while they are experiencing the service encounter during the consumption stage as well as during the post-purchase stage. Consider the evaluations made when buying a ticket to the Sziget Music Festival in Budapest online. Firstly, evaluation takes place when the ticket is bought, evaluating the speed of the transaction, the ease of navigation through the website, the method of payment, the security of the transaction and the speed of receiving a receipt via e-mail. This may be negative but is then improved by a positive evaluation of the speed of ticket arrival in the post, the inclusion of details of the bands that are playing, and discount vouchers for trains, buses and camping equipment. The actual festival experience will then be evaluated during the event and also re-evaluated afterwards through discussions with friends, reading reviews and post-purchase communication from the organizers.

From a marketer's point of view, this opens up several opportunities to directly influence that evaluation; particularly in face-to-face or telephone service interactions. Hence, the restaurant manager who visits diners' tables and asks, 'How is your dinner this evening?' is able to catch problems and change evaluations in a way that the manufacturer of a packaged good cannot.

Post-choice considerations

The post-purchase evaluation of services, therefore, is a complex process. It begins soon after the customer makes the choice of the service firm he or she will be using and continues throughout the consumption and post-consumption stages. The evaluation is influenced by the unavoidable interaction of a substantial number of social, psychological and situational variables. Service satisfaction relies not only on the properties of the four elements of the servuction system – contact personnel, servicescape, other customers and internal organization systems – but also on the synchronization of these elements in the service production/consumption process.

The success or failure of a service firm can be at least partly attributed to management's ability or inability to manipulate the customer experience as the output of a collection of interpersonal interactions (client versus client, client versus employee) and human–environment interactions (employee versus working environment and supporting facilities, customer versus service environment and supporting facilities). A number of proposed models attempt to describe the process by which consumers evaluate their purchase decisions.

expectancy disconfirmation model
The model in which consumers evaluate services by comparing expectations with perceptions.

Post-choice models: The expectancy disconfirmation model. How does service satisfaction arise during the consumption and post-purchase stages? A number of approaches have been suggested, but perhaps the simplest and most powerful is the expectancy disconfirmation model. The concept of this model is straightforward. Consumers evaluate services by comparing expectations with perceptions (see Figure 4.4). The service organization's performance is perceived by the consumer on elements such as the past experience, corporate image, brand name and reputation of the service organization (Robledo, 2001), its service quality and all elements of the marketing mix (Andreassen, 1995).

The expectancy disconfirmation model, therefore, proposes that consumers often have preconceived ideas and expectations of the service they are going to receive even before purchase and consumption take place. Therefore, the preconceived expectations of the service will affect their dissatisfaction or indeed satisfaction of the service received. Dissatisfaction will arise if the preconceived ideas and expectations are not met. Conversely, satisfaction will arise if the preconceived ideas and expectations are met or exceeded. It is important to note here, that the preconceived expectations are in the mind of the consumer and, as all consumers are different, they may not necessarily reflect the unsatisfactory or satisfactory service delivered by the service organization itself (Prenshaw et al., 2006). Ultimately customer service is achieved through the effective management of customer perceptions and expectations.

It is the perceived service that matters, not the actual service. One of the best examples that reinforce this issue involves a high-rise hotel. The hotel was receiving numerous complaints concerning the time guests had to wait for elevator service in the lobby. Realizing that from an operational viewpoint, the speed of the elevators could not be increased, and that attempting

Figure 4.4

Expectation management model

Source Robledo, M.A. (2001) 'Measuring and Managing Service Quality: Integrating Customer Expectations', *Managing Service Quality*, Vol. 11, No. pp. 22–31.

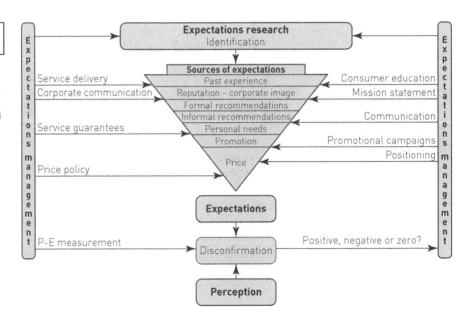

to schedule the guests' elevator usage was futile, management installed mirrors in the lobby next to the elevator bays. Guest complaints were reduced immediately – the mirrors provided a means for the guests to occupy their waiting time. Guests were observed using the mirrors to observe their own appearance and that of others around them. In reality, the speed of the elevators had not changed; however, the perception was that the waiting time was now acceptable.

It is necessary for organizations to understand what perceptions their consumers have towards the service offered in order to focus their attention on areas that will improve the overall perception of the service. A good example of this is based on research conducted for the transportation services in the capital of Norway. Results found that frequent travellers were dissatisfied with 1' the time travelling, 2' price level and 3' the physical environment of the station/platform. One of the recommendations was to improve the physical environment such as constructing additional bus shelters. This may improve the overall satisfaction of bus travellers. A decrease in price level was not recommended as this would not improve the overall impression of the service provided (Andreassen, 1995).

Consumer expectations should be managed through consumer education, communications, and so on (see Figure 4.4) in order to produce satisfaction without altering in any way the quality of the actual service delivered. For example, visit www.hotelformula1.com and you will see from the home page that not only do Hotel Formula1 want you to 'sleep well at the best prices' but they also 'guarantee cleanliness'. Hotel Formula 1, therefore, are managing the customer expectations to place price and cleanliness first on their list of priorities because they do not have services such as swimming pools, health clubs and full-service restaurants, which are associated with the higher-priced hotels. Economy-minded hotels, therefore, are carving out a niche in the market by providing the basics. The result is that customers know exactly what they will get ahead of time and are happy not only with the quality of the service received but also with the cost savings.

Post-choice models: The perceived-control perspective. Another model that assists in describing the post-purchase stage is the perceived-control perspective. The concept of control has drawn considerable attention from psychologists. They argue that in modern society, in which people no longer have to bother about the satisfaction of primary biological needs, the need for control over situations in which one finds oneself is a major force driving human behaviour (Bateson, 1984). Rather than being treated as a service attribute, as implied by multi-attribute models, perceived control can be conceptualized as a superfactor – a global index that summarizes an individual's experience with a service. The basic premise of this perspective is that during the service experience, the higher the level of control over the situation perceived by consumers, the higher their satisfaction with the service. Higher satisfaction is also gained when consumers are engaged in a higher

perceived-control perspective A model in which consumers evaluate services by the amount of control they have over the perceived situation.

state of arousal due to heightened stimulation such as scents, colours and sounds (Mattila and Wirtz, 2006).

In a slightly different way, it is equally important for the service firm itself to maintain control of the service experience. If the consumer gets too much control, the economic position of the firm may be affected as consumers tip the value equation in their favour, even to an extent that the firm may begin to lose money. On the other hand, if the service employees take complete control, consumers may become unhappy and leave. Even if this does not happen, the operational efficiency of the firm may be impaired. This three-cornered struggle among the service firm, its employees, and consumers is described in Figure 4.5.

Services can be thought of as a consumer's giving up cash and control in exchange for benefits, with each party seeking to gain as much advantage as possible. But it would appear that no one can truly win in such a 'contest'. In fact, the concept of control is much broader than implied. Behavioural control, the ability to control what is actually going on, is only part of the idea. Research shows that cognitive control is also important. Thus, when consumers perceive that they are in control, or at least that what is happening to them is predictable, the effect can be the same as that achieved by behavioural control. In other words, it is the perception of control, not the reality, which is important.

Managerially, this concept raises a number of interesting ideas. The first idea raised is the value of the information given to consumers during the service experience in order to increase their sense that they are in control and that they know what will happen next. This is particularly important for professional service firms, which often assume that simply doing a good job will make their clients happy – they forget that their clients may not have heard from them for more than a month and might be frantic due to the lack of contact and little or no information. For example, if a customer buying tickets for the Sziget Music Festival had not received them within two weeks they would become concerned, dissatisfied and stressed. However, if the ticket seller had sent e-mails to say the order had been accepted and another to say the tickets were being dispatched the dissatisfaction could be avoided. This form of communication is not expensive for the organization and it

Figure 4.5

The perceived behavioural control conflicts in the service encounter

Source Adapted from John E. G. Bateson, 'Perceived Control and the Service Encounter,' In John A. Czepiel, Michael R. Solomon, and Carol F. Suprenant, eds., *The Service Encounter* (Lexington, MA: Heath, 1985), pp. 67–82.

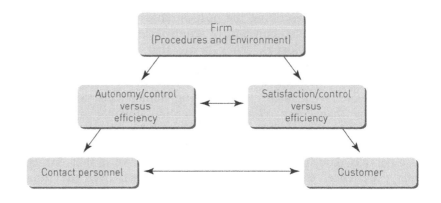

forms a relationship between the supplier and the consumer. It is equally important to an airline that delays a flight after passengers have boarded but fails to let them know what is happening or how long the delay will be.

Similarly, if a firm is due to make changes in its operation that will have an impact on consumers, it is important that those consumers be fore-warned. If they are not, they may perceive themselves to be 'out of control' and become dissatisfied with the service received to the extent that they change suppliers.

The control perspective raises interesting issues about the trade-off between predictability and choice. Operationally, one of the most important strategic issues is the amount of choice to give the consumer. Because both choice and predictability (standardization) can contribute to a sense of control, it is crucial to determine what the more powerful source of control is for the consumer.

Post-choice models: The script perspective – All the world's a stage and all the people players. A number of theories in psychology and sociology can be brought together in the ideas of a *script* and a *role*. A role is defined as 'a set of behaviour patterns learned through experience and communication, to be performed by an individual in a certain social interaction in order to attain a maximum effectiveness in goal accomplishment' (Solomon et al., 1985: 101). The principal idea proposed is that in a service encounter, customers perform roles, and their satisfaction is a function of role congruence – whether the actual behaviours by customers and staff are consistent with the expected roles. In the case of staff, their roles are boundary-spanning as they have contact with customers, other staff and management, as well as meeting all their demands and fulfilling their work-based tasks (Chung and Schneider, 2002). Customers see the member of staff as the face of the organization, indeed 'customer-contact employees are typically the first and only representative of retail-service organizations with whom customers interact' (Coote et al., 2004: 547). Therefore the two-way encounter between staff and consumer is crucial to any service organization.

role congruence The property of actual behaviours by customers and staff being consistent with their expected roles.

The role congruence, therefore, focuses on the post-purchase phases of a service encounter. The described interaction is two-way, so role congruence is expected to exert an impact on the customer as well as on the service provider. In other words, satisfaction of both parties is likely when the customer and the service provider engage in behaviours that are consistent with each other's role expectation; otherwise, both performers may be upset by the interaction.

The key managerial tasks implied by role theory perspectives are (1) to design roles for the service encounter that are acceptable and capable of fulfilling the needs of both the customers and the service providers and (2) to communicate these roles to both customers and employees so that both have realistic perceptions of their roles as well as those of their partners in their interactions.

Role is assumed to be *extra-individual*. Hence, every individual is expected to display the same predetermined set of behaviours when he or she takes up a certain role, either as a customer or as a service provider. Because role theory originally was not directly concerned with the perception of participants in the service encounter, it is incompatible with the concepts of service evaluation and customer satisfaction. Consider two customers, one an introvert and one an extrovert; both may have completely different perceptions and evaluations of interactions with the same chatty service provider. The introvert may not like the 'intrusive nature' of the service provider; but the extrovert may be delighted with the easy flowing conversations that the staff member provides. In this case, *intra-individual* variables must be employed in order to explain the differences in customer evaluation and satisfaction.

The role idea can, however, be adapted for use in service situations. This adaptation draws on the psychological idea of a script. The script theory and role theory perspectives appear on the surface to be similar. Script theory argues that rules, mostly determined by social and cultural variables, exist to facilitate interactions in daily repetitive events, including a variety of service experiences. The script for service organizations is not a full word-for-word manual which dictates what is to be said and done in each service encounter (Lyons, 2006). However, it is a guide to work with that expresses the routines and core competencies of the organization which in turn provide 'rules' that shape the participants' expectations in these types of interactions. Furthermore, the rules must be acknowledged and obeyed by all participants if satisfactory outcomes are to be generated. For example, patrons of a fine dining restaurant will have behavioural expectations of their waiter that are consistent with the service setting. Similarly, the waiter will have expectations of the patron's behaviour as well. If one participant deviates from the rules, the other co-actors in the service setting will be uncomfortable. Therefore, a satisfied customer is unlikely given a dissatisfied service provider, and a dissatisfied customer is unlikely given a satisfied service provider.

Despite the similarity of the role theory and script theory perspectives, basic differences exist between them. First, the script theory perspective has a wider range of concerns (including the impact of the service setting) and hence is concerned with the whole service experience rather than with only the interpersonal service encounter. Second, scripts are by definition intra-individual and are a function of an individual's experience and personality. Finally, consumer scripts can be revised by service providers who educate consumers about the service process.

The expectancy disconfirmation model, the perceived-control perspective, and the script perspective may not totally reflect reality, but because they are the result of much research in marketing and psychology, they at least allow us to make logical deductions about consumer behaviour when making marketing decisions. Moreover, since all the models described here have both strengths and weaknesses, they should be considered complementary rather than mutually exclusive. Managerial insights can be developed more effectively through a combination of these various perspectives as we continue to learn about consumer decision processing.

script theory Argues that rules, mostly determined by social and cultural variables, exist to facilitate interactions in daily repetitive events, including a variety of service experiences.

Organizational buying behaviour

The purchases discussed so far have been about services that a consumer would buy for themselves or their friends and family. When a person is buying on behalf of an organization they behave differently than they would when buying for their household. This is because the purchaser often feels detached from the purchase as it is for the organization and not for them. Similarly the organizational buyer has to also deal with the demands and requirements that their organization has for the service being purchased, while at the same time negotiating with suppliers for the best deal. Most importantly, the organizational buyer is not the only person involved in the purchase decision. Often, especially in medium and large organizations, purchasing expensive services or equipment requires a team effort. The team is known as the buying centre. The team members of the buying centre are (1) the initiator, (2) the gatekeeper,

buying centre All the members of the team that play some role in the purchase decision of goods and services for and on behalf of the organization.

1	The Initiator	A person who identifies a need or who has an idea for a purchase. The initiator often plays other roles (e.g., the role of the user) in the buying process.
2	The Gatekeeper	A person in the organization who controls the flow of information. Many times, this person could serve in the role of administrative assistant to other people in the buying centre.
3	The Influencer	A person in the organization who may have important technical or practical knowledge about the product category. This person could also be a resident expert. The influencer could also be a person who mixes regularly with the key decision-makers of an organization
4	The Decider	The person who makes the final decision. The person will determine whether specifications for bids are acceptable or be in charge of identifying acceptable vendor and/or service providers.
5	The Buyer	This person physically buys the service or product. They often negotiate the best deals in terms of price and specifications.
6	The User	The person or persons who consume the product or service. In some cases, the final user may have had little or no involvement in the decision-making process.

Table 4.3

Decision making unit

Source Adapted from Arnould, Price and Zinkhan, 2004: 547.

(3) the influencer, (4) the decider, (5) the buyer, (6) the user (see Table 4.3). It is important to note that there can be considerable role sharing throughout organizational buying processes. It should also be noted that in smaller organizations, such as a family business, the team members in the buying centre may be only two people. The following scenario illustrates how the roles are intertwined. The Facilities Manager (the initiator) commissioned research into the physical environment of his organization. He was shocked how many complaints there were about the plant and flower displays. The Facilities Manager took a tour around the organization and noticed that virtually all the plants were dying or in a poor state of health. Additionally, the plant containers were all different shapes and colours, none of which fitted the corporate colours of green, purple and silver. The Facilities Manager recognized that improvements needed to be made. Therefore, a short report was drafted requesting the services of interior landscapers who specialize in project design, installation, maintenance and aftercare for plants and containers. The report was put together for the Managing Director (the decider). However, the Facilities Manager asked for advice from the Managing Director's Personal Assistant (the influencer and gatekeeper) with regard to specific budgets to adhere to, colour schemes to suggest and the most appropriate time to submit the report. The Personal Assistant chose all the paintings displayed in the

---

Figure 4.6

Organizational buying behaviour

Source From Sheth/Mittal/Newman, *Customer Behavior*, 2nd edition. © 2004 South-Western, a part of Cengage Learning, Inc. Reproduced by permission. www.cengage.com/permissions.

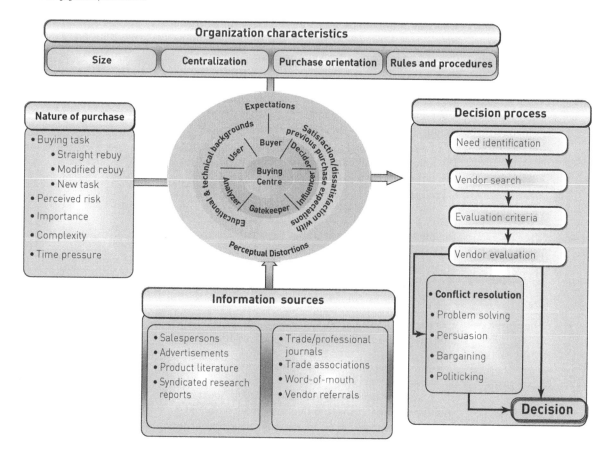

Conference Rooms, hence he has a reputation for style and design and becomes an influencer. Additionally, the Personal Assistant is a gatekeeper as such persons are known to have considerable power in accepting or rejecting information between the decision maker and other team members in the buying centre. The Facilities Manager also spoke to the Procurement Officer (an influencer) who gathered information about interior landscape service organizations from salespeople, product brochures and advertisements. Six months later, three thousand members of staff arrived at their organization on Monday morning to be greeted by beautiful plant displays throughout the building. The staff and the Facilities Manager (the users) all have the benefits that plants bring to health and well-being, by reducing dust and noise pollution.

Not all purchases take several months from the initial idea being recognized to the services being used. The nature of the purchase can be very different as some purchases may take longer, such as choosing the right service organization to maintain a major High Street bank's cash machines. However, some purchases are quick and easy to make, such as window cleaning services. There are three classes of organizational purchases. The buy classes are (1) *new task buys*, (2) *straight re-buys* and (3) *modified buys*. The decision process involved for a new task buy brings with it considerable uncertainty and risk. Therefore, the buying centre includes many people, as shown in the example earlier for the services of interior landscapers. The buying centre will develop the criteria and specifications required for the purchase. Many people from the buying centre will also be involved in inviting vendors to submit written proposals or watching potential suppliers present their bids. Some, or all members of the buying centre, will evaluate and choose the most appropriate supplier. The buying centre is more important at this stage as the users will feedback their satisfaction or dissatisfaction with the purchase made. This extensive decision process and involvement of the entire buying centre is not appropriate for straight re-buys as it would be inefficient in terms of costs and time for purchases that are frequently needed and the organization is satisfied with the service it currently receives. Therefore, straight re-buys will involve fewer people from the buying centre. Similarly the decision process will not involve as many stages. A modified buy, as the name suggests, may be required to improve the energy efficiency for electricity or gas services. Therefore, the basic service required is the same, but modifications need to be introduced to ensure that corporate targets are met.

Like all purchasing decisions made by consumers (see Figure 4.1) organizations also proceed along a linear decision-making process (see Figure 4.6, Organizational Buying Behaviour). This model not only shows details of the decision process, it brings together the components of the buying centre and the nature of the purchases. Similarly, it adds to the sources of information that the buying centre can draw upon to gather data about the services, prices and after-sales care available.

Summary

This chapter has presented consumer and organizational decision process issues as they relate to service consumers. The consumer decision process model consists of three main stages: the pre-purchase stage, the consumption stage and the post-purchase stage. The pre-purchase stage consists of the events that occur prior to the consumer's acquisition of the service and includes stimulus reception, problem awareness, information search, and evaluation of alternatives. The outcome of the pre-purchase stage is a choice that takes place during the consumption stage. The consumption stage includes the activities of buying, using and disposing of the product. The post-purchase stage refers to the process by which the consumer evaluates his or her level of satisfaction with the purchase.

Although the consumer decision process model applies to both goods and services, unique considerations arise with respect to services in each of the three stages. Compared with their considerations when purchasing goods, consumers of services during the pre-purchase stage of the decision process (1) perceive higher levels of risk to be associated with the purchase; (2) tend to be more brand loyal; (3) rely more on personal sources of information; (4) tend to have fewer alternatives to consider; and (5) often include self-provision as a viable alternative.

The consumption stage is more complex for services in comparison with that of goods as the production, acquisition and use of services become entangled in a single process. Moreover, due to the extended service delivery process, many believe that the consumer's post-choice evaluation occurs during and after, rather than only after, the use of services. From a marketer's point of view, this provides the opportunity to directly influence the consumer's evaluation during the service delivery process. Because of the client/company interface, the service provider is able to catch problems and change evaluations in a way that the manufacturer of a packaged good cannot.

Similarly, the post-purchase evaluation of services is also a complex process. The evaluation process begins soon after the customer makes the choice of the service firm he or she will be using and continues throughout the consumption and post-consumption stages. The evaluation is influenced by the unavoidable interaction of a substantial number of social, psychological and situational variables. Service satisfaction relies not only on the technical quality of the service and the four elements of the servuction system (contact personnel, servicescape, other customers and internal organizational systems), but also on the synchronization of these elements in the service production/consumption process.

Models that assist in our understanding of the consumer's post-purchase evaluation process include the expectancy disconfirmation model, the perceived-control perspective and the script perspective. Briefly, the expectancy disconfirmation model defines satisfaction as meeting or exceeding customer expectations. The perceived-control perspective proposes that during the service experience, the higher the level of control over the situation perceived by consumers, the stronger will be their satisfaction with the service. The script perspective proposes that in a service encounter, customers perform roles, and their satisfaction is a function of role congruence – whether or not the actual behaviours by customers and staff are consistent with the expected roles. Models such as these help us understand how consumer evaluations are processed and indicate areas where service marketers can focus their efforts in pursuit of the ultimate goal of providing customer satisfaction.

Organizational purchase decisions are often more complex and formal involving more than one person and a number of roles (the buying centre). The complexity of the decision is partly determined by the buy class of the purchase, which can be a straightforward rebuy, a modified rebuy or a new task decision. As with consumer purchase decisions a number of organizational buying models exist that help marketers to understand the process and the influences on these decisions.

Discussion questions

1 Discuss the value of consumer behaviour models to services marketing.

2 Describe and provide examples of the types of risks associated with visiting Centre Parks.

3 Discuss why perceived risk is generally greater for services than for goods purchases.

4 Define and discuss the following terms: search attributes, experience attributes, and credence attributes.

5 Evaluate, using service examples, the usefulness of the multi-attribute models (the linear compensatory approach and the lexicographic approach).

6 Explain why consumers are more brand loyal for services, such as Centre Parks, than they are for products.

7 Why do personal sources of information tend to be more important for consumers of services?

8 Discuss the managerial implications of the client/company interface during the consumption stage.

9 Explain the relevance of the perceived-control model as it relates to the post-consumption stage.

References and further reading

Andreasen, A. R. (1995) *Marketing Social Change: Changing Behaviour to Promote Health, Social Development, and the Environment*, San Francisco, CA: Jossey-Bass.

Arnould, E., Price, L. and Zinkhan, G. (2004) *Consumers*, 2nd ed., New York: McGraw Hill.

Bateson, J. E. G. (1984) 'Perceived control and the service encounter', in *The Service Encounter*, eds John A. Czepiel, Michael R. Solomon and Carol F. Suprenant, Lexington, MA: Lexington Books, pp. 67–82.

Bateson, John E. G. (1992) *Managing Services Marketing: Text and Readings*, 2nd ed., Fort Worth, TX: Dryden Press.

Bauer, R. A. (1960) 'Consumer behaviour as risk taking', in *Dynamic Marketing for a Changing World*, ed. R.S. Hancock, Chicago: American Marketing Association, pp. 389–398.

Chung, B. G. and Schneider, B. (2002) 'Serving multiple masters: role conflict experienced by service employees', *Journal of Services Marketing* 16 (1): pp. 70–87.

Coote, L. V., Price, E. and Ackfeldt, A.-L. (2004) 'An investigation into the antecedents of goal congruence in retail-service settings', *Journal of Services Marketing* 18 (7): 547–559.

Guseman, D. (1981) 'Risk perception and risk reduction in consumer services', in *Marketing of Services*, eds J. Donnelly and William R. George, Chicago: American Marketing Association, pp. 200–204.

Hogg, G., Laing, A. and Winkelman, D. (2003) 'The professional service encounter in the age of the Internet: an exploratory study', *Journal of Services Marketing* 17 (5): 476–494.

Hong-Youl Ha (2006) 'An integrative model of consumer satisfaction in the context of e-services', *International Journal of Consumer Studies* 30 (2): 137–149.

Jaakkola, E. (2007) 'Purchase decision-making within professional consumer services. Organizational or consumer buying behaviour', *Marketing Theory* 7 (1): 93–108.

Kaplan, L., Szybilo, G. J. and Jacoby, J. (1974) 'Components of perceived risk in product purchase; a cross-validation', *Journal of Applied Psychology* 59: 287–291.

Lyons, P. (2006) 'Performance scripts creation: Processes and applications', *Journal of European Industrial Training* 30 (2): 152–164.

MacInnis, D. J., Moorman, C. and Jaworski, B. J. (1991) 'Enhancing and measuring consumers' motivation, opportunity, and ability to process brand information from ads', *Journal of Marketing* 55 (4): 32–53.

Mattila, A. S. and Wirtz, J. (2006) 'Arousal expectations and service evaluations', *International Journal of Service Industry Management* 17 (3): 229–244.

Nicosia, F. and Mayer, R. N. (1976) 'Toward a sociology of consumption', *Journal of Consumer Research* 3 (2): 65–75.

Odekerken-Schroder, G., De Wulf, K., Kasper, H., Kleijnen, M., Hoekstra, J. and Commandeur, H. (2001) 'The impact of quality on store loyalty: a contingency approach', *Total Quality Management* 12 (3): 307–322.

Prenshaw, P. J. Kovar, S. E. and Burke, K. G. (2006) 'The impact of involvement on satisfaction for new, non-traditional, credence-based service offerings', *Journal of Services Marketing* 20 (7): 439–452.

Reid, R. D. and Bojanic, D. C. (2006) *Hospitality Marketing Management*, London: Wiley.

Robledo, M. A. (2001) 'Measuring and managing service quality: integrating customer expectations', *Managing Service Quality* 11 (1): 22–31.

Sheth, J. and Mittal, B. (2004) *Customer Behavior: A Managerial Perspective*, 2nd ed., Thomson.

Solomon, M. R., Suprenant, C. F., Czepiel, J. A. and Gatman, E. G. (1985) 'A role theory perspective on dyadic interactions: the service encounter', *Journal of Marketing* 49 (1): 99–111.

Svensson, G. (2006) 'The interactive interface of service quality: a conceptual framework', *European Business Review* 18 (3): 243–257.

Walker J.L. (1995) 'Service encounter satisfaction: conceptualized', *Journal of Services Marketing* 9 (1): 5–14.

White R. (2007) 'Search marketing', *WARC Best Practice*, June.

Wicken, G. (2001) 'A deeper understanding of European internet users', *Admap Magazine*, September, Issue 420.

www.thebonviveur.co.uk/.

www.casamiaonline.com/.

Chapter 5
Researching service markets

Companies with deep knowledge about their customers, competitors and operations will be the winners of this age.

(Sisodia, 1992: 63)

Chapter objectives

There is, undoubtedly, a need for an increased use of **marketing information** within the service industries in order to improve all aspects of decision making and marketing activity planning. This chapter details why the information is needed, how it can be obtained and how it should be used in a practical and realistic way.

After reading this chapter, you should be able to:

marketing information
Any facts, figues or data that can support maketing decision making.

- Understand the importance of information in developing and maintaining successful service marketing strategies.

- Appreciate the variety of sources of information and the advantages and disadvantages of each.

- Recognize the range of data generation methods and select appropriate ones for given situations

- Understand the importance of managing information and the potential drawbacks involved.

Services in context
Researching young readers

In many industries, launching a new product without first finding out whether or not consumers want to buy it is inconceivable. Months of research can precede the unveiling of a new toy or magazine, but in children's book publishing, consumer research remains something of a luxury.

Publishers often rely on instinct or on knowledge of what has worked previously, but consumer research can offer a more objective approach. 'No one is suggesting every cover or storyline can, or should, be market-tested', says Catherine Hunt, head of media and insight at HarperCollins. 'But it can be hard for any industry, including publishing, to be objective about a product and its potential audience.'

Cost is often cited as the main obstacle to carrying out consumer research. However, there are ways to undertake consumer research without it being expensive. The marketing team at Puffin, for example, limits its activity to one major research project each year. Marketing director Kirsten Grant says: 'It is a substantial investment but you do see the returns. It gives us a real handle on how our consumers spend their time, how they see things, how they buy things and what interests them.' The company's past research projects have included examining what would entice teenagers to read more. It found there was a demand from this age group for more online publications. Consumer research was instrumental in the launch and development of Egmont Press's 2Heads list. It revealed what kinds of stories children enjoy and how titles would be perceived by parents. Working alongside research company Kids Industries, Egmont visited schools and spoke to around 800 children and parents.

Sarah Radford, senior consultant at Kids Industries, says that because the children's publishing market is crowded, publishers need to be able to offer titles that stand out and are 100% right for their readers. 'Consumer research can tell you what will and what won't work.'

Other publishers successfully using in-house research include Scholastic who regularly visits schools to gain feedback on ongoing projects and book covers, while Puffin invites classes into its offices. 'They can see how the publishing machine works, meet authors and give us feedback on some new designs and ideas', says Adele Minchin, Puffin's publicity director. Though not as structured as commercial research projects, the feedback can still be valuable.

HarperCollins (HC) has a media and insight research team based at its head office. Catherine Hunt, its head, says it was created following some company research that indicated a lack of understanding of who the HC consumer really was. 'This is a creative industry, so you can't treat our products the same as most manufacturers, but this research helps us to put the *consumer* at the heart of what we do.' Alison Ruane, children's marketing director at HarperCollins, adds: 'We won't just say: "This book will suit a girl aged eight to 12 years", but: "This girl, who is aged eight to 12 years, has these aspirations, does this with her spare time, and this is what she does when she's not reading." Your marketing becomes smarter.'

'It challenges your assumptions about the market', Ruane says. 'You know as much as you think you do, but we are not children. When you ask for opinions from your *consumers*, you have to be prepared for that. You'll think something is spot on and when it comes back, it's not.'

Carrying out market research can also give a publisher leverage with booksellers. 'Retailers might say they are not sure if a series will work or if the cover is right. We can show them the series and design will work [and] we are confident the product is right because that is what children have told us', Ruane adds.

So, while it might take time and some extra expense, market research can help to ensure that a book launch is not a guessing game. And each individual piece of research also adds to the bigger picture of building up a young reader profile.

Source: Adapted from: Caroline Horn, 'Researching young readers', *Bookseller*, 8/17/2007 Supplement, pp. 11–12.

Introduction

In order to gain and sustain competitive advantage all organizations need to gather, analyse and use information from a variety of sources. At the very least a knowledge of existing and potential markets, business trends, competitors and the effectiveness of marketing programmes is critical to the success of any organization. This requires a focused continuous gathering and use of information against which to measure the achievement of objectives.

The relationship between information use and the marketing value chain is illustrated in Figure 5.1.

Because of the failure to focus on information issues, few organizations know what information they have or need. For sectors where there is a high level of customer contact and hence the service industry, a firm's ability to deliver quality service depends largely on its ability to collect, process and distribute information. Berkley and Gupta's (1995) list of what they suggest as areas of prime importance in a service-based industry highlight the complexity and variety of

competitive advantage A distinctive or unique competence when compared with that offered by competing firms.

marketing value chain Each activity in maketing planning adds value to the offering to the customer.

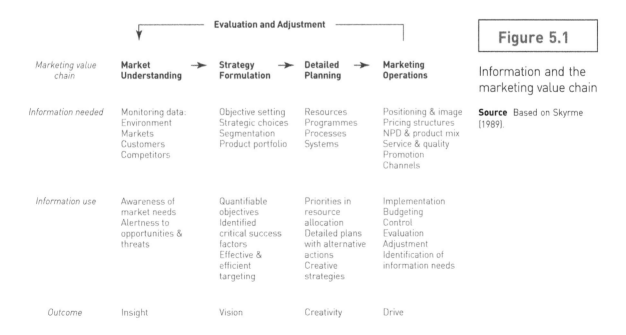

Figure 5.1

Information and the marketing value chain

Source Based on Skyrme (1989).

Marketing value chain	Market Understanding	Strategy Formulation	Detailed Planning	Marketing Operations
		Evaluation and Adjustment		
Information needed	Monitoring data: Environment Markets Customers Competitors	Objective setting Strategic choices Segmentation Product portfolio	Resources Programmes Processes Systems	Positioning & image Pricing structures NPD & product mix Service & quality Promotion Channels
Information use	Awareness of market needs Alertness to opportunities & threats	Quantifiable objectives Identified critical success factors Effective & efficient targeting	Priorities in resource allocation Detailed plans with alternative actions Creative strategies	Implementation Budgeting Control Evaluation Adjustment Identification of information needs
Outcome	Insight	Vision	Creativity	Drive

information needs within service organizations. These are: demands and capacities, service specifications, service history, market trends, service standards, customer instructions, process information, knowledge, job status, security, quality control, internal quality measures, external quality measures, complaints and compliments, service recovery and customer defections.

Much of the information generated in the service industry results from people-to-people interaction between employees and customers, customers and customers and employees and employees. This type of qualitative data is highly valuable but more difficult to systematically collect, analyse and use and this may be one of the reasons why many organizations have not initiated systematic efforts in realizing the benefits of formal marketing information systems (Sisodia, 1992).

Although the main uses for marketing information are for continuous improvement of all marketing activities, to gain competitive advantage, to build customer loyalty and so on, within some service areas, such as not-for-profit and public services, there are additional benefits to be gained from having access to valid and reliable data. This data will often provide the evidence required to secure continued political and financial support from a number of important stakeholder groups.

Glazer (1997) argues that information itself is the key strategic asset to be maximized as well as the guiding principle around which corporate

marketing information systems A formal or informal process for managing the information gathered by an organization.

B2B services in action
Market research: The unutilized potential in B2B marketing

Amazingly, most B2B companies conduct very little market research. Or, to put it more precisely, they concentrate on various technical statistical data but make no effort to find out the emotional responses within their target group towards their industry's services.

Now, it's not wrong to find out how large your target group is, what age group and gender the decision makers are, what is the size/turnover/purchase quantity of the average client, which technical requirements they have and things like that. These are useful data too. However, such technical information seldom avails itself to make a difference in the market in terms of creating demand for the services of a particular company.

In consumer marketing, market research is predominantly about the emotional responses of the target group. We understand that this is so because the consumer isn't making his decisions rationally but through emotional

impulses. It is assumed that the B2B market services 'factual' needs and that the decision-making process is equally completely rational. However, any decision involving human behaviour also involves emotion. It is true that the B2B market is much more rational, its decision-making process far more logical than is the case with consumers, but it is also moved by emotion.

Being emotional has in a way become a sin for the thinking person, especially so within the B2B sector wherein feelings are the antitheses of scientific rationality. Logical thinking is the keyword within the B2B industries because it is the ideal which is sought within a profession.

However, if emotion has no influence or value then why isn't B2B purchasing and selling done by computers? Those work solely on data with absolutely no ability to emit or sense any form of emotion.

Emotions are an inherent part of judgement, relationship building and, indeed, professionalism and are the key to conducting meaningful marketing research. Clever market research can find out the emotional influence on decisions and through this knowledge allow B2B services to ensure that marketing materials, approach, service concept and prospecting all align with every wish and viewpoint of a target group. For example:

● How do they see your salespersons and their actions, behaviour, knowledge, service attitude and so on?

● Which problem do the members of your target group consider their biggest, the one they want to solve now...but to which they don't believe a solution exists?

● What addition to your service concept would be just what they want or the thing they look for as a sign of reliability, trustworthiness or exceptional level of innovation in a company within your industry?

● What things do they see as proof of the opposite?

● Which of the qualities and (possibly unique) benefits of your services /products are they actually aware of...and how well do they truly understand those qualities?

● What areas of their own responsibilities and/ or knowhow are they sensitive about, so much so that you should avoid ever mentioning those in your marketing?

● What makes them want to find out more about the products/services of another provider within your industry? What things in your online/printed promotional materials would tell them not to bother contacting you at all...and why?

The result can provide those few sentences that can be used in marketing knowing that those are the best messages to convey and create exactly the type of image you want in the eyes of the average target person.

In-depth marketing research can provide something of concrete pragmatic value, which guarantees with absolute certainty that you have maximized your pull on the market and created a uniquely positive brand or image in the eyes of your target group.

And then you have it: Accurate information guaranteed to maximize the efficiency of your marketing thus optimizing the cost...and all arrived at with the principles of exact sciences.

Source: Adapted from Harry Kafka (2007). *HDK Consultants Ltd,* http://www.competitivebranding.com/marketresearch.html.

structures or departments are organized and that the focus of this information should be the customer who becomes central to everything the firm undertakes. Indeed, we are now starting to see a convergence between market research, competitor intelligence and customer relationship management. This convergence is driven by the recognition that the ability to understand markets and customers in order to predict their needs and position products and services to meet those needs in innovative ways is critical to a firm's success (Simpson, 2005). Despite this, very few service organizations make the best use of the information available and fewer still undertake regular marketing research. This is particularly true in organizational markets (see B2B Services in Action). The value of pertinent, reliable, timely information in providing competitive advantage has grown with increasing competition and improvements in information-based technologies. The many advantages of applying information technology in these areas are illustrated in Figure 5.2 and it becomes clear that service organizations of all sizes can no longer afford to neglect this valuable resource.

competitor intelligence
Information gathered on the specific activities of competing organizations.

marketing research
Information gathered to address a particular marketing problem or requirement.

The following sections take the reader through these sources of information, how they can be accessed, generated, applied and managed, in the context of the service environment.

The information required

recurrent monitoring data Data gathered form the continuous scanning of the firm's environment.

Before beginning any data gathering exercise it is necessary to have clearly defined objectives. This is as important for recurrent monitoring data gathered from a continuous scanning of the environment as it is for one-off market research projects and there is a need to detail why the information is needed and how it will be used. Once these objectives have been set it is then possible to determine the information required in order to make each marketing decision.

Source Sisodia, 1992 'Marketing information and decision support systems for services' in *The Journal of Services Marketing*, vol. 6(1) pp. 51–64

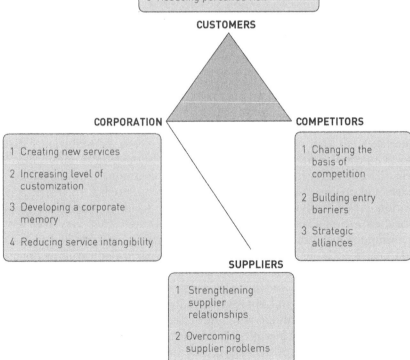

Figure 5.2

Information technology and the extended strategic triangle

The first stage in any research exercise is to check if the information required already exists and is in some usable form. For example, data may be routinely gathered and stored during each customer transaction, whether this is a purchase, a complaint, a recommendation or an enquiry. Many hotels now use systems which not only reserve rooms but also collect valuable information on customer preferences such as smoking/non-smoking room, breakfast order, morning paper and use of hotel facilities. This information can then be used to better serve the individual customer by anticipating their needs or can be aggregated and analysed to form the basis for future service developments and improvements. A drawback with such internal data, however, is that it is only gathered from existing customers and does not provide an insight into those not choosing to use the service or those who prefer competitors' offerings. A further disadvantage is the depth of information provided. Such internal systems often show what is happening but do not explain why. If insufficient or inappropriate date is available through these systems, it is necessary to ascertain whether or not the information can be obtained in time, at an acceptable cost and whether the likely benefits of its use will outweigh the resource requirements of producing it. For all organizations, however, there will always be a minimum amount of primary research that needs to be undertaken on a regular basis in order to provide sufficient information on which to base decisions.

Although information generated within the organization is a good starting point, it is important not to rely on this to the neglect of external data. Xu and Kaye (1995) argue that 80 per cent of information should be generated from outside the organization rather than the current practice of 80 per cent from internal sources (internal data). This highlights the need for monitoring information gathered from a variety of external sources in order to better understand market trends, competitor activity and any wider social, economic or technological changes which could affect the business. The four main types of information available, therefore, can be categorized as internal or external and primary or secondary. Secondary data (data which already exists for another purpose) is likely to be cheaper and quicker to obtain but may be out-of-date or too general. Primary data requiring marketing research can be costly but is tailored to the needs of the decision maker.

primary research Fist-hand data collected for a specific purpose.

external data Information gathered outside the operations of the organization.

internal data Information created within the organization through day-to-day operations.

secondary data Information that already exists in some form and has been gathered for a previous purpose.

Services marketing information needs

The four main marketing research areas of market analysis, consumer research, promotion studies and performance evaluation can be expanded upon to provide a more comprehensive checklist of information needs (Table 5.1).

Setting objectives. Realistic objective-setting requires hard, quantifiable data which can be largely historically based but also require a knowledge of the current financial and other organizational resource constraints along with an understanding of current market conditions. For example, in setting service use objectives for next year the local leisure centre manager will need to analyse data on past use from their internal transaction systems and also consider wider leisure and health trends, use of competing facilities and knowledge of planned funding changes.

Macro-environment analysis. The economic, social, legal, technological, demographic and political environments require monitoring on a continual basis. The regular scanning of a number of key sources of information to build up a market intelligence database is a relatively cost-effective way to gain useful insights and a precursor to an accurate forecasting system. Most of this information is available free of charge or at relatively low cost through media scanning, web resources and a variety of published reports from international, national and local agencies.

Customer analysis, segmentation and targeting strategy. A detailed knowledge of customers and markets is the most valuable resource an organization can have. In service organizations customers will include individuals, organizations or both and within these a range of different types with distinct characteristics. The complexity of these customer groups means that a detailed knowledge of their preferences and behaviours is of greater importance if their various needs are to be met. Only once the characteristics within these groups have been identified can the market be usefully segmented and only when those segments have been quantified and assessed can a targeting strategy be developed. The more detailed the knowledge of each customer, the closer the organization can get to a customized offering creating greater satisfaction and long-term customer relationships.

central customer information file Main store of information containing data on customer history, characteristics, preferences.

Glazer (1997) argues that an organization's information system should be based around a central customer information file (CIF) which contains information on customer characteristics, customer responses to firm decisions and customer purchase history. This needs to be built upon continually and becomes a vital part of the organization's memory utilizing past, present and likely future actions of customers, potential customers and lost customers.

Table 5.1

Checklist of service industry marketing information needs

Setting objectives	✓
Macro-environment analysis	✓
Customer analysis, segmentation and targeting strategy	✓
Customer satisfaction	✓
Customer expectations	✓
Competitor analysis and positioning	✓
Tactical marketing decisions	✓
Long-term planning	✓

Customer satisfaction measurement. This requires primary research before and after (and potentially during) each service encounter as well as the monitoring of repeat business levels, customer complaints, front line staff comments and so on. Quantitative measures are needed for meaningful comparison with other services and qualitative data to provide insight into areas for improvement. Care must be taken to ensure that the methods employed will produce useful information that can be used to improve the offering rather than data gathering for its own sake and 'to look like we care'.

A well known tyre and exhaust service firm in the UK routinely calls customers within seven days of using their services to assess satisfaction levels. However, on a number of occasions when the customer was not happy the caller continued with their script, thanked the customer and hung up the phone. Going through the motions of conducting satisfaction surveys in order to portray a caring image does little for that image and wastes an opportunity for collecting and using valuable data (both negative and positive). A similar experience is common in restaurants with the 'is everything all right with your meal?' question but an often dismissive response if there is a problem.

quantitative measures Numerical information, data in number or coded form usually consisting of large samples.

Customer expectations. It is imperative to ascertain these before any service is delivered to the customer, before an existing service is improved or before a new service is developed, as expectations have a great effect on levels of satisfaction and future purchase behaviour. High expectations may sell more tickets for one event but if those expectations are not met then future business will be lost. The expectations of the event need to be gleaned from those who did not attend as well as those who did as these market perceptions create the event organization's relative competitive position.

Competitor analysis and positioning. An understanding of the industry structure coupled with regular competitor intelligence can be used in a number of ways. Market share can be estimated from financial data and used to inform generic strategies. An understanding of competitor reactions to strategic moves can inform future plans, and recognition of best practice through benchmarking can enable the organization to learn from others in the industry. A thorough understanding of competitive offerings provides an insight into the decision-making process of the prospective customer and can suggest which benefits to emphasize in promotional material.

Marketing tactical decisions. Information from a variety of sources such as monitoring the services of others, using expert panels, customer feedback and so on can be used to inspire idea generation, aid portfolio planning, and maintain product innovation for competitive advantage.

As part of this process, research is needed to ascertain the market perceptions of related brand images prior to creating new brands, developing brand extensions or re-imaging existing brands.

In order to set customer-value-based pricing strategies and structures, information is also needed on the perceived benefits received and costs incurred for each market segment and stakeholder group. An understanding of the price elasticity of the service using supply and demand estimates is vital if price is to be used effectively in yield management and a competitive distribution strategy can only be initiated once customer preferences for the 'where, when and how' of the service purchase have been identified.

Quite often a large proportion of the marketing budget of service organizations is spent on marketing communications. In order to monitor the effectiveness of this spend, information is needed on the reach, impact, and short- and long-term effects on attitude and purchase behaviour of each promotional component and on the integrated communications strategy as a whole. This requires pre-campaign testing as well as monitoring of post-campaign results.

Long-term planning. A strategic rather than operational use of information is required in the long term in order to provide the basis for planning several years. This strategic orientation requires the development of a 'learning organization' making use of historic information, learning from mistakes and successes and forecasting ahead.

learning organization
A firm which uses information to learn from mistakes and successes and to plan for the future.

The development of appropriate long-term objectives and clear strategic paths to achieve them can be achieved only by the effective use of the information gathered from all the above activities in marketing decision-making.

The availability and location of information: Types and sources of data

In order to provide management decision makers with relevant, timely and reliable information it is important to utilize a variety of types and sources of data. However, it needs to be borne in mind that the exact data required will always be determined by the objectives of the research which in turn are determined by the needs of the decision maker: for example, to ascertain why sales have fallen this year, to justify continued investment or to identify new target markets.

The cheapest and most easily accessible type of data is that which is generated by the day-to-day running of the organization. The usefulness of this type of data can be greatly enhanced by systematic and consistent report generation using database and query software. This internal data is often the starting point of a developing marketing information system, however, caution is required as it is easy to become over-reliant on internal data to the neglect of vital external sources.

Quantitative internal data includes information on sales, accounts, customer records, costings and so on. Internally generated qualitative data might include sales staff reports, minutes of meetings, feedback from customer service staff, customer complaints/compliments and so on.

Data gathered from outside the organization are vital for decision making in a market-focused competitive firm. External data in the form of market intelligence, continuous market scanning and recurrent stakeholder surveys should be the priority of the service organization's information gathering activities.

The starting point for external data is to make use of information which already exists in some form. This secondary data can be quantitative such as government statistics, online data, industry surveys, published market research reports, trade or association data, published financial data, or qualitative including news reports/articles, trade journals, other media, competitor sales literature, trade directories, CD-ROMs and websites. The continuous monitoring of identified key external sources creates longitudinal data, which can be used to anticipate customer trends, competitor reactions, or economic fluctuations and is vital for forecasting and hence long-term planning decisions.

To complement these existing sources and to provide a richer picture of the organization's proximate macro-environment (customers, competitors, suppliers, publics) it is necessary to generate first-hand data. As this process will be comparatively costly and time-consuming it is important to have clear objectives for the research and to ensure that it can be carried out reliably (in-house or outsourced) within the given budget and time constraints. Again this primary information can be either quantitative or qualitative or preferably a combination of the two. Quantitative data tend to result from larger-scale surveys, resident panels, visitor profiles and so on and require the application of correct sampling procedures to ensure validity and reliability. Qualitative data are normally smaller scale but give more depth of information and are useful for ascertaining opinions, feelings and attitudes and for identifying initial problem areas for further investigation. This richer information can be gathered using observation, focus groups, in-depth interviews with customers and potential customers and through recording service staff feedback and utilizing management notes and commentary. The internet now provides the opportunity for gathering both secondary and primary information in an accessible, inexpensive and potentially innovative manner (see E-Services in Marketing).

qualitative data 'Wordy' information often gathered on opinions and attitudes in some depth but using smaller samples.

E-services in action
The internet as an information source: Present and future

Present

The internet is a knowledge-producing venue and therefore a wonderful new medium for research, with four clear advantages.

1 *Cost* – In today's environment, price, and thus cost, dictates the nature of the research. To the degree that a research venue promises lower costs, researchers take it seriously. The cost savings in inter-net research can be tremendous, because of the reduced costs to recruit, reward respondents, and administer the process.

2 *Speed* – The internet reaches thousands of respondents almost simultaneously. This allows interviews to be conducted virtually overnight, with quotas filled more rapidly than ever before. What researcher ever disliked bigger base sizes in the sample at no extra cost?

3 *Simplicity* – The internet reduces the complexity of research to template format. A number of services today promote DIY research, ranging from the simple to the complex, from simple questionnaires to conjoint analyses.

4 *Process simplification* – The internet simplifies the research process, often dramatically. Stimuli are presented in a standardised format, except perhaps for the settings of different browsers, which can make some visual stimuli appear different across respondents. Respondents' ratings are electronically acquired and stored, in many cases tabulated almost immediately upon the end of fieldwork. This simplification puts research into the hands of many, making it very affordable and accessible.

▶

Future

The internet offers the opportunity to move away from a one-way, or stimulus-response (SR) approach. The internet is a dynamic tool, allowing two-way interaction. From the researcher's side the internet can present the stimuli, and acquire data, whether these data be ratings or behaviours that co-vary with the stimulus (for example, search time for a stimulus, response time to a stimulus, exploratory behaviour, and change in the nature of selected stimuli from a set of choices). Given this existing, rapidly maturing power of the internet, we may expect to see some, if not all, of the following in the near future.

Real-time dialogue with consumers using artificial intelligence

An entire field content analysis has already emerged to deal with text information. Artificial intelligence models, implemented on the internet, will soon make their appearance. In the past decade, some more sophisticated methods have appeared that go further, to holding a reasonably intelligent conversation with respondents. As internet research matures, we may expect to see this type of artificial intelligence used more widely in dialogues with consumers, perhaps to understand their needs, but also to acquire information about their wants.

Ethnographic information using cameras to record, the internet to transmit data, and programs to analyse it

The era of small sensors is here. Cameras attached to computers, or which project to computers, are already popular. Radio frequency identifying devices (RFIDs) are another major technology that can be used to passively monitor behaviour of products and of people. At the same time, these technologies generate the need to automatically code and analyse the behaviour they monitor. The combination of large-scale volumes of visual data from free-ranging respondents (for example, in stores), sent to a central processor to code and analyse, may represent a new breakthrough in ethnography.

Real-time content mining and subsequent consumer interactions

The internet is filled with content, especially with respect to news and business issues. Corporate communications are always looking to identify weak signals in the environment from communications about companies. As computer programs sweep the net to acquire daily information about companies, there is a need to identify how consumers respond to this information, and in some cases adjust content and tonality of subsequent communication, at that specific time of interaction, to accord with the preferences of that individual consumer. New tools will be developed to determine what type of information represents an opportunity, what represents a threat and what is irrelevant to individuals. The technology will combine databases about consumer preferences with classification of consumers into segments, with each segment attuned to a different type of message. These research-based tools will be used both in informational communications of news events, and in sales-oriented communication of product/services.

A consumer psychologist analysing video footage.

Real-time ideation to identify business trends

We can imagine a world in which the components of a new idea/product/service lie within the minds of thousands of people, none of whom knows the new idea completely. With internet-enabled programs it may be possible to extract the components of the new idea, and have consumers themselves filter and amplify the components, until the idea emerges in a more complete shape. The ability to tap the minds of thousands of consumers overnight, and have them act as filters and amplifiers, represents a new trend whose importance is beginning to be recognized.

All in all, the future is quite exciting for the internet. The best advice is to stay tuned. As the saying goes, 'You ain't seen nothin' yet.'

Sources: Howard Moskowitz, 'Online Research: Prospects For A New Era', *Admap*, October 2004, Issue 454, pp. 140–142.
C. Cleveland, 'Quali-Quant techniques with Socrates and Aristotle', in: *Quester Text Processing*, ch. 3, Genesis Institute, 2001.
http://www.rfidjournal.com/.
L. Flores, 'Making idea generation and innovation available on the decision-maker desktop', Working Paper, Amiens Graduate School of Business, 2002.

Any successful marketing information system needs to combine internal and external sources and use both quantitative and qualitative data in order to provide statistical reliability plus in-depth insights in a meaningful and useable manner. Most organizations will start with internal and secondary information as this is quick and cheap to obtain. The scanning of external data regularly to build up market intelligence begins to give a market focus, but the core research activity should always centre on gathering customer information and it is not sufficient for this to come from internal systems. The gathering of external primary data is vital for organizations who tend to have a variety of stakeholders with changing needs and who operate in a highly competitive environment. It is this information that will enable the anticipation of future needs, the development of innovative offerings and hence a sustainable competitive advantage.

Methods for obtaining first-hand information: Generating data

In determining the parameters of primary research, the focus throughout should again be on 'fitness for purpose'. How will the final report be used? Who will read it and what decisions will be based on it? Starting at the end helps to focus on the objectives and not get carried away with an 'it would be nice to know' research agenda.

For all research projects there will be a range of tools and techniques which can be applied and need to be evaluated and selected. The quantitative/qualitative mix needs to be considered, as does the sampling methods and sample size. These again will depend upon the depth of information required and the levels of reliability and accuracy expected. Even if the research is to be outsourced to an agency, the initial decisions of methods and size should be considered.

A useful technique suggested by Smith and Fletcher (2001) is to start by detailing the ideal research design and then to trade down from this based on constraints of time, budget, expertise and so on. These constraints lead to what they call a 'five-way trade off' consisting of precision, depth of understanding, credibility, practicality and cost. Once the practical design has been achieved it is necessary to assess what sources of error have been introduced and whether these are acceptable.

The main techniques for gathering first-hand data are discussed below.

Surveys

The use of questionnaires to generate largely quantitative data are often used to gain customer opinions. These can be administered in a number of ways to meet the needs of the research undertaken, using either a trained interviewer (face-to-face or telephone) or self-completion by the respondent (hard copy, e-mail or online).

Online surveys are growing in popularity and are often used in the business-to-business market where customer access to the internet is close to 100 per cent. An example of this trend is the MIA Tracker system developed by the Meetings Industry Association. Event venues subscribe to an online software system that automatically solicits the opinions of event organizers on the venue shortly after each event. A further benefit is that as a syndicated research tool it can also provide each subscribing organization with information for competitive benchmarking (Meetings Industry Association/Catlow Consulting, 2002).

survey Used to gather data from a standard set of questions usually from larger samples and often quantitative.

A variation on the one-off survey is one that is repeated at regular intervals to provide longitudinal data. These surveys usually recruit a panel of consumers, businesses, or residents, who are used each time a survey is conducted. This type of research is very useful for tracking changes over time and often gives far better response rates. One disadvantage, however, is that the respondents' reported behaviour and attitudes may be influenced by the knowledge that they are regularly questioned and this variation on the 'Hawthorne effect' can be very difficult to recognize and quantify.

Any quantitative survey requires robust sampling procedures and recognition of any error or bias inherent in the process. These errors can be created by the number and type of non-response, by the interviewer technique, by initial sample size and selection, or by data entry and analysis procedures. The subsequent use of the data for decision-making must always allow for levels of reliability and validity and can be improved by making use of a number of sources of information rather than be reliant on the results of a single quantitative survey.

Focus groups/interviews

When information is required on attitudes, opinions or motivations it is often difficult or inappropriate to use quantitative techniques. Prompted but not controlled expression direct from the respondent can provide very rich insightful data that can lead to further areas for study or provide substance to the findings of parallel quantitative research. The depth of data generated from group discussions or in-depth interviews with customers, lapsed customers and prospective customers often provides the key to problem areas which would otherwise not have been anticipated by the researchers. Although guided in discussion areas, the respondents are not forced into making choices from pre-selected responses as with quantitative research, so there is no second guessing of the outcomes. However, the richness and unstructured nature of the data generated leads to problems in analysis and interpretation and requires skilled and experienced researchers if the findings are to be reliable and objective. Figure 5.3 shows an example of a focus group interview schedule.

> **interview** One-to-one, paired or group posing of structured questions by interviewer.

Internet chat rooms and discussion groups can be set-up as virtual focus groups with either an overt facilitator whose role is recognized by the participants or with a covert facilitator who poses as an ordinary participant. These e-groups can provide the opportunity to monitor attitude changes over time in a longitudinal study.

> **focus group** Facilitator-led discussion involving 6–12 participants to gather qualitative data.

A useful variation on focus groups is in soliciting expert opinion. Here the members of the discussion group are chosen based on their experience and knowledge of the topic rather than on the basis of being representative of a larger segment or population. The soliciting of expert opinion can be used in idea generation and product innovation as well as in recognizing the causes of previously identified problems. Experts can be drawn from any of the company's stakeholder groups and often involve suppliers and distributors. For example, a post-service mixed expert focus group may consist of the service providers, representatives from the partners involved, local government and local community representatives. The diversity of views expressed and the differing objectives of each group help to generate innovative ideas and solutions. In some situations it is possible to create discussion groups consisting of direct competitors if the topic is of mutual benefit and the findings are to be shared.

Customer group's attitudes to TV advertising campaign

1. Warm-up/Explanation of focus group rules.

2. Attendees' opinions of the product/brand itself.
   Why they use it, level of satisfaction

3. Knowledge of the advertisement for the service.
   Unprompted response initially. Where/when they
   saw the ad/What was remembered about it.

4. Discussion of advertisement's features.
   Attitudes, perceptions, image, knowledge, changes in attitude.

5. Their purchase behaviour and the ad.
   Trial, increased use, recommendation and so on.

6. Opinions of relationship between the ad and the service.
   Was the ad appropriate? Did the ad affect attitude to the service?

Figure 5.3

Example of an
interview schedule

Observation

Observing customer behaviour can provide detailed information on how the service is used and give clues to the benefits gained as well as helping to gauge levels of enjoyment or satisfaction. Observing behaviour as it happens provides very reliable information as it does not depend upon the respondent's memory or desire to be seen in a certain light. However, the recording and interpretation of that behaviour require a high level of skill and objectivity. Figure 5.4 shows an example of an observation checklist.

participant observation
The researcher takes on the role of the participants during the activity being researched while observing/recording their behaviour.

Participant observation has been used to investigate young people's social behaviour as a precursor to developing leisure services such as night clubs. The observer joins the group being observed on a social occasion and records their movements, purchases and conversation. The information is then combined with other sources to provide a detailed picture of prospective customer characteristics and their preferences.

Covert observation of the customer experience is a variation on the 'mystery shopper' technique pioneered in the retail industry. Here a trained researcher experiences the service and records the positive and negative aspects of it. This technique can be combined with experimentation by the observer setting up certain situations. For example, they may play the role of a dissatisfied customer and record how they are dealt with by customer service staff or they may stipulate particular dietary or mobility needs when booking and experience how these are implemented.

Conducting experiments

Although not often used within marketing research practice, experiments can supply valuable data which are not easily obtained through the other methods discussed. An experiment requires the observation, recording of the effects of changes made and a comparison of these changes in a before and after situation or through using a control group. In marketing research one of the main difficulties in conducting experiments is in controlling the other factors that could have an effect on the observed variable and the ethical dimensions involved in treating one group of customers, say, differently from another in order to learn from their responses.

Experiments can be conducted in a 'laboratory' (or 'created' environment) where external factors are more easily controlled but where the responses may differ from those experienced in the 'real world'. Examples of laboratory experiments might include taste tests, pupil dilation measured as response to visual stimuli (ads, logos, etc.), or monitoring how customers navigate a website and complete a set task (Essawy, 2006).

The field experiment maintains the logic and scientific basis of the laboratory experiment but places it in the 'context of purchase

SOURCE © ISTOCK.COM/MARCIN BALCERZAK

Focus groups provide invaluable information on both products and services.

or consumption, most commonly using a 'before-and-after, with control group' design' (Ryals and Wilson, 2005).

An example of the use of field experiments is provided by Ryals and Wilson (2005: 349). In this case an ICT (information and communication technology) service provider wished to test the hypothesis that the introduction of desk-based account managers (DBAMs) to work alongside the existing field sales force would save cost without decreasing revenue or customer satisfaction. A pilot study was defined to test this hypothesis, introducing 12 DBAMs into a set of accounts for a trial period, with measurement in both this experimental group and a control group of employee satisfaction, customer satisfaction, sales cost and revenue. The findings showed that DBAMs proved able to sell products to a much higher value than had been anticipated and that the DBAMs played an important role at earlier stages of the decision-making process. As a result, the ICT firm significantly reduced its cost-to-revenue ratio by replacing around 20 per cent of its field sales staff

Observation date: _____						
Please record your observations in the appropriate cells.						
Attendance	**10am**		**12noon**		**2pm**	
Record number of males, females and total in your observation area	M F Total		M F Total		M F Total	
Age groups *(Number in each age group)*	0–14 15–24 25–34 35–44 45–54 55+		0–14 15–24 25–34 35–44 45–54 55+		0–14 15–24 25–34 35–44 45–54 55+	
Visitor types	Family Family and friends Friends Individual Other	☐ ☐ ☐ ☐ ☐	Family Family and friends Friends Individual Other	☐ ☐ ☐ ☐ ☐	Family Family and friends Friends Individual Other	☐ ☐ ☐ ☐ ☐
Involvement *Tick one 'A' scale variable to indicate involvement level*	Anticipation Arousal Action Aggression	☐ ☐ ☐ ☐	Anticipation Arousal Action Aggression	☐ ☐ ☐ ☐	Anticipation Arousal Action Aggression	☐ ☐ ☐ ☐

Figure 5.4

Example of observation tool checklist for theme park

Source Adapted from O'Neill, M.A., Getz, D. and Carlsen, J. 'Evaluation of service quality at events: The 1998 Coca-Cola Masters Surfing event at Margaret River, Western Australia', *Managing Service Quality* 9(3): 158–166.

▶

| Expenditure Any evidence of spending on additional products? If yes, which ones? Tick boxes. If other items, note below other | Soft drinks Sweets/ Crisps Burgers/ hotdog Souvenirs T-shirts Toys Other (if yes, what?) | ☐ ☐ ☐ ☐ ☐ ☐ ☐ | Soft drinks Sweets/ Crisps Burgers/ hotdog Souvenirs T-shirts Toys Other (if yes, what?) | ☐ ☐ ☐ ☐ ☐ ☐ ☐ | Soft drinks Sweets/ Crisps Burgers/ hotdog Souvenirs T-shirts Toys Other (if yes, what?) | ☐ ☐ ☐ ☐ ☐ ☐ ☐ |
| Environment Any evidence environmental impacts? If yes, what type? | Litter Food waste Plastics Cans Other Vegetation trampling Other | ☐ ☐ ☐ ☐ ☐ ☐ ☐ | Litter Food waste Plastics Cans Other Vegetation trampling Other | ☐ ☐ ☐ ☐ ☐ ☐ ☐ | Litter Food waste Plastics Cans Other Vegetation trampling Other | ☐ ☐ ☐ ☐ ☐ ☐ ☐ |

with desk-based account managers. It also estimated an eight-figure increase in annual revenue as a result of the change of strategy.

In order to undertake a thorough evaluation of current service offerings, to gain a deeper understanding of potential markets or to generate new ideas, it is important to use a combination of the techniques discussed in this section. This holistic use of sources of information provides triangulation of findings and therefore improves reliability while giving a much greater depth of understanding of the issue being researched. The use of marketing research combining a range of methods is not limited to the private sector. The Child Support Agency in Australia successfully used a variety of information sources to underpin a new strategic framework. The information gathered is used continuously to measure performance and to assist in the development of new strategies. Examples of the studies used include:

- research into client compliance, that is determining the factors that influence parent's ability to meet their child support responsibilities;
- client satisfaction research – including both qualitative and quantitative research;
- research with clients to shape the development and marketing of products and services that support client independence;
- staff satisfaction research based on an holistic model of organizational health;
- research to determine the defining characteristics of high-performing staff;

- research regarding the community perception of the Child Support Agency and the role of government in the administration of child support; and
- research into client perceptions of e-business and electronic service delivery.

These studies use both quantitative and qualitative research methodologies, including the use of online surveys and automated responses using the telephony system (Wearne et al., 2004).

Effectively executed market research is a key vehicle for understanding customer perceptions of service quality and success. It is critical therefore that service marketers use both formal and informal methods of data collection and use these to ensure that services are consistently improved upon and sustainable competitive advantage gained. However, much marketing research requires specialist knowledge and skills that may be outside the capability of smaller service firms. The 'buying in' of this through the use of market research agencies may be one solution. Indeed, information generation, gathering, analysis and interpretation is a growing sector of the service industries (see Global Services in Action).

Interpreting the information: Analysing, managing and using the data

The importance of bringing information from a number of sources together in order to provide substantiated reliable evidence on which to base future decisions has been highlighted above. This process will require the application of a number of techniques for analysing qualitative and quantitative data and the use of information technology for analysis, storage, manipulation and retrieval.

The data analysis process for complex information from a variety of sources requires an initial clarification of the decision maker's goals. This sets the objectives for the analysis and presentation of results. It is then necessary to check and clearly acknowledge the data validity and reliability. Once this is done the data can be reduced through the use of statistical methods for quantitative data or through techniques such as content analysis for qualitative data. The reduced data can then be investigated to identify trends, shapes and patterns and these can in turn be used to develop and build models to explain behaviours. The final stage is to present the findings in an objective and useable manner to those who will be using it to inform strategic marketing decisions.

Although the procedure outlined above is valid for each project being

SOURCE © ISTOCK.COM

undertaken, there also needs to be a system in place to manage the continual flow of information from market intelligence, internal records, ad hoc projects and so on. The complexity, competitiveness and volatility of many services creates a greater need for marketing information to be managed within a bespoke system and this system development is a key stage in the

---

Global services in action
The global market research industry 2006: A summary

The annual ESOMAR report on the global market research industry shows healthy growth and a number of emerging trends.

Industry report

The industry's performance surpasses expectations and underlines the health of the sector, which has shown continuous growth since ESOMAR began compiling the annual industry study in 1988. Worldwide industry turnover exceeds US$ 24.6 billion in 2006 with a growth rate of 6.8 % (4% after inflation) on 2005.

Europe is the leading region with 43% market share, followed by North America (36%), Asia Pacific (14%), Latin America (5%) and the Middle East & Africa (2%). Growth remains stable in Europe at 5.0% and, notably, Germany expands at more than double the pace of France and the UK. North America witnesses healthy acceleration with growth of 6.6, despite much reported downward pressure on prices due to ongoing adoption of online research, but it is emerging markets such as Brazil, China, India and Russia which are showing the highest growth rates.

Top five markets

The world's five largest markets for market research in 2006, based on turnover are ranked as indicated in Table 5.2.

Over two thirds of global market research turnover is generated in the five largest national markets – the US, UK, France, Germany and

Table 5.2

Top five markets

Country	Turnover (US$m) 2005	Turnover (US$m) 2006	Absolute growth rate (%) 2005/06	Net growth rate after inflation (%) 2005/06
USA	7,722	8,232	6.6	3.3
UK	2,411	2,369	2	0.1
France	2,247	2,214	2.5	0.8
Germany	2,185	2,206	5	3.1
Japan	1,405	1,380	4.3	3.9

NOTES: ESOMAR estimates. Rounded figures presented. Growth rates calculated in local currencies. Exchange rate fluctuations eliminated.

Japan. All of the Top Five have grown continuously in the last five years, underlining their strong fundamentals.

Market research turnover

'Our latest Global Market Research report provides clear indication that the market research sector has an increasingly important role in everyday practical and strategic business activities', confirmed Véronique Jeannin, ESOMAR's Director General.

'Market researchers are expanding their remit to meet the growing and varying needs of their clientele who require more comprehensive research and advisory services worldwide, whilst still being able to provide that necessary crucial local market insight.'

Online research

Online research spending is estimated to be above US$ 3bn in 2006, an increase of around 14% on the year before. Speed and low costs remain the key drivers of adoption – and rising levels of online data collection are helping boutique agencies and consultancies to compete with the larger players.

Three of the Top Five rank among the top ten countries with the highest online research spend as percentage of total spend – the UK (13%), the US (19%), and Japan (28%) the second ranked country after Australia in terms of the highest proportion of online spend.

Source: adapted from www.esomar.org [accessed 10/11/2007].

Region	Turnover (US$m) 2005	Turnover (US$m) 2006	Absolute growth (%) 2005/06	Net growth after inflation (%) 2005/06
Europe	10,475	10,597	5.0	2.8
North America	8,306	8,884	6.6	3.4
Asia Pacific	3,330	3,530	8.7	6.6
Latin America	971	1,221	17.1	11.3
Middle East & Africa	343	385	14.4	9.5
World	23,425	24,618	6.8	4.0

Table 5.3

Market research turnover

Source Rounded figures presented. Growth rates calculated in local currencies. Exchange rate fluctuations eliminated.

development of an information-based decision-making culture within service organizations.

As we have seen, the information needs of service organizations are great and cannot afford to be overlooked as they will be faced with the need to monitor an ever larger and rapidly changing marketing environment. To handle the increasing external and internal information flow and to improve its quality companies have to take advantage of the opportunities offered by information technology (IT) and information systems. Managing marketing information by IT has become one of the most vital elements of effective marketing (Talvinen and Saarinen, 1995).

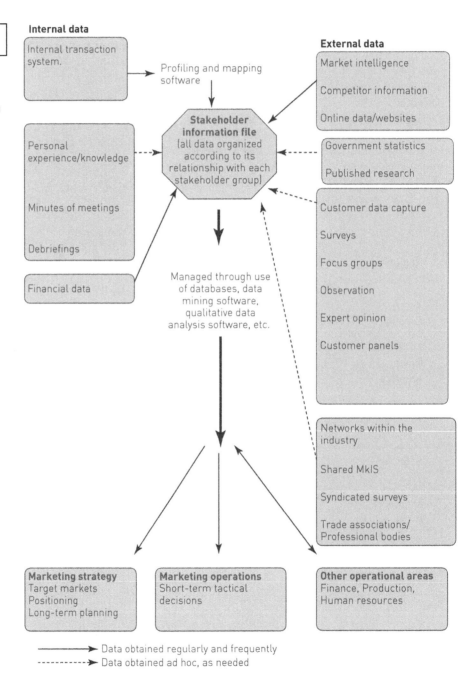

Figure 5.5

Marketing information management within services organizations

The marketing information system must ensure a continuous flow of pertinent information to the decision-maker without restricting the creativity and freedom needed for service development. A semi-informal system, similar to that suggested by Wright and Ashill (1998) is better suited to the smaller firm, but whether formal or informal the system needs to incorporate the 80 per cent external data suggested by Xu and Kaye (1995), the accessing of online information and the sharing of information within industry groups (Wood, 2001), be centred around Glazer's (1997) 'customer interface file', make use of Talvinen's strategic partnerships and cross-functional networks and incorporate the informal creative insights that abound within the services sector.

Figure 5.5 illustrates the key areas that a marketing information system should incorporate, although, it is recognised that the needs of each organization will differ and that the system needs to remain flexible and fluid.

What can go wrong: Pitfalls to avoid

Although, generally, the benefits of collecting, managing and using marketing information far outweigh the costs and inconveniences involved, there are a number of issues (listed in Table 5.4) which can affect the effectiveness of its use and the acceptance of its importance within the organization.

Information overload. In the present information age a scarcity of information is rarely the problem. It is the sheer abundance of information which can have a detrimental effect as information consumes attention and decision makers have many demands upon their time. One way to overcome information overload is to recognize the short shelf-life of information and to focus on becoming a 'market-driven learning organization'. This requires acceptance of the idea that what is known at any time is always less important than the ability to learn (Glazer, 1997).

information overload
Decision making adversely affected by mismanaged quantity of data.

Stifling creativity. Many of the arguments against information systems and formalized research and planning stem from the fear that they will in some

Information overload
Stifling creativity
Information cost vs. effectiveness gains
Skills, training and personnel shortages
Privacy and data protection issues

Table 5.4

Marketing information pitfalls

way prevent artistic flair, intuition and creativity and therefore innovation, or compromise artistic integrity.

Information cost vs. effectiveness gains. In setting up a marketing information system it is possible for its 'champions' to become carried away with the importance of the system while losing sight of the needs of the decision makers it serves. It is imperative that the users control the inputs to the system and this is achieved by designing information around end use and fitness for purpose rather than being driven by 'the machine'.

Skills, training, personnel. An efficient and effective marketing information system is dependent upon those who manage and use it. This will inevitably mean that existing staff will need to be informed of its benefits and should be given ownership through being involved in the design and set-up stages. This requires a certain amount of internal marketing and is undoubtedly helped if there is a 'champion of the system' to move it forward. Once initiated, the system requires staff with skills in data gathering, data input, analysis and interpretation and in report preparation and presentation and this may require some investment in training.

Privacy and data protection. In collecting and using information on individuals, the organization needs to be aware of the legislation that governs its use to ensure that they are not infringing the far-ranging data protection laws. Although there are legislative requirements, the ethical use of information goes beyond these. For example, these might include issues around unsolicited direct marketing material, the use of photographs taken of customers, or 'small print' opt-out clauses. One way to help ensure that the use of information does not alienate customers is to use the principles of 'permission marketing' (Godin, 1999). The basic premise of permission marketing is that customers are marketed to only if they have asked to be and in doing so their information is being used only with their express permission.

Summary

In order to succeed through strategic competitive advantage, service organizations need to make use of marketing information. To do this it is necessary to first identify clearly and precisely their information needs in terms of the marketing decisions to be taken. Once the needs have been identified the sources of information can be investigated and if necessary, primary data collected. The information collected on a continuous and on an ad hoc basis then needs to be organized within a marketing information system. This system needs to be organized so that decision makers can access a broad range of information, creating a holistic view of specific marketing problems.

Discussion questions

1 Discuss the sources of information and data gathering methods that would be appropriate for:

   a. Evaluating customer satisfaction within a high-class restaurant.

   b. Comparing competitor offerings in website design services.

   c. Identifying trends in the European travel insurance industry.

2 Explain, using examples from a service sector of your choice, the potential disadvantages of marketing information collection and use.

3 Discuss the advantages and disadvantages relating to accessibility, cost, reliability and ethics of a variety of sources of competitor intelligence in the private health care sector. How could this information be used?

Case link

See Case 4: House concerts: Service demands under your own roof.

4 Compare the value and importance of organization-based (internal) information with market-based (external) information in relation to:

   a. public sector library services

   b. a major charity.

5 Discuss the challenges in undertaking customer research for the market discussed in the 'House Concerts' case study.

References and further reading

Berkly, B. J. and Gupta, A. (1995) 'Identifying the information requirements needed to deliver quality service', *International Journal of Service Industry Management* 6 (5): 5–31.

Essawy, M. (2006) 'Testing the usability of hotel websites: the springboard for customer relationship building', *Information Technology & Tourism* 8: 47–70.

Getz, D. (1998) 'Information sharing among festival managers', *Festival Management and Event Tourism: An International Journal* 15 (1/2): 71–83.

Glazer, R. (1997) 'Strategy and structure in information-intensive markets: the relationship between marketing and IT', *Journal of Market Focused Management* 2: 65–81.

Godin, S. (1999) *Permission Marketing: Turning Strangers Into Friends, and Friends Into Customers*, New York: Simon & Schuster.

KAFKA, h. (2007) 'About HDK Conjsultants Ltd and Harry Kafka', http://www.competitivebranding.com/HDK.html, accessed 20 August 2008.

Meetings Industry Association/Catlow Consulting (2002) http://www.miatracker.org/, accessed 25 Oct. 2002.

O'Neill, M.A., Getz, D. and Carlsen, J. (1999) 'Evaluation of service quality at events: The 1998 Coca-Cola Masters Surfing event at Margaret River, Western Australia', *Managing Service Quality* 9(3): 158–166.

Poria, Y. and Harmen, O. (2002) 'Exploring possible uses of multi-user domains in tourism research', *Tourism Today* 2002, pp. 15–33.

Ryals, L. and Wilson, H. (2005) 'Experimental methods in market research: from information to insight', *International Journal of Market Research* 47 (4): 345–364.

Simpson, H. (2005) 'Client-driven convergence of the market research, CRM and competitive intelligence industries', *ESOMAR Innovate! Conference*, Paris, February 2005. Available from www.warc.com.

Sisodia, R. S. (1992) 'Marketing information and decision support systems for services', *Journal of Services Marketing* 6 (1): 51–64.

Skyrme, D. J. (1989) 'The planning and marketing of the market intelligence function', *Marketing Intelligence & Planning* 7 (1/2): 5–10.

Smith, D. V. L. and Fletcher, J. H. (2001), *Inside Information: Making Sense of Marketing Data*, Chichester: Wiley.

Talvinen, J. M. (1995) 'Information systems in marketing. Identifying opportunities for new applications', *European Journal of Marketing* 29 (1): 8–25.

Talvinen, J. M. and Saarinen, T. (1995) 'MkIS support for the marketing management process: perceived improvements for marketing management', *Marketing Intelligence & Planning* 13 (1):18–27.

Wearne, N., Argal, C. and Bycroft, P. (2004) 'Market research, accountability, outcome focus and service standards. How market research has significantly improved the reformation of the Australian government public sector', *ESOMAR, Public Sector Research*, Berlin, May 2004.

Wood, E. (2001) 'Marketing information systems in tourism and hospitality SMEs: A study of internet use for market intelligence', *International Journal of Tourism Research* 3: 283–299.

Wright, M. and Ashill, N. (1998) 'A contingency model of marketing information', *European Journal of Marketing* 32 (1/2):125–144.

Xu, X. and Kaye, R. G. (1995) 'Building market intelligence systems for environment scanning', *Logistics Information Management* 8 (2): 22–29.

Part two

Service strategy:
Managing the
service
experience

Service Strategy: Managing the Service Experience is dedicated to topics that pertain to managing the service experience. In this part, you will learn about the strategic issues that affect both the marketing mix and the components of the servuction model including process, pricing, promotion, physical evidence and people (employee and customer) issues. Part two concludes by outlining the need for organizations not only to recruit customers but to manage the customer relationship to form long-lasting relations.

Chapter 6
Service development and innovation

The world is turning into a service economy. The more service organizations there are, the more competitors there are. To maintain market share, in a competitive environment, organizations need to provide good service and adapt to the needs of the consumer. However, organizations that want stay ahead of the competition do so by crafting exciting, innovative and creative environments for their customers.

Alexandra J. Kenyon

Chapter objectives

In this chapter we discuss service development and innovation as they relate to the purchase of services.

After reading this chapter, you should be able to:

- Understand the reasons why service organizations need to develop and change.
- Discuss the seven new service categories of innovation.
- Understand the new service development process.
- Understand how to create an environment for innovation and creativity.

Services in context
Enterprise – Rent a Car – Innovative company, innovative research, innovative quality control

When you think of Rent a Car, the global companies that spring to mind are Hertz, Avis, Budget and Europcar. However, there is a worldwide company that focuses on local markets. Enterprise was founded in 1957 by Jack Taylor. Initially he founded a simple leasing company but being the entrepreneur that he is, Jack Taylor has added many more services over the years. Usually, people rent a car when they go on holiday – but there are many other occasions when a car is needed. Enterprise recognized those 'other' occasions and now specializes in renting cars to customers who need a car for a short business trip, or because their own car is being repaired or has been stolen. The business is now thriving with a £4.6 billion turnover, fleet of over 602,000 cars and 6,000 branches worldwide. Enterprise declares it is their people that make the difference. Their staff provides a service that makes it an organization where customer satisfaction and customer referrals are remarkable.

The company's culture encourages innovation, creativity and excellent customer service. Brice Adamson, UK/Ireland Managing Director states, 'We actively encourage our people to make decisions and build their confidence at finding innovative business solutions to day-to-day concerns.' This clearly shows that the organization believes and trusts their staff to seek improvements and make suggestions to develop and improve the performance of the organization. Additionally, sales personnel are rewarded for their improvements as profit bonuses are correlated directly with the overall performance of each branch. So staff are

motivated to go the extra mile, think of ways to improve customer service and feel confident that their thoughts and ideas are valued.

Valued personnel are also promoted. Promotion within the company depends on four key areas of the business:

1 Demonstration of profitability and cost control,

2 Fleet growth,

3 Development of the team and

4 Above-average scores on the Enterprise Service Quality Index (ESQi).

The ESQi is an innovative way to ensure that quality standards are monitored. Excellent service quality is one of the key aims for Enterprise. However, they were worried that by being a flexible, fast-moving organization their desire to grow may make their staff lose sight of the need to provide excellent service. Many organizations that expand quickly often forget the basic features of service quality and Enterprise did not want this to happen. Therefore, the introduction of ESQi gave them the opportunity to measure customer satisfaction at every branch. ESQi is an independent customer survey. The score from the ESQi is important as it provides information to establish bonuses and staff promotion. Over 200,000 surveys are conducted worldwide each month. Complete customer satisfaction in 2004 was running at 81 per cent – this makes Enterprise very proud of their staff. Moreover, Enterprise has an innovative approach to business that encourages ideas from the front-line staff, which in turn gives personnel confidence and reward.

Introduction

Service organizations have a major role to play in the economic and employment activity of most countries. In fact in many Western countries manufacturing is declining and the service industry is growing. Customer services and distribution facilities account for one of the largest sources of jobs in the UK and Germany with over 20 per cent of employment in service organizations (Fagan, O'Reilly and Halpin, 2005). This means that service organizations have a lot to offer employers and service workers in addition to the overall economy of each country. Service organizations, however, must not be complacent. They need to recognize that they exist in a highly competitive marketplace and customer expectations change on a regular basis. Therefore, to succeed and remain competitive, service organizations need to provide high-quality services and, more importantly, create new and innovative approaches to their organizations to meet these demands.

Why service organizations change

All service organizations need to change and develop to maintain their market position, stay ahead of the competition or fulfil the changing needs of their customers. Therefore, it is natural that news services and products are launched onto the market and existing, unprofitable ones are withdrawn. The introduction and withdrawal of services and products is known as the product life cycle. The product life cycle is one of the most common marketing concepts that service businesses use when developing their business. Services and products go through distinct stages. The stages are described below and shown in Figure 6.1, Product Life Cycle.

product life cycle
How a service or product progresses through a sequence of stages from introduction to growth, maturity and decline.

product development
A means to enable the introduction of new designs, processes and the marketing of new services.

Product development. During the product development stage the new service delivery mechanisms or distribution ideas are conceived. Also during this stage the ideas are researched and assessed. Often discussions take place as to the potential profitability of the new idea and often the service or product is tested to ensure that the delivery mechanisms and distribution channels are relevant to the target audience. New service and product developments do not have to be major service innovations such as introducing a call-centre; they can be minor service improvements such as changing menu items in a café. However, all ideas need to be developed and researched before they are introduced to the customer. Clearly during the product development stage no sales are made, as customers are not aware

---

Figure 6.1

Product Life Cycle

Source Adapted from Capon, C. (2008) *Understanding Strategic Management*, London: Prentice Hall.

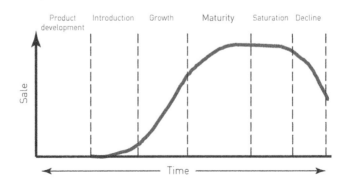

of the new services or products. However, research, development and testing costs money.

Introduction. During the introduction stage of the product life cycle service organizations launch their new ideas onto the market. If the new service is a major innovation it is likely that there will be a great deal of media activity; TV advertising, press releases or 'launch parties' may be held. If the service is a minor style change such as a bank offering credit cards with pictures of animals and birds, media activity will be less. As shown in Figure 6.1 the amount of sales are low during the introduction stage as it takes time before customers become aware of and take advantage of the new service.

introduction During this stage of the product life cycle, costs are high due to research and development costs and sales are low as few customers are aware of the new developments.

Growth. During the growth period more customers become aware of the new service on offer and sales rise. As sales rise, the revenue increases and the service organization will begin to recoup the money it spent on research and development. During the growth stage service organizations need to monitor competitor activity. Often following the introduction of a new service or product, competitors react by launching similar services or products or cut prices on their existing services.

growth When services and products are introduced to the market, sales are slow to begin with but grow as more customers become aware of the new developments.

Maturity. During the maturity stage of the product life cycle, sales reach their peak and profits are incurred. Sales growth will be more difficult as competitors will have often joined the market for the new services and products. Additionally, consumers may be starting to tire of the service offer and they begin to look around for the latest and more exciting service offerings.

maturity A period during the product life cycle where sales are at their height.

Saturation. The saturation stage of the product life cycle occurs when there are many competitors seeking the same customers. The market begins to be 'flooded' with similar and 'copy-cat' products and services. Currently the retail mobile phone market in the UK is reaching saturation point. There are many retailers who offer the basic service. Therefore, retailers are beginning to expand their product range, to change contracts from 12 months to 18 months and to include a variety of accessories.

saturation The saturation stage of the product life cycle occurs when there are many competitors seeking the same customers and the marketplace is flooded with similar services and products.

Decline. Decline in the product life cycle occurs as fashions and technology change. During this period service organizations withdraw services and products from their range as sales decline and become unprofitable. When internet access became popular at the turn of the twenty-first century households in the UK would 'pay per minute'. Most internet service providers withdrew this facility in favour of contracts where customers are charged a monthly fee and may use the internet as often as they like. The reason for the withdrawal was based on declining 'pay per minute' sales, new technology becoming available and the increasing desire for extensive internet use by the consumer.

decline When an organizations services are no longer preferred by customers, sales are low and profits are reducing.

However, Figure 6.1, Product Life Cycle displays the different stages over a period of 'time'. It is important to note that 'time' from the development of the service or product idea to the decline and withdrawal of the service or product can vary. For example, from the initial development stage of minor service innovations such as changing the restaurant menu to its withdrawal may take only three to four months. However, major service innovations such as introducing a clothes catalogue to complement High Street retail outlets may take several years from development to withdrawal. Similarly, the six stages shown in Figure 6.1 are represented as equally divided stages. However, the life cycle of a new service or product does not move equally through the sequence of stages. For example, Pizza Hut's pizzas have been at the maturity stage of the product life cycle for many decades but they keep introducing new initiatives to entice existing and new customers. In the US, Pizza Hut has launched a Pizzone which is their equivalent of a calzone pizza. Currently, it is in the growth stage in the US. If it is successful in the US, Pizza Hut may offer it on the menu in the UK.

Case link

For the product life cycle of airline services, see Case 5: Fine Dining in the Sky.

Different points of service organizations can be at different stages of the product life cycle and it should not be used as a method of accurately forecasting the future (Bowie and Buttle, 2004). During the later half of 2007 the banking market worldwide began to feel the effects of the 'credit crunch' following effects of the sub-prime housing market in the US. Many marketers from UK banks made the decision to withdraw some of their mortgage services. The reason for withdrawing services was a result of the economic downturn and not because their services were in the decline stage of the product life cycle. Therefore, marketers always need to ensure they understand the marketplace and the many factors driving their decision. The following section considers some of the factors that drive change in the services industry.

Drivers for change in the service industry

A service organization's competitive position is constantly being challenged by its competitor's activity and the rising demands of its customers. However, it is not only competitors and customers that drive service organizations to develop new services in order to protect their market share. There are many other factors that must not be overlooked, to ensure that the organization remains competitive. Naturally, marketers will research their own sales figures, customer satisfaction indicators, customer retention ratios and profitability to establish how their organization is performing. They also need to consider other external factors when planning their organization's future. Table 6.1, Drivers for Service Change provides an essential guide for marketers to consider.

Table 6.1		
Opportunities	Regulations	Perishability
Seasonal patterns	Fashions	Competitors

Drivers for service change

Opportunities

Many opportunities are available to service organizations. Opportunities emerge if a competitor withdraws from the market or their own market research discovers a need that is currently not being met. Additionally, it could be that new technological advancements provide a mechanism to enhance service delivery. Microsoft launched the Table Top PC in 2007 which is a 30-inch interactive flat screen that sits on coffee tables, desks and even on restaurant tables. Restaurant owners can display their menus with high-definition pictures of their starters, main courses, sweets, drinks, crisps, peanuts, wine labels, cocktails – in fact everything that the restaurant owner has on offer. Customers merely touch the picture of the meal they would like to order and the information whizzes straight to the kitchen. Technological opportunities enable the marketer to enhance service delivery and enable their customers to have fun with the latest innovative Table Top PC. See Global Services in Action for more examples of technology used in service organizations.

Global services in action
British Airways: Small innovations mean big changes in the eyes of the customer

The early 1900s brought a major product and service innovation into the world of travel. British Airways was one of the pioneers in terms of offering daily international travel. Naturally, this was a huge investment of money, people, staff training and marketing as it brought countries of the world closer to UK citizens.

Over the years British Airways has included many changes and innovative ideas to its customers worldwide. For example, it has joined forces with American Express (AMEX) to create a joint credit card for use specifically by their frequent flyers. Regular travellers have also been able to join the AirMiles programme. Both of these innovations were beneficial to the customer as they were given rewards for their repeat custom. From 1 December 2003 they provided a comission-based incentive for travel agents. Bookings made through travel agents received a commission of 1 per cent. These innovations are low-level process innovations. Clearly both customers and travel agents benefit from these tangible innovations. However, international air travel is an experiencial service with many intangible elements – such as convenience, comfort or safety. Service and process innovations have recently been included for the Club World customer. One of the service innovations is found in the Elemis Travel Spa which customers can use at the airport or on arrival at their destination. Customers can enjoy spa treatments or simply take a shower so that they are refreshed for the rest of the day. Process innovations include 'Fast Bag Drop' whereby customers leave their luggage at the airport desk having checked themselves in through the online service or by using the self-service kiosk. An innovative feature in British Airways cabins is the 'Z' bed. The 'Z' bed positions itself in such a way that it supports the knees and back of the passenger and is ideal for sleeping on or watching the in-flight entertainment.

These innovations include minor service, product and process innovations, but they make a big difference to how customers experience convenient and relaxing travel with British Airways.

Source: http://www.britishairways.com.

Regulations

Many changes in service organizations are forced upon them by regulations and legal changes imposed by the government of the country in which the organization operates. Marketers can use the enforced changes as positive PR and according to Malcolm Wicks, MP, Minister of State for Energy UK (2006), 'Reporting on environmental matters is a sensible way to reduce risks and develop opportunities.' Reporting on environmental and social issues are requirements in many countries within Europe. There are regulations that require organizations to declare their corporate and social responsibilities (Kenyon, 2008). Many organizations do this through their financial reports. However, many service organizations shout about how their new service developments contribute to the health and well-being of our world. For example, Marks and Spencer states clearly in their advertising that their food range includes 'Oakham Gold free-range chicken' and 'Organic free-range chicken'. Marks and Spencer and the farming communities have joined forces to improve animal welfare standards. Marks and Spencer were awarded the Compassion in World Farming Award for Investment and Innovation in Farm Animal Welfare Research 2005–2006 and received commendation from the Royal Society for the Prevention of Cruelty to Animals (RSPCA) in their Alternative Awards. Marks and Spencer are required to report, as part of their year-end financial review, details of how their business is progressing in terms of corporate and social responsibilities, but they have gone further and embraced the regulations and used them to help animal welfare, gain recognition from the RSPCA and respect from their customers.

Perishability

As shown in Chapter 2, perishability occurs when there are vacant seats in a restaurant or low usage of transportation systems outside the morning and evening 'rush hours'. Therefore, new services should be developed to use the spare capacity. These may include 'early bird' menus and special offers in restaurants or mother and toddler swimming classes at local sports centres. B&Q International, the home improvement store, offer 10 per cent discount on all products bought on Wednesdays by customers over the age of 65. They recognized Wednesday as a day when the store was not running a full capacity. Therefore, they introduced a special 'discount day' for their older customers.

Seasonal patterns

Many service organizations are affected by the seasons. This is particularly acute for the travel and hospitality industry. La Manga Golf Urbanization in Spain, part of the Hyatt Group, has a different target audience during the different seasons. For example, during the summer-time there are fewer guests playing golf due to exceptionally high temperatures. Therefore, during the summer-time La Manga Golf Urbanization appeals to families by including events and festivals that will appeal to children and early teenagers. During the spring and autumn season, the weather is perfect for playing golf and their target audience during these periods are ladies, gentlemen and golf societies that wish to take advantage of the many golf competitions open to guests.

Fashions

Changing fashions acutely affect service industries. This is clear in the retail industry as fashion houses constantly keep up with the latest trends. Additionally other service organizations are driven by changing fashions. Consider the changes in hairstyles over the past 50 years. In the 1950s women backcombed their hair into bouffant styles and beehives. In the 1970s high pony tails and shaggy perms were the main hairstyles because of the disco craze. The 1990s brought us the 'messed-up' styles for both men and women and the beginning of the twenty-first century has encouraged women to have straight, sleek and long hairstyles. Because of the changing fashions, hair salons have had to adapt both in their skills and in the equipment required to create the styles that their customer's desire.

Competitors

Service organizations keep a constant watch over their competitors' activities. The banking markets in the UK were not innovative until they were jolted into action following the launch of First Direct, the world's first telephone-only bank. First Direct took 650,000 affluent customers onto their books in fewer than seven years. At first UK banks ignored First Directs' 'no branch banking' innovation; but after five years there were 15 competitors offering telephone banking. On this occasion First Direct were clearly market leaders in their field. However, other UK banks followed the leader and also began to provide 'virtual' banking for their own customers. The UK banking world has been very active in terms of offering new service developments including internet and mobile telephone banking.

The drivers for the service industry are varied and often external to the organization. It is clear that marketers need to continually scan their environment for clues as to the latest trends in fashions, competitor activity and technology. Additionally, they need to research what consumers want and what governments may impose upon them in the form of new regulations or legal obligations. Whichever driver is identified, marketers can use it as an advantage to introduce new services for their customers.

The new service categories of innovation

Service organizations that subscribe to the marketing concept clearly understand their target market and provide a professional service to their customers. Organizations have a range of strategic options available to them to grow; these are:

- Sell more existing services to existing customers.
- Sell existing services to new customers.

- Sell new services to existing customers.
- Sell new services to new customers.

The intensity and investment in the service being offered will be different depending upon the strategic option chosen. For example, B&Q International chose the strategy of selling more existing services to existing customers when they introduced the 10 per cent discount to their over-65 customers. Little investment was required in terms of infrastructure or staff training. However, a bank wishing to sell new services to existing customers by introducing an online banking service would have to make a large investment in terms of infrastructure, staff recruitment and training. New service developments do not just make limited changes to the product's characteristics such as the introduction of a diet range of drinks to the Pepsi range of carbonated drinks. The strategic options available to service organizations usually include changes to how and when the service is delivered and also the client interface (OECD, 2000). These characteristics are called the continuum of new service development. The continuum of new service development can be anything from a minor adaptation to an existing service to major developments such as e-commerce or a call centre.

The continuum of innovative service developments can be classed into seven categories (Lovelock and Wirtz, 2007):

Case link

For an example of new service development, see Case 5: Fine Dining in the Sky.

continuum of new service development A range of service developments from major overhauls to minor style changes.

1. Major service innovations
2. Major process innovations
3. Product-line extensions
4. Process-line extensions
5. Supplementary service innovations
6. Service improvements
7. Style changes

Major service innovations

major service innovations Radical changes to service delivery mechanisms.

Major service innovations include new products and services for consumers that have not been defined and therefore have not been targeted before. The launch of First Direct Banking was revolutionary and so was eBay's on-line auction. Another major service innovation was Skype. In 2003 Niklas Zennström and Janus Friis launched the new internet service. Previously, consumers in different locations could use the telephone network or e-mail. Zennström and Friis created a piece of software that made communication easy, fun and *free*. People around the world who want to talk to each other need only to download the software onto their PC. They can then talk to each other – and see each other through a webcam – for free. This is one of the most innovative services of the twenty-first century due to the benefits it brings in international communications and because it was launched by two individuals and is not an extension of a service provided by a multi-billion-pound, global organization.

Major process innovations

Major process innovations as the name implies introduce new ways of delivering the existing core products and services. The Polish Open University (POU) has two modes of study in two different languages. For example, undergraduate students from Poland or anywhere in the world can study their degree on-campus in Warsaw, Krakow and Legnica. POU's major process innovation is the opportunity for students from all over the world to study their degree through e-learning. E-learning delivers the existing core products and services that a student would experience through on-campus study. E-learning is done via on-screen lectures, interactive workshops, chat facilities and revision exercises. Therefore, tuition is provided to enable a student to attain a degree award; however, the service is delivered through virtual media instead of a face-to-face experience in lecture theatres and classrooms. POU also deliver the degree programmes in Polish and English, thus widening their target audience to students who do not speak Polish. Major process innovations have also led to a number of retailers that supply their products and service solely online. For example, www.asos.com (As Seen On Stars) provides an extensive

major process innovations Radical introductions of new processes to new markets.

E-services in action
www.asos.com interactive innovative services

There are many 'e-tailers' that have images of their clothing and accessories online. However, www.asos.com (As Seen On Stars) has some very innovative ideas. One of the creative ideas they have is to show photographs of celebrities and fashion icons on their website. They then show items of clothing that they have for sale which are very similar to the clothes worn by 'superstars'. Customers are excited that they can buy merchandise similar to that that their favourite stars are wearing. Another interactive idea that is very creative is the way in which clothes and accessories are displayed. Clothes are displayed on a moving image. The moving image is of a model, wearing the clothes and accessories, walking down a catwalk.

This innovative idea makes the consumer feel they are buying clothes after being at a fashion show. They have one other innovative idea specifically designed to encourage sales. Once a customer has made a purchase, other images immediately appear. The other images are of items of clothing, shoes or handbags that other customers have bought. These innovative ideas make the buying experience much more exciting than merely viewing two-dimensional items.

Source: http://www.asos.com.

SOURCE © MROZ/DREAMSTIME.COM

range of clothing and accessories. They do not have 'bricks and mortar' outlets; only an online portal. They are able to move quickly with the changing fashions and their unique selling point is to show famous celebrities wearing the latest trends and then offering alternative clothing similar to that worn by the celebrity. The internet has enabled many service organizations to invest in their online portal rather than paying fixed costs such as the rent and rates associated with High Street stores. See E-Services in Action for more innovative ideas provided by www.asos.com.

As the names *major service innovations* and *major process innovations*, imply these service developments offer new services and facilities to a new 'type' of customer. Innovations as sophisticated as First Direct, eBay or POU E-earning are few and far between as they will need dedication and commitment from across the entire organization including departments such as Research and Development, Information Technology, Marketing, HR, Finance and Training. Additionally, to implement major service or major process innovations takes time. Often there are many years between the initial innovative idea and the actual launch of the new service or delivery process.

innovation An all-encompassing term used for major and incremental changes in services, products and processes.

Innovation does not always have to radical, complex or have long lead times. The following categories show other types of innovations that can be naturally progressive or minor improvements to hold customers' interest.

Product-line extensions

product-line extensions Introducing new products to the existing product mix.

Product-line extensions refer to new service additions where the core product of the organization stays the same. British Airways (BA) introduced BA CityFlyer in 2007. BA CityFlyer is a subsidiary of BA and makes short flights within eight European countries. BA has extended their product-line by introducing BA CityFlyer but has kept the core product of air passenger transportation the same.

Process-line extensions

process-line extensions Introducing new process delivery mechanisms to existing ones.

Process-line extensions require less innovation than major process innovations. Therefore, process-line extensions can be implemented within a short time-frame. Top Shop has a fabulous range of clothing for men and women. They have also recently introduced a Personal Shopper at their large city stores. Personal shoppers are usually in the haute couture houses or up-market department stores such as Harvey Nicholls or Harrods. However, Top Shop have trained their staff to help customers choose clothes appropriate to their physique and style. The service is free and is an additional way of moving consumers through the process from entering to leaving the store. With the aid of a personal shopper, customers can benefit from the advice given and the personal shopper can easily collect clothes and accessories in different sizes while the customer is still in the changing rooms. At the other end of the spectrum, supermarkets such as Asda (Walmart) and Morrisons have introduced 'self-scanning fast lanes' which have no staff at all. The self-scanning fast lane checkouts help speed customers through the buying process as customers scan their shopping items in front of a laser beam which detects the barcode. The process-line extensions described here have been quick to implement and staff training can be conducted on-site with existing staff as required. See Global Services in Action for examples of the service innovations that British Airways have introduced.

Supplementary service innovations

Supplementary service innovations occur regularly and they are add-ons to the existing core service. Taxi drivers are now able to respond to the request of customers easily due to innovative technology. The headquarters of taxi firms can use a satellite system to locate their drivers while they are on the move. Taxi drivers receive a message via a monitor attached to their GDS system advising that a customer wants to order a taxi. Taxi drivers near to the location can immediately advise their headquarters that they can respond. They do this by pressing a small keyboard attached to the GDS system. Upon arrival at the destination the taxi driver calls the customer from his mobile telephone. The customer's telephone number is shown on his GDS monitor. This system is extremely useful. The customers perceive an efficient supplementary service built around the existing core service that their local taxi rank offers.

supplementary service innovations Add-ons to the existing core service.

Service improvements

Service improvements are innovations which are the most common type of service innovations. The changes are modest and include minor changes to the existing core service or supplementary services. Hard Rock Café is very innovative in terms of its themed restaurants. They are always busy and customers often have to wait for a table. When customers have advised the *maître de* of their arrival they are given a 1960s, 1970s or 1980s LP cover. The LP cover is a marker for each customer so that waiting staff can easily find their guests when they need to be escorted to their table (Veggie Hound, 2008).

service improvements The most common type of innovation. They include service improvements which deal with service delivery.

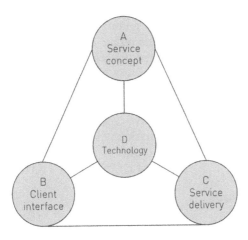

Figure 6.2

Dimensions of innovation in services

Source Adapted from den Hertog and Bilderbeek (2000) 'The new knowledge infrastructure: the role of technology-based knowledge-intensive business services in national innovation systems', in Boden, M., Miles, I., eds, *Services and the Knowledge-Based Economy*, London: Continuum, 222–246.

Style changes

style-changes Simple
changes to existing
styles – such as the
introduction of new staff
uniforms.

Style changes are also simple innovations, which require little product testing or major changes to processes. The changes can include minor redecoration to introduce new colour schemes. The Hogshead pub chain repainted the interior of its bars to reflect the different seasons. Staff uniforms often change each year to include fashion changes and helpful design features. Drivers for the bus and coach service GoFirst have recently received new uniforms. The jackets are dark blue with gold buttons embossed with GoFirst's logo. Each jacket has also got an inside pocket, conveniently designed for the mobile phone issued to all staff, for use in emergencies.

The above service developments can be summarized into four dimensions. Figure 6.2, Dimensions of Innovation in Services shows how all the innovations are interlinked. The reason for this is that in practice innovations are a mixture of minor and major innovations *and* service and product features.

Dimension (A) – Service concept. This innovation dimension considers combining services currently conducted by several organizations (Van der Aa and Elfring, 2002). For example, JCDecaux is an outdoor advertising company that produces revolutionary innovations in movable outdoor media. It also combines services usually left to contract cleaning companies. The service that JCDecaux usually delivers is to provide advertising/PR for bus shelters. JCDecaux added an additional innovative service concept to their portfolio by providing the cleaning and maintenance of the bus shelters. If the bus shelters are clean and in an excellent state of repair, JCDecaux's advertising/PR displays will also be in tiptop condition.

Dimension (B) – Client interface. Throughout this book the importance of the customer/client interface has been discussed. Examples of client interface innovations include providing the National Lottery or bingo online. Customers can play the Lotto or bingo online, thus having no contact with the customer service personnel of the National Lottery or at the bingo hall. Additionally, changes in the client interface include service organizations such as Yellow Pages providing business telephone numbers online in addition to the hard-copy book delivered to each household in the UK.

SOURCE COURTESY OF YELL.COM

Yell.com – the online client interface of the Yellow Pages.

Dimension (C) – Service delivery system. Innovative delivery systems include online supermarket shopping, where all groceries are bought online and delivered to the customers' homes at a time that is convenient to them.

Dimension (D) – Technological options. Changes in technology offer marketing managers endless possibilities. Examples of innovations using technology include real-time technology where stores such as Virgin Megastores can track sales and trends of the latest music, video and games. This enables store managers to order the right number of items, decrease waste and become more profitable – see B2B services in Action for more details of real-time technology.

Clearly, innovation and change enable service organizations to differentiate themselves from the competition. However, service developments are easy to replicate. Therefore, marketing managers need to monitor the marketplace and try to anticipate the changing needs of their customers. There are a number of ways that changes can be generated and ideas created and these are outlined in the following section.

B2B services in action
Test and test again: State of the art airport but baggage handling disaster

Her Majesty The Queen opened Terminal 5 at Heathrow in March 2008. Terminal 5 is spectacular in design and it creates a modern environment second to none. BAA is the supplier of security, commercial retail accommodation, fire services and baggage handling and they constructed Terminal 5. Prior to the opening of Terminal 5 BAA invited 15,000 volunteers to help 'test' the new services and facilities. Volunteers were in Terminal 5 for over six hours. Each volunteer was given an 'imaginary role' and groups of up to 2,250 volunteers acted out scenarios so that BAA could ensure that Terminal 5 was safe, secure and 'runs like clockwork' (BBC, 2008). However, as soon as the fanfares at the opening ceremony had died away, disaster struck. Within the first five days of operation 500 flights had been cancelled and over 23,000 bags had been lost (Thomson, 2008).

Problems began before customers arrived. Personnel were not able to find parking spaces and there were problems getting staff through the electronic security systems. Once they were inside the building they had to find a lift that was working as 18 did not! However, it was when customers arrived that the situation went from bad to worse. The baggage handling system and IT that supports it were

unable to cope with the 40,000 customers that were coming through Terminal 5. For BA that meant a loss of £16 million due to 'missing' luggage and flight cancellations. Willie Walsh, BA's Chief Executive stated that if he had the chance to open Terminal 5 again, knowing what he knows now he would ensure there was more staff training and IT testing. He felt that they had compromised on pre-testing.

Sources: BBC (2008) 'Volunteers test out Heathrow T5' (internet), http://news.bbc.co.uk/1/hi/england/london/7008412.stm (accessed 16th May 2008). R. Thomson (2008) 'Update: lack of software testing to blame for Terminal 5 fiasco, BA executive tell MP's' (internet), www.computerweekly.com/Articles.aspx (accessed 16th May 2008).

New service development process

There are several trends emerging in the service industry. These include (1) heightened customer expectations and awareness of the range of competitors that can suit their needs, (2) advances in the internet and e-commerce, both

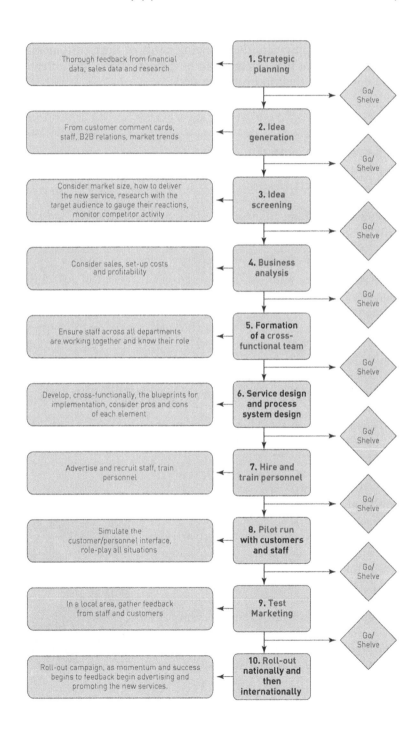

Figure 6.3

New service developments

Source Adapted from Ilam and Perry 2002.

strategic planning
A deliberate course of action to move the organization forward into the future.

idea generation
Ideas are generated through research, new technologies, front-line staff, suppliers and staff.

idea screening Ideas need to be screened for effectiveness, cost and potential.

business analysis
The way an organization improves its future activities based on past performance and research on how it can innovate its current activities to satisfy the needs of the customer.

cross-functional team
A group of people who work towards a common goal but are from different departments in the Organization.

hire and train personnel
During the implementation of major new services and process developments, new staff need to be hired and trained.

enhanced due to technological advances and (3) new competitors joining the marketplace due to de-regulations and organizations no longer requiring High Street facilities to be noticed. Service organizations, therefore, need a systematic approach to use when researching and developing new process delivery systems or product innovations. Some of the innovations outlined in this chapter, such as introducing e-commerce or call centres must be launched in a systematic way. The launch of major service innovations may take several years and will include all departments of the service organization in one form or another. Even minor service changes, such as redecorating retail outlets, will require careful thought about planning, timing and the disruption the redecoration process will have on the day-to-day running of the business. Figure 6.3 shows a linear process of new service development.

The flow diagram shows all the steps that organizations will go through during new service development. One of the most important elements of the systematic approach shown in Figure 6.3, is testing and receiving feedback from staff and customers. Introducing new products and services always has an element of risk; therefore, to keep risk to a minimum, researching and testing new services is of the utmost importance. See B2B Services in Action for an example of how more testing of the service could have improved baggage handling at Terminal 5 Heathrow Airport.

pilot run During NSD – new service development – services and processes are piloted to ensure that adjustments are made before the actual service goes 'live' to the public.

test marketing During NSD – new service development – services, processes and products are trialled with customers and staff to ensure delivery will run smoothly when it is rolled out to the public.

roll-out During NSD – new service development – this is the final part of the process when the new service goes 'live' to the public.

Environment for innovation and creativity

So far we have discussed the reasons why the marketing manager must develop service organizations to ensure that their market position is protected and that they continue to satisfy the needs of the consumer. Figure 6.4 shows that idea generation comes from a variety of sources such as staff, customers or relationships that organizations have with their suppliers. The creative ideas, therefore, are the seeds that enable service organizations to move forward strategically. Service organizations that are leaders in their field encourage creativity as they view it as an important part of their development. Figure 6.4 shows how creativity and innovation are linked and how idea generation turns into growth.

Clearly new ideas and improved services and products lead towards growth in service organizations. Therefore, creating an environment that encourages idea generation is an important asset to the organization. For organizations to take advantage of this important asset they need to ensure that their staff have freedom to express their ideas. They should also provide a culture within the organization that is open to ideas and actively gives people 'time to think' of new ideas and improvements (Ekvall, 2000). An organization needs to enable a number of activities to occur if they wish to encourage an environment that will be creative and help to develop strategic growth (see Table 6.2).

Organizations that empower their staff and encourage feedback from their customers and suppliers are creating an open and honest environment. This type of environment will encourage idea generation and business growth.

Figure 6.4

Idea generation as a strategic tool

Source Adapted from Cook, 1998.

Table 6.2

Organizational activities to encourage innovation and creativity

Source Isaksen et al., 2001: 175.

Challenge and involvement	Degree to which people are involved in daily operations, long-term goals, and visions. When there is a high degree of challenge and involvement, people feel motivated and committed to making contributions. The climate is dynamic, electric, and inspiring. People find joy and meaningfulness in their work. In the opposite situation, people are not engaged, and feelings of alienation and apathy are present. Individuals lack interest in their work and interpersonal interactions are dull and listless.
Freedom	Independence in behaviour exerted by the people in the organization. In a climate with much freedom, people are given the autonomy and resources to define much of their work. They exercise discretion in their day-to-day activities. Individuals are provided the opportunity and take the initiative to acquire and share information about their work. In the opposite climate, people work within strict guidelines and roles. They carry out their work in prescribed ways with little room to redefine their tasks.
Trust/ Openness	Emotional safety in relationships. When there is a high degree of trust, individuals can be genuinely open and frank with one another. People count on each other for professional and personal support. People have a sincere respect for one another and give credit where credit is due. Where trust is missing, people are suspicious of each other, and therefore, they closely guard themselves, their plans, and their ideas. In these situations, people find it extremely difficult to openly communicate with each other.
Idea time	Amount of time people can use (and do use) for elaborating new ideas. In the high idea-time situation, possibilities exist to discuss and test suggestions not included in the task assignment. There are opportunities to take the time to explore and develop new ideas. Flexible timelines permit people to explore new avenues and alternatives. In the reverse case, every minute is booked and specified. The time pressure makes thinking outside the instructions and planned routines impossible.

Playfulness/ Humour	Spontaneity and ease displayed within the workplace. A professional yet relaxed atmosphere where good-natured jokes and laughter occur often is indicative of this dimension. People can be seen having fun at work. The climate is seen as easy-going and light-hearted. The opposite climate is characterized by gravity and seriousness. The atmosphere is stiff, gloomy, and cumbrous. Jokes and laughter are regarded as improper and intolerable.
Idea support	Ways new ideas are treated. In the supportive climate, ideas and suggestions are received in an attentive and professional way by bosses, peers, and subordinates. People listen to each other and encourage initiatives. Possibilities for trying out new ideas are created. The atmosphere is constructive and positive when considering new ideas. When idea support is low, the automatic 'no' is prevailing. Fault-finding and obstacle-raising are the usual styles of responding to ideas.
Debate	Occurrence of encounters and disagreements between viewpoints, ideas, and differing experiences and knowledge. In the debating organization, many voices are heard and people are keen on putting forward their ideas for consideration and review. People can often be seen discussing opposing opinions and sharing a diversity of perspectives. Where debate is missing, people follow authoritarian patterns without questioning them.
Risk-taking	Tolerance of uncertainty and ambiguity in the workplace. In the high risk-taking case, bold initiatives can be taken even when the outcomes are unknown. People feel as though they can 'take a gamble' on their ideas. People will often 'go out on a limb' to put an idea forward. In a risk-avoiding climate, there is a cautious, hesitant mentality. People try to be on the 'safe side' and often 'sleep on the matter'. They set up committees, and they cover themselves in many ways.

Summary

This chapter has demonstrated why creativity and innovation play a key role in moving service organizations forward. It has discussed why service organizations must not be complacent in the highly competitive market place. To succeed, service organizations should consider the key drivers for change in their industry and provide opportunities for staff, customers and suppliers to suggest ideas that could be implemented into their future plans. Once ideas for future change have been generated, service organizations should follow a rigorous service development process. The service development process provides key stages that service organizations use to test ideas before they roll out the new services, processes or products to their customers.

Discussion questions

1 Discuss the different stages of the product life cycle. Consider an organization of your choice and discuss where it is in the product life cycle and why.

2 What is meant by the continuum of innovative service developments?

3 Choose an organization and give examples of innovative activities it has introduced.

4 Consider the innovative activities that airlines have developed over the years. What innovations do you suggest that could differentiate an airline business from its competitors?

Case link

See Case 5: Fine Dining in the Sky.

5 There are many drivers of innovation. Give examples of drivers that organizations have used to grow and develop their business.

6 Define and explain the dimensions of service innovation.

7 Why is it crucial to have an organization that encourages innovation and creativity?

8 Give examples of activities you would recommend to an organization to encourage innovation and creativity.

Further reading and references

Alam, I. and Perry, C. (2002) 'A customer-oriented new service development process', *Journal of Services Marketing* 16 (6): 515–534.

BBC (2008) 'Volunteers test out Heathrow T5', http://news.bbc.co.uk/1/hi/england/london/7008412.stm, accessed 16 May 2008,

Bowie, D. and Buttle, F. (2004) *Hospitality Marketing: An Introduction*, Oxford: Elsevier Butterworth-Heinemann.

Capon, C. (2008) *Understanding Strategic Management*, London: Prentice Hall.

Cook, P. (1998) 'The creativity advantage – is your organization the leader of the pack?', *Industrial and Commercial Training* 30 (5): 179–184.

den Hertog, P. and Bilderbeek, R. (2000) 'The new knowledge infrastructure: the role of technology-based knowledge-intensive business services in national innovation systems', in Boden, M., Miles, I., eds, *Services and the Knowledge-Based Economy*, London: Continuum, 222–246.

De Jong, J. P. J., Bruins, A., Dolfsma, W. and Meijaard, J. (2003) *Innovation in service firms explored: what, how and why?* EIM Business & Policy Research.

Ekvall, G. (2000) 'Management and organizational philosophies and practices as stimulants or blocks to creative behaviour: a study of engineers', *Creativity & Innovation Management* 9 (2): 94–99.

Fagan, C., O'Reilly, J. and Halpin, B. (2005) *Job Opportunities for Whom? Labour Market Dynamics and Service-Sector Employment Growth in Germany and Britain*, London: Anglo-German Foundation for the Study of Industrial Society.

Isaksen, S. G., Lauer, K. J., Ekvall, G. and Britz, A (2001) 'Perceptions of the best and worst climates for creativity: preliminary validation evidence for the situational outlook questionnaire', *Creativity Research Journal* 13 (2): 171–184.

Kenyon, A. J. (2008) 'Exploring corporate and social responsibilities: a retailer's challenge', *CIRCLE – The 5th International Conference on Consumer Behaviour*, Cyprus.

OECD (2000) *Promoting innovation and growth in services*, Paris: Organization for Economic Cooperation and Development.

Thomson, R. (2008) 'Update: Lack of software testing to blame for Terminal 5 fiasco, BA executive tell MPs', www.computerweekly.com/Articles.aspx, accessed 16 May 2008.

Van der Aa, W. and Elfring, T. (2002) 'Realizing innovation in services', *Scandinavian Journal of Management* 18 (2): 155–171.

Veggie Hound (2008) 'Hard Rock Café', http://veggiehound.wordpress.com/tag/contemporary-lounge/, accessed 10 May 2008.

Wicks, M. (2006) 'Minister of State for Energy UK Corporate Social Responsibility', http://www.berr. gov.uk/pressroom/Speeches/page31561.html, accessed 3 April 2008.

Chapter 7
Service delivery process

Choose Me, Hear Me, Stuff Me, Stitch Me, Fluff Me, Name Me, Dress Me, Take Me Home.

Build-a-Bear Workshop's World-Class Service Process

Chapter objectives

The main objective in this chapter is to familiarize you with operations concepts and to explain the importance of balancing operations and marketing functions in service operations.

After reading this chapter, you should be able to:

- Discuss the stages of operational competitiveness.

- Appreciate the relationship between operations and marketing as it pertains to developing service delivery systems.

- Describe the types of operational models that facilitate operational efficiency.

- Consider the challenges associated with applying peak efficiency models to service organizations and recommend strategies that overcome some of these difficulties.

- Explain the art of service blueprinting as it relates to the design of service delivery systems.

Services in context
Build-a-Bear Workshop

Service firms can strategically view their operations along a continuum ranging from a necessary evil to the other extreme, where operations are viewed as a key source of competitive advantage. Clearly, Build-a-Bear Workshop have used their world-class service delivery systems to create a compelling service experience for its customers. Build-a-Bear Workshops offer an experience-based business model where customers and their children or grandchildren can make and accessorize their own teddy bears. Given the option of purchasing a bear off the shelf at the local discount toy store or accompanying a child to a Build-a-Bear Workshop where they can be personally involved in creating the bear as a family, many customers are enthusiastically opting for the latter choice.

Build-A-Bear Workshop, Inc., is the only global company that offers an interactive make-your-own stuffed animal retail-entertainment experience. Founded in St Louis in 1997, the company currently operates more than 240 stores in the UK, United States and Canada. The addition of franchise stores in Europe, Asia and Australia make Build-A-Bear Workshop the leader in interactive retail. In November 2004, the company expanded the make-your-own concept from stuffed animals to dolls with the opening of its first Friends 2B made® stores, where guests can make their own doll friends. In April 2006, Build-A-Bear Workshop acquired The Bear Factory, a UK-based stuffed animal retailer, and Amsbra, Ltd, the company's franchisee in the UK, adding company-owned stores in the United Kingdom and Ireland. Build-a-Bear Workshop (NYSE: BBW) posted total revenue of $362 million in fiscal 2005.

Build-a-Bear's competitive advantage has been its service delivery system consisting of the clever process of *Choose Me, Hear Me, Stuff Me, Stitch Me, Fluff Me, Name Me, Dress Me, and Take Me Home*. As described by the company's website (www.buildabear.com), the process of making a teddy bear flows as follows:

Choose Me – guests select from a variety of bears, dogs, cats, bunnies, monkeys and a series of limited edition offerings.

Hear Me – guests are then able to select from several sound choices that are placed inside their new stuffed friend. Examples of sounds include giggles, growls, barks, meows and recorded messages such as 'I Love You' and songs like 'Let Me Call You Sweetheart'.

Stuff Me – guests, with the help of master Bear Builder associates, fill their new stuffed friends with just the right amount of stuffing for customized huggability. Each guest then selects a satin heart, makes a wish, and places the heart inside their new furry friend.

Stitch Me – stuffed friends are stitched up but not before a store associate places a barcode inside the stuffed animal so that if lost, the furry friend can be reunited with its owner. The company believes that thousands of bears have been returned to their owners through their exclusive Find-a-Bear ID tracking programme.

Fluff Me – guests are now able to fluff their new friends to perfection with the use of cool-air hair dryers and brushes at the purposely designed bear spa.

Name Me – guests stop at the Name Me computer where they enter their names, and the birth date and name of their new friend. Guests can then select between customized birth certificates or a story that incorporates the owner's name and the stuffed animal's name.

Dress Me – guests are now directed to the bear apparel boutique where Pawsonal Shoppers help guests select from hundreds of choices the perfect outfit and accessories for their new friend.

Take Me Home – guests end their experience at the Take Me Home station where they are given their customized birth certificate or story and a Buy Stuff Club Card to apply towards future purchases. Finally, each new furry friend is placed within a Club Condo carrying case that is specifically designed as a handy travel carrier and new home.

As testament to the effectiveness of Build-a-Bear Workshop's extraordinary delivery system, the company has received numerous awards such as 2005 Customer First Awards, 2006 Pinnacle Award, 2006 Best International Campaign and ICSC 2004 Hot Retailer Award. The company has also been profiled in books such as *Revolutionize Your Customer Experience and Customer Service Excellence 2004: Exemplary Practices in Retail*.

Sources: http://www.buildabear.com, accessed 29 February 2008.
http://www.traffordcentre.co.uk/news, accessed 29 February 2008.

Introduction

The servuction model introduced in Chapter 1 clearly demonstrates that consumers are an integral part of the service process. Their participation may be active or passive, but they are always there. If the consumer is an active participant in the service factory, it is clear that if the factory is changed, consumer behaviour will have to be changed. Moreover, changes to the visible part of the service firm will be apparent to the consumer.

For example, when supermarkets first opened, petrol was not part of the product offering. The introduction of petrol to the product mix presented two new challenges to consumers. First, from a psychological standpoint, the initial thought of buying fuel at the same location as food products was resisted. Petrol stations at the time were generally dirty, grimy places staffed by burly men who had years of grit built up under their fingernails. A petrol station was hardly the place one wanted to buy food. The second challenge, having customers fill their own tanks, created a change in operations that required a change in consumer behaviour. Consumers had to learn how to work a petrol pump, and the supermarket and petrol pump manufacturers had to develop pumps and monitoring procedures for this new type of self-service operation. This has now changed further with the introduction of 'pay-at-the-pump' services where customers deliver and pay for fuel without having to visit the shop or kiosk. Indeed recent research by Meuter, Bitner, Ostrom and Bown (2005: 63) concludes that a 'key obstacle to persuading customers to try a new SST [self-service technology] is that it often involves a significant behaviour change on the part of the customer. In a self-service situation, customers are coproducing the service and have responsibility for the delivery of the service and their own satisfaction.'

Managers of service firms must understand the interactive nature of services and the involvement of the consumer in the production process. As we discussed in Chapter 4, consumers appear to develop a script for frequently used services. This script is similar to a theatrical script in that it helps guide the consumer through the service experience. Changes in the service factory process will imply changes in the consumer script – the way in which the consumer participates in the process.

New developments coming from either the service factory or the consumer imply major changes in the consumer script as well as changes in the scripts of contact personnel. This chapter highlights the trade-offs between the search for operational efficiency and the need to create marketing effectiveness. In the service factory, many of the traditional methods for increasing operational effectiveness cannot be implemented behind closed doors. In fact, changes made to increase the service operation's efficiency can often downgrade the final service product. This chapter focuses on the positive things marketing can achieve to help improve the efficiency of service operations.

Stages of operational competitiveness

Without a successful operation, the firm is out of business, because it will have nothing to offer the customer. However, firms setting out to construct a service operation can choose from a large range of operational options. Strategically, the service firm can choose to use its operations as the key component of its competitive strategy or view its operations as a necessary evil. The manner in which 'operational competitiveness' is embraced by various service firms can be described by four stages:

Stage 1: Available for service

Stage 2: Journeyman

Stage 3: Distinctive competencies achieved

Stage 4: World-class service delivery

(Chase and Hayes, 1991)

Stage 1: Available for service

Operations for a firm with this level of competitiveness are viewed as a 'necessary evil'. Operations are at best reactive to the needs of the rest of the organization and deliver the service as specified. As its mission, the operations department attempts primarily to avoid mistakes. Back-office support is minimized to keep costs down. Technological investment is also minimized, as is investment in training for front-line personnel. Management designs any skill out of the work done by these personnel and pays them the minimum wage whenever possible.

Stage 2: Journeyman

This level of competitiveness is often provided by the arrival of competition. It is no longer enough just to have an operation that works. The firm must now seek feedback from its customers on the relative costs and perceived qualities of the service. At this point, the operations department becomes much more outward-looking and often becomes interested in benchmarking.

Technology for firms at this stage tends to be justified on the basis of the cost savings possible. The back office is now seen as a contributor to the service but tends to be treated as an internal service function. In the management of front-line employees, the emphasis shifts from controlling workers to managing processes. Employees are often given procedures to follow, and management consists of ensuring that these procedures are followed.

Stage 3: Distinctive competence achieved

By this stage, operations have reached a point where they continually excel, reinforced by the personnel management function and systems that support the customer focus. By this time, the firm has mastered the core service and understands the complexity of changing such operations. The back office is now seen to be as valuable as the front-of-house personnel. Technology is no longer seen as a source of cost advantage alone, but also as a way of enhancing the service to customers.

Perhaps the biggest changes come about in the workforce and in the nature of front-line management. Front-line workers are allowed to select from alternative procedures and are not tied down in the same way. The role of front-line management is to listen to customers and become coaches to the front-line workers.

Stage 4: World-class service delivery

To sustain this level of performance, operations not only have to continually excel but also become a fast learner and innovator. The back office, once seen as a second-class citizen, now must be proactive, develop its own capabilities, and generate opportunities. Technology is seen as a way to break the paradigm – to do things competitors cannot do (See Global Services in Action).

Global services in action
Video to DVD to download LOVEFiLM

Traditional players in the film rental industry have gradually lost ground over the past few years through not embracing changes in service delivery as quickly as newer and small rivals. Once market leader in the UK and US, Blockbuster is now stuggling to survive against their rapidly expanding rival, LOVEFiLM. LOVEFiLM, based in the UK, has grown from being a small national operator to having a global presence in a few years. This has been achieved by embracing new technology and retaining the level of customer service

and personalization associated with a small firm but rolling this out to an intenational audience.

The global delivery of services often depends upon the nature of the product. For the film rental industy, changes in technology, from bulky videos to slimmer CDs to downloads to streaming, have increased the potential for global growth at limited cost.

LOVEFiLM builds its growing reputation on value for money, choice, innovation and a source of movie and home entertainment information.

They aim to deliver a quality service by listening to customers and continually improving their experience through new service ideas.

With over 65,000 DVDs to choose from, LOVEFiLM also launched the first UK mass-market movie download service in 2005. Short films and full-length feature films are available from major Hollywood studios including Universal, Warner Bros., Sony, Momentum, Icon, Celluloid Dreams and Contender.

A survey of LOVEFiLM customers revealed that they care about new technologies and are adopting them at a surprisingly fast rate:

- Only 20 per cent of members had never watched a video online.
- Awareness of next-generation DVD technology is high – HD-DVD (73%), Blu-Ray (58%).
- Customers are interested in downloading more full-length films and TV shows, not video clips and short films.

So, what next for LOVEFiLM?
Their goals are to:

- Offer the best choice, service and convenience.

- Help customers find the movies they will enjoy watching by building their community.
- Create a highly personalized platform for all home entertainment needs.
- Deliver superb value for money, better than the High Street.
- Develop and operate a world-class platform to bring on-demand home entertainment to a mass market.
- Have fun and share their passion for entertainment!

Sources: http://news.bbc.co.uk/1/hi/business/7228008.stm, accessed 29 Feb. 2008.
http://www.lovefilm.com, accessed 29 Feb. 2008.

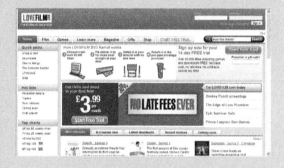

The workforce itself must be a source of innovators, not just operators. To achieve this, the front-line supervisors must go beyond coaching to mentoring. As mentors, they need to be accountable for the personal development of the workforce so that employees can develop the skills necessary for them to innovate for the firm.

Overall, the purpose of this chapter is to highlight the fact that operations management problems in services cannot be solved by the operations function alone. As pointed out by the four stages noted earlier, the search for operations efficiency can be crucial to long-term competitiveness. However, efficiency must be balanced against the effectiveness of the system from the customer's point of view. Table 7.1 provides a quick glimpse into the major trade-offs between efficiency and effectiveness when developing operations for low-customer-contact versus high-customer-contact services.

Frequently, it is too easy to view the customer as a constraint: 'If we could get rid of all these customers, we could run a good service operation!' Such a negative perspective ignores a golden opportunity. Customers in a service operation can be used to help operations. Such a positive view does, however, require that operations personnel recognize the importance of their marketing counterparts.

More importantly, such a view also requires that marketing personnel have an intimate knowledge of the operations system and its problems. It is not enough to propose new products that can be delivered through the system. The impact of such products on the whole system must be considered.

	Decision	High-contact system	Low-contact system
Table 7.1 Major design trade-offs in high- and low-contact systems **Source** Richard C. Chase, 'Where Does the Customer Fit in a Service Operation?' *Harvard Business Review* (November–December 1978), pp. 137–142. Reprinted by permission of *Harvard Business Review*. Copyright ©1978 by the President and Fellows of Harvard College.	Facility location	Operations must be near the customer.	Operations may be placed near supply, transportation, or labour.
	Facility layout	Facility should accomodate the customer's physical and psychological needs and expectations.	Facility should enhance production.
	Product design	Environment as well as the physical product define the nature of the service.	Customer is not in the service environment so the product can be defined by fewer attributes.
	Process design	Stages of production process have a direct immediate effect on the customer.	Customer is not involved in the majority of processing steps.
	Scheduling	Customer is in the production schedule and must be accommodated.	Customer is concerned mainly with completion dates.
	Production planning	Orders cannot be stored, so smoothing production flow will result in loss of business.	Both backlogging and production smoothing are possible.
	Worker skills	Direct workforce makes up a major part of the service product and so must be able to interact well with the public.	Direct workforce need have only technical skills.

Quality control	Quality standards are often in the eye of the beholder and, hence, variable.	Quality standards are generally measurable and, hence, fixed.
Time standards	Service time depends on customer needs, so time standards are inherently loose.	Work is performed on customer surrogates (e.g., forms), and time standards can be tight.
Wage payments	Variable output requires time-based wage systems.	'Fixable' outputs permits output-based wage systems.
Capacity planning	To avoid lost sales, capacity must be set to match peak demand.	Storable output permits setting capacity at some average demand level.
Fore-casting	Forecasts are short-term, time-oriented.	Forecasts are long term, output oriented.

Marketing and operations: Balance is critical

In a broad sense, one way of viewing the relationship between marketing and operations is to think of it as the marrying of consumers'needs with the technology and manufacturing capabilities of the firm. Such a marriage will obviously involve compromises since the consumers'needs can seldom be met completely and economically. In a goods firm, this partnership requires marketing's understanding of the capabilities of manufacturing and of research and development. The task of marketing goods is made somewhat easier because the different functions can be separated by means of an inventory.

In a service firm, this marketing problem is magnified. Significant aspects of the operation are the product because they create the interactive experience that delivers the bundle of benefits to the consumer. For example, a restaurant experience is not based solely on the quality of the food. The physical environment and interactions with contact personnel throughout the experience also affect consumer perceptions of the quality of service delivered. A successful compromise between operations efficiency and marketing effectiveness is, therefore, that much more difficult to achieve. Success in services marketing demands a much greater understanding of the constraints and opportunities posed by operations. Dabholkar and Overby (2004) found that 'service process is closely linked with service quality evaluations, whereas service outcome is closely linked with customer satisfaction evaluations'. Customer perceptions and experiences of overall quality are therefore largely determined by the appropriateness, efficiency and method of service delivery.

The importance of service delivery processes takes on greater importance in organizational markets where users often require a greater level of support and interaction with the service provider. Indeed Kumar and Kumar's (2004) research suggests that these service providers must focus on the organizational culture and values of their customers as much as on the service design.

To introduce these complexities, we will first adopt the perspective of an operations manager and ask, 'What would be the ideal way to run the system from an operations perspective?' The impact on marketing and the opportunities for marketing to assist in the creation of this ideal are then developed.

As pointed out in Chapter 1, the key distinctive characteristic of services is that the product is an experience. That experience is created by the operating system of the firm's interaction with the customer. Thus, the operating system of the firm, in all its complexity, is the product. For a marketing manager, this imposes constraints on the strategies that can be employed, but it also presents new and challenging opportunities for improving the profitability of the firm.

Chapter 4 provided one base on which to build an understanding of the product design problem for services. An understanding of consumer behaviour has always been a necessary condition for successful marketing. One way of viewing the product design process is to think of it as the process of combining such an understanding with the technological and manufacturing skills of the organization. To be an effective services marketer, a knowledge of consumer behaviour is not sufficient in itself to produce economically successful products. Successful managers also need a keen understanding of operations and human resource concepts and strategies.

As we discussed in Chapter 2, it is possible for goods producers to separate the problems of manufacturing and marketing by the use of inventory. Even so, there are many areas of potential conflict, as shown in Table 7.2. Although the issues are characterized as conflicts, they can be reconceptualized as opportunities. In each area it is clear that a better integration of marketing and manufacturing plans could yield a more efficient and profitable organization. For example, the determination of the extent of the product line should be seen as a compromise between the heterogeneous demands of consumers and the manufacturing demand of homogeneity. If marketing managers have their way, too many products will probably be developed, and the operation will become inefficient. As long as this is compensated for by higher prices, then a successful strategy can be implemented. In contrast, if the operations people have their way, everyone would be driving the same model of car, painted the same colour, which is less attractive for consumers. As long as this is compensated for by lower costs, and hence lower prices, a successful strategy can emerge.

Marketing and operations are in a tug of war that should be resolved by compromise. In the service sector, the possible areas of conflict or compromise are much broader because the operation itself is the product. Again, there is no single solution since operational efficiency and marketing effectiveness may push in opposite directions.

Problem area	Typical marketing comment	Typical manufacturing comment
1. Capacity planning and long-range sales forecasting	'Why don't we have enough capacity?'	'Why didn't we have accurate sales forecasts?'
2. Production scheduling and short-range sales forecasting	'We need faster response. Our lead times are ridiculous.'	'We need realistic customer commitments and sales forecasts that don't change like wind direction.'
3. Delivery and physical distribution	'Why don't we ever have the right merchandise in inventory?'	'We can't keep everything in inventory.'
4. Quality assurance	'Why can't we have reasonable quality at reasonable costs?'	'Why must we always offer options that are too hard to manufacture and that offer little customer utility?'
5. Breadth of product line	'Our customers demand variety.'	'The product line is too broad – all we get are short, uneconomical runs.'
6. Cost control	'Our costs are so high that we are not competitive in the marketplace.'	'We can't provide fast delivery, broad variety, rapid response to change, and high quality at low cost.'
7. New product introduction	'New products are our lifeblood.'	'Unnecessary design changes are prohibitively expensive.'
8. Adjunct services such as spare parts, inventory support, installation, and repair	'Field service costs are too high.'	'Products are being used in ways for which they weren't designed.'

Table 7.2

Sources of cooperation/conflict between marketing and operations

To polarize the issues, the perspective adopted in this chapter is that of the operations manager, just as in Chapter 4 the consumer's position was presented. The focus is on the requirements for operational efficiency and the ways that marketing can help achieve those requirements. We stress that in the drive for competitive advantage in the marketplace, marketing demand may in the end mean less operational efficiency. As the level of customer contact increases, the likelihood that the service firm will operate efficiently decreases. Customers ultimately determine:

- the type of demand,
- the cycle of demand,
- and the length of the service experience.

Meanwhile, the service firm loses more and more control over its daily operations. This is the nature of the service business.

In a perfect world, service firms would be efficient

Operating a service firm at peak efficiency would be an ideal situation. Thompson's *perfect-world model* provides us the direction needed to achieve this ultimate goal. However, in reality, peak efficiency is often unattainable. The *focused factory* and *plant-within-a-plant* concepts provide managers with alternative strategies that enhance the efficiency of the firm while taking into consideration marketing effectiveness.

Thompson's perfect-world model

The starting point for this discussion is the work of J. D. Thompson (1967). Thompson, who started from an organizational perspective, introduced the idea of a technical core – the place within the organization where its primary operations are conducted. In the service sector, the technical core consists of kitchens in restaurants, garages in auto service stations, work areas at dry cleaners, and operating theatres in a hospital. Thompson proposed in his perfect-world model that to operate efficiently, a firm must be able to operate 'as if the market will absorb the single kind of product at a continuous rate and as if the inputs flowed continuously at a steady rate and with specified quality'. At the centre of his argument was the idea that uncertainty creates inefficiency. In the ideal situation, the technical core is able to operate without uncertainty on both the input and output side, thereby creating many advantages for management.

The absence of uncertainty means that decisions within the core can become programmed and that individual discretion can be replaced by rules; the removal of individual discretion means that jobs are 'de-skilled' and that a lower quality of labour can be used. Alternatively, the rules can be programmed into machines and labour replaced with capital. Because output

technical core The place within an organization where its primary operations are conducted.

perfect-world model J. D. Thompson's model of organizations proposing that operations''perfect' efficiency is possible only if inputs, outputs and quality happen at a constant rate and remain known and certain.

and input are fixed, it is simple to plan production and to run at the high levels of utilization needed to generate the most efficient operations performance.

All in all, a system without uncertainty is easy to control and manage. Performance can be measured using objective standards. Furthermore, since the system is not subject to disturbances from the outside, the causes of any problems are also easy to diagnose.

The focused factory concept

Obviously, such an ideal world as proposed by Thompson is virtually impossible to create, and even in goods companies the demands of purchasing the inputs and marketing's management of the outputs have to be traded off against the ideal operations demands. In goods manufacturing, this trade-off has been accomplished through the focused factory. (Skinner, 1974). The focused factory focuses on a particular job; once this focus is achieved, the factory does a better job because repetition and concentration in one area allow the workforce and managers to become effective and experienced in the task required for success. The focused factory broadens Thompson's perfect-world model in that it argues that focus generates effectiveness as well as efficiency. In other words, the focused factory can meet the demands of the market better whether the demand is low cost through efficiency, high quality, or any other criterion.

focused factory An operation that concentrates on performing one particular task in one particular part of the plant; used for promoting experience and effectiveness through repetition and concentration on one task necessary for success.

The plant-within-a-plant concept

The idea of a focused factory can be extended in another direction by introducing the plant-within-a-plant (PWP) concept. Because there are advantages to having production capability at a single site, the plant-within-a-plant strategy introduces the concept of breaking up large, unfocused plants into smaller units buffered from one another so that they can each be focused separately.

plant within a plant The strategy of breaking up large, unfocused plants into smaller units buffered from one another so that each can be focused separately.

In goods manufacturing, the concept of buffering is very important. 'Organizations seek to buffer environmental influences by surrounding their technical core with input and output components' (Thompson, 1967). A PWP can thus be operated in a manner close to Thompson's perfect-world model if buffer inventories are created on the input and output sides. On the input side, the components needed in a plant can be inventoried and their quality controlled before they are needed; in this way, it can appear to the PWP that the quality and flow of the inputs into the system are constant. In a similar way, the PWP can be separated from downstream plants or from the market by creating finished goods inventories. Car manufacturers are good examples. Finished goods are absorbed downstream by an established retail dealership system that purchases and holds the manufacturer's inventory in regional markets until sold to the final consumer.

buffering Surrounding the technical core with input and output components to buffer environmental influences.

The alternatives proposed by Thompson to buffering are smoothing, anticipating and rationing. Smoothing and anticipating focus on the uncertainty introduced into the system by the flow of work; smoothing involves

smoothing Managing the environment to reduce fluctuations in supply and/ or demand.

anticipating Mitigating the worst effects of supply and demand fluctuations by planning for them.

rationing Direct allocations of inputs and outputs when the demands placed on a system by the environment exceed the system's ability to handle them.

managing the environment to reduce fluctuations in supply and/or demand, and anticipating involves mitigating the worst effects of those fluctuations by planning for them. Finally, rationing involves resorting to triage when the demands placed on the system by the environment exceed its ability to handle them. Successful firms preplan smoothing, anticipating and rationing strategies so that they can be more efficiently implemented in times of need.

Applying the efficiency models to service firms

The application of operations concepts to services is fraught with difficulty. The problem can be easily understood by thinking about the servuction model presented in Chapter 1. From an operational point of view, the key characteristics of the model are that the customer is an integral part of the process and that the system operates in real time. Because the system is interactive, it can be (and often is) used to customize the service for each individual.

To put it bluntly, the servuction system itself is an operations nightmare. In most cases it is impossible to use inventories and impossible to decouple production from the customer. Instead of receiving demand at a constant rate, the system is linked directly to a market that frequently varies from day to day, hour to hour, and even minute to minute. This creates massive problems in capacity planning and utilization. In fact, in many instances supply and demand match up purely by accident.

It is clear from this simplified model that services, by their very nature, do not meet the requirements of the perfect-world model. The closest the servuction model comes to this ideal state is the part of the system that is invisible to the customer. Even here, however, the customization taking place may introduce uncertainty into the system. Providing that all customization can take place within the servuction system itself, then the part invisible to the customer can be run separately. It can often be located in a place different from the customer-contact portion of the model (Matteis, 1979). However, when customization cannot be done within the servuction system, uncertainty can be introduced into the back office.

Instead of 'the single kind of product' desired by the perfect-world model, the service system can be called upon to make a different 'product' for each customer. Indeed, one could argue that since each customer is different and is an integral part of the process, and since each experience or product is unique, the uncertainty about the next task to be performed is massive.

The Thompson model requires inputs that flow continuously, at a steady rate, and at a specified quality. Consider the inputs to the servuction system: the physical environment, contact personnel, other customers and the individual customer. The environment may remain constant in many service encounters, but the other three inputs are totally variable, not only in their quality, but also in their rate of arrival into the process.

Moreover, contact personnel are individuals, not inanimate objects. They have emotions and feelings and, like all other people, are affected by things happening in their lives outside of the work environment. If they arrive in a bad mood, this can influence their performance throughout the day. That bad mood then directly affects the customer, since the service worker is a visible part of the experience being purchased.

Customers can also be subject to moods that can affect their behaviour towards the service firm and towards one another. Some moods are predictable, like the mood when a home team wins and the crowds hit the local bars. Other moods are individual, specific and totally unpredictable until after the consumer is already part of the servuction system.

Finally, customers arrive at the service firm at unpredictable rates, making smoothing and anticipation of incoming demand difficult. One minute a restaurant can be empty, and in the next few minutes, it can be full. One need only consider the variability of demand at tills in a supermarket to understand the basics of this problem. Analysis of demand can often show predictable peaks that can be planned for in advance; but even this precaution introduces inefficiency into the firm since the firm would ideally prefer the customers to arrive in a steady stream. Worse still are the unpredictable peaks. Planning for these peaks would produce large amounts of excess capacity at most times. The excess would strain the entire system, undermining the experience for customer and contact personnel alike.

Within the operations management and marketing literature of the past decade, a growing list of strategies has emerged regarding overcoming some of the problems of service operations. These strategies can be classified into six broad areas:

1　isolating the technical core,
2　minimizing the servuction system,
3　production-lining the whole system,
4　creating flexible capacity,
5　increasing customer participation, and
6　moving the time of demand.

Isolating the technical core

Isolating the technical core of the service firm and minimizing the servuction system have been combined because they are closely related from an operations viewpoint and because their marketing implications are similar. This approach proposes the clear separation of the servuction system, which is characterized by a high degree of customer contact, from the technical core. Once separation is achieved, different management philosophies should be adopted for each separate unit of operation. In other words, let's divide the service firm into two distinct areas – high customer contact and no/low customer contact, and operate each area differently.

In the servuction system, management should focus on optimizing the experience for the consumer. Conversely, once the technical core (no/low contact area) has been isolated, it should be subjected to traditional production-lining approaches (Matteis, 1979). In summary, high-contact systems should sacrifice efficiency in the interest of the customer, but low-contact systems need not do so (Chase, 1981; Chase and Tansik, 1983).

Isolating the technical core argues for minimizing the amount of customer contact with the system. 'Clients...pose problems for organizations...by disrupting their routines, ignoring their offers for service, failing to comply with their procedures, making exaggerated demands, and so forth' (Danet, 1984). Operating efficiency is thus reduced by the uncertainty introduced into the system by the customer (Bitner, Nyquist and Booms, 1985).

decoupling
Disassociating the technical core from the servuction system.

Examples of decoupling the technical core from high-contact areas of the servuction system include suggestions from operations experts such as handling only exceptions on a face-to-face basis, with routine transactions as much as possible being handled by telephone or, even better, by post or e-mail – mail transactions have the great advantage of being able to be inventoried (Chase, 1981). The introduction of ATMs by the majority of High Street banks serves this function with day-to-day opeations being carried out by the customer without service staff intervention but with the ability to offer a high level of customer service on a face-to-face basis when needed through specialist advisers located in the branches (see E-Services in Action). In addition, the degree of customer contact should be matched to customer requirements, and the amount of high-contact service offered should be the minimum acceptable to the customer. Overall, operational efficiency always favours low-contact systems, but effectiveness from the customer's point of view may be something completely different.

At this point, the need for marketing involvement in the approach becomes clear, as a decision about the extent of customer contact favoured by the customer is clearly a marketing issue. In some cases, a high degree of customer contact can be used to differentiate the service from its competitors; in such cases, the operational costs must be weighed against the competitive benefits. Consider the competitive advantages that a five-star restaurant has over a fast-food franchise.

Conversely, in some situations, the segment of the firm that the operations group views as the back office is not actually invisible to the customer. For example, in some financial services, the teller operation takes place in the

---

E-services in action
Fujitsu and La Caixa – Improving ATM services

Since its foundation in 1904, 'La Caixa' has grown to become the third largest Spanish Financial Institution (by assets) and one of the biggest savings banks in Europe. 'La Caixa' Group has over 5,000 branches, more than 25,000 employees, over 10 million clients and the biggest ATM network of the Spanish financial system.

'La Caixa' bought the first ATMs in 1979, and by 1985 it had 235 units. Nowadays, 'La Caixa' Group's ATM network, almost all of it built by Fujitsu, has more than 7,210 units, through which more than 460 million operations were processed in 2005.

The multi-channel management strategy of 'La Caixa' is based on the intensive use of new technologies. This delivers innovative services and improves customer service by enabling distribution channels to complement each other and work efficiently. The customer is the centre of attention and must have an integrated experience when using the different distribution channels.

Due to high volume of transactions and the extensive market coverage of 'La Caixa', the self-service channel is an essential element of the bank's ability to provide services to its customers. This channel is one of the means available for the customers to do their operations quickly and efficiently, in accordance with the Financial Institution's service objective. In this sense, an ATM that is stopped or not working implies inconveniences for the customer and the loss of a great number of operations.

In order to deliver an enhanced level of service to 'La Caixa' and its customers in the self-service channel, Fujitsu developed an incident management model that links the network's availability to contractual conditions. This meant ATMs could be fixed within the required timescales, even outside of the typical branch hours. Fujitsu also established a Self-Service Management Centre (Centro de Gestión de Autoservicio – CGA) to enable the continuous improvement of the service delivery, the software and the system management.

Fujitsu has continued to work closely with 'La Caixa' to deploy innovative technology in order to continuously enhance its service delivery and support the evolution of its 5,000 branches using a 'retail store' model.

In particular, Fujitsu has introduced new communications and advertising methods into bank branches using its 'Digital Media Networks' (DMN). 'La Caixa' is the first financial organization in Spain to use dynamic multimedia technology to present company information, product details and special offers to customers. As well as reducing launch time for campaigns by up to 83 per cent, DMN enables businesses to run up to three times more advertising campaigns than normal, adapting them to the needs of each branch, and thereby improving the image of the bank and its branches.

'La Caixa' is also set to be the first organization in Spain to introduce Fujitsu's pioneering PalmSecure security technology into its ATM network. Unlike other biometric systems, PalmSecure identifies people using their palm vein pattern, which is unique to each person, so that they can interact with the ATM more easily and safely. As these veins are two or three millimetres under the surface of the skin, it is almost impossible to forge them and they do not vary even in a wide range of temperatures.

Source: Adapted from material aviailable at http://www.fujitsu.com/uk/casestudies/fs_la-caixa.html. Accessed February 2008.

SOURCE © ISTOCK.COM/ROMAN MILERT

administrative offices. Operationally, this means that staff members can leave their paperwork to serve customers only when needed. Unfortunately, customers view this operationally efficient system negatively. A customer waiting to be served can see a closed teller window and observe staff who apparently do not care because they sit at their desks without offering to assist the customer. However, the reality is that these tellers may be very busy, but the nature of the administrative work is such that they may not give this impression to customers.

Even if it is decided that part of the system can be decoupled, marketing has a major role in evaluating and implementing alternative approaches. Any change in the way in which the servuction system works implies a change in the behaviour of the customer. A switch from a personal service to a web-based, postal or telephone system clearly requires a massive change in the way the customer behaves in the system. An alternative to the use of self-service technology is to outsource some of the service delivery process to specialist firms. B2B Services in Action illustrates the growth in these specialized service fims that provide a range of service delivery functions on an international basis.

Sometimes decoupling the system to become more efficient does not go over well with customers. For example, the closure of many rural and local post offices in the UK due to changed consumer behaviour involving more online and postal operations rather than visits to the local post office has resulted in a national outcry and numerous petitions. Even those who rarely use their post office see it as a 'traditional institution' and part of 'the British way of life' serving a vital social function in towns and villages. However, with the change to online payments and banking, a single transaction in a post office can cost the post office up to £8 (Marston, 2008). Maintaining these face-to-face opportunities is therefore important in some service operations even when they are inefficient and underutilized.

B2B services in action
The growing service delivery support industry

The complexity of delivering services in a global market has created a growing industry in global business support. These service providers offer a variety of services to businesses which help them extend their reach while improving the local delivery of their products. These operators are now far more than mere 'call-centre' providers in that they offer a broad range of services including finance and accounting; human resources; supply-chain management; market, business and financial research, and analytical services. One such example is WNS, originally an Indian-based company but now operating on a global scale serving a diverse client base. WNS Global Services is a recognized leader in business process outsourcing (BPO). Their proposition is simple: 'We deliver value to our clients by bringing operational excellence and deep industry and functional knowledge to their critical business processes.'

Their client industries include travel, insurance, financial services, healthcare, professional services, manufacturing, distribution and retail. Their offering is the provision of essential corporate functions, such as finance and accounting, human resources (payroll and benefits administration), research and analytics on a global scale.

For example, WNS recently launched a new delivery centre in Bucharest, Romania enhancing their clients' global delivery model with multi-lingual nearshore operation.

The 150-seat facility in Bucharest further expands WNS' global delivery capability and serves as a nearshore delivery centre for global clients with European operations. The centre is able to provide multi-lingual services in French, German, Italian and Spanish for clients across a range of industries. At the outset, the centre will deliver finance and accounting (F&A) and customer support services. With the launch in Romania, WNS has expanded its global delivery footprint to 14 delivery centres and is developing plans for additional centers in the region.

'Our expansion into Eastern Europe is a key step in enhancing our global footprint and providing comprehensive, integrated solutions to our clients', said Neeraj Bhargava, CEO of WNS Global Services. 'The ability to deliver services in an array of languages supports our clients' needs for standardization, consolidation, and transformation for improved performance of their business processes.'

Eric Selvadurai, Managing Director – Europe, WNS said, 'As a location, Bucharest provides a strong combination of language skills and talent, while still providing a competitive advantage for clients operating in the European Union. Language capability is a key delivery component for those who are increasingly looking to benefit from global delivery models.'

Sources: http://www.sharedxpertise.com/file/4040/ wns-launches-delivery-center-in-bucharest.html, accessed 29 Feb. 2008. http://www.wnsgs.com, accessed 29 Feb. 2008.

Production-lining the whole system

The production-line approach involves the application of hard and soft technologies to both the 'front' and 'back' of the service operation (Levitt, 1972). Hard technologies involve hardware to facilitate the production of a standardized product. Similarly, soft technologies refer to rules, regulations and procedures that should be followed to produce the same result. This kind of approach to increasing operational efficiency is relatively rare, and, indeed, fast-food firms provide a classic example in which customization is minimal, volume is large, and customer participation in the process is high.

Generating any kind of operational efficiency in such a high-contact system implies a limited product line. In the case of fast food, the product line is the menu. Moreover, customization must be kept to a minimum since the whole operating system is linked straight through to the consumer. The primary problem is how to provide efficient, standardized service at an acceptable level of quality while simultaneously treating each customer as unique (Suprenant and Solomon, 1987). Past attempts to solve this problem illustrate its complexity. Attempts at forms of routine personalization such as the 'have-a-nice-day' syndrome have had positive effects on the perceived friendliness of the service provider but have had adverse effects on perceived competence. Consequently, an apparently simple operations decision can have complex effects on customer perceptions.

production-line approach The application of hard and soft technologies to a service operation in order to produce a standardized service product.

hard technologies Hardware that facilitates the production of a standardized product.

soft technologies Rules, regulations and procedures that facilitate the production of a standardized product.

In fast food chains, customization must be kept to a minimum.

The servuction system applied to fast food also depends for its success on a large volume of customers being available to take the standardized food that is produced. Since the invisible component is not decoupled and food cannot be prepared to order, the operating system has to run independently of individual demand and assume that, in the end, aggregate demand will absorb the food produced. This is why pre-made sandwiches are stacked in bins as they wait to be absorbed by future demand in the marketplace.

Such an operating system is extremely demanding of its customers. They must preselect what they want to eat. They are expected to have their order ready when they reach the order point. They must leave the order point quickly and carry their food to the table. Finally, in many cases, these same customers are expected to clear their own tables.

Creating flexible capacity

As pointed out in Chapter 2, the few times that supply matches demand during service encounters occur primarily by accident. One method used to minimize the effects of variable demand is to create flexible capacity (supply) (Sasser, 1976). However, even in this area, strategies that start as common-sense operational solutions have far-reaching marketing implications as these new initiatives come face to face with the service firm's customer base. For example, a few of the strategies to create flexible capacity mentioned in Chapter 2 included (1) using part-time employees; (2) cross-training employees so that the majority of employee efforts focus on customer-contact jobs during peak hours; and (3) sharing capacity with other firms.

Although these strategies are fairly straightforward from an operational point of view, consider their marketing implications. Part-time employees appear to be a useful strategy because they can be used to provide extra capacity in peak times without increasing the costs in off-peak times. There are, however, a number of marketing implications. For example, part-time employees may deliver a lower-quality service than full-time workers; their dedication to quality may be lower, and their training probably less comprehensive. They are used at times when the operation is at its busiest, such as Christmas or during tourist seasons, when demand is fast and furious, and this may be reflected in their attitudes of frustration, which can be highly visible to customers and negatively influence customer perceptions of the quality of service delivered.

In a similar way, the other two possible solutions for creating flexible capacity also have major marketing implications. First, focusing on customer-contact jobs during peak demand presupposes that it is possible to identify the key part of the service from the customer's point of view. Secondly, the dangers of sharing capacity are numerous. For example, the television show *'Cheers'* provided ample examples of the problems associated with the upscale and upstairs customers of Melville's Restaurant as they mixed with *Cheers'* everyday clientele such as Norm and Cliff. Confusion may be produced in the customer's mind over exactly what the service facility is doing, and this could be particularly critical during changeover times when customers from two different firms are in the same facility, each group with different priorities and different scripts.

Increasing customer participation

The essence of increasing customer participation is to replace the work done by the employees of the firm with work done by the customer. Unlike the other strategies discussed, which focus on improving the efficiency of the operation, this approach focuses primarily on reducing the costs associated with providing the service to the customer. This strategy, too, has its trade-offs.

Consider for a moment our earlier discussions about consumer scripts. Increasing consumer participation in the service encounter requires a substantial modification of the consumer's script. Moreover, the customers are called upon to take greater responsibility for the service they receive. For example, the automatic teller machine (ATM) is seen by many operations personnel as a way of saving labour. In fact, the substitution of human labour with machines is a classic operations approach, and the ATM can definitely be viewed in that light. From a customer's point of view, such ATMs provide added convenience in terms of the hours during which the bank is accessible. However, it has been shown that for some customers, an ATM represents increased risk, less control of the situation and a loss of human contact (Schneider, 1980).

Such a switching of activities to the customer clearly has major marketing implications since the whole nature of the product received is changing. Such changes in the customer's script, therefore, require much customer research and detailed planning.

Moving the time of demand to fit capacity

Finally, yet another strategy utilized to optimize the efficiency of service operations is the attempt to shift the time of demand to smooth the peaks and valleys associated with many services. Perhaps the classic example of this problem is the mass transit system that needs to create capacity to deal with the rush hour and, as a consequence, has much of its fleet and labour idle during non-rush hours. Many mass transit authorities have attempted to reduce the severity of the problem by inducing customers through discounts and give-aways to travel during off-peak periods. Once again, operations and marketing become intertwined. Smoothing demand is a useful strategy from an operations point of view; however, this strategy fails to recognize the change in consumer behaviour needed to make the strategy effective. Unfortunately, because much of the travel on the mass transit system is derived from demand based on commuter work schedules, little success in the effort to reallocate demand can be expected (Lovelock and Young, 1979).

The art of blueprinting

One of the most common techniques used to analyse and manage complex production processes in pursuit of operational efficiency is flowcharting. Flowcharts identify:

- the directions in which processes flow,
- the time it takes to move from one process to the next,
- the costs involved with each process step,
- the amount of inventory build-up at each step, and
- the bottlenecks in the system.

blueprinting The flowcharting of a service operation.

The flowcharting of a service operation, commonly referred to as blueprinting, is a useful tool not only for the operations manager but for the marketing manager as well (Shostack, 1987).

Because services are delivered by an interactive process involving the consumer, the marketing manager in a service firm needs to have detailed knowledge of the operation. Blueprinting provides a useful systematic method for acquiring that knowledge. Blueprints enable the marketing manager to understand what parts in the operating system are visible to the consumer and hence part of the servuction system – the fundamental building blocks of consumer perceptions.

Identifying the components of an individual firm's servuction system turns out to be more difficult than it first appears. Many firms, for example, underestimate the number of points of contact between them and their customers. Many forget or underestimate the importance of telephone operators, secretarial and cleaning staff, or accounting personnel. The material that follows describes the simple process of flowcharting these numerous points of contact. Service flowcharts, in addition to being useful to the operations managers, allow marketing managers to better understand the servuction process.

The heart of the service product is the experience of the consumer, which takes place in real time. This interaction can occur in a building or in an environment created by the service firm, such as the complex environments that are created at Disney World, Legoland and Center Parcs. In some instances, such as lawn care, the service interaction takes place in a natural setting. It is the interactive process itself that creates the benefits desired by the consumer. Designing that process, therefore, becomes key to the product design for a service firm.

The interactive process that is visible to consumers develops their perception of reality and defines the final service product. However, as the servuction model discussed in Chapter 1 demonstrated, the visible part of the operations process, with which the consumer interacts, must be supported by an invisible process.

The search for operational efficiency is not unique to service firms, but it does pose some interesting problems. A change in the service operation may be more efficient, but it may also change the quality of interaction with the consumer. For example, students at many universities are now able to register for classes through automated telephone services or online forms. This type of operation offers increased efficiency but sometimes minimizes the quality of the student/adviser interaction. A detailed blueprint provides a means of communications between operations and marketing and can highlight potential problems on paper before they occur in real time.

An example of a simple blueprint

Figure 7.1 shows a simple process in which, for now, it is assumed that the entire operation is visible to the customer. It represents the blueprint of a cafeteria-style restaurant and specifies the steps involved in getting a meal. In this example, each process activity is represented by a box. In contrast to a goods manufacturer, the 'raw materials' flowing through the process are the customers. Due to the intangibility of services, there are no inventories in the process, but clearly, inventories of customers form at each step in the process while they wait their turn to proceed to the next counter. A restaurant run in this manner would be a single long chain of counters with customers progressing along the chain and emerging after paying, as in a motorway service station, IKEA restaurant or university cafeteria. In Figure 7.1, the cost calculation by each stage represents the cost of providing personnel to service each counter.

To calculate the service cost per meal, or the labour costs associated with providing the meal on a per-meal basis, the following calculations are made. First, the process time is calculated by dividing the activity time (the time required to perform the activity) by the number of stations, or locations performing the activity. In our example, the process and activity times are the same because only one station is available for each activity.

Second, the maximum output per hour for each location is calculated on the basis of the process time. Simply stated, the maximum output per hour is the number of people that can be served at each station in an hour's time. For example, the process time at the salad counter is 30 seconds. This means that two people can be processed in a minute, or 120 people (2 people × 60 minutes) in an hour. Another easy way to calculate the maximum output per hour is to use the formula: 60 (60 ÷ process time). In our example, the salad counter calculation would be 60 (60 ÷ 30) = 120.

Finally, to calculate the service cost per meal, total labour costs per hour of the entire system are divided by the maximum output per hour for the system (total labour costs divided by maximum output per hour). Total labour costs per hour are calculated by simply adding the hourly wages of personnel stationed at each counter. In our example, total labour cost per hour equals $50.00 (8 + 8 + 8 + 8 + 8 + 10). Maximum output per hour

service cost per meal The labour costs associated with providing a meal on a per-meal basis (total labour costs/ maximum output per hour).

process time Calculated by dividing the activity time by the number of locations at which the activity is performed.

activity time The time required to perform one activity at one station.

stations A location at which an activity is performed.

maximum output per hour The number of people that can be processed at each station in one hour.

	Appetizer counter	Salad counter	Hot-food counter	Dessert counter	Drinks counter	Cashier
	$8/hr	$8/hr	$8/hr	$8/hr	$8/hr	$10/hr
Number of stations	1	1	1	1	1	1
Activity time	15 sec	30 sec	60 sec	40 sec	20 sec	30 sec
Process time	15 sec	30 sec	60 sec	40 sec	20 sec	30 sec
Maximum output/hr	240	120	60*	90	180	120

*Bottleneck   Service cost per meal $= \dfrac{50}{60} = \$0.83$

Figure 7.1

Blueprint for cafeteria-style restaurant

is determined by selecting the lowest maximum output calculated in the second step. Hence, the service cost per meal in our example is $50.00 ÷ 60 customers, or $0.83 per meal.

Why would you use the lowest maximum output per hour? This step is particularly confusing for some students. The lowest maximum output in the system is the maximum number of people who can be processed through the entire system in an hour. In our example, 240 customers can be processed through the appetizer counter in an hour; however, only 120 customers can be processed through the salad counter in the same amount of time. This means that after the first hour, 120 customers (240 − 120)are still waiting to be processed through the salad counter. Similarly, only 60 customers can be processed through the hot-food counter in an hour's time. Since 60 is the lowest maximum output per hour for any counter in the system, only 60 customers can actually complete the entire system in an hour.

The service operations manager's perspective

The first thing the blueprint does is provide a check on the logical flow of the whole process. Clearly, a service blueprint makes it immediately apparent if a task is being performed out of sequence. At this point, we shall place a constraint on our example system that the till is fixed and cannot be moved to another point in the process. All other stations can be moved and resequenced.

bottlenecks Points in the system at which consumers wait the longest periods of time.

Once the different steps have been identified, it is relatively easy to identify the potential bottlenecks in the system. Bottlenecks represent points in the system where consumers wait the longest periods of time. In Figure 7.1, the hot-food counter is an obvious bottleneck since it represents the longest process time – the time to process one individual through that stage. A balanced production line is one in which the process times of all the steps are the same and inventories or, in our case, consumers flow smoothly through the system without waiting for the next process.

To solve this particular bottleneck problem, we could consider adding one extra station, in this case an extra counter, to the hot-food stage. The process time would drop to 30 seconds (60 seconds divided by 2). The bottleneck would then become the dessert counter, which has a process time of 40 seconds and a maximum turnover rate of 90 persons per hour. Costs would go up by $8.00 per hour; however, the service cost per meal would go down to $0.64 per meal. These changes are illustrated in Figure 7.2.

The creative use of additional counters and staff may produce a model such as that shown in Figure 7.3, which combines certain activities and uses multiple stations. This particular layout is capable of handling 120 customers per hour compared with the original layout presented in Figure 7.1. Although labour costs rise, the service cost per meal falls because of the increase in the number of consumers that are processed through the system in a shorter period of time. Further changes to this particular setup would be fruitless. Adding counters at the bottlenecks created by both the dessert/drinks and cashier counters would actually increase the service cost per meal from $0.48 ($58.00 ÷ 120 meals) to $0.50 ($68.00 ÷ 137.14 meals).

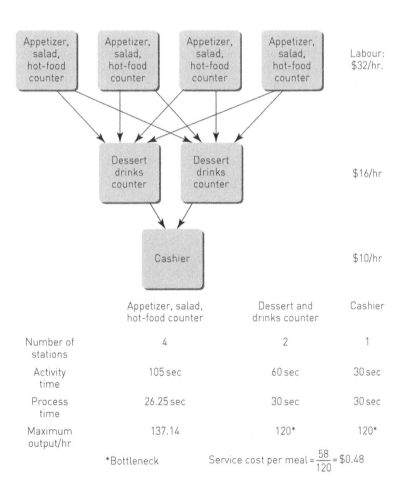

Figure 7.2

Modified blueprint for cafeteria-style restaurant

Appetizer counter $8/hr → Salad counter $8/hr → Hot-food counter $8/hr → Dessert counter $8/hr → Drinks counter $8/hr → Cashier $10/hr

Hot-food counter $8/hr

	Appetizer counter	Salad counter	Hot-food counter	Dessert counter	Drinks counter	Cashier
Number of stations	1	1	2	1	1	1
Activity time	15 sec	30 sec	60 sec	40 sec	20 sec	30 sec
Process time	15 sec	30 sec	30 sec	40 sec	20 sec	30 sec
Maximum output/hr	240	120	120	90*	180	120

*Bottleneck   Service cost per meal $= \dfrac{58}{90} = \$0.64$

Figure 7.3

Alternate blueprint for cafeteria-style restaurant

Appetizer, salad, hot-food counter × 4   Labour: $32/hr.

Dessert drinks counter × 2 $16/hr

Cashier $10/hr

	Appetizer, salad, hot-food counter	Dessert and drinks counter	Cashier
Number of stations	4	2	1
Activity time	105 sec	60 sec	30 sec
Process time	26.25 sec	30 sec	30 sec
Maximum output/hr	137.14	120*	120*

*Bottleneck   Service cost per meal $= \dfrac{58}{120} = \$0.48$

The service marketing manager's perspective

A marketing manager dealing with the process illustrated in Figure 7.1 has some of the same problems as the operations manager. The process as defined is designed to operate at certain production levels, and these are the service standards that customers should perceive. But if the process is capable of processing only 60 customers per hour, there may be a problem. For example, lunch customers who need to return to work quickly might purchase their lunches at a competing restaurant that serves its customers more efficiently. Also, it is clear that the bottleneck at the hot-food counter will produce lengthy, possibly frustrating, waits within the line.

The marketing manager should immediately recognize the benefits of changing the system to process customers more effectively. However, the blueprint also shows the change in consumer behaviour that would be required in order for the new system to operate. In Figure 7.1, the consumer goes from counter to counter, has only one choice at each counter, will probably have to wait in line at each counter, and will definitely have to wait longer at the hot-food counter. Moreover, the wait at each stage will certainly exceed the time spent in each activity. In the process proposed in Figure 7.3, the consumer visits fewer stations but is frequently faced with a choice between different stations. Clearly, depending on the format chosen, the script to be followed by consumers will be different. In addition, the restaurant itself will look completely different.

The use of the blueprinting approach allows the marketing and operations personnel to analyse in detail the process that they are jointly trying to create and manage. It can easily highlight any conflict between operations and marketing managers and provide a common framework for their discussion and a basis for the resolution of their problems.

Using service blueprints to identify the servuction process

Blueprints may also be used for a different purpose. Consider Figure 7.4, which shows a much more detailed blueprint for the production of a discount brokerage service. This chart is designed to identify the points of contact between the service firm and the customer. The points above the line are visible to the consumer, and those below are invisible. In assessing the quality of service received, according to the servuction model, the customer refers to the points of contact when developing perceptions regarding the value of service quality received.

To illustrate, consider the customers to be proactive rather than reactive. Consider them as worried individuals looking for clues that they have made the right decision rather than as inanimate raw materials to which things are done. The points of contact are the clues that develop the servuction process.

Besides illustrating a more complicated process, Figure 7.4 has a number of added features. First, each of the main features is linked to a target time. In the top-right corner, for example, the time to mail a statement is targeted as five days after the month's end. In designing a service, these target times should initially be set by marketing, and they should be based on the consumers' expected level of service. If the service is to be offered in a competitive

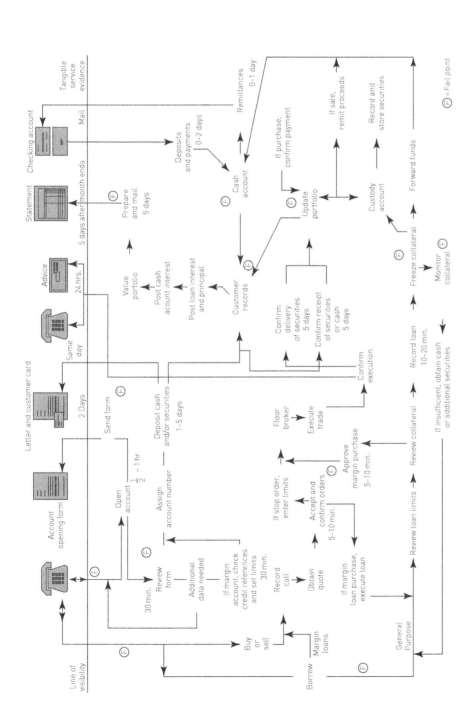

Figure 7.4

Flowchart of a discount brokerage service

Source G. Lynn Shostack, 'Service Design in the Operating Environment', pp. 27–43, 1984, reprinted with permission from *Developing New Services*, William R. George and Claudia Marshall, eds., published by American Marketing Association, Chicago. L 60606.

marketplace, it may be necessary to set standards higher than those of services currently available. Once the standards have been set, however, the probability of achieving them must be assessed. If the firm is prepared to invest enough, it may be feasible to meet all of the standards developed by marketing; doing so, however, affects the costs and, therefore, the subsequent price of the service. The process should, then, be an interactive one.

Figure 7.4 also highlights the potential fail points, 'F.' Fail points have three characteristics:

fail points Points in the system at which the potential for malfunction is high and at which a failure would be visible to the customer and regarded as significant.

1 the potential for operations malfunction is high,

2 the result of the malfunction is visible to consumers, and

3 a system malfunction is regarded by consumers as particularly significant.

A marketing blueprint or an operations blueprint?

Although the idea of a blueprint is attractive to both marketing and operations, it may well be that a marketing blueprint should be prepared in a different way. The blueprints we have discussed so far have an internal focus – although they identify clearly the tangible points of contact with the client, they start from the organization and look outward.

An alternative way to develop a blueprint would be to start from consumer scripts. Consumers, individually or in groups, would be asked to describe the process or steps they follow in using a service. Obviously, such an approach cannot cover the invisible part of the service firm, but it can provide a much better understanding of the points of contact. The process as described by the consumer may differ greatly from that perceived by the firm.

Consumers asked to describe a flight on KLM, for example, might start with their experience with the travel agent. They might then describe the process of getting to the airport, parking and entering the terminal. If the signs for KLM and the entrance to its specific terminal are confusing, this will be reflected in consumers' perceptions of the airline. A parking lot that is littered or poorly lit will also deter customers. Although the airline may not have direct control over these points of contact, it could be a wise investment for the airline to use its own staff to improve the parking lot. McDonald's long ago learned the value of removing the litter not only from its own property but also from the adjoining roadways. McDonald's recognized that their customers' experiences began long before they entered the actual restaurant.

Constructing the service blueprint

The first step in the design of a service blueprint (Hoffman and Howe, 1991) is to elicit scripts from both employees and consumers. The primary objective of this task is to break down the service system into a sequence of events followed by both parties. Too often, management makes the mistake of developing a one-sided blueprint based on its own perception of how the sequence of events should occur. This one-sided approach fails to recognize that consumer perceptions, not management's, define the realities of the encounter. Similarly, employee scripts are equally important in identifying

one-sided blueprint An unbalanced blueprint based on management's perception of how the sequence of events *should* occur.

those parts of the service system not observable to the consumer. Hence, both scripts are necessary to develop a successful blueprint.

Script theory suggests that consumers possess purchasing scripts that guide their thinking and behaviour during service encounters. The scripts contain the sequence of actions that consumers follow when entering a service interaction. Experts believe that 'these action sequences, or cognitive scripts, guide the interpretation of information, the development of expectations, and the enactment of appropriate behavior routines' (Leigh and Rethans, 1983).

Similarly, service employees also have scripts that dictate their own behaviour during interactions with the customer. Convergent scripts, those that are mutually agreeable, enhance the probability of customer satisfaction and the quality of the relationship between the customer and the service operation. Divergent scripts point to areas that need to be examined and corrected because consumer expectations are not being met and evaluations of service quality could decline.

Obtaining consumer and employee scripts is a potentially powerful technique for analysing the service encounter. Scripts provide the dialogue from which consumer and employee perceptions of the encounter can be analysed and potential or existing problems identified. Overall, scripts provide the following:

- the basis for planning service encounters,
- goals and objectives,
- development of behavioural routines that maximize the opportunities for a successful exchange, and
- evaluation of the effectiveness of current service delivery systems.

The procedure used to develop a two-sided blueprint is to present employees and customers with a script-relevant situation, such as the steps taken to proceed through an airline boarding experience. Respondents are requested to note specific events or activities expected in their involvement in the situation. In particular, employees and consumers are asked to pay special attention to those contact activities that elicit strong positive or negative reactions during the service encounter. Script norms are then constructed by grouping together commonly mentioned events and ordering the events in their sequence of occurrence.

To facilitate the process of identifying script norms, the blueprint designer can compare the frequency of specific events mentioned by each of the groups. The value of this process is the potential recognition of gaps or discrepancies existing between employee and consumer perceptions. For example, consumers may mention the difficulties associated with parking, which employees may not mention since many report to work before the operation is open to customers.

The second step of the blueprint development process is to identify steps in the process at which the system can go awry. By asking employees and customers to further focus on events that are important in conveying service satisfaction and dissatisfaction, fail points can be isolated. The consequences of service failures can be greatly reduced by analysing fail points and instructing employees on the appropriate response or action when the inevitable failure occurs.

After the sequence of events/activities and potential fail points has been identified, the third step in the process involves specifying the timeframe of

convergent scripts
Employee/consumer scripts that are mutually agreeable and enhance the probability of customer satisfaction.

divergent scripts
Employee/consumer scripts that 'mismatch' and point to areas in which consumer expectations are not being met.

two-sided blueprint A blueprint that takes into account both employee and customer perceptions of how the sequence of events actually occurs.

script norms Proposed scripts developed by grouping together events commonly mentioned by both employees and customers and then ordering those events in their sequence of occurrence.

service execution. The major cost component of most service systems relates to the time required to complete the service; consequently, standard execution time norms must be established.

Once the standard execution times of the events that make up the service encounter have been specified, the manager can analyse the profitability of the system, given the costs of inputs needed for the system to operate. The resulting blueprint allows the planner to determine the profitability of the existing service delivery system as well as to speculate on the effects on profitability when changing one or more system components. Consequently, the service blueprint allows a company to test its assumptions on paper and to minimize the system's shortcomings before the system is imposed on customers and employees. The service manager can test a prototype of the delivery system with potential customers and use the feedback to modify the blueprint before testing the procedure again.

Blueprinting and new-product development: The roles of complexity and divergence

Blueprints may also be used in new-product development. Once the process has been documented and a blueprint has been drawn, choices can be made that will produce 'new' products. Although the processes in Figures 7.1, 7.2, and 7.3 are for the same task, from the consumer's point of view they are very different. The two blueprints define alternatives that are operationally feasible; the choice between which of the two to implement is for marketing.

Strategically, the decision may be to move the line separating visibility and invisibility. Operationally, arguments have been made for minimizing the visible component by isolating the technical core of the process. From a marketing point of view, however, more visibility may create more differentiation in the mind of the consumer. For example, a restaurant can make its kitchen into a distinctive feature by making it visible to restaurant patrons. This poses constraints on the operations personnel, but it may add value in the mind of the consumer.

complexity A measure of the number and intricacy of the steps and sequences that constitute a process.

divergence A measure of the degrees of freedom service personnel are allowed when providing a service.

New-product development within service firms can be implemented through the introduction of complexity and divergence (Shostack, 1987). Complexity is a measure of the number and intricacy of the steps and sequences that constitute the process – the more steps, the more complex the process. Divergence is defined as the degrees of freedom service personnel are allowed when providing the service. As an example, Figures 7.5 and 7.6 illustrate the blueprints for two florists who differ dramatically in their complexity and divergence. Although they perform equivalent tasks from an operations viewpoint, they can be very different from a marketing viewpoint and, therefore, constitute new products.

Figure 7.5 presents a traditional florist. The process, as in our restaurant example in Figure 7.1, is linear and involves a limited number of steps and so is low in complexity. However, the generation of flower arrangements under such a system calls for considerable discretion or degrees of freedom to be allowed the florist at each stage – in the choice of vase, flowers and display – and produces a heterogeneous final product. The system is, therefore, high in divergence.

Figure 7.6 provides the blueprint for a second florist that has attempted to standardize their final product. Because the objective of this system is to deskill the job, the system is designed to generate a limited number of standardized arrangements. The divergence of the system is therefore reduced, but to achieve this, the complexity of the process is increased significantly.

In developing products in the service sector, the amount of manipulation of the operation's complexity and divergence are the two key choices. Reducing divergence creates the uniformity that can reduce costs, but it does so at the expense of creativity and flexibility in the system. Companies that wish to pursue a volume-oriented positioning strategy often do so by reducing divergence. For example, a builder of swimming pools who focuses on the installation of prefabricated vinyl pools has greatly reduced the divergence of his operations. In addition to lowering production costs, reducing divergence increases productivity and facilitates distribution of the standardized service. From the customer's perspective, reducing divergence is associated with improved reliability, availability and uniform service quality. However, the downside of reduced divergence is the lack of customization that can be provided individual customers.

volume-oriented positioning strategy A positioning strategy that reduces divergence to create product uniformity and reduce costs.

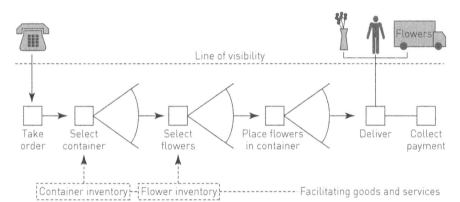

Figure 7.5

Park Avenue florist

Source G. Lynn Shostack, 'Service Positioning through Structural Change', *Journal of Marketing* 51 (January 1987), pp. 34–43. Reprinted by permission of the American Marketing Association.

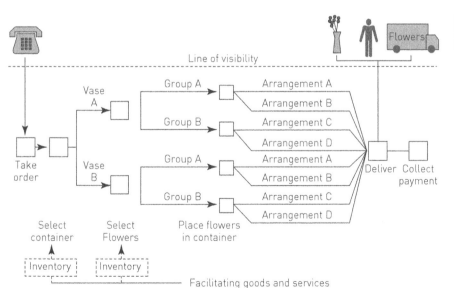

Figure 7.6

Florist services: Alternative design

Source G. Lynn Shostack, 'Service Positioning through Structural Change', *Journal of Marketing* 51 (January 1987), pp. 34–43. Reprinted by permission of the American Marketing Association.

niche positioning strategy A positioning strategy that increases divergence in an operation to tailor the service experience to each customer.

On the other hand, increasing divergence creates flexibility in tailoring the experience to each customer, but it does so at increased expense, and consumer prices are subsequently higher. Companies wishing to pursue a niche positioning strategy do so through increasing the divergence in their operations. For example, our pool builder may increase the divergence of his operation by specializing in the design and construction of customized pools and spas that can be built to resemble anything from a classical guitar to an exclamation mark! Profits, under this scenario, depend less on volume and more on margins on each individual purchase. The downside of increasing divergence is that the service operation becomes more difficult to manage, control and distribute. Moreover, customers may not be willing to pay the higher prices associated with a customized service.

specialization positioning strategy A positioning strategy that reduces complexity by unbundling the different services offered.

unbundling Divesting an operation of different services and concentrating on providing only one or a few services in order to pursue a specialization positioning strategy.

Reducing complexity is a specialization positioning strategy often involving the unbundling of the different services offered. Hence, our hypothetical pool builder may restrict himself to the installation of a single type of prefabricated pool and divest operations that were focused on supplemental services such as maintenance and repair as well as the design of pools and spas. The advantages associated with reduced complexity include improved control over the final product and improved distribution. However, risks are involved if full-service competitors, offering one-stop convenience, continue to operate. The full-service competitor appeals to consumers wishing to work with a provider that offers a number of choices.

penetration strategy A positioning strategy that increases complexity by adding more services and/ or enhancing current services to capture more of a market.

Increasing complexity is utilized by companies that pursue a mass market or penetration strategy. Increasing complexity translates into the addition of more services to the firm's offering as well as the enhancement of current ones. Within this scenario, our pool builder would offer customized pools and spas and a wide variety of prefabricated vinyl pools. In addition to installation, other services such as general pool maintenance and repair would be offered. Firms pursuing a penetration strategy often try to be everything to everybody and often gloss over individual consumer needs. Moreover, when providing such a broad range of services, the quality of the provider's skills are bound to vary depending upon the task being performed, leaving some customers less than satisfied. Hence, firms that increase complexity of their operations by offering enhanced and/or additional services run the risk of becoming vulnerable to companies that pursue more specialized types of operations.

Summary

The primary objective of this chapter was to highlight the idea that for a service firm to be successful, its marketing and operations departments must work together. In a broad sense, one could view the functions of marketing and operations as the marriage of consumers' needs with the technology and manufacturing capabilities of the firm. This marriage entails many compromises that attempt to balance operational efficiency with the effectiveness of the system from the consumer's point of view. To be effective, operations personnel must recognize the importance of their marketing counterparts, and vice versa.

Firms operating at peak efficiency are free from outside influences and operate as if the market will consume the firm's production at a continuous rate. Uncertainty creates inefficiency. Hence, in an ideal situation, the technical core of the firm is able to operate without uncertainty on either the input or output side. Although the attempt to operate at peak efficiency is a worthy goal, it likely represents an unrealistic objective for most service firms. The production of most services is an operations nightmare. Instead of receiving demand at a constant rate, service firms are often linked directly to a market that frequently varies from day to day, hour to hour and even minute to minute. Service customers frequently affect the time of demand, the cycle of demand, the type of demand and the duration of many service transactions.

Plans to operate at peak efficiency must be altered to cope with the uncertainties inherent in service operations. Strategies that attempt to increase the efficiency of the service operation by facilitating the balance of supply and demand include minimizing the servuction system by iso-

lating the technical core; production-lining the whole system utilizing hard and soft technologies; creating flexible capacity; increasing customer participation; and moving the time of demand to fit capacity.

Service blueprints can be developed that identify the direction in which processes flow and the parts of a process that may both increase operational efficiency and enhance the customer's service experience. Operational changes made to the service blueprint often require changes in consumer behaviour and, in some instances, lead to new service products. New service development is achieved through the introduction of complexity and divergence. Reducing divergence standardizes the service product and reduces production costs, whereas increasing divergence enables service providers to tailor their products to individual customers. Similarly, reducing complexity is consistent with a specialisation positioning strategy, while increasing complexity is appropriate for firms pursuing a penetration strategy.

Note

1 Much of this chapter is adopted from Chapters 3 and 4 of John E. G. Bateson, *Managing Services Marketing*, 2nd ed. (Fort Worth, TX: The Dryden Press, 1992), pp. 156–169, 200–207.

Discussion questions

1 Explain how the inability to inventory services affects the operational efficiency of most service firms.

2 Compare Thompson's perfect-world model to the focused factory and plant-within-a-plant concepts.

3 What is buffering? How do the strategies of anticipating, smoothing and rationing relate to buffering?

4 Discuss some specific examples of how the customer's involvement in the service encounter influences the operational efficiency of the average service firm.

5 What does it mean to isolate the technical core of a business? Give both consumer and B2B examples of this.

6 Discuss the steps for developing a meaningful blueprint for the service offered by LOVEFiLMS (Global Services in Action). What are the limitations of this service delivery tool?

7 Use examples to discuss the difficulties in service delivery in multinational markets. How can these difficulties be overcome? Illustrate your answer by references to the case study, 'Westin Hotels in Asia: Global Distribution'.

Case link

See Case 6: Westin Hotels in Asia: Global Distribution.

Further reading and references

Bitner, M. J., Nyquist, J. D. and Booms, B. H. (1985) 'The critical incident technique for analyzing the service encounter', in *Service Marketing in a Changing Environment*, Thomas M. Block, Gregory D. Upah and Valerie A. Zeithaml, eds., Chicago: American Marketing Association, pp. 48–51.

Chase, R. B. (1981) 'The customer contact approach to services: Theoretical base and practical extensions', *Operations Research* 29 (4): 698–706.

Chase, B. and Hayes, R. H. (1991) 'Beefing up operations in service firms', *Sloan Management Review* (Fall): 15–26.

Chase, R. B. and Tansik, D. A. (1983) 'The customer contact model for organization design', *Management Service* 29 (9): 1037–1050.

Dabholkar, P. A. and Overby, J. W. (2005) 'Linking process and outcome to service quality and customer satisfaction evaluations', *International Journal of Service Industry Management* 16 (1): 10–27.

Danet, B. (1984) 'Client-organization interfaces', in *Handbook of Organization Design*, 2nd ed., P. C. Nystrom and W. N. Starbuck, eds., New York: Oxford University Press.

Hoffman, K. D. and Howe, V. (1991) 'Developing the micro service audit via script theoretic and blueprinting procedures', in *Marketing Toward the Twenty-First Century*, Robert L. King, ed. University of Richmond: Southern Marketing Association, pp. 379–383.

Kumar, R. and Kumar, U. (2004) 'A conceptual framework for the development of a service delivery strategy for industrial systems and products', *Journal of Business &Industrial Marketing* 19 (5): 310–319.

Levitt, T. (1972) 'Production-line approach to services', *Harvard Business Review* 50 (5): 41–52.

Leigh, T. W. and Rethans, A. J. (1983) 'Experience with script elicitation within consumer making contexts', in *Advances in Consumer Research*, Volume Ten, Alice Tybout and Richard Bagozzi, eds., Ann Arbor, MI: Association for Consumer Research, pp. 667–672.

Lovelock, C. H. and Young, R. F. (1979) 'Look to consumers to increase productivity', *Harvard Business Review* (May–June): 168–178.

Marston, C. (2008) 'Last post for rural post office?', www.news.bbc.co.uk, accessed 19 Feb. 2008.

Matteis, R. J. (1979) 'The new back office focuses on customer service', *Harvard Business Review* 57: 146–159.

Meuter, M. L., Bitner, M. J., Ostrom, A. L. and Brown, S. W. (2005) 'Choosing among alternative service delivery modes: an investigation of customer trial of self-service technologies', *Journal of Marketing* 69 (2): 61–83.

Sasser, W. E. (1976) 'Match supply and demand in service industries', *Harvard Business Review* 54 (5): 61–65.

Schneider, B. (1980) 'The service organization: Climate is crucial', *Organizational Dynamics* (August): 52–65.

Shostack, G. L. (1987) 'Service positioning through structural change', *Journal of Marketing* 51 (January): 34–43.

Skinner, W. (1974) 'The focused factory', *Harvard Business Review* 52 (3)(May–June): 113–121.

Suprenant, C. F. and Solomon, M. (1987) 'Predictability and personalization in the service encounter', *Journal of Marketing* 51: 86–96.

Thompson, J. D. (1967) *Organizations in Action*, New York: McGraw-Hill.

Chapter 8
The pricing of services

Pricing of services has long been given less attention than product pricing. However, as services have become an increasingly important part of the economy – and a bigger source of profit for many companies – the need to understand service pricing has grown. Without such an understanding many product-orientated managers are in danger of leaving money on the table.

(Doctors, Reopel, Sun and Tanny, 2004: 23)

Chapter objectives

The purpose of this chapter is to familiarize you with the special considerations needed when pricing services.

After reading this chapter, you should be able to:

- Describe how consumers relate value and price.

- Understand the special considerations of service pricing as they relate to demand, cost, customer, competitor, profit, product, and legal considerations.

- Discuss the circumstances under which price segmentation is most effective.

- Explain satisfaction-based, relationship, and efficiency approaches to pricing.

Services in context
The big players can get it wrong

Ticket pricing at premier league matches in the UK has often been the subject of controversial debate. The rising prices at some clubs has made watching your team play equivalent to the cost of a meal in a high-class restaurant or a night out at the opera or London theatre. With raised prices comes changes in consumer behaviour. Not just in the numbers and demographics of those attending, but in raised expectations of value through entertainment and a greater propensity to criticize and respond to poor performance.

For example, in 1968 the average age of fans standing in the Stretford End (at Manchester United's Old Trafford stadium) was 17. The cost of admission for under-16s was eight shillings (40p). Forty years on, the average age of fans sitting in the Stretford End is over 40. And the ticket price is £33 (£16.50 for under-16s, which is more than three times the relative cost of the 1967 entrance fee, allowing for inflation).

The hike in ticket prices at Old Trafford has disenfranchised some of United's traditional support. For a man proud of his working-class roots, Sir Alex Ferguson should listen to the concerns of those whose passion for United rivals his own. 'If you want Old Trafford to be a "cauldron" of intensity and fervour for the home team, why not make it affordable again to people on a normal wage?' writes a supporter from Salford who describes himself as 'a normal working-class fan being gradually priced out'.

Chelsea Football Club also risked alienating their supporters when in 2005 they neglected to apply promised discounts for European matches. The Club ended up repaying fans around £200,000. More recently Chelsea, despite financial losses, have attempted to freeze ticket prices over the past few years. 'We understand that our ticket prices are at the higher end and we are sensitive to the economic demands on our supporters', said Chelsea's chief executive, Peter Kenyon. 'This decision, taken after regular dialogue with the fans' forum, achieves a good balance between those demands and the needs of our business. With the success we have had we believe Chelsea offers good value on and off the pitch.'

Kenyon said: 'A major issue recently, both at Chelsea, and in football generally, has been ticket prices and the effect this has, or could have, on attendances.'

For many of the big clubs in European football, match ticket sales are not the main driver of profitability, with the big money being made in sponsorship and media deals. However, the spectacle of the match and the success of the team is often made or destroyed by the enthusiasm of the crowd. High ticket prices lead to lower attendance and a poorer match day atmosphere. This in turn affects audience enjoyment and ultimately team performance. The pricing strategy therefore has a direct impact upon the product offering as the supporters' presence and participation creates the match experience for other spectators in the stadium but also for those listening on the radio or watching via television and internet.

Sources: M. Scott (2007) 'Chelsea make losses but deny owner is losing interest', www.guardian.co.uk, 20 Feb. 2007, accessed 25 March 2008.
G. Tynan (2005) 'Kenyon admits European ticket pricing mix-up', www.independent.co.uk, 24 Sept. 2005, accessed 25 March 2008.
J. White (2008) 'Football's money men making loudest noise', www.telegraph.co.uk, 5 Jan. 2008, accessed 25 March 2008.
H. Winter (2008) 'Alex Ferguson must listen to heartbroken fans', www.telegraph.co.uk, 5 Jan. 2008, accessed 25 March 2008.

Introduction

Of the traditional marketing mix variables that are utilized to influence customer purchase decisions, the development of effective pricing strategies perhaps remains the most elusive. Pricing is often a perplexing issue for practitioners and researchers alike. Consider the following sample of expressed opinions regarding pricing practices over the past 50 years that reflect both the confusion and frustration associated with pricing decisions:

> Pricing policy is the last stronghold of medievalism in modern management. [Pricing] is still largely intuitive and even mystical in the sense that the intuition is often the province of the big boss.
>
> (Dean, 1947)

> [P]erhaps few ideas have wider currency than the mistaken impression that prices are or should be determined by costs of production.
>
> (Backman, 1953)

> For marketers of industrial goods and construction companies, pricing is the single judgment that translates potential business into reality. Yet pricing is the least rational of all decisions made in this specialised field.
>
> (Walker, 1967)

> Many managing directors do not concern themselves with pricing details; some are not even aware of how their products are priced.
>
> (Marshall, 1979)

> Pricing is approached in Britain like Russian roulette – to be indulged in mainly by those contemplating suicide.
>
> (Chief Executive, 1981)

> Perhaps it is reasonable that marketers have only recently begun to focus seriously on effective pricing. Only after managers have mastered the techniques of creating value do the techniques of capturing value become important.
>
> (Nagle and Holden, 1995)

> Too often, pricing is the undiscussed subject in many companies. Senior managers need to take a fresh look at their pricing strategies in the face of unprecedented price pressures.
>
> (Coulson-Thomas, 2007)

Today, price remains one of the least researched and mastered areas of marketing. Research and expertise pertaining to the pricing of services is particularly lacking. Many of the concepts developed for goods apply equally to services. This chapter focuses on how the pricing approaches apply and on how, to a greater or lesser extent, service pricing policies differ from those of goods.

Perceptions of value

Buyers' perceptions of value represent a trade-off between the perceived benefits of the service to be purchased and the perceived sacrifice in terms of the costs to be paid (see Figure 8.1). Total customer costs include more than simply the monetary price paid for the service. Other costs include time costs, energy costs, and psychic costs, which reflect the time and trouble the customer has to endure to acquire the

monetary price The actual dollar price paid by the consumer for a product.

time costs The time the customer has to spend to acquire the service.

energy costs The physical energy spent by the customer to acquire the service.

psychic costs The mental energy spent by the customer to acquire the service.

product value The worth assigned to the product by the customer.

service value The worth assigned to the service by the customer.

personnel value The worth assigned to the service-providing personnel by the customer.

image value The worth assigned to the image of the service or service provider by the customer.

service. Similarly, total customer value extends beyond product value and includes service value, personnel value, and image value (Kotler, 1994).

For example, a customer who wishes to purchase a new mobile phone must pay the monetary price for the phone plus the monthly charges for the services received. In this example, the customer chose a Sony Ericsson phone due to its advanced functions and styling (product value) and the quality associated with the Sony name (image value). In addition, Sony's warranty (service value) was competitive with leading alternatives. The customer bought the system at Carphone Warehouse because of the sales representative's superior product knowledge (personnel value) compared with the dismal quality of information received at alternative purchase locations.

In addition to the monetary cost, the customer incurred time and energy costs while shopping at various locations and questioning sales representatives about the various brands and packages available. Additional time costs were incurred waiting for the phone to be set up. The activation and registration, which should have taken 15 minutes, took an hour. In addition, the customer was out of contact with her office during this time and kept on-hold on a help-line for 20 minutes. Each of these events added to the psychic cost (e.g., worry and aggravation) of the whole experience.

Overall, if the signal sent by total customer cost is an indicator of sacrifice relative to value, then price will have a negative or repelling effect and may reduce demand. If the signal sent by the price is an indicator of benefit or value, then price will be an attractor and may increase demand. Because of the perceived connection between cost and benefit, buyers have both lower and upper price thresholds. For example, buyers might be discouraged from buying when the price is perceived to be too low simply because they see a low price as an indicator of inferior quality.

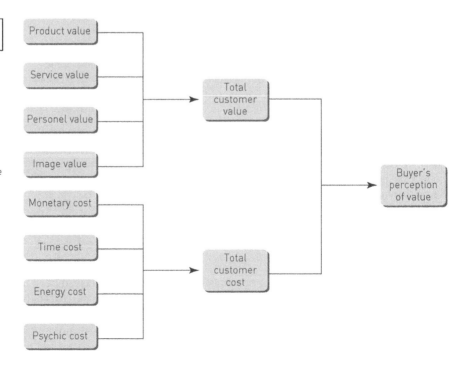

Figure 8.1

Buyer's perception of value

Source Philip Kotler; Kevin Lane Keller, *Marketing Management*, 12th Edition, © 2006, p. 141. Adapted by permission of Pearson Education, Inc., Upper Saddle River, NJ.

Consumers exchange their money, time and effort for the bundle of benefits the service provider offers. Economic theory suggests that consumers will have a reservation price that captures the value they place on these benefits. As long as the total cost to the consumer is less than the reservation price, he or she will be prepared to buy. If the consumer can purchase the service for less than the reservation price, a consumer's surplus will exist. The eight dimensions of value described here and shown in Figure 8.1 provide direction for how service firms can differentiate themselves from competitors.

Special considerations of service pricing

The ultimate pricing challenge faced by most firms is determining a price that sells the service while at the same time offering a profitable return. When pricing services, many of the same market conditions that are considered for pricing goods should be examined. 'The difference between price setting and strategic pricing is the difference between reacting to market conditions and proactively managing them' (Nagle and Holden, 2002). The literature suggests that price determination should be based on demand, cost, customer, competitive, profit, product and legal considerations (Lewison, 1997). While these market conditions are the same for goods and services, the contents of the considerations differ. For example, Tahar and El Basha (2006) propose that when pricing services the three dimensions of consumer heterogeneity should be considered alongside the distinctive characteristics of service. These three dimensions are 'value of information', 'price sensitivity' and 'differing transaction costs'. The discussion that follows highlights some of these key differences (see Table 8.1).

Demand considerations

There are a number of demand considerations that differentiate the pricing of services from the pricing of goods. First, demand for services tends to be more inelastic. Cost increases are often simply passed along to consumers. Second, consumers of services often implicitly bundle prices. For example, the demand for food services at a theme park are impacted by the price of the theme park's hotel and ticket prices. Consequently, the cross-price elasticity of services should be taken into careful consideration. Finally, due to the supply and demand fluctuations inherent in services, price discrimination strategies should also be investigated.

Demand for services tends to be more inelastic. In general, consumers of services are more willing to pay higher prices if doing so reduces their level of perceived risk. Perceived risk is a function of consequence (the degree of importance and/or danger associated with the purchase) and uncertainty (the variability in service performance from customer to customer or from day to day). The service characteristics of intangibility, inseparability, heterogeneity and perishability contribute greatly to heightened levels of perceived risk.

Experts in the field suggest ten factors that influence customer price sensitivity (see Table 8.2). In short, price sensitivity decreases as:

Table 8.1	**Demand considerations**	
	D1:	The demand for services tends to be more inelastic than the demand for goods.
Unique differences associated with service prices	D2:	Due to the implicit bundling of services by consumers, cross-price elasticity considerations need to be examined.
	D3:	Price discrimination is a viable practice to manage demand and supply challenges.
	Cost considerations	
	D4:	With many professional services (and some others), the consumer may not know the actual price they will pay for the service until the service is completed.
	D5:	Cost-oriented pricing is more difficult for services.
	D6:	Services tend to be characterized by a high fixed/variable cost ratio.
	D7:	Economies of scale tend to be limited.
	Customer considerations	
	D8:	Price tends to be one of the few cues available to consumers during prepurchase.
	D9:	Service consumers are more likely to use price as a cue to quality.
	D10:	Service consumers tend to be less certain about reservation prices.
	Competitive considerations	
	D11:	Comparing prices of competitors is more difficult for service consumers.
	D12:	Self-service is a viable competitive alternative.
	Profit considerations	
	D13:	Price bundling makes the determination of individual prices in the bundle of services more complicated.
	D14:	Price bundling is more effective in a services context.
	Product considerations	
	D15:	Compared to the goods sector, there tend to be many different names for price in the service sector.
	D16:	Consumers are less able to stockpile services by taking advantage of discount prices.
	D17:	Product-line pricing tends to be more complicated.
	Legal considerations	
	D18:	The opportunity for illegal pricing practices to go undetected is greater for services than goods.

1 the perceived number of substitutes decrease;
2 the perceived unique value of the service increases;
3 switching costs increase;
4 the difficulty in comparing substitutes increases;
5 the extent to which price is used as a quality cue increases;
6 the expenditure is relatively small in terms of dollars or as a percentage of household income;
7 the less price sensitive consumers are to the end-benefit;
8 shared costs for the expenditure increase;
9 the price is perceived as fair compared to similar services purchased under similar circumstances; and
10 the customer's ability to build an inventory decreases.

(Hoffman and Turley, 1999)

Price sensitivity factors	Proposed relationship
Perceived substitute effect	Price sensitivity increases when the price for Service A is higher than the price of perceived substitutes.
Unique value effect	Price sensitivity increases as the unique value of Service A is perceived to be equal to or less than the unique value of perceived substitutes.
Switching costs effect	Price sensitivity increases as switching costs decrease.
Difficult comparison effect	Price sensitivity increases as the difficulty in comparing substitutes decreases.
Price-quality effect	Price sensitivity increases to the extent that price is not used as a quality cue.
Expenditure effect	Price sensitivity increases when the expenditure is large in terms of dollars or as a percentage of household income.
End-benefit effect	The more price sensitive consumers are to the end benefit, the more price sensitive they will be to services that contribute to the end benefit.

Table 8.2

Factors influencing customers' price sensitivity

▶

Shared-cost effect	Price sensitivity increases as the shared costs with third parties decreases.
Fairness effect	Price sensitivity increases when the price paid for similar services under similar circumstances is lower.
Inventory effect	Price sensitivity increases as the customers' ability to hold an inventory increases.

inelastic demand The type of market demand when a change in price of service is greater than a change in quantity demanded.

Clearly, price sensitivities will vary across different types of services, but in general the demand for services tends to be inelastic. Different groups of consumers will likely weigh the importance of each price sensitivity factor differently (see B2B Services in Action). Service firms must assess which of the factors are more salient to their target market's purchasing decisions.

Cross price elasticity considerations need to be examined. Consumers of services often implicitly bundle prices. In other words, consumers may figure that the total cost of going to the movies includes the tickets and refreshments. Therefore, total revenues may be maximized by carefully considering the cross-price elasticities of the total product offering. This is particularly true in cases where the price of the core service offering influences the demand of supplemental services. Cross-price elasticity of demand measures the responsiveness of demand for a service relative to a change in price for another service. If this relationship is negative, then the two services are said to be complementary. For example, if movie ticket prices increase substantially, consumers are likely to purchase less popcorn. If the relationship is positive, however, then the two services are called substitutes, and consumption of one is at the expense of the consumption of the other. For example, the increase in cinema tickets will likely decrease the demand for DVD rentals. Multi-product considerations dominate many service industries such as business services, personal services, professional services and the hospitality industry. The golf industry provides a prime example of the effects of cross-price elasticities. Consumers have different price sensitivities for greens fees, buggy fees, range fees and food and beverage expenses. If consumers perceive the price of admission (greens fees) as good value, they are likely to purchase additional revenue-generating products in the form of buggies, practice range balls and food and beverages. In contrast, if the price of admission is perceived as low in value, consumer price sensitivities for supplemental services are likely to increase. Consumers often forego some or all of these additional services in order to keep their total expenses in line. In effect, the higher price of admission often leads to overall lower consumer expenditures and reduces the revenue stream for the firm.

cross-price elasticity A measure of the responsiveness of demand for a service relative to a change in price for another service.

complementary The result of negative cross-price elasticity in which the increasing price of one service decreases the demand for another service.

substitutes The result of positive cross-price elasticity in which the increasing price of one service increases the demand for another service.

price discrimination Charging customers different prices for essentially the same service.

Price discrimination is a viable practice to manage demand and supply challenges. Price discrimination involves charging customers different prices for essentially the same service (see Global Services in Action). This unique aspect of service pricing relates to both the perishability

B2B services in action
Airfares: Pricing and the business traveller

Many services are characterized by a high fixed/variable cost ratio. The airline industry is a typical example. The three major costs to an airline are the fleet, labour and fuel. Fleet and labour costs are primarily fixed, whereas fuel costs are variable. Perhaps more importantly, fuel costs are beyond an airline's control; however, the airline has some influence over the other two expenses.

The traditional airline business model bases its economic vitality on its high-fare business travellers. Business travellers generally account for three-quarters of an airline's revenues but only half of the passenger total. In the past, business travellers who booked last-minute fares paid on average five times the price of the lowest leisure ticket price. However, fares for budget airlines grew by 10 per cent in the last year and now account for one in eight business travel bookings, according to a survey by Hogg Robinson Group (HRG).

According to the international corporate services company, traditional carriers have responded to the growth of the low-cost carriers in the business sector by reducing the cost of their economy fares by an average 5 per cent. This heightened competition across the airline industry has kept overall average price increases below those seen in previous years despite an increase in the number of travellers.

HRG's air trends survey was compiled from actual flights booked and ticket rates paid by an indicative sample of over 250,000 business travellers booking from the UK between May 2006 and June 2007. The findings reveal that:

- The average cost of economy seats on major airlines has dropped by 5 per cent;
- Budget airlines have increased their market share on popular routes, allowing them to increase fares by an average of 10 per cent;
- Prices for business class tickets have gone up by 4 per cent despite marginal change in the number of travellers choosing this class.

'Of the low cost carriers, easyJet's business-friendly routes have helped it to increase its market share to almost 20 per cent on popular routes, despite the fact that it continues to be the most expensive of the budget airlines surveyed. The additional volume of bookings has given easyJet the confidence to increase its prices during the last year, with return flights to popular destinations such as Edinburgh and Amsterdam now costing more than £100', stated HRG.

Mike Platt, HRG's Group Industry Affairs Director, said: 'During the last year we have booked over 90,000 flights on low-cost carriers and we are seeing more businesses choose this option for domestic and some short haul flights. It is also interesting to see business class ticket prices increasing by almost 4 per cent despite ticket sales remaining static, reflecting the airlines' confidence in the popularity of the business class cabin.'

Although economy class has suffered as a result of the increase in business customers using budget airlines, economy class continues to account for the largest proportion of business travellers.

SOURCE CORBIS

HRG's survey looked at the different classes chosen by business travellers and found the following trends:

- The number of people travelling on low-cost carriers has risen by an astonishing 33 per cent, to represent over 12 per cent of the total market.
- As a consequence of increased competition from budget airlines the economy-class share of the overall market dropped by 4 per cent to 59 per cent.
- First, business and premium economy shares of the market are relatively static at 0.3 per cent, 28 per cent and 0.8 per cent respectively.

HRG's survey also looked at the most popular destinations for business travellers over the last year and found that bookings to long-haul destinations had increased significantly:

- The number of travellers going to the Far East and Australia increased by over 30 per cent.
- 28 per cent more business travel bookings were made to the Middle East.
- Business travel to Africa has increased by 23 per cent.
- Bookings to South America were up by 12 per cent.

Platt said, 'With such steep increases in bookings it is no surprise to see that ticket prices have risen on the most popular routes. Africa is becoming an important business destination, with prices up by 14 per cent, being largely driven by the popularity of Johannesburg. The cost of tickets to South America is also up, by a more modest 5 per cent, and we expect to see ticket prices continue to rise on these routes as they become more important business destinations.'

Source: Adapted from Eyefortravel.com, 20 Sept. 2007, accessed 25 March 2008.

and simultaneous production and consumption of services. Price discrimination is a viable practice in service industries due in part to differences in the demand elasticities held by customers and the need of the organization to balance demand and supply for its service products.

The viability of price discrimination is enhanced by the fact that in some services customers readily accept that prices often drop significantly before the opportunity to sell the service passes completely (e.g., last-minute concert tickets). Alternatively more proactive service providers will manage demand and cash flow by using price to encourage early purchase. Advance pricing rewards the customer for taking a greater risk through paying in advance of the service use through a lower price (Shugan and Xie, 2000). For example, low-cost airlines offer cheaper deals the further in advance of the flight you buy and many event ticket agencies now offer an early booking discount. The risk to the cutomer is that their plans may change, they may be ill on the day and so on. Therefore, in many service settings, consumers have become quite accustomed to different customers paying different amounts for the same service (e.g. hotels). In addition, online services have now emerged that allow consumers to name their own price for airline tickets and car rentals. Service providers accept these proposals in order to cover at least some portion of their fixed costs. Some revenue is deemed better than no revenue in these situations.

Effective price segmentation benefits consumers and providers alike. Consumers often benefit from options that offer lower prices, and providers are often able to manage demand and increase capacity utilization. The interaction that creates the service experience, which is what the consumer buys, takes place in real time. Since consumers must, in most cases, come to the service setting to be part of the experience, capacity utilization depends on when they arrive. For most services, consumers tend to arrive unevenly and unpredictably, as at a supermarket, bank or restaurant. The result is often periods of low utilization of capacity because of the impossibility of matching capacity to demand.

Capacity, in turn, represents the bulk of the costs for a service. The restaurant has to be open, staffed, and resourced even at times when it has

---

Global services in action
Ethnic pricing ... Is this ethical?

The practice of *ethnic pricing*, giving discounts to people of certain nationalities, has been routine in countries such as India, China and Russia. Other countries also offer ethnic pricing but are not very public about it due to ethical and legal ramifications. According to the *Wall Street Journal*, airline passengers throughout Europe could obtain discount fares on airline tickets based on the origin of their passport or those of their employers. Brenden McInerney, a passenger attempting to book a Lufthansa flight to Japan, accidently learned of the practice and was not too happy about it. His wife could fly to Japan for 1,700 marks; however, Mr McInerney's ticket was priced at 2,700 marks! The reason given by the airline: Mr McInerney is an American, while his wife is Japanese. The airline eventually capitulated and Mr McInerney was finally given the same fare after he complained.

Lufthansa did not deny its involvement with ethnic pricing. Dagmar Rotter, a spokesperson for the airline, stated that the airline was only reacting to the competition from the national carrier of Japan that also flies out of Germany. 'The others started it ... we only offer it [ethnic pricing] after the market forced us to do so.'

Other European airlines such as Swissair and Air France also practised ethnic pricing. Swissair offered 'guest-worker' fares to passengers from Turkey, Portugal, Spain, Greece and Morocco flying to these same destinations. However, it did not offer discount fares to Japanese flying to Japan. A Swissair spokesperson argued that if the discounts were not provided to the 'guest-workers' from Southern Europe and the Mediterranean rim, they would never be able to afford to go home to visit their families. Similarly, Air France offers discounted rates to citizens of Vietnam, China, South Korea and Japan, but only for its flights that were departing from Germany. An Air France spokesperson noted: 'In Germany everybody seems to be doing it ... it seems to be something very specific to the German market.'

British Airway's involvement was readily apparent when it offered its travel package 'Ho, Ho, Ho' for British citizens in Turkey. 'Short of stuffing, need some pork sausages, fretting about Christmas pud? Not to worry – show your British passport and you can take 48 per cent off normal fares to Britain.'

One way that companies make these policies less obvious is to offer discounts through 'locally' available media. For example several London visitor attractions ensure that Londoners pay less by distributing coupons and special offers through local schools, newspapers and letterbox leafleting.

Whatever the method used, discriminatory pricing is here to stay whether it be based on age, usage levels, location, payment method, time of booking or, more controversially, nationality.

Source: Adapted from 'Ethnic Pricing Means Unfair Air Fares', *Wall Street Journal*, 5 December 1997, pp. B1, B14.

no customers. The result is a very low level of variable costs for services and a high value attributable to incremental customers, even at discount prices. As a result, pricing is called upon to try to smooth demand in two ways:

- creating new demand in off-peak, low-capacity utilization periods,
- flattening peaks by moving existing customers from peaks to less busy times.

The following are several criteria for effective price segmentation:

1. Different groups of consumers must have different responses to price.

If different groups of consumers have the same response to price changes, then the price segmentation strategy becomes counterproductive. For example, for years theatres have offered matinees at a reduced fee. This strategy helped the theatre create demand for unused capacity during the day and also helped to smooth demand during the evening shows. Moreover, this approach has attracted market segments such as families with children and individuals on fixed incomes, who may not otherwise attend the higher-priced evening shows. This strategy has been effective because the price change did not create the same response for everyone. If most consumers had shifted their demand to the afternoon shows at lower rates, the theatre would have overutilized capacity in the afternoons and would be generating lower total revenues for the firm.

2. The different segments must be identifiable, and a mechanism must exist to price them differently.

Effective price segmentation requires that consumer segments with different demand patterns be identifiable on the basis of some readily apparent common characteristic such as age, family-life cycle stage, gender, and/or educational status. Discriminating based on a convoluted segmentation scheme confuses customers and service providers, who must implement the strategy. Common forms of segmentation identification include college ID cards, low-income passport schemes and driving licences.

3. No opportunity should exist for individuals in one segment who have paid a low price to sell their tickets to those in other segments.

For example, it does the theatre little good to sell reduced-price seats in the afternoon to buyers who can turn around and sell those tickets that evening in the car park to full-paying customers. Sometimes you just can't win! A local municipal golf course was trying to do 'the right thing' by offering its senior citizen customers coupon books for rounds of golf priced at a reduced rate. Soon after the promotion began, some senior citizen customers were seen in the car park selling their coupons at a profit to the golf course's full-price customers.

4. The segment should be large enough to make the exercise worthwhile.

The time and effort involved in offering a price segmentation

Strategic price segmentation? Half price theatre tickets are sold in London's Leicester Square.

scheme should be justified based on the return it brings to the business. Having little or no response to the firm's effort signals that either consumers are uninterested, eligible customers are few, or the firm's price segmentation offer is off its mark.

5. The cost of running the price segmentation strategy should not exceed the incremental revenues obtained. The objectives of engaging in price segmentation efforts may be to reduce peak demand, fill periods of underutilized capacity, increase overall revenues, or achieve nonprofit issues, such as making your service available to individuals who otherwise may not be able to take advantage of the services the firm offers. If the cost of running the price segmentation strategy exceeds the returns produced, management needs to reconsider the offering.

6. The customers should not be confused by the use of different prices. Phone companies and electric utilities often offer customers reduced rates that are based on the time of usage. Frequently, however, these time-related discounts change as new promotions arise. Customers caught unaware of the change often end up paying higher rates than expected, which negatively impacts customer satisfaction. Other pricing strategies such as those employed by mobile telecommunications networks simply frustrate the customer. Recently, some of these companies have offered 'simple pricing' as a point of differentiation in their advertising. Other firms are offering higher-priced 'peak rates' and lower-priced 'nonpeak' rates that vary throughout the day, and customers must be aware at all times which rate they will be paying in order to take advantage of this particular type of pricing strategy.

(adapted fom Bateson, 1992)

Cost considerations

Cost considerations should also be taken into account when formulating service pricing strategy. First, service pricing is often not finalized until after provision. Consequently, the consumer experiences greater price uncertainty. Second, since services have no cost of goods sold (nothing tangible was produced), cost-based pricing is more difficult for services. Third, many service industries, such as the airlines discussed in B2B Services in Action, are often characterized by a high fixed/variable cost ratio, which leads to further pricing challenges. Finally, the mass production of services leads to limited economies of scale.

Consumers may not know the actual price they will pay for a service until after the service is completed. Although consumers can usually find a base price to use as a comparison during prepurchase evaluation, many services are customized during delivery. Consumers may not know the exact amount they will be charged until after the service is performed. For example, a patient may know what a standard car sevice costs, but may not know what will be charged for replacement parts, loan car or valeting. A client may know how much a solicitor charges for an hour of work but may not know how many hours it will take to finalize a will. In contrast to goods that are produced, purchased and consumed, services are often purchased (implied), produced and consumed simultaneously, and then actually paid for when the final bill is presented. The final price is sometimes the last piece of information revealed to the customer.

Cost-based pricing is more difficult for services. Many service managers experience difficulties accurately estimating their costs of doing business. This difficulty arises for several reasons. First, when producing an intangible product, the cost of goods sold is either a small or nonexistent portion of the total cost. Second, labour needs are difficult to accurately forecast in many service settings due in part to fluctuating demand. Third, workforce turnover is typically high in many service industries. This, coupled with the fact that finding good personnel is an ongoing challenge, leads to further difficulty in estimating the costs associated with a particular service encounter. These factors make what is often considered the most common approach to pricing, cost-oriented pricing, difficult at best for service firms. Consequently, the difficulties associated with controlling and forecasting costs are a fundamental difference between goods and services pricing.

Unfortunately, traditional cost accounting practices, which were designed to monitor raw material consumption, depreciation and labour, offer little in helping service managers understand their own cost structures. A more useful approach, activity-based costing (ABC), focuses on the resources consumed in developing the final product (Chaffman and Talbott, 1991). Traditionally, overheads in most service firms have been allocated to projects based on the amount of direct labour charged to complete the customer's requirements. However, this method of charging overhead has frustrated managers of specific projects for years. Consider the following example:

Let's say that ABC Company charges £2.00 for overheads for every pound of direct labour charged to customers. As the manager of ABC Company, you have just negotiated with a customer to provide architectural drawings of a deck for £1,000. The customer wants the drawing in three days. Realizing that using your best architect, whom you pay £20 an hour, will result in a loss for the project, you assign the architect's apprentice, who makes £7 an hour. The results of the project are as follows:

activity-based costing Costing method that breaks down the organization into a set of activities, and activities into tasks, which convert materials, labour and technology into outputs.

Time Required	40 hours
Apprentice's Rate	£7 per hour
Direct Labour	£280
Overheads @ £2	£560
Project Cost	£840
Revenue	£1000
Profit	£160

If the firm's best architect had completed the job, the following results would have been submitted:

Time Required	20 hours
Architect's Rate	£20 per hour
Direct Labour	£400
Overhead @ £2	£800
Project Cost	£1200
Revenue	£1000
Profit/Loss	(£200)

This traditional approach used in service firms makes little sense. Intuitively, it does not make sense that a job that took a shorter period of time should be charged more overhead. Moreover, this type of system encourages the firm to use less-skilled labour, who produce an inferior product in an unacceptable period of time as specified by the customer. The firm produces a profit on paper but will most likely never have the opportunity to work for this customer again (or his/her friends, for that matter). Even more confusing is that salary increases and promotions are based on profits generated, so the manager is rewarded for using inferior labour. Something is definitely wrong with this picture!

Activity-based costing focuses on the cost of activities by breaking down the organization into a set of activities, and activities into tasks, which convert materials, labour and technology into outputs. The tasks are thought of as 'users' of overheads and identified as cost drivers. The firm's past records are used to arrive at cost-per-task figures that are then allocated to each project based on the activities required to complete the project. In addition, by breaking the overall overhead figure into a set of activities that are driven by cost drivers, the firm can now concentrate its efforts on reducing costs and increasing profitability.

For example, one activity in the firm's overall overhead figure is ordering materials. Ordering materials is driven by the number of purchase orders submitted. Company records indicate that overhead associated with ordering materials cost the firm £10,400 during the period. During this same period, 325 purchase orders were submitted. Hence, the activity cost associated with each purchase order is £32.00. Similar calculations are made for other overhead items. Overheads are then allocated to each project based on the activities undertaken to complete the project. Table 8.3 presents examples of overhead items and their cost drivers.

cost drivers The tasks in activity-based costing that are considered to be the 'users' of overhead.

Services are typically characterized by a high fixed/variable cost ratio. The United Parcel Service (UPS) is a prime example. On the retail side of the business, the company maintains 3,400 UPS stores; 1,100 mail boxes etc.; 1,000 UPS customer centres; 17,000 authorized outlets; and 45,000 UPS drop boxes. Packages and documents collected at these retail sites are then funnelled to 1,748 operating facilities where they are distributed to a delivery fleet consisting of 88,000 package cars, vans, tractors and motorcycles; 270 UPS jet aircraft; and 304 chartered aircraft. As a result of this infrastructure, the company handles more than 3 billion packages and 5.5 per cent of the United States' GDP annually (UPS, 2004).

In comparison to UPS' massive fixed costs, the variable costs associated with handling one more package are practically nil. The challenges faced by businesses that have a high fixed/variable cost ratio are numerous. First, what prices should be charged to individual customers? How should the firm sell

fixed costs Costs that are planned and accrued during the operating period regardless of the level of production and sales.

variable costs Costs that are directly associated with increases in production and sales.

Table 8.3	Activity pools	Cost driver
	General administration	Direct labour £
Activity-based costing	Project costing	No. of timesheet entries
	Accounts payable/receiving	No. of vendor invoices
Source Adapted from Beth M. Chapman and John Talbott, 'Activity-Based Costing in a Service Organization', *CMA Magazine* (December 1990/ January 1991), 15–18.	Accounts receivable	No. of client invoices
	Payroll/mail sorting and delivery	No. of employees
	Recruiting personnel	No. of new hires
	Employee insurance processing	Insurance claims processed
	Proposals/RFPs	No. of proposals
	Client sales meeting/sales aids	Sales £
	Shipping	No. of project numbers
	Ordering	No. of purchase orders
	Copying	No. of copies
	Blueprinting	No. of blueprints

Cost driver	Fixed overhead cost	Total base	Cost per driver
Direct labour £	73	1,016,687	0.07
No. of time entries	10	13,300	0.78
No. of vendor invoices	29	2,270	12.60
No. of client invoices	10	1,128	9.22
No. of employees	18	67	271.64
No. of new hires	8	19	410.53
Insurance claims filed	3	670	3.88
No. of proposals	29	510	56.08
Sales £	41	3,795,264	0.01
No. of project numbers	5	253	20.55
No. of purchase orders	10	325	32.00
No. of copies	16	373,750	0.04
No. of blueprint m^2	8	86,200	0.09
Total overhead cost	260	-	-

off unused capacity? For example, should an airline sell twenty unsold seats at a reduced rate to customers who are willing to accept the risk of not reserving a seat on the plane prior to the day of departure? Does selling unused capacity at discounted rates alienate full-fare paying customers? How can companies offer reduced prices to sell off unused capacity without full-fare paying customers shifting their buying patterns?

Service economies of scale tend to be limited. Due to inseparability and perishability, the consumption of services is not separated by time and space. Inventory cannot be used to buffer demand, and the physical presence of customers and providers is frequently necessary for a transaction to take place. Consequently, service providers often produce services on demand rather than in advance. Therefore, it is difficult for service providers to achieve the cost advantages traditionally associated with economies of scale. Some services are also more likely than goods to be customized to each customer's specifications and/or needs. Customization limits the amount of work that can be done in advance of a customer's request for service.

Customer considerations

Customer considerations take into account the price the customer is willing to pay for the service. In comparison to goods, the price of the service tends to be one of the few search attributes available to consumers for alternative evaluation purposes. As a result, the price of the service is often used as a quality cue – the higher the price, the better the perceived quality of the service. Services that are priced too low may very well be perceived as inferior in quality and bypassed for more expensive alternatives. Finally, service customers tend to be less certain about reservation prices.

Price tends to be one of the few cues available to consumers during prepurchase. Due to the intangible nature of services, services are characterized by few search attributes. Search attributes are informational cues that can be determined prior to purchase. In contrast, the tangibility of goods dramatically increases the number of search attributes available for consumers to consider. For example, the style and fit of a suit can be determined prior to purchase. In contrast, the enjoyment of a dinner is not known until after the experience is complete.

Pricing research has noted that the informational value of price decreases as the number of other informational cues increase. Similarly, others have found consumer reliance on price to be U-shaped. Price is heavily used if few cues are present, loses value as more cues become present, and then increases in value if consumers are overwhelmed with information (Monroe, 1973).

Service consumers are more likely to use price as a cue to quality. Service providers must also consider the message the service price sends to customers. Much work has been devoted to understanding whether price can be an indicator of quality. Some studies that have been performed seem to imply that consumers can use price to infer the quality of the product they are considering. Conflicting studies seem to indicate that they cannot. For example, classic studies in the field have presented customers with identical products, such as pieces of carpet, priced at different levels. The respondents' judgement of quality seemed to indicate that quality followed price. However, very similar studies later found little relationship between price and perceived quality (Bateson, 1992).

Price plays a key informational role in service consumer decision processes. Decision theory suggests that consumers will use those cues that are most readily available in the alternative evaluation process to assess product quality. Due to the importance of its role, price should be a dominant cue for consumers attempting to evaluate service quality prior to purchase. Studies suggest that price is more likely to be used as a cue to quality under the following conditions:

- when price is the primary differential information available;
- when alternatives are heterogeneous; and
- when comparative price differences are relatively large.

Clearly, these conditions exist in many service purchase scenarios.

Service consumers tend to be less certain about reservation prices.
A consumer's reservation price is the maximum amount that the consumer is willing to pay for a product. Ultimately, a consumer's reservation price for a service determines whether a purchase or no purchase decision is made. If the reservation price exceeds the price charged for the service, the consumer is more inclined to purchase that particular service. However, if the reservation price is lower than the actual price charged, then the consumer is precluded from purchasing that particular service offering.

Research has noted the lack of service consumer certainty regarding reservation prices. Consumers' reservation prices are determined in part by their awareness of competitive prices in the market. For some services, the lack of pricing information available and the lack of purchasing frequency may lead to less certainty regarding the reservation price of the service under consideration (Guitinan, 1987).

reservation price The price a consumer considers to capture the value he or she places on the benefits.

Competitive considerations

Service pricing strategy is affected by two unique competitive considerations. First, comparing prices of service alternatives is often difficult, which may make competitive-based pricing less of an important consideration for services compared to goods. In addition, a unique competitor must be considered when pricing services – the self-service consumer. Consumers are often willing to provide self-service to save money and customise the end result among other perceived advantages.

Comparing prices of competitors is more difficult for service consumers. Actual price information for services tends to be more difficult for consumers to acquire than it is for goods. Further, when service price information is available to consumers, it also tends to be more difficult to make meaningful comparisons between services. For example, although base service prices can sometimes be determined in advance, competing services are not sold together in retail stores the way that many competing goods are in supermarkets, discount or department stores. Consumers have to either individually visit geographically separated service firms or contact them to compare prices. Comparative shopping has therefore required more time and effort. The internet has changed this, however, for many services with the growth in price comparison sites for everything from financial and insurance services to medical services and music lessons.

Self-service is a viable competitive alternative. One result of the inseparability of production and consumption for services is the possibility of the customer actively participating in the service delivery process, commonly referred to as self-service option. The availability of self-service options has an effect on customer perceptions of the service. Initially, self-service options invariably provided the service customer with some form of price reduction (self-service restaurants). Today, the literature suggests that service customers often are seeking other benefits besides lower prices when purchasing self-service options. These benefits might include greater convenience, more control, less human contact, faster service time, greater efficiency and greater independence. Self-service options must be considered in the formation of pricing strategy.

Profit considerations

Price bundling often increases the profit opportunities for service firms. Compared to goods, services are more amenable to price bundling; however, price bundling makes the determination of individual prices in the bundle of services more complicated. *Price bundling* involves pricing a group of services at a price that is below their cost if bought separately. In general, price bundles are perceived as a better value for the customer and typically generate additional revenues for the selling firm (see E-Services in Action).

Price bundling makes the determination of individual prices in the bundle of services more complicated. Bundling, the practice of marketing two or more goods and/or services for a single price, is a useful strategic pricing tool that can help services marketers achieve several different strategic objectives. However, it also complicates the alternative evaluation process for consumers. Consumers experience difficulty when attempting to calculate how much each component of the bundle is contributing to the total cost. For example, a consumer evaluating available alternatives for a trip to Jamaica might have a hard time comparing the costs associated with an all-inclusive hotel package bundled with airfare and transfers to a traditional pay-as-you-go holiday alternative.

Price bundling is more effective in a service context. A wide variety of services make use of price bundling as a strategic approach to pricing. Many service organizations bundle their own service offerings together, as with broadband, phone and TV packages offered by one service provider. Other service organizations choose to form strategic alliances with other firms and bundle services that each provides. For example, the travel industry bundles hotel charges, airline tickets and transfer services into a single price. Regardless of the form or type of bundling, this strategy essentially creates a new service that can be used to either attract new customers, cross-sell existing customers, or retain current customers. Bundling has proliferated in the service sector primarily because of high fixed/variable cost ratios, the degree of cost sharing and the high levels of

---

E-Services in action
Bundle and build broadband business

The number of worldwide consumer broadband connections will reach 364 million by 2010. At the end of 2005, 12 per cent of households worldwide had a broadband connection and by 2010 it is estimated that figure will nearly double to reach 21 per cent. The mature market segment of Asia/Pacific and Japan will continue to account for nearly 40 per cent of worldwide broadband connections. In this region, it is predicted that three-quarters of households will have broadband connections by 2010 compared with around half of North American and Western European households.

'The rapid rise in consumer broadband penetration in recent years has been largely driven by price cuts of more than ten per cent a year as well as increased service speeds', said Susan Richardson, principal research analyst at Gartner. 'In that time it has become one of the key revenue generators for operators, helping to counter declining revenue from services such as traditional voice and legacy data services. However, as penetration in some markets heads towards saturation point, telecom carriers are facing up to the fact that a continued focus on acquiring new customers will not be enough to make price cutting profitable in the future.'

Western Europe

Broadband has achieved mass-market penetration in Western Europe with France, Germany and the UK leading in terms of absolute numbers. Denmark, the Netherlands and Switzerland had the highest consumer broadband household penetration rates in 2005.

Household broadband penetration by country (per cent)

	2005	2007	2010
Denmark	45.8	57.8	68.1
France	33.2	44.6	53.4
Germany	23.1	38.3	49.9
Netherlands	45.6	59.0	67.4
Switzerland	42.4	51.4	59.5
United Kingdom	35.5	55.6	64.4
Total Western Europe	30.7	44.7	55.0

Source Gartner (2006).

Growth in Western Europe began to slow down towards the end of 2006 and although some way off saturation point, service providers will need to take steps to safeguard future revenues. 'Providers are going to have to work harder to both attract new customers and increase average revenue per user (ARPU)', said Ms Richardson. 'As competitive pressure from alternative operators increases, features such as greater speeds will no longer be a differentiation factor but a means to deliver

▶

the kinds of web-based applications, voice and video services which users will demand.'

Strategies adopted by providers to maximize future revenues will vary from country to country according to the relative maturity and sophistication of the market. In the Nordic countries for example, absolute penetration levels will be about 70 per cent, while many southern European countries will have potential penetration levels below 50 per cent and consequently lower saturation points.

Broadband service providers are advised to reduce their focus in consumer markets on price cuts and to develop additional services within their offerings that address new user needs. This includes additional download bandwidth and storage for online music, photo storage, wireless connectivity, firewall protection and security services. 'Without value-add, providers have to resort to price as a short-term differentiator, which leads to price reductions. With service differentiation, the competition is no less intense, but by giving the customer more value wrapped into the price they already pay providers can maintain their revenues.'

Ms Richardson highlighted the importance of building profitable bundled services by carefully modelling customer usage patterns. 'Given the tremendous growth in broadband penetration we have seen in Western Europe in recent years, a slowdown is inevitable', concluded Ms Richardson. 'However, by developing additional services and focusing on the kind of service innovation continuum we have seen in countries like France, providers can enjoy long and successful relationships with customers for years to come.'

Source: Adapted from C. Swedemyr (2008) www.gartner.com.

interdependent demand. For example, the demand for a hotel restaurant is directly related to the demand for hotel rooms.

Product considerations

Service pricing strategy recognizes three unique service product considerations. First, price is called by many different names in the service sector. As a result, price may be perceived differently in some sectors compared to others. Second, since service products are unable to be inventoried, service consumers should be less price sensitive and less prone to delay their purchases until a better price is offered some time in the future. Finally, the common practice of price lining used for tangible products makes less sense to service consumers.

Compared to the goods sector, there tend to be many different names for price in the service sector. One of the interesting aspects of pricing in a service context involves the many different names that are used to express price in different service industries. For example, in the financial services industry the term *price* is rarely if ever used. Instead, customers pay service charges, interest, fees and commissions. Similarly, travellers pay airfares or bus fares, apartment dwellers pay rent, hotel occupants are charged a room rate, and the list goes on and on.

Upon further examination, many of the terms used for price in the service sector incorporate the benefit(s) customers receive. For instance, customers pay fares for the benefit of transportation, rents and room rates for occupancy, and service charges for processing requests. Is price by any other name still a price, or does incorporating the benefit into the term used for price alter consumer perceptions and affect price sensitivities?

Consumers are less able to stockpile services by taking advantage of discount prices. Retail pricing researchers note that pricing policies and strategies can have a direct impact on inventory decisions and planning (Subrahmanyan and Shoemaker, 1996). Goods are often discounted to reduce over-abundant inventories. Consumers take advantage of the discounts and often engage in forward buying. Forward buying enables consumers to build their own inventories of goods and reduces the amount of defections to competitive brands. In contrast, services cannot be stored. Consequently, service consumers cannot stockpile service offerings. When consumers need or want a service, they must pay the prevailing price.

> **forward buying** When retailers purchase enough product on deal to carry over until the product is being sold on deal again.

Product-line pricing tends to be more complicated. Product-line pricing, the practice of pricing multiple versions of the same product or grouping similar products together, is widely used in goods marketing. For example, beginner, intermediate and expert level tennis rackets are generally priced at different price points to reflect the different levels of quality construction. Consumers of goods can more easily evaluate the differences among the multiple versions offered since tangibility provides search attributes. Search attributes assist consumers in making objective evaluations. In contrast, consider the difficulty of real estate consumers when faced with the choices offered by Century 21 Real Estate. The company offers home sellers three levels of service that are priced at increasing commission rates of 6, 7 and 8 per cent. Customers, particularly those who sell homes infrequently, lack the expertise to make an informed decision. The performance levels associated with the three levels of service offered cannot be assessed until after the contract with the real estate agent has been signed and the customer has committed to the commission rate.

> **product-line pricing** The practice of pricing multiple versions of the same product or grouping similar products together.

Traditionally, product-line pricing provides customers with choices and gives managers an opportunity to maximize total revenues. However, the product-line pricing of services more often than not generates customer confusion and alienation. Industries struggling with the price lining of their services include telecommunications (BT, Vodafone), insurance (e.g., multiple policy variations), and financial services (e.g., multiple types of current and savings accounts and mortgage options).

Legal considerations

When developing pricing strategy, marketers must consider not only what is profitable but also what is legal. In general, the opportunity to engage in and benefit from illegal pricing practices in the service sector is predominantly attributed to intangibility, inseparability and heterogeneity. As discussed in Chapter 5, intangibility decreases the consumer's ability to objectively evaluate purchases, while inseparability reflects the human element of the service encounter that can potentially expose the customer to coercive influence techniques.

The opportunity for illegal pricing practices to go undetected is greater for services than for goods. Is it legal for chemists to charge excessive prices for vaccinations during a flu epidemic, or for repair services to triple their hourly rate to repair homes in neighbourhoods damaged by severe weather? Although not illegal, it could be argued that these practices are unethical and though they may creat short-term profits they are likely to cause longer-term customer alienation. In contrast, identifying excessive service pricing practices is not as clear for 'everyday' types of purchase occasions.

Service consumers are more vulnerable to illegal pricing practices. The pricing implications of service consumer vulnerability are twofold. First, consumer vulnerability and perceived risk are directly related. Consumers feeling particularly vulnerable are willing to pay higher prices for a service if it lowers their perceived risk. Second, dubious service providers that abuse the customer's trust by taking advantage of vulnerable consumers through excessive prices may benefit in the short term, but once they are discovered, the long-term success of their firms is doubtful. To consumers, the issue is one of fairness and dual entitlement. Cost-driven price changes are perceived as fair because they allow sellers to maintain their profit entitlement. In contrast, demand-driven prices are often perceived as unfair. They allow the seller to increase their profit margins purely at the expense of the increasing consumer demand (Czinkota et al., 2000).

dual entitlement Cost-driven price increases are perceived as fair, whereas demand-driven price increases are viewed as unfair.

Emerging service pricing strategies

Traditional pricing strategies such as penetration pricing, competitive pricing and premium pricing offer little benefit to service customers or service providers. For example, competitive pricing has led to disappearing profit margins in industries such as car rental and health insurance and to customer confusion and mistrust in industries such as long-distance telephone service. At the core of the pricing problem is a lack of understanding of the special considerations in the pricing of intangibles and how consumers use and benefit from the services they are purchasing. Service marketers should create pricing strategies that offer a compromise between the overly complex and the too simplistic, both of which neglect the variations in consumer needs (Berry and Yadav, 1996).

To effectively price services, the service firm must first understand what its target market truly values (see E-Services in Action) and not rely on unsustainable price cutting as a means of competition. Three alternative pricing strategies that convey value to the customer include satisfaction-based, relationship, and efficiency pricing (see Table 8.4).

Satisfaction-based pricing

satisfaction-based pricing Pricing strategies that are designed to reduce the amount of perceived risk associated with a purchase.

The primary goal of satisfaction-based pricing is to reduce the amount of perceived risk associated with the service purchase and to appeal to target markets that value certainty. Satisfaction-based pricing can be achieved through offering guarantees, benefit-driven pricing and flat-rate pricing.

Service guarantees are becoming a popular way of attracting customers (Hart, Schlesinger, and Maher, 1992). The guarantee assures customers that if they are less than satisfied with their purchase, they can invoke the guarantee, and a partial or full refund will occur. Offering guarantees signals to customers that the firm is committed to delivering quality services and is confident in its ability to do so. In instances where competing services are priced similarly, the service guarantee offers a differential advantage.

Benefit-driven pricing focuses on the aspects of the service that customers actually use. The objective of this approach is to develop a direct association between the price of the service and the components of the service that customers value. For example, online computer services such as information databases typically use benefit-driven pricing strategies. This is evident by their practice of charging customers for the services they actually use rather than merely their time online.

The concept of flat-rate pricing is fairly straightforward. Its primary objective is to decrease consumer uncertainty about the final price of the service by agreeing to a fixed price before the service transaction occurs. With flat-rate pricing, the provider assumes the risk of price increases and overruns. Flat-rate pricing makes the most sense when:

- the price is competitive;
- the firm offering the flat rate has its costs under control and operates efficiently; and
- the opportunities to engage in a long-term relationship and to generate additional revenues with the customer are possible.

benefit-driven pricing A pricing strategy that charges customers for services actually used as opposed to overall 'membership' fees.

flat-rate pricing A pricing strategy in which the customer pays a fixed price and the provider assumes the risk of price increases and cost overruns.

Pricing strategy	Provides value by ...	Implemented as ...
Satisfaction-based pricing	Recognizing and reducing customers' perceptions of uncertainty, which the intangible nature of service magnifies.	Service guarantees Benefit-driven pricing Flat-rate pricing
Relationship pricing	Encouraging long-term relationships with the company that customers view as beneficial.	Long-term contracts Price bundling
Efficiency pricing	Sharing with customers the cost saving that the company has achieved by understanding, managing, and reducing the costs of providing the service.	Cost-leader pricing

Table 8.4

Satisfaction-based, relationship, and efficiency pricing strategies

Source Leonard L. Berry and Manjit S. Yadav, 'Capture and Communicate Value in the Pricing of Services', *Sloan Management Review* (Summer 1996), 41–51. © 1996 by Massachusetts Institute of Technology. All rights reserved. Distributed by Tribune Media Services.

Relationship pricing

relationship pricing
Pricing strategies that encourage the customer to expand his/her dealings with the service provider.

The primary objective of relationship pricing is to enhance the firm's relationship with its targeted consumers. For example, in the banking industry, relationship pricing strategies can be utilized to further nurture the relationship between the bank and its existing current account customers by offering special savings accounts, deals on safe-deposit boxes and special rates on certificates of deposit. Two types of relationship pricing techniques include long-term contracts and price bundling.

long-term contracts
Offering prospective customers price and non-price incentives for dealing with the same provider over a number of years.

Long-term contracts offer prospective customers price and non-price incentives for dealing with the same provider over a number of years. UPS recently entered into long-term shipping contracts with Land's End and Ford Motor Company. Because of its customers' long-term commitments, UPS has been able to transform its business with these clients from discrete to continuous transactions. UPS now has operations and personnel dedicated solely to providing services to these specific customers. Since transactions are now continuous, economies of scale have developed, and cost savings that can be passed to the customer plus opportunities for improving the firm's profit performance have emerged.

price bundling The practice of marketing two or more products and/or services in a single package at a single price.

Since most service organizations provide more than one service, the practice of bundling services has become more common. Price bundling, broadly defined, is the practice of marketing two or more products and/or services in a single package at a single price. Common examples include hotels putting together weekend packages that include lodging, meals and sometimes entertainment at an inclusive rate. Airlines routinely price vacation packages that include air travel, car rental and hotel accommodations.

Price bundling flows logically from the issues discussed earlier in the chapter. Individual services have low marginal costs and high shared costs. Moreover, the services offered by most businesses are generally interdependent in terms of demand. For example, the demand for the hotel's food service is directly related to the demand for hotel rooms.

mixed bundling Price-bundling technique that allows consumers to either buy Service A and Service B together or purchase one service separately.

Generally, services are concerned with mixed bundling, which enables consumers to buy either Service A and Service B together or purchase one service separately. The simplest argument for bundling is based on the idea of consumer surplus. Bundling makes it possible to shift the consumer surplus from one service to another service that otherwise would have a negative surplus (i.e., would not be purchased). Thus, the combined value of the two services is less than the combined price, even though separately only one service would be purchased.

Three reasons have been suggested for why the sum of the parts would have less value than the whole. First, information theory would argue that the consumer finds value in easy access to information. Consumers of one financial service institution have a lower information cost when buying another service from the same institution than when buying that service from a different institution. A second case argues that the bundling of Service B with Service A can enhance a consumer's satisfaction with Service A, for example, a ski resort that offers a ski-rental-and-lessons package. The reservation price for the lessons is likely to be the same whether or not the skis are rented because the value of the lessons depends on the skills and needs of the skier. However, the reservation price of the ski rental will be enhanced, at least for novices, by lessons. The final argument is that the addition of Service B to Service A can enhance the total image of the firm. A financial-planning service offering both investment advice and tax advice enhances its credibility in both services.

Efficiency pricing

The primary goal of efficiency pricing is to appeal to economically minded consumers who are looking for the best price. 'Efficiency pricers almost always are industry heretics, shunning traditional operating practices in search of sustainable cost advantages' (Berry and Yadav, 1996). Ryanair and its relentless efforts to reduce costs is one such example. Ryanair reduces costs by flying shorter, more direct routes to less congested, less expensive airports. No meals are served, passengers are seated on a first-come, first-served basis, encouraged to bring hand baggage only and to check in online.

Efficiency pricing is focused on delivering the best and most cost-effective service available for the price. Operations are streamlined, and innovations that enable further cost reduction become part of the operation's culture. The leaner the cost structure, the more difficult it is for new competitors to imitate Southwest's success. Understanding and managing costs are the fundamental building blocks of efficiency pricing.

efficiency pricing
Pricing strategies that appeal to economically minded consumers by delivering the best and most cost-effective service for the price.

Some final thoughts on pricing services

Pricing services is a difficult task. Consumers are purchasing an experience and often feel uneasy about or do not understand what they are paying for. Similarly, service providers do not have a cost-of-goods-sold figure upon which to base their prices. Confused and bewildered, many providers simply look to what the competition is charging, regardless of their own cost structures and competitive advantage. In contrast, successful service providers tend to abide by the following pricing guidelines (Berry and Yadav, 1996):

- The price should be easy for customers to understand.
- The price should represent value to the customer.
- The price should encourage customer retention and facilitate the customer's relationship with the providing firm.
- The price should reinforce customer trust.
- The price should reduce customer uncertainty.

A further complication which occurs more often in services is the cost of 'free' services. These range from attending a festival in the local park to choosing a state school to using the health authority's 'quit smoking' drop-in sessions.

Although the customers do not pay directly for these services, they incur costs and consequently

SOURCE © ISTOCK.COM

assess value. In offering and evaluating these types of service the provider needs to consider how the customer/user perceives the costs involved and how these then affect their evaluation of service value and quality.

Summary

Successful service pricing depends on recognizing the value that a customer places on a service and pricing that service accordingly. Customer perceptions of value represent a trade-off between the perceived benefits obtained from purchasing the product and the perceived sacrifice in terms of cost to be paid. Total customer costs extend beyond monetary costs and include time, energy and psychological costs. Similarly, total customer value extends beyond product value and includes service, personnel and image value.

When developing service pricing strategies, managers should take into account a number of considerations including demand, cost, customer, competitive, profit, product and legal considerations. Table 8.1 provides a summary of each of these considerations.

Overall, traditional pricing strategies and cost accounting approaches offer little benefit to either service consumers or service providers. Three alternative pricing strategies that convey value to the customer include satisfaction-based, relationship and efficiency pricing. The primary goal of satisfaction-based pricing is to reduce the perceived risk associated with the purchase of services and to appeal to target markets that value certainty. Satisfaction-based pricing strategies include offering guarantees, benefit-driven pricing and flat-rate pricing. The goal of relationship pricing is to enhance the firm's relationship with its targeted consumers. Relationship pricing techniques include offering long-term contracts and price bundling. In comparison, efficiency pricing appeals to economically minded consumers and focuses on delivering the best and most cost-effective service for the price. Understanding and managing costs are the fundamental building blocks of efficiency pricing.

Discussion questions

1 Discuss the factors that comprise consumer perceptions of value. How do these differ for a paid-for service compared to a free service?

2 Consider the role of price as an indicator of quality to consumers. Use examples to illustrate your points.

3 Evaluate the effectiveness of charging lower prices for advance bookings or lower pricing for last-minute bookers in the airline industry. Refer to the case study regarding easyJet to illustrate your answer.

Case link

See Case 7: Yield management in Budget airlines: The case of easyJet.

4 Discuss the differences between traditional methods of allocating overhead expenses and activity-based costing.

5 Using examples, explain why self-service does not have to be charged at a lower price.

6 Compare the advantages and disadvantages of discriminatory pricing in a service sector of your choice.

7 Discuss and illustrate the basic concepts behind satisfaction-based, relationship, and efficiency pricing.

References and further reading

Alden, John, 'What in the world drives UPS?', *International Business* (1998), 11 (2): 6–7.

Backman, J. (1953) *Price Practices and Price Policies*, New York: Ronald Press, 1953.

Bateson, J. E. G. (1992) *Managing Services Marketing*, 2nd ed., Fort Worth, TX: Dryden Press, pp. 357–365.

Berry, L. L. and Yadav, M. S. (1996) 'Capture and communicate value in the pricing of services', *Sloan Management Review* (Summer): 41–51.

Chaffman, B. M. and Talbott, J. (1991) 'Activity-based costing in a service organization', *CMA Magazine* (December 1990/January 1991): 15–18.

Chief Executive (1981) 'Finding the right price is no easy game to play', *Chief Executive* (September): 16–18.

Coulson-Thomas, C. (2007) *Pricing for Profit . . . the Critical Success Factors*, Peterborough: Policy Publications.

Czinkota et al. (2000) *Marketing: Best Practices*, Fort Worth, TX: Dryden Press.

Dean, J. (1947) 'Research approach to pricing', in *Planning the Price Structure*, Marketing Series No. 67, American Marketing Association.

Doctors, R., Reopel, M., Sun, J. and Tanny, S. (2004) 'Capturing the unique value of services: Why pricing of services is different', *Journal of Business Strategy* 25 (2): 23–28.

Guiltinan, J. P. (1987) 'The price bundling of services: A normative framework', *Journal of Marketing* 51 (2): 74–85.

Hart, C. W. L., Schlesinger, L.A. and Maher, D. (1992) 'Guarantees come to professional service firms', *Sloan Management Review* (Spring): 19–29.

Hoffman, D. K. and Turley, L. W. (1999) 'Toward an understanding of consumer price sensitivity for professional services', in *Developments in Marketing Science*, Charles H. Noble, ed., Miami, FL: Academy of Marketing Science, pp. 169–173.

Kelley, Jim, 'From lip service to real service: Reversing America's downward service spiral', *Vital Speeches of the Day* (1998), 64 (10): 301–304.

Kotler, P. (1994) *Marketing Management*, 8th ed., Englewood Cliffs, NJ: Prentice Hall.

Lewison, D. (1997)*Retailing*, 6th ed., Upper Saddle River: Prentice Hall.

Marshall, A. (1979) *More Profitable Pricing*, London: McGraw-Hill.

Monroe, K. B. (1973) 'Buyers' subjective perceptions of price', *Journal of Marketing Research* 10 (February): 70–80.

Nagle, T. T. and Holden, R. K. (1995) *The Strategy and Tactics of Pricing*, Englewood Cliffs, NJ: Prentice Hall.

Nagle, T. T. and Holden, R. K. (2002) *The Strategy and Tactics of Pricing*, 3rd ed., Upper Saddle River: Prentice Hall.

Shugan, S. M. and Xie, J. (2000) 'Advance pricing of services and other implications of separating purchase and consumption', *Journal of Service Research* 2 (3) (February): 227–239.

Subrahmanyan, S. and Shoemaker, R. (1996) 'Developing optimal pricing and inventory policies for retailers who face uncertain demand', *Journal of Retailing* 72 (1): 7–30.

Tahar, A. and El Basha, H. (2006) 'Heterogeneity of consumer demand: opportunities for pricing of services', *Journal of Product & Brand Management* 15 (5): 331–340.

UPS (2004) www.ups.com, accessed 30 January 2005, 'Only Santa delivers more in one day than UPS', Press Release (December 13, 2004); http://pressroom.ups.com/ups.com/us/press_releases/, accessed 30 January 2005

Walker A. W. (1967) 'How to price industrial products', *Harvard Business Review* 45: 38–45.

Chapter 9

Developing the service communications mix

Customer collaboration means putting the customer at the centre of the communications; making sure you have their permission before you communicate with them; ensuring all your media are fully integrated and focused; and that there is genuine creativity. Only then will customers stop asking: You talkin' to me?

(Chartered Institute of Marketing, 2004: 14)

Chapter objectives

The purpose of this chapter is to provide an overview of communications mix strategies as they apply to the marketing of services.
    After reading this chapter, you should be able to:

- Discuss factors that influence the development of the organization's communications mix.

- Describe the goals of the communications mix during prepurchase, consumption, and postpurchase stages.

- Appreciate the special problems associated with developing the service communications mix.

- Understand the importance of integrating marketing communications.

- Explain the special problems encountered by professional service providers.

Services in context
The rise and fall of advertising icons

Given the intangible nature of services, service products are often abstract in the minds of potential customers. Consequently, one of the principal guidelines for communicating with customers about a service is to make it more concrete. Creating a character or icon to represent the brand or product is one way to achieve this. When long lived, these icons become part of modern culture, are used intertextually within other aspects of life and are held dear by many consumers (Kenyon, 2006). Think of the nostalgia and affection associated with icons such as Nestle's 'Milky Bar Kid', 'Kellogs' 'Tony the Tiger' and the ubiquitous 'Ronald McDonald' not to mention the Dulux Dog and the, now global, Andrex puppy. Despite their success, however, changes in consumer culture, media fragmentation and the need to constantly innovate in communications are leading to the demise of the enduring icon. Ronald McDonald is in semi-retirement, and even the Marlboro cowboy is no more. It's becoming increasingly difficult to survive the tests of time and geography.

The agencies charged with developing such ideas suggest that the main change is short-termism in client, agency and consumer attention spans. Ideas with universal resonance are very difficult to find. 'Great domestic campaigns are hard enough, but obviously the more people you are trying to please, the harder it is to come up with something unifying', observes John Lowery, chief European planning officer for advertising network Grey.

He points out that the majority of global advertising icons have some childish or infantile element to them – it's an immensely powerful territory with almost universal appeal but limited application.

But even outstanding campaigns can take years to bed in. 'It's hard to predict what is going to work well because advertising really takes place in the minds of the consumers, who are so cynical and informed these days that they tend to do what they want with communication. When clients are in their jobs for just a couple of years and the whole organization is driven by quarterly reporting, it can be much harder to take a longer-term view', observes Lowery.

Advertising fads also play a part. 'These devices tend to be seen by the advertising industry and consumers, to some extent, as clunky 1950s advertising. They do have a real drawback, which is that they can make it harder to introduce detailed messages because the icon drowns out more subtle communication', says David Bain, planning director of FCB Banks Hoggins O'Shea.

And when a brand changes agency, as they tend to do with increasing frequency, the last thing the new agency wants is to run the same old ads. Bain states that 'they have been replaced by either a distinctive tone of voice as in VW or Nike advertising, or by the almost ubiquitous use of celebrities, which, of course, allow you to establish your values much more quickly.'

He says that contemporary brand icons need to be given a post-modern twist. The recent campaigns for Carphone Warehouse featuring an anthropomorphic mobile called Mobly, demonstrate this. While Mobly observes many of the conventions of the classic 1950s advertising icon, to play it straight would switch off today's consumers so the convention is subverted in the ads by treating Mobly with callous disregard.

A more traditional and relatively new contender is the Churchill Insurance dog, a lugubrious bulldog originally voiced by comedian Vic Reeves with the simple catchphrase 'Oh, yes' in answer to customer queries. The bulldog was used for the first time in advertising in 1994 and in less than two years, the Nodding Dog™ brand was born. In 2005, despite a refresh of the brand, the bulldog remains and nodding Churchill bulldogs can be seen in the rear window of many a car.

Other successes in the insurance industry are the Aflac duck, a well loved icon in the US and Japan who, according to Aflac Inc., 'has done more for the life and disability insurer's brand recognition in less than five years than most advertising symbols have done for their brand over decades'. The now demised 'telephone on wheels' used by Direct Line insurance for several years and still part of the brand was also a success. However, the search for ways to represent tangibility in communicating services does now appear to have moved away from the often culturally constrained and quickly outdated icon. Indeed the intangible aspects are often the focus of advertisements today with an increasing use of subtle, surreal and at times obtuse advertisements. Ads now need to entertain the cynical consumer often by mimicking or parodying art, comedy or soap opera.

SOURCE IMAGE COURTESY OF THE ADVERTISING ARCHIVES

Sources: A. Benady (2004) 'Soft, strong and very long-lived', published 26 Apr. 2004, *Financial Times*, www.ft.com.
Churchill Insurance (2008), www.churchill.com. http://www.aflac.com, accessed 26 April 2005.
A. J. Kenyon (2006) 'Exploring intertextuality: young people reading alcohol advertising', *Euro Med Journal of Business* 3 (Autumn): 50–63.

Introduction

Marketing communications represent all of the elements in a service brand's marketing mix that facilitate establishing shared meanings with the brand's stakeholders (Masterman and Wood, 2006). Communications strategy is, therefore, both a key component of and a means of integrating the service marketing mix. In general, the primary role of a service organization's communications strategy is to inform, persuade, or remind consumers about the service being offered. Consumers cannot be expected to use a service they do not know about; therefore, a primary objective of communications strategy is to create consumer awareness and to position the service offering in the consumer's evoked set of alternatives. Moreover, even when awareness of the service product exists, consumers may need additional encouragement to try it and information about how to obtain and use the service. Finally, people forget. Just because they have been told something once does not mean that they will necessarily remember it over the course of time (Bateson, 1992).

Communicating the service offering may be accomplished through non-personal sources, such as television advertising or printed information in magazines and newspapers, or through personal sources on a face-to-face

nonpersonal sources
Sources such as mass advertising that consumers use to gather information about a service.

personal sources
Sources such as friends, family and other opinion leaders that consumers use to gather information about a service.

basis through all the individuals who come into contact with the consumer in the prepurchase, consumption and postpurchase stages. In addition, the communications mix can be designed to influence customer expectations and perceptions of the service.

Communications objectives and strategies vary, depending upon the nature of the target audience. Separate communications strategies are necessary for current users of a service in order to influence or change their patterns of service use, and for nonusers in order to attract them to the service. However, in order to make the most of the wide variety of methods and media available, consistency of message is required. This allows for a synergy to develop through maximizing the number of contacts (or touch points) with each customer. This use of a consistent message across a variety of complementary methods and media is at the heart of 'integrated marketing communications' (Hartley and Pickton, 1999).

integrated marketing communications (IMC) Combining a variety of complementary communications methods and media to deliver a consistent message.

Developing a communications strategy: The basics

The development of a sound communications strategy is based on the fundamentals of marketing strategy – identifying a target market, selecting a positioning strategy and tailoring a communications mix to the targeted audience that reinforces the desired positioning strategy. The threefold objectives of communications strategy – *inform*, *persuade*, and *remind* – change in priority over the course of the product's life cycle and whether the company is targeting current users or nonusers. Communications mix elements will also change under the same considerations.

Selecting target markets

Developing a communications strategy follows a common pattern whether the organization is producing goods or services. The service organization must first analyse the needs of consumers and then categorize consumers with similar needs into market segments. Each market segment should then be considered based on profit and growth potential and the segment's compatibility with organizational resources and objectives. Segments that become the focus of the organization's marketing efforts become target markets.

target markets The segments of potential customers that become the focus of an organization's marketing efforts.

Developing the organization's positioning strategy

Once the target market is selected, successful service organizations establish a positioning strategy, which differentiates them from competitors in consumers' eyes. Effective positioning is particularly critical for service organizations where intangibility clouds the consumer's ability to differentiate one service provider's offering from the next. For example, competing airlines that fly the same routes may stress operational elements such as the percentage of 'on-time' arrivals, while others stress service elements such as the friendliness and helpfulness of the flight crew and the quality of the food served.

positioning strategy The plan for differentiating the organization from its competitors in consumers' eyes.

Ultimately, positioning involves a strategic manipulation of the organization's marketing mix variables: *product*, *price*, *promotion*, *place*, *physical evidence*, *people* and *processes*. Each of these marketing mix variables is controllable. When effectively combined, the marketing mix can offset the effects of the uncontrollable factors that exist in every organization's operating environment such as technological advances, consumer needs, new and existing competitors, governmental regulations, economic conditions and the effects of seasonality that are constantly changing the environment in which the organization operates. Organizations that fail to alter their positioning strategy to reflect environmental changes in order to differentiate themselves from competitors often falter in the long run (see Table 9.1) (Kotler, 1997).

Developing the communications budget and mix

The organization's promotion, or communications mix, communicates the organization's positioning strategy to its relevant markets, including consumers, employees, stockholders and suppliers. The term communications mix describes the array of communications tools available to marketers. Just as marketers need to combine the elements of the marketing mix (including communications) to produce a marketing programme, they must also convey the message by selecting the most appropriate communication vehicles from the growing number available (see E-Services in Action).

The elements of the communications mix have traditionally been categorized under four main headings: personal selling, media advertising,

communications mix The array of communications tools available to marketers.

personal selling The two-way element of the communications mix in which the service provider influences a consumer via direct interaction.

media advertising A one-way communications tool that utilizes such media as television and radio to reach a broadly defined audience.

Table 9.1	Product differentiation	Personnel differentiation
Differentiation approaches for effective positioning	Features	Competence
	Performance	Courtesy
	Conformance	Credibility
Source Adapted from Philip Kotler, *Marketing Management*, 9th ed. (Englewood Cliffs, NJ: Prentice-Hall, 1997), p. 283.	Durability	Reliability
	Reliability	Responsiveness
	Repairability	Communication style
	Design (integrates the above)	
	Image differentiation	**Service differentiation**
	Symbols	Delivery (speed, accuracy)
	Written, audio/visual media	Installation
	Atmosphere	Customer training
	Events	Consulting service
		Repair
		Miscellaneous service

publicity and public relations, and sales promotion. Personal selling is clearly a two-way form of communication. The remainder have been seen as one-way communications, going only from the marketer to the customer. However, with the evolution of new media such as the internet, e-mail and direct response TV a wide variety of methods now exist with the propensity for two-way communication. Using more than one communications tool or using any one tool repeatedly increases the chances that existing and potential customers will be exposed to the organization's message, associate it with the organization, and remember it. By reinforcing its message, the organization can ensure that existing customers as well as potential ones become more aware of 'who' the organization is and what it has to offer. The organization's communications mix often lays the foundation for subsequent contact with potential consumers, making discussions with consumers easier for the provider and more comfortable for the consumers.

It is important at this stage of developing the organization's communications mix to determine the communications budget. Budget-setting techniques typically covered in most introductory marketing classes include the percentage-of-sales technique, the incremental technique, the all-you-can-

publicity and public relations A one-way communications tool between an organization and its customers, vendors, news media, employees, stockholders, the government and the general public.

sales promotion A one-way communications tool that utilizes promotional or informational activities at the point of sale.

E-services in action
Social media – Ignore at your peril

Social media can take many different forms, including text, images, audio and video. Teens are creating and sharing online content at a startling rate. What is truly astonishing is the creative effort ploughed into its more popular forms: blogs, podcasts and vlogs (video blogs). Every 24 hours, visitors to the popular video search engine YouTube (www.youtube.com) upload over 65,000 new videos, and users view 100 million video clips per day according to a July 2006 survey.

Today, almost anyone can become a content producer, content sharer or content commentator with a ready audience of their friends and their friends' friends. It is easy to understand the rapid spread of information across this heavily interconnected actively sharing universe.

The market is constantly evolving and is characterized by the frequent emergence of overnight sensations – from Bebo to Second Life. Furthermore, the market is defined in different ways by different people, depending on their personal web usage and their interpretation of the term 'personal space'. As such, the market may be considered to include blogs, forums, chat rooms, photo-sharing sites such as Flickr, dating services, video-upload sites such as YouTube, or 'contact' sites such as Friends Reunited, as well as the dedicated 'spaces' providers such as MySpace, Orkut, Windows Live Spaces, Bebo, Hi5, Faceparty, Facebook and Friendster and Badoo.

Users often apply their own structure and parameters when considering the shape of the spaces market. For example, those interested in music may place MySpace at the centre of their spaces universe, while Facebook is now the place they connect with their friends. Windows Live Spaces, meanwhile, is increasingly seen as a leader in digital memories (often communication centred around personal photos) and keeping in touch with closer networks.

For others, the market is defined by the market leader. Orkut dominates personal spaces usage in Brazil to the extent that it represents the benchmark against which all other providers are judged. MySpace dominated usage and collective consciousness a year ago in other markets such as the UK, US and Canada, but the rise of Facebook has now overtaken it. This illustrates how unsettled this market remains, along with the power wielded by users themselves in shaping each brand's success – if your friends move the conversation onto another network, you will move with them.

The challenge for marketers

The move towards social networking creates unprecedented marketing opportunities for advertisers to reach both consumers and their networks (a recent Jupiter survey suggested that one-third of existing online advertisers will launch social networking profiles for their brands in the next 12 months). However, social networks are distinctive in that the users create and spread the content-their voice can be heard directly and immediately – and so advertisers are treading with caution into this space. Some of the main hesitations from advertisers are as follows:

Relevance – is our brand relevant in this environment?

Control – will our brand message be manipulated?

Context – we can't manage the context.

Intrusion – will users perceive branded messages as intrusive?

There is an awareness that a community has power and can quickly generate support for a brand but also, more frighteningly, against one. So because individuals create the content, own the spaces, are connected to one another, and share ideas and content on a massive scale, many of the traditional marketing rules no longer apply.

Currently, advertisers have two basic ways to use social networking sites as ad vehicles. One is through traditional internet marketing methods, such as banner ads, skyscrapers and video rolls. The other way is to use the sites to create profiles for brands the same way their mostly youthful users create profiles

about themselves. The goal, marketers say, is to create a 'brand experience' that will attract users.

Savvy advertisers know that young people use social networking sites to establish their identities and to communicate with friends about their interests and social lives. What the marketers are hoping is that people who use the sites for these purposes will incorporate an advertiser's brand messaging into their communications with each other. For example, a movie studio might place a trailer for a new film on a networking site, where technically savvy users can grab a snippet and send it to a friend, thereby creating an implicit word-of-mouth endorsement for the movie, says Dawn Winchester, executive vice president of client services for the New York-based ad agency R/GA.

Advertisers are increasingly targeting consumers on social networking sites such as MySpace.

The same kind of scenario can be created for other brands that users like and are willing to share information about with their friends.

What does this mean for marketing professionals? Simply stated, it's where your audience hangs out if you are trying to reach savvy, relationship-rich young people. Check out the social media space and know where you're headed so you can realize its potential.

Sources: C. Vogt and S. Knapman 'The anatomy of social networks', *Market Leader*, Spring 2008, Issue 40, available from www.warc.com.
J. Wolfe 'Space Race', *The Advertiser*, August 2006, www.ana.net.
A. Watlington 'An Introduction to Social Media – Where the Teens Are', *Web Marketing Today*, 11 Jan. 2007, 14: 28.

afford approach, competitive parity and the objective-and-task method (Boone and Kurtz, 1993). After the budget has been established, the target audience or audiences, objectives and budgets are divided among the different areas of the communications mix. Each area does not have to be assigned the same task or audience as long as they collectively meet the overall objectives of the organization's communications strategy. Once they do, information delivery can be planned and executed and the results monitored.

Defining communications objectives

The objectives of an organization's communications mix often relate directly to the service offering's stage within the product life cycle (PLC) (see Table 9.2). In

Product life cycle stage	Communication content	Communication objectives
Introduction	Informational	Introduce the service offering Create brand awareness Prepare the way for personal selling efforts Encourage trial
Growth and maturity	Informational and persuasive	Create a positive attitude relative to competitive offerings Provoke an immediate buying action Enhance the firm's image
Maturity and decline	Persuasive and reminder	Encourage repeat purchases Provide ongoing contact Express gratitude to existing customer base Confirm past purchase decisions

Table 9.2

Communication content and objectives

general, the major communications objectives within the introduction and growth stages of the PLC are to inform the customer. Informational communications introduce the service offering and create brand awareness for the organization (see B2B Services in Action). Informational communications also encourage trials and often prepare the way for personal selling efforts to be conducted later.

As professional and public service providers are now beginning to promote their services, informational communications objectives tend to be the first step. Informational communications tend to be less obtrusive than other forms of communication, and in many ways, the information being conveyed often provides a public service to consumers who otherwise might not have access to or knowledge of the range of services available. Legal and educational services that advertise are typical examples. Although many of us poke fun at many of the ads that solicitors place on TV and radio, they do serve their purpose. Many of the clients who contact these services are lower-income, lower-educated clients who, by their own admission, have stated that if it were not for the advertisements, they would not know where to turn (based on a customer satisfaction study conducted by K. Douglas Hoffman for Rainmaker Marketing's North Carolina Lawyer Referral Service). Information-based communications are also ruling the web, with the majority of service organizations, no matter how small, now having websites and exponential growth in other online information sources such as product comparison sites.

Communications objectives during the growth and maturity stages of the PLC tend to lean towards informational and persuasive content. Objectives during this stage include creating a positive attitude towards the service offering relative to competitive alternatives, attempting to provoke an immediate purchase action and enhancing the organization's image. Professional service associations often discourage the use of persuasive advertising among their members as it often pits one professional member against another. Many in professional associations believe that members engaged in persuasive communications ultimately cheapen the image of the entire industry. As a result, promotional messages that are primarily information-based are viewed as a more acceptable and tasteful method of promotion.

Finally, communications objectives during the maturity and decline stages of the PLC tend to utilize persuasive and reminder communications. The communications objectives during this phase of the PLC are to influence existing customers to purchase again, to provide ongoing contact with the existing client base in order to remind clients that the organization still values their relationship, and to confirm clients' past purchase decisions, thereby minimizing levels of felt cognitive dissonance. As with informational communications, reminder communications tend to be less obtrusive and more acceptable to professional and public sector organizations than persuasive communications.

Dividing the communications objectives and target audiences

Once the overall objectives and target audiences for the entire communications mix have been set, it is necessary to divide the tasks among advertising, selling, publicity and public relations, and sales promotions. This is a process of matching the tasks to the capabilities of the different communications channels.

Targeting nonusers. If the objective is to reach nonusers of the service, then the choice of communications channel is reduced to media advertising, selling performed by a sales force rather than a service provider, and publicity and public relations (see B2B Services in Action).

B2B services in action
An XL Corporate Market!

XL Capital is one of the leading Corporate Insurers in Europe and has a market value of $10 billion, but nobody, apart from their clients, knew them. The clean and solid balance sheet of XL Capital put them into a preferred position as the market changed after 9/11 and capacity became limited. In this environment, XL positioned itself based on its fundamental financial strength and started to communicate through print and TV focusing on corporate customers and prospects. After one year, brand awareness and reputation increased dramatically and XL was recommended by brokers considerably more often than before.

Campaign objectives

- Increase brand awareness, build reputation and thereby increase the likelihood of making it onto potential customers' shortlists.
- Reach 10% spontaneous brand awareness and 50% aided brand awareness in Europe by the end of 2003.
- Increase brand reputation to 30%, achieving a 3% increase for the two main indicators 'secure/solid' and 'high reputation' compared to 2002.

Target audience

- CEOs and CFOs of large multinational companies in Europe.
- Risk managers of large multinational companies in Europe.
- Insurance brokers.

The target audience is predominately male, 35+ years old, with a high level of education and a high income. They are frequent travellers.

Creative strategy

XL Capital is one of the few insurance companies that focuses exclusively on corporate insurance and its financial background is excellent. For CEOs and CFOs, risk managers and brokers, security/solidity has become the most important criteria for selecting a corporate insurance provider.

XL Capital positioned itself as 'The B2B financial specialist with fundamental financial strength'. A tagline, 'fundamental strength – capital and people', became the foundation of every communication activity.

The XL logo was revised; it had to become the symbol of a strong financial service company. For that reason the colour was changed from black/gold-orange to platinum and the XL letters were spaced out to increase legibility.

In the print campaign the Fundamental Strength message was expressed by transforming the new logo into a 3-D symbol of such strength. This 3-D logo was also placed at XL Capital's client branches around the world as an icon of protection and security.

The TV commercial focused more on the people element of the Fundamental Strength message and demonstrated how XL employees are different from their industry peers. The new logo was used as a symbol of strength at the end of the commercial.

▶

Media strategy

In order to increase brand awareness the focus of the media strategy was to build reach rather than gain high contacts. The objective was to get 80 per cent to 90 per cent reach within active periods. A total of three active waves were executed, all timed before the renewal phase of insurance contracts. Having studied the information pattern of the target group and their receptiveness to advertising, ads were placed in selective media reaching the target audience during business time.

A mix of media was used as this provides more reach than a single media-strategy. 30 per cent of the budget was invested in Pan-European media and 70 per cent in individual countries. To reach the CEOs and CFOs, business press and business TV was used combined with strategic airport billboards (Frankfurt, Paris). In addition, risk managers and brokers were targeted through trade press.

Evidence of results

Spontaneous brand awareness increased by 11 per cent, from 1 per cent to 12 per cent compared to the previous year.

Aided brand awareness also increased substantially compared to the previous year, XL Ins experiencing a 35 per cent increase and XL Re seeing a 50 per cent increase.

The percentage of potential clients stating lack of knowledge about XL as the reason for not doing business with the company decreased by 7 per cent, from 43 per cent to 36 per cent.

The percentage of potential clients stating lack of recommendation by a broker as the reason for not doing business with the company also decreased by 7 per cent.

XL considerably improved its reputation, achieving substantially higher scores with regards to the indicators 'secure/solid' and 'high reputation'.

Sources: Adapted from: European Association of Communications Agencies (2004)' Euro Effies Finalist: Fundamental Strength', available from www.warc.com. www.xl.com. NFO Infratest Financial Research 2004.

One way of assigning tasks across the array of communications channels is to consider the degree to which the message can be targeted at specific audiences. Media advertising itself varies along this dimension. At the broadcast, 'shotgun' level, television can reach a very wide audience but is not especially selective except in the variation of audiences across channels by time of day. However, this is changing with the proliferation of digital TV channels allowing for the targeting of smaller audiences with particular viewing characteristics. National print media such as newspapers and magazines offer more selective focus, as they themselves tend to be targeted at more specific segments of consumers. Trade magazines are even more specific in their readership. Direct mail offers the most focused of the impersonal media. The choice among these media must be based on the cost per thousand members of the target audience and the risk and cost of reaching the wrong segments.

When the service provider has a broadly defined audience and little to lose in reaching the wrong segments, television advertising may work out to be the least expensive vehicle on a cost per person basis. However, television and other forms of mass media are unlikely to be efficient for a specialty service such as an upscale restaurant with a tightly defined target audience and a high cost associated with attracting the wrong segment.

Public relations and publicity can be either broad or tightly focused, depending on how they are used. Editorial comment can be solicited in broad or narrow media including websites. Public relations carries with it the advantages and disadvantages of not being paid advertising. On the positive side, it is given more credence by the consumer; on the negative side, it is much more difficult to control. The content may not be designed, or the coverage may be limited.

Much media advertising and public relations and publicity are one-way forms of communication. They cannot respond to consumers' enquiries or tailor the message to the particular characteristics of the receiver. Personal or telemarketing is far more expensive per member of the target audience, but it does offer the flexibility of altering the message during the presentation. If the message is difficult to communicate or a great deal of persuasion is needed, personal communication may be most appropriate. A sales force can be highly targeted and trained to make complex arguments interactively, responding to the inputs of consumers during the process. A similar process can also now be achieved electronically through the use of specialized software and web development reducing costs whilst maintaining 'personalized' contact with a wide and geographically dispersed target audience (see Global Services in Action).

Targeting users. Users can be reached through all the channels we have discussed, and they can be further reached by communications through the service provider. The role of the service provider is multifaceted. Different providers are called upon to perform different communication functions. The classifications of these providers and functions are described next (Booms and Nyquist, 1981).

Type 1 service staff are required to deal with customers quickly and effectively in 'once only' situations where large numbers of customers are present. The exchanges consist of simple information and limited responses to customer requests. Effective communication requires the ability to establish customer relationships very quickly, deal efficiently with customer problems, and convey short, rapid messages that customers can easily understand. Typical examples include front-line personnel at fast-food restaurants or dry cleaners and patient representatives whose job is to obtain and process insurance information.

Type 2 service staff deal with numerous, often repeat customers in restricted interactions of somewhat longer duration. The information provided is mixed – partly simple and partly more complex – and requires some independent decision making on the part of the staff member. Communication in this category requires effective listening skills, the ability to establish trust, interpreting customer information and making decisions in customer relationships that are often ongoing over a period of time. Communications are generally more intense than in type 1 situations. Typical examples include relationships with

type 1 service staff
Service staff that are required to deal with customers quickly and effectively in 'once only' situations where large numbers of customers are present.

type 2 service staff
Service staff that deal with numerous, often repeat customers in restricted interactions of somewhat longer duration.

SOURCE GETTY

Richard Branson abseils into a press conference for the launch of Virgin Mobile in France.

suppliers or customer relationships such as with a customer who requests floral designs from a florist on a regular basis, a loyal customer of a seamstress/tailor, or an effective *maitre d'* at a fine dining establishment.

type 3 service staff
Service staff required to have more highly developed communication skills because of more extended and complex interactions with customers.

Type 3 service staff are required to have more complex communication skills. Interactions with consumers are repeated over time, extensive flow of communication is required, and communication tasks are complicated and often nonrepeatable. Effective communication requires the ability to listen and process complicated information, to think creatively in face-to-face interactions with consumers and to provide information in a clear and understandable manner. Typical examples include staff members who are likely to be qualified as professionals.

Any service organization may have employees in one, two, or all three of these categories. Thus, a bank may have cashiers performing type 1 communications, a loan officer engaged in type 2 and a commercial loan officer engaged in type 3. A travel company may have an agent engaged in both type 2 (when writing tickets and booking arrangements) and type 3 communications (when planning trips) and a receptionist handling type 1 communications.

Each type of communication requires a different set of skills from the providers and places different levels of stress on them. It is clearly important that the correct communications role be assigned to the correct person within the organization. Type 1 is predominantly an operations role, whereas type 3 is a mixed selling and operations role.

Global services in action
Marriott International, Inc.

Believe it or not, Marriott International, Inc., one of the world's leading hospitality companies, started out as a root beer stand in Washington DC in 1927. Over the years, the proud owners of that root beer stand, J. Willard and Alice S. Marriott, have done very well. The hospitality giant opened its first international hotel in Acapulco, Mexico in 1969. Marriott International, Inc. is now a leading hospitality company with nearly 2,800 lodging properties in the United States and 66 other countries and territories. The company employs 143,000 individuals worldwide and reported 2005 financial year-end sales of US$11.6 billion.

One of the challenges faced by international service marketers is developing promotional campaigns that meet the needs of local clientele. In order to customize the pro-

motional plan for the international market, the international marketer should consider issues related to positioning and advertising copy. The most important category of adaptations is based on local behaviour, tastes, attitudes and traditions – all reflecting the marketer's need to gain customers' approval. The product itself may not change at all but its positioning may need to be adjusted. For example, a Marriott property in one location may be positioned as a weekend getaway for adults, while another location in a more conservative country may stress family values in its communication strategy.

Frequently, the copy in advertisements needs to be adjusted to appeal to the international customer. While some advertisements may share common graphic elements, the copy in the ad will be customized for the local culture. Marriott used similar ads to reach the business traveller in the US, Saudi Arabia, Latin America and German-speaking Europe. However, the copy was modified based on needs of the local consumer. While the common theme, 'When You Are Comfortable, You Can Do Anything', was used worldwide, local emphases in the creative copy varied; for example, the Latin version stressed comfort, the German version focused on results.

Similarly, ads for hotel properties marketed in countries such as Saudi Arabia need to be sensitive to local moral standards. While a global creative approach can be used, the copy and the images used in promotions may require some adjusting. For example, if a Western-based Marriott advertisement showed a man and a woman embracing with bare arms visible, this version used around the world may be adjusted for Saudi Arabia to show the man's arm clothed in a dark suit sleeve, and the woman's hand merely brushing his hand. In the end, international service promotions should be carefully tailored to fit the needs and expectations of local markets.

In order to maintain this degree of 'local' adaptation in its communications Marriot, along with Accenture, have developed a web-based system. The new platform reflects Marriott's global scale and supports 16 global sites, each created in local language and with information appropriate to travellers in specific regions. These sites provide a direct and easy way for guests to interact with Marriott and make the most of their stay at a Marriott property

Sources www.marriott.com, accessed 27 April 2005; adapted from K. Douglas Hoffman et al., *Marketing Principles & Best Practices* (Mason, OH: Thomson South-Western, 2006), pp. 121–122. www.accenture.com, accessed 20 March 2008. www.Marriott.com, accessed 20 March 2008.

When a communications mix that includes the service provider is developed, the final objectives for the staff will probably fall within one of the three service categories. However, it is important to recall the position of the employee providing the service. The service provider is not simply a salesperson; he or she is an integral part of the operations process and a part of the experience purchased by the customer. An apparently simple decision – for example, to have a bank cashier sell services – can have profound negative consequences. It could well be that the decision produces role conflict for the teller. Role/self-conflict could be caused by the tellers' wanting to see themselves not as salespeople but as bankers. Direct conflict between the two roles can arise when the operations role demands fast service and minimization of the time spent with each customer but the selling role demands the opposite. In addition, the script may break down for both the service provider and the customer as the teller tries to do something new. The customer may be expecting a brisk, businesslike transaction when suddenly, the teller wants to build rapport by talking about the weather (before starting the sell).

Potentially, such a decision can also diminish operational efficiency as the transaction time per customer rises. This problem is illustrated by the experiences of FedEx before it centralized its telephone customer contact system. In times of peak demand, especially if those times were unpredicted, everyone in the FedEx depots answered telephones, including the field sales-persons based at the depots. The result was that the various depot employees changed the service communication from type 1 to type 3. It also meant that calls took much longer than usual, and the telephone bottleneck consequently worsened.

The communications mix as it relates to consumer behaviour considerations

Consumer behaviour is important because it imposes constraints on the objectives set for services. It is perhaps best to consider behaviour during the three phases discussed in Chapter 4 – prepurchase, consumption and postpurchase (Bateson, 1995).

The preconsumption choice stage

Consumers will try to minimize risk taken in the purchase phase. Risk is some combination of consequences and uncertainty, so these are the two dimensions that the organization's communications objectives can attempt to minimize. In each case, the objective must be to ensure that the company's service is the one perceived to be the least risky alternative. For example, an internet company can reduce consumer fears of ordering by taking the lead and communicating customer-friendly return policies. However, in a recent survey of dot.com sites, two out of three do not explicitly state whether it's the seller or the buyer who is responsible for shipping costs associated with returned items.

financial consequences The perceived monetary consequences of a purchase decision by a consumer.

social consequences The perceived consequences of a consumer's purchase decision among the consumer's peers or the public in general.

performance consequences The perceived consequences of a consumer's purchase decision should the service perform less than 100 per cent effectively.

Communication can obviously impart information that is a key factor in reducing the uncertainty in all risky decisions. It can also offer reassurance. Consequences are generally of three basic types: financial, social, and performance. Financial consequences can be reduced by communications that ensure that consumers correctly understand the likely financial consequences of a purchase, particularly if a money-back guarantee is offered. Concerns about social consequences can be reduced by highlighting for consumers that other people are using the service and that it would not be embarrassing for them to use it. Performance consequences need to be made explicit and clearly communicated to ensure that consumers understand what would happen if the performance were not 100 per cent successful. Clearly, most services are perceived as more risky on the social and performance dimensions, and communications have a key role to play in reassuring customers.

The communications mix can, for example, be based on generating positive word-of-mouth references. This key communications area for services traditionally managed using public relations and publicity can now make use of the burgeoning and highly influential social e-media (E-Services in Action) and viral marketing techniques (Godin and Gladwell, 2001). It has also been shown to be a key method in reducing consumers' perceived risk.

The rational mathematician model assumes that consumers are rational decision makers using a choice matrix of attributes, brand or company scores, and importance weights like those described in the example presented in Chapter 4. Services in the evoked set are scored using the matrix, and the one with the highest score is chosen. Communications can be used to try to influence the choice in the following ways:

- To ensure that the organization's service offering is in the evoked set.
- To alter the weights consumers attach to different attributes to favour those in which the company is strong.
- To alter the score on a given attribute for the company, particularly if a gap exists between performance and consumers' perceptions.
- To alter the score on a given attribute given to a competitor, particularly if a gap exists between performance and consumers' perceptions.
- If the company is not in the evoked set, to build enough awareness of the offering to stimulate inclusion.

It is important to remember the difference between actual and perceived performance. If actual performance is higher than perceived performance, communications may be more effective than if the reverse were the case. Alternatively, marketing communication can be used to maintain a situation that is favourable to the organization. Consumers need to be reminded that an organization does well on particular attributes and that those attributes are important.

rational mathematician model A model that assumes consumers are rational decision makers using a choice matrix of attributes, brand or company scores, and importance weights.

The consumption stage

During the consumption stage, the service consumer is more or less an active participant in the production process. It is important that consumers perform that production role successfully. From the organization's point of view, successful performance will improve the efficiency of the operation and the satisfaction of other customers. From the consumer's point of view, successful performance will ensure a high level of perceived control and, in all probability, a high level of satisfaction in the post-consumption phase.

Communications, in the broadest sense, can be used to ensure successful performance by giving the consumer a clear script (see Figure 9.1). Although this can be done through promotion, the presence of the consumer in the actual service setting creates the opportunity for a much broader range of communications channels. Point-of-sale signs, service providers, and the environment itself can all be used to teach the consumer the script.

In times of operational change, managing the consumer's script takes on even more importance. An example can be seen in a bank that is changing from multiple-line queuing to single-line queuing. No longer may consumers wait in front of a specific teller window. Instead, they must form a single line and go to the first free window available to them when they arrive at the head of the line. Operationally, this offers shorter and more predictable waiting times.

However, such a shift requires a script change. Arriving at the bank without prior warning of the change, the consumer finds a new experience, one that no longer conforms to the existing script. Because it is not immediately obvious how the new system works, the customer may feel a loss of control. The line seems to be extremely long, and worse still, it is no longer possible to choose a specific, favourite cashier. Clearly, the script needs to be modified.

It is fairly obvious how elements of the communications mix can be used to achieve script modification. The bank can use media advertising or leaflets to describe the new process. Contact personnel outside the bank can explain the new system to customers before they enter. Public relations can be used to generate consumer comment about the benefits of the new system. Inside the building, the layout and signs displayed can clearly signal the desired customer behaviour. Finally, service providers can personally reassure customers and reinforce the new script.

The postconsumption evaluation stage

Chapter 4 also introduced the disconfirmation model of consumer satisfaction. This model hypothesises that consumers determine satisfaction by comparing their prior expectations of performance with the perceived actual performance.

Consumer expectations come from a number of sources, some within the control of the service organization, and some beyond its control. Expectations arise either from previous experience with the organization and/or its competitors or from some form of communication. The latter can encompass all aspects of the communications mix. Communications, designed to influence prepurchase choice behaviour, can set expectations in the customer's mind about the quality of service that will be received. Indeed, setting

---

Figure 9.1

Teaching the consumer the script: Wendy's Hamburgers

Source Bateson and Hoffman, *Managing Services Marketing*, 4th ed. © 1999 South-Western, a part of Cengage Learning, Inc. Reproduced by permission. www.cengage.com/permissions.

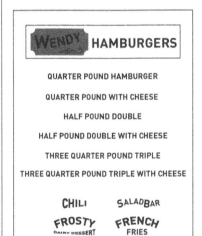

Your recipe for a great Hamburger.

At Wendy Restaurants we don't tell you how to have your hamburger. You tell us.

The order-taker will want to know what size hamburger you'd like. A glance at the menu will help you to make up your mind. With cheese or without?

Then you've a choice of what goes on top. Mayonnaise, Ketchup, Pickle, Fresh Onion, Juicy Tomato, Crisp Lettuce, Mustard. Choose as many as you like – or have the lot – all at no extra charge.

The rest is up to us. In no time at all you'll have a pure beef hamburger that's hot, fresh and juicy – and made just the way you like it.

such expectations may be a key aspect of an organization's communications strategy.

In Chapter 4, you learned that, based on studies of consumer behaviour, word-of-mouth communication can be expected to have an increased role in the service industry because of the high levels of perceived risk associated with the purchase of many services. Such word-of-mouth communication can be random, or it can be orchestrated through the public relations component of the communications mix. Service organizations often strategically place customer testimonials in their promotional campaigns for this very reason.

Special problems of the service communications mix

Intangibility and inseparability present special challenges that should be considered when developing a communications strategy. Firstly, since services are often consumed as a shared experience, mistargeted communications are likely to result in unanticipated consequences. Secondly, an organization's communications are often interpreted as an explicit service promise that consumers use to base their initial expectations. Thirdly, since employees often produce the service in close proximity to customers, employees should be considered as much a target audience as customers. Finally, service providers produce the service and also must sell the service. When the service provider is engaged in selling activities, production halts. When the service provider is producing services, future customers are not being cultivated. How should service providers balance the activities of selling and operations? (George and Berry, 1981)

Mistargeted communications

Segmentation is one of the basic concepts of marketing. In essence, it suggests that an organization's marketing efficiency can be improved by targeting marketing activities at discrete groups of consumers who behave differently in some way towards the organization. Although segmentation is applied in both goods and services companies, the consequences of reaching an inappropriate segment with a part of the communications mix are far less serious for goods companies than for services. If the wrong group of consumers buys a particular brand of soap, for example, it does not really affect the company making the soap; sales are still being generated. Or a product may have been developed for the youth market, but through some quirk of the advertising execution, the product has attracted some senior citizens. For example, take the Pepsi advertisement that portrayed the youthful effects of Pepsi being delivered to a senior citizen's home by error instead of to the student house. Let's say that the ad is interpreted by senior citizens that Pepsi will make them feel young again. Clearly, this was not Pepsi's (who targets the younger generation) original intent. Members of this group who misinterpreted the message visit the supermarket, buy the product and use it in their homes. The negative consequences associated with the elder segment's use of the product are nil.

Suppose, however, that some of the wrong segment decides to buy the services of a restaurant. An upscale concept has been developed, but to launch the restaurant, management decides to have a price promotion, and the advertising agency develops inappropriate advertising. Or, through poor management, publicity activity is unfocused and produces feature articles in the wrong media. The result is that the restaurant gets two types of customers: upscale, middle-aged couples and price-conscious groups of students. The former were the original target, and the latter were attracted by inappropriate marketing tactics. Unfortunately for the restaurant and for many other services, the other customers are part of the product. The result is that neither segment enjoys the experience because of the presence of the other, and neither type of customer returns. Hence, the consequences of mistargeted communications for certain types of service organizations, because of the shared consumption experience, are clearly more significant than the consequences experienced by traditional goods-producing organizations.

mistargeted communications
Communications methods that affect an inappropriate segment of the market.

Managing expectations

The service organization's communications strategy can play a key role in formulating customer expectations about its services (see Global Services in Action). Organisations may reinforce pre-existing ideas or they may dramatically alter those ideas. Expectations can be set by something as explicit as a promise ('Your food will be ready in five minutes') or as implicit as a behaviour pattern that sets a tone. Often such expectations are created unwittingly, as when a server promises to 'be right back'. Such a statement can be viewed both as a binding contract by a customer and as a farewell salutation by the service provider.

Perceived service also has many service sources. Technical service quality is an objective level of performance produced by the operating system of the organization. It is measurable with a stopwatch, temperature gauge, or other measuring instrument. Unfortunately, this is not the level of performance the customer perceives. Perception acts as a filter that moves the perceived service level up or down.

technical service quality
A level of service quality measured by technology such as speed of transactions per hour at an ATM or consistent temperature within a shopping centre, hence performance is measured mechnically.

Perception is itself influenced by the same factors that dictate expectations. For example, communications can create warm feelings towards the organization that raises perceived service levels. Inappropriately dressed and ill-behaving staff can deliver high levels of technical service quality but be poorly perceived by the consumer, who will downgrade the perceived service level.

Many sources of expectations are under the direct control of the organization. Only past experience and competitors' activities cannot be directly influenced in one way or the other. Given such control, the organization must determine the objectives of the communications mix.

In the absence of competition, reduced expectations will result in higher satisfaction levels, provided that levels of perceived service are maintained. Therefore, one strategy would be to reduce expectations as much as possible.

Regardless of the service actually delivered, the customer would then be satisfied.

Unfortunately, communications must also play the more traditional role of stimulating demand. It is inconsistent to think of achieving this by promising average service, even if doing so might minimize customers' expectations (for the few customers who use the service!).

In competitive terms, organizations make promises and strive to build expectations that will differentiate them in the marketplace and cause customers to come to them and not to their competitors. The temptation is, therefore, to promise too much and to raise expectations to an unrealistic level. It is perhaps fortunate that the variability in services is well known to most consumers and that they consequently discount many of the promises made by service organizations. When the promises are taken seriously, however, the result is often dissatisfied customers.

It is probably more effective to attempt to match customers' expectations to the performance characteristics of the service delivery system. In such a scenario, the behaviour of the customer is most likely to conform to the script required by the operating system. There is little point, for example, in encouraging McDonald's customers to specify how well they want their hamburgers done. Not only would the customers be disappointed, but any attempt to meet their demands would destroy the efficiency of the operating system (Bateson, 1992).

Internal marketing communications

The staff of service organizations frequently forms a secondary audience for any organization's communications campaign. Clearly, communications seen by the staff, if they empathize with it, can be highly motivating. However, if communications are developed without a clear understanding of the operational problems, it can imply service performance levels that are technically or bureaucratically impossible; that is, it can set expectation levels unrealistically high. This has a doubly detrimental effect on the staff since (1) it shows that people who developed the communications (the marketing department) did not understand the business and (2) it raises the prospects that customers will actually expect the service to operate that way, and the staff will have to tell them that the reality differs from the level of service portrayed in the organization's communications. In both cases, the impact will be a negative influence on staff motivation, which will, in turn, negatively influence customer satisfaction. A classic example involved American Airlines. The company ran an ad that featured a flight attendant reading a young child a story during the flight. As a result, passengers expected the flight attendants to tend to their children, and flight attendants were miffed by the implication that they were supposed to be babysitters in addition to all of their other duties.

The bottom line is that in order for service organizations to succeed, they must first sell the service job to the employee before they sell the service to the customer (Sasser and Albeit, 1976). For years, communications from British Airways have shown smiling employees going to great lengths to please the customer. Although the communications are clearly targeted towards customers, they also send a message to employees regarding appropriate role behaviour. In the end, service communications not only provide a means of communicating with customers, but also serve as a vehicle to communicate, motivate, and educate employees, the internal audience (George and Berry, 1981).

Selling/operation conflicts

Another consideration unique to the service sector is that the individuals who sell the service are often the same people who provide the service. In many instances, the service provider is much more comfortable providing the service than marketing his or her own abilities. However, in some cases, providers become so involved in the communications aspects of their organization that they no longer actively participate in the operations end of the business.

The conflicts associated with selling versus operations are at least two-fold. First are the economic considerations. Typically, service providers are paid for providing services and are not paid for time spent on communications activities. Clearly, the provider must engage in marketing activities in order to generate future customers, but the time spent on marketing does not generate revenues for the provider at that particular moment. Moreover, the time spent on communications activities is often while an ongoing project is being conducted. This means that the time dedicated to communications activities must be considered when estimating completion dates to customers. Often the organization's communications efforts must occur while previously sold services are being processed in order to avoid shut-down periods between customer orders.

The second conflict that arises is often role-related. Many professional service providers believe that communications activities such as personal selling are not within their areas of expertise. Consequently, some providers feel uncomfortable with communications activities, and, even more disturbing, some providers feel that this type of activity is beneath them. Many areas of public sector service have been plagued by this problem through the years. However, increased competition has lead to recognition of the need for marketing training directed at public service providers whether this is healthcare, education or policing. Many of these institutions, particularly the good ones, now embrace the importance of the organization's communications efforts.

General guidelines for developing service communications

After a review of the literature that directly examines the specifics of promoting services, several common themes emerge that create guidelines for communicating services. Many of these guidelines have developed directly as a result of the intangibility, inseparability, heterogeneity and perishability inherent in service products.

Develop a word-of-mouth communications network

Consumers of services often rely on personal sources of information more than nonpersonal sources to reduce the risk associated with a purchase. Given the importance of nonpersonal sources, communications should be developed that facilitate the development of a word-of-mouth network. Advertising that features satisfied customers, use of e-mail, blogs and promotional strategies that encourage current customers to recruit their friends are typical. Other communications strategies such as presentations for community and professional groups and sponsorship of community and professional activities have also been effective in stimulating word-of-mouth communications. Encouraging the target audience to carry the message to others in known as 'viral' or 'buzz' marketing and has increased greatly with the use of new media. Consider the forward-to-a-friend amusing e-mails received regularly, the use of YouTube video clips and the growing use of event and experiential marketing to engage customers and get them talking.

Promise what is possible

In its most basic form, customer satisfaction is developed by customers' comparing their expectations to their perceptions of the actual service delivery process. In times of increasing competitive pressures, organizations may be tempted to overpromise. Making promises the organization cannot keep initially increases customer expectations and then subsequently lowers customer satisfaction as those promises are not met.

Two problems are associated with overpromising. First, customers leave disappointed, and a significant loss of trust occurs between the organization and its customers. Moreover, disappointed customers are sure to tell others of their experience, which increases the fallout from the experience. The second problem directly affects the service organization's employees. Working for organizations that make false promises places employees in compromising and often confrontational positions. Front-line personnel are left to repeatedly explain to customers why the company cannot keep its promises. Given the link between employee satisfaction and customer satisfaction, creating expectations that cannot be met can have devastating long-term effects.

Make tangible the intangible

In Chapter 1, we discussed that the distinction between goods and services is unclear and presented the scale of market entities – a continuum that assesses the tangible properties of the market entity, ranging from tangible dominant to intangible dominant. Interestingly, tangible dominant market entities, such as perfume, utilize image development in their advertising schemes. From a basic viewpoint, perfume is simply liquid scent in a bottle. The customer can pick it up, try it on and smell the fragrance. Hence, the perfume is tangible dominant. As with many tangible-dominant products, the advertising tends to make them more abstract in order to differentiate one product from another. For example, when you think of the fragrance Calvin Klein, what images come to mind? The company uses these images to differentiate its product from competitive offerings.

In contrast, services, being intangible dominant are already abstract. Hence, one of the principal guidelines for advertising a service is to make it more concrete. This explains why corporations utilize tangible symbols to represent their companies. For example, Legal and General have the umbrella, McDonalds have the golden arches, and as discussed in the opening vignette Churchill have 'the nodding dog' and Aflac has 'The Duck'. Insurance products are already abstract, so it becomes the advertisement's objective to explain the service in simple and concrete terms. In addition to tangible symbols, other organizations have made tangible their service offerings by using numbers in their advertisements, such as, 'We've been in business since 1925', or 'Nine out of ten customers would recommend us to a friend'.

In making tangible the intangible (Hill and Ghandi, 1992), the scale of market entities should be turned on its end (see Figure 9.2). The advertising of tangible-dominant products tends to make them more abstract in order to differentiate them from one another. In contrast, the advertising of intangible-dominant products should concentrate on making them more concrete through the use of physical cues and tangible evidence. The advertising of products in the middle of the continuum often utilizes both approaches. McDonald's, for example, promotes 'food, folks, and fun' in one of its advertisements. Food and folks are concrete, and fun is abstract. Recent research by Grove, Carlsen and Dorsch (2002) suggests that a variety of service firms would benefit through using integrated marketing communications to enhance the tangibility of their offerings. One simple tool suggested to achieve this is to provide clear clues/links within advertising that direct consumers to public relations initiatives, websites and sales promotions.

Feature the working relationship between customer and provider

As you should well understand by now, service delivery is an interactive process between the service provider and the customer. Because of inseparability, it is appropriate in the organization's advertising to feature a

---

Figure 9.2

The impact of intangibility: Different communication strategies for different products

Source Adapted from G. Lynn Shostack, 'Breaking Free from Product Marketing', *The Journal of Marketing* (April 1977).

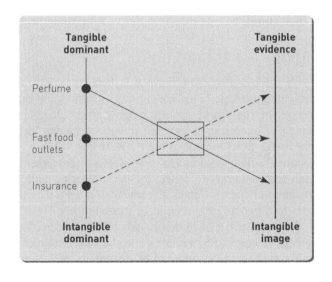

company representative and a customer working together to achieve a desired outcome. Many financial institutions, legal organizations and insurance companies use advertising that commonly shows a company representative and a customer interacting in a friendly and reassuring manner. The advertising of services, in particular, must concentrate not only on encouraging customers to buy, but also on encouraging employees to perform. Clearly, advertising that illustrates the inseparability of the service delivery process should target both the customer and the organization's service providers.

Reduce consumer fears about variations in performance

The organization's advertising can also minimize the pitfalls of heterogeneity in the customer's mind. To enhance the perception of consistent quality, the organization's advertising should provide some form of documentation that reassures the customer. Typical examples include stating the organization's performance record through numbers as opposed to qualitative testimonials. The use of 'hard' numbers in advertisements reduces the consumer's fear of variability and also tangibilizes the service, as mentioned earlier.

Determine and focus on relevant service quality dimensions

The reasons customers choose among competing services are often closely related to the five dimensions of service quality – reliability, responsiveness, assurance, empathy and the quality of the tangibles associated with the service. However, it is common that some features are more important to customers than others. For example, 30 per cent of airline customers have listed 'safety' as one of their top five considerations when choosing an airline (Miller, 1991). Consequently, it would be appropriate for airlines to emphasise the assurance dimension of service quality by featuring the airline's safety record, maintenance and training programmes, as well as any certified aspects of their particular airline operation. One advertising campaign that backfired promoted a hotel as one of the tallest hotels in the world. Although this reinforced the tangible dimension of service quality, this particular tangible component was not very important to customers in choosing hotels. In fact, many customers who had even the slightest fear of heights avoided the hotel for fear of being placed on an upper floor.

Differentiate the service product via the service delivery process

A dramatic difference exists between what the service provides and how it is provided. Identifying the various inputs into the process, which contributes to a competitive or quality advantage, and stressing these inputs in the organization's advertising is likely to be a successful approach. On the surface, it appears somewhat difficult to differentiate one tax accountant from the next. However, if we consider the process of obtaining a consultation, which consists of calling to make an appointment, interacting with staff at the front desk, the appearance of the office in the reception area where the client is waiting, the appearance of the accountant's office, the interaction between the client and the accountant, and the payment procedures, several potential areas for differentiation arise. Outlining the various inputs within the service delivery process may indicate key competitive and/or quality advantages that traditionally have been overlooked.

Make the service more easily understood

Services can be more fully explained to potential customers via the communications mix by presenting the service as a series of events. When questioned, consumers often break down the service experience into a series of sequential events. Understanding the sequence permits the service provider to view the service from the customer's perspective. For example, bank customers may first view the external building, parking facilities, landscaping and cleanliness of the grounds. When entering the bank, customers notice the interior furnishings, odours, music, temperature and service personnel. While conducting bank transactions, the appearance and demeanour of specific contact personnel become additional quality cues. Hence, perceptions of quality are assessed at each stage of the service encounter. Advertising developed from the sequence-of-events perspective considers the customer throughout the process and highlights the organization's strengths in each area.

E-marketing communication for services

Although a variety of 'traditional' marketing communication methods and media are available to service providers it is becoming increasingly important to integrate these with newer methods. The majority of these involve some form of electronic communication whether this is via the internet, e-mail or mobile telecommunications. These newer methods and media tend to be less restrictive in time and place and can often be more easily personalized and targeted. The e-marketing tools that are most appropriate for services are described below along with a discussion of their uses, advantages and disadvantages (the following section is adapted form Masterman and Wood, 2006).

Websites and 'brochureware'

A service organization's website can serve many functions for many different target groups. It can be a source of information for employees, investors, partners and researchers as well as for current and prospective customers. The website can communicate about the organization and its service offerings in an interactive way allowing the internet users to select the type of information they wish to access and creating a dialogue between the organization and the user when needed. At its most simple the website can be merely an online version of a printed brochure. However, to make use of the unique properties of the internet, websites should be far more sophisticated using regularly updated information of interest to the various target groups and displaying this using multimedia images, text and sound. Interactivity can be used to gather data from visitors, respond to requests and to take orders. Effective websites generate loyal visitors who return on a regular basis to access new information. This does not necessarily mean that they are loyal to the company or its products but it does mean that a relationship has been created that can be leveraged in the future

The internet as a marketing communication tool is particularly important as it is most often used in the information search and evaluation stages of the decision-making process. An internet user is actively searching for information on a type of product or service and will gather that information easily from a number of websites in order to compare and make a decision. There is often, therefore, a clearer link between this form of communication and purchase behaviour than with other methods.

The characteristics of a good business website can be summarized as:

1 Clear strategic objectives for the site which fit with other communication methods.
2 Customer-led rather than product-driven providing different areas for different customer groups.
3 Value added content updated regularly and customized for different user groups.
4 Content management ensuring a dynamic rather than static site.
5 Data quality management.
6 Professional design and usability projecting a consistent corporate image.
7 High interactivity and functionality allowing customers to contact key personnel in the organization and each other.
8 Easy to navigate and quick to download with regular usability testing.
9 E-communications strategy to complement the website.
10 Effective marketing of the website.

(adapted from Hart, 2003: 284)

Other internet tools

As well as the use of websites, the internet offers other communication opportunities. These are generally forms of advertising using the internet and the websites of others as the host. Internet advertising uses a variety of techniques including banner ads, pop-ups and click-throughs. It also encompasses the use of search engine listings and directories to encourage visitors to the website. A further aspect of the internet is the opportunity for partnership marketing through joint or consortium websites, referral sites and online agencies or e-tailers.

Search engines, as well as being a useful navigational tool, also offer paid-for advertising in the form of 'featured sites' which appear more prominently in search result listings when particular 'adwords' are used in the search term. These are relatively expensive but are often necessary when first launching a new website. One benefit of these bought search terms is that usually they are only paid for by click-through rate (user sees the listing and clicks to enter the website) rather than by the number of times they are viewed. Search engine marketing (SEM), therefore, requires an understanding of the users' search behaviour and has accordingly moved from the realm of web designer to marketer (Smith and Taylor, 2004).

The art of obtaining natural listings on search engines or search engine optimization (SEO) has become a business in its own right with agencies specializing in website design that makes use of the various ways search engines search and generate results lists. Search engine providers constantly refine their systems in order to overcome some of the unethical practices used to get a website to the top of the list. For example, one of the more important factors looked for when ranking searched-for websites is the number of relevant sites linking into the website. The practice of link farms and link exchange programmes which create vast numbers of links regardless of relevance is frowned upon by search engine providers and can lead to websites being banned from the search listings. However, encouraging relevant and useful sites to link to the organization's website should be part of the continual website management process. Most websites will provide web links for free if the link adds value to their own site visitors and if the link is reciprocated. The other side to this process is to discourage non-relevant sites from linking to a site. This is hard to enforce, although larger organizations have managed to do so through the legal system. For example, universal studios have successfully prevented other websites from linking directly to movie clips and images on their site although they have not been able to prevent sites from linking to their homepages.

To check the number and type of websites with links to your own site you can simply type 'link:' followed by the website URL into the search engine. Although there are a number of factors which can be incorporated into website design to increase its chances of a good search engine listing, most search engines are wise to any tricks and scams and will penalize for them. The best rule of thumb is that 'content is king' and if the content is right then the search engine listing will follow (Grant and McBride, 2000).

A related alternative to web links and advertising is the use of referral websites. A website is chosen that clearly targets a desirable market for the event and a referral link is negotiated. The link is paid for on a piece rate each time a user clicks through to the event organization's website. Payment can be made simply on click through or on purchase made. This type of referral agreement encourages the linking website to give more prominence to the link and therefore encourages more visitors and limits costs by only being paid for when it is used. For example, a referral link to a visitor attractions website may be negotiated with an accommodation or travel provider, a special interest group or the websites of other attractions.

Smaller organizations may choose not to have their own website but to join a web marketing consortium of similar or related organizations or to make greater use of online directories and agencies. These options reduce the costs to the organization and can increase value to the visitor through the ease of accessing a range of information in one place.

The benefits of using the internet as an advertising medium are that it can very precisely target relevant customer groups through the selection of the carrying websites. This overcomes the disadvantage of the untargeted nature of the internet generally in that through online advertising, web links and referrals, the visitors to the website can to some extent be controlled and monitored.

The effectiveness of online advertising can be easily monitored through various web metric programmes giving an indication of online customer behaviour as well as simple counts. Media cynical consumers have a greater trust in the integrity of search engine listings and links from credible websites than in traditional media messages, as these appear as more objective information rather than promotion. The often more effective method of web links, referrals and shared sites can cost relatively little and can also help the organization to form valuable partnerships.

A final benefit is the opportunity offered to recoup some of the costs of website design and maintenance through selling advertising space and links on the organization's own website.

One of the main drawbacks in online advertising is that, on a medium which is based on user choice and selection, unsolicited advertisements can be viewed as intrusive and annoying. This is certainly the case for pop-up ads, the use of which now appears to be in decline. Pop-up ads can delay the visitor's access to a website and can be difficult to close and therefore block other information. The visitor loses patience not necessarily with the advertiser but with the hosting website. Many websites are therefore no longer allowing this type of internet advertising and have limited advertisers to banner and feature ads which are more suitably integrated into the website content. This loses the attention-getting benefits of pop-ups but is likely to result in more genuine interest click-throughs.

The annoyance factor of internet advertisements has led to a proliferation in ad-blocking software available at little or no cost to the internet user (O'Connor and Galvin, 2001). This software can block pop-ups and can detect ad content in banner ads and prevent it from being displayed. This is a benefit to the internet user wasting download time on graphic ads, but is bad news for the web-based ad agencies and those organizations spending a growing proportion of their communications budget on internet ads that may never be seen.

Internet PR

As well as being used as an advertising medium, the internet should also be incorporated into the communications plan as a valuable platform for public relations. Features, reviews and news can be generated around the company. Its employees and products should be regularly fed to other websites in the same way as it would be issued to the print, TV and radio media. These websites will add the information to their content, creating additional exposure, interest and credibility. News should also be a permanent feature of the organizations' website and should include all current media releases plus relevant news from further afield providing a source of information and therefore extra value for the visitor.

One of the main benefits of internet PR is that information can be uploaded and accessed almost immediately by a global audience. There is no production time lag and therefore new and updated information is available as it happens and at no extra cost (Ihator, 2001). This can be very useful in pre-empting or counteracting negative publicity.

Any media releases can include a web link for further information and can therefore be used to generate website traffic. This can encourage new target markets and again increase exposure and interest.

One of the disadvantages of publicity generally is the lack of control over content that the organization has. Information may be provided to relevant websites in a ready-to-use format but is likely to be edited and added to by many in order to present an objective viewpoint. This enhances the credibility of the website as a source of information but also means that negative publicity may also be included. This problem is no different from the traditional media but is exacerbated by the ungoverned, unfiltered nature of much of the internet. Monitoring and controlling what is published on the internet about the organization is very difficult. It is impossible to prevent publication of what could be untrue rumours and stories so it is doubly important to monitor and respond to these, where necessary, as quickly as possible through websites with accepted credibility for each targeted public

E-mail marketing

Contacting and being contacted by potential and existing customers by e-mail has seen exponential growth as a communications medium. Very few companies worldwide are now without e-mail capability and the majority of individuals in a large number of countries around the world can be contacted via work or home e-mail addresses. E-mail marketing is often linked to internet marketing in that access to and interaction with a website creates the initial e-mail contact by registering with the site, information requests, queries or online ordering. However, target market e-mail addresses can be requested at any point of contact, for example, through sales promotion participation, and are routinely included in organization contact details.

E-mail marketing is therefore the use of an electronic medium for direct marketing as it entails personalized contact with a target audience. Successful e-mail marketing uses carefully targeted messages to ensure that recipients only receive offers and information of interest. These can include graphics and audio to gain attention but these should be used carefully due to file size and company filters of attachments. Requests via e-mail for information, advice, quotations, tickets and so on need to be responded to quickly and in a personalized manner. E-mail is viewed by many as an alternative to the telephone rather than the postal system and therefore an almost immediate response is expected.

E-mail communications can be tailored to the needs of individual customers and can be effective at all stages of the decision-making process. However, the response to e-mailed information is improved if the recipient is already aware of the organization or the product. This may be as a past customer or through visiting the website or through being exposed to advertising and sales promotions. E-mails should therefore be integrated with the rest of the communications campaign and maintain a consistent overall message and image.

E-mail is also one of the cheapest and quickest methods for reaching a large number of recipients with a personalized message and also provides the opportunity for direct response.

The problems with using e-mail stem largely from its overuse and misuse. Inbox clutter and e-mail spam (unsolicited e-mails) create target audiences who are quick to press the delete button. In order to cut through this clutter the sender needs to be recognized by the recipient through previous contacts and the sender needs to recognize that recipients have given permission for their e-mail address to be used in this way. The headline of the e-mail needs to get the reader's attention and the body text should be short and relevant to the reader, with links to the website in order to gain further information or take advantage of the offer. E-mails should always include a signature, name and contact details rather than being sent anonymously from the company and should always offer the opportunity to unsubscribe or opt out.

The database used for e-mailings requires constant updating and cleaning to ensure the legality of the contacts being made and the effectiveness of correct targeting. Repeated opt-out and permission renewal requests can help in filtering out the less likely prospects.

A disadvantage of direct e-mail over direct postal mail is its intangibility and transience. Although images can be sent via e-mail, samples and free gifts cannot. The text or image can be viewed and deleted in a matter of seconds whereas as letters, brochures, programmes, merchandise sent by post may remain 'on display' in the home or office for days or weeks.

Companies that use e-mail to replace other personal selling methods may be saving money but will lose out on the relationship building and persuasive benefits of telephone or face-to-face contact. This is particularly true in business-to-business communications where e-mail has its uses but can never take the place of phone calls and personal visits.

A final word of caution is also needed in launching a large-scale e-mail campaign without estimating the resources needed to respond. The speed of design and implementation and the low cost of this method mean that large-scale campaigns can be instigated by relatively small companies. If successful, this can lead to an audience response that cannot be dealt with and subsequently may result in bad publicity, negative word-of-mouth and a detrimental effect on company image.

E-viral marketing

Closely related to the use of direct e-mail is the use of e-mail as the conduit for word-of-mouth (or word-of-mouse) campaigns. This type of creation or encouragement of word-of-mouth is known as viral marketing. The premise behind viral marketing is that the market itself will spread information if it is presented in the right way. In order to do this the organization needs to use or create an idea linked to the product or organization and then communicate that idea to a small but carefully selected target audience (opinion leaders in the form of individuals, groups or websites). The idea for an e-viral campaign can be text, a graphic, audio or video clip or website link but it needs to be attention-getting. This can be achieved through the use of humour, shock, enlightenment information, special offers, or interaction.

The targeted audience (or seeds) finds something of interest in the idea and therefore passes on the information to others, these others then pass it on and so on, and the virus spreads. Although not limited to e-mail, this method is one of the fastest for spreading word-of-mouth as each recipient can forward on the information quickly and at no cost to many contacts. There are also many sites which gather viral marketing examples (e.g. www.viralbank.com, and www.viralmeister.com) and therefore extend the life and exposure of these campaigns.

E-mails received from friends and colleagues are far more likely to get through the inbox clutter and gain the recipient's attention. The credibility of the forwarder source adds to the credibility of the sponsoring organization and at the same time endorses the brand. This voluntary spreading of a message creates exponential and self-perpetuating exposure for very little cost, with the possibility of reaching a large global audience within weeks of seeding. There are approximately 891 million electronic mail boxes around the world (Perry and Whitaker, 2002).

Although this technique entails insubstantial media costs, there are other costs in the initial set-up of e-viral campaigns. One of these costs is in the research needed to identify suitable 'seeds' or opinion leaders, to understand their preferences and contacts and to gain their permission to send them the 'idea' e-mails. The second cost is in the creative development of a suitable 'idea'. In developing the idea there needs to be a clear focus on the characteristics of the targeted opinion leaders in order to create something innovative and of value.

Care needs to be taken to avoid the creativity of the campaign from obscuring the product being offered. A successful creative idea may lead to exponential spreading of the message and interest, involvement and loyalty to that message without achieving attitudinal or behavioural changes towards the brand, product or organization. This can happen if the idea is memorable and likeable but is not explicitly associated with the product.

A possible disadvantage of e-viral campaigns is that the message can get lost amongst inbox clutter and, worse, be perceived as spam, chain e-mail or one of the many e-mail scams. One way to overcome this is to use a pull-seeding mechanism using the websites dedicated to virals (e.g. The Lycos Viral Chart, Viralbank and puchbaby.com) which attract an audience willing to send them on (Howell, 2003).

Internet communities

A more sophisticated and value-laden focused use of the internet than the organization website is the creation of internet communities. An internet community replicates social behaviour in hyperspace (Hoey, 1998) allowing individuals with shared interests to interact, gather information and learn from each other. An internet community can provide a 'one-stop shopping mall', providing, on regular visitation, access to everything that they need or want to know about a particular topic, brand or event (Wills, 1997). Such internet communities can be encouraged via use of part of one organization's website or can be created by a group of organizations with shared target audiences. Examples include the use of fan or supporter websites to connect audiences with interests in sports, music and film. Glastonbury Music Festival (www.glastonburyfestivals.co.uk) has managed to create a sense of community within their website through the inclusion of message boards, information openness and web casts.

The use of internet communities provides a forum for word-of-mouth information to be spread but with some degree of control and the ability to monitor what is being said. The monitoring of discussion boards and forums is now a recognized and useful new addition to marketing research tools (Poria and Harmen, 2002) and provides the additional benefit of the opportunity to respond immediately to users' comments.

When created sensitively, these virtual communities are seen as a useful resource by the user and therefore create extra value to the brand of participating organizations. The information provided in such forums is generally viewed by users as being objective and credible as it is not issued direct from the organization and is therefore more effective.

In order to prevent misuse of the forums and possible offence to users, the content needs to be regularly monitored and policed. The censoring of posted messages, however, has a negative impact on the credibility of the content and therefore needs to be handled openly with clear guidelines published for users. Most message boards require registration to ensure the users with anonymity and security and in registering, the user agrees to abide by the forum's rules. For example, an excerpt from the terms and conditions for the efestivals forums includes an agreement not to 'post any material which is knowingly false and/or defamatory, inaccurate, abusive, vulgar, hateful, harassing, obscene, profane, sexually oriented, threatening, invasive of a person's privacy, or otherwise violative of the law' (efestivals, 2004). These types of forum will often use an independent moderating team who monitor content for any breach of the published terms.

As with internet PR, it is not possible to have complete control of this form of communication and posted messages and chat room comments may include negative comments. However, the opportunity to respond to these in a public environment is likely to be beneficial to the corporate image and will help to create a long-term positive image of the openness and responsiveness of the organization.

Mobile telecommunications

The use of mobile or cell phones as a marketing medium is increasing alongside the improvements in technology. As more and more of the billions of mobile phones worldwide are able to send and receive text, graphics and video, connect to the web through WAP and Blue Tooth technology, the more opportunities there are for these to be used for highly targeted and high-impact one-to-one marketing communications.

The location-based marketing benefits of mobile phones also offer a number of possibilities. Mobile phone technology means that the location of users can be pinpointed accurately when they use their phones and they can therefore be sent location-relevant messages. For example, Guinness have used this information to guide customers to pubs holding Guinness promotions. Tour organizers are beginning to use this technology to provide personalized routes around cities and to transmit focused messages as the visitor passes particular locations.

Mobile phones therefore provide a personal level of interactivity with the service itself and with other forms of promotion. For example, text response numbers can be used to elicit requests for further information or to buy in response to TV, radio, outdoor ads or to take part in sales promotions.

Mobile phone partnership marketing is a growing area where network operators form partnerships with other organizations to create a branded phone service. Existing examples of this include the *Financial Times* newspaper in the UK, MTV in Sweden and Hesburger restaurant chain in Finland. Performers are already beginning to take advantage of this additional branding tool with the highly successful Hong Kong based music duo, Twins, recently launching a branded phone service. The Twins SIM card provides access to Twins news, concert details, ringtones, e-cards and loyalty scheme (Moore and Ahonen, 2004). Other brands are sure to follow this trend.

The main advantages of mobile phone marketing communications are due to the importance of this communication device to the consumer. The mobile phone is highly personal, more so than the fixed-line phone which is often a shared resource (family, friends, office) or e-mail. Most users keep their phone within arm's reach day and night and respond quickly to voice, text and multimedia messages. Although SMS and MMS messaging is still used largely by the youth market, penetration into other demographic groups is rapidly increasing helped on by popular TV shows which ask for text message interaction and voting.

Messages sent to mobile phones can be very precisely targeted and timed for maximum impact. Timing becomes an important aspect of message delivery, as unlike direct mail and e-mail the message is likely to be viewed or listened to as soon as it is transmitted.

The interconnectedness of mobile phones makes them ideal as conduits for viral campaigns. The increasing convergence of technology means that the mobile phone is now also used as a browser and camera, allowing for the development of more innovative ways to communicate with each individual user.

The personal nature of the mobile phone, although increasing the impact and responsiveness of this medium, can also be a disadvantage. Unwanted messages will be seen as highly intrusive and can have a very negative affect on the recipients' attitudes to the brand. Ill-targeted messages and those where explicit permission has not been sought are most likely to be viewed negatively. It is, therefore, important to tailor any messages to the precise needs of each target group, to regularly renew permissions and to provide easy opt-outs.

The newness of the technology in mobile telephony has created barriers to use in some target groups and a mistrust of making purchases or sending personal details via this method. This can be overcome with assurances of security and privacy and through the gradual adoption of the newer aspects of the technology.

E-marketing reviewed

The possibilities for e-marketing communications are constantly expanding with the introduction of new technologies, the convergence of established technology and the discovery of new and creative ways of using these technologies. The internet has had a major impact on marketing communication emphasis through the use of websites and e-mail. This medium has empowered consumers through information and choice and has led to opportunities for communicating in a more open, objective and therefore credible manner. This communication is more effective when customers and other interested parties contribute to the communications message. This can be done through the passing on of messages of interest (e-viral) or through contributing to forums and discussions (internet communities).

Summary

This chapter has provided an overview of communications mix strategies as they apply to the marketing of services. Communications strategy is one of the key components of an organization's overall marketing mix. Its role is to inform, persuade and/or remind consumers about the services being offered. The components of the communications mix include personal selling, media advertising, publicity and public relations, and sales promotion. It is vital that a variety of these are used in order to maximize the contact with the target audience, reinforcing a consistent message in an integrated and high-impact manner. The service organization's budget is allocated among each component of the communications mix. Depending on the target audience and the organization's objectives, some components of the mix will be utilized more often than others.

The objectives of an organization's communications mix often relate directly to the service offering's stage within the product life cycle. For instance, the content of communications during the introduction stage tends to be informational to create consumer awareness. As the service moves into the growth and maturity stages of its life cycle, the content of the communication tends to be informational and persuasive to help position the service among competing alternatives. The content of the communications mix switches to persuasive and reminder as the organization progresses through the maturity stage and into the decline stage.

It is vital that service organizations utilize e-communications within in any marketing communications plan. These provide highly targeted and personalized methods for reaching large and geographically dispersed target customers. However, despite their advantages there are also drawbacks to be aware of.

Discussion questions

1 Discuss the options available for positioning and differentiating service organizations.

2 Explain the benefits of integrating the four elements of the communications mix.

3 Compare the communication skills necessary to conduct type 1, type 2, and type 3 service transactions.

4 Discuss the relevance of the rational mathematician model as it relates to developing communications strategy.

5 Explain the problems associated with mistargeted communications. Why do they occur?

6 Discuss the need for service employees to be considered when developing communications materials.

7 Discuss using examples how insurance companies make their services more easily understood.

8 Discuss the ways in which a service provider could integrate e-communications with more traditional methods. Use the Kulula.com case study to support your arguments.

Case link

See Case 17: Kulula.com.

9 Discuss the differences between e-mail marketing and e-viral marketing. Choose a service organization and consider how they could use these marketing tools.

References and further reading

Bateson, J. E. G. (1992) *Managing Services Marketing,* 2nd ed., Fort Worth, TX: Dryden Press.

Bateson, J. E. G. (1995). *Managing Services Marketing,* 3rd ed. Fort Worth, TX: Dryden Press.

Booms, B. H. and Nyquist, J. L. (1981) 'Analyzing the customer/organization communication component of the services marketing mix', in *Marketing of Services,* James H. Donnelly and William R. George, eds, Chicago: American Marketing Association, pp. 172–177.

Boone, L. E. and Kurtz, D. L. (1993 *Contemporary Marketing,* 8th ed., Fort Worth, TX: Dryden Press.

Chartered Institute of Marketing (2004) 'You talkin' to me? Communication in the age of consent', www.shapethe agenda.com, January.

Efestivals (2004) www.efestivals.co.uk/forums, accessed October 2004.

Fox, J. (1994) *Starting and Building Your Own Accounting Business,* New York: John Wiley & Sons.

George, W. R. and Berry, L. L. (1981) 'Guidelines for the advertising of services', *Business Horizons* 24 (4)(July–August): 52–56.

Glastonbury Festival (2004) www.glastonburyfestival.co.uk, accessed July 2004.

Godin, S. and Gladwell, M. (2001) *Unleashing the Ideavirus,* Hyperion.

Grant, D. and McBride, P. (2000) *Guide to the Internet: Getting Your Business Online,* : Butterworth-Heinemann.

Grove, S. J., Carlsen, L. and Dorsch, M. J. (2002) 'Addressing services' intangibility through integrated marketing communication: an exploratory study', *Journal of Services Marketing,* 16 (5): 393–411.

Hart, S. (2003) *Marketing Changes,* Thomson.

Hartley, B. and Pickton, D. (1999) 'Integrated marketing communications requires a new way of thinking', *Journal of Marketing Communications* 5: 97–106.

Hill, D. H., and Gandhi, N. (1992) 'Service advertising: a framework to its effectiveness', *Journal of Services Marketing* 6 (4): 63–77.

Hoey, C. (1998) 'Maximising the effctiveness of web-based marketing communications', *Marketing Intelligence and Planning 16* (1): 31–37.

Howell, N. (2003) 'Catching the bug', *New Media Age,* 10 April, pp. 31–32.

Ihator, A. S. (2001) 'Communication style in the information age', *Corporate Communications: An International Journal, 6* (4): 199–204.

Kenyon, A. J., Wood, E. H. and Parsons, A. (2008) 'Exploring the audience's role: a decoding model for the 21st century', *Journal of Advertising Research* 48 (2) (June): 276–286.

Kotler, P. (1997) *Marketing Management,* 9th ed., Englewood Cliffs, NJ: Prentice Hall.

Kotler, P. and Bloom, P. N. (1984) *Marketing Professional Services,* Englewood Cliffs, NJ: Prentice Hall.

Masterman, G. and Wood, E. H. (2006) *Innovative Marketing Communications: Strategies for the events industry,* Oxford: Elsevier.

Miller, C. (1991) 'Airline safety seen as new marketing issue', *Marketing News,* 8 July, pp. 1, 11.

Moore, A. and Ahonen, T. (2004) 'Mobile marketing: how to succeed in a connected age', *Market Leader* 24 (Spring).

O'Connor, J. and Galvin, E. (2001) *Marketing in the Digital Age,* 2nd ed., Englewood Cliffs, NJ: Prentice Hall.

Perry, Richard and Whitaker, Andrew (2002) *Viral Marketing – in a week,* Reading: Hodder & Stoughton.

Poria, Y. and Harmen, O. (2002) 'Exploring possible uses of multi-user domains in tourism research', *Tourism Today,* pp: 15–33.

Reedy, J., Schullo, S. and Zimmerman, K. (2000) *Electronic Marketing,* Fort Worth, TX: Dryden Press.

Sasser, W. E. and Albeit, S. P. (1976) 'Selling jobs in the service sector', *Business Horizons* (June): 64.

Smith, P. R. and Taylor, J. (2004) *Marketing Communications: An Integrated Approach,* 4th ed., London: Kogan Page.

Zunin, L. and Zunin, N. (1972) *Contact: The First Four Minutes,* Los Angeles: Nash Publishing.

Chapter 10
Managing the firm's physical evidence

We have moved away from marketplaces to marketspaces, themed environments designed to stimulate our senses while motivating us to empty our wallets.

(Solomon, 2004: 8)

Chapter objectives

This chapter will provide you with an understanding of the importance of the service firm's physical evidence regarding customer perceptions of the quality of services provided.

After reading this chapter, you should be able to:

- Appreciate the strategic role of physical evidence as it relates to the marketing of service firms.

- Outline the stimulus–response model.

- Discuss the major components of the servicescapes model.

- Describe the use of sensory cues when developing tactical design strategies.

- Compare design considerations for low-versus high-customer-contact firms.

Services in context
Portmeirion, the fairy tale hotel

Clough Williams-Ellis fantasized about opening the perfect hotel and restaurant. His imaginings became reality in 1925 when he began to build Portmeirion in North Wales. The beautiful and dream-like village sports Castell Deudraeth, which overlooks the estuary, the Portmeirion Hotel which looks onto the shore, and the self-catering cottages that make up the village. Castell Deudraeth is a prime example of how a firm's servicescape differentiates it from competitors and packages the services within.

In 1926 the Portmeirion Hotel was transformed from a derelict house to an eclectic hotel which has been added to many times over the years. In its first year a tower-like wing was built and lime-washed in yellow which made the hotel stand out like a magical castle.

Additional buildings and improvements were made to complement the inspirational ideas of Williams-Evans. The dinning room is shaped like, and has the atmosphere of, a beautiful ocean liner and is fuelled with stunning curvilinear art deco. The dining room was inspired and designed by Sir Terence Conran. Every other room in the hotel is enthused with quality furnishings; each has a theme of its own. For example, The Bridge House Room 4 is a twin bedroom, which as it name suggests has been built on top of an arched bridge. It is situated on the first floor overlooking the village square to the west and the estuary to the south. The fabric used for the bedding, cushions and curtains are traditional crewel work from Kashmir and the decor reflects this Eastern flavour. The Bridge House Room 4, therefore, has a luxurious, exotic feel because of the physical evidence provided in the décor and furnishings. The Salutation Room, situated in the Triumphal Arch, is a double room with views over the village centre. This room has a country style theme with blue and yellow flowers incorporated in the soft furnishings. This room reflects the fact that it was originally the loft of a Victorian stable block and provides a traditional, relaxing feel in the bedroom.

Portmeirion Hotel is not the only hotel to use physical evidence to create a theme. The Sea Spray Boutique Hotel in Brighton has used physical evidence to a greater extent by creating, among others, a Salvador Dali room, a Marrakech double room, an Oriental suite, and a saucy Boudoir room.

Sources: http://www.portmeirion-village.com/en/accommodation3.php?PID = 201&sM_id = 3&ptype = 6. www.brighton.co.uk/themed_hotel_rooms. http://www. portmeirion-village.com.

SOURCE IMAGE COURTESY OF THE PORT MEIRION HOTEL

Introduction

Managing the firm's physical evidence includes everything tangible, from the firm's physical facilities, to brochures and business cards and even the way the organization's personnel are dressed. A firm's physical evidence affects the consumer's experience throughout the duration of the service encounter. Therefore, consumers can have negative or positive feelings about an organization based on just the physical evidence of the reception area or external car park facilities because these physical clues give a 'suggestion' as to the whole service encounter. Consider the average consumer's visit to a High Street bank. Physical stimuli such as prominent large windows have a positive psychological effect on a consumer's visit as the bank will feel light, airy and open. However, consumers feel that bandit screens are intimidating and make the bank personnel seem austere and remote. Consumers prefer approaching staff who are seated at a reception desk, with additional chairs on which they can sit and chat openly about their banking needs (Greenland and McGoldrick, 2005). The same could be said about all service encounters. People who are collecting welfare or child benefit payments would also prefer an open, friendly environment where they feel welcomed.

The consumer experience of a service provider begins prior to the service actually taking place. Prior to entering the bank, customers begin to evaluate it based on advertising they may have seen on television, on the internet or in the telephone directory. As the consumer approaches the bank, the ease with which the bank can be found, the bank's signage, and the building itself all enter into the consumer's evaluation process. Similarly, the cleanliness of the ATM, the front entrance and the foyer has an affect on the consumer's expectations and perceptions.

Upon entering, the bank's furnishings and the bank's counter top should be spotless to create an ambience of order and precision expected of an organization that deals with a consumer's finances. Additionally, when customers are waiting for their turn to see a cashier at the bank, they will look for tangible cues that will advise them when it is their turn to move to the cashier. The cues could be visual, sound or gesture, all of which are part of the physical environment. Visual cues often take the form of cashier desks being numbered and an LCD sign showing which cashier is available. Alternatively, the same principle can be used with a voice recording stating which cashier desk is available. Additional evaluations occur as consumers ask questions such as – Is there a pen? Is the cashier smart? Is the cashier cheerful? Does the cashier greet me in an appropriate manner? Is the cash till, that holds my cash and cheques, tidy?

As the banking transaction takes place, how the cash, foreign currency or statements are presented is yet another indicator of the bank's quality. The final part of the consumer experience is the farewell from the cashier; did the cashier say thank-you and, most of all, did they mean it? After consumers have left the bank they will subconsciously or consciously make comparisons of the service they received with their own expectations and with previous visits they have made to this bank and other banks.

It is not just banks that should plan carefully their physical surroundings; all service organizations need to understand the value that physical

Banks are removing physical barriers to increase the quality of service provided for their customers.

cues have on the overall service experience their customers encounter. In fact service organizations should take pride in the physical evidence that they provide. The Square & Compass, a local pub in Dorset, was awarded first place in 'Britain's 10 best pubs with Gardens' (Crump, 2008). As the name of the pub implies, The Square & Compass was a local hostelry to quarrymen who would call for a beer or cider on their way home from work. The Newman family have been landlords of the pub for 101 years and have an amazing beer garden. The beer garden has stone sculptures dotted around and every table is a 'mini Stonehenge'. Wandering in and out of the stone sculptures are hens and geese that are happy to share their garden with customers enjoying a drink at the pub. There is a stone-carving festival in midsummer and the view from the gardens over the village rooftops is breathtaking. The Newman family have taken great care to ensure the physical evidence of their beer garden is so inviting that it will encourage people to explore the garden and venture inside for refreshments.

The strategic role of physical evidence

tangibles Items that are part of the firm's physical evidence, such as business cards, stationery, billing statements, reports, employee appearance, uniforms and brochures.

facility exterior The physical exterior of the service facility; includes the exterior design, signage, parking, landscaping and the surrounding environment.

facility interior The physical interior of the service facility; includes the interior design, equipment used to serve customers, signage, layout, air quality and temperature.

Due to the intangibility of services, service quality is difficult for consumers to objectively evaluate. As a result, consumers often rely on the tangibles or physical evidence that surrounds the service to help them form their evaluations (see Table 10.1). The role of physical evidence, therefore, in the marketing of intangibles is multifaceted. Physical evidence can fall into three broad categories: (1) facility exterior, (2) facility interior and (3) other tangibles. Examples of the elements that compose the facility exterior include the exterior design, signage, parking, landscaping and the surrounding environment. For example, the facility may be built on a mountainside, overlooking a lake. The facility interior includes elements such as the interior design, equipment used to serve the customer directly or used to run the business, signage, layout, air quality and temperature. Other elements that form part of the firm's physical evidence, which in turn attract the consumer, include the use of colours, temperature, music, scents and attractive design (Bitner, 2000)

The extensive use of physical evidence varies by the type of service firm (see Figure 10.1). Service firms such as hospitals, sporting events and child-care facilities often make extensive use of physical evidence in facility design and other tangibles associated with the service. In contrast, service firms such as express mail drop-off or dry cleaners use limited physical evidence. Regardless of the variation in usage, all service firms need to recognize that the physical evidence helps to shape the value proposition of the organization in the mind of the consumer. The physical evidence, therefore:

- packages the service with tangible clues that communicate an image to the consumer;
- facilitate, through design, the flow of activities that consumers and employees need to accomplish;

- socialize customers and employees alike in terms of their respective roles, behaviours and relationships; and
- differentiate the firm from its competitors and communicate this image to the core target market.

(Bitner 2000)

For example, nurseries, such as École International Malherbe near Paris, offer a service to the infants that is an interactive experience with carefully managed physical evidence. The physical environment, therefore, comprises

Table 10.1

The importance of physical evidence

Source Adapted from Hoffman, Kelley and Chung (2003) 'A CIT Investigation of Servicescape Failures and Associated Recovery Strategies', *Journal of Services Marketing* 17 (4): 322–340.

An organization's exterior appearance, interior design, and other tangibles create a package that surrounds the service. In a study of 1,540 hospitality-related service failures, 123 of the failures were attributed to problems associated with the hospitality firms' management of their physical evidence. Typical problems are described below.

Facility-based failures
Mechanical problems

Core mechanical problems (e.g., core service is not available due to catastrophic
    mechanical problems such as airline engine problems)
Mechanical problems relating to the core (e.g., core service is available; however, inoperative equipment relating to the core inconvenienced the customer such as bar code scanners, heating systems, ice machines)

Cleanliness issues

Foreign object (nonliving/nonhuman-related) (e.g., foreign objects such as plastic, wood and glass found in food, bedding or changing rooms)
Foreign object (human-related) (e.g., foreign objects such as hair, blood, fingernails and used band-aids found in food, cafés or changing rooms)
Foreign object (insect/animal-related) (e.g., foreign objects such as ants, flies, mice and worms found in food, hotel restaurants, or stock rooms)
General cleanliness issues (e.g., hotel room or plane not cleaned or deteriorating conditions)
Smells (e.g., strange and/or offensive odours)

Design issues

Poor facility planning (e.g., undesirable view from room, sleeping quarters located next to hotel ballrooms and/or elevators, slippery walkways, insufficient access for mothers with prams or wheelchair users)

play, relaxation and learning environments. Sensory and exploratory play is extremely important for the development of infants and nurseries have sand pits, sponges, cooking areas, brightly coloured mobiles and music to appeal to the senses of the children. The theme created by using cues in the physical environment features strongly at École International Malherbe in the décor, play areas and directed activities.

Packaging

The firm's physical evidence plays a major role in packaging the service. The service itself is intangible and, therefore, does not require a package for purely functional reasons. However, utilizing the firm's physical evidence to package the service does send quality cues to consumers and adds value to the service in terms of image development. Image development, in turn, improves consumer perceptions of service while reducing both levels of perceived risk associated with the purchase and levels of cognitive dissonance after the purchase.

The firm's exterior appearance, interior elements and other tangibles create the package that surrounds the service. The firm's physical facility forms the customer's initial impression concerning the type and quality of service provided. For example, local delicatessen stores often have a theme, such as 'Traditional', 'Italian' or 'Gourmet'. Many delicatessens utilize specific types of architectural designs that communicate to customers their firms' offerings. The firm's physical evidence also conveys expectations to consumers. Consumers will have one set of expectations for a restaurant with mood lighting in dining rooms, soft music, and linen tablecloths and napkins and a different set of expectations for a restaurant that has bright lighting, cement floors, plastic tablecloths, paper serviettes and loud popular music.

Facilitating the service process

Another use of the firm's physical evidence is to facilitate the flow of activities that produce the service. Physical evidence can provide information to customers on how the service production process works. Take for instance a trip to the airport. Physical evidence is helpful in facilitating the flow of travellers. For example, physical evidence includes signage that specifically

Figure 10.1

Variations in usage of physical evidence

Source Mary J. Bitner, 'Servicescapes: The Impact of Physical Surroundings on Customers and Employees', *Journal of Marketing* 56, 2 (April 1992), p. 60. Reprinted with permission of the American Marketing Association.

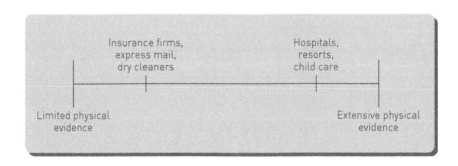

instructs consumers who wish to find their way to the café, duty free shop or internet wifi zone; menus that explain the restaurant's offerings and advises whether the restaurant is self-service or waiter service; and physical structures that direct the flow of consumers while waiting for their flight, and barriers, such as the baggage check-in desk, that separate the technical core of the business from the travellers. All of these clues help 'move the traveller through the service encounter' in a stress-free manner.

Socializing employees and customers

Organizational socialization is the process by which an individual adapts to and comes to appreciate the values, norms and required behaviour patterns of an organization. The firm's physical evidence plays an important part in the socialization process by conveying expected roles, behaviours and relationships among employees and between employees and customers. The purpose of the socialization process is to project a positive and consistent image to the public. However, the service firm's image is only as good as the image each employee conveys when interacting with the public (Solomon, 2004). Therefore, it is important to ensure that each employee knows their role; more about the value of employees in shown in Chapter 11.

socialization The process by which an individual adapts to the values, norms and required behaviour patterns of an organization.

Physical evidence, such as the use of uniforms, facilitates the socialization of employees towards accepting organizational goals and affects consumer perceptions of the calibre of service provided. Studies have shown that the use of uniforms:

- aids in identifying the firm's personnel,
- presents a physical symbol that embodies the group's ideals and attributes,
- implies a coherent group structure,
- facilitates the perceived consistency of performance,
- provides a tangible symbol of an employee's change in status (e.g., military uniforms change as personnel move through the ranks), and
- assists in controlling the behaviour of errant employees.

(Solomon, 2004)

A means for differentiation

The effective management of the physical evidence can also be a source of differentiation. For example, several airlines are now expanding the amount of leg room available for passengers. In addition, the appearance of personnel and facilities often has a direct impact on how consumers perceive that the firm will handle the service aspects of its business. Numerous studies have shown that well-dressed individuals are perceived as being more intelligent, better workers and more pleasant. Similarly, beautifully designed facilities are going to be perceived as having the advantage over poorly designed facilities.

Differentiation can also be achieved by utilizing physical evidence to reposition the service firm in the eyes of its customers. Upgrading the firm's

organizm The recipients of the set of stimuli in the service encounter; includes employees and customers.

environmental psychology The use of physical evidence to create service environments and its influence on the perceptions and behaviour of individuals.

stimulus–response model A model developed by environmental psychologists to help explain the effects of the service environment on consumer behaviour; describes environmental stimuli, emotional states, and responses to those states.

facilities often upgrades the image of the firm in the minds of consumers and may also attract more desirable market segments, which further aids in differentiating the firm from its competitors. B2B Services in Action shows just how a flight with one organization can be a whole new experience based on additional space, services and fabulously designed casinos and restaurants – all at 15,000 feet in the air! However, it is important to note that too many elaborate features and upgrades may alienate some customers who believe that the firm may be passing on the costs of the upgrade to consumers through higher prices. This is precisely why many offices are decorated professionally, but not lavishly.

The stimulus–resonse model

As already outlined, physical evidence influences the emotions and behaviours of consumers (Gilboa and Rafaeli, 2003). Therefore, creative use of the service environment can affect the perceptions and behaviours of individuals or organizms. The effect is referred to as environmental psychology. Mehrabrian and Russell (1974) presented a categorization of human emotions which was later developed by Donovan and Rossiter (1982) to form the stimulus–response model. The stimulus–response

B2B services in action
The Airbus A380: The world's largest passenger plane

One of the primary roles of a firm's physical evidence is to provide a means of differentiation among competing alternatives. A current example can be found in the B2B airline industry where European-based Airbus is attempting to differentiate its products from American-based Boeing. On 27 April 2005, Airbus unveiled its giant Airbus A380 as a direct attempt to increase passenger plane sales to the world's air carriers. According to French President, Jacques Chirac, 'A new page in aviation history has been written. It is a magnificent result of European industrial cooperation.'

The new jumbo jetliner, which weighs 308 tons, took Airbus 11 years to build and costs approximately $13 billion. Boeing had passed on making the new jumbo jet in favour of concentrating its business efforts on the construction of smaller, long-range jets like its Boeing 787 Dreamliner. However, Airbus believes that A380 improvements will reduce per-passenger costs by as much as 20 per cent and is ideal for

airlines flying between the world's airport hubs. Airbus has currently received 154 orders for the A380 from 15 different carriers including Virgin, Lufthansa and Air France.

The Airbus A380 is huge! Due to enter service for Singapore Airlines in 2006, the A380 is 80 feet tall (equivalent to a seven-storey building), 239 feet long, boasts a wingspan of 262 feet, and can fly approximately 8,000 nautical miles. In comparison, a Boeing 747 is 64 feet tall, 232 feet long, includes a wingspan of 211 feet, and flies 7,670 nautical miles. The Airbus A380 can carry up to 840 passengers on two decks or, if preferred, the space can be redesigned to include shops, a casino, and restaurant on the lower deck with passenger space maintained above.

Source: Laurence Frost, 'Biggest Bird Takes to the Sky: Airbus A380 Makes Aviation History with Maiden Flights', *The Coloradoan* (28 April 2005): D8-D7. Laurence Frost is a writer for the Associated Press.

model is presented in Figure 10.2 and is often used to help explain the effects the service environment has on consumer behaviour (Machleit and Eroglu, 2000; Moye and Kincade (2002).

The physical environment, consciously or unconsciously, influences how people feel. Therefore, the environmental stimuli in cafés, hairdressing salons, rock concert, retail stores, or dentist offices make consumers and employees feel certain emotions. The emotions are then interpreted and can be reflected in the way consumers and employees behave (see Figure 10.2). The Mediating Emotions are central to the model and it is these emotions that drive consumer behaviour. The responses of employees and customers to the set of stimuli are influenced by three basic emotional states: pleasure–displeasure, arousal–nonarousal, and dominance–submissiveness. The pleasure–displeasure emotional state reflects the degree to which consumers and employees feel satisfied with the service experience. The arousal–nonarousal state reflects the degree to which consumers and employees feel excited and stimulated. The third emotional state, dominance–submissiveness, reflects feelings of control and the ability to act freely within the service environment. Ideally, service firms should utilize physical evidence to build environments that appeal to pleasure and arousal states, and stay away from creating atmospheres that create submissiveness.

Consumers and employees respond to the set of environmental stimuli that are characterized as approach behaviours or avoidance behaviours. Consumer 'approach' and 'avoidance' behaviours and outcomes can be demonstrated in any combination of the following four ways (Ghosh, 1994):

1 a desire to stay (approach) or leave (avoid) the service establishment,

2 a desire to further explore and interact with the service environment (approach) or a tendency to ignore it (avoidance),

3 a desire to communicate with others (approach) or to ignore the attempts of service providers to communicate with customers (avoid), or

4 feelings of satisfaction (approach) or disappointment (avoidance) with the service experience.

stimuli The various elements of the firm's physical evidence.

responses (outcomes) Consumers' reactions or behaviours in response to stimuli.

pleasure–displeasure The emotional state that reflects the degree to which consumers and employees feel satisfied with the service experience.

arousal–nonarousal The emotional state that reflects the degree to which consumers and employees feel excited and stimulated.

dominance–submissiveness The emotional state that reflects the degree to which consumers and employees feel in control and able to act freely within the service environment.

approach/avoidance behaviours Consumer responses to the set of environmental stimuli that are characterized by a desire to stay or leave an establishment, explore/ interact with the service environment or just ignore it, or feel satisfaction or disappointment with the service experience.

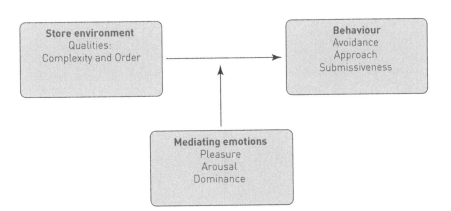

Figure 10.2

Stimulus–response model

Source Adapted from A. Mehrabian and J. A. Russell, *An Approach to Environmental Psychology*, Cambridge, MA: MIT Press, 1974.

In addition to the stimulus–response model, Russell (1980) went on to say that emotional responses lay in two areas, pleasant/unpleasant and arousing/sleepy; see Russell's Model of Affect, Figure 10.3. Feelings of pleasure/displeasure are subjective responses to the environment, dependent upon whether the consumer likes or dislikes the environment. States of arousal and sleepiness are internal states that occur dependent upon high and low levels of adrenaline in the bloodstream (Lovelock and Wirtz, 2007). Marketers should use the pleasant/unpleasant and arousing/sleepy dimensions when they decide how to ensure that their environment will stimulate their consumers. For example, a local Greek restaurant that encourages the plate smashing tradition would stimulate arousal and be exciting and it would heighten its guests' adrenaline. However, the surroundings and services offered by a physiotherapist should make the customers feel pleasantly relaxed. Alternatively, store environments such as Primark or other low-cost retailers often create an unpleasant feeling as the adrenalin and stress levels are raised as shoppers find the servicescape untidy and noisy and the flow of movement between goods is not logical. The 'rushed' feeling consumers have in low-cost stores are created so that customers move through the service encounter quickly. Stores do not wish customers in low-cost outlets to dwell and linger for prolonged periods. These experiences described are plotted in Figure 10.3, Russell's Model of Affect.

The development of servicescapes

servicescapes All the non-living features that comprise the service environment.

The framework presented in Figure 10.4 shows the fundamentals of the stimulus–organizm–response model that directly applies to the influence of the service firm's physical evidence on consumers' and employees' subsequent behaviours. The term servicescapes refers to the use of physical evidence to design service environments. Due to inseparability, the model recognizes that the firm's environment is likely to affect consumers and employees alike. However, the facility should be designed to meet the needs of those individuals who spend the most time within the

| **Figure 10.3**

Russell model of affect

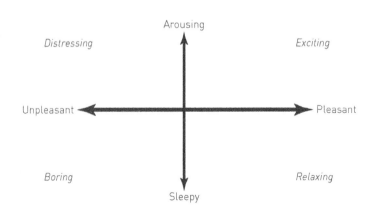

confines of the facility. Global Services in Action highlights the importance of ensuring that every physical element of the service encounter is considered with care, and more importantly that all physical elements must be interrelated.

Remote, self-service, and interpersonal services

Figure 10.5 presents a continuum of facility usage by service type. Some services, such as mail order, online facilities for paying household gas and electric bills, call centres, online banking or online retailers such as www. ebay.co.uk are described as remote services. In remote services, employees have a physical presence; they pack the mail order products, or take the telephone calls. The service, therefore, is at a *remote* location. Consequently, facility design should facilitate the employees' efforts and enhance motivation, productivity and employee satisfaction. See E-Services in Action for details of how Google provides the ultimate remote service.

At the other end of the spectrum are services and goods that customers can acquire on their own and service their own requirements through self-service. Self-service environments are dominated by the customer's physical presence and include services such as ATMs, miniature golf courses, postal kiosks and self-service car washes. The environment of

remote services
Services in which employees are physically present while customer involvement in the service production process is at arm's length.

self-services Service environments that are dominated by the customer's physical presence, such as ATMs or postal kiosks.

Figure 10.4

Comprehensive stimulus–response model

Source M. J. Bitner (1992) 'Servicescapes: The impact of physical surroundings on customers and employees', *Journal of Marketing* 56 (April): 57–71.

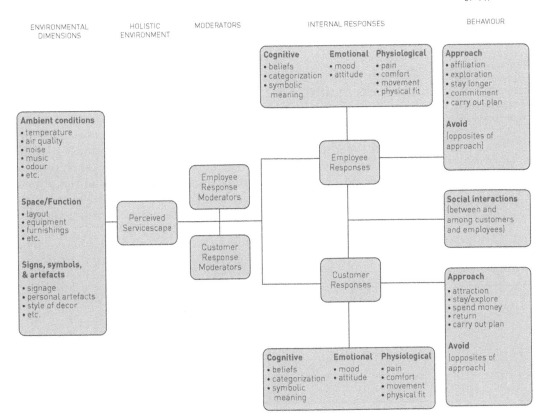

self-service establishments should be constructed to enhance customer attraction and satisfaction.

In contrast to remote and self-service environments, many services such as restaurants, hospitals, beauty salons, nail bars, hotels, banks and airlines are interpersonal services, where the physical space is shared jointly by consumers and employees. The environment of interpersonal services should be developed with the needs of both parties involved and should facilitate the social interaction between and among customers and employees.

interpersonal services Service environments in which customers and providers interact.

Physical environmental dimensions

The servicescapes model depicted in Figure 10.6 (p. 274) immediately recognizes the set of stimuli that are commonly utilized when developing service environments. In broad terms, the set of stimuli include ambient conditions; space/function; and signs, symbols, and artifacts. Ambient conditions reflect the distinctive atmosphere of the service setting and include elements such as lighting, air quality, noise and music, such as low lighting and soft music to create a romantic atmosphere. Environmental dimensions that pertain to the use of space/function include elements such as the layout of the facility, equipment and the firm's furnishings, such as hygienically clean equipment at a dentist's surgery. Signs, symbols, and artefacts include signage that directs the flow of the service process, personal artefacts which lend character and individuality that personalize the facility, and the style of decor, such as themed, contemporary, or traditional in a coffee shop.

ambient conditions The distinctive atmosphere of the service setting that includes lighting, air quality, noise and music.

space/function Environmental dimensions that include the layout of the facility, the equipment and the firm's furnishings.

signs, symbols and artefacts Environmental physical evidence that includes signage to direct the flow of the service process, personal artefacts to personalize the facility, and the style of decor.

Holistic environment

The holistic environment portion of the servicescapes model pertains to the perceptions of the servicescape that employees and consumers form based on all of the physical and environmental dimensions; in other words, the holistic environment. The holistic environment, therefore, is a perceived overall image of the service organization based on the physical evidence. This is referred to in the model as the perceived servicescape. The perceived servicescape is difficult to define precisely, and perceptions

holistic environment Overall perceptions of the servicescape formed by employees and customers based on the physical environmental dimensions.

perceived servicescape A composite of mental images of the service firm's physical facilities.

Figure 10.5

Facility usage

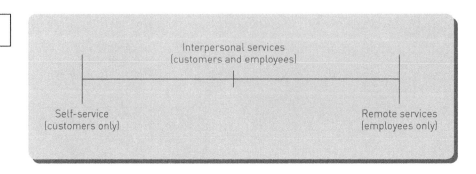

of the same establishment will vary among individuals; operatic music may be sheer enjoyment for some consumers, but for others it may spoil their satisfaction of the service encounter. Essentially, the perceived servicescape is a composite of mental images of the service firm's physical facilities.

Strategically managing the perceived servicescape helps to establish a positioning strategy that differentiates one service organization from their competitors. Additionally, the perceived servicescape influences the

---

Global services in action
Disneyland in Paris

Disneyland is a prime example of how a firm's servicescape differentiates itself from competitors and packages the services within. Disneyland's servicescape has been purposely designed to reinforce its image as the Magic Kingdom. Adults and children alike are captivated by the sights and sounds that comprise the Disney environment. Disneyland Paris (originally named Euro Disney) opened in 1992 and whichever Disneyland you have visited or seen on the television, they have a basic servicescape – although each one has some small adaptations based on the country in which it is built. The servicescape familiarity is helpful to customers as they can develop ideas with regard to the service experience based on past visits or by assessing the physical evidence presented to them through advertisements or brochures.

But... somehow Disneyland Paris does not seem to sit well in its environment because it is, well, ... so American in its feel, shape and commercialization. Maybe it's the pink pastel towers of the magical and mythical Disneyland Hotel that are awe-inspiring as they abruptly appear, like magic, out of the plains of Merne-la-Vallee. The bright colours, the sounds and the smells somehow seem out of place.

But, once inside it is impossible not to get swept along with the American myths, Hollywood pizzazz, Mickey Mouse and all his friends. Everything in Disneyland is make-believe. The physical evidence is all larger than life; even the hotels and cafés seem to be made out of brightly coloured sweets and toffees.

It is easy to move around Disneyland Paris as there is clear signposting – in French and English. And the designers and marketing managers at Disneyland Paris have tried to include some of France's own cultural icons. American-born Disney characters in their bright coloured uniforms join the parade to entertain their guests and thank them for joining in the fun. But the floats were created by the French-Romanian designer Petrika Ionesco and Daniel Ogier designed the period costumes for some of the musicians, dancers and actors. Whilst 'France' has been included in the design elements, Disneyland Paris is still projecting American Dream-like fun during the parade.

Upon close inspection there are some other European icons in Disneyland Paris such as Can-Can girls who appear in the Lucky Nugget Diamond Lil's saloon. And two of the attractions are more aligned to European culture – Space Mountain has had a 'name change' to De la Terre à la Lune ('From the Earth to the Moon') and Cinderella's Golden Carousel is called Lancelot's Merry-Go Round. So the physical evidence at Disneyland is one of the main elements in the marketing mix that makes it unique.

Source: www.disneylandparis.co.uk.

economic customers
Consumers who make purchase decisions based primarily on price.

customer decision process when choosing among competing alternatives. The service organizations must develop the servicescape with its target market in mind. Economic customers, who make purchase decisions based on price, will avoid service establishments that appear to have spent large amounts of money on plush surroundings, extravagant furnishings and tailored staff uniforms. It is likely that the economic consumer will perceive the establishment to be a high-priced provider. Economic customers tend to be attracted to environments that are simple yet reflect quality and those that are clean and modern. Some hairdressers such as Notaufnahme (translated to mean 'accident and emergency') in Berlin use this type of environment. Notaufnahme is a hairdressing business that appeals to those customers who feel a haircut is more a functional service than a service where they wish to feel pampered. The hairdresser's shop is functional, neat and tidy, no appointment is necessary and there is a self-service coffee vending machine for consumers and staff. The Notaufnahme has recycled hospital beds, so that consumers can relax while waiting for their haircut. The price of the haircut is low, due to the 'no frills' service environment and easy availability. In contrast, personalized customers want to be pampered and attended to and are much less price sensitive when choosing among providers. Therefore, organizations catering to personalized shoppers create environments that reflect the status their customers seek by investing more in items such as

personalized customers
Consumers who desire to be pampered and attended to and who are much less price sensitive.

Figure 10.6

The servicescapes model: A framework for understanding environment-user relationships in service organizations

Source Mary J. Bitner, 'Servicescapes: The Impact of Physical Surroundings on Customers and Employees,' *Journal of Marketing* 60, no. 2 (April 1992), 60. Reprinted with permission of the American Marketing Association.

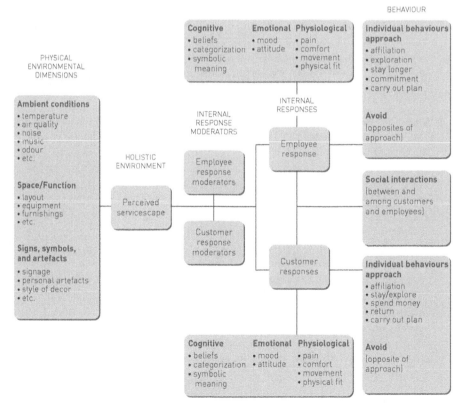

marble foyers, glass and brass fixtures, and furnishings that encourage customers to shop at a leisurely pace. For example, Clipso in London has a personalized service, where stylists spend time discussing needs with their customers. The physical environment is very modern and the gallery of award-winning collections, by stylists, gives inspiring ideas. Similarly, firms that wish to service apathetic customers, who seek convenience, or ethical customers, who support smaller or local organizations, need to ensure that the physical environment fits the type of service encounter their target audience requires.

apathetic customers
Consumers who seek convenience over price and personal attention.

ethical customers
Consumers who support smaller or local firms as opposed to larger or national service providers.

E-services in action
Google.com's servicescape: When less is more

One of the secrets behind Google's success has been the thoughtful management of its own servicescape. The components of an online servicescape consist of the website's layout of text and graphics; colours; product depictions; use of flash media, streaming video and audio; and advertisements, just to name a few elements. In the early days of the internet, it seemed like the fancier the website the better. Web designers were literally in a race to outdo one another for bragging rights. However, in the end, all that really mattered was whether the website effectively served customers.

Google's success story is extraordinary! Google entered the search engine market in 1998, long after its counterparts Yahoo and Excite. However, Google made three great decisions that eventually led to it being named Global Brand of the Year. First, Google found the right technology for the right price. The company's two young co-founders, Sergey Brin and Larry Page, built their own system from commodity hardware parts and were able to pack in eight times as much server power in the same space as competitors. Second, Google's search strategy is innovative. Instead of being based solely on keyword searches, a Google search is based on the site's popularity. As a result, a Google search is directed more by human input than technology. The end result is that users typically receive more relevant information. Finally, Google.com provides an excellent example of how sometimes 'less is more'. Google uses simple graphics, allows no advertising on its home page, and within its website allows only banner advertisements without graphics. Consequently, Google's servicescape downloads faster than competitive offerings and is easier to read since it is less distracting.

As a testament to Google's effectiveness, the company performs 250 million searches on its 4 billion and growing web pages a day. Customers can 'google' in 88 languages and many customers are doing just that! Google is the fourth most visited US website and is ranked in the top three in most European countries. In the past few years, Google's revenue growth and employee expansion rate have been in the triple digits. Today, it is estimated that Google powers 54 per cent of all searches worldwide.

Source: Judy Strauss, Adel El-Ansary and Raymond Frost, *E-Marketing*, Fourth Edition (Upper Saddle River, NJ: Pearson Prentice Hall, 2006), p. 241.

SOURCE © 2008 GOOGLE

Internal response moderators

internal response moderators The three basic emotional states of the SOR model that mediate the reaction between the perceived servicescape and customers' and employees' responses to the service environment.

The moderators in the servicescape model are both the customer and the employee. The internal response moderators of the servicescapes model therefore pertain to the three basic emotional states of pleasure–displeasure, arousal–nonarousal, and dominance–submissiveness shown in the stimulus–response model. The three response moderators mediate the reaction between the perceived servicescape and customers' and employees' responses to the service environment. For example, if a customer desires to remain in a state of nonarousal and spend a nice, quiet evening with someone special, that customer will avoid bright, loud and crowded service establishments. He or she would, in turn, be attracted to environments that are more peaceful and conducive to conducting conversation. Similarly, the employees' responses to the firm's environment will also be affected by their own emotional states. Sometimes employees look forward to engaging in conversations with customers. Other days, employees would just as soon minimize conversations and process customers as raw materials on a production line. Response moderators help explain why services are characterized by heterogeneity as the service varies from provider to provider, and even from day to day with the same provider.

Internal responses to the environment

Theory asserts that customers and employees are exposed to the set of stimuli that make up the firm's perceived servicescape and the responses to these stimuli are moderated by emotional states. Customers and employees internally respond to the firm's environment at different levels – cognitively, emotionally and physiologically.

cognitive responses The thought processes of individuals that lead them to form beliefs, categorize and assign symbolic meanings to elements of their physical environment.

beliefs Consumers' opinions about the provider's ability to perform the service.

Cognitive responses. Cognitive responses are the thought processes of individuals and, according to the model, include beliefs, categorization and symbolic meaning. In the formation of beliefs, the firm's environment acts as a form of non-verbal communication and influences a consumer's beliefs about the provider's ability to perform the service. For example, the waiting area at the check-out is often ineffective, boring and frustrating for consumers. Consumers have a perceived 'waiting time' in their minds (Pruyn and Smidts, 1998). If the 'waiting time' is exceeded, consumers become angry and frustrated. If the 'waiting time' is acceptable, consumers remain satisfied with the overall experience. Therefore, organizations need to improve the consumers' environment and to manage lengthy waiting times. For example, consumers often have a number of 'waiting experiences' when they wish to watch a football match. Large stadiums manage the waiting times so as to avoid cognitive notions of poor service at the football ground. Improvements to the environment include numerous entrances and ticket collection points, so as to avoid bottlenecks and large, clear signage to ensure free movement of football fans (Hightower Jr. et al., 2002). If the provider's waiting areas are crowded, with no signage advising football fans where to queue or advice about their seating, they are more likely to attribute poor service to the provider. Hence, physical evidence assists customers with beliefs about the provider's success, price for services and competence. Employees form similar types of beliefs about the firm based on the overall perceived servicescape.

Categorization is the second type of cognitive response. Bars and night-clubs operate within a number of environments. Some are high-class establishments, and others cater strictly to local clientele or specific market segments. The process of categorization facilitates human understanding at a quicker pace. Consumers assess the physical evidence and often quickly categorize new service establishments with existing types of operations. They then access the appropriate behaviour script for the type of operation and act accordingly.

Individuals also infer symbolic meaning from the firm's use of physical evidence. For example, Hemingway's is a bar in Zagreb – Croatia. The bar has the name of a famous writer known for his brilliance and liberty, but also known for being a heavy drinker. The bar has memorabilia, photographs, expensive spirits, chintz furniture – all typical of Hemingway and his era. The physical evidence may translate into a number of symbols, such as individuality, youthful success, shattered dreams, or other meanings, depending on individual interpretation. Symbolic meaning through the use of physical evidence aids in differentiation and positioning.

categorization
Consumer assessment of the physical evidence and a quick mental assignment of a firm to a known group of styles or types.

symbolic meaning
Meaning inferred from the firm's use of physical evidence.

Emotional responses. In addition to forming beliefs, individuals will also respond to the firm's physical environment on an emotional level. Emotional responses do not involve thinking; they simply happen, often inexplicably and suddenly. Specific songs, for example, may make individuals feel happy, feel sad, or recreate other past feelings that were associated with the particular piece of music. Scents have similar effects on individuals. Obviously, the goal of effective physical evidence management is to stimulate positive emotions that create atmospheres in which employees love to work and customers want to spend their time and money.

emotional responses
Responses to the firm's physical environment on an emotional level instead of an intellectual or social level.

Physiological responses. In contrast to cognitive and emotional responses, physiological responses are often described in terms of physical pleasure or discomfort. Typical physiological responses involve pain and comfort. Environments in which music is played very loudly may lead to employee and customer discomfort and movement away from the source of the noise. Instead of being arousing, environments that are brightly lit may cause eye discomfort. In contrast, a dimly lit restaurant may cause eye strain as customers struggle to read their menus. All these responses determine whether a customer will approach and explore the firm's offerings or avoid and leave the premises to minimize the amount of physiological discomfort. Because of the duration of time spent in the firm's facility, employees might find the physical environment particularly harmful if mismanaged. Adequate work space, proper equipment to get the job done and appropriate ambient conditions such as temperature and air quality are directly related to employees' willingness to continue to work,

physiological responses
Responses to the firm's physical environment based on pain or comfort.

their productivity while at work, their job satisfaction and their positive interactions with co-workers.

Behavioural responses to the environment

Individual behaviour. As stated in the section on the fundamentals of the stimulus–organizm–response (SOR) model, individual responses to environmental stimuli are characterized as approach and avoidance behaviour. In retail settings, the store's environment influences approach behaviour such as:

- shopping enjoyment,
- repeat visits,
- favourable impressions of the store,
- money spent,
- time spent, and
- willingness of consumers to stay and explore the store.

In other instances, environmental stimuli have been purposely managed to discourage unwelcome market segments. For example, convenience stores have cleverly used 'elevator music' (e.g., Muzak – boring music) outside their stores to repel unwelcome neighbourhood gangs that 'hang out' in the store's parking lot and deter desired clientele from entering the store.

Social interactions. Due to the inseparability inherent in interpersonal services, the firm's servicescape should encourage interactions between employees and customers, among customers, and among employees. The challenge in creating such an environment is that often, what the customer desires, employees would prefer to forego so that they can complete their tasks with a minimum of customer involvement. Environmental variables such as physical proximity, seating arrangements, facility size and flexibility in changing the configuration of the servicescape define the possibilities and place limits on the amount of social interaction possible.

Consider the seating arrangements of a Japanese steakhouse, which combines different groups of customers at one table as opposed to traditional seating arrangements in which each party has its own table. Obviously, for better or worse, 'community seating' at a Japanese steakhouse encourages interaction among customers. In addition, each table is assigned its own chef who actively interacts with the customers during the production process. SMS or text massaging is often being used in nightclubs so that clubbers can find out the 'latest' place to be or find the love of their life. Therefore, nightclubs collect mobile phone numbers and then send text messages advertising drinks promotions, information about the latest DJ or inviting clubbers to the VIP lounge. This enables clubs to begin interacting with guests before they arrive at the club. Mobile dating is also used to encourage social interaction as flirting messages can be transmitted to large TV screens. Also interaction can take place between staff at a nightclub and customers without there being physical proximity. Clubbers can order drinks to be sent to people at another table or text song requests to the DJ. Text messages and large TV screens add to the physical environment and the number of social interactions that can take place in nightclubs.

Specific tactics for creating service atmospheres

When developing the facility's atmosphere, the service firm must consider the physical and psychological impact of the atmosphere on customers, employees and the firm's operations. Just as the firm cannot be all things to all people, the atmosphere developed will likely not appeal to all consumers. Therefore, firms should develop facilities with a particular target market in mind. Kotler as long ago as 1973 began suggesting that organizations should answer the following questions before implementing an atmosphere development plan:

1 Who is the firm's target market?
2 What does the target market seek from the service experience?
3 What atmospheric elements can reinforce the beliefs and emotional reactions that buyers seek?
4 How do these same atmospheric elements affect employee satisfaction and the firm's operations?
5 Does the suggested atmosphere development plan compete effectively with competitors' atmospheres?

Ultimately, individuals base their perceptions of a firm's facilities on their interpretation of sensory cues. The following section discusses how firms can utilize the senses of sight, sound, scent, touch and taste in creating sensory appeal that enhances customer and employee attraction responses (Lewison, 1991). Baker et al. (2002) state that all of the design appeals give clues as to the type of experience the customer will have. Indeed they go on to say that the design elements have a stronger and more persuasive effect than sound or employee interaction! However, as each of the chapters in this book identify, it is not individual elements that provide an excellent service for the customer, but all of the elements combined.

Sight appeals

The sense of sight conveys more information to consumers than any other sense and, therefore, should be considered as the most important means available to service firms when developing the firm's atmosphere. Sight appeals can be defined as the process of interpreting stimuli, resulting in perceived visual relationships. On a basic level, the three primary visual stimuli that appeal to consumers are size, shape, and colours. Consumers interpret visual stimuli in terms of visual relationships, consisting of perceptions of harmony, contrast and clash. Harmony refers to visual agreement and is associated with quieter, plushier and more formal business settings. In comparison, contrast and clash are associated with exciting, cheerful and informal

sight appeals Stimuli that result in perceived visual relationships.

size/shape/colours The three primary visual stimuli that appeal to consumers on a basic level.

harmony Visual agreement associated with quieter, plushier and more formal business settings.

contrast/clash Visual effects associated with exciting, cheerful and informal business settings.

business settings. Hence, based on the size, shape and colours of the visual stimuli utilized and the way consumers interpret the various visual relationships, extremely different perceptions of the firm emerge. For example, consider how different target markets might respond to entering a Chucky Cheese restaurant for the first time. Some segments would find the environment inviting, while others might be completely overwhelmed by too much stimuli.

Size perceptions. The actual size of the firm's facility, signs and departments conveys different meanings to different markets. In general, the larger the size of the organization and its corresponding physical evidence, the more consumers associates the firm with importance, power, success, security and stability. For many consumers, the larger the firm, the lower the perceived risk associated with the service purchase. Such consumers believe that larger firms are more competent and more likely to engage in service recovery efforts when problems do arise. Still other customers enjoy the prestige often associated with conducting business with a larger, well known, firm. On the flip side, other customers may view large firms as impersonal and uncaring and seek out smaller, niche firms that they view as more personal, intimate and friendly. Generally, high ceilings and large windows convey feelings of spaciousness, whereas low ceilings are associated with cosyness and intimacy (Ching, 1996). Hence, depending on the needs of the firm's target market, size appeals differently to different segments.

Shape. Shape perceptions of a service firm are created from a variety of sources, such as the use and placement of shelves, mirrors and windows, and even the design of wallpaper. Studies show that different shapes arouse different emotions in consumers. Vertical shapes or vertical lines are perceived as 'rigid, severe, and lend[ing] a masculine quality to an area. It expresses strength and stability...gives the viewer an up-and-down eye movement...tends to heighten an area, gives the illusion of increased space in this direction' (Mills and Paul, 1982). In contrast, horizontal shapes or lines evoke perceptions of relaxation and restfulness. Diagonal shapes and lines evoke perceptions of progressiveness, pro-activeness and movement. Curved shapes and lines are perceived as feminine and flowing. Utilizing similar and/or dissimilar shapes in facility design will create the desired visual relationship of harmony, contrast, or clash. For example, the use of several different shapes in one area might be utilized for emphasis.

Colour perceptions. The colour of the firm's physical evidence often makes the first impression, whether seen in the firm's brochure, the business cards of its personnel, or the exterior or interior of the facility itself (see E-Services in Action). It has long been recognized that white, yellow, orange, red, pink, purple, green, blue, brown, grey and black are colours which are easily recognized and little effort or thought is involved

(Davies and Corbett, 1995). It should be noted that black and white attract the least attention from the 11 recognizable colours (Evans et al., 1997). Service organizations should consider the speed at which colour is recognized to help consumers identify signage, staff uniforms or displays in the quickest time. Key physical cues, therefore, should be made from colours such as green that have a quick response time (1.92 seconds) and not peach which has the slowest response time (2.63 seconds) (Jansson et al., 2004). Psychological impact of colour upon individuals is the result of three properties: hue, value and intensity. *Hue* refers to the actual family of the colour, such as red, blue, yellow, or green. *Value* defines the lightness and darkness of the colours. Darker values are called *shades*, and lighter values are called *tints*. *Intensity* defines the brightness or dullness of the hue.

Hues are classified into warm and cool colours. Warm colours include red, yellow and orange hues, while cool colours include blue, green and violet hues. Warm and cool colours symbolize different things to different consumer groups, as presented in Table 10.2. In general, warm colours tend to evoke consumer feelings of energy and informality. For example, red commonly evokes feelings of love and romance and behaviour such as passion or excitement, yellow evokes feelings of sunlight and warmth leading to optimistic responses, and orange evokes feelings of openness and friendliness

Warm Colours			Cool Colours		
Red	**Yellow**	**Orange**	**Blue**	**Green**	**Violet**
Love	Sunlight	Sunlight	Coolness	Coolness	Coolness
Romance	Warmth	Warmth	Aloofness	Restfulness	Shyness
Sex	Cowardice	Openness	Fidelity	Peace	Dignity
Courage	Openness	Friendliness	Calmness	Freshness	Wealth
Danger	Friendliness	Gaiety	Piety	Growth	
Fire	Gaiety	Glory	Masculinity	Softness	
Sin	Glory		Assurance	Richness	
Warmth	Brightness		Sadness	Go	
Excitement	Caution				
Vigor					
Cheerfulness					
Enthusiasm					
Stop					

Table 10.2

Perceptions of colour

Source Dale M. Lewison, *Retailing*, 4th ed. (New York: Macmillan, 1991), p. 277.

which encourages verbal expressions. Studies have shown that warm colours, particularly red and yellow, are a better choice than cool colours for attracting customers in retail settings. Warm colours are also said to encourage quick decisions and to work best for businesses where low-involvement purchase decisions are made.

In contrast to warm colours, cool colours are perceived as aloof, icy and formal. For example, the use of too much violet may dampen consumer spirits and depress employees who have to continuously work in the violet environment. Although cool colours do not initially attract customers as well as warm colours, cool colours are preferred when the customer needs to take time to make decisions, such as the time needed for high-involvement purchases. For example, cool colours are a good choice for banks or insurance offices where consumers and staff need to remain calm and focused on their purchases. Despite their different psychological effects, when used together properly, combinations of warm and cool colours can create relaxing, yet stimulating atmospheres.

The value of hues also psychologically affects the firm's customers. Offices painted in lighter colours tend to look larger, while darker colours may make large, empty spaces look smaller. Lighter hues are also popular for fixtures such as electrical face plates, air conditioning vents and overhead speaker systems. The lighter colours help the fixtures blend in with the firm's environment. On the other hand, darker colours can be used to grab consumers' attention. Retailers are often faced with the problem that only 25 per cent of their customers ever make it more than halfway into the store. Some retailers have had limited success in attracting more customers farther into the store by painting the back wall in a darker colour that attracts the customer's attention.

The intensity of the colour also affects perceptions of the service firm's atmosphere. For example, bright colours make objects appear larger than do duller colours. However, bright colours are perceived as harsher and 'harder', while duller colours are perceived as 'softer'. In general, children appear to prefer brighter colours, and adults tend to prefer softer tones.

The location of the firm. The firm's location is dependent upon the amount of customer involvement necessary to produce the service. While low-customer-contact services should consider locating in remote sites that are less expensive and closer to sources of supply, transportation and labour, high-customer-contact services have other concerns. Typically, when evaluating locations for the firm, there are three questions that need to be addressed.

Case link

For tactics to attract customers, see Case 8: Activating E-Bank Users.

First, how visible is the firm? Customers tend to shop at places of which they are aware. The firm's visibility is essential in creating awareness. Ideally, firms should be visible from major traffic arteries and can enhance their visibility by facing the direction of traffic that maximizes visibility. If available, sites that are set back from the street (which permit customers to gain a broad perspective) while still remaining close enough to permit customers to read the firm's signs are preferable.

The second question about a location under consideration pertains to the compatibility of the site being evaluated with its surrounding environment. Is the size of the site suitable for the size of the building being planned? More importantly, what other types of businesses are in the area? For example, it would make sense for a law office specializing in healthcare matters to locate close to a major hospital, which is generally surrounded by a number of private medical practices as well.

The third question concerns whether the site is suited for customer convenience. Is the site accessible? Does it have ample parking or alternative parking options nearby? Do customers who use mass transit systems have reasonable access to the firm?

The firm's architecture. The architecture of the firm's physical facility is often a three-way trade-off among the type of design that will attract the firm's intended target market, the type of design that maximizes the efficiency of the service production process and the type of design that is affordable. The firm's architecture conveys a number of impressions as well as communicates information to its customers, such as the nature of the firm's business, the firm's strength and stability and the price of the firm's services.

The firm's sign. The firm's sign has two major purposes: to identify the firm and to attract attention. The firm's sign is often the first 'mark' of the firm the customer notices. All logos on the firm's remaining physical evidence, such as letterhead, business cards and note cards, should be consistent with the firm's sign to reinforce the firm's image. As Keller and Lehmann (2003) state, the brand, contained in the logo, represents the identity, image and expectatation of service quality of the organization, all rolled into one small symbol. Ideally, signs should indicate to consumers the who, what, where and when of the service offering. The sign's size, shape, colouring and lighting all contribute to the firm's projected image.

The firm's entrance. The firm's entrance and foyer areas can dramatically influence customer perceptions about the firm's activities. Worn carpet, scuffed walls, unprofessional artwork, torn and outdated reading materials, and unskilled and unkempt personnel form one impression. In contrast, neatly appointed reception areas, the creative use of colours, distinctive furnishings, and friendly and professional staff create a much different, more positive impression. Other tactical considerations include lighting that clearly identifies the entrance, doors that are easy to open, flat entryways that minimize the number of customers who might trip, non-slip floor materials for rainy days, and doors that are wide enough to accommodate customers with disabilities as well as large materials being transported in and out of the organization. Countryman and Jang (2006) found that three physical attributes, colour, lighting and style of a hotel foyer had a significant effect on the overall impression of the hotel; this finding clearly suggests that from a hospitality and lodging perspective, design and atmospherics must be placed at the top of the agenda.

Lighting. The psychological effects of lighting on consumer behaviour are particularly intriguing. Our response to light may have started when our parents put us to bed, turned out the lights and told us to be quiet and go to sleep. Through repetitive conditioning, most individuals' response to dimly lit rooms is that of a calming effect. The repetitive conditioning is also used when consumers visit service outlets. 'For example, a customer entering a store with tile floors, the smell of popcorn, fluorescent lighting, and Top-40 music may access from memory a 'discount store' schema and infer that the store's merchandise is low priced and of average quality and that the store has minimal service.' (Baker et al., 2002: 122). Lighting, therefore, can set the mood, tone and pace of the service encounter. Consumers talk more softly when the lights are low, the service environment is perceived as more formal, and the pace of the encounter slows. In contrast, brightly lit service environments are louder, communication exchanges among customers and between customers and employees are more frequent, and the overall environment is perceived as being more informal, exciting and cheerful. Consumers also 'feel special' when lighting is inviting and warm; dull and basic lighting gives negative feelings, so much so that consumers may be put off approaching the merchandise (Kerfoot et al., 2003).

Sound appeals

sound appeals Appeals associated with certain sounds, such as music or announcements.

Sound appeals have three major roles: mood setter, attention grabber and informer. Proactive methods for purposely inserting sound into the service encounter can be accomplished through music and announcements. Music helps set the mood of the consumers' experience while announcements can be used to grab consumers' attention or to inform them of the firm's offerings. Sound can also be a distraction to the consumers' experience; consequently, sound avoidance tactics should also be considered.

Music. Music is an inexpensive addition to the physical evidence of a service environment and studies have shown that background music affects the state of mind and behaviour of customers many ways. For example, music makes consumers, who have to wait in a queue, less irritable (Grewal et al., 2003). Also, patients in a hospital waiting room found that music increased feelings of relaxation and decreased feelings of stress (Tansik and Routhieaux, 1999). Positive feelings and mood, therefore, enhance the customer's perception of the organization. Music often influences the amount of time spent in stores (Areni, 2003; Maso et al., 1993) and organizations that play background music are thought to care more about their customers than organizations that have no music (Milliman, 1982).

Studies have shown that in addition to creating a positive attitude, music directly influences consumer buying behaviour. Playing faster tempo music increases the pace of consumer transactions. Slowing down the tempo of the music encourages customers to stay longer. The type of music played also enhances the perception of the environment in which it is played. North and Hargreaves (1998) played four different musical styles (easy listening, classical, pop or silence) to students while they ate their lunch in the school cafeteria. The student's perceptions changed with each different type. One surprising result was that students stated they would be prepared to pay more for their lunch when classical music was being played. Still other studies have indicated that consumers find music distracting when considering high-involvement purchases, yet found that listening to music during low-involvement purchases made the choice process easier. Moreover, employees tend to be happier and more productive when listening to background music, which in turn leads to a more positive experience for customers.

Table 10.3 displays the impact of background music on consumer and provider behaviour in a restaurant setting. As can be concluded by the numbers, the pace of service delivered and the pace of consumer consumption is affected by the tempo of the music. Although the estimated gross margin was higher when the restaurant played slow music, the restaurant should also consider the additional number of tables that would turn if faster-paced music was played throughout the day. Indeed, different music, such as ethnic music, can even encourage more patrons to choose ethnic entrées from the menu (Feinstein et al., 2002)!

Announcements. Another common sound in service establishments is the announcements made over intercom systems, such as to alert restaurant patrons when their tables are ready, to inform airline passengers of their current location and to page specific employees within the firm. The professionalism in which announcements are made directly influences consumer perceptions of the firm.

Sound avoidance. When planning the firm's facilities, it is as important to understand the avoidance of undesirable sounds as it is to understand the creation of desirable ones. Desirable sounds attract customers, and undesirable sounds distract from the firm's overall atmosphere. Music has two components – volume and pitch. Music that is too loud or at a very high pitch can be very irritating (Lin, 2004). But it is not just music that creates noise. Within a restaurant setting, sounds that should be strategically masked include those emanating from kitchen and toilet areas. Obviously,

Variables	Slow music	Fast music
Service time	29 min.	27 min.
Customer time at table	56 min.	45 min.
Customer groups leaving before seated	10.5 per cent	12.0 per cent
Amount of food purchased	$55.81	$55.12
Amount of bar purchases	$30.47	$21.62
Estimated gross margin	$55.82	$48.62

Table 10.3

The impact of background music on restaurant patrons

Source R. E. Milliman, 'The Influences of Background Music on the Behavior of Restaurant Patrons', *Journal of Consumer Research* 13 (September 1986), p. 288; see also R. E. Milliman, 'Using Background Music to Affect the Behavior of Supermarket Shopper', *Journal of Marketing*, Summer 1982, pp. 86–91.

listening to a toilet flush throughout dinner does little to add to the enjoyment of the customer's dining experience. Similarly in the dentist's waiting room, the noise that drills make when creating holes for fillings would make consumers fearful for their appointment. Adding doors and passageways or installing durable hallway carpets can eliminate the distracting sounds of clicking heels, drills or flushing toilets. Strategically placing loud central air conditioning units in areas away from those where the staff and customers conduct the majority of their business, and installing lower ceilings and sound-absorbing partitions, can reduce unwanted sounds even further.

Scent appeals

scent appeals Appeals associated with certain scents.

The atmosphere of the firm can be strongly affected by scents, and the service manager should be aware of this fact. When considering scent appeals, often known as olfactory cues, as was the case with sound appeals, service managers should pay as much attention to scent avoidance as to scent creation. Stale, musty, foul odours affect everyone and are sure to create negative impressions about the firm. Poor ventilation systems that fail to remove odours and poorly located trash receptacles are common contributors to potential odour problems.

Scents are included in avoid/approach strategies that organizations can employ. Pleasant smells such as lavender give consumers a more relaxed mood. On the other hand grapefruit heightens arousal and is stimulating on the senses (Mattila and Wirt, 2001). Therefore, pleasurable scents can often induce customers to make purchases and can affect the perception of products that don't naturally have their own scent. Hirsch (1991) found that the smell of fresh bread coming from a bakery encourages 300 per cent more sales. Indeed, many bakeries bake on the premises now, rather than have bread delivered each day. Although this particular example is related to bread which is a tangible product, it does seem to indicate that scents do influence consumer perceptions regarding products such as services that do not naturally smell on their own. Experts in scent creation note that a firm should smell like it's supposed to, according to target market expectations. Hospitals should smell clean and antiseptic, and perhaps older, established law firms should even smell a little musty.

Touch appeals

touch appeals Appeals associated with being able to touch a tangible product or physical evidence of a service, such as shaking hands with service providers.

The chances of a product selling increase substantially when the consumer handles it. But how does one touch an intangible product? Service firms such as mail-order retailers have a tangible component that can be shipped to customers. One of the reasons that non-store retailing now accounts for 10 per cent of all retail sales, and is increasing, is because of the liberal return policies that were implemented to increase touch appeals. For example, Spiegel, an American online women's clothes retailer, will send the customer the merchandise for inspection, and if the customer does not want it, the customer simply picks up the phone, notifies Spiegel, and places the returning product outside the door. Spiegel notifies UPS to pick up the package and pays for all costs associated with the return.

For purer services with a smaller tangible component, touch appeals can be developed through the use of 'open houses' where the public has a chance to meet the people providing the service. Shaking hands and engaging in face-to-face communications with potential and existing customers is definitely a form of touch appeal. Clearly, firms engaged in creating touch appeals are perceived as more caring, closer to their customers, and genuinely concerned and interested in their customers' welfare.

Taste appeals

Taste appeals, the final sensory cue, are the equivalent of providing the customer with samples. Within the service sector, the usefulness of taste appeals when developing service atmospheres is dependent upon the tangibility of the service. Service firms such as car washes, dry cleaners and restaurants may use taste appeals to initially attract customers. While sampling the firm's services, the customer will have the opportunity to observe the firm's physical evidence and form perceptions regarding the firm and its performance capabilities. Consequently, firms that use samples should view this process as an opportunity rather than as catering to a bunch of people who want something for free.

taste appeals The equivalent of providing the customer with free samples.

Design considerations for high- versus low-customer-contact service firms

One final topic that deserves special attention is the design considerations for low-customer-contact versus high-customer-contact firms. High-customer-contact firms include self-service and interpersonal services, while low-customer-contact firms include remote services. Depending on the level of contact, strategic differences exist regarding facility location, facility design, product design, and process design. However, remember that the last service encounter should be the best one that the consumer receives, as this encounter will be the one that remains in the memory (Chase and Dasu, 2001).

Facility location

The choice location for the firm's service operation depends upon the amount of customer contact that is necessary during the production process. If customers are an integral part of the process, convenient locations located near customers' homes or workplaces will offer the firm a differential advantage over competitors. For example, with all other things being equal, the most conveniently located car washes, dry cleaners and hairstylists are likely to obtain the most business.

In contrast, low-contact businesses should consider locations that may be more convenient for labour, sources of supply and access to major transportation routes. For example, mail-order facilities have little or no customer contact and can actually increase the efficiencies of their operations by locating closer to sources of supply and major transportation alternatives, such as close to interstate highways for trucking purposes or airports for overnight airline shipments. In many cases, these types of locations are less expensive to purchase or rent since they are generally in remote areas, where the cost of land and construction is not as expensive as it is inside city limits where other businesses are trying to locate close to their customers.

Facility layout

In regard to the layout of the service operation, high-contact service firms should take the customers' physical and psychological needs and expectations into consideration. When a customer enters a high-contact service operation, that customer expects the facility to look like something other than a dusty, musty, old warehouse. Attractive personnel, clearly marked signs explaining the process, enough room to comfortably move about the facility and a facility suited to bring friends and family are among consumers' expectations. In contrast, low-contact facility layouts should be designed to maximize employee expectations and production requirements. Clearly, designing facilities for high-contact services is often more expensive than designing for their low-contact counterparts.

Product design

'Home away from home' — hotel rooms have all the creative comforts of your own bedroom.

Since the customer is involved in the production process of high-contact services, the customer will ultimately define that product differently from one produced by a low-contact service. In services such as restaurants, which have a tangible product associated with their service offering, the customer will define the product by the physical product itself as well as by the physical evidence that surrounds the product in the service environment. High-contact services that produce purely intangible products, such as education and insurance, are defined almost solely by the physical evidence that surrounds the service and by the thoughts and opinions of others.

In low-contact services, the customer is not directly involved in the production process, so the product is defined by fewer attributes. Consider our mail-order operation in which the customer never physically enters the facility. The customer will define the end product by the physical product itself (a pair of boots), the conversation that took place with personnel when ordering the boots, the quality of the mail-order catalogue that featured the boots, the box in which the boots were packaged, and the billing materials that request payment.

Process design

In high-contact operations, the physical presence of the customer in the process itself must also be considered. Each stage in the process will have a direct and immediate effect on the customer. Consequently, a set of mini-service encounters and the physical evidence present at each encounter will contribute to the customer's overall evaluation of the service process. For example, a hotel guest is directly involved in the reservation process; the check-in process; the consumption process associated with the use of the hotel room itself; the consumption processes associated with the use of hotel amenities such as the restaurant, pool, and health club; and the check-out process.

In contrast, since the customer is not involved with many of the production steps in low-contact services, their evaluation is based primarily on the outcome itself.

Summary

The effective management of physical evidence is particularly important to service firms. Due to the intangibility of services, consumers lack objective sources of information when forming evaluations. As a result, customers often look to the physical evidence that surrounds the service when forming evaluations.

A firm's physical evidence includes, but is not limited to, facility exterior design elements such as the architecture of the building, the firm's sign, parking and landscaping, and the surrounding environment of the firm's location; interior design elements such as size, shape and colours, the firm's entrance and foyer areas, equipment utilized to operate the business, interior signage, layout, air quality and temperature; and other physical evidence that forms customer perceptions, including business cards, stationery, billing statements, reports, the appearance of personnel and the firm's brochures.

From a strategic perspective, the importance of managing the firm's physical evidence stems from the firm's ability to: (1) package the service; (2) facilitate the flow of the service delivery process; (3) socialize customers and employees alike in terms of their respective roles, behaviours and relationships; and (4) differentiate the firm from its competitors.

From a theoretical perspective, the firm's environment influences the behaviour of consumers and employees alike due to the inseparability of many services. When designing the firm's facilities, consideration needs to be given to whether the firm is a remote service, an interpersonal service, or a self-service. The subsequent design should reflect the needs of the parties who are dominating the service production process. Decisions about facility location, layout, product design and process design in particular may result in different outcomes, depending on whether the customer is actively involved in the production process. Figure 10.3 illustrates the theoretical framework that helps us to further understand how individuals are affected by the firm's environmental dimensions, which ultimately leads to approach and/or avoidance behaviours.

Finally, numerous tactical decisions must be made when designing the firm's environment. Individuals base perceptions of the firm's services on sensory cues that exist in the firm's environment. Specific tactical decisions must be made about the creation and sometimes the avoidance of scent appeals, sight appeals, sound appeals, touch appeals and taste appeals. The design and management of the firm's sensory cues are critical to the firm's long-term success.

Discussion questions

1 Discuss the strategic role of physical evidence.

2 Discuss the relevance of remote, self-service, and interpersonal services to facility design.

3 How should the servicescape of a firm that targets ethical shoppers be designed?

4 Discuss how internal response moderators relate to the characteristic of heterogeneity.

5 Some service organizations have bricks and mortar outlets and e-services through online portals. Both have a physical appearance. What are the differences between actual (bricks and mortar outlets) and virtual (e-services)?.

6 What is the impact of music on customer and employee behaviour?

7 Develop strategies for a service firm that would enhance the firm's touch and taste appeals.

8 Discuss the use of employee uniforms as physical evidence.

9 What are the major design differences between high-customer-contact and low-customer-contact services?

Further reading and references

Areni, C. S. (2003) 'Exploring managers' implicit theories of atmospheric music: comparing academic analysis to industry insight', *Journal of Services Marketing* (17) (2): 161–184.

Baker, J., Parasuraman, A., Grewal, D. and Voss, G. B. (2002) 'The influence of multiple store environment cues on perceived merchandise value and patronage intentions', *Journal of Marketing* 66 (April): 120–141.

Bitner, M. J. (1992) 'Servicescapes: The impact of physical surroundings on customers and employees', *Journal of Marketing* 56 (2): 60.

Bitner, M. J. (2000) 'The servicescape', in Swartz, T. A. and Iacobucci, D., *Handbook of Services Marketing and Management*, California: Sage Publications, pp. 37–51.

Chase R. B and Dasu, S. (2001) 'Want to perfect your company's service? Use behavioral science', *Harvard Business Review* 79 (6): 78–84.

Ching, F. (1996) *Architecture: Form, Space, and Order*, New York: Van Nostrand.

Countryman, C. C. C. and Jang, S. (2006) 'The effects of atmospheric elements on customer impression: the case of hotel lobbies', *International Journal of Contemporary Hospitality Management* 18 (7): 534–545.

Crump, V. (2008) 'Britain's 10 Best Pubs with Gardens', http://travel.timesonline.co.uk/tol/life_and_style/travel/best_of_britain/article3860597.ece, accessed 9 June 2008.

Davies, I. and Corbett, G. (1995) 'A practical field method for identifying basic colour terms', *Languages of the World* 9: 25–36.

Donovan, R. J. and Rossiter, J. R. (1982) 'Store atmosphere: an environmental psychological approach', *Journal of Retailing* 58 (1): 34–57.

Ecole International Malherbe, http://www.ecole-malherbe.com/, accessed 21 September 2007.

Evans, M. J., Moutinho, L. and Van Raaij, V. F. (1997) *Applied Consumer Behaviour*, Harlow: Addison-Wesley.

Feinstein, A., Harrah, W. F. and Hinskton, T. S. (2002) 'Exploring the effects of music atmospherics on menu item selection', *Journal of Foodservice Business Research* 5 (4): 3–25.

Ghosh, A. (1994) *Retail Management*, 2nd ed., Fort Worth, TX: Dryden Press.

Gilboa, S. and Rafaeli, A. (2003) 'Store environment, emotions and approach behaviour: applying environmental aesthetics to retailing', *International Review of Retail, Distribution and Consumer Research* 13 (2): 195–211.

Greenland, S. and McGoldrick, P. (2005) 'Evaluating the design of retail financial service environments', *International Journal of Bank Marketing* 23 (2): 132–152.

Grewal, D., Baker, J., Levy, M. and Voss, G. B. (2003) 'The effects of wait expectations and store atmosphere evaluations on patronage intentions in service-intensive retail stores', *Journal of Retailing* 79: 259–268.

Hawse, Douglas K. and McGinley, Hugh (1988) 'Music for the eyes, colour for the ears: an overview', in *Proceedings of the Society for Consumer Psychology*, David W. Schumann, ed., Washington, DC: Society for Consumer Psychology, pp. 145–152.

Hightower Jr., H., Brady, M. K. and Baker, T. L. (2002) 'Investigating the role of the physical environment in hedonic service consumption: an exploratory study of sporting events', *Journal of Business Research* 55 (9): 697–707.

Hirsch, A. R. (1991) 'Nostalgia: a neuropsychiatric understanding', Paper presented at the Annual Meeting of the Association for Consumer Research Conference, Chicago, IL.

Jansson, C., Marlow, N. and Bristow, M. (2004) 'The influence of colour on visual search times in cluttered environments', *Journal of Marketing Communications* 10 (1): 183–193.

Kerfoot, S., Davies, B. and Ward, P. (2003) 'Visual merchandising and the creation of discernible retail brands', *International Journal of Retail and Distribution Management* 31 (3): 143–152.

Keller, K. L. and Lehmann, D. R. (2003) 'Brands and Branding: Research Findings and Future Priorities', http://bear.cba.ufl.edu/CENTERS/MKS/invited/BRANDS%20AND%20BRANDING.pdf, accessed 06.10.07.

Kotler, P. (1974) 'Atmospherics as a marketing tool,' *Journal of Retailing* (Winter 1973–1974): 48.

Kristen. A and Zemke (1991) *Delivering Knock Your Socks Off Service*, New York: AMACOM.

Le Meurice, http://www.lemeurice.com/rooms_suites/index.html, accessed 23 September 2007.

Lewison, D. M. (1991) *Retailing*, 4th ed., New York: macmillan.

Lin, I. Y. (2004) 'Evaluating a servicescape: the effect of cognition and emotion', *Hospitality Management*, 23: 163–178.

Lovelock, C. H. and Wirtz, J. (2007) *Services Marketing People, Technology, Strategy*, 6th ed., Englewood Cliffs, NJ: Prentice Hall.

Machleit, K. A. and Eroglu, S. A (2000) 'Describing and measuring emotional response to shopping experience, *Journal of Business Research* 49: 101–111.

Mason, J. B., Mayer, M. L. and Ezell, H. F. (1994) *Retailing*, 5th ed., Homewood, IL: Irwin.

Mason, J. B., Mayer, M. L. and Wilkinson, J. B. (1993) *Modern Retailing: Theory and Practice*, 6th ed., Homewood, IL: Irwin.

Mattila, A. S. and Wirtz, J. (2001) 'Congruency of scent and music as a driver of in-store evaluations and behaviour, *Journal of Retailing* 77: 273–289.

Mehrabian, A. and Russell, J. A. (1974) *An Approach to Environmental Psychology*, Cambridge, MA: MIT Press.

Milliman, R. E. (1982) 'Using background music to affect the behaviour of supermarket shoppers', *Journal of Marketing* 46 (3): 86–91.

Mills, K. H. and Paul J. E. (1982) *Applied Visual Merchandising*, Englewood Cliffs, NJ: Prentice Hall.

Mintel (2006) 'Hotels', http://academic.mintel.com/sinatra/oxygen_academic/search_results/showand/display/id = 173615, accessed 20 September 2007.

Moye, L. N. and Kincade, D. H. (2002) 'Influence of usage situation and consumer shopping orientations on the importance of the retail environment', *International Review of Retail, Distribution and Consumer Research* 12 (1): 59–79.

North, A. C. and Hargreaves, D. J. (1998) 'The effect of music on atmosphere and purchase intentions in a cafeteria', *Journal of Applied Social Psychology* 28 (24): 2254–2273.

Pruyn, A. and Smidt, A. (1998) 'Effects of waiting on the satisfaction with the service: beyond objective time measures', *International Journal of Research in Marketing* 15 (4): 321–334.

Russell, J. A. (1980) 'A circumplex model of affect', *Journal of Personality and Social Psychology* 39 (6): 1161–1178.

Schein, E. (1968) 'Organizational socialization and the profession of management', *Industrial Management Review* 9 (Winter): 1–16.

Solomon, M. R. (2004) 'For services, the play's (still) the thing', *Managing Service Quality* 12 (1): 6–10.

Tansik, D. A. and Routhieaux, R. (1999) 'Customer stress-relaxation: the impact of music in a hospital waiting room', *International Journal of Service Industry Management* 10 (1): 88–81.

Chapter 11
People issues: Managing service employees

I have never given away more than I got back!

(Chairman Robert Wegman, Wegmans Food Markets Inc.)

Chapter objectives

The purpose of this chapter is to discuss the key issues that will help you understand the many challenges associated with managing employees within the service experience. Service business, by its very definition, is a people business and requires talented managers who can navigate the thin line between the needs of the organization, its employees and its customers.

After reading this chapter, you should be able to:

- Discuss the importance of contact personnel as boundary spanners.

- Explain the sources of conflict in boundary-spanning roles and the consequences of role stress.

- Appreciate the concepts of empowerment and enfranchisement and understand the contingency empowerment approach.

- Describe the relevance of employee satisfaction as it relates to the service-profit chain.

Services in context
Best Workplaces in Europe 2007

For more than 25 years Great Places to Work® Institute has been asking the question 'Who is the best company to work for?' Every year, hundreds of companies have carried out a Culture Audit® and asked their staff to complete a comprehensive employee survey to see if they could receive the coveted award of being the Best Workplace in Europe. In 2007 over 1000 companies from 15 European countries took part. Overall, Ferrari, Italy received the prestigious award. Ferrari won the award as their success is built around the fact that they strive for excellent team spirit and enable their staff to work in a high-trust environment. These are just two key elements that are at the centre of the organization's business strategy. 98 per cent of staff at Ferrari, Italy agreed that 'my work has special meaning: this is not just a job' – an accolade that many organizations would be proud of.

Each one of the top ten Best Workplaces in Europe has their own values and staff rewards. For example, Piscines Ideales, Greece has company values that include respect, comaradeirie, teamwork, pride, focus on quality, learning and professional development.

Clearly the 99 staff at Piscines Ideales who install and maintain swimming pools are central to the organization's business. Indeed, each member of staff receives 'little things' such as a celebratary birthday cake, or a laptop for the children of a Piscines Ideales employee when they go to university, or if an employee gets married, a wedding gift of one month's salary. One employee at Piscines Ideales, Greece said 'We work with fun and we help each other with our heart'.

The employees at Beeverbrooks, UK, a jewellry retailer, also celebrate together at Christmas – that's 59 Christmas parties – one for each store. Beeverbrooks, UK has a mission statement that includes phrases such as 'be energentic, create fun and smile' and 'clebrate our success'. All 718 staff are trained each week and promotion comes from within the company itself. This again shows the commitment that organizations have to their service personnel. Andarr, Netherlands is a management consultacy business and also has an employee-centric culture. The staff at Andarr obviously like their working environment as 95 per cent said they expect to work there 'for a long time' and 100 per cent said they felt that Andarr is a 'friendly place to work' – praise indeed.

'Rewarding and training staff like this costs money' – the marketing, HR and finance managers will probably cry. But as this chapter and the following three chapers demonstrate, investing in staff and the service they provide reaps rewards – and the rewards are often cost-effective ones!

Often managers of service organizations complain of high staff turnover. When comparing the 100 Best Workplaces in Europe with staff turnover by European country, the 100 Best have significantly less. For example, staff turnover for 100 Best Workplaces in Europe is 8.5 per cent. Staff turnover in the Netherlands is 22 per cent, UK 17.9 per cent, Sweden 11.7 per cent, Austria 10 per cent. Reducing staff turnover saves an organization a great deal of money – money spent on advertising, recruiting and training

Piscines Ideales is an 'ideal' workplace for its 99 employees.

new personnel. Absenteeism is another problem that many organizations complain about. The average absenteeism rate for the 100 Best Workplaces in Europe is 2.5 per cent. This is much lower when comparing absenteeism rates by European country. For example, absenteeism rates are as high as 8.0 per cent Netherlands, 8.0 per cent Sweden, 6.8 per cent Norway, 4.5 per cent UK. Everyone knows that absenteeism costs money. Consider Ivan, a person who earns €46,920 per year. The official statistical bureau for Belgium states that on average absenteeism is 6.6 per cent compared with 2.5 per cent of the Best Workplaces in Belgium. The Best Workplaces in Belgium, therefore, save the costs associated with the reduced 4.1 per cent absen-teeism. Returning to Ivan, who earns €46,920 – those associated savings amount to €1,924. If an organization has 500 employees earning the same as Ivan, that amounts to nearly one million € of costs saved!

It is important for companies to be employee-centric. This chapter will consider just how important service personal are to an organization's success, as it is the staff that represent the organization's brand values, they are the face of the organization and therefore they should be trained, managed and rewarded accordingly.

Source: 100 Best Workplaces in Europe 2007 – Building a better society by helping companies transform their workplaces – Great Place to Work® Institute.

Introduction

Employee satisfaction and customer satisfaction are clearly related. Let's say it again another way: If you want to satisfy your customers, employee satisfaction is critical! The public face of a service firm is its contact personnel. Be they factory workers, police administrators, nurses or civil servents – service personnel often perform a complex and difficult job (Nickson, Warhurs and Dutton 2005). Lower-ranking service personnel represent the face of the brand and are often the first contact that consumers have with an organization. The employee, therefore, plays an important role in the success and profitability of the organization. In addition to that, the roles that service personnel play are often the most complex. For example, in the healthcare community, the individuals most responsible for patient care and patient perceptions of the service quality they receive are the nurses. And consider just how they have to be adaptable to each patient's individual needs. Similarly, in the education system, a classroom primary school teacher is responsible for the day-to-day education, welfare and care of between 20 and 30 children, who all have different requirements and abilities. When a fireman or woman is called out to a house that is on fire, it is unlikely that each house fire is the same; therefore, they will need to make on-the-spot decisions that will help to save lives. The list of complex situations goes on and on. Consider any service industry, and look to the individuals who are the most responsible for customer interactions and the quality of service delivered, and unfortunately you will most likely see the lowest-paid and least-respected individuals in the company. This makes no sense because, as we have seen in previous chapters, the staff help to create the intangible experience that the consumer enjoys.

It is little wonder, therefore, that service jobs often have extremely high levels of staff turnover. Think back to the health care example: high staff turnover rates often lead to low patient satisfaction because the quality and continuity of care received is low (Newman et al., 2002; Kramer and Schmalenberg, 2004). Therefore, high turnover rates are not only a waste of money, but can also affect the quality of care and safety the patient needs. And it is not just patients who require care and good service quality. Tourists from around the world will be descending on London for the Olympic Games in 2012 and Roger Blitz is worried about the staff turnover in the hospitality industry, especially as there is a 'shortage in skilled chefs, . . . and more than half of managers lack minimum managerial qualifications'. So the UK has a huge task ahead in order to ensure that staff in the service industries are motivated, highly trained and welcoming.

The importance of service personnel

This chapter highlights the importance of contact personnel to the service firm and explains their particular role in creating customer satisfaction. Strategically, service personnel are an important source of product differentiation. It is often challenging for a service organization to differentiate itself from other similar organizations in the benefits bundle it offers or its delivery system (see B2B Services in Action). For example, one extreme view is that many airlines offer similar bundles of benefits and fly the same types of aircraft from the same airports to the same destinations. Their only hope of a competitive advantage is, therefore, from the service level – the way things are done. Some of this differentiation can come from staffing levels or the physical systems designed to support the staff. Often, however, the deciding factor that distinguishes one airline from another is the poise and attitude of the service providers. Virgin Atlantic take their customer service and customer satisfaction very seriously through regular staff reviews and research. Virgin are one of the top ten Super Brands in terms of Customer Service with 92 per cent of their customers satisfied and 85 per cent of cutomers recommending Virgin Atlantic to friends and family (Virgin, 2008).

Despite the strategic importance of personnel, it often seems that personnel, customers and the service firm itself are in pursuit of different goals representing the classic confrontation between marketing, human resources and operations. Inevitably, clashes occur that have profound long-term effects on how customers view the organization and how the service providers view customers in subsequent transactions. It is a self-perpetuating nightmare. As stated above, front-line staff have to deal with the individual needs of all of their customers, even the 'customers from hell', or as Lovelock (1994) coined the phrase – 'jaycustomers'. Jaycustomers are those people who misbehave in a thoughtless or deliberate manner. And not only do front-line service staff have to deal with Jaycustomers but they also have to be adaptable enough to respond to the behaviour of eight different types of jaycustomer (see Figure 11.1)

Figure 11.1 shows the different types of jaycustomers, how they behave and what motivates them. Each jaycustomer is primarily motivated to act in some way if they feel an injustice to them has occurred. They then feel that they wish to restore the balance; possibly with a financial reward.

1 *Compensation letter writers* – These consumers write following a service encounter. The complaints, often very trivial, are sent to a central customer service department and the request in the letter is for financial gain or other monetary recompense.

2 *Undesirable customers* – These include customers who go outside the normal behaviour that is expected when experiencing a service encounter. For example, some families let their children 'run riot' in a restaurant to the annoyance of the staff and other customers.

3 *Property abusers* – These include consumers who steal or vandalize property. Many hotel guests take bathrobes or towels as 'souvenirs' or try to run away with merchandise from a music event.

4 *Service workers* – Some people, who are service personnel 'by day', take advantage when their role is reversed and they become the customer. Service workers often alter their behaviour as they know how to get quick service or are rude to the member of staff who is serving them. These jaycustomers have learnt the skills from watching their own customers gain financial rewards.

5 *Vindictive customers* – These customers are rude to service staff when both parties are in a different location. For example, customers approach service personnel and physically or verbally abuse them or their organization outside work hours.

6 *Oral abusers* – Often these jaycustomers need an ego-boost as they seem to feel that they can shout or verbally attack a member of staff who they feel is beneath them, does not know their job or is poor at their job.

Figure 11.1

The eight forms and motives of jaycustomers

Source Harris and Reynolds, (2004) 'Jaycustomer behaviour: an explosion of hypes and motives in the hospitality industry', *Journal of Services Marketing*, Vol. 18, No. 5 p344.

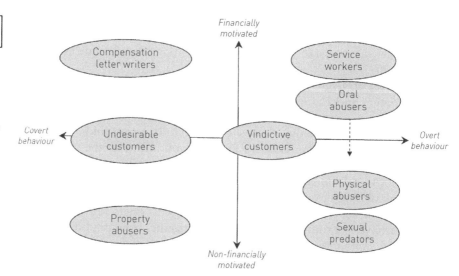

7 *Physical abusers* – These customers can be known to physically hit, punch or push staff or fellow customers. For example, customers may physically abuse each other if one customer does not wait his/her turn in a queue.

8 *Sexual predators* – Often male customers who become over-familiar, rude, or lewd to female service personnel or even attempt to physically touch or abuse the member of staff.

Unfortunately, staff experience 'jaycustomer behaviour' on a regular basis. It has long been observed by marketing managers that the 'customer is King'. But in circumstances like these, service personnel need to have the support of their colleagues and management to be able to respond to these types of behaviour appropriately.

Service personnel as boundary spanners

Service personnel often experience the pressures and tensions of their role as boundary spanners. As boundary spanners, service personnel perform the dual functions of interacting with both the firm's external environment and its internal organization and structure. In simpler terms, the boundary-spanning role has been defined as one that links an organization with the outside world. Boundary spanners therefore communicate on a regular basis to customers and suppliers from outside the organization as well as colleagues and managers

boundary-spanning roles
The various parts played by contact personnel who perform dual functions of interacting with the firm's external environment and internal organization.

B2B services in action
It's all about the personal service

Strategically, service personnel are an important source of product differentiation. It is often challenging for a service organization to differentiate itself from other similar organizations in the benefit bundle it offers to its customers. Industrial flooring is one such product that to many customers is just another commodity product. There are hundreds of industrial flooring services, from those that offer ceramic tiling to those that offer seamless resin floors. Seamless industrial flooring now accounts for 90 per cent (Mintel, 2007) of all flooring seen in warehouses, schools, call centres and sports arenas. Indeed the preparation and installing of resin flooring are likely to rise over the next five years (Mintel, 2007).

Therefore, there are many organizations that offer preparation and installation services from big businesses such as Altro, who employ over 507, to aSurface, a family-run business in South East England. So how do businesses choose an industrial flooring organization will provide a good service within budget?

- Will the biggest be the best?
- Will smaller companies not have the expertise?
- Will big companies rip me off to pay for the big company cars and big salaries?
- Will smaller companies charge more because they can't buy the resin and curing agents at competitive prices?

All these questions, and more, must go through the minds of organizations when they request pitches for industrial flooring jobs. Perhaps organizations should consider what

▶

an additional asset good customer service would bring when choosing the business that will prepare and install their industrial flooring.

G Tec Resin Flooring Limited is a small business in West Yorkshire, England, that has been trading for six years. Alistair Mitchell has many roles to play in keeping his G Tec Resin Flooring Limited flourishing within a highly competitive marketplace. Like many people working in the service sector, Alistair has to wear many hats; one day he is the advertising manager and the next he will be installing epoxy resin flooring in a car showroom. He also deals with financial matters such as buying resin and curing materials for the industrial flooring, to completing tax returns and visiting the accountant. Clearly he needs to be professional and friendly with all of his business-to-business contacts, but one of the roles he particularly enjoys is pitching for new business.

When pitching for new business the ability for service personnel to understand the needs of their 'potential customer' is paramount. During the pitching process, personnel are 'the face' of the organization they represent. The way they talk, behave and interact during the pitch are the main factors that customers and clients use to judge the organization as a whole – see introduction to this chapter. Not only that, but service industry personnel have to quickly evaluate the needs of their 'potential customers' during the pitch. Therefore, Alistair has to fulfil two roles. Firstly, he has to demonstrate his expertise. Secondly he has to ask the right questions, listen carefully to the answers and then try to understand the needs of his 'potential customer'.

For example, the last time he pitched for business was for resin flooring at a European chocolate biscuit factory. Initially, he met the senior manager and accountants. For this Alistair interacted in a business-like manner; he brought financial reports and showed samples of previous work he had done. These customers wanted to see that Alistair was a

man who knew the business, could demonstrate past successes and who behaved in a manner appropriate for a deal worth several thousands pounds. After the formal meeting, Alistair asked to view the site. At this point he changed from his suit and tie into his overalls and hard hat. Alistair wanted to discuss the amount of heavy goods traffic likely to pass over each area of the surface in the biscuit factory to assess the amount of spillage. These discussions he had with the factory manager and his team. Because the factory manager and his team were 'on the ground' on a daily basis, Alistair judged they would be the most knowledgeable people with whom to discuss actual specifications. The final part of the pitch was back with the senior manager.

Alistair said, 'I certainly thought I'd provided a really good service. I think I impressed the senior manager by the fact that I'd gone to discuss job specifications with the factory manager and his team ... and because I met with them we discovered a few changes that would keep my price competitive. No other organizations pitching for the business did that. Perhaps the senior manager thought I was a down-to-earth sort of person because I started talking to him about the dog in his family photograph ... I've got the same type of dog, you see, and before you know it we were laughing about how our dogs do the same silly things. Whichever reason it was, a week later I got the job!'

Personnel providing a service should take pride in their work, be efficient and cooperative. And Alistair is sure it is the personal touches and friendly service that he gives that keep his business successful. He also says that he gets free publicity through positive word of mouth!

Sources: Altro (2007) 'Talking Beyond the Surface', www.altrotransflor.com, accessed 10 January 2008. aSurface (2008) 'The Resin Floor and Sanding Specialists', http://www.asurface.co.uk/~about-asurface. asp, accessed 10 January 2008.
Mintel (2007) 'Industrial Flooring (Industrial Report)', September 2007. http://academic.mintel.com.

within their department. They also have to span the boundaries between their own department and as well as colleagues and managers from different departments within the organization and with managers from supplier organizations (Hoe, 2006). The B2B Services in Action case study highlights the fact that boundary spanners have many duties and some managers feel that the personal service provided is the greatest function they can perform.

Employees in boundary-spanning roles create these links for the organization by interacting with nonmembers of the organization. As such, boundary-spanning personnel have two main functions:

- information transfer, and
- representation.

Boundary spanners collect information from the environment and feed it back into the organization, and they communicate with the environment on behalf of the organization. Boundary-spanning personnel are also the organization's personal representatives.

Individuals who occupy boundary-spanning roles can be classified by the degree of inseparability and intangibility of the service encounter.

The above table highlights how different personnel in service organizations have a wide variety of roles to play. Staff who have high contact/non-qualified roles work for service firms where the customers' purchase decision is entirely discretionary. They are subordinate to the organization and to the customer. Examples of subordinate service roles include waiters, door supervisors, drivers, and others who operate at the very base of the organization and yet are the organization's primary contact personnel with the outside world. At the same time the customer experiences the dominant power in the relationship between staff and customer (Menon and Bansal, 2007).

On the other hand, personnel who have highly qualified and professional roles occupy the dominant power role. These boundary spanners have a different status, not only in the mind of the consumer, but also in the minds of colleagues within their organizations and suppliers external to their organization. Their status, therefore, is quite different from that of the

subordinate service roles The parts played by personnel who work in firms where customers' purchase decisions are entirely discretionary, such as waitresses, bellmen and drivers.

	High contact	Low contact
Highly professional	Education Dentistry	Data storage manager Barrister
Qualified/trained	Hairdressing Travel agent	Plumbing Call centre staff
Non-qualified	Taxi driver Waiter/waitress Laundering	Decorating Gardener Cleaner

Table 11.1

Range of skills and people-based boundary spanners

Case link

For the role played by company culture, See Case 18: Nando's International.

subordinate provider. Due to their professional qualifications, personnel with professional service roles have a status that is independent of their place in the organization. Customers, or as they are more often called, clients, do not feel superior to professionals because clients acknowledge the professionals' expertise on which they wish to draw.

Sources of conflict in boundary-spanning roles

professional service roles The parts played by personnel who have a status independent of their place in an organization due to their professional qualifications.

Employees who occupy boundary-spanning roles are often placed in situations that produce conflict and stress. Common sources of stress include person/role conflicts consisting of *inequality dilemmas, feelings versus behaviour,* and *territorial conflicts*; organization/client conflicts; and inter-client conflicts.

person/role conflict A bad fit between an individual's self-perception and the specific role the person must play in an organization.

Person/role conflicts. For services to operate successfully, both customers and contact personnel must conform to a script or role. Each must play his or her part. A person/role conflict indicates that playing such a role may be inconsistent with an individual's self-perception. Some customers may wish boundary spanners to be subservient, a role that an employee normally would not desire to play, especially with certain types of customers. Boundary-spanning personnel are often called on to suppress their personal feelings and are asked to smile and be helpful. This is particularly difficult when front-line staff feel that customers are 'over-demanding', 'unreasonable', 'refuse to listen', 'always want everything their way, immediately' and even 'arrogant'' (Mahesh and Kasturi, 2006: 146). Staff with few qualifications and/or limited training often have to bear the brunt of aggressive customers who treat service staff in a subservient manner because of the role they are in. Highly professional staff, however, are much more likely to be able to operate within their own self-image and to feel less obligated to maintain a pleasant 'bedside manner'. Person/role conflicts can be categorized into three types:

SOURCE © ISTOCK.COM

Dentists are more likely to operate within their own self-image so feel less obligated to maintain a 'bedside manner'.

1 *Inequality dilemmas.* Although it is important to put the customer first, this can sometimes result in service personnel feeling belittled or demeaned. These feelings can be magnified if customers make a point of establishing their personal superiority over the server.

2 *Feelings versus behaviour.* Contact personnel are required to hide their true feelings and present a 'front' or 'face' to the customer. This can result in role stress as the server does not identify with the role he or she is acting out.

3 *Territorial conflict.* Contact personnel will often try to establish their own personal space, which they can defend against clients and other servers. Trespassing on this space can lead to reactions that conflict with the server's own role.

Organization/client conflicts. Contact personnel can sometimes receive conflicting instructions, one set from the client who wants a service performed in a particular way, the other from the organization that wants the service performed in a different way. This three-cornered fight between what the customers want, what the organization provides and what the member of staff can provide at that moment often means that a compromise needs to be made. Customer-orientated businesses deal with the organization/client conflict by empowering their staff and giving them the opportunity to be able to bypass the 'rule book' if necessary. Table 11.2 gives examples of situations and solutions in times of conflict.

Empowering staff in this way to resolve organization/client conflicts helps staff feel more independent, less subservient and more creative

organization/client conflicts Disagreements that arise when a customer requests services that violate the rules of the organization.

Complaint	Acknowledgement	Action
Guest advises – No towels in the bathroom in the hotel bedroom	Complaint ownership – taking immediate action to resolve customer complaints, even if the complaint is not directly related to their area of responsibility	Receptionist takes ownership and immediately takes towels to bedroom
Customer arrives to pick up their dog at the Mucky Pups Grooming Salon. Their dog is still being groomed. Complains to the dog grooming service	Concession Reducing customer's bill/ money off next visit to appease the customer	Owner of the dog grooming salon offers a 'free bath and fluff out' when the customer brings their dog back for its regular clipping
Elderly couple complain to platform cleaner that the train has moved platform and they won't be able to get to the train ahead of the crowds	'Do whatever it takes' – using judgement and skill, staff can go beyond the call of duty to pacify customers (Lashley, 1997)	Platform cleaner uses radio phone to advise the conductor of the situation. Conductor reserves seats for the elderly couple and platform cleaner helps them with their luggage

Table 11.2

Resolving organization/client conflict

(Klidas, van den Berg and Wilderom, 2007). More information regarding empowerment is shown later in this chapter.

However, such compromises or actions, if mishandled or not acceptable in the eyes of the customer, may leave the server feeling badly treated or downhearted. Conflicts between the demands of the organization and those of the client are the most common source of conflict for boundary-spanning personnel. Conflicts of this type arise when the client or customer requests services that violate the rules of the organization. Such a violation can be as simple as a request for a second bread roll in a restaurant or as complex as a request that a bank stay open later than their regular hours to accommodate a customers' availability to visit the local branch to discuss a savings plan.

The reaction to the organization/client conflict is often related to the employee's role within the organization. Subordinate service personnel are often unable to change the rules and regulations of the company. Moreover, they are unable to explain why the rules and regulations exist in the first place. However, subordinate service personnel appear to be well aware of the rules and regulations that prevent them from giving good service. In many cases, when faced with an organization/client conflict, subordinate service personnel will side with the client and away from the organization to resolve the conflict. In contrast, professional service personnel, with their higher status and clearer understanding of the purpose of specific rules and regulations, are more able to control what happens.

inter-client conflicts
Disagreements between clients that arise because of the number of clients who influence one another's experience.

Inter-client conflicts. Conflicts between clients, or inter-client conflicts, arise because many service delivery systems have a number of clients who influence one another's experiences. Because different clients are likely to have different needs, they tend to have completely different scripts for themselves, the contact personnel and other customers. When customers do conflict, it is usually the boundary-spanning personnel who are asked to resolve the confrontation. For example, it is the waiter who is generally requested to ask other diners not to talk, sing or laugh too loud. Attempts to satisfy all of the clients all of the time can escalate the conflict or bring the boundary-spanning personnel into a battle. Other conflicts occur when a busy manicurist receives very unpleasant looks, if not a walk-out from clients, because her current client is slow in choosing her nail art and furthermore asks for jewels and rings to be added.

Employee reaction and effectiveness in resolving inter-client conflicts appear to be once again related to the employee's role within the organization. Employees in subordinate roles start from the weakest position since they have low status with clients. Clients may simply disregard responses made by subordinate service providers. Professionals may face the same problems; for example, consider the patient in the hospital waiting room, demanding preferential treatment. In a case such as this, however, the professional can invoke his or her status and expertise to resolve the situation.

The implications of role stress for boundary-spanning personnel

The consequences of conflict and stress are dissatisfaction, frustration and turnover in personnel. When faced with potential conflict and stress in their jobs, employees attempt a variety of strategies to shield themselves. The simplest way of avoiding conflict is to avoid the customers. This is exemplified by the waiter who refuses to notice a customer who wishes to place an order. This strategy allows the employee to increase his or her personal sense of control over the encounter. An alternative strategy is to move into a people-processing mode where customers are treated as inanimate objects to be processed rather than as individuals. This reduces the requirement of the boundary-spanning personnel to associate or empathize with an individual.

Boundary-spanning personnel also employ other strategies to maintain a sense of control over the encounter. Physical symbols and furniture are often used to boost the employee's status and, hence, his or her sense of professional legitimacy. Examples of physical symbols that give qualified and non-qualified front-line staff status are uniforms, specialized equipment and technology, all of which help to identify the member of staff, but also to aid them in their delivery of the service they are employed to provide (Cobb-Walgren and Mohr, 1998). In an extreme case, the employee may over-act the role and force the customer into a subservient role, as is the case with some waiters and waitresses. Interestingly, a national restaurant franchise called Dick's Last Resort encourages employees to be overly demanding as part of their overall theme. In fact the restaurant's theme could easily be: 'Dick's Last Resort...Where the Customer Is Always Wrong!'

An alternative strategy employees use to reduce organization/client conflict is to side completely with the customer. When forced to obey a rule with which they disagree, boundary-spanning personnel will proceed to list for the customer all the other things about the organization with which they disagree. In this way, employees attempt to reduce stress by seeking sympathy from the customer.

The tasks that boundary spanners perform are highly complex. However, as service personnel are the main people who provide fantastic service, they are the ones who are trusted the most. Customers also want to trust organizations that provide e-services. E-Services in Action considers boundary spanners who are in remote locations, but who still need to be trusted by the customer.

Reducing role stress with marketing

Traditionally, marketing can either cause or reduce role stress. Marketing can, without making major strategic changes, help to reduce service employee stress levels, and it's in the firm's best interest to do so. Clearly, unhappy, frustrated and disagreeable service personnel are visible to customers and will ultimately affect consumer perceptions of service quality (Kotler, Bowen and Makens, 2003). Strategies such as ignoring the customer or

E-services in action
The e-face of the brand

Many retailers offer services through bricks and mortar High Street stores. E-tailing is a growing service offering, both as a stand-alone delivery mechanism or to support High Street stores. This section highlights the fact that the customer/ service interface is paramount because staff represent the face of the brand. This can also be said for internet services. Customers buying online trust a retailer's service credibility through the interface. Features such as construction, the level of information provided, the design and the ease with which the customer can navigate around the website are all important factors in maintaining trust throughout the e-tail transaction. Therefore, it is important that online retailers understand which features, shown on their website, are attractive and create that all-important trust in the minds of their customers.

Online 'customer service representatives' are one of the features that appear on e-service providers. The online persona tends to be represented in three forms:

1 A static photograph of a typical service representative – see One Complete Service (industrial contract cleaners) and Vodafone.

2 Human-like character – some of which can be animated so the online persona smiles, blinks 'naturally', has eye movement and other changeable facial expressions – and also speaks! See IKEA Help Assistant (named Anna on most European sites, but Anny on the Czech Republic site).

3 Cartoon-like characters – animated characters – see Vodafone on-line help interface.

Just as service staff are boundary spanners, when dealing with customers face-to-face, on-screen 'customer service representatives' also build a relationship with customers in what would otherwise seem a very impersonal experience. The experience can be enhanced as a relationship is formed and the on-screen persona encourages the customer to ask questions and/or discuss problems. On-screen personas, particularly the 'animated human-like online characters', induce feelings in the customer because of their life-like behaviour. The induced feelings encourage and motivate customers through the transaction. From the limited studies to date, human-like characters are seen as trustworthy, likeable and appropriate – but cartoon-like characters are seen as a more positive persona when customers are making online payments. It seems that even computer-generated human-like personas are not trusted with 'private' information. Additionally, human-like characters also seem to take on a 'big brother is watching you' role!

Sources: A. Kolsaker and C. Payne (2002) 'Engendering trust in e-commerce: a study of gender-based concerns', *Marketing Intelligence and Planning* 20 (4): 206–214.

J.T. Lou and P. McGoldrick, S. Beatty and K.A. Keeling (2006) 'On-screen characters: their design and influence on consumer trust', *Journal of Services Marketing* 20 (2): 112–124.

M.C. Roy, O. Dewit and B.A. Aubert (2001) 'The impact of interface usability on trust in web retailers', *Internet Research: Electronic Networking Applications and Policy* 11 (5): 388–398.

http://www.ocs.co.uk/Contact_Us.

simply processing the customer as a raw material through the service delivery system will most likely generate negative customer perceptions. Customers obviously do not like being ignored by waiters or treated as if they were inanimate objects. If contact personnel attempt to maximize their sense of control over their encounters, it will most likely be at the expense of the amount of control felt by customers. In addition, although customers may sympathize with a service provider's explanation that the organization stops them from providing excellent service, customers will still develop negative perceptions about the organization.

Reducing person/role conflicts. Marketing can reduce the conflict between the individual and the assigned role by simply being sensitive and by actively seeking input from employees about the issue. A promotional gimmick dreamed up at the head office may look great on paper. For example, a medieval-theme day in the hotel almost certainly will have great public relations value, but how will the staff feel when they are called upon to wear strange and awkward (not to mention uncomfortable) costumes? How will these costumes affect the employees' relationships with customers during the service encounter?

To improve the quality of service, a change in operating procedure may be needed. However, it is important to ensure that service providers are well trained in the new script. Should they not be, they may well become extremely embarrassed in the presence of customers. This situation can be aggravated if the new service is advertised in such a way that the customers are more aware of the new script than the staff.

Reducing organization/client conflicts. Similarly, marketing can help reduce conflicts between the organization and its clients. It is crucial, for example, that customer expectations be consistent with the capabilities of the service system. Customers should not ask for services the system cannot provide. Advertising is one of the main causes of inflated expectations, as the temptation is to exaggerate claims in advertising to maximize the impact. Consider, for example, the advertisement that depicted a flight attendant reading a young child a story while the plane was in flight. A number of passengers took the advertisement literally, either because they believed it or because they could not resist the temptation, and called upon the flight attendants to read stories to their children.

Reducing inter-client conflicts. Conflicts between clients can be avoided if the clients are relatively homogeneous in their expectations. Due to the inseparability of services, customers often share their service experiences with other customers. Hence, successful service firms recognize the importance of effective segmentation, which minimizes the chances that two or more divergent groups will share the encounter simultaneously. As long as all the clients share the same script and expect the same standard of service, the chances of inter-client conflicts are much reduced.

The importance of human resources for service firms

Personnel constitute the bulk of the product of most service firms (see Global Services in Action). However, marketing theory is ill-equipped to provide insights into the problem of where contact personnel fit into the hierarchy of the service firm. Human resources, by comparison, is a field of study focused on this and similar problems. Human resource policies come from the mission and objectives of the organizations. Therefore, if an organization understands the value of service orientation and performance it will achieve

---

Global services in action
Dell offshore tech support: Lost in translation

The interactions between a service firm's personnel and its customers define 'moments of truth'. Moments of truth represent the service firm's greatest opportunity for gains and losses. This is why employee selection and training are so important to service firms. One service firm that is currently struggling with this issue is Dell, Inc. of Austin, Texas.

To outsource tech support offshore, or not, that is the question for Dell, Inc. What began as a way for the company to cut costs, the off-shoring of Dell's tech support to India has become somewhat of a political incident. During the tech recession, Dell laid off nearly 5,700 workers. Most of these employees were tech support personnel working in Texas. Since this time, most of the growth in Dell's workforce has occurred in overseas call centres based in India. To say the least, the average Texan is not too happy about this 'motivated by cost savings' turn of events.

Dell is now faced with the decision about whether to recall some of these lost jobs back to America. Dell customers have complained about the quality of support received from Indian-based call centres. Meanwhile, upset Indians are bristling at the thought that 'their thick accents' and 'scripted responses' have motivated Dell to move some of its tech support positions back to America. However, it does appear that Dell has done just this, particularly for its large-scale corporate clients. In fact, delivering customer support from North America–based locations appears to have become a major selling point for Dell's corporate clients.

The off-shoring of customer tech support has become a thorny issue. On the one hand, India provides the cost savings that drives Dell's value proposition. On the other hand, more and more corporate customers are shopping tech firms based on the issue of the location of technical support. In the meantime, many industry observers are wondering whether the quality of technical support has really declined due to its India-based location or whether Dell has become the victim of a well organized e-mail and bulletin board campaign that promotes protectionism. Commenting on Dell's dilemma, *The Economist* writes, 'It may be its [Dell] customer service has become genuinely poorer as a result – though multi-regional, multi-racial America has its fair share of different accents, too. Which customers, after all, can claim happy experiences with Texan call centres?'

Source: Patrick Thibodeau, 'Offshore Tech Support Still Stirs Controversy', *Computerworld* (2 May 2005), 39 (18): 7; 'Lost in Translation', *The Economist* (29 November 2003), 369 (8352): 58.

greater customer satisfaction, competitive advantage, growth and, to satisfy the stakeholders, more profit (Lytle and Timmerman, 2006).

As shown in Global Services in Action, it is important to ensure that personnel understand how effective, or not, their service is to the customer experience. And because service firms often involve the customer as a co-producer, they operate open systems, where the effects of human resource practices and policies as well as the organization's climate are visible to customers. The organization's Culture and Climate must be at the heart of an organization's business strategy, which in turn should have the emphasis on customer service. If services are part of the culture and climate of an organization, they become the axel around which the whole of the organization pivots. This philosophy is demonstrated in Figure 11.2.

climate Employee perceptions of one or more organizational strategic imperatives.

As can be seen in Figure 11.2, service orientation is at the centre of an organization's strategy. Therefore, organizations that understand that their service personnel are one of their main priorities will be successful performers in the marketplace and be profitable. In an ideal world all organizations and their service personnel should have a passion for service. A passion for service leads to a climate that sets service values as the key strategic imperative (see Tables 11.3 and 11.4). Service orientation within a firm can then be measured using the following criteria established by Lytle and Timmerman (2006: 137):

1 Servant leadership
2 Service vision
3 Customer treatment
4 Employee empowerment
5 Service training
6 Service rewards
7 Service failure prevention
8 Service failure/recovery
9 Service technology
10 Service standards communication.

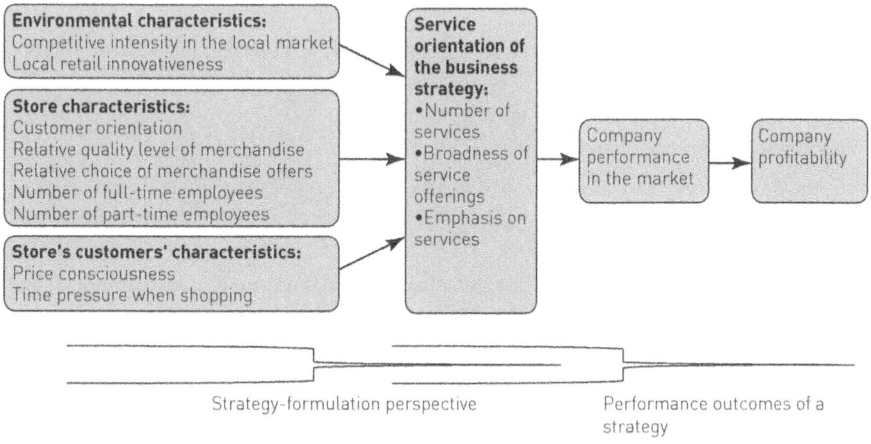

Figure 11.2

The content of a service-oriented business strategy

Source Homburg et al., (2002), 'Service Orientation of a Retailer's Business Strategy: Dimensions, Antecedents and Performance Outcomes', *Journal of Marketing*, Vol. 66, Issue 4 p88.

The above criterion continues with the idea that service delivery, training and rewards are important issues for human resource managers. When service commitment is high, the service firm displays a passion for doing things directly related to the provision of service. Employees speak often and

Table 11.3	**High passion for service**
Descriptions of staffing issues in firms with a high, moderate, and low passion for service	There is not enough staff to whom we can delegate responsibilities. Management is running lean at the top. There aren't enough people for cross-training.
	Moderate passion for service
Source Benjamin Schneider and David E. Bowen, *Winning the Service Game* (Boston, MA: Harvard Business School Press, 1995), p. 130.	There is nobody to replace someone who takes a vacation. We have been reduced to a skeleton staff, but the work must still go out. Unusually heavy workloads are our biggest problem.
	Low passion for service
	When people leave, they are not replaced. Every day there is another staffing problem. Our receptionist has so many duties she sometimes can't even answer the phone.

Table 11.4	**High passion for service**
Descriptions of training in firms with a high, moderate, and low passion for service	There is cross-training in operations to improve service. Seminars are held for both in-house personnel and customers.
	Moderate passion for service
Source Benjamin Schneider and David E. Bowen, *Winning the Service Game* (Boston, MA: Harvard Business School Press, 1995), p. 135.	We can't learn other jobs because there is nobody here to relieve us while we are being trained. Some people get terrific training; others get none. We need more sales training.
	Low passion for service
	We have to go through hell to get permission to attend a training seminar. No one is being trained to use the PCs; automation is occurring without the necessary training. I'm taking a real estate course, and my company won't pay for it even though we are a mortgage bank.

favourably about the service delivery process and the product offered to consumers, as well as about the concern for and/or responsiveness of the firm to customer opinions. In addition, when service passion is strong, employees speak favourably about performance feedback, internal equity of compensation, training and staff quality, which is communicated to customers throughout the service delivery process.

Creating the right type of organization

Human resource management practices are the key drivers available to senior management for creating the type of organization that can be a source of sustainable competitive advantage. Often, however, front-line customer contact jobs are designed to be as simple and narrow as possible so that they can be filled by anyone – in other words, 'idiot-proof' jobs. Employers place few demands on employees, selection criteria are minimal and wages are low. The result is the classic cycle of failure of the industrial model as discussed in Chapter 1. Fewer and less-knowledgeable contact personnel are available, and hence, the customer gets less and lower-quality help. Customers vent their feelings of impatience and dissatisfaction on the staff, which, in turn, demotivates the employees, especially the most conscientious ones, since they are already aware of the poor service they are being forced to give. The best staff leave and are replaced with poorly trained recruits and the cycle continues. Current human resource theory is looking for ways to break out of the industrial model mindset, and, in particular, how to use empowerment and enfranchisement to break the cycle of failure.

Empowerment and enfranchisement

One of the most powerful tools for breaking free of the old logic is the use of employee empowerment and enfranchisement. Empowerment means giving discretion to contact personnel to 'turn the front line loose'. Empowerment is the reverse of 'doing things by the book'. Enfranchisement carries this logic even further by first empowering individuals and then coupling this with a reward system that recognizes people for their performance.

Rewarding employees is the most powerful way to encourage customer-oriented behaviours. Rewards can be extrinsic (e.g., pay) or intrinsic, such as enjoying the job itself, receiving recognition from co-workers and supervisors and/or accomplishing challenging and meaningful goals. Effective reward systems pass the seven tests listed below (Shneider and Bowen, 1995). Interestingly, in many instances, pay alone does not pass these effectiveness tests.

> *Availability* – Rewards must be available and substantial. Not having enough rewards or large enough rewards is likely to discourage desired behaviours rather than encourage them.
>
> *Flexibility* – Rewards should be flexible enough that they can be given to anyone at any time.
>
> *Reversibility* – If rewards are given to the wrong people for the wrong reasons, they should not be lifelong. Bonuses are better than pay increases that become lifetime annuities.

empowerment Giving discretion to front-line personnel to meet the needs of consumers creatively.

enfranchisement Empowerment coupled with a performance-based compensation method.

Contingent – Rewards should be directly tied to desired performance criteria.

Visibility – Rewards should be visible, and their value should be understood by all employees. For example, pay is not visible and is often shrouded in secrecy.

Timeliness – This is not to say that employees are rats, but rats are trained to receive food pellets immediately following the execution of a desired behaviour (e.g., pushing a bar). However, in this instance, employees are not that much different. Rewards should be given immediately following desired behaviours.

Durability – The motivating effects of a reward should last for a long time. The motivational effects of plaques and medallions last longer than the short-term effects of pay.

The most significant and successful enfranchisement programmes have occurred in the field of retailing. Here, advocates argue that it can improve sales and earnings dramatically while at the same time require less supervision from corporate management. Perhaps the most commonly used example is Nordstrom, which pays salespeople a commission not only on what they sell but also on the extent to which they can exceed their superiors' projected sales forecasts. At the same time, Nordstrom's management frees salespeople from normal constraints and publicly celebrates associates' outstanding service accomplishments.

When to empower and enfranchise

Managing boundary spanners is and always has been a challenging area. One of the ways that service personnel can provide a better, friendlier service is to be given greater freedom to adapt to the needs of the customer. Empowerment and enfranchisement are ways in which service personnel can be given that adaptability. Yip (2000) states that empowered employees have greater levels of satisfaction in their roles because they have the power, knowledge and greater abilities to provide a successful service encounter.

The benefits. Empowerment clearly brings benefits. Empowered employees are more customer-focused and are much quicker in responding to customer needs. They will customize the product or remix it in real time (Melhem, 2004) Empowered employees are more likely to respond in a positive manner to service failures and to engage in effective service recovery strategies.

Employees who are empowered tend to feel better about their jobs and themselves. This is automatically reflected in the way they interact with customers. They will be genuinely warmer and friendlier. Empowerment, therefore, can not only reduce unnecessary service recovery costs, but can also improve the quality of the product.

If close to the front line, an empowered employee is in a position continuously exposed to both the good and the bad aspects of the service delivery system. This employee can be the key to new service ideas and may often be a cheaper source for market research than going to the customer directly. If the organization truly gives their staff the freedom and flexibility that empowerment brings, staff will be able to answer positively to the following questions:

1 I am allowed to do anything to do a high-quality job.
2 I have the authority to correct problems when they occur.
3 I am allowed to be creative when I deal with problems at work.
4 I go through a lot of red tape and rigid rules to change things.
5 I have a lot of control over how I do my job.
6 I don't need to get management approval before I handle problems.
7 I have a lot of responsibility in my job.
8 I am not encouraged to handle job-related problems by myself.
9 I can make changes on my job whenever I want.
10 I cannot take charge of problems that require immediate attention.
11 I cannot feel free to meet my customers' needs under the bank's regulations.
12 The work load reduces the service I provide to my customers

(Melhem, 2004: 92)

The costs. Unfortunately, empowerment and enfranchisement do carry costs. The balance between benefits and costs determines the appropriateness of the approach. Empowerment increases the costs of the organization. But a greater investment is needed in remuneration and recruitment to assure that the right people are empowered. A low-cost model of using inexpensive and/or part-time labour cannot cope with empowerment, so the basic costs of the organization will be higher.

If costs are higher, marketing implications also arise. By definition, an empowered employee will customize the product. This means that the service received will vary from one encounter to the next, depending on the employee. The delivery is also likely to be slower because the service is customized. Moreover, since customers are treated differently, other customers may perceive that some customers are receiving preferential treatment. Finally, empowered employees, when attempting to satisfy customers, sometimes give away too much and make bad decisions. For example, a bellman who notices that a businessman forgot his briefcase at the front desk should make every attempt to return the briefcase to its owner. However, tracking the owner to the airport and hopping on the next available flight to the owner's destination is far beyond the call of duty and 'worlds' beyond what is economically feasible.

The balance of empowerment and enfranchisement, therefore, comes down to the benefit concept of the organization. A branded organization that guarantees consistency of product and service dare not empower for fear of the inconsistency that doing so would produce. For example, Subways European head office is in Amsterdam and their target is to have 4,000 quick food restaurants open across Europe by 2010 (Subway, 2008). One of its key differential advantages is to offer the same level of service, quality and efficiency across the world. Therefore, high levels of empowerment would begin to dissolve the Subway experience.

An organization that competes on the basis of value driven by a low cost base cannot afford to empower because of the costs involved. Equally, a high-cost service organization using a non-routine and complex technology almost certainly has to empower because its ability to use an industrial approach is severely limited.

Levels of empowerment

Empowerment is not for every firm. Firms can indeed be successful without fully empowering their employees. However, empowerment approaches vary by degree and include suggestion involvement, job involvement and high involvement. Each of the three levels of empowerment fall along a continuum that ranges from control-oriented to involvement-oriented approaches (see Figure 11.3).

suggestion involvement
Low-level empowerment that allows employees to recommend suggestions for improvement of the firm's operations.

quality circles
Empowerment involving small groups of employees from various departments in the firm who use brainstorming sessions to generate additional improvement suggestions.

Suggestion involvement falls near the control-oriented point of the empowerment continuum. Suggestion involvement empowers employees to recommend suggestions for improving the firm's operations. Employees are not empowered to implement suggestions themselves but are encouraged to suggest improvements for formal review. Firms that utilize suggestion involvement typically maintain formal suggestion programmes that proactively solicit employee suggestions. Quality circles often involve small groups of employees from various departments in the organization brainstorming ideas to generate additional suggestions. Including suggestions programmes and quality circles shows that organizations truly appreciate their workforce by giving them the opportunity to make suggestions for better service quality (Klages and Löffler, 2002). And, if the suggestions are implemented, staff are motivated because they feel their ideas have been heard and acted upon.

Figure 11.3

Levels of empowerment

Source Adapted from David E. Bowen and Edward E. Lawler III, 'The Empowerment of Service Workers: What, Why, How, and When', *Sloan Management Review* (Spring 1992), 31–39. © 1992 by Massachusetts Institute of Technology. All rights reserved. Distributed by Tribune Media Services.

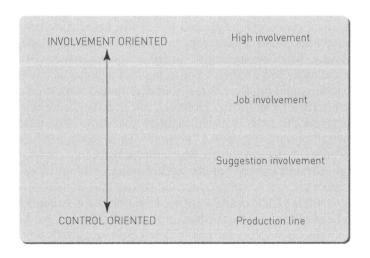

Job involvement typically falls in the middle of the empowerment continuum, between control-oriented and involvement-oriented approaches. Job involvement allows employees to examine the content of their own jobs and to define their role within the organization. Firms engaged in job involvement use teams of employees extensively for the betterment of the firm's service delivery system. In contrast to suggestion involvement, employees engaged in job involvement use a variety of skills, have considerable more freedom and receive extensive feedback from management, employees and customers.

job involvement Allows employees to examine the content of their own jobs and to define their role within the organization.

However, higher-level decisions and reward allocation decisions remain the responsibility of the firm's upper management.

High involvement falls at the involvement-oriented end of the empowerment continuum. Essentially, the goal of high involvement is to train people to manage themselves. Extensive training is utilized to develop skills in teamwork, problem solving, and business operations. Moreover, employees control the majority of the reward allocation decisions through profit sharing and employee ownership of the firm. In sum, virtually every aspect of a high-involvement firm is different from those of a control-oriented firm.

high involvement Allows employees to eventually learn to manage themselves, utilizing extensive training and employee control of the reward allocation decisions.

How much to empower: A contingency approach

When deciding to choose a) suggestion involvement, b) job involvement or c) high-involvement empowerment strategies, the firm must consider several factors in order to select the correct strategy. Table 11.5 provides a rating system to help managers assess their particular situations. According to the table, managers should rate their firms on five contingencies:

1 the firm's basic business strategy,
2 its tie to the customer,
3 technology,
4 the business environment, and
5 types of leadership.

The basic business strategy of the firm pertains to whether the firm produces a standardized, low-cost, high-volume product or whether it produces a differentiated, customized, personalized product. As the product becomes more standardized, lower levels of empowerment are suggested. Production-lining the service delivery system will make the system more efficient, thereby controlling costs and increasing the standardization of product produced.

basic business strategy A firm's fundamental approach as to whether it produces a standardized, low-cost, high-volume product or a differentiated, customized, personalized product.

The firm's tie to the customer refers to the type of relationship the firm has with its customers. If the relationship involves discrete transactions that occur over a short time period, control-oriented approaches should dominate. In contrast, if the customer–client relationship is long-term, such as that with an insurance agent, broker, or CPA, employees should be empowered to meet the individual needs of clients.

tie to the customer The degree of involvement the firm has with its customers.

technology The level of automation a firm utilizes.

Similarly, if the technology utilized to carry out the firm's operations is simple and routine and the business environment within which the firm operates is predictable, then the costs associated with empowered employees

business environment The social, technological and financial environment in which a firm operates and markets.

outweigh the benefits. If, on the other hand, the technology is nonroutine and complex and the business environment is volatile, empowered employees are necessary for coping with client concerns and the constantly changing environment.

Finally, empowered employees need different kinds of leadership. Theory Y managers, who coach and facilitate rather than control and manipulate, are needed to work with employees who have high growth needs and strong interpersonal skills – the needs and skills of empowered employees. In contrast, firms governed by Theory X managers believe that employees are working primarily to collect a paycheck. Theory X managers work best with employees who have low growth needs, low social needs and weak interpersonal skills. Theory X managers fit best with control-oriented organizations.

The contingency approach, presented in Table 11.5, rates each of the five factors (basic business strategy, tie to the customer, technology, business environment and types of people) on a scale from 1 to 5, where lower numbers favour a control-oriented approach and higher numbers favour an empowerment approach. Upon adding the scores of the five factors together, firms scoring in the 5–10 range are recommended to pursue a very control-oriented, production-line approach. Firms scoring in the 11–15 range are advised to implement a suggestion involvement strategy. Firms rating in the 16–20 range are urged to utilize a job involvement approach, and firms that score in the 21–25 range are encouraged to implement a high-involvement empowerment approach. The selection of empowerment strategy should be

---

Table 11.5

The contingencies of empowerment

Source David E. Bowen and Edward E. Lawler, III, 'The Empowerment of Service Workers: What, Why, How, and When' *Sloan Management Review* (Spring 1992), pp. 31–39. ©1992 by Massachusetts Institute of Technology. All rights reserved. Distributed by Tribune Media Services.

Contingency	Production-line approach		Empowerment
Basic business strategy	Low cost, high volume	1 2 3 4 5	Differentiation, customized, personalized
Tie to the customer	Transaction, short time period	1 2 3 4 5	Relationship, long time period
Technology	Routine, simple	1 2 3 4 5	Nonroutine, complex
Business environment	Predictable, few surprises	1 2 3 4 5	Unpredictable, many surprises
Types of people	Theory X managers, employees with low growth needs, low social needs, and weak interpersonal skills	1 2 3 4 5	Theory Y managers, employees with high growth needs, high social needs, and strong interpersonal skills

dependent upon the firm and the market in which it operates. Different types of firms have different needs.

Pulling it all together

Ultimately, the use of empowerment and enfranchisement is to break free from the shackles imposed by the industrial management model and move to values embraced by the market-focused management approach. As we introduced in Chapter 1, the market-focused management model champions the notion that the purpose of the firm is to service its customers. By following this approach, the service delivery process becomes the focus of the organization and the overall key to successfully differentiating the firm from its competition. People become the key to success.

The market-focused management approach recognizes that employee turnover and customer satisfaction are clearly related. As a result, the recruitment and training of front-line personnel is emphasized. Pay is directly tied to performance throughout every level of the organization. The benefits of superior training and education programmes are clear. Better-trained and better-paid employees provide better service, need less supervision and are more likely to stay on the job. In turn, customers are more satisfied, return to make purchases more often, purchase more when they do return and tell their friends of the positive experience. The elements discussed in this chapter are clearly beneficial to organizations that have the service orientation at the heart of their business strategy. The benefits are summarized in Figure 11.4.

Figure 11.4 brings together all the elements discussed in this chapter with regard to service orientated businesses. Clearly, there are benefits to each of the main stakeholders – customers, staff and of course shareholders who want a return on their investment. The final benefit, therefore, for the organization shown in this model is higher profit margins. Therefore, a

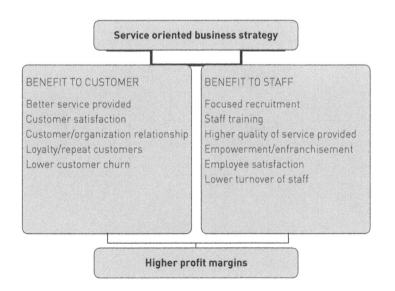

Figure 11.4

Benefits of service oriented business strategy

market-focused company that is service-led can reap the rewards through higher financial returns.

The service–profit chain

service–profit chain
Logical process ensuring that satisfied employees provide excellent customer service which leads to bottom-line profit.

The benefits of the market-focused management model are illustrated in the service–profit chain presented in Figure 11.5. The links in the chain reveal that employee satisfaction and customer satisfaction are directly related. Employee satisfaction is derived from a workplace and job design that facilitates internal service quality. Hiring, training and rewarding effective personnel are also major contributors to internal service quality.

Satisfied employees remain with the firm and improve their individual productivity. Hence, employee satisfaction is linked with increases in the firm's overall productivity and decreases in recruitment and training costs. Moreover, the increase in productivity coupled with a sincere desire to assist customers results in external service value. Employee attitudes and beliefs about the organization are often reflected in their behaviours. Given the customer's involvement in the production process, these behaviours are visible to the customer and ultimately influence the customer's satisfaction.

Customer satisfaction is directly related to customer loyalty, which is demonstrated through repeat purchases and positive word-of-mouth referrals to other customers. The net effects of customer retention are increased revenues and profitability for the firm.

Simultaneously, employees are also rewarded for their efforts. The outcomes associated with employee satisfaction – external service values, customer satisfaction, customer loyalty, revenue growth and increased profitability – reinforce the company's commitment for continually improving internal service quality. As the recipients of internal quality improvements and positive customer responses, employees directly experience the fruits of their efforts. Employee satisfaction is subsequently reinforced and the integrity of the service–profit chain is maintained.

Figure 11.5

The service-profit chain

Source James L. Heskett, Thomas O. Jones, Gary W. Loveman, W. Earl Sasser, Jr., and Leonard A. Schlesinger, 'Putting the Service-Profit Chain to Work', *Harvard Business Review* (March–April 1994), 164–174. Reprinted by permission of *Harvard Business Review*. Copyright © 1994 by the President and Fellows of Harvard College.

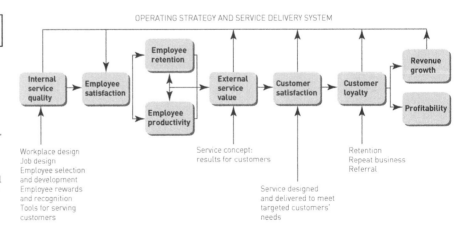

The service–profit chain provides the logic behind the change in perspective which has led to the new services model. The major lessons to be learned by the chain are two-fold. First, a firm must satisfy its employees in order for customer satisfaction to become a consistent reality. Second, the chain proclaims the simple fact that service and quality pay off!

Summary

Successful service firms develop a seamless relationship among marketing, operations and human resources. This chapter has focused on some of the human resource issues that must be considered when marketing services. Much has been written about the fact that, for many service firms, personnel constitute the bulk of their product. It is thus important that the place of personnel within the organization be understood. By drawing on the concept of organizational behaviour and, in particular, the concepts of boundary-spanning roles, empowerment and enfranchisement, this chapter has provided a solid framework on which to develop the marketing implications of personnel as a key component of the firm's overall product offering.

As boundary spanners, service personnel perform the dual functions of interacting with both the firm's external environment and its internal organization and structure. Employees who occupy boundary-spanning roles are often placed in situations that produce conflict and stress. There are five common types of stress: inequality dilemmas, feelings versus behaviour, territorial conflict, organization/client conflicts and inter-client conflicts.

Because service firms often involve the customer as a co-producer, they operate open systems, where the effects of human resource practices and policies as well as the organization's climate are visible to customers. Current human resource theory is looking for ways to break out of the industrial model mindset, and, in particular, how to use empowerment and enfranchisement to break the cycle of failure. When deciding among empowerment strategies, the firm must consider the following:

1 the firm's basic business strategy,
2 its tie to the customer,
3 technology,
4 the business environment, and
5 types of leadership.

The selection of empowerment strategy should be dependent upon the firm and the market in which it operates. Different types of firms have different needs. Ultimately, the use of empowerment and enfranchisement is to break free from the shackles imposed by the industrial management model and move to values embraced by the market-focused management approach. The benefits of the market-focused management model are illustrated in the service–profit chain. The major lessons to be learned by the chain are two-fold. First, a firm must satisfy its employees in order for customer satisfaction to become a consistent reality. Second, the chain proclaims the simple fact that service and quality pay off!

Discussion questions

1 Relate the concepts of intangibility, inseparability, heterogeneity and perishability to the importance of personnel in the service firm.

2 What are boundary-spanning personnel? Discuss the five types of conflict that they generally encounter.

3 How can marketing be utilized to reduce the amount of stress and conflict experienced by boundary-spanning personnel?

4 Which organizations should avoid empowerment approaches?

5 In what type of organizations should implement a job-involvement empowerment approach?

6 Discuss the benefits and costs associated with empowerment and enfranchisement.

7 What is climate? Why is organizational climate of particular importance to service firms?

8 Define enfranchisement. Summarize the seven tests of reward effectiveness.

References and further reading

Altro (2007) 'Talking Beyond the Surface', www. altrotransflor.com, accessed 10 January 2008.

aSurface (2008) 'The Resin Floor and Sanding Specialists', http://www.asurface.co.uk/-about-asurface.asp, accessed 10 January 2008.

Blitz, R. (2007) 'Tourism told to raise its game for Olympics', Published 18 Sept. 2007, http://search.ft.com/ftArticle?queryText = %22high + staff + turnover %22 + %22services% 22andy = 11andaje = trueandx = 21andid = 070918001008andct = 0, accessed 3 January 2008.

Bowen, D. E. and Lawler, III, E. E. (1992) 'The empowerment of service workers: what, why, how, and when', *Sloan Management Review* (Spring): 31–39.

Cobb-Walgren, C. J. and Mohr, L. A. (1998) 'Symbols in service advertisements', *Journal of Services Marketing* 12 (2): 129–151.

The Economist (2003) 'Lost in translation', 29 November, 369 (8352): 58.

Harris, L. C. and Reynolds K. L. (2004) 'Jaycustomer behaviour: an exploration of types and motives in the hospitality industry', *Journal of Services Marketing* 18 (5): 339–357.

Heskett, J. L., Jones, T. O., Loveman, G. W. Sasser, Jr., W. E. and Schlesinger, L. A. (1994) 'Putting the service-profit chain to work', *Harvard Business Review* (March–April): 164–174.

Hoe, S. L. (2006) 'The boundary spanner's role in organizational learning: unleashing untapped potential', *Development and Learning in Organizations* 20 (5): 9–11.

Homburg, C., Hoyer, W. D. and Fassnacht, M. (2002) 'Service orientation of a retailer's business strategy:

dimensions, antecedents, and performance outcomes', *Business Journal of Marketing* 66 (4): 86–101.

Klages, H. and Löffler, E. (2002) 'Giving Staff of Local Authorities a Voice: A Checklist of Success Factors for Staff Surveys – Local Governance, 2002' mediaworks.uwe.ac.uk.

Klidas, A., van den Berg, P. T. and Wilderom, C. P. M. (2007) 'Managing employee empowerment in luxury hotels in Europe', *International Journal of Service Industry Management* 18 (1): 70–88.

Kolsaker, A. and Payne, C. (2002) 'Engendering trust in e-commerce: a study of gender-based concerns', *Marketing Intelligence and Planning* 20 (4): 206–214.

Kotler, P., Bowen, J., Makens, J. (2003) *Marketing for Hospitality and Tourism*, 3rd edn ed., Engelwood Cliffs, NJ: Prentice Hall.

Kramer, M. and Schmalenberg, C. (2004) 'Essentials of a magnetic work environment: part 1', *Nursing* 34 (6): pp. 50–54.

Lashley, C. (1997) *Empowering Service Excellence: Beyond the Quick Fix*, London: Cassell.

Lou, J. T., McGoldrick, P. Beatty, S. and Keeling, K. A. (2006) 'On-screen characters: their design and influence on consumer trust', *Journal of Services Marketing* 20 (2): 112–124.

Lovelock, C. H. (1994) *Product Plus: How Product + Service = Competitive Advantage*, New York: McGraw-Hill.

Lytle, R. S. and Timmerman, J. E. (2006) 'Service orientation and performance: an organizational perspective', *Journal of Services Marketing* 20 (2).

Mahesh, V. S. and Kasturi, A. (2006) 'Improving call centre agent performance: a UK-India study based on the agents' point of view', *International Journal of Service Industry Management* 17 (2): 136–157.

Melhem, Y. (2004) 'Empowerment; Services; customer service management', *Banking Employee Relations* 26 (1): 72–93.

Menon, K. and Bansal, H. S. (2007) 'Exploring consumer experience of social power during service consumption', *International Journal of Service Industry Management* 18 (1): 89–104.

Mintel (2007) 'Industrial Flooring (Industrial Report)', September, http://academic.mintel.com.

Newman, K., Maylor, U. and Chansarkar, B. (2002) 'The nurse satisfaction, service quality and nurse retention chain', *Journal of Management in Medicine* 16 (4): 271– 291.

Nickson, D. Warhurs, C. and Dutton, E. (2005) 'The inportance of attitude and appearance in the service encounter in retail and hospitality', *Managing Service Quality* 15 (2): 195–208.

Roy, M. C., Dewit, O. and Aubert, B. A. (2001) 'The impact of interface usability on trust in web retailers', *Internet Research: Electronic Networking Applications and Policy* 11 (5): 388–398.

Schneider, B. and Bowen, D. E. (1995) *Winning the Service Game*, Boston, MA: Harvard Business School Press.

Subway (2008) 'European Franchising (2008) Poised for worldwide growth. The SUBWAY sandwich chain is poised for tremendous growth around the world. SUBWAY's European Regional Director Kevin Graham reports', *Journal for European Franchise Opportunities*, http://www.europeanfranchising.net/franchise/Subway-Sandwiches/Poised-for-worldwide-growth/1115, accessed 11 January 2008.

Thibodeau, P. (2005) 'Offshore tech support still stirs controversy', *Computerworld* (2 May), 39 (18): 7.

Virgin (2008) 'Responsible Business Practice', http://www.virgin-energy.co.uk/RBP/Customers/Awards.aspx?L3_GenericContent_NavigateToPage = 2, accessed 3 January 2008.

Yip J. S. L. (2000) 'Quality service success – property management development to empowerment: a Hong Kong analysis', *Structural Survey* 18 (4): 148–154.

Chapter 12

People issues: Managing service consumers

Use your good judgement in all situations. There will be no additional rules.

(Nordstrom, Inc., Employee Handbook)

Chapter objectives

The purpose of this chapter is to explore the special role of the service consumer. Due to the impact of inseparability, the consumer's role in service production can both facilitate and hinder the exchange process. Hence, it is critical to develop a strategic understanding of how the consumer can be effectively managed within the service encounter.

After reading this chapter, you should be able to:

- Discuss strategies for managing consumer participation within the service encounter.

- Describe approaches that manage consumer waiting time.

- Explain appropriate methods for dealing with difficult customers.

- Understand the fundamental components of an electronic customer relationship management (CRM) system.

Services in context
Customers' inseperability from the service – and from each other

Consumers and service providers interact with each other during the service encounter. The need for excellent service delivery processes were discussed in the previous chapter. Service encounters can happen every day, such as buying a bus ticket or a sandwich for lunch. They can also be regular encounters such as a visit to the barber for a shave or to the games store to rent a Play Station game. And, of course, they can be special purchases such as visiting a travel agent to arrange a honeymoon or visiting a car showroom to buy a Mini Cooper. All of these examples show the interdependency between customer and provider. During the more complex service encounters the inseparability between the customer and the provider becomes more pronounced. However, in some encounters the customer becomes a 'part-time' member of staff. Instances where customers 'become' staff include using day-to-day services such as ATMs to 'self-serving' a side order from the salad bar. It is also important to remember that the customer and provider do not work in isolation as there are many other customers interacting in and participating in the service encounter. Encounters where customer-to-customer interactions are essential and pre-planned by the provider include quiz nights at the local pub to karaoke competitions at holiday resorts. And just imagine what it would be like if there was only one spectator at the 100 metres men's final at the Olympic Games!

Customer-to-customer interactions are not always pre-planned by the provider. There are three typologies to describe customers interacting with each other in the service environment. The typologies are helpseeker, reactive helper and proactive helper. Helpseekers asks 'strangers' within a service environment for basic information. An example of this is when a lady is buying a garment for a gentleman in a retail store. The female helpseeker asks a male customer basic product advice about size. Alternatively, grandparents may ask other customers, who have children with them. For example, Bratz dolls are the latest craze for five-year-olds so grandparents may approach customers with children to ensure they buy the 'right' doll for their grand-daughters Isobel and Lucy. Reactive helpers are the 'experts' that helpseekers interact with. This customer-to-customer interaction can be pleasing or embarrassing for the reactive helper. Some reactive helpers will feel honoured to be asked their opinions about size or the latest trend in dolls for five-year-olds. However, other reactive helpers, providing value judgements, when asked 'Does this dress suit me?' are embarrassed to provide an opinion to a complete stranger. It is interesting to note that cross-gender requests solicit positive reactions. Helpseeker females appear to be the 'damsel in distress' when interacting with a male reactive helper. And helpseeker men appear to be a 'little boy lost' while interacting with female reactive helpers

The proactive helper has an 'inner desire' to guide others, especially strangers that are in the same environment. An example of this could be when two customers are admiring cars on a garage forecourt. The proactive helper will discuss the merits of the cars as they have facts and information and wish to pass on their knowledge. Proactive helpers also have good price comparison knowledge and actively advise other customers of them. For example, thinking back to the grandparents who were going to buy a Bratz doll for Isobel and Lucy, a customer overhearing them discuss their dilemma may approach the grandparents, advise them that Bratz dolls are appropriate and recommend they buy the dolls from the indoor market as they are £5.00 cheaper.

▶

During a field experiment at a garden centre, customers were asked what motivated them to interact with other customers rather than 'go it alone' or interact with the service provider. Answers included:

'You're outside the four walls of your house and you're meeting new people and it sort of brightens up your day, doesn't it, to meet new people.'

(Helpseeker)

'I enjoy talking about the garden.'

(Proactive helper)

'Contact. Just contact with another person.'

(Reactive helper)

And the benefits of talking with other customers are shown in Table 12.1.

Clearly, as demonstrated in Chapter 2 there is inseparability between the customer and the staff employed by the service provider. This case study shows there is also inseparability within the customer-to-customer interface. Front-line staff should be made aware of this, particularly in the body language displayed by helpseekers. Staff should then actively approach customers in need of help and join in conversation when helpseekers have approached reactive helpers. As staff become more involved, customers enjoy the service encounters more.

Sources: A.J. Kenyon (2008) 'Workshop case study – Leeds Metropolitan University'.
C. Parker and P. Ward (2000) 'An analysis of role adoptions and scripts during customer-to-customer encounters', *European Journal of Marketing* 34 (3/4): 341–359.
M.A. McGrath and C. Otnes (1995) 'Unacquainted influencers: When strangers interact in the retail setting', *Journal of Business Research* 32 (3): 261–272.

Table 12.1	Consequence of interaction	Example of response in that category
Consequence of interacting with other customers **Source** Parker and Ward, (2000) 'An analysis of role adoptions and scripts during customer-to-customer encounters', *European Journal of Marketing*, Vol. 34, No. 3/4 p352.	1. Increased enjoyment of service experience	'I think it makes it more enjoyable, it can brighten up your day'
	2. Improved/increased purchase	'I wouldn't have spent £20 on a shrub unless I'd been sure and he (the other customer) reassured me'
	3. Social involvement	'Because you don't feel that you're just, how shall I put it, just somebody who's trotting around in their own little world, shut off from the world, doing your own thing, because there's been that interaction'
	4. Increased knowledge	'Because I've learned something new … I'm always interested in learning something new'
	5. Negative (e.g. irritation, embarrassment)	'Other customers can lose your concentration; having to deal or speak with them you can forget what you're doing for yourself and that's a major irritation'

Introduction

Ultimately, the success of many service encounters depends upon how effectively the service organization manages its clientele. As mentioned in previous chapters, the service encounter can be viewed as a three-way fight for control among the customer, the employee and the organization itself. The procedures and systems established by the organization to balance this arrangement are not created simply to add to the bureaucracy of the encounter but are primarily put in place to ensure profitability.

Unlike the goods manufacturer, who may seldom see an actual customer while producing the good in a secluded factory, service providers are often in constant contact with their customers and must construct their service operations with the customer's physical presence at the top of their mind. This interaction between customer and service provider defines a critical incident. Critical incidents represent the greatest opportunity for both gains and losses in regard to customer satisfaction and customer retention.

During the customer's interaction with the service provider, the customer provides input into the service production process. As such, the customer often plays a key role in the successful completion of the service encounter. The customer's involvement in the production process may vary from (1) a requirement that the customer be physically present to receive the service, as in dental services, a haircut, or surgery; (2) a need for the customer to be present only to start and stop the service, as in dry cleaning and auto repair; and (3) a need for the customer to be only mentally present, as in participation in college courses that are transmitted via the internet. Each scenario reflects different levels of customer contact, and as a result each service delivery system should be designed differently.

The focus of this chapter is on four consumer management areas of particular importance:

1 the management of consumer participation in the service process;
2 the management of consumer waiting periods;
3 dealing with difficult customers – managing to keep your cool while those around you are losing theirs; and
4 an introduction to an electronic CRM system.

Managing customer participation

Overall, as customer participation increases, the efficiency of the operation decreases. The customer's involvement in the production process creates uncertainties in the scheduling of production. For example, the customer has a direct impact on the type of service desired, the length of the service delivery process and the cycle of service demand. Attempting to manage consumer participation in the production process with efficient operating procedures is a delicate art.

Increasing consumer participation in the service delivery process has become a popular strategy to increase the supply of service available to the

co-produce Service produced via a cooperative effort between customers and service providers.

firm and to provide a form of service differentiation. By allowing consumers to co-produce at least part of their own service, contact personnel are freed to perform other duties, such as serving other customers or engaging in non-customer-related activities (such as completing paperwork). Increasing customer participation is associated with a number of advantages and disadvantages. The primary advantage to the customer and the service firm is that customers can customize their own service and produce it faster and less expensively than if the firm had produced it. Customers making their own salads at Pizza Hut's salad bar or picking their own strawberries are classic examples. On the other hand, increased levels of customer participation are also associated with the firm's losing control of quality; increased waste, which increases operating costs; and customer perceptions that the firm may be attempting to distance itself from its customers (Parker and Ward, 2000; Bateson, 1985).

When making the transition from a full-service to a self-service operation, the firm needs to be sensitive to the reasons the customer may have for preferring one format over another. Guidelines have evolved that help facilitate this transition and avoid insensitivity.

Develop customer trust

Efforts to increase customer participation throughout the production process should not be interpreted as the firm's way of distancing itself from the customer. The firm should provide information to the customer that explains why self-service opportunities are being provided and the potential customer benefits. When it is readily apparent that the only reason the firm is offering self-service options is to benefit the firm, customers will quickly flock to full-service competitors.

Promote the benefits and stimulate trial

The typical benefits associated with self-service are convenience, customization and cost savings to the customer. Self-service petrol stations provide a cost savings, self-service salad and dessert bars allow customers to customize their own salads and ice cream sundaes and automatic teller machines (ATM) provide 24-hour service and extend the bank's services in hundreds of convenient locations.

To promote new self-service options, customers will need to feel they can trust the new technology (Turner, Safar and Ramaswamy, 2006). Many banks and home-service providers such as gas and electricity use voice recognition software. Customers using it for the first time may not feel convinced that a machine will 'hear' them correctly. However, when they begin to receive statements following a request to their bank or receive a bill from the electricity company showing their latest meter reading, customers soon begin to trust the new technology. And one of the greatest benefits is that customers can provide meter readings, request statements and move money from their bank to the electricity company 'hands free' using their own mobile phones.

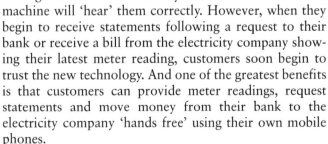

Case link

For an example of self-service, see Case Study 9: Champions League Final Moscow.

Understand customer habits

Organizations are transferring from full-service to self-service more often. The problem with this is that organizations tend to forget why customers might prefer using full-service options in the first place. Despite the convenience of ATMs, many customers like the personalization of dealing with a particular teller. Friendships and trust develop between customers and service employees, something that cannot be replaced by machines. In addition, many bank customers will use an ATM for withdrawals, but refuse to make deposits through the same ATM. The thought of handing over cheques and cash to a machine seems to be too much of a risk for some customers.

Pre-test new procedures

All new self-service options should be thoroughly pre-tested, not only by the firm's employees but particularly by customers who do not have the advantage of full information. For example, the British postal system attempted to enlist the help of its customers by requesting them to use extremely long postal codes when addressing envelopes. The plan was a disaster. The postal codes were far too long to remember, and the public basically vetoed any further development of the project by simply refusing to participate.

Pre-testing helps in identifying and correcting potential problems before new procedures are fully introduced. In many instances, the company may have only one or two chances to prove to customers the benefits of self-service alternatives, many of which are often offered on the corporate website. However, if the website and/or on-site processes are flawed and/or difficult to understand, the firm may lose its chance to convince customers of the advantages. For example, more customers might use ATMs if the screens did not face the sun and were easier to read, if the machines had not initially frequently 'eaten' the customers' ATM cards and if customers did not have to be gymnasts to use drive-through ATMs from their vehicles because the machine was not within easy reach.

Understand the determinants of consumer behaviour

When considering consumer benefits of self-service alternatives, firms should understand the determinants of consumer behaviour. Why would a customer use an ATM instead of a bank teller? Or why would customers like to select and cook their own steaks in a fine dining restaurant? The consumer benefits promoted by the firm should be defined by the customer. For example, customers who work shifts other than the traditional 8 to 5 slot enjoy the 24-hour accessibility of ATMs. Other customers may simply be in a hurry, and the ATM provides a faster means of service. At self-service 'cookeries', the experience of selection and preparation may facilitate social interaction and/or be ego driven. Clearly not all customers behave the same and even though e-tailers/e-businesses and e-buying is relatively new – there are clearly different consumers groups. See E-Services in Action for alternative typologies of online shopping behaviour around the world.

E-services in action
Developing an effective web strategy: The typology of online shoppers

Online shopping continues to be a phenomenal success all over the world. As more advanced technology is introduced consumers can shop not only from their PCs but from their television, PDA or mobile phones. Table 12.2 just hints at the growing trend in internet activity between 2000 and 2007.

Shoppers use the internet for many reasons such as (1) can't be bothered to 'go' shopping, to (2) time saving, to (3) more bargain hunting opportunities. Online shopping is big business – but many consumers still like the bricks and mortar stores. What is interesting is that customers often shop in physical locations at the weekend and then make comparisons by moving to online shopping on Mondays. In fact most online shopping happens on Mondays (Moskalyuk, 2004). It is these interesting facts that organizations with online shopping facilities need to know. A recent study with net shoppers in Asia showed that there are six different behavioural activities. These typologies are outlined in Table 12.3.

Understanding these typologies enables organizations to promote their products and services to the different segments. For example, some customers are clearly 'information

gatherers' who need good websites to provide up-to-date information that will in drive the customer to the bricks and mortar stores.

The experience the different shoppers have online is important as it progresses over time through four unique stages: (1) Functionality – 'The site works well'; (2) Intimacy – 'The site understands my particular set of needs'; (3) Internalization – 'Visiting the site is part of my daily life'; and (4) Evangelism – 'I love to tell others about the site.'

Clearly the challenge for organizations is to build a relationship with the customer through face-to-face and virtual interactions. The marketing managers must ensure that the two faces of the organization are in harmony but allow for different segmentation types.

Sources: A. K. Kau, Y. E. Tang and S. Ghose (2003) 'Typology of online shoppers', *Journal of Consumer Marketing* 20 (2): 139–156.
R. A. Mohammed, R. J. Fisher, B. J. Jaworski and A. Cahill (2002) *Internet Marketing: Building Advantage in a Networked Economy* (Boston, MA: McGraw-Hill Irwin), pp. 622–624.
R. Zemke and T. Connellan (2001) *E-service* (New York: AMACOM).

Table 12.2 World internet usage and population statistics	World regions	Population (2007 est.)	Population % of world	Internet usage, latest data	% Population (penetration)	Usage % of world	Usage growth 2000–2007
	Africa	941,249,130	14.2 %	44,361,940	4.7 %	3.4 %	882.7 %
	Asia	3,733,783,474	56.5 %	510,478,743	13.7 %	38.7 %	346.6 %
	Europe	801,821,187	12.1 %	348,125,847	43.4 %	26.4 %	231.2 %
	Middle East	192,755,045	2.9 %	33,510,500	17.4 %	2.5 %	920.2 %

North America	334,659,631	5.1 %	238,015,529	71.1 %	18.0 %	120.2 %
Latin America/ Caribbean	569,133,474	8.6 %	126,203,714	22.2 %	9.6 %	598.5 %
Oceania / Australia	33,569,718	0.5 %	19,175,836	57.1 %	1.5 %	151.6 %
WORLD TOTAL	**6,606,971,659**	**100.0 %**	**1,319,872,109**	**20.0 %**	**100.0 %**	**265.6 %**

NOTES: (1) Internet Usage and World Population Statistics are for December 31, 2007. (2) Demographic (Population) numbers are based on data from the *US Census Bureau*. (3) Internet usage information comes from data published by *Nielsen//NetRatings*, by the *International Telecommunications Union*, by local NIC, and other reliable sources) Information in this site (www.internetworldstats.com) may be cited, giving the due credit to www.internetworldstats.com. Copyright © 2000–2008, Miniwatts Marketing Group. All rights reserved

Typology	Behaviour
On-off shopper	On-off shoppers surf the internet and collect online information and yet prefer to shop offline. They look for advertisements, are frequent users of bookmarks and use the same search engine on a regular basis. They are experienced navigators and seek out the best deals. Their profile tends to be single, aged 15–24; there is no gender difference.
Comparison shopper	Comparison shoppers are excellent surfers who actively seek comparative information about product features, prices and brands before making purchase decision. They also actively look out for price or other promotional offers. This group is more likely to be male aged 25–29
Traditional shopper	Traditional shoppers buy from bricks and mortar stores. They do not search for bargains or comparisons. They are more likely to be aged 40–49.
Dual shopper	Dual shoppers do search for information, but do not seek deals exclusively. They particularly search for information about brands and their product features. They are more likely to be 15–24 years old and male.
e-laggard	Females tend to be e-laggards and older (35 years and above). Information seeking is not their area of interest and they are not navigation savvy.
Information surfer	These surfers are more likely to be married. They browse websites for banner advertisements and look specifically for promotional offers. They are good navigators and make regular online purchases

Table 12.3

Behavioural activities

Teach consumers how to use service innovations

Many of today's self-service options are technology driven, and in many cases, customers are left to fend for themselves in attempts to use these new alternatives. An 'on your own' approach does not exactly encourage customers to try new self-service methods. For customers to be taught, employees must first know how to use the technology themselves. Nothing will turn off customers faster than employees who have no idea how to use the new systems themselves.

Monitor and evaluate performance

Finally, if a firm's self-service option enjoys an initial success, it should be continuously monitored and evaluated throughout the year. Does demand fluctuate? What are the possible causes? Has demand increased, decreased, or levelled off? What other services do consumers want self-service access to? Customer surveys and focus groups will not only define satisfaction with today's services but will also provide insight pertaining to the needs of tomorrow. Currently, in many service environments modern technology is trying to make the service experience quick and easy. This is because customers are cash rich and time poor. Therefore, convenience a key factor – but not always. Customers would like convenience for some services but are prepared to wait for others. Figure 12.1, A Model of Service Convenience shows different service characteristics. All service encounters will include these service characteristics (see Chapter 2). Customers will want some service encounters to be convenient, quick and easy. But for some transactions customers will be prepared, even happy, to wait. Consider queuing to buy a ticket. Consumers purchasing a ticket to see Schalke vs Barcelona for

---

Figure 12.1

A model of services convenience

Source L. L. Berry, K. Seiders and D. Grewal (2002) 'Understanding Service Convenience', *Journal of Marketing* 66 (July): 4.

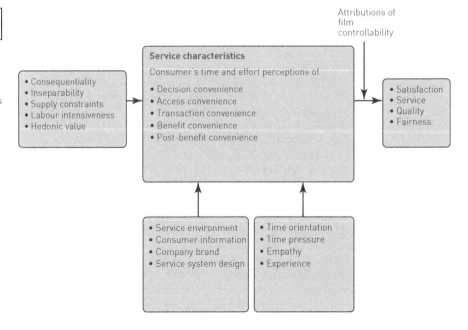

the UEFA Champions League Quarter Final will wait for hours outside the ticket bureau without complaint. This is because the service characteristics appeal to the customer's hedonic values. Therefore, *perception* of the time and effort elements, shown in the service convenience section of the model, will not be driven by the need for a fast, efficient service. The post-benefit factors of getting to the Quarter Final will certainly compensate for the time and effort spent buying the ticket. Compare this example with buying a train ticket to get to work. Consumers want the fast, efficient, convenient service and will complain vehemently if they have to wait. This is because they want a quick transaction; spending a lot of time and effort is not compensated in the same way as buying a ticket to watch your favourite football team in the UEFA Champions League Final.

Generally, customers wishing to purchase highly valued services such as a wedding gown will not want nor expect a fast and efficient service. A golf lesson or haircut can also be highly valued. These service encounters are prized, hence consumers are tolerant of wait-time due to the inseparability of the service. However, some consumers may decide that convenience is paramount and so forego the service encounter because of time pressure. For example, consumers often have to make a reservation at popular restaurants. By making a reservation the customer has transaction convenience (see Figure 12.1). Due to the inseparability of the dining experience customers need to remain calm and be patient if they have to wait beyond the time when they booked their meal. However, if the customer does not feel that the post-benefit of waiting compensates for their delay they will take their business to a less popular restaurant, which lacks the pizzazz of the restaurant they had originally chosen, but is quick and convenient. Consumers waiting for a burger at a fast-food take-away want quick access and a quick transaction and do not want to wait. Clearly an organization will decide upon their service delivery mechanisms and account for the challenges of customers having to wait. Below are some strategies that organizations can consider.

Managing consumer waits

In addition to managing consumer participation, service managers are often faced with managing other customer-related challenges as well. Because production and consumption occur simultaneously, several customers often share a common service experience. As a result, demand often outpaces supply and queues develop that must be effectively managed to minimize customer dissatisfaction. Due to the unpredictability of consumer demand inherent in many service operations, the only cases in which the supply of available service and consumer demand balance exactly – *is by accident*. As a result, consumers of services often find themselves waiting for service.

Effectively managing consumer waits is particularly crucial due to the importance of first impressions on consumer perceptions of the service experience. First impressions are often long-lasting and can dramatically affect customer evaluations of the total experience, regardless of how good the service was after the wait. A dental patient waiting until 4:00 p.m. for an appointment that was supposed to begin at 2:00 p.m. will most likely care little about how friendly the staff and the dentist are by the time the appointment actually begins.

Over the years, through trial and error, eight principles of waiting have developed to help service firms effectively manage consumer waits (Maister 1984). Service firms sensitive to these principles have developed strategies to deal with consumer waits and to minimize the negative effects associated with delays. In fact, in some instances, effective management of consumer waits has actually led to increased profit opportunities.

Principle No.1: Unoccupied waits feel longer than occupied waits

Waiting around with nothing to do makes every minute seem so much longer. Successful service firms have learned to manage consumer waits by occupying the consumer's time. Restaurants can occupy consumer waits by offering to let the consumer wait in the lounge area, which also increases the profit-making opportunity for the firm. Similarly, golf courses offer driving ranges, and the medical community tends to offer reading materials. Ideally, tactics utilized to occupy consumers should be related to the ensuing service encounter. Trivial attempts to occupy consumer waits, such as forcing the customer to listen to Muzak when placed on hold during a phone call, are sometimes met with customer resistance and frustration.

Principle No.2: Pre-process waits feel longer than in-process waits – post-process waits feel longest of all

The waiting period before the service starts feels longer to customers than waiting while the service is in process. For example, doctors often move waiting patients into empty examining rooms to convey the sense that the service has started. Realistically, the physician has simply changed the location of the wait. Effective techniques to manage pre-process waits include simply acknowledging the customer. For example, wait-staff are often too busy to serve customers as soon as they are seated. Phrases such as 'I'll be with you as soon as I can' acknowledge the customer's presence and convey the message that the service has started. Other phrases such as 'your order is being processed' are also effective in keeping the customer informed of the status of the order.

Post-process waits feel the longest of all waits. In many instances, the service has been delivered, and now the customer is simply waiting for the check or bill. It's baffling to customers to be subjected to delays when the customer simply wants to give the service establishment money. Another example of customer impatience regarding post-process waits can be experienced during deplaning procedures at the airport. On your next flight, listen to the sounds of passengers releasing their seatbelts as soon as (or before) the plane comes to a full stop. The door to the plane is not open, no one is leaving the plane, yet people are literally fighting for positions to get themselves off the plane as quickly as possible.

Principle No.3: Anxiety makes the wait seem longer

Have you ever noticed how much longer traffic lights take to change when you are in a hurry? This is because anxiety expands consumer perceptions of time. Effective service firms manage the anxiety levels of their customers by attempting to identify and then removing anxiety-producing components of the service encounter. The use of focus groups is particularly helpful in effectively identifying anxiety producers because many consumers' fears may be irrational and/or overlooked by providers who fully understand the service delivery process. Often, information is one of the most effective tools in relieving consumer anxiety. For example, informing delayed airline passengers that connecting flights are being held for them, notifying waiting movie-goers that seats are available and assisting new students in finding the right lines during registration will remove much of the anxiety felt by these consumer groups.

Principle No.4: Uncertain waits are longer than known, finite waits

While waiting in a doctor's office, the wait 'before' the stated appointment time passes much more quickly than the time spent waiting 'beyond' the appointment time. Restaurants have learned this lesson the hard way. In the not-so-distant-past, it seemed that restaurants would purposely underestimate their wait-times to encourage patrons not to leave the restaurant to dine at a competitor's establishment. This strategy resulted in angry, frustrated customers who felt they had been purposely misled and lied to for the sake of greed. By the time the customers were seated, they were so consumed with anger that the food, service and atmosphere of the encounter became irrelevant, regardless of their quality. Moreover, many of these patrons would vow never to return. Today, it seems that restaurants overestimate their waits to provide consumers with a realistic time-frame from which to develop expectations. Other service providers simply make and keep appointments, which eliminates the customer's wait altogether. Other providers, such as Disney, provide finite waiting times stated on signage that is strategically placed at certain points along the line (e.g., 10 minutes from this point).

Principle No.5: Unexplained waits are longer than explained waits

It is human nature to want an explanation. You can almost see the disappointment in people's faces when the slow speed during a traffic jam

SOURCE © ANTONIO ODUIAS/ DREAMSTIME.COM

Uncertain waits are longer than known, finite waits.

on the road resumes its normal pace without an explanation. Customers want to know why they have to wait, and the earlier the information is provided, the more understanding the consumer becomes, and the shorter the perception of the wait.

Due to the inseparability of services, customers sometimes have a difficult time understanding why all the service providers in the factory are not serving customers. Banks are a good example. Bank cashiers must sometimes perform operational duties, such as balancing the cash drawer, which prohibits them from serving customers. However, since all bank cashier stations are visible to the customers, customers often question why all the bank cashiers are not actively serving the bank's customers.

Effective management may try to minimize this problem in one of two ways. First, management may consider educating consumers about the realities of the bank teller's duties, which extend beyond interactions with customers. Second, management may consider developing a physical facility where the teller is out of sight when performing non-customer-related duties. This type of problem extends beyond the banking industry. Airlines, grocery stores and other businesses that grant their employees rest breaks that are visible to the customer face similar challenges.

Principle No.6: Unfair waits are longer than equitable waits

Effective consumer management should strive to provide a level playing field that is fair for all consumers. The majority of consumers are not unreasonable. Most restaurant consumers understand that larger parties will wait longer than smaller parties and those parties with reservations will be seated sooner than those who arrive unannounced. However, probably nothing will ignite a serious confrontation faster than consumers who feel they have been passed over by other customers who entered the service experience at a later time under the same set of circumstances.

Lines such as those found at McDonald's and drive-through banks are classic examples of why consumers become frustrated. In each instance, the customer must pick the line he or she thinks will move fastest. Inevitably, the other lines move faster, and customers who entered the lines at a later time are served first, 'out of order'. From a fairness perspective, methods that form a single line, such as those used at KFC or Burger King, and many banks, are preferable. Customers are served in the order in which they enter the service process.

Another classic example of unfair service is the priority that telephone calls receive over customers who are physically standing in line. The person on the telephone usually takes priority. This is the equivalent of that person walking up to the front of the line and bypassing all of the other customers who have been patiently awaiting their turn. Management needs to consider the costs of having employees returning phone calls at a more appropriate time versus the cost of alienating existing customers and placing employees in an awkward and often indefensible position.

Principle No.7: The more valuable the service, the longer the customer will wait

Why else would you wait in a doctor's office for two hours? Is it any wonder that the word 'patient' is a form of the word 'patience'? The amount of time customers are willing to wait is often situational. When the service is considered valuable and few competitive alternatives exist, customers will be willing to wait much longer than if the reverse were true.

Perceived value of the service tends to increase with the title and status of the provider. Students will tend to wait longer for a full professor who is late for class than they will wait for an assistant lecturer, and they will wait for a dean or chancellor of the university even longer. Similarly, customers are willing to wait much longer for their meals at upscale restaurants than at fast-food establishments. When managing consumer waits, the firm must understand the value its customers place on its services and the time they consider to be a reasonable wait because it does vary from sector to sector and within sectors.

Principle No.8: Solo waits are longer than group waits

It is amusing to consider the amount of customer interaction typically displayed in a grocery store line. Generally, there is none at all, even though we are standing within inches of one another. However, note what happens when a delay occurs, such as a price check on an item or a customer who takes too long keying in their pin code – the rest of the line quickly bonds together like old friends! Group waits serve the function of occupying customers' time and reduce the perceived wait. When managing consumer waits, the practicality of actively encouraging consumers to interact may be considered.

Case link

For examples of managing waiting times, see Case 9: Champions League Final Moscow.

Managing uncooperative customers

Since services are often a 'shared experience', one of the primary challenges is to manage different market segments with different needs within a single service environment (see Global Services in Action). Customers are not always saints, and disruptive behaviour impacts not only on other customers but service personnel as well. For further insight into the realities of dealing with customers, visit customerssuck.com for a wide variety of often humorous (sometimes frightening) provider stories about their customers.

Few companies ever sit down with employees to discuss how to deal with difficult customers, despite the fact that employees have to act as 'the police' when dealing with difficult customers (Lovelock, 2004). The lack of discussion about dealing with difficult customers may be a result of the lack of attention paid to the subject in institutions of higher learning. Despite the importance of the customer as the central theme that runs throughout the field of marketing, little, if any, discussion occurs on how to interact with a real, live customer in most colleges and universities. Here's your chance to be part of the cutting edge.

Five customer profiles have been developed, representing the worst that customers have to offer (Zemke and Anderson, 1990). By categorizing unreasonable customers into one of the five profiles, contact personnel are more easily able to depersonalize the conflict and handle customer complaints more objectively. In reality, the worst customer of all is a little of all five types. The characteristics of each of the five 'customers from hell' and suggestions for ways to deal with them are discussed next.

Egocentric Edgar

Egocentric Edgar is the guy Carly Simon had in mind when she wrote the song, 'You're So Vain'. Edgar doesn't believe he should stand in line for any reason. He'll push his way to the front and demand service on a variety of things that demand little immediate attention. If your company's creed is 'We are here to serve', Edgar interprets that message as, 'Your Company exists to serve my needs and my needs alone, and right now!'

Another of Edgar's nasty characteristics is that he will walk over front-line employees to get to whom he'll call 'the man in charge'. Edgar treats front-line employees as well-worn speed bumps that deserve just that much consideration. Once he gets to the top, Edgar uses the chance to belittle upper management and prove he knows how things should be done.

Dealing with Edgar is particularly troublesome for providers who are new on the job, unsure of their own abilities and easily pushed around. The key to dealing with Edgar is to not let his ego destroy yours, while at the same time appealing to his ego. Because Edgar believes you are incapable of performing any task, take action that demonstrates your ability to solve his problem. This will surprise Edgar. In addition, never talk policy to Edgar. Edgar thinks he is special and that the rules that apply to everyone else should not apply to him. Policy should still apply to Edgar, but just don't let him know that you are restating policy. Phrases such as, 'For you Edgar, I can do the following...' where 'the following' is simply policy; this will appeal to Edgar's ego while still managing him within the policies of the organization.

By agreeing with Bad-Mouth Betty on minor issues, it shows that the customer is being heard.

Bad-Mouth Betty

Bad-Mouth Betty lets you know in no uncertain terms exactly what she thinks of you, your organization, and the heritage of both. If she cannot be right, she will be loud, vulgar, and insensitive. She is crude not only to service employees but also to other customers who are sharing her unpleasant experience.

Dealing with Betty consists of at least four options. First, since Betty is polluting the service environment with her foul mouth, attempt to move her 'offstage' so as to not further contaminate the service environment of your other customers. Once isolated, one option is to ignore her foul language and listen to determine the core of the problem and take appropriate action. This is a difficult option to undertake, particularly if her language is excessively abusive and personal in nature. A second option is to use selective agreement in an attempt to show Betty that you are listening and possibly on her side. Selective agreement involves agreeing with Betty on minor issues such as, 'You're right; waiting 10 minutes for your Egg McMuffin is a long time'. However, agreeing with Betty that your boss really is a '****' is not advisable since Betty is likely to use this to her advantage at a later date. The last option that every good service firm should seriously consider is to 'force the issue'. In other words, let Betty know that you would be more than willing to help her solve her problem but that you don't have to listen to her abusive language. If Betty continues to be crude, hang up, walk away, or do whatever is necessary to let her know she is on her own. In most cases, she will return the call, or walk over and apologize, and let you get on with your job.

> **selective agreement** A method of dealing with a dissatisfied customer by agreeing on minor issues in order to show that the customer is being heard.

Hysterical Harold

Hysterical Harold is a screamer. If he doesn't get his way, his face will turn colours and veins will literally pop out from his neck. 'Harold demonstrates the dark side...of the child inside all of us. He is the classic tantrum thrower, the adult embodiment of the terrible twos. Only louder. Much louder'. (Bateson, 1992).

Dealing with Harold is much like dealing with Betty in many ways. These two occupy the 'other customers' slot of the servuction model and negatively affect everyone else's service experience. Consequently, move Harold offstage and give your other customers a chance to enjoy the remainder of their encounter. When Harold has a problem, Harold has to vent. When offstage, let him vent and get it off his chest. This is when you can finally get to the heart of the matter and begin to take action. Finally, take responsibility for the problem. Do not blame the problem on fellow employees, upper management, or others who may ultimately be responsible. Offer an apology for what has occurred and, more importantly, a solution to Harold's problem.

Dictatorial Dick

Dictatorial Dick is claimed to be Egocentric Edgar's evil twin. Dick likes to tell everyone exactly how they are supposed to do their jobs because he has done it all before. Just so you don't get confused, Dick will provide you with a written copy of his instructions, which is copied to your boss, your boss's boss and his lawyer. Dick will most likely make you sign for your copy.

If his brilliant instructions do not produce the desired outcome, then it's your company's fault or, more likely, your fault because you were too incompetent to fully understand Dick's brilliance. Or perhaps Dick's paranoia will set in, which makes him believe that you deliberately sabotaged his plan to make him look bad. You wouldn't do that, would you?

Dealing with Dick would test anyone's patience. The main key is to not let him push you around. Employees should stick to their game plans and provide service in the manner they know is appropriate and equitable for all concerned. Since other customers are likely to be present, employees need to be consistent in how they deal with individual customers. Dick should not be treated as the 'squeaky wheel' who always gets the grease. The best strategy for dealing with Dick is to tell him in a straightforward fashion exactly what you can do for him. If reasonable to do so, fulfilling his request will break up Dick's game plan and resolve the conflict.

Freeloading Freda

Freeloading Freda wants it all for free. Give her an inch and she'll take the plates, the silverware and everything else that's not nailed down. Freda will push your return policy to the limits. If her kid's shoes begin to wear out in a year or two, she'll return them for new ones. In need of a cocktail dress, Freda will buy one on Thursday and return it bright and early Monday morning, punch stains and all. Question her credibility, and Freda will scream blue murder to anyone and everyone who will listen – including the news media and the Better Business Bureau.

Dealing with Freda, in many cases, involves biting your tongue and giving her what she wants. Despite popular beliefs, the Fredas of the world probably represent only 1 to 2 per cent of your customers, if that. Most customers are honest and believe that they should pay for the goods and services they consume. Another possibility is to track Freda's actions and suggest possible legal action to persuade her to take her business elsewhere. Managers of competing firms often share information regarding the Fredas of the world to avoid their excessive abuses. Finally, recognize that Freda is the exception and not the common customer. Too often, new policies are developed for the sole purpose of defeating Freda and her comrades. These new policies add to the bureaucratization of the organization and penalize the customers who follow the rules. The filing of lengthy forms to return merchandise or invoke service guarantees is a common example of penalizing the majority of customers by treating them as suspected criminals rather than as valued customers.

Hellish thoughts

When dealing with 'customers from hell', it is difficult for employees not to take these sorts of confrontations personally. The consumer profiles introduced here should help employees prepare for the various types of difficult customers and provide strategies for minimizing the amount of conflict that actually occurs. Viewing customers as distinct profile types helps depersonalize the situation for the employee – 'Oh, it's just Edgar again'. This is not to say that each customer shouldn't be treated as an individual, but simply that customer complaints and behaviour shouldn't be taken overly personally. In closing, one word of warning: Employees who truly master the art of dealing with difficult customers are rewarded by becoming these customers' favourite provider, the one they request by name time after time. No good deed goes unpunished!

Organizations have to take these complainants seriously and try to win them round. If a service organization is able to delight all its customers, so much that the customers wish to show their appreciation by voicing their delight to other customers, employees can take pride in their work and welcome customers – instead of dreading them! See Global Services in Action.

Customer relationship management (CRM) – An introduction

Given the dynamic growth of e-services as presented in Chapter 3, a number of electronic mechanisms exist that comprise customer relationship management systems. The last section of this chapter is dedicated to explaining the pros and cons of CRM systems as well as introducing their basic electronic component parts.

The origins of CRM

Customer relationship management is fast becoming the new tool for marketing success. CRM began as a tool, hyped-up by IT specialists who wanted to increase business-2-business sales. However, see B2B in Action for details of how it has progressed. In the initial stages of CRM development, service organizations were sceptical of it because they felt that relationships with their customers developed through long-term face-to-face contact. However, whilst CRM is still in its infancy, service organizations are beginning to realize the benefits that the technology can bring to managing and servicing their customers to the benefit of all.

CRM is an expression commonly used – but to mean a variety of themes. It can be an all-embracing term to 'beef up' selling or to express a way to build trust and loyalty. It is also an expression used by organizations that identify and interact with the needs of their customer. All these expressions fail to include profit as the major driver for investing in technology to identify and maintain profitable customers. Profit at the end of the day is paramount to an organization's success. And existing customers have the greatest impact on the bottom line. This is because identifying and recruiting new customers in an expensive business. Indeed it costs between five to ten times more money to acquire new customers than it does to keep existing customers (Flanagan and Safdie, 1998; Masnick, 1997). Indeed this is also true of internet businesses. E-businesses initially spent time acquiring a customer base. They now realize that the cost of acquiring new customers is becoming so expensive then they compare it to the cost of retailing their exiting e-buyers (Shaw, 2002). Profit also varies from existing customer to exiting customer – and sometimes the most profitable customer goes unnoticed. Take for example a retired gentleman that visits a coffee bar each day, Monday to Friday. He buys a café latte, a fruit juice and a sandwich. Therefore, on average he spends £6.50 each visit, which equates to £32.50 per week. Two female and two male students burst into

customer relationship management The process of identifying, attracting, differentiating, and retaining customers where firms focus their efforts disproportionately on their most lucrative clients.

the coffee shop after their Strategy Lecture on Wednesday and after their final Marketing Workshop on Friday. They are lively, boisterous and full of fun and the owner of the coffee shop looks forward to their visits. Each student celebrates their day with a grande cappuccino which costs £2.60, which equates to £5.20 per week. Clearly the retired gentleman is the most profitable, but he remains unnoticed by the owner due to his quiet demeanour. Imagine an organization that has thousands of quiet steady customers – who like the retired gentleman go unnoticed. And as stated by Shaw (2002), Flanagan and Safdie (1998) and Masnick (1997), existing customers should not go unnoticed. CRM can help organizations identify their profitable customers, encourage loyal behaviour and make more sales. Additionally, see Global Services in Action, to see how employees only have to spend a few moments with customers to begin the relationship and make the customer feel special.

B2B services in action
Customer relationship management: Is it working?

Customer relationship management (CRM) is the process of identifying, attracting, differentiating and retaining customers. The idea sounds great, but is it working? According to some studies, only 30 per cent of CRM implementations are successful. Consequently, the logical question becomes: 'What leads to CRM success?'

Implementing a successful CRM system involves matching the needs of the firm with the CRM products offered by CRM vendors. Some CRM software specializes in data mining, which permits the firm to better define its current and potential market segments. Other software collects and analyses information obtained from customers who visit websites. Additional CRM software can be linked to enterprise management software to obtain a 360-degree view of the customer's relationship with the firm including accounting, shipping, invoice processing, marketing research and customer service information. Other CRM software options enable firms to match specific customers with specific customer service representatives while routing other customers to automated phone systems. When selecting CRM vendors, experts suggest that if the vendor cannot explain how their software enables

the company to manage the types of relationships it wants with its customers, then it is time to talk to another vendor.

Ultimately, effective CRM systems accomplish the following worthwhile tasks:

- Gathers, processes, and analyses customer information.
- Provides insight into how and why customers make purchases.
- Streamlines company processes, which facilitate the customer's interaction with the firm.
- Provides access to customer information throughout the firm.

In the end, to be a successful service firm, the firm should know its customers well, build lasting relationships with its most valued customers, develop processes that effectively manage these relationships, and actively monitor customer relationships over time. An effective CRM system if properly implemented can accomplish just that.

Source: Camille Schuster, 'Customer Relationship Management Can Work for You, But Is It?' *Business Credit* 107 (4) (April 2005): 65–66.

CRM – What it means to the customer and the organization

CRM for the customer means 'knowing me for who I am and what I do'. Customers like to feel like an individual and not one out of a thousand. If they are regular business travellers and visit the same hotel, they like to be called by their name and they will feel the hotel cares if they always receive the same newspaper automatically delivered to their door in the morning. Customer relationship management can monitor and track information down to the individual. Similarly, hotel visitors are encouraged to 'charge' drinks, meals, coffees and purchases at the spa and fitness centres to their room. By doing this, hotels can obtain a detailed summary of individual behaviour and spending patterns. Future visits by the same business traveller can be given 'special offers' or upgrades if they are seen to be a profitable customer. This scenario describes the interactions between the customer and the organization and these are called:

Global services in action
Golfing breaks – Where service is first class

To get a 'hole in one' when on a golfing holiday would eclipse poor service, shoddy accommodation and bad weather. Sadly many golfers do not get a 'hole in one'. Therefore, golf resorts need to provide a range of excellent amenities to ensure that all guests enjoy their stay. Conde Nast Traveller allows guests to take part in a poll to acknowledge the incredible service, challenging course, accommodation or fine dining experiences they have received while on their golfing holiday. In 2007 customers provided Conde Nast with their views, and awarded Dromoland Castle in County Clare, Ireland and Four Seasons Resort The Lodge at Koelle, Lanai Hawaii 100 per cent for the 'Best In Service Award'. James Potter was delighted with the service he received at Dromoland Castle. The employees delighted him in many ways. These included being personally greeted by Executive Chef David McCann as he entered the Earl of Thomond Dining Room and trusting the 50 (ish) year-old local woman with his children for a few hours whilst he joined in with the Irish ballads being sung in the Castle's library/bar. The service at Dromoland Castle was charming and James Potter felt he was treated better than Royalty. Each time a customer interacts with an employee a relationship is born. Organizations need to nurture these small relationships and build on them so that all customers feel as though they are treated like Royalty. The relationship will flourish; customers will become loyal and hopefully tell their family and friends.

Source: J. M. Potter (2007) 'Fit for a King; Families get the royal treatment at Ireland's luxurious Dromoland Castle', *Boston Herald*, 25 January 2007.

Golfers expect the level of service to be in full swing and never under par.

1 *Customer interaction platform* – where the customer has touchpoints with the organization – such as the bar, restaurant, spa or use of internet in room and so on. Every point of contact that the customer has with the organization is useful information and should be integrated into the CRM system.

2 *Customer information platform* – this is the platform where the service organization stores all of the information it has about all their customers, such as service history, frequency of visits and length of visit.

3 *Platform integration process* – this is the final data 'churning' stage. The customer interaction platform and the customer information platform are integrated and analysis can identify consumer behaviour that is very profitable, profitable and unprofitable. From this information, organizations can concentrate on the profitable and very profitable customers and encourage their behaviour patterns further.

(Boxwell, 2000)

Limitations of CRM practices

Technology greatly enhances CRM processes by identifying current and potential customers, differentiating between high-value and low-value customers and customizing offers to meet the needs of individual high-value customers. However, there are limitations. First, customers do not like hearing that some customers are valued more than others, especially when they are not the ones receiving the 'white glove' treatment. Many companies are well aware of potential customer ill-will and are fairly protective about discussing the outcomes of their CRM practices. Meanwhile, in service operations where service discrimination is common such as airlines, banks, retail stores, hotels and telecommunication companies, customer satisfaction is taking a 'nosedive' and customer complaints are on the rise (see Figure 12.2).

Another concern relating to CRM practices involves privacy issues. How much should a company really know about its customers? When discussing its new customer information system, the Vice President of Continental Airlines recently boasted: 'We even know if they [the customers] put their eyeshades on and go to sleep.' Ironically, in this day and age of high-tech CRM systems, experts are now suggesting that if customers want better service, they should protect their privacy. In doing so, it is recommended that customers avoid filling out surveys and be protective about credit card

Figure 12.2

Satisfaction takes a nosedive...

Source Diane Brady, 'Why Service Stinks', *Business Week* (October 23, 2000), pp. 120–121.

and social security information. But the more companies know about their customers, the better they will be able to categorize them, and the more likely the customer will feel like a valued customer.

CRM is also limited by its focus on past purchase patterns. In reality, what someone spends today is not necessarily a good predictor of what their behaviour will be tomorrow. Questions are being asked such as how many potential profitable customers are being eliminated today because their current purchasing behaviour has them slotted and treated as 'commoners'. Spurned by such treatment, how many of these customers defect to another provider that appreciates their potential and treats them appropriately. Life situations and spending habits do change over time. The question is how CRM systems track these changes in behaviour.

Service discrimination also leads to some interesting ethical questions. Should only the wealthy be recipients of quality service? Is this a form of red-lining – the practice of identifying and avoiding unprofitable types of neighbourhoods or types of people?

red-lining The practice of identifying and avoiding unprofitable types of neighborhoods or types of people.

Summary

Due to the impact of inseparability, the consumer's role in service production can both facilitate and hinder the exchange process. Hence, it is critical to develop a strategic understanding of how the consumer can be effectively managed within the service encounter. The focus of this chapter has been on four consumer management areas of particular importance:

1 the management of consumer participation in the service process;
2 the management of consumer waiting periods,
3 dealing with difficult customers – managing to keep your cool while those around you are losing theirs; and
4 an introduction to an electronic CRM system.

Increasing consumer participation in the service delivery process has become a popular strategy for increasing the supply of service available to the firm and for providing a form of service differentiation. Increasing customer participation is associated with a number of advantages and disadvantages. The primary advantage to the customer and the service firm is that customers can customize their own service and produce it faster and less expensively than if the firm had produced it. On the other hand, increased levels of customer participation are also associated with the firm's losing control of quality; increased waste, which increases operating costs; and customer perceptions that the firm may be attempting to distance itself from its customers. When making the transition from a full-service to a self-service operation, the firm needs to be sensitive to the reasons the customer may have for preferring one format over another. Guidelines were presented within this chapter to help facilitate this transition and avoid insensitivity to customers' underlying needs.

In addition to managing consumer participation, service managers are often faced with managing other customer-related challenges as well. Because production and consumption occur simultaneously, several customers often share a common service experience. As a result, demand often outpaces supply and queues develop that must be effectively managed to mini-mize customer dissatisfaction. Eight 'prin-ciples of waiting' are presented that are designed to help service managers mini-mize customer frustrations associated with 'waiting for service'.

Since services are often a 'shared expe-rience', one of the primary challenges is to manage different market segments with different needs within a single service envi-ronment. Customers are not always saints, and disruptive behaviour impacts not only upon other customers but service person-nel as well. Five customer profiles were presented, representing the worst that customers have to offer. By categorizing unreasonable customers into one of the five profiles, contact personnel are more easily able to depersonalize the conflict and han-dle customer complaints more objectively.

Discussion questions

1 Discuss the pros and cons of increasing customer participation in the service delivery process.

2 Consider the Case Study – Champions League Final, Moscow – how many points of contact will fans have been involved in during the service delivery process?

Case link

See Case 9: Champions League Final, Moscow.

3 When transitioning from a full-service to a self-service operation, this chapter has offered a number of guidelines to facilitate the change. Select four of these guidelines and discuss their importance as it pertains to increasing customer participation.

4 Despite the best attempts of many service firms to balance supply and demand, the only time the balance truly occurs may be by accident. Explain why this is so.

5 Select four of the eight 'principles of waiting' and discuss their significance to managing the consumer's experience.

6 How does profiling disruptive customers assist customer contact personnel in dealing with 'customers from hell'?

7 Why is the management of consumer waits and customer participation particularly important for service firms?

8 Select one of the profiles of 'customers from hell'. Describe the profile of this customer and offer suggested methods for dealing with this type of individual.

References and further reading

Bateson, J. E. (1985) 'Perceived control and the service encounter', in John Czepiel, Michael R. Solomon and Carol F. Suprenant, eds, *The Service Encounter*, Lexington, MA: Heath, 67–82.

Bateson, J. E. G. (1992) *Managing Services arketing: Text and Readings*, Fort Worth, TX: Dryden Press.

Berry, L. L., Seiders, K. and Grewal, D. (2002) 'Understanding service convenience', *Journal of Marketing* 66 (July): 4.

Boxwell, L. (2000) 'Customer Relationship Management', http://start.it.uts.edu.au/pgproj/crm.pdf, accessed 31 November 2007.

Brady, D. (2000) 'Why service stinks', *Business Week* (23 October): 118–128.

Flanagan, T., Safdie, E. (1998) *Building a Successful CRM Environment*, Natick, Mass.: The Applied Technology Group.

Kau, A. K., Tang, Y. E. and Ghose, S. (2003) 'Typology of online shoppers', *Journal of Consumer Marketing* 20 (2): 139–156.

Lovelock, C. and Wirtz, J. (2004) *Services arketing People, Technology, Strategy*, 6th edn ed., Engelwood Cliffs, NJ: Prentice Hall.

Maister, D. H. (1984) 'The psychology of waiting in lines', Boston: Harvard Business School Note 9-684-064, Rev. May, pp. 2–3.

Massnick, F. (1997) 'Customer service can kill you', *Management Review* 86 (3): 33–35.

McGrath, M. A. and Otnes, C. (1995) 'Unacquainted influencers: when strangers interact in the retail setting', *Journal of Business Research* 32 (3): 261–272.

Mohammed, R. A., Fisher, R. J., Jaworski, B. J. and Cahill, A (2002) *Internet Marketing: Building Advantage in a Networked Economy*, Boston, MA: McGraw-Hill Irwin.

Moskalyuk. A. (2004) 'Most online shopping happens on Mondays', http://blogs.zdnet.com/ITFacts/?p = 6544, accessed 13 February 2008.

Parker, C. and Ward P. (2000) 'An analysis of role adoptions and scripts during customer-to-customer encounters', *European Journal of Marketing* 34 (3/4): 341–359.

Potter J. M. (2007) 'Fit for a King; Families get the royal treatment at Ireland's luxurious Dromoland Castle', *Boston Herald* (25 January).

Schuster, C. (2005) 'Customer relationship management can work for you, but is it?', *Business Credit* 107 (4) (April): 65–66.

Shaw, M. (2002) *E-Business Management: Integration of Web Technology with Business Models*, London: Klvwer Academic Publishers.

Turner, C. W., Safar, J. A. and Ramaswamy, K. (2006) 'The effects of use on acceptance and trust in voice authentication technology', *Human Factors and Ergonomics Society Annual Meeting Proceedings Computer Systems*, pp. 718–722.

Zemke, R. and Anderson, Kristen (1990) 'Customers from Hell', *Training* 26 (February): 25–31.

Zemke, R. and Connellan, T. (2001) *E-service New York*, New York: AMACOM Ron.

Chapter 13

Customer relationship marketing

[Relationship marketing] RM offers more common sense in marketing, and it makes important phenomena visible in the confusing world in which marketers search for meaning.

(Evert Gummesson, 2002: 20)

Chapter objectives

Relationships are inherent within many service marketing encounters and, therefore, the relatively new paradigm of relationship marketing is a vital part of successfully marketing a range of consumer and business services. Although relationship marketing includes the development of relationships with all stakeholders, including competitors, this chapter will focus on the importance of creating and maintaining relationships with customers.

After reading this chapter you should be able to:

- Understand the concept of relationship marketing for services.

- Compare the characteristics of transaction marketing with relationship marketing.

- Describe the levels of relationship marketing and the ladder of loyalty.

- Discuss the methods used to develop and manage services marketing relationships.

- Understand some of the pitfalls inherent in relationship marketing strategies.

Services in context
Visibility, credibility and profitability

Relationship marketing involves building deep networks strongly rooted in a bond or connection that is developed over time with other people. These relationships don't just spring up full grown; they must be nurtured. As they grow, fed by mutual trust and shared benefits, they evolve through three phases: visibility, credibility and profitability (VCP).

Dr Ivan Misner (Founder and Chairman of BNI, the world's largest business networking organization) says, 'The VCP model describes the process of creation, growth and strengthening of business, professional and personal relationships; when fully realized, such a relationship is mutually rewarding and thus self-perpetuating.'

The first phase of growing a relationship is visibility, where you and another individual become aware of each other. The greater your visibility, the greater will be your chances of being accepted by other individuals or groups as someone to whom they should refer business.

Next is credibility – the quality of being reliable and worthy of confidence. Credibil-ity grows when appointments are kept, promises are acted upon, facts are verified and services are rendered. Once you have credibility, the relationship can mature and you can move onto profitability.

Whether business or personal, the mature relationship can be defined in terms of its profitability. Is it mutually rewarding? Do both partners gain satisfaction from it? If it doesn't profit both partners to keep it going, the relationship will probably not endure.

Visibility and credibility are important in the relationship-building stages of the referral marketing process, but it is only when you have established an effective referral-generation system that you will have entered the profitability stage of your relationships with many people. All of this is critical to successful relationship marketing and networking and these three phases are the key to keeping your networking connections.

Source: Adapted from Business Wire, 17 march 2008.

Introduction

Although it can be argued that relationship marketing has always been around, especially within B2B (Peter Turnbull), the main shift towards this new paradigm occurred over the past 20 years with a recognition that marketing is all about relationships and the development of these can lead to higher profits, growth and success. As the opening quotation suggests, this is 'common sense'. However, some of the aspects of relationship building and management are complex. These relate to areas of loyalty, trust and commitment, to resource allocation, to the ideas of permission marketing, privacy and data protection along with the application of new technologies to database marketing. This chapter provides an overview of the relationship marketing paradigm and its development and focuses on the methods used to create, develop and manage relationships in service organizations.

What is customer relationship marketing?

Relationship marketing is a natural development of a customer orientation in that through a focus on customer and other stakeholder needs, characteristics and behaviour an organization is in a stronger position to develop a mutually beneficial relationship with those customers. This 'relationship' increases the levels of involvement of both parties through shared interests and when developed further can lead to long-term loyalty and support.

The paradigm of customer relationship marketing grew from business-to-business marketing where one-to-one relationships with clients are often necessary in order to create the product to specification, draw up contracts and work together to install and maintain the product. Since the 1980s a number of authors have developed the theoretical and practical understanding of this area in consumer markets and in services. Although the definitions of relationship marketing have proliferated with this increase of academic research and writing (e.g. Berry, 1983; Grönroos, 1990; Gummesson, 1996; and Bruhn, 2003) the preferred definition here is:

> relationship marketing is a marketing orientation that seeks to initiate and develop close interactions with selected stakeholders for mutual value creation through cooperative and collaborative efforts.
>
> (in Wood and Masterman , 2006 and adapted from Sheth and Parvatiyar, 1995 and Bruhn, 2003).

customer relationship marketing Marketing paradigm that focuses on customer retention.

Relationship marketing is a move away from a focus on one-off transactions or sales to an emphasis on customer retention. This is achieved through higher levels of customer service and quality and through repeated and varied customer contacts. The goals of relationship marketing are therefore longer term, aiming to develop customer involvement, commitment, trust and loyalty. These goals require customers and other stakeholders to have a higher level of involvement with the service provider through some degree of empowerment.

customer retention Focusing the firm's marketing efforts towards the existing customer base.

customer involvement Participation and interest in the brand and/or organization.

In practical terms this means that the customer makes a valued input to the organization (other than simply purchasing the service) and receives extra value in exchange. The customer input may be simply information about themselves and their purchases or could be extended to comments, advice, suggestions, support and advocacy. The additional value gained in exchange may range from receiving personalized information and services to special offers for repeat customers, to reward points, free gifts or upgrades. For example, the relationship developed between a hairdresser and their client can be deepened through the amount of personal attention received, such as remembering how she takes her coffee to having records of the colour of her highlights and past treatments. In exchange for this the client is likely to develop trust and commitment to the salon, patronize the salon more often and promote their services through positive word of mouth and referrals.

SOURCE ISTOCK

The relationship between the customer and their hairdresser is essential, especially when it comes to making the big day perfect.

The move towards relationship marketing has come about as a result of a number of social and technological trends. The increasing level of competition in most markets creates greater demands on organizations to differentiate what they offer in a meaningful and lasting way. This has lead to many products and services being viewed by customers as homogenous. Customers have increasing difficulty in differentiating between competing offerings and therefore demand higher levels of service and quality at all points of contact. Many customers are looking for value over and above the product offering through engagement with the organization, its brand, its communications and its stakeholders. Organizations have realized that there are diminishing returns from one-off transactions and have started to recognize the lifetime value of the customer. Even organizations with large customer bases have been able to facilitate this through the developments in information technology. Database advances, the internet and telecommunications all allow the organization and the customer to better understand each other and therefore, to develop repeated contacts and long-term relationships. However, an over-reliance on technology can have a negative effect on a relationship and whenever possible should not completely replace interpersonal contact. Hotel booking websites can be efficient and pleasant to use but often a call to the hotel allows the customer to request additional services or non-standard features not available through automated booking systems. Through this and through the direct contact once at the hotel, a more meaningful and longer-lasting relationship with the hotel can be fostered. Technology can still be used to record theses additional requests and used to make the customer feel more valued next time they book. For example, being greeted with 'Welcome back, Mrs Davis. We've ordered the *Guardian* for you and would you like your usual table at dinner? – makes the customer feel appreciated and encourages a longer-term profitable relationship.

> **lifetime value** The worth of a customer from initial purchase to eventual defection to competitor or ceasing to use the service.

Difference between traditional and relationship marketing

In understanding relationship marketing it is useful to compare the characteristics of this with traditional (or transactional) marketing thinking.

> **traditional/transactional marketing** Focus on one-off sales.

The initial difference is that rather than viewing the results of marketing as a number of single exchanges, relationship marketing outcomes are seen as a series of interdependent purchase episodes. These purchase episodes, therefore, become the basis of the relationship. This perspective then helps to reduce the marketing inefficiencies created through generating one-off transactions, each of which requires a greater amount of effort and resources than is needed for encouraging repeat business and long-term retention. A customer who continues to use a gardening service once a month over several years is more profitable than several customers who use the service only once. Efficiencies are gained in a number of ways: through customer/provider understanding, knowing what the customer wants and expects; through less costly means of communication and less wasted communication; through increasing levels of service; through recommendation and word of mouth; and through a positive role in developing the business. For example, the gardening services client may, over the years, increase the service from lawn mowing to general garden maintenance and may have additional requirements for tree pruning, landscaping and so on. The client's needs can be better understood by the gardener who has built up a relationship in terms of personal contact, experience and feedback. The client in turn is likely to recommend the service to others and may suggest other services that could expand the business, for example garden design and patio construction.

A further difference between relationship marketing and traditional marketing (see Table 13.1) is in the level of customer service. In order to build a lasting relationship there must be a high level of quality customer service. The series of transactions is a minimal prerequisite, therefore, and what is required is the creation of feelings of security, trust (predictability, dependability and faith) and commitment (dialogue, investment and relevance). Customer service is a key component in creating service quality, satisfaction and above all, loyalty.

Relationship marketing values the customer over the lifetime of the relationship and every customer, therefore, has a 'potential' lifetime value. A lapsed customer is lost revenue and a sale to new customer has greater costs

Table 13.1	Traditional marketing	Relationship marketing
Traditional and relationship marketing compared	Focus on single sale	Focus on customer retention
	Quality is primary concern of operations	Quality is concern of all
	Orientation on features	Orientation on benefits
	Short-term	Long-term
	Little emphasis on customer service	High level of customer service
	Limited customer commitment	High customer commitment
	Moderate customer contact	High customer contact
	Passive consumers	Active consumers
	Competition/conflict	Co-operation/partnership
	Need satisfaction	Customer retention
	Customer satisfaction	Empowering customers

than an additional sale to an existing customer. There is clearly therefore an undeniable logic to relationship marketing (Gummesson, 2002) in any business but even more so in services where there is often greater opportunity for ongoing contact and a greater need to develop mutual understanding.

Developing customer relationships: The relationship ladder

Several authors (Payne, Peck and Clark, 1998; Little and Marandi, 2003) recognize that developing meaningful relationships with customers requires an understanding of the different levels of relationship and the factors which help to deepen or move relationships to the next level. The relationship between service provider and customer can help to overcome the intangibility of the service by reducing the perceived level of risk and creating trust. For example, the relationship between a client and their hair stylist develops over time and creates a bond of mutual understanding and trust when managed well. A service such as this contains considerable personal risk in terms of such things as affecting the client's level of self-confidence, feelings of attractiveness and so on. Many people will therefore continue to use one trusted hair stylist. The relationship isn't developed immediately and involves a number of contacts and differing techniques and may be developed with more than one person. For example, the politeness of the receptionist when booking an appointment and greeting the client upon arrival, the pre-service consultation and the during-service chat all help to deepen the relationship. However, this level of relationship development is not possible with all types of service and all types of market segments.

Levels of relationship marketing

Kotler and others have recognized that relationships with customers can be on a number of levels, ranging from one-off transactions to longer-term involvement and commitment. These are: basic, reactive, accountable, proactive and partnership marketing.

Basic marketing. At the basic level a relationship consists merely of the transaction and service use. For example, stopping at a service station on a motorway, buying and eating a meal and driving on. Here the provider merely 'sells' the service.

Reactive marketing. At this level the service provider sells the service but also encourages the customer to get back in touch if they have any problems or questions. For example, this may be the level of relationship offered by a tyre and exhaust centre. The exhaust is replaced and the customer told to contact them if anything goes wrong with it in the next year.

Accountable marketing. A stronger relationship is developed if the provider calls the customer after the sale to ensure satisfaction and seek comments. The provider is therefore creating a level of accountability for the service provided and is committing to acting upon the comments received. For example, most car breakdown service operators issue a brief questionnaire a few days after a client has used the service. This requests details about the level of service received and the customer's level of satisfaction with the service. The information is used to manage outsourced service providers (local garages) and to ensure the customer of a commitment to service improvement. Others, such as KwikFit (automotive repairs), phone the customer a few days after purchase to gather similar types of information and to ensure satisfaction with the service received.

Proactive marketing. Here the customer is contacted from time to time between service use in order to inform them of improved services or new offers. In order for this to be successful, the organization needs to maintain an up-to-date database and have gained permission from each customer to contact them. BT regularly contact existing customers by phone and mail in order to inform them of new and improved services and many mobile telecommunications companies let their customers know of new call plans and service changes by text message. A monthly or quarterly newsletter (by post or e-mail) can also serve the same purpose. For example, a local garden centre may mail out a newsletter with seasonal gardening tips, special offers and feature stories to opted in customers. Many theatres regularly send their programme and details of upcoming special events to customers who have previously booked with them.

opted-in Permission given for contact.

Partnership marketing. In order to achieve this higher level of relationship the service organization needs to work with their customers continuously to help improve their performance. The customer, therefore, becomes a 'partner' in the business and in return feels valued and is rewarded. This requires contact which is not merely related to a sale or even future sales but is designed to create a greater level of interest and involvement in the organization and its products. For example, a local theatre may encourage customers to become 'friends of' the theatre through some form of membership (free or subscribed to). These friends of the theatre are then contacted regularly for feedback on performances, invited to special shows and offered the opportunity to volunteer as stagehands or ushers. Although this may appear easier for organizations with fewer customers, it can also be achieved with larger customer groups. For example, most of the larger festival organizers encourage an ongoing 'community' through clever use of their websites. Here previous festival visitors, prospective visitors and those who would like to go but are unable to get tickets can share views, photos and tips throughout the year using discussion forums, blogs and chat rooms (see www.Glastonbury.co.uk). Large retailers also aim to achieve partnership marketing through a combination of loyalty schemes and sophisticated data gathering and use (see E-Services in Action) and even global organizations, such as the Harley-Davidson owners

loyalty scheme Rewards for continued business with the organization designed to encourage repeat purchases.

group, can achieve this through creating added value and online communities (see Global Services in Action).

The types of relationship marketing described above can be applied to different situations (see Table 13.2). For example, it may not always be possible or appropriate to aim for partnership marketing – in some situations customers are too diverse and contact too expensive for this to be feasible or it may be that customers value their privacy or do not want to be 'hassled' by companies requesting feedback or constantly sending out details of special offers. Indeed an important part of relationship marketing is recognizing which customers want which type of relationship. One particular client may

---

Global services in action
H.O.G.: A global community

H.O.G. (Harley Owner's Group) is the world's largest and most successful factory-sponsored owners club. With a simple philosophy encapsulated in their invitation to Harley-Davidson motorbike devotees:

> Your mission – if you choose to accept it – will be a simple one: 'To Ride and Have Fun.'

The community spirit is encouraged through statements such as 'We like to think of Harley-Davidson – from the top corporate officer to the newest Harley owner and rider – as one big, happy family. The Harley Owners Group® helps us turn that philosophy into reality.'

The 'unique' concept of the Harley Owners Group was created in 1983 and within six years, H.O.G. membership grew to more than 90,000. By the year 2000, it exceeded 500,000 members.

As well as joining the global community of Harley owners there is also the opportunity to join a local 'chapter'. Chapters are encouraged to sponsor and organize a variety of activities, for members only, creating additional value through ensuring that there are plenty of opportunities 'to ride and have fun'. The consumption of mass quantities of great food and riding are, apparently, a central theme. Local H.O.G.® chapters are described as families, 'a collection of diverse individuals united by a common passion'. The creation of a chapter is linked in to the distribution network with each one sponsored by an authorized Harley-Davidson dealer.

The website screenshot demonstrates the tone of the organization and its global reach.

Much of this service has been made possible by a sophisticated loyalty system developed by arvato. In order to improve the experience for H.O.G. members worldwide while making cost savings and increasing the size and value of the membership base, they worked with Harley-Davidson to implement a consolidated system. This involved a multilingual contact centre, integrated fulfilment, subscription renewals, online payment options, member surveys, event management and retention programmes. Some of the results of the new system were reduced contact centre spend, lost calls captured, an increase in membership, increased spend

'Your mission – if you choose to accept it – will be a simple one: "To Ride and Have Fun."'

SOURCE © LINDA MORLAND/ DREAMSTIME.COM

per head by 50 per cent and member satisfaction rating up from 50 per cent to 80 per cent.

The problems solved by the improved system were largely a result of international differences and lack of control. The main isues were summarized as:

- A fragmented approach to customer management.
- Poor customer service adversely affecting brand perception.
- Inconsistent customer communication channels.
- Limited payment options offered to members with little or no tracking in place.
- Delivery inefficiencies on fulfilment and deadlines.
- Costs spiralling out of control in each of the local markets.
- Mismanagement of events.

Bringing in an outsourced loyalty management organization (arvatoloyalty) helped in a number of ways including:

- Controlled payment methods.
- Efficient reporting.
- Access to statistics, revenue streams for effective planning.
- Event support to execute strategies.
- Analysis to benchmark future communication and rollout new initiatives.
- Gaining a true insight into customers.

Sources: www.arvatoloyalty.com www.harley-davidson.com.

	High profit margin	Medium profit margin	Low profit margin
Type of service **Type of market**			
Many customers	Accountable marketing	Reactive marketing	Basic marketing
Medium number of customers	Proactive marketing	Accountable marketing	Reactive marketing
Few customers	Partnership marketing	Proactive marketing	Accountable marketing

Table 13.2

Relationship marketing level and type of service/market

respond well to regular contact and may be encouraged through this to spend more with the company whereas another client may be happier dealing with a company who leaves them alone. Customers need to know that they can control the relationship and request or decline contact as needed. Companies that recognize this take the time to find out how often a customer would like to be contacted and in what form this should take. They also regularly ask them if this is still okay and offer easy opt outs. Indeed some of the more

opt-outs Opportunity to withdraw personal information and to cease contact.

E-services in action
Tescos – data warehouse and CRM

If, like many people, you're a Tesco online shopper, you will already be receiving regular e-mails detailing the supermarket's latest offers, which have been tailored to your own buys. Such specific targeting is made possible by sophisticated IT systems, which analyse vast quantities of data across literally billions of transactions every month. Clearly, the closer online promotions match customer preferences, the better the response rates. This level of intelligent data mining has helped Tesco become the UK's number-one internet retailer

As with other online retailers, Tesco.com relies on in-store advertising and marketing to the supermarket's Clubcard loyalty scheme's customer base to persuade customers to shop online. NMA (2005) quotes Nigel Dodd, marketing director at Tesco.com as saying: 'These are invaluable sources as we have such a strong customer base.' However, for non-food goods the supermarket does also advertise online using keyword targeted ads.

For existing customers, e-mail marketing and direct mail marketing to provide special offers and promotions to customers are important.

According to Humby (2003), e-retailer Tesco.com use what he describes as a 'commitment-based segmentation' or 'loyalty ladder' which is based on recency of purchase, frequency of purchase and value, which is used to identify six life-cycle categories which are then further divided into target communications:

- 'Logged-on'
- 'Cautionary'

- 'Developing'
- 'Established'
- 'Dedicated'
- 'Logged-off' (the aim here is to winback).

Tesco then use automated event-triggered messaging created to encourage continued purchase. For example, Tesco.com have a touch strategy which includes a sequence of follow-up communications triggered after different events in the customer life-cycle. In the example given below, communications after event 1 are intended to achieve the objective of converting a website visitor to action; communications after event 2 are intended to move the customer from a first-time purchaser to a regular purchaser and for event 3 to reactivate lapsed purchasers.

- Trigger event 1: Customer first registers on site (but does not buy).
- Auto-response (AR) 1: Two days after registration e-mail sent offering phone assistance and £5 discount off first purchase to encourage trial.
- Trigger event 2: Customer first purchases online.
- AR1: Immediate order confirmation.
- AR2: Five days after purchase e-mail sent with link to online customer satisfaction survey asking about quality of service from driver and picker (e.g. item quality and substitutions).
- AR3: Two weeks after first purchase – Direct mail offering tips on how to use service and

▶

£5 discount on next purchases intended to encourage re-use of online services.

- AR4: Generic monthly e-newsletter with online exclusive offers encouraging cross-selling.
- AR5: Bi-weekly alert with personalized offers for customer.
- AR6: After two months – £5 discount for next shop.
- AR7: Quarterly mailing of coupons encouraging repeat sales and cross-sales.
- Trigger event 3: Customer does not purchase for an extended period.
- AR1: Dormancy detected – Reactivation e-mail with survey of how the customer is finding the service (to identify any problems) and a £5 incentive.
- AR2: A further discount incentive is used in order to encourage continued usage to shop after the first shop after a break.

As well as this sophisticated online system, retailers such as Tesco also employ customer insight teams to drive value by data mining their loyalty card data.

The interesting part of these roles is customer insight, which is about understanding customers through qualitative and quantitative research to answer questions such as:

- Characteristics: Who are they? (profiling)
- Needs: What do they want?
- Behaviours: What do they do (response and purchase histories)?
- Beliefs: What do they think (about us, about our competitors, about life)?
- Value: What are they worth?

Despite the obvious benefits and success of Tesco's use of technology there is also a word of caution. Technology provides the modern marketer with a multitude of techniques for data gathering, analysis, planning, implementation and performance measurement. As techniques they are greatly to be welcomed. At the same time, they keep marketers in their offices and far away from consumers. This is especially ironic for service marketers, as the nature of that business requires closer identification with the customer's point of view. Techno-marketing provides the illusion of control and leads to the subconscious business philosophy that marketers are cattle farmers. Customers are assets to be milked and to be managed according to their lifetime value. Smart marketers do not follow trends; they create new ones. They start by recognizing that customers are not cattle, they are us. So service marketers should transcend technology and rediscover empathy by living the customer's life and experiencing their own services.

Sources: T. Ambler (2007) 'Call centres, CRM and cows: why modern service marketing is not like cattle farming', *Market Leader*, Winter, Issue 39; available from www.warc.com.
P. Hill (2008) 'Gamble of the week: the secret of Tesco's success', *Money Week*, April (www.moneyweek.com). *Tesco case study sources: Humby (2003), NMA (2005), Hitwise (2005), Wikipedia (2005).*
C. Humby and T. Hunt (2003) *'Scoring points. How Tesco is Winning Customer Loyalty'*, Kogan Page, London, UK. NMA (2005) 'New media age. Delivering the good', *New Media Age*, article by Nic Howell, 5 May 2005. Wikipedia (2005). Tesco – Wikipedia. www.davechaffey.com.

recent and successful segmentation systems use level and type of contact required as one of the key criteria.

Ladder of customer loyalty

ladder of loyalty Stages in developing customer relationships.

Although it may not be possible with all customers, the aim of relationship marketing is to move customers up the ladder of loyalty (Payne et al. 1998).

This ladder metaphor recognizes that as customers stay with a business through repeat transactions and deeper levels of involvement, a level of loyalty develops. This loyalty leads to competitive advantage (through customer advocacy and input) and increased profitability through repeat business, reduced customer defection and fewer costs in reaching new customers.

The ladder of loyalty begins with prospective customers with an emphasis on gaining new custom. 'Prospects' become 'customers' and the marketing emphasis switches to developing and enhancing relationships and through this, customer retention. Through repeat business and greater involvement, customers become 'clients'. As the relationship deepens, clients become 'supporters', then 'advocates' and finally 'partners'. At any stage customer can be lost but this is less likely the further up the ladder they are. There are obvious analogies with personal relationships (see Figure 13.1) and as with these, the relationship is stronger if there is trust and commitment on both sides. Inevitably, however, people change, and the relationship may no longer be valuable to customer or business and the relationship ends.

Loyalty, however, is not an end in itself. It may be that customers are loyal to more than one brand (polygamous) or that they are loyal to certain aspects of the brand and not to others. The ideas of instrumental and emotional loyalty suggest that there is both a rational attachment to the positive benefits of regular patronage but also the potential for more affective loyalty to what the brand stands for, to tradition or nostalgia. For example, Barclays bank has a long history and tradition in the UK and customers remain loyal due to this and the fact that their parents and even grandparents had bank accounts with Barclays. This emotional loyalty suggests that they would stick with the bank even though they may know that other banks offer a service better suited to their needs. Instrumental loyalty on the other hand focuses on loyalty to the services offered. Instrumentally loyal customers will stay with the bank only if it appears to offer them the best services, lowest costs, greatest convenience and so on. Emotional loyalty, therefore, although more difficult to develop, can be stronger and longer-lasting.

Organizations that develop some form of reward for loyalty in terms of frequent flyer points, money off vouchers, free gifts and so on. also run the risk of encouraging customers who are loyal to the reward scheme but not the organization or brand. This type of loyalty is easily eroded by a competitor who appears to offer greater value in return for repeat custom.

Some customers may give the appearance of being loyal but in fact this may be due to negative relational motives and risks or costs involved in switching supplier. As soon as a competitor reduces those risks the customer is liable to leave for a better offer. The personal banking industry again illustrates this. Changing bank accounts can be a risky and stressful undertaking and previously there were charges involved in setting up new accounts and/or closing old ones. With new banking regulations, the arrival of telephone and internet banking, customers were suddenly given far more choice and the newer banks competed by offering to switch your account for you at no charge and with none of the previous hassle of having to contact each direct debit and standing order recipient. The older banks soon found out that their once loyal customers were leaving in droves and the only thing that had kept them 'loyal' was the fear and cost of change.

emotional loyalty
Attachment due to non-rational reasons.

instrumental loyalty
Attachment due to rational reasons.

Perhaps a better measurement, therefore, of the strength of a relationship is the degree of trust in and commitment to the organization by the customer rather than merely the duration of the relationship or the number of transactions made. Little and Marandi (2003: 54) suggest that in order for trust and commitment to develop, a firm must adopt certain characteristics and behaviours. The eight prerequisites are:

1 Develop a customer orientation – focus on customer needs and benefits and anticipate and respond to changes in these;

2 Create a cohesive and strong brand image and organizational reputation;

3 Enable a culture of information sharing (company to customer) and confidentiality (customer details);

4 Avoid opportunistic behaviour – don't take advantage of the relationship at the customer's expense;

5 Share power – listen and respond to customers, involve them in decision making;

6 Value the relationship and demonstrate this to the customer through tangible and intangible rewards;

7 Implement a customer care and recovery strategy; and

8 Keep any promises made.

cross-selling
Encouraging a customer to buy an additional service during a transaction.

Developing trust and commitment takes time to develop but can be lost through seemingly trivial actions. For example, there is a fine line between 'sharing information' in terms of new services and special offers and cross-selling in an opportunistic manner. One customer may see these as

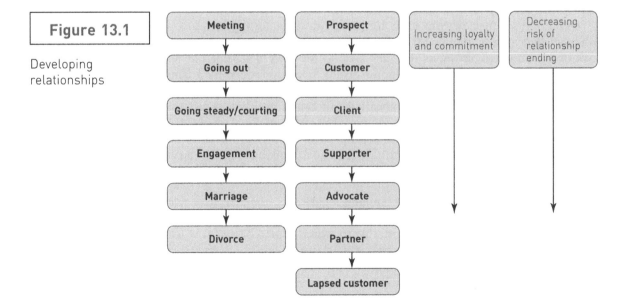

Figure 13.1

Developing relationships

informative and useful whereas another may see them as intrusive and pressuring – for example, the bank whose customer service staff are trained to 'suggest' the need for a personal loan to every customer who has rung to enquire about their balance. Relationship marketing, therefore, requires organization-wide dedication and a shared understanding which in turn requires careful planning of internal and external communications.

Database marketing and relationships

A key aspect of relationship marketing for many service organizations involves the creation, use and maintenance of a customer database or CRM system. This captures customer data each time they have contact with the organization and can be used on a personal level in individualized contacts or to more accurately segment customers so that each communication, although not personalized, is better tailored to their needs. For example, Tesco sends out hundreds of versions of their newsletter with each version tailored to a customer group developed through analysing the vast amount of information gathered at point-of-sale and through their loyalty scheme and stored in their data warehouse (see E-Services in Action). The database of contacts is therefore vital and can be used not only to underpin communication methods but to aid the development of other aspects of the organization's marketing strategy (product development, marketing research, pricing structures, etc.). An often quoted example is

customer database
Electronic storage of customer information.

CRM system Software that manages customer information and contact.

Wal-Mart's use of data-mining software to interrogate their vast amount of customer data. The software discovered that on Friday evenings men aged between 25 and 35 were purchasing six-packs of beer along with packs of nappies. The beer was apparently their reward (self-awarded) for picking up the nappies on the way home from work. Wal-Mart used the information to change their in-store display and sell more nappies and beer.

data-mining Software used to analyse and interrogate large amounts of customer data.

The database is built by the gathering of information at points of contact with customers and potential customers. This information can be gained in a variety of ways, through purchase transactions, requests for information, participation in sales promotions,

SOURCE © FRANCIS BRETT

Fathers reward themselves with beer for remembering to buy nappies.

registration on websites, memberships, complaints, recommend-a-friend schemes and so on. It is important when gathering the information to explicitly ask for permission to use it to contact that individual in the future. For new start-up organizations or those with small current customer contacts the database can be supplemented by bought-in lists. These can be purchased or rented from one of the many list brokers and can be highly targeted in whom they include. Lists purchased from specialist agencies should only include those who have given permission for their information to be passed on; however, bought-in lists will never be as accurate or focused as the organization's own database.

privacy policy Details of how customer data will be used.

In many countries consumer information and privacy protection are becoming more stringently enforced through revised laws and regulations. However, those organizations that have already recognized that loyalty and long-term relationships are built through consumer trust have been proactive in developing and prominently displaying their privacy policies, in using opt-ins for further contacts and making opt-outs easy to select. These organizations were seeking customer permission long before there was any legal requirement to do so and in this way have gained a competitive advantage over those that continued to use personal information in a less scrupulous manner. For example, Amazon sends out regular e-mails to previous customers advising them of special offers or new products (tailored to their previous purchase behaviour) but clearly display the 'opt-out' link. Knowing that opting out is easy creates trust and encourages customers to remain on the mailing list rather than vice versa.

Service marketers using databases as part of their customer relationship strategy must therefore not simply comply with consumer information protection legislation but should actively use their ethical and sensitive handling of customer data as a competitive advantage in developing trust and loyalty.

When not to develop a relationship

Although relationship marketing uses the tools of database marketing, cross-selling and loyalty rewards, these are not sufficient to create real commitment, trust and interdependence (O'Malley and Tynan, 2000). Collecting customer information electronically provides an understanding of the behaviours and preferences of large target markets but can lead to the neglect of real qualitative communication with the customer base. The reaction to the use of out-sourced call-centres for handling customer contact in many industries is testament to this. Although the cross-selling of related products and merchandise can be used to personalize offers and add value, it can also be perceived as intrusive and pushy, tilting the balance of perceived value away from the customer. Customers need to be in control of how and when they are contacted and the extent to which the relationship develops. The increased use of the internet to book holidays, buy insurance, or apply for mortgages, for example, is partly due to the desire for control. Customers are free to choose when and where and with whom they make the transaction. The growth in internet purchasing of services also suggests that there are many customers who prefer a less 'personal', more anonymous relationship with their service provider.

Customers are either 'active partners' or passive targets, but not both. Although service organizations may claim that their customers are viewed as the former, their actions often suggest the latter (O'Malley and Tynan, 1998). Relationship targeting is not about controlling or manipulating the customer as is often the case with direct marketing, database marketing and technology-enabled customer contact, but a focus on mutual benefit and responding to customer needs in the longer term.

Relationship marketing also requires resources in terms of staff training, communication, system management and rewards. It is therefore necessary to ensure that there will be an appropriate return on this investment at some future point (see B2B Services in Action). A small number of major clients may expect a closer relationship with personal visits, corporate hospitality and involvement in the organization and will respond accordingly with repeat contracts and increased business. This intensity of relationship, however, will not be financially viable for larger customer bases and smaller-scale transactions.

corporate hospitality Entertaining clients in a social atmosphere in order to deepen a relationship.

Some customers may not respond well to certain approaches whereas others will. A simple difference might be in the use of first name or title and last name in a telephone conversation. The pizza delivery company that answers the call with, 'Good evening Miss Taylor. Is it the usual with extra chilli or something special as it's your birthday?', may be making good use of their customer database but is also likely to be seen as overly 'informed' and personal by the customer. Gaining permission in a transparent manner and ensuring that the customer manages and has control of the relationship are therefore vital.

B2B services in action
Don't ignore the small but simple customer

B2B suppliers often find it tricky to apply mass modelling techniques to their marketing strategies because of their relatively small customer bases. If these businesses get the bulk of their income from a few, high-value customers, it might not even be cost-effective to manage some of the low-value accounts at all. This quandary presents a marketing challenge – how do you create different customer relationship management (CRM) strategies for high-and low-value customers so you get – the maximum profit from each?

Russell Biggar, a partner in Stirling-based Intelligent Customer Development (ICD) Part-

nership, believes, 'If a company is serious about retaining and developing a customer base, they've got to respect each of their customers and develop an appropriate treatment strategy. Adopting a common relationship with the small customers who still want to buy but don't want an intense relationship.' Biggart recommends that a business has to organize itself appropriately, or otherwise the customer base will start to suffer from attrition. While some customers may be measured by sales volume, the relational model is more about how companies can develop services to meet the needs of the customers.

▶

'A lot of organizations haven't realized that building a relationship with their customers ultimately ends up with the customers staying with them longer, buying more of their services and contributing continually to the profit of that organization', he says.

This development of relationships with the most profitable clients is often referred to as 'key account management'. However, an alternative to the conventional account management principle, although specifically applicable to high-value customers, is 'partnership management'. Here the vendor and the customer examine areas in their relationship – such as ordering processes, communications and training – where resources can be shared to reduce costs. This approach has the added benefit of securing customer retention by building a closer relationship between customer and supplier. This fact is not lost on John Matthews (Research Director with Infact Research):

'Going back four or five years, companies were focused on getting new customers. Customer retention was an afterthought. In the current climate, new customers are very difficult to get, but there's still not much evidence that companies know how to retain them.'

However, this doesn't mean merely focusing on larger currently profitable customers, as many B2B service organizations may have unrealized profit embedded in their small and medium-size customers, especially if this group requires minimal servicing. At the same time, many of the high-value customers could have a low opinion of their vendors. Says one CRM consultant, 'You'd be amazed how many key accounts don't think much of their suppliers. You need to work on those accounts as soon as you identify them, because they're going to leave when a competitor comes along.'

Says Biggart: 'You may find that some of your small to medium-size customers buy simple products that don't need any kind of complicated support, such as the involvement of a salesperson. And because they don't need much servicing they may be more profitable than bigger clients.'

Biggart's consultancy examined one blue-chip company's customer portfolio and found that medium-size customers were actually producing 40 per cent of its overall profit. 'We also found that there was competition sniffing around the small to medium-size companies and that the competition had identified that these customers were highly profitable and more likely to move because there was no strong relationship between supplier and customer'. Another potential scenario is that a low-spending customer could be a big company that has a lot of influence in the marketplace.

In summary B2B service organizations need to:

- Gain maximum profit by developing different CRM strategies for different value customers.
- Realize that the biggest spenders are not always the most profitable – look at each account carefully.
- Not just look at what a customer or client is worth – don't forget to account for potential value.

Source: Adapted From: I. Sclater (2003) 'Relationship building', *Marketing Business*, September.

Summary

Relationship marketing is vital within service industries as it emphasizes the importance of customer contact, personalization and a longer-term view of customer value. The shift towards relationship marketing has been led by business-to-business marketing practice and is a logical development of the customer focus of marketing as opposed to a sales/transaction focus. The aim of relationship marketing is to develop high levels of customer service and contact and through this create active, empowered consumers who are, to varying degrees, 'partners' in the business. To do this the organization needs to engender loyalty and through this mutual trust and commitment resulting in longer-term customer retention

There are five types or level of relationship marketing (basic, reactive, accountable, proactive and partnership). Each of these may be appropriate depending upon the size of market segment, value of service and customer response.

Relationship marketing recognizes that customers can be classified according to their relationship stage and that these can be developed from prospect to customer, client, supporter, advocate and finally, partner. At the partnership level, trust and commitment are high and the likelihood of defection is low. Both the organization and the customer gain increased value from the relationship.

The ability to develop personalized relationships with large customer groups has been enabled through the use of database technology, telecommunications and the internet. However, this has brought with it new challenges in terms of information use, privacy and potential loss of 'real' interaction.

In order for relationship marketing to be successful, the customer must be able to control the nature of the relationship and perceive real value in continuing or deepening it.

Discussion questions

1 'Services marketing has always been about relationships with customers.' Discuss this statement referring to the differences between 'traditional' marketing and relationship marketing. Use the case study 'BUPA' to illustrate your discussion.

Case link

See Case 10: BUPA: Ethical relationships.

2 Compare the importance of relationship marketing in personal banking and corporate finance.

3 Using examples, explain the differences between the five types of relationship marketing.

4 Critically apply the 'ladder of loyalty' to a service that you are familiar with. What techniques are used to move customers from one level to the next?

5 From your own experience and using examples, discuss the ways in which service providers can develop trust and commitment.

6 Discuss the potential pitfalls in relationship marketing. How might these be avoided?

References and further reading

Ambler, T. (2007) 'Call centres, CRM and cows: why modern service marketing is not like cattle farming', *Market Leader* 39 (Winter), available from www.warc.com.

Arnold, M. J. and Tapp, S. R. (2003) 'Direct marketing in non-profit services: investigating the case of the arts industry', *Journal of Services Marketing* 17 (2): 141–160.

Berry, L. L. (1983) 'Relationship marketing', in AMA (ed.), *Emerging Perspectives on Services Marketing*, Chicago: AMA, pp.25–28.

Bruhn, M. (2003) *Relationship Marketing: Management of Customer Relationships*, Harlow: Pearson Education.

Curtis, J. (2001) 'The weakest link?', *Marketing Business* (April): 38–40.

Evans, M., Patterson, M. and O'Malley, L. (2005) 'The direct marketing–direct consumer gap: qualitative insights', *Qualitative Market Research: An International Journal* 4 (1): 17–24.

Fletcher, K. (2003) 'Consumer power and privacy. The changing nature of CRM', *International Journal of Advertising* 22 (2).

Grönroos, C. (1990) 'Relationship approach to marketing in service contexts: the marketing and organizational behavior interface', *Journal of Business Research* 20 (1): 3–11.

Gummesson, E. (1996) 'Relationship marketing and imaginary organizations. A synthesis', *European Journal of Marketing* 30 (2): 31–44.

Gummesson, E. (2002) *Total Relationship Marketing*, New York: Butterworth-Heineman.

Little, E. and Marandi, E. (2003) *Relationship Marketing Management*, London: Thomson.

O'Malley, L. and Tynan, C. (1998) 'Concept, metaphor or reality?: the prognosis for consumer-organizational relationships', in J. Sheth and A. Menon, eds, *New Frontiers in Relationship Marketing Theory and Practice*, Atlanta, GA: Emory University.

O'Malley, L. and Tynan, C. (2000) 'Relationship marketing in consumer markets. Rhetoric or reality?', *European Journal of Marketing* 34 (7): 797–815.

Payne, A. Christopher, M., Peck, H. and Clark, M. (1998) *Relationship Marketing for Competitive Advantage: Winning and Keeping Customers*, London: Butterworth-Heinemann.

Sheth, J. N. and Parvatiyar, A. (1995) 'Relationship marketing in consumer markets. Antecedents and consequences', *Journal of the Academy of Marketing Science* 23 (4): 255–271.

Tapp, A. (2000) *Principles of Direct and Database Marketing*, Harlow: Pearson Education.

Wood, E. H. (2004) 'Marketing information for the events industry', in *Festival and Events Management: An International Arts and Cultural Perspective*, Oxford: Elsevier.

Wood, E. H. and Masterman. G. (2006) *Innovative Marketing Communications: Strategies for the events industry*, Oxford, Elsevier.

Part three
Assessing and improving service delivery

Assessing and Improving Service Delivery, focuses on customer satisfaction and service quality issues. Methods for tracking service failures and employee recovery efforts as well as customer retention strategies are presented. Ideally, assessing and improving the service delivery system will lead to 'seamless' service provided without interruption, confusion, or hassle to the customer. The final chapter will consider the changing environment and how marketing managers need to think about consumer trends and behaviour to succeed in business over the long term.

Chapter 14

Defining and measuring customer satisfaction

If you can't measure it, goes the old cliché, you can't manage it. In fact, if you can't measure it, managers seem unable to pay attention to it.

Fortune Magazine

Chapter objectives

The objectives of this chapter are to introduce you to the importance and benefits of customer satisfaction and the special factors to consider in measuring customer satisfaction.

After reading this chapter, you should be able to:

- Define customer satisfaction and understand the benefits associated with satisfied customers.

- Appreciate various methods for measuring customer satisfaction and discuss the limitations of customer satisfaction measurements.

- Discuss factors to consider when investing in customer satisfaction improvements.

- Understand the many factors that influence customer expectations.

Services in context
The UK Customer Satisfaction Index

A major new UK-wide survey rating UK customers' satisfaction with the service they receive from organisations such as banks, retailers, hotels and utilities was announced by the Institure of Customer Service in 2005.

The ICS UK Customer Satisfaction Index enables consumers to make an immediate comparison between each organisation included in the survey. The new survey also allows UK organisations to benchmark their performance against the best in the country.

'Customer service is increasingly important in the UK, as the traditionally mild-mannered British consumer has learned to expect superb service and to vote with their feet if they're not satisfied', said Institute of Customer Service (ICS) Director Robert Crawford.

'An independent Customer Satisfaction Index will give customers valuable information, while showing companies where they could improve and how they stand against the best in the country. A similar survey in the US is seen as one of the major market features that keeps organisations on their toes, and customers in touch', added Crawford.

It's no secret that customers are attracted to – and stay with – organisations that do best that which matters most to them. So it's in any organisation's interests to give as much customer satisfaction as possible, as efficiently as it can.

The UKCSI allows customers and organisations to:

- see how different UK sectors perform
- find out how the best organisations perform
- discover whether customer satisfaction is improving.

Why have a Customer Satisfaction Index?

Successive UK governments – along with most forward-thinking organisations – agree that focusing on the customer has a direct effect on:

- bottom- line performance
- profitability or more efficient use of resources
- retaining customers and earning their trust
- lower costs per customer
- customer endorsements and recommendations
- staff satisfaction and turnover
- reputation.

If an organisation wants to succeed, it has to be the best at what matters most to its customers. So what exactly does matter most?

The Institute of Customer Service commissioned a major piece of research to find out customers' priorities – which factors determine how satisfied they are with products and services. The study also shows how important these priorities are in relation to each other and how they vary from sector to sector and place to place.

The results highlighted 20 separate customer priorities, which can be grouped into five attributes:

- Professionalism
- Problem-solving
- Timeliness
- Quality/efficiency
- Ease of doing business.

How the Customer Satisfaction Index is calculated

The UKCSI is based on the results of an online questionnaire that is completed by a representative sample of UK adults. Customers are asked to rate organisations across various sectors on each of the factors considered most important. They are also asked about any complaints they've made and how the organisation handled them.

The ICS research found that the top ten from these priorities are:

- Overall quality of the product or service
- Being treated as a valued customer
- Speed of service
- Friendliness of staff
- Handling of problems and complaints
- Handling of enquiries
- Competence of staff
- Ease of doing business
- Being kept informed
- Helpfulness of staff.

Satisfaction scores are collected every six months when the survey is repeated, while importance scores are the ones generated by the customer priorities research. This research is reviewed every two to three years.

The sectors covered by the survey are:

Automotive
Car manufacturers and dealerships
Finance – banks
Banks and building societies
Finance – insurers
Insurance companies and large brokers
Government depts/agencies
Central departments such as DSS, agencies such as the DVLA and publicly owned services such as Royal Mail
Leisure and tourism
Gyms, health clubs, bars, restaurants, tourist attractions, etc.
Local government
Local authority services, and police and fire services
Retail – food
Supermarkets and convenience stores
Retail – non-food
High Street shops, out-of-town stores, etc.

Services
Hairdressers, plumbers, electricians, solicitors, estate agents, etc.
Telecoms
Fixed or mobile telephones
Transport
Buses, trains, air travel
Utilities
Gas, electricity and water suppliers.

The top performers in the January 2008 results included Audi, Mercedes Benz, first direct, Alliance & Leicester, John Lewis, Marks & Spencer, Waitrose, Virgin Atlantic and P&O. The worst performers were telecoms and government services. Both sectors performed particularly badly when it came to handling complaints, with people grumbling that staff showed lack of interest, were dismissive and were too ready to pass them on to someone else.

Importance of customer satisfaction

There is strong evidence, mainly from the US, that customer satisfaction is the most important factor in determining growth of the economy and individual organisations.

ICS executive director Robert Crawford claims that the index is proving to be an economic

Alliance & Leicester were top performers in the survey.

SOURCE © ALEX SEGRE/ALAMY

indicator and will become all the more so as it gets bigger, with more of a track record.

'Despite the much-publicized credit crunch most commentators believe there will still be economic growth in 2008 in the UK', he says. 'The UKCSI figures support that. They show customers are happier with service', says the survey .

Sources: Institute of Customer Service (2005) UK Customer Satisfaction Index, announced 23 September 2005, www.instituteofcustomerservice.com. www.ukcsi.com.
'Customers happier with service says survey' 10/1/2008, www.uksci.com/pressreleases.
'Customers – what they really, really want', 23/04/2008, www.ukcsi.com/pressreleases.

Introduction

Customer satisfaction is one of the most studied areas in marketing. Between 1970 and 1990 more than 15,000 academic and trade articles were published on the topic (Peterson and Wilson, 1992). In fact, the *Journal of Advertising Research* has suggested that customer satisfaction surveys may be the fastest growing area in market research. Such devotion to the subject is certainly understandable given that satisfaction is a central theme of the marketing concept and is frequently included in the mission statements and promotional campaigns of successful organisations.

From a historical perspective, a great deal of the work in the customer satisfaction area began in the 1970s, when consumerism was on the rise. The rise of the consumer movement was directly related to the decline in service felt by many consumers. The decline in customer service and resulting customer dissatisfaction can be attributed to a number of sources. First, skyrocketing inflation in many Western economies during this period forced many firms to slash service in the effort to keep prices down. In some industries, deregulation led to fierce competition among firms who had never had to compete before. Price competition quickly became the attempted means of differentiation, and price wars developed. Firms once again slashed costs associated with customer service to cut operating expenses.

As time went on, labour shortages also contributed to the decline in customer service. Service workers who were motivated were difficult to find, and who could blame them? The typical service job included low pay, no career path, no sense of pride and no training in customer relations. Automation also contributed to the problem. Replacing human labour with machines indeed increased the efficiency of many operating systems, but often at the expense of distancing customers from the firm and leaving customers to fend for themselves. Finally, over the years, customers have become tougher to please. They are more informed than ever, their expectations have increased and they are more particular about where they spend their disposable income.

Researchers in the field of consumer satisfaction clearly recognized the connection between the study of satisfaction and the consumer movement. The connection between the marketing concept, satisfaction and consumerism continues to be one of the driving forces behind the study of customer satisfaction.

The importance of customer satisfaction

The importance of customer satisfaction cannot be overstated. Without customers, the service firm has no reason to exist. Every service business needs to proactively define and measure customer satisfaction. It is naïve to wait for customers to complain in order to identify problems in the service delivery system or to gauge the firm's progress in customer satisfaction based on the number of complaints received. Consider the following figures gathered by the Technical Assistance Research Program (TARP) (Albrecht and Zwenke, 1985):

- The average business does not hear from 96 per cent of its unhappy customers.
- For every complaint received, 26 customers actually have the same problem.
- The average person with a problem tells 9 or 10 people. Thirteen per cent will tell more than 20.
- Customers who have their complaints satisfactorily resolved tell an average of five people about the treatment they received.
- Complainers are more likely to do business with you again than noncomplainers: 54–70 per cent if resolved at all, and 95 per cent if handled quickly.

The TARP figures demonstrate that customers do not actively complain to service firms themselves. Instead, consumers voice their dissatisfaction with their feet, by defecting to competitors, and with their mouths, by telling your existing and potential customers exactly how they were mistreated by your firm. Based on the TARP figures, a firm that serves 100 customers per week and boasts a 90 per cent customer satisfaction rating will be the object of thousands of negative stories by the end of a year. For example, if 10 dissatisfied customers per week tell 10 of their friends of the poor service received, by the end of the year (52 weeks) 5,200 negative word-of-mouth communications will have been generated.

The TARP figures are not all bad news. Firms that effectively respond to customer complaints are the objects of positive word-of-mouth communications. Although positive news travels at half the rate of negative news, the positive stories can ultimately translate into customer loyalty and new customers. A firm should also learn from the TARP figures that complainers are the firm's friends. Complainers are a free source of market information, and the complaints themselves should be viewed as opportunities for the firm to improve its delivery systems, not as a source of irritation.

What is customer satisfaction/ dissatisfaction?

Although a variety of alternative definitions exist, the most popular definition of customer satisfaction/dissatisfaction is that it is a comparison of customer expectations to perceptions regarding the actual service encounter.

(Alternative definitions are provided in Table 14.1.) Comparing customer expectations with their perceptions is based on what marketers refer to as the expectancy disconfirmation model. Simply stated, if customer perceptions meet expectations, these are said to be confirmed expectations, and the customer is satisfied. If perceptions and expectations are not equal, then these are said to be disconfirmed expectations.

Although the term 'disconfirmation' sounds like a negative experience, it is not necessarily so. There are two types of disconfirmations. If actual perceptions were less than what was expected, the result is a negative disconfirmation, which results in customer dissatisfaction and may lead to negative word-of-mouth publicity and/or customer defection (see B2B Services in Action). In contrast, a positive disconfirmation exists when perceptions exceed expectations, thereby resulting in customer satisfaction, positive word-of-mouth publicity and customer retention.

Every day, consumers utilize the disconfirmation paradigm by comparing their expectations with perceptions. While dining at a resort restaurant on the west coast of Florida, our waiter not only provided everything we requested but also was very good at anticipating needs. My three-year-old niece had had enough fun and sun for the day and was very tired. She crawled up into a vacant booth located directly behind our table and went to sleep. The waiter, noticing her absence from our table, and on his own initiative, placed a white tablecloth over her to use as a blanket. This particular incident combined with other incidents throughout the evening lead to a positive disconfirmation of our expectations. That evening's great service reinforced the notion that with so much poor service all around, customers really do notice when the service is excellent.

expectancy disconfirmation model The model in which consumers evaluate services by comparing expectating with perceptions.

confirmed expectations Customer expectations that match customer perceptions.

disconfirmed expectations Customer expectations that do not match customer perceptions.

negative disconfirmation A nonmatch because customer perceptions are lower than customer expectations.

positive disconfirmation A nonmatch because customer perceptions exceed customer expectations.

The benefits of customer satisfaction

Although some may argue that customers are unreasonable at times, little evidence can be found of extravagant customer expectations (Berry, Parasuraman and Zeithaml, 1994). Consequently, satisfying customers is not an

		Table 14.1
Normative deficit definition	Compares actual outcomes to those that are culturally acceptable.	
Equity definition	Compares gains in a social exchange – if the gains are inequal, the loser is dissatisfied.	
Normative standard definition	Expectations are based on what the consumer believes he/she *should* receive – dissatisfaction occurs when the actual outcome is different from the standard expectation.	
Procedural fairness definition	Satisfaction is a function of the consumer's belief that he/she was treated fairly.	

Alternative satisfaction definitions

Source Keith Hunt, 'Consumer Satisfaction, Dissatisfaction, and Complaining Behavior', *Journal of Social Issues* 47 (1) (1991): 109–110.

impossible task. In fact, meeting and exceeding customer expectations may reap several valuable benefits for the firm. Positive word-of-mouth generated from existing customers often translates into more new customers. For example, consider the positive publicity generated for the firms listed in the Top 10 Most Admired Companies (see Table 14.2). In comparison, as a potential employee, would you have any reservations about working for the Bottom 10? Satisfied

---

B2B services in action
J. D. Power & Associates to the rescue

Tired of waiting in automated telephone queues? You're not alone. One recent call to an award-winning customer service centre to set up a service appointment was particularly frustrating. After waiting 30 minutes and 30 seconds in the queue, a customer was told by the customer service representative that his call would have to be transferred to another department. This was the second call to the service centre for the same problem. The first time the appointment was made, the company failed to appear or call. Adding to the frustration, the recorded message played while on hold, touted their superior service record, and promoted a sale that had ended days before. This scenario, and thousands like it, begs the question: *Is anyone listening?*

Customer relationship management systems code incoming callers based on their profitability and then route calls directly to customer service representatives or automated telephone queues based on the caller's code level. For customers, the minutes spent listening to the messages played in automated queues can seem like hours. Douglas Faneuil, the ex-Merrill Lynch aide who testified in the Martha Stewart trial, lightened up the mood of the courtroom as he explained that Martha Stewart threatened to dump Merrill because she hated the company's hold music. Merrill Lynch, like General Motors, IBM and Dell, plays classical music. Wal-Mart plays country, the Salvation Army plays hymns, and Microsoft callers listen to silence – apparently believing in this case that 'nothing' is better than 'something'.

To date, there are approximately 100,000 call centres worldwide. Realizing the need for a rating system, J. D. Power & Associates have begun evaluating call centres based on how long callers are kept on hold and how satisfied customers are when they hang up. The top 20 per cent of performers will hold the designation 'Certified by Power'; the remainder of firms will receive feedback regarding how to improve their service. For Power, the call centre market holds much potential. Company fees range from $20,000 to $100,000 per review. Interestingly, research already conducted by J. D. Power and Associates has not indicated any difference in service between onshore and offshore call centres.

Source: Brian Hindo and Ira Sager, 'Your Call is Important', *Business Week*, 23 February 2004, Issue 3871: 14; *Brain Hindo and Ira Sager, 'Call Centers from 'A' to 'F', Business Week, Issue 3864: 13.*

Is anyone listening?

current customers often purchase more products more frequently and are less likely to be lost to competitors than are dissatisfied customers.

Companies who command high customer satisfaction ratings also seem to have the ability to insulate themselves from competitive pressures, particularly price competition. Customers are often willing to pay more and stay with a firm that meets their needs than to take the risk associated with moving to a lower-priced service offering. Finally, firms that pride themselves on their customer satisfaction efforts generally provide better environments in which to work. Within these positive work environments, organizational cultures develop where employees are challenged to perform and rewarded for their efforts. Table 14.3 provides an example of the types of attributes that are key in building great corporate reputations and the companies that excel at particular key attributes.

In and of themselves, customer satisfaction surveys also provide several worthwhile benefits. Such surveys provide a formal means of customer feedback to the firm, which may identify existing and potential problems. Satisfaction surveys also convey the message to customers that the firm cares about their well-being and values customer input concerning its operations (Peterson and Wilson, 1992). However, the placement of customer feedback forms by some companies makes customers wonder if they really want the feedback (see Figure 14.1).

The Top Ten – Quality of products and services	
1	Anheuser-Busch
2	Deere
3	Procter & Gamble
4	BMW
5	United Parcel Service
6	Fluor
7	Caterpillar
8	Nestlé
9	Apple
10	Daimler
The Bottom Ten – Quality of products and services	
1	Hanwha
2	SABIC
3	Sanmina-SCI
4	Old Mutual
5	CNP Assurances
6	Asahi Breweries
7	Poste Italiane
8	SABMiller
9	ONEX (Celestica)
10	Fortis

Table 14.2

World's most and least admired companies, 2008

Source FORTUNE, 'World's Most Admired Companies' © 2008 Time Inc. All rights reserved.

Table 14.3	Attributes	Most admired companies
	1 Innovativeness	Apple; Proctor & Gamble
Nine key attributes of reputation	2 People management	General Electric; BMW
	3 Social reposnsibility	United Parcel Service; Anheuser-Busch
Source FORTUNE, 'World's Most Admired Companies' © 2008 Time Inc. All rights reserved.	4 Quality of management	Proctor & Gamble; General Electric
	5 Financial soundness	Exxon Mobil; United Parcel Service
	6 Use of corporation assets	Exxon Mobil; Berkshire Hathaway
	7 Long-term investment value	Berkshire Hatahaway, Exxon Mobil
	8 Quality of products/services	Anheuser-Busch; Deere
	9 Global competitiveness	Nestlé; Proctor and Gamble

Figure 14.1

United Wings customer feedback form

United Wings Air Line ✈

Many thanks for taking the time out to provide us with your feedback. With your help, we strive to improve the quality of service for our most valued customers.

Date: / /   Flight No. ☐   Departure city ☐   Destination city ☐

✈ What is the purpose of your air travel? ☐

✈ Overall, how satisfied are you with the air line?

☐ Satisfied ☐ Somewhat satisfied ☐ Neutral ☐ Somewhat dissatisfied ☐ Dissatisfied

✈ Please rate the United Wings Air Line on the following:

	Excellent	Good	Average	Poor	Very poor
Flight reservation:	☐	☐	☐	☐	☐
Check-in/boarding:	☐	☐	☐	☐	☐
Aircraft interior:	☐	☐	☐	☐	☐
Flight crew	☐	☐	☐	☐	☐
Snacks/beverages:	☐	☐	☐	☐	☐

✈ Would you purchase your next flight with us?

☐ Yes ☐ No

✈ What could we do to improve the quality of your flight?

✈ Contact details:

Name:
Address:
Email:
Contact number:

Please tick here if you would not like to receive promotional material from us. ☐

Other benefits are derived directly from the results of satisfaction surveys. Satisfaction results are often utilized in evaluating employee performance for merit and compensation reviews and for sales management purposes, such as the development of sales training programmes. Survey results are also useful for comparison purposes to determine how the firm stacks up against the competition. When ratings are favourable, many firms utilize the results in their corporate advertising (Peterson and Wilson, 1992).

Measures of customer satisfaction are derived via indirect and direct measures. Indirect measures of customer satisfaction include tracking and monitoring sales records, profits and customer complaints. Firms that rely solely on indirect measures are taking a passive approach to determining whether customer perceptions are meeting or exceeding customer expectations. Moreover, if the average firm does not hear from 96 per cent of its unhappy customers, it is losing a great many customers while waiting for the other 4 per cent to speak their minds.

Direct measures of satisfaction are generally obtained via customer satisfaction surveys. Avis-Europe successfully use these to respond quickly to customer feedback (see Figure 14.2). However, to say the least, customer satisfaction surveys are not standardized among firms. For example, the scales used to collect the data vary (e.g., 5-point to 100-point scales), questions asked of respondents vary (e.g., general to specific questions), and data collection methods vary (e.g., personal interviews to self-administered questionnaires). The following section discusses the use of various scales.

indirect measures Tracking customer satisfation through changes in sales, profits and number of customer complaints registered.

direct measures The proactive collection of customer satisfaction data through customer satisfaction surveys.

The scale of 100 approach

Some firms request customers to rate the firm's performance on a scale of 100. In essence, the firm is asking customers to give the firm a grade. However, the problems with this approach are readily apparent. Let's say that the firm scores an average of 83. What does the 83 mean – the firm received a B–? Does an 83 mean the same thing to all customers? Not likely. More importantly, what should the firm do to improve its satisfaction rating? The 83 does not provide specific suggestions for improvements that would lead to an increased customer satisfaction rating.

The 'very dissatisfied/very satisfied' approach

Other firms present customers with a 5-point scale, which is typically labeled utilizing the following format:

1 Very dissatisfied
2 Somewhat dissatisfied
3 Neutral
4 Somewhat satisfied
5 Very satisfied

Avis-Europe successfully use customer satisfaction surveys to improve their service.

Figure 14.2

Customer
Satisfaction taken
seriously at Avis
Europe

Source http://www.avis-
europe.com accessed 20 May
2008.

We aim to make Avis first choice of our customers by continually improving our service and so ensuring customer satisfaction and loyalty. This is especially important in ensuring brand differentiation and improving customer loyalty, in an increasingly price competitive market environment. We have made further good progress this year.

We monitor customer satisfaction principally through customer surveys and the level of complaints and each country Managing Director takes personal responsibility for monitoring and improving customer satisfaction scores.

Each month we distribute over 30,000 surveys and we receive over 5,000 replies. In line with our environmental objectives we have continued to increase the number of surveys sent out electronically wherever possible and this doubled in the year to reach 80 per cent. Of those returned, some 80 per cent are received back in less than three days, enabling us to pass comments on to the relevant business area for appropriate action with minimal delay.

Our four key measures of customer satisfaction are:

- overall satisfaction;
- willingness of customers to recommend Avis ('Net Promoter Score');
- customer complaints; and
- perception of station performance.

In 2007, overall satisfaction levels, which reflect customer satisfaction 'overall with the rental experience' rose by a further 2 per cent, continuing the steady improvement we have seen over the past seven years. The net promoter score, which measures the willingness to recommend Avis to a friend, improved again, by 4 per cent. The number of adjustments made to customer invoices reduced by 2 per cent in 2007. The station performance score, which records the overall efficiency of the running of a station, improved by over 1 per cent against last year.

During 2007 we continued to focus strongly on introducing further customer service initiatives, to differentiate the brand and continue to make the rental process faster, simpler and clearer for customers.

2007 saw further increases in the number of people signing up to the Avis Preferred service, underlining the improving trend in customer satisfaction and loyalty. Avis Preferred sign-ups increased by 69 per cent, while the number of active Avis Preferred customers increased by 17 per cent.

For Avis Preferred customers we began our 'Three Minute Promise' programme. Under this programme we guarantee customers their keys and mental agreement within three minutes of entering the service station.

If we fail, the customer receives a retail voucher for €30. We piloted the programme in France in 2007. The service is now available in 390 stations across six countries. This has provided real differentiation in the market place. In addition, our new significantly enhanced website, which improves ease of use and is designed to increase the number of customers booking directly, was rolled out across the Group in 2007.

We remain the only car rental company to have achieved the ISO 10002 CMSAS 86:2000 standard for Quality Management Customer Satisfaction Complaint Handling and were re-accredited in January 2008. The standard covers all our European offices and demonstrates that we follow best practice in all aspects of complaint management and continual improvement of performance.

Firms utilizing this format generally combine the percentage of 'somewhat satisfied' and 'very satisfied' responses to arrive at a satisfaction rating. Similarly, firms that utilize a 10-point scale with anchor points of 'very dissatisfied' and 'very satisfied' define customer satisfaction as the percentage of customers rating their satisfaction higher than 6. Although this approach provides more meaning to the satisfaction rating itself, it still lacks the diagnostic power to indicate specific areas of improvement. In other words, regardless of whether a firm uses a 100-point, 10-point, or 5-point scale, the interpretive value of the information is restricted by its quantitative nature. Qualitative information is needed to highlight specific areas for improvement. This is exactly the problem Federal Express encountered when it set up its first customer satisfaction measurement programme. Initially, customer satisfaction was measured on a 100-point scale and transaction success was defined as whether the package actually arrived the next day. Upon further qualitative examination, Federal Express determined that transaction success as defined by the customer was a much broader concept (see Table 14.4). The company now proactively improves its customer satisfaction ratings by continually improving upon those activities that were identified by its customer base – termed 'The Hierarchy of Horrors'.

The combined approach

The combined approach utilizes the quantitative scores obtained by the 'very dissatisfied/very satisfied' approach and adds a qualitative analysis of feedback obtained from respondents who indicated that they were less than 'very satisfied'. Customers who indicate that they are less than 'very satisfied' are informing the firm that the delivery system is performing at levels lower than expected.

1	Wrong day delivery (package delivered a day later than promised)
2	Right day late delivery (package delivered on the promised day, but after the promised deadline)
3	Pick-up not made (failure to make a pick-up on the day requested)
4	Lost package
5	Customer misinformed by Federal Express (mistaken or inaccurate information on rates, schedules, etc.)
6	Billing and paperwork mistakes (invoice errors, overcharges, missing proof-of-delivery documents)
7	Employee performance failures (courtesy, responsiveness, etc.)
8	Damaged packages

Table 14.4

Fedex's 'hierarchy of horrors'

Source AMA Management Briefing, *Blueprints for Service Quality: The Federal Express Approach* (New York: AMA Membership Publications Division, 1991).

By prompting customers to suggest how the firm could perform better, the firm can then categorize and prioritize the suggestions for continuous improvement efforts.

The combined approach provides two valuable pieces of information. The quantitative satisfaction rating provides a benchmark against which future company satisfaction surveys should be compared. In addition, the quantitative rating provides the means of comparing the firm's performance against its competition. Complementing the quantitative rating, the qualitative data provide diagnostic information and pinpoint areas for improvement. Combining the qualitative and quantitative data outperforms either approach used alone.

Understanding customer satisfaction ratings

After a consultant conducted a customer satisfaction survey for a regional engineering firm, the results revealed to upper management were that the firm commanded an 85 per cent customer satisfaction rating. Immediately, upper management wanted to know whether 85 per cent was a 'good' satisfaction rating or not. To effectively utilize customer satisfaction ratings, it is necessary to understand the factors that may influence customer responses.

Despite the lack of standardization among satisfaction studies, they share one common characteristic. 'Virtually all self-reports of customer satisfaction possess a distribution in which a majority of the responses indicate that customers are satisfied and the distribution itself is negatively skewed' (Peterson and Wilson, 1992: 67). Figure 14.3 depicts the negatively skewed distribution of customer satisfaction results.

Typically, customer satisfaction ratings are fairly high. Table 14.5 displays a sample of customer satisfaction results across various industries. As can be seen from the table, it is not unusual to see results in the 80–90 per cent range. Repeated findings such as these have led some researchers to conclude that 'to feel above average is normal'.

Figure 14.3

Conceptual distribution of satisfaction measurements

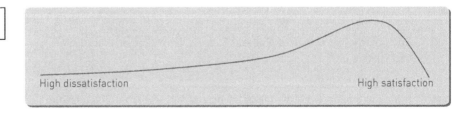

High dissatisfaction   High satisfaction

Source Robert A. Peterson and William R. Wilson, 'Measuring Customer Satisfaction: Fact and Artifact', *Journal of the Academy of Marketing Science*, 20, 1 (1992), p. 61.

Factors influencing customer satisfaction ratings

Satisfaction ratings may be influenced by numerous confounding factors that occur during the data collection process. This section provides explanations for inflated satisfaction results and reinforces the notion that obtaining accurate measures of customer satisfaction is not an easily accomplished task.

Customers are genuinely satisfied. One possible reason for high satisfaction scores is simply that customers are satisfied with the goods and services they typically purchase and consume – that's why they buy these products from the firm in the first place! Intuitively, this makes good sense. If the majority of customers were neutral or dissatisfied, they would most likely defect to competitive offerings of goods and services. Of course, this explanation assumes that competitors in the market are better at providing goods and services than the original supplier (see E-Services in Action).

Response bias. Another possible explanation for inflated satisfaction results may be response bias. Some experts argue that the reason ratings are so high is that companies hear from only satisfied customers. In contrast, dissatisfied customers do not believe that the firm's survey will do them any good; therefore, the questionnaire is discarded.

response bias A bias in survey results because of responses being received from only a limited group among the total survey population.

Other experts discount this explanation. Their argument is that it makes more sense for highly dissatisfied customers to express their opinion than it does for highly satisfied customers to do so. This position is supported by prior research, which indicates that dissatisfaction itself is more action-oriented and emotionally intense than satisfaction (Ritchins, 1983). Others argue that it is possible that highly dissatisfied customers and highly satisfied customers are more likely to respond than are those

Sample	Percentage satisfied
British Airways customers	85
HMO enrollees	92
Sears' customers	84
Children's instructional programmes/parents	82
Medical care	84
Clothing/and white goods/adults	82
Shoes/students	83

Table 14.5

Sampling of satisfaction results

Source Robert A. Peterson and William R. Wilson, 'Measuring Customer Satisfaction: Fact and Artifact', *Journal of the Academy of Marketing Science* 20 (1) (1992): 61.

E-services in action
Humanizing the net via innovative e-service

What is e-service? Strictly speaking, *e-service* pertains to customer service support provided on the net. E-service plays a critical role in online customer satisfaction. Ultimately, e-service humanizes the net by providing various customer service activities while simultaneously reducing the online firm's operating costs. Examples include the following:

- *Electronic order confirmation* – Noted as one of the easiest and most cost-effective methods to increase customer satisfaction, electronic order confirmation notifies customers within seconds or minutes that their order has been received by detailing the item purchased, quantity selected, cost of the item, shipping charges and order availability.

- *Package tracking services* – Once an order has been placed, effective e-tailers also notify customers when their purchases have been shipped and provide an expected delivery date. In addition, the best companies also provide package tracking identification numbers so that customers can track the physical movement of their purchases through a shipper's website (for example, FedEx or Parcelforce).

- *Electronic wallets* – According to one study, two-thirds of all shopping carts are left at the virtual checkout counter. Checking out online can be a lengthy process as customers enter their credit card information, phone numbers, billing address, shipping address, etc. Electronic wallets have been designed for repeat customers where the customer's credit card and desired shipping preferences are stored on the company's server and automatically appear when the customer places an order. For example Amazon use a '1-click' puchase option for registered customers.

- *Co-browsing* – In order to facilitate the social aspects of online shopping, e-tailers that offer co-browsing opportunities enable users to access the same website simultaneously from two different locations. Live text boxes are also provided so that users can chat online while making their purchase decisions.

- *Live text chats* – In addition to enabling customer-to-customer communications, live text chats are also facilitating customer-to-e-tailer communications. Innovative outsourcing firms, such as liveperson.com, staff a number of major e-tailers' live text chats and respond to customer enquiries online, often in under 60 seconds.

- *Merchandise return services* – 25 per cent of all merchandise purchased online is returned and the rate is higher in some industries, such as apparel. Today, many e-tailers include supply return authorizations with their shipments to facilitate the return process. Other e-tailers outsource their return activities, which enables customers to print return labels from the e-tailer's website and drop returns off at the Post Office.

- *Collaborative filtering* – This software program facilitates suggestive selling by monitoring the purchasing behaviour of like-minded customers online and then suggesting in real time what other customers have purchased. For example, based on Customer A's past purchase behaviour, Amazon.com will suggests to Customer A book titles of interest based on what others have purchased who also purchased the same title as Customer A.

Source: Adapted from Rafi A. Mohammed, Robert J. Fisher, Bernard J. Jaworski and Aileen Cahill (2002) *Internet Marketing: Building Advantage in a Networked Economy*, Boston, MA: McGraw-Hill Irwin. Zemke and Connellan, e-Service, AMACOM.

who are more neutral. Although these additional explanations are intriguing, they fail to explain the traditional response distribution depicted in Figure 14.3.

Data collection method. A third explanation for inflated satisfaction scores is the data collection method used to obtain results. Prior research suggests that higher levels of satisfaction are obtained via personal interviews and phone surveys compared with results from mail questionnaires and/or self-administered interviews. In fact, studies indicate that as much as a 10 per cent difference exists between questionnaires administered orally and self-administered questionnaires. The reason is that respondents to personal interviews and phone surveys may feel awkward expressing negative statements to other 'live' individuals as opposed to expressing them anonymously on a self-administered questionnaire.

data collection method The method used to collect information, such as questionnaires, surveys and personal interviews.

Research on data collection modes' effects on satisfaction ratings has produced some interesting results. The data collection mode does indeed appear to influence the level of reported satisfaction; however, the negatively skewed distribution of the satisfaction ratings remains unchanged, regardless of the data collection mode.

Question form. The way the question is asked on the questionnaire, or the question form, has also been offered as a possible explanation for inflated satisfaction ratings. It does appear that the question's being asked in positive form ('How satisfied are you?') as opposed to negative form ('How dissatisfied are you?') does have an impact on satisfaction ratings. Asking a question in the positive form appears to lead to greater reported levels of satisfaction than does posing the question in a negative form.

question form The way a question is phrased, i.e., positively or negatively.

Table 14.6 presents results from a study about the effects of stating the same question in two forms. In one version, the question asked respondents 'how satisfied' they were, and in the other version, the question asked 'how dissatisfied' they were. Results reveal that 91 per cent of respondents reported feeling 'very' or 'somewhat satisfied' when the question was stated in its positive form but only 82 per cent when stated in the negative form. Similarly, 9 per cent of respondents expressed that they were somewhat or very dissatisfied when asked in the positive form, compared with nearly 18 per cent when asked in the negative form.

Response category	'Satisfied'	'Dissatisfied'
Very satisfied	57.4%	53.4%
Somewhat satisfied	33.6%	28.7%
Somewhat dissatisfied	5.0%	8.5%
Very dissatisfied	4.0%	9.4%

Table 14.6

Responses by question form

Source Robert A. Peterson and William R. Wilson, 'Measuring Customer Satisfaction: Fact and Artifact', *Journal of the Academy of Marketing Science* 20 (1) (1992): 65.

question context The placement and tone of a question relative to the other questions asked.

Context of the question. The question context may also affect the satisfaction rating. Question context effects pertain to the ordering of questions and whether questions asked earlier in a questionnaire influence answers to subsequent questions. For example, in a study concerning satisfaction with vehicles, asking a general satisfaction question (e.g., 'In general, how satisfied are you with the products in your house?') prior to a specific vehicle satisfaction question (e.g., 'How satisfied are you with your Citroen?') increased the tendency towards a 'very satisfied' response for the specific question.

Timing of the question. Satisfaction ratings may also be influenced by the timing of the question relative to the date of purchase. Customer satisfaction appears to be highest immediately after a purchase and then begins to decrease over time. Again, regarding car purchases, researchers have noted a 20 per cent decline in satisfaction ratings over a 60-day period. It is not clear whether the initial ratings are inflated to compensate for feelings of cognitive dissonance or the latter ratings are deflated. Some consideration has been given that there may be different types of satisfaction measured at different points in time.

timing of the question The length of time after the date of purchase in which questions are asked.

Another possible explanation is that satisfaction rates may decay over time as customers reflect upon their purchase decision. Prior research indicates that the influence of negative events, which are more memorable than positive events, carries more weight in satisfaction evaluations over time. Consequently, satisfaction surveys distributed longer after purchases provide respondents the opportunity to take retribution as they recall such negative events.

social desirability bias A bias in survey results because of respondents' tendencies to provide information they believe is socially appropriate.

Social desirability bias. Social desirability bias describes a respondent's tendency to provide information that the respondent believes is socially appropriate. In satisfaction surveys, some researchers argue that respondents tend to withhold critical judgement because to do otherwise would be socially inappropriate. This would explain high satisfaction ratings and the shape of the distribution of results. Although the explanation is intriguing, widespread empirical support is lacking.

Mood. One more factor that could possibly influence customer satisfaction ratings is the mood of the customer while completing the survey. An abundance of research demonstrates the influence of positive mood states towards prosocial behaviours (Hoffman, 1992). More specifically, prior research has shown that respondents in positive mood states make more positive judgements, rate products they own more favourably, tend to see the brighter side of things and are more likely to rate strangers favourably. Hence, consumers in positive moods should give higher marks to service personnel and service firms than their neutral- or negative-mood counterparts.

Are customer satisfaction surveys worth it?

Given the number of factors that may distort the 'true' customer satisfaction ratings, one may wonder whether it is worth spending the time and money to measure satisfaction at all. Customer satisfaction ratings may fall under the category of the Hawthorne effect, that is, in and of themselves, satisfaction surveys might increase customer satisfaction regardless of the good or service being evaluated. Furthermore, due to the already high levels of customer satisfaction that already exist for most firms, it may not make sense to attempt to increase satisfaction levels across the board. However, two areas of satisfaction that do deserve special attention are (1) company attempts to maintain satisfaction over time to counter the decay effect, and (2) concentration on the tail of the satisfaction distribution – those customers who are dissatisfied. In and of themselves, satisfaction ratings cannot be interpreted with much meaning. Consequently, benchmarking with past satisfaction measures and comparisons with competition provide more meaningful feedback to companies.

> **benchmarking** Setting standards against which to compare future data collected.

All in all, despite all the possible complications and given the benefits derived from customer satisfaction, when firms use satisfaction surveys in conjunction with other measures, such as those described later in this chapter, the information provided is invaluable.

Customer satisfaction: How good is good enough?

How much satisfaction is enough? At 98 per cent, a company that completes 1,000 transactions per week upsets 20 customers per week, who tell 9 or 10 of their friends. Given this scenario, the bottom line translates into 200 negative stories per week and 10,400 negative stories per year. Although these numbers provide support for continuous improvements that enhance customer satisfaction ratings, we tend to forget that for every percentage of satisfaction improvement, very real investment costs are involved.

For example, if a firm currently boasts a 95 per cent customer satisfaction rating, is it worth a $100,000 investment to improve satisfaction to 98 per cent? (Babich, 1992). It depends. Pete Babich, the quality manager for the San Diego division of Hewlett-Packard, was faced with this exact question. Hewlett-Packard defines customer satisfaction as the customer's willingness to refer Hewlett-Packard products to friends. Hewlett-Packard has found that 70 per cent of its purchases are made because of previous positive experiences with the product or referrals from others.

Although Babich found an abundance of anecdotal evidence that retaining customers was much less expensive than seeking out new customers, this information failed to answer his original question: Is it worth $100,000 investment to improve satisfaction to 98 per cent? As a result, Babich proceeded to develop a customer satisfaction model that would predict market share changes over time as they related to customer satisfaction ratings.

The model is based on an algorithm that can easily be converted into a spreadsheet and that is built upon a number of assumptions. First, in this particular example, the model assumes a closed market of three firms that begin at period 'zero' with equal market shares (i.e. 33.3 per cent). The three firms offer comparable products and prices and compete for a growing customer base. Next, the model assumes that satisfied consumers will continue to buy from the same firm and that dissatisfied customers will defect to other firms in the market. For example, dissatisfied customers of Firm A will buy at Firm B or Firm C during the next time period. The length of the time period varies, depending on the product (e.g. eye test versus lawn care).

The direction of customer defection depends upon the firm's market share. In other words, if Firm C's market share is higher than Firm B's market share, Firm C will obtain a higher share of Firm A's dissatisfied customers. This logic is based on the premise that dissatisfied customers will be more particular the next time around and will conduct more research and seek out referrals from others. In this case, due to Firm C's higher market share, Firm C would be the beneficiary of more positive referrals.

Results generated from the customer satisfaction model when given three different scenarios are presented in Figure 14.4. Panel (a) illustrates the scenario of how a firm with a 95 per cent customer satisfaction rating would stack up against firms commanding 90 per cent and 91 per cent customer satisfaction ratings. Clearly, the firm with 95 per cent satisfaction dominates the market after 12 time periods. Panel (b) of the figure illustrates how that same firm with a 95 per cent satisfaction rating would compete with firms commanding 98 per cent and 99 per cent ratings. In this scenario, the 95 per cent firm controls less than 10 per cent of the market after 24 time periods. This scenario dramatically illustrates the impact of the competition's satisfaction ratings.

Finally, Panel (c) illustrates the effect of customer satisfaction on market share at lower customer satisfaction levels. In this scenario, Firms A, B, and C command satisfaction ratings of 90 per cent, 82 per cent, and 80 per cent, respectively. In essence, this panel illustrates the effect of increasing the dissatisfaction levels of Panel (a) by 2. In this scenario, Firm A once again achieves market dominance, but at a much faster rate.

What does Peter Babich's customer satisfaction model tell us? First, firms with higher customer satisfaction ratings make the firm more resistant to competitors' efforts to improve their market share. Secondly, if the firm knows what a 1 per cent improvement in market share does for its bottom line, then comparing the 1 per cent increase in market share to the investment needed to improve customer satisfaction gives the firm the necessary information to make a business decision. Finally, the model points out the necessity of knowing not only your own firm's satisfaction rating, but also your competitors'.

Should a firm invest $100,000 to improve customer satisfaction ratings from 95 per cent to 98 per cent? It depends upon several factors:

- the satisfaction ratings of the firm's competitors,
- the dollar investment necessary to increase customer satisfaction relative to the impact of increasing the firm's market share,
- the number of time periods required to recoup the investment, and
- the opportunity costs associated with other uses of the $100,000.

Does customer satisfaction translate into customer retention?

High satisfaction ratings do not necessarily mean that a firm is going to retain a customer forever (Lowenstein, 1993). In fact, according to one group of consultants, on average, 65 per cent to 85 per cent of customers

(a)

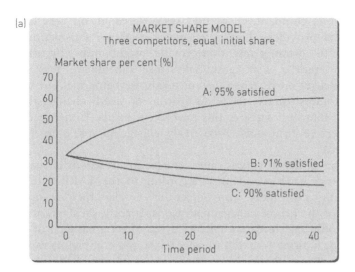

(b)

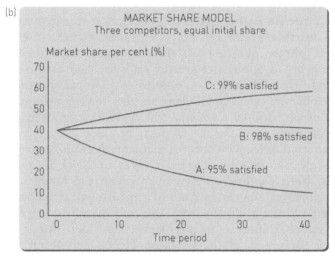

(c)

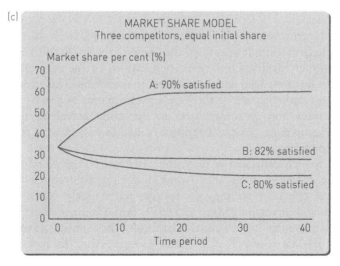

Figure 14.4

Customer
satisfaction model:
Three scenarios

Source Adapted from Peter
Babich, 'Customer
Satisfaction: How Good is
Good Enough', *Quality
Progress* (December 1992),
pp. 65–67.

who defect to competitors say they were 'satisfied' or 'very satisfied' with their former providers. Five criticisms of customer satisfaction research as they relate to customer retention provide insights into why firms with high satisfaction ratings may potentially lose customers. First, satisfaction research focuses on whether current needs are being met but fails to investigate customers' future needs. As customers' needs change, they will seek out a firm that best satisfies this new set of needs. Consequently, the progressive service firm must proactively engage in assessing its customers' future needs.

A second criticism of customer satisfaction research is that it tends to focus on registered complaints. According to the TARP figures presented earlier, many customers who defect never relay their complaints to an employee or the firm's management. Consequently, satisfaction research that examines only registered complaints overlooks a great deal of information. In addition, limiting research to only registered complaints most likely also overlooks many of the problems that need to be remedied in order to lower defection rates.

A third criticism is that customer satisfaction research tends to focus on global attributes and ignores operational elements. For example, firms often phrase questions in their customer satisfaction questionnaires using broad, global statements such as 'The firm provides good service' and 'The firm has good employees.' Global statements such as these overlook the operational elements that make up these statements. Examples of operational elements that measure employee performance may include such items as eye contact, product knowledge, courteous actions and credibility. Operational elements pertaining to good service might include the amount of time it takes to check in and check out at a hotel, the cleanliness of the facility and the hours of operation. Utilizing global attributes instead of operational elements in surveys fails to provide the company with the information it needs for developing effective solutions to problems. Consider, for example, the operational usefulness of the Sheraton Hotels and Resorts Guest Satisfaction Survey conducted by J. D. Power and Associates, presented in Table 14.7.

A fourth criticism of customer satisfaction research is that it often excludes the firm's employees from the survey process. Employee satisfaction drives customer loyalty. Employees' perceptions of the service delivery system need to be compared with customers' perceptions. This process provides feedback to employees about the firm's performance and assists in ensuring that employees and customers are on the same wavelength. As internal customers, employees often contribute valuable suggestions for improving the firm's operations.

Finally, a fifth criticism is that some firms are convinced that customers may not know what they want and that sometimes ignoring the customer is the best strategy to follow, particularly when it comes to new product innovation (Martin, 1995). Some believe that firms can go overboard listening to customers, thereby becoming slaves to demographics, market research and focus groups. And, in fact, listening to customers often does discourage truly innovative products. As evidence,

SHERATON HOTELS & RESORTS GUEST SATISFACTION SURVEY	**Table 14.7**

Sheraton Hotels and Resorts Guest Satisfaction Survey

Source J. D. Power and Associates, Agoura Hills, CA 91301.

MAKE YOUR ANSWERS COUNT!   *Correct Mark* ☒ ☑

1. How likely are you to...

	Very Likely	Somewhat Likely	Somewhat Unlikely	Very Unlikely
Return to this hotel if you are in the same area again?	☐	☐	☐	☐
Recommend this hotel to a friend or colleague planning to visit the area?	☐	☐	☐	☐
Stay at a Sheraton hotel again?	☐	☐	☐	☐

2. How satisfied were you with...   Outstanding ←——————————————→ Unacceptable

- Your overall experience as a guest in this hotel   ☐ ☐ ☐ ☐ ☐ ☐ ☐ ☐ ☐ ☐
- The value for the price paid   ☐ ☐ ☐ ☐ ☐ ☐ ☐ ☐ ☐ ☐
- Cleanliness and maintenance of hotel   ☐ ☐ ☐ ☐ ☐ ☐ ☐ ☐ ☐ ☐
- Responsiveness of staff to your needs   ☐ ☐ ☐ ☐ ☐ ☐ ☐ ☐ ☐ ☐
- Knowledge of staff

Check-in
- Accuracy of reservation   ☐ ☐ ☐ ☐ ☐ ☐ ☐ ☐ ☐ ☐
- Speed/efficiency of check-in   ☐ ☐ ☐ ☐ ☐ ☐ ☐ ☐ ☐ ☐
- Staff friendliness at check-in

Guest Room
- Size of room   ☐ ☐ ☐ ☐ ☐ ☐ ☐ ☐ ☐ ☐
- Comfort of bed   ☐ ☐ ☐ ☐ ☐ ☐ ☐ ☐ ☐ ☐
- Room décor/furnishings   ☐ ☐ ☐ ☐ ☐ ☐ ☐ ☐ ☐ ☐
- Ability to work in guest room   ☐ ☐ ☐ ☐ ☐ ☐ ☐ ☐ ☐ ☐
- Cleanliness of guest room   ☐ ☐ ☐ ☐ ☐ ☐ ☐ ☐ ☐ ☐
- Maintenance of guest room   ☐ ☐ ☐ ☐ ☐ ☐ ☐ ☐ ☐ ☐
- Cleanliness of bathroom   ☐ ☐ ☐ ☐ ☐ ☐ ☐ ☐ ☐ ☐
- Bath/shower water pressure

Hotel Services (If Used)
- Helpfulness of bell staff   ☐ ☐ ☐ ☐ ☐ ☐ ☐ ☐ ☐ ☐ ☐ N/A
- Hotel safety/security   ☐ ☐ ☐ ☐ ☐ ☐ ☐ ☐ ☐ ☐ ☐ N/A

Food and Dining (If Used)
- Food quality   ☐ ☐ ☐ ☐ ☐ ☐ ☐ ☐ ☐ ☐ ☐ N/A
- Speed/efficiency of service   ☐ ☐ ☐ ☐ ☐ ☐ ☐ ☐ ☐ ☐ ☐ N/A
- Room service speed/efficiency   ☐ ☐ ☐ ☐ ☐ ☐ ☐ ☐ ☐ ☐ ☐ N/A

Check-Out
- Speed/efficiency of check-out process   ☐ ☐ ☐ ☐ ☐ ☐ ☐ ☐ ☐ ☐
- Accuracy of billing   ☐ ☐ ☐ ☐ ☐ ☐ ☐ ☐ ☐ ☐

3. Please rate...
- Delivery of Sheraton promise 'I'll take care of you'   ☐ ☐ ☐ ☐ ☐ ☐ ☐ ☐ ☐
- This experience compared to other Sheraton hotels   ☐ ☐ ☐ ☐ ☐ ☐ ☐ ☐ ☐

4. Are you a member of the Starwood Preferred Guest Program?   ☐ Yes   ☐ No

5. If you are a member of the Starwood Preferred Guest Program, how satisfied were you with the benefits you received during your stay?   ☐ ☐ ☐ ☐ ☐ ☐ ☐ ☐ ☐ ☐ ☐ N/A

6. Please mark any problem you experienced during your stay. (MARK ALL THAT APPLY)

☐ Air conditioner/heater	☐ Hotel maintenance	☐ Reservation date	☐ Room maintenance
☐ Bathroom cleanliness	☐ Noise	☐ Reservation rate	☐ Room readiness
☐ Check-in	☐ No reservation	☐ Responsiveness of staff	☐ Sink/tub/toilet
☐ Guest room cleanliness	☐ Number of towels	☐ Room assignment	☐ Other

7. Did you contact anyone in the hotel to resolve the problem?   ☐ Yes   ☐ No

8. Was the problem resolved to your satisfaction?   ☐ Yes   ☐ No

9. Which of the following best describes the reason for your stay?   ☐ Business   ☐ Both Business/Leisure   ☐ Leisure   ☐ Meeting/Conference

10. Your gender: ☐ Female   ☐ Male

Please write in your e-mail address: ☐☐☐

Additional comments: _____

Please return in the enclosed envelope to: J.D. Power and Associates, 30401 Agoura Road, Suite 200, Agoura Hills, CA 91301

90 per cent of so-called new products are simply line extensions of existing products.

Listening to customers does have its drawbacks. Customers often focus on current needs and have a difficult time projecting their needs into the future. In addition, consumers sometimes pick up cues from the person asking questions and attempt to answer questions in a direction that will please the interviewer. Other problems include the consumer being in a hurry, not fully understanding what is being asked, not wanting to be rude and so cheerfully agreeing with whatever is being asked, and most importantly, not making decisions using real money.

The list of products consumers initially rejected that went on to be huge successes is impressive. Products such as the Chrysler minivan, fax machines, VCRs, FedEx, CNN, Compaq PC servers, cellular phones, personal digital assistants, microwave ovens and even Birdseye frozen foods were all rejected by customers during initial survey attempts. In contrast, products that surveyed customers indicated would be great successes, such as McDonald's McLean, KFC's skinless fried chicken, Pizza Hut's low-calorie pizza and New Coke, among others, turned out to be flops.

The problem is not so much listening to what customers have to say as it is companies feeling paralysed to make strategic moves without strong consumer support. Of course, customers should not be completely ignored. However, some marketers argue that the best consumer information is obtained through detached observation instead of through traditional survey techniques: 'Ignore what your customers say; pay attention to what they do' (Martin, 1995). Controversially, Williams and Visser (2002) go further and argue that customer satisfaction is unimportant and only focused on by 'middle managers' – the real benefit, they state, lies in understanding customer behaviour and ceasing to reward customer dissatisfaction.

Customer satisfaction: A closer look

So far, this chapter has provided a broad overview of customer satisfaction. This section takes a closer look at customer expectations and how they relate to customer satisfaction and service quality assessments (see Global Services in Action). This section further defines customer satisfaction and provides the transition into the next chapter, which focuses solely on service quality issues.

Types of customer expectations

At first glance, comparing expectations with perceptions when developing customer satisfaction evaluations sounds fairly straightforward. Expectations serve as benchmarks against which present and future service encounters are compared. However, this relatively simple scenario becomes a bit more confusing when you realize that there exist at least three different types of expectations (Zeithaml, Berry and Parasuraman, 1993).

Predicted service is a probability expectation that reflects the level of service customers believe is likely to occur. For example, bank customers tend to conduct their banking business at the same location over time. Customers become accustomed to dealing with the same bank personnel and, over time, begin to anticipate certain performance levels. It is generally agreed that customer satisfaction evaluations are developed by comparing predicted service to perceived service received (see Figure 14.5).

predicted service The level of service quality a consumer believes is likely to occur.

probability expectation A customer expectation based on the customer's opinion of what will be most likely when dealing with service personnel.

Global services in action
Global customer satisfaction: The influence of colours, numbers, smells and animals

Throughout the world, the case can be made that customer satisfaction is achieved by meeting and/or exceeding customer expectations. Consequently, increases in customer satisfaction may be strategically achieved by lowering customer expectations prior to arrival, and/or managing perceptions as the customer experiences the service encounter. However, the most complicated task of achieving global satisfaction is understanding the basis of different cultures' expectations and perceptions. Consider, for example, the differences in the meaning of colours, numbers, smells and animals around the world.

Colours symbolize different ideas among the world's nations. Where white is the colour of birth in the West, it symbolizes mourning in the East. In contrast, black is an everyday colour in the East, but symbolizes death in the West. In fact, the colour of mourning varies greatly around the world – purple in Brazil, yellow in Mexico and dark red on the Ivory Coast. In America, green suggests freshness and good health; however, in countries with dense green jungles, green suggests disease. When projecting masculinity, blue is the colour of choice in America and red is seen as the manly colour in the United Kingdom and France. Red is interpreted as a sign of good

fortune in China but is associated with death in Turkey. If trying to project a more feminine image, pink is the most feminine colour in many Western countries, but it is yellow that is more feminine in other parts of the world.

Service marketers must also carefully consider the meanings of smells, numbers and animals when communicating with international markets. While the smell of a lemon is associated with freshness in America, the same smell is associated with illness in the Philippines. In the UK, the number 13 is considered unlucky; however, the unlucky number in Japan is 4, and in Ghana, Kenya and Singapore it is 7. In contrast, 'lucky 7' is a common phrase in Anglo countries. Finally, care should be taken when using animals to create various images. Although the owl may symbolize wisdom in many countries, it translates to bad luck in India (similar to a black cat in the UK). Moreover, a company might align itself with a fox to symbolize its intellect ('smart as a fox'), but in Japan that same company would be associated with witches.

Source: Adapted from Jean-Claude Usunier and Julie Anne Lee, *Marketing Across Cultures*, 4th ed. (Harlow, England: Prentice Hall, 2005), p. 264.

desired service The level of service quality a customer actually wants from a service encounter.

ideal expectation A customer's expectation of what a 'perfect' service encounter would be.

perceived service superiority A measure of service quality derived by comparing desired service expectations and perceived service received.

adequate service The level of service quality a customer is willing to accept.

minimum tolerable expectation A customer expectation based on the absolute minimum acceptable outcome.

perceived service adequacy A measure of service quality derived by comparing adequate service and perceived service.

zone of tolerance Level of quality ranging from high to low and reflecting the difference between desired service and adequate service; expands and contracts across customers and within the same customer, depending on the service and the conditions under which it is provided.

Desired service is an ideal expectation that reflects what customers actually want compared with predicted service, which is what is likely to occur. Hence, in most instances, desired service reflects a higher expectation than predicted service. For example, our bank customer's desired service is that he not only receive his predicted service but that the cashiers call him by his first name and enthusiastically greet him as he enters the bank. Comparing desired service expectations to perceived service received results in a measure of perceived service superiority (see Figure 14.5).

In contrast, adequate service is a minimum tolerable expectation and reflects the level of service the customer is willing to accept. Adequate service is based on experiences or norms that develop over time. For example, most adult consumers have dined at hundreds, if not thousands, of restaurants. Through these experiences, norms develop that consumers expect to occur. Hence, one factor that influences adequate service is predicted service. Encounters that fall below expected norms fall below adequate service expectations. Comparing adequate service with perceived service produces a measure of perceived service adequacy.

The zone of tolerance

Because services are characterized by heterogeneity, consumers learn to expect variation in service delivery from one location to the next and even with the same provider from one day to the next. Consumers who accept this variation develop a zone of tolerance, which reflects the difference between desired service and adequate service (see Figure 14.6). The zone of tolerance expands and contracts across customers and within the same customer depending on the service and the conditions under which the service is provided. Other factors, such as price, may influence the zone of tolerance. Typically, as the price increases, the customer's zone of tolerance decreases as desired service needs begin to dominate, and the customer becomes less forgiving of sloppy service.

Figure 14.5

Comparison between customer evaluation of service quality and customer satisfaction

Source Adapted from Valerie A. Zeithaml, Leonard L. Berry, and A. Parasuraman, 'The Nature and Determinants of Customer Expectations of Service', *Journal of the Academy of Marketing Science* 21, 1 (1993), pp. 1–12.

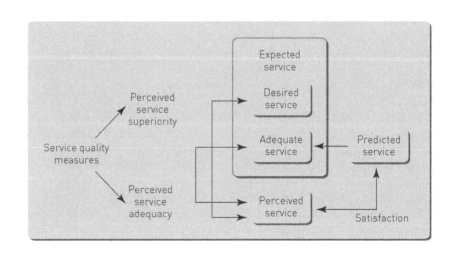

Another interesting characteristic of the zone of tolerance is that desired service is less subject to change than adequate service. One way to picture the zone of tolerance is to compare it with a projector screen located at the top of a whiteboard. The metal canister bolted to the wall that holds the screen represents the desired service level. The desired service level represents what the customer believes the ideal service firm should provide to its customers. Its movement is less subject to change than the rest of the screen. The screen itself represents the zone of tolerance, and the metal piece with the handle at the bottom of the screen represents the adequate service level. Adequate service fluctuates based on circumstances surrounding the service delivery process and changes the size of the zone of tolerance accordingly.

Factors influencing service expectations: Desired service and predicted service

Desired service expectations are developed as a result of six different sources (see Figure 14.7). The first source, enduring service intensifiers, are personal factors that are stable over time and that increase a customer's sensitivity to how the service should best be provided. Two types of enduring service intensifiers include the customer's derived expectations and personal service philosophies. Derived expectations are created from the expectations of others. For example, if your boss requests that you find someone to pressure-wash the office building, your expectations of the provider performing the job will most likely be higher than if you had hired the provider on your own initiative. In the attempt to satisfy your boss's expectations, your sensitivity to the calibre of service significantly increases.

enduring service intensifiers Personal factors that are stable over time and increase a customer's sensitivity to how a service should best be provided.

derived expectations Expectations appropriated from and based on the expectations of others.

personal service philosophies A customer's own internal views of the meaning of service and the manner in which service providers should conduct themselves.

Figure 14.6

The zone of tolerance

Source Valerie A. Zeithaml, Leonard L. Berry, and A. Parasuraman, 'The Nature and Determinants of Customer Expectations of Service', *Journal of the Academy of Marketing Science* 21, 1 (1993), pp. 1–12.

Similarly, the customer's personal service philosophies, or personal views of the meaning of service and the manner in which service providers should conduct themselves, will also heighten his or her sensitivities. Customers who work in the service sector are particularly sensitive to the calibre of service provided. These customers hold their own views regarding exactly how service should be provided; they want to be treated the way they believe they treat their customers.

The second factor influencing desired service expectations is the customer's own **personal needs**, including physical, social and psychological needs. Simply stated, some customers are needier than others. Some customers are very particular about where they are seated in a restaurant, while others are happy to sit nearly anywhere. In a hotel, some customers are very interested in the hotel's amenities, such as the pool, sauna, dining room and other forms of available entertainment, while others are simply looking for a clean room. This is one of the reasons that

personal needs A customer's physical, social and psychological needs.

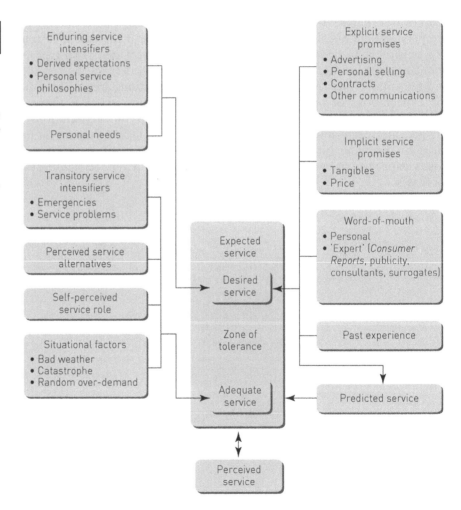

Figure 14.7

Factors influencing expected service

Source Adapted from Valerie A. Zeithaml, Leonard L. Berry, and A. Parasuraman, 'The Nature and Determinants of Customer Expectations of Service', *Journal of the Academy of Marketing Science* 21, 1 (1993), pp. 1–12.

managing a service firm is particularly challenging. Customers have a variety of needs, and no two customers are alike in every way.

The other four factors that influence desired service expectations also influence predicted service expectations and include (1) explicit service promises, (2) implicit service promises, (3) word-of-mouth communications and (4) past experience (see Figure 14.7).

Explicit service promises encompass the firm's advertising, personal selling, contracts and other forms of communication. Due to the lack of a tangible product, consumers of services base their evaluations of the service on various forms of information available. The more ambiguous the service, the more customers rely on the firm's advertising when forming expectations. If a hotel stresses modern and clean rooms, customers expect the rooms to be exactly the way they were pictured in the advertisement. Similarly, if a builder states that a customer's new house will be completed in December, the customer takes this as the builder's promise, and the standard is established on which the customer will base subsequent evaluations.

explicit service promises Obligations to which the firm commits itself via its advertising, personal selling, contracts and other forms of communication.

Implicit service promises also influence desired service and predicted service. The tangibles surrounding the service and the price of the service are common types of implicit service promises. As the price increases, customers expect the firm to deliver higher-quality services. In the absence of a tangible product, the price becomes an indicator of quality to most consumers. For example, customers would probably have higher expectations for service at a higher-priced hair salon than they would for 'Cheap Charlie's Barber Shop'. Similarly, if the tangibles surrounding a service are plush, customers interpret those tangibles as a sign of quality. In general, the nicer the furnishings of the service establishment, the higher customer expectations become.

implicit service promises Obligations to which the firm commits itself via the tangibles surrounding the service and the price of the service.

Word-of-mouth communications also play an important role in forming customer expectations. As discussed in Chapter 4, customers tend to rely more on personal sources of information than on nonpersonal ones when choosing among service alternatives. Since services cannot be evaluated fully before purchase, customers view word-of-mouth information as unbiased information from someone who has been through the service experience. Sources of word-of-mouth information range from friends and family to consultants to product review publications such as *Consumer Reports*.

word-of-mouth communications Unbiased information from someone who has been through the service experience, such as friends, family, or consultants.

Finally, past experience also contributes to customer expectations of desired and predicted service. Service evaluations are often based on a comparison of the current service encounter to other encounters with the same provider, other providers in the industry and other providers in other industries. In the education system, student desires and predicted service expectations of lecturers are likely to be based on past experience in other classes with the same lecturer and on other classes with other lecturers.

past experience The previous service encounters a consumer has had with a service provider.

Factors influencing service expectations: Adequate service

Adequate service reflects the level of service the consumer is willing to accept and is influenced by five factors: (1) transitory service intensifiers,

(2) perceived service alternatives, (3) customer self-perceived service roles, (4) situation factors and (5) predicted service (see Figure 14.7).

Transitory service intensifiers.

transitory service intensifiers Personal, short-term factors that heighten a customer's sensitivity to service.

In contrast to enduring service intensifiers, transitory service intensifiers are individualized, short-term factors that heighten the customer's sensitivity to service. For example, customers who have had service problems in the past with specific types of providers are more sensitive to the quality of service delivered during subsequent encounters. Another example is the need for service under personal emergency situations. Typically, consumers are willing to wait their turn to see a doctor. However, under personal emergency conditions, consumers are less willing to be patient and expect a higher level of service in a shorter period of time. Hence, the level of adequate service increases, and the zone of tolerance becomes narrower.

Perceived service alternatives.

perceived service alternatives Comparable services customers believe they can obtain elsewhere and/ or produce themselves.

The level of adequate service is also affected by the customer's perceived service alternatives. The larger the number of perceived service alternatives, the higher the level of adequate service expectations, and the more narrow the zone of tolerance. Customers who believe that they can obtain comparable services elsewhere and/or that they can produce the service themselves expect higher levels of adequate service than those customers who believe they are not able to receive sufficiently better service from another provider.

Self-perceived service role.

self-perceived service role The input a customer believes he or she is required to present in order to produce a satisfactory service encounter.

As has been discussed on numerous occasions, the service customer is often involved in the production process and can directly influence the outcome of the service delivery system. When customers have a strong self-perceived service role, that is, when they believe that they are doing their part, their adequate service expectations are increased. However, if customers willingly admit that they have failed to complete forms or provide the necessary information to produce a superior service outcome, then their adequate service expectations decrease, and the zone of tolerance increases.

Situational factors.

situational factors Circumstances that lower the service quality but that are beyond the control of the service provider.

As a group, customers are not unreasonable. They understand that from time to time situational factors beyond the control of the service provider will lower the quality of service. If the power goes out in one part of town around dinner time, restaurants in other parts of town will be overrun by hungry patrons. As a result, lengthy waits will develop as the service delivery system becomes backed up. Similarly, after a hurricane, flood, or other natural disaster occurs, the customer's insurance agent may not be as responsive as under normal circumstances. When circumstances occur beyond the control of the provider and the customer has knowledge of these circumstances, adequate service expectations are lowered, and the zone of tolerance becomes wider.

Predicted Service. The level of service that consumers believe is likely to occur, is the fifth and final factor that influences adequate service expectations. Predicted service is a function of the firm's explicit and implicit service promises, word-of-mouth communications and the customer's own past experiences. Taking these factors into consideration, customers form judgements regarding the predicted service that is likely to occur and set adequate service expectations simultaneously.

predicted service The level of service quality a consumer believes is likely to occur.

The link between expectations, customer satisfaction and service quality

When evaluating the service experience, consumers compare the three types of expectations (predicted service, adequate service and desired service) to the perceived service delivered. Customer satisfaction is calculated by comparing predicted service and perceived service. Perceived service adequacy, which compares adequate service and perceived service, and perceived service superiority, which compares desired service and perceived service, are measures of service quality (refer to Figure 14.5). Other major differences between service quality and customer satisfaction as well as issues related to service quality measurement are discussed in greater detail in Chapter 15.

Summary

Customer satisfaction research is one of the fastest-growing areas in market research. Defined as a comparison of perceptions and predicted service expectations, customer satisfaction has been associated with such benefits as repeat sales, more frequent sales, increased sales per transaction, positive word-of-mouth communications, insulation from price competition and pleasant work environments for employees. Customer satisfaction questionnaires send the signal to consumers that the firm cares about its customers and wants their input. In addition, data collected from questionnaires facilitates the development of employee training programmes, identifies strengths and weaknesses in the firm's service delivery process and provides information to be used in employee performance reviews and compensation decisions.

Firms use a variety of methods to track customer satisfaction. Moreover, a number of factors can dramatically increase or decrease the firm's satisfaction ratings. The main lessons to be learned are that (1) customer satisfaction surveys that collect qualitative and quantitative data are more useful than those that collect either qualitative or quantitative data alone; and (2) regardless of the methods used, such as the timing of the questions, the context of the questions, the data collection method and a variety of other research issues, the firm must be consistent in its approach in order to make meaningful comparisons over time. Overall, customer satisfaction ratings tend to be negatively skewed, and responses indicating above-average performance tend to be the norm.

Despite its problems, customer satisfaction assessment is a valuable management exercise. However, firms should not attempt to increase their satisfaction ratings without carefully considering (1) the satisfaction ratings of competing firms, (2) the cost of an investment in increasing market share relative to the impact on the firm's bottom line, (3) the number of time periods it takes to recoup such an investment and (4) the opportunity costs associated with the use of the firm's funds. Finally, one of the driving forces behind customer satisfaction is the customer's expectations. Three types of expectations and the factors influencing each type were presented. The three types of expectations form the basis for both customer satisfaction and service quality assessments, which are discussed in Chapter 12.

Discussion questions

1 Discuss the differences among a confirmation, a positive disconfirmation, and a negative disconfirmation.

2 Explain what is meant by the description that most satisfaction scores are negatively skewed? Use examples to illustrate why this score distribution occurs.

3 Discuss how the form of a question may influence satisfaction scores.

4 Debate whether a company should always attempt to achieve 100 per cent customer satisfaction?

5 Discuss the relationship between customer satisfaction and customer retention with reference to the case study 'Ticketing'.

Case link

See Case 11: Ticketing.

6 Consider the drawbacks of listening to customers and assessing customer satisfaction. How might these be overcome?

7 Define and explain the relevance of the terms *predicted service*, *desired service*, and *adequate service* as they pertain to customer satisfaction and service quality.

8 What are the factors that influence customer expectations? How can understanding these help to improve customer satisfaction?

References and further reading

Albrecht, K. and Zemke, R. (1985) *Service America! Doing Business in the New Economy*, Homewood, IL: Business One Irwin.

Babich, P. (1992) 'Customer satisfaction: how good is good enough', *Quality Progress* (December): 65–67.

Berry, L. L., Parasuraman, A. and Zeithaml, V. A. (1994) 'Improving service quality in America: lessons learned', *Academy of Management Executive* 8 (2).

Hoffman, K. D. (1992) 'A conceptual framework of the influence of positive mood states on service exchange relationships', in *Marketing Theory and Applications*, Chris T. Allen et al., eds., San Antonio, TX: American Marketing Association Winter Educator's Conference, p. 147.

Hunt, K. (1991) 'Consumer satisfaction, dissatisfaction, and complaining behavior', *Journal of Social Issues* 47 (1): 109–110.

Lowenstein, M. W. (1993) 'The voice of the customer', *Small Business Reports* (December): 57–61.

Martin, J. (1995) 'Ignore your customer', *Fortune*, 1 May, pp. 121–126.

Peterson, R. A. and Wilson, W. R. (1992) 'Measuring customer satisfaction: fact and artifact', *Journal of the Academy of Marketing Science* 20 (1): 61.

Richins, M. L. (1983) 'Negative word-of-mouth by dissatisfied consumers: a pilot study', *Journal of Marketing* 47 (Winter): 68–78.

Williams, R. and Visser, R. (2002) 'Customer statisfaction: it is dead but it will not lie down', *Managing Service Quality* 12 (3): 194–200.

Zeithaml, V. A., Berry, L. L. and Parasuraman, A. (1993) 'The nature and determinants of customer expectations of service', *Journal of the Academy of Marketing Science* 21 (1): 1–12.

Chapter 15

Defining and measuring service quality

It's just the little touches after the average man would quit that makes the master's fame.

(Orison Swett Marden, founder, *Success* magazine)

Chapter objectives

The major objectives of this chapter are to introduce you to the concepts of service quality, service quality measurement, and service quality information systems.

After reading this chapter, you should be able to:

- Contrast service quality as it compares to customer satisfaction.

- Identify the gaps that influence consumer perceptions of service quality and discuss factors that influence the size of each service quality gap.

- Understand the basic concepts of SERVQUAL.

- Describe the components of a service quality information system.

Services in context
WOW! Awards

The WOW! Award™ is part of The National Customer Service Awards which was set up nine years ago. The National Customer Service Awards helps organizations to reward service staff for their outstanding contribution for innovation, best practice and service excellence – all of which are vital in today's fast-moving service industry.

The 2007 awards were held at the Grosvenor House Hotel, Park Lane, London on 18 September 2007. Over 1500 Customer Service Professionals from all over the UK and from many different companies from the public sector, airlines, retailers and librarians. The WOW! Awards™ is an extra special award as it is the only category where individuals or businesses are nominated by their customers. This enables true service quality to be acknowledged and rewarded by the people who really count.

There are six simple rules which need to be met in order for a business or individual to receive the WOW! Award:

1 The WOW! Award is only awarded to businesses. Much as we would like to see great service in every walk of life we can only accept nominations for genuine businesses. The business can be of any size from a one-man business to a multi-million pound business.

2 The experience must relate to something that happened here in the UK. The purpose of the WOW! Awards is to recognize and promote UK businesses.

3 The relationship between you and the business that you nominate must be a normal customer relationship. Please don't nominate a business that you have any personal involvement with.

4 The experience must be one that has happened to you personally. We expect you to be honest in how you tell the story. Please tell the story in your own words the way that it really happened. Your story may be published and used to promote 'The WOW! Awards' so we need to be sure that we've got it right.

5 The story has to be one of exceptional customer service for the business to receive an award. We do get lots of stories of good service. But we are looking for stories that make us go 'WOW!'

6 The story should be a recent one. Please do not send us stories of experiences that happened more than one year ago.

One organization that was nominated with a staggering 471 nominees was Haringey Council, London and they are the first UK local authority to start using the WOW! Awards. Like all councils Haringey has to manage many service providers including libraries, schools, tourist attractions, hospital, street lighting, refuse collection and so on. Out of the 471 nominees several came in for street cleaning, police and libraries and curators at their tourist sites. Chris McLean, Corporate Customer Focus Manager, said 'The WOW! Awards have been a real boost for customer services staff in Haringey, and winning the National Customer Service award has shown that we can compete with the best. I'd certainly encourage other local authorities to get involved.' Clearly having a culture for providing quality services across a wide range of disciplines is exceptionally good management. Other service organizations that have also been involved in the WOW! Awards are NSN

Productions Limited who source live music entertainment for large indoor and outdoor events and Autotrader which provides a magazine and an online portal for customers buying and selling cars.

Sources: http://www.nsn-productions.com/. http://www.thewowawardswebs.co.uk/autotrader/. http://whttp://www.thewowawards.co.uk/users/ businessesusingwow.aspx. www.thewowawards.co.uk/haringeycouncil.

Introduction

One of the few issues on which service quality researchers agree is that service quality is an elusive and abstract concept that is difficult to define and measure because of the intangibility and inseparability elements, described in Chapter 2. This particular problem is challenging for academicians and practitioners alike. For example, traditional measures of productivity such as Gross Domestic Product (GDP) do not account for increases in service quality delivered. However, as Figure 11.2 showed in Chapter 11, if service quality is at the heart of an organization's business strategy it can actually increase an organization's performance (Homburg et al., 2002) Therefore, good service quality pays dividends in terms of loyal customers, loyal staff and increased profits. Conversely, poor service quality can create very expensive problems! For example, if a mail-order company sends you the wrong product, the pounds spent on phone calls and return mailings to correct the mistake will add to the GDP.

Other governmental institutions, such as the Bureau of Labour Statistics (BLS), have attempted to account for increases in quality by adjusting the consumer price index. For example, if a car costs more this year than last but includes quality improvements such as an air bag, better gas mileage and cleaner emissions, the BLS will subtract the estimated retail value of the improvements before calculating the consumer price index. However, the BLS does this for only a few industries and without the help of customers who are the true evaluators of quality improvements. Efficiency measures are also of no help. A retail store that stocks lots of merchandise may please more customers and make more money while decreasing the firm's efficiency rating.

The productivity of education and government services is notoriously difficult to measure. Increases in quality, such as improving the quality of education and training government employees to be more pleasant throughout their daily interactions with the pubic, do not show up in productivity measures. However, it is readily apparent that increases in quality can have a dramatic impact on a firm's or industry's survival.

It is important that marketers, operations managers and human resources managers work hand-in-hand to ensure that excellent service quality is provided to enhance the customer experience. Operations managers often wish to increase productivity by reducing waiting times and long queues. But speedy service may make customers feel as though they are being rushed along a production line. Collaboration between the marketing, operations and human resources departments is imperative in the service industry to achieve the vision and goals of the organization that are not detrimental to customer experience. Exciting promotional campaigns such as all-leather sofas on sale for £45.00 coincided with the new Ikea store in Edmonton, North London. The store was due to open at midnight but queues started forming from 6.00 pm. By midnight over 4,000 men, women and children were waiting for the doors to open. When the store did open there was chaos – queue jumpers rushed past those who had been waiting patiently, some families lost one another in the crush and roads around North London were at a standstill. This chaos created poor service delivery as human resources had not recruited seasonal sales personnel. And the operations department had not planned for appropriate car-parking facilities and check-out procedures.

What is service quality?

Perhaps the best way to begin a discussion of service quality is to first attempt to distinguish service quality measurement from customer satisfaction measurement. Most experts agree that customer satisfaction is a short-term, transaction-specific measure, whereas service quality is an attitude formed by long-term, overall evaluation of performance.

Without a doubt, the two concepts of customer satisfaction and service quality are intertwined. However, the relationship between these two concepts is unclear. Some believe that customer satisfaction leads to perceived service quality, while others believe that service quality leads to customer satisfaction. Indeed customers who are satisfied become loyal and for customers to be satisfied, service quality is key (Lovelock and Wirtz, 2004).

One plausible explanation is that satisfaction assists consumers in revising service quality perceptions (Cronin, Jr. and Taylor, 1992). The logic for this position consists of the following:

1 Consumer perceptions of the service quality of a firm with which he or she has no prior experience are based on the consumer's expectations.

2 Subsequent encounters with the firm lead the consumer through the disconfirmation process and revised perceptions of service quality.

3 Each additional encounter with the firm further revises or reinforces service quality perceptions.

4 Revised service quality perceptions modify future consumer purchase intentions towards the firm.

To deliver a consistent set of satisfying experiences that can build into an evaluation of high quality requires the entire organization to be focused on the task. The needs of the consumer must be understood in detail, as must the operational constraints under which the firm operates. Service providers must be focused on quality, and the system must be designed to support that mission by being controlled correctly and delivering as it was designed to do.

The difference in quality perspectives between goods and services

service quality An attitude formed by a long-term, overall evaluation of a firm's performance.

Service quality is one of the key elements of differentiation and it is definitely a fundamental element to achieving success and survival. Particularly where a small number of firms that offer nearly identical services are competing within a small area, such as banks might do, establishing service quality may be the only way of differentiating oneself. Service quality differentiation can generate increased market share and ultimately mean the difference between financial success and failure.

Ample evidence suggests that the provision of quality can deliver repeat purchases as well as new customers. Full details of the value of retaining existing customers through customer relationship management (CRM) were shown in Chapter 13. Briefly, repeat customers yield many benefits to the service organization. The cost of marketing to them is lower than that of marketing to new customers. Once customers have become regulars of the service, they know the script and are efficient users of the servuction system. As they gain trust in the organization, the level of risk for them is greatly reduced. This means they are more likely to consolidate their business with the firm. For example, insurance customers tend to move current policies to, and purchase new policies from, the one provider they feel serves their needs the best. Goods manufacturers have already learned this lesson over the past decade and have made producing quality goods a priority issue. Improving the quality of manufactured goods has become a major strategy for both establishing efficient, smoothly running operations and increasing consumer market share in an atmosphere in which customers are consistently demanding higher and higher quality. Goods quality improvement measures have focused largely on the quality of the products themselves, and specifically on eliminating product failure. Initially, these measures were based on rigorous checking of all finished products before they met the customer. More recently, quality control has focused on the principle of ensuring quality during the manufacturing process, on 'getting it right the first time' and on reducing end-of-production-line failures to zero. The final evolution in goods manufacturing has been to define quality as delivering the right product to the right customer at the right time, thus extending quality beyond the product itself and using external as well as internal measures to assess overall quality.

However, service quality cannot be understood in quite the same way. The servuction system depends on the customer as a participant in the production process, and normal quality-control measures that depend on eliminating defects before the consumer sees the product are not available. Consequently, service quality is not a specific goal or programme that can be achieved or completed but must be an ongoing part of all management and service production on a daily basis. However, some organizations try to include guaranteed service quality – see Global Services in Action – Restaurant Promises.

Global services in action
Restaurant promises

Providing a quality service is one of the goals that restaurant owners strive for. This chapter highlights the link between customer satisfaction and service quality. The gaps in service highlighted in Table 15.1 also demonstrate that an organization has to adhere to the promises it makes to customers so that disappointment and termination of their business does not ensue.

Therefore, some restaurants support their business with guarantees to try to advise their guests what they offer. There are in fact several types of service guarantee, from single-attribute-specific to multi-attribute-specific guarantees.

Single-attribute-specific guarantees focus on one key element of the service provided – for example, postal services often offer 'overnight delivery guaranteed'. The single attribute that Domino's Pizza offered was 'delivery within 30 minutes or the pizza for free'. Sadly due to circumstances such as traffic congestion and peak order times Domino's Pizza had to

withdraw their service guarantee. Marriott have recently launched a 'Look No Further Best Rate Guarantee' which gives customers the opportunity to find a better price at any Marriott hotel. Customers who do find a better price through another travel agent, for example, will receive their room booking at the lower price and 25 per cent off the lower price. This is also a single-attribute guarantee that implies that the Marriott offers its customers a fair price everyday.

Multi-attribute-specific guarantees are less specific in outcome. Marriott (Minneapolis) again takes up the challenge of guaranteeing the intangible elements that make a visit to a hotel a success. Their multi-attribute-specific guarantee is:

'Our quality commitment to you is to provide:

- A friendly, efficient check-in.
- A clean, comfortable room, where everything works.
- A friendly, efficient check-out.
- If we, in your opinion, do not deliver on this commitment, we will give you $20 in cash. No questions asked. It is your interpretation.'

To succeed in this type of guarantee, front-line personnel need to be aware of the promise and be trained and empowered to achieve the service expectations this guarantee implies.

When the launch of the guarantee takes place, marketing managers must work together with operations and HR departments to ensure that all staff within the organization are fully briefed and committed. Naturally, while the guarantee is in place, the implications of it need to be monitored. Competitors may start price wars and introduce counter-guarantees, customers may use the umbrella of the guarantee as an easy way to 'complain' and staff may feel stressed as they are the deliverers of the guarantee. These are areas which need to

first class
service
guaranteed

LPCB

UKAS
QUALITY
MANAGEMENT
007

ISO 9001:2000

LPS 1048-1 :
Issue 4 : September 2003

FIRST CLASS

First class service may be promised but is not always guaranteed.

be monitored – but crucially, success of the guarantee can be judged by retention of customers, higher profit margins and reduced values of compensation offered to customers.

Sources: L. Fabien (2005) 'Design and implementation of a service guarantee', *Journal of Services Marketing* 19 (1): 33–38.

J. Wirtz and D. Kum (2001) 'Designing service guarantees – is full satisfaction the best you can guarantee?' *Journal of Services Marketing* 15 (4): 282–299.
C. Brune, 'E-business Misses the Mark on Customer Service', *Internal Auditor* 57 (3) (June 2000): 13–15; 'Rainer: Top Companies Lax in Replying to Email', http://www.nua.ie/surveys (3 August 2000).

Diagnosing failure gaps in service quality

Many difficulties are inherent in implementing and evaluating service quality. In the first place, perceptions of quality tend to rely on a repeated comparison of the customer's expectation about a particular service. If a service, no matter how good, fails repeatedly to meet a customer's expectations, the customer will perceive the service to be of poor quality. Second, unlike goods marketing, where customers evaluate the finished product alone, in services, the customer evaluates the process of the service as well as its outcome. A customer visiting a hairdresser, for example, will evaluate service based not only on whether he or she likes the haircut, but also on whether the hairdresser is friendly, competent and personally clean.

Figure 15.1

Conceptual model of service quality

Source Adapted from A. Parasuraman, Valerie Zeithaml, and Leonard Berry, 'A Conceptual Model of Service Quality and Its Implications for Service Quality Research', *Journal of Marketing* 49 (Fall 1985), pp. 41–50.

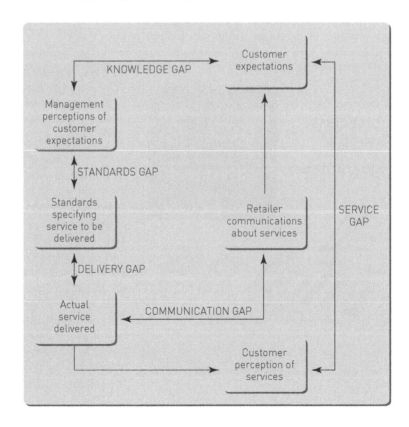

1 The knowledge gap	The difference between what service providers believe customers expect and customers' actual needs and expectations.	External gaps
2 The standards gap	The difference between management's expectations of customer expectations and the quality standards established for service delivery	Internal gaps
3 The delivery gap	The difference between specified delivery standards and the service provider's actual performance on these standards.	Internal gaps
4 The internal communications gap	The difference between what the company's advertising and sales personnel think are the product's features, performance and service quality level and what the company is actually able to deliver.	Internal gaps
5 The perceptions gap	The difference between what is actually delivered and what customers perceive they received (because they are unable to evaluate service quality accurately).	External gaps
6 The interpretation gap	The difference between what a service provider's communication offers (in advance of service delivery) actually promise and what a customer thinks was promised by these communications.	External gaps
7 The service gap	The difference between what customers expect to receive and their perceptions of the service that is actually delivered.	External gaps

Table 15.1

The seven service delivery gaps

Source Lovelock and Wirtz, 2004: 424.

Conceptually, the service quality process can be examined in terms of gaps between expectations and perceptions on the part of management, employees and customers – see Figure 15.1 (Parasuraman, Zeithaml and Berry, 1985). This conceptual model has been with us for over 20 years but it is important to reflect on this model, as it is the foundation for most literature and empirical research for gaps in service quality. Indeed, few authors have provided a satisfactory 'new and improved' version to totally replace it. The most important gap, the service gap, is between customers' expectations of service and their perception of the service actually delivered. Ultimately, the goal of the

service gap The distance between a customer's expectations of a service and perception of the service actually delivered.

service firm is to close the service gap or at least narrow it as far as possible. Consequently, examining service quality gaps is much like the disconfirmation of expectations model discussed in Chapter 13. However, it is important to remember that service quality focuses on the customer's *cumulative attitude* towards the firm. The cumulative attitude is collected by the consumer from a number of successful or unsuccessful service experiences.

Before the firm can close the service gap and exceed customer expectation, it must close or attempt to narrow four other gaps shown in Figure 15.1.

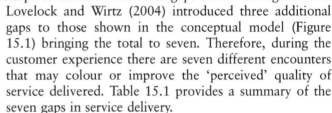

Lovelock and Wirtz (2004) introduced three additional gaps to those shown in the conceptual model (Figure 15.1) bringing the total to seven. Therefore, during the customer experience there are seven different encounters that may colour or improve the 'perceived' quality of service delivered. Table 15.1 provides a summary of the seven gaps in service delivery.

Case link

For more on service quality, see Case 12: The service is all part of the Craic.

Hence, the service gap is a function of the knowledge gap, the specifications gap, the delivery gap, and the communications gap. As each of these gaps increases or decreases, the service gap responds in a similar manner. The internal gaps occur as different departments fail to deliver an appropriate service within the organization itself, whereas the external gaps are the service gaps that occur between the organization and the customer. Front-line staff are close to the customer and it is the inseparability, intangibility and invariability service characteristics that make it so difficult to manage 'perceived' service quality.

The knowledge gap

The most immediate and obvious gap is usually between what customers want and what managers think customers want. Often managers think they know what their customers want but are, in fact, mistaken. Banking customers may prefer security to a good interest rate. Some restaurant customers may prefer quality and taste of food over an attractive arrangement of the tables or a good view from the window. A hotel may think that its customers prefer comfortable rooms, when, in fact, the majority of them spend little time in their rooms and are more interested in on-site amenities.

When a knowledge gap occurs, a variety of other mistakes tends to follow. The wrong facilities may be provided, the wrong staff may be hired and the wrong training may be undertaken. Services may be provided that customers have no use for, while the services they do desire are not offered. Closing this gap requires minutely detailed knowledge of what customers desire and then building that response into the service operating system.

Three main factors influence the size of the knowledge gap. First, the firm's research orientation, which reflects its attitude towards conducting consumer research, can dramatically influence the size of the gap. Information obtained from consumer research defines consumer expectations. As the firm's research orientation increases, the size of the knowledge gap should decrease. The amount of upward communication is a second factor that influences the size of the knowledge gap. Upward communication refers to the flow of information from front-line personnel to upper levels of the

knowledge gap
The difference between what consumers expect of a service and what management perceives that consumers expect.

research orientation
A firm's attitude towards conducting consumer research.

upward communication
The flow of information from front-line personnel to upper levels of the organization.

organization. Front-line personnel interact with customers on a frequent basis, so they are often more in touch with customer needs than is top management. Consequently, as the flow of upward communication increases through the organization, the smaller the knowledge gap should become. Finally, the levels of management in the organization can also influence the size of the knowledge gap. As the organizational hierarchy becomes more complex and more levels of management are added, higher levels of management tend to become more distant from customers and the day-to-day activities of the organization. As a result, when the levels of management increase, the size of the knowledge gap tends to increase.

levels of management
The complexity of the organizational hierarchy and the number of levels between top management and the customers.

The standards gap

Even if customer expectations have been accurately determined, the standards gap may open between management's perception of customer expectations and the actual standards set for service delivery, such as order processing speed, the way cloth napkins are to be folded, or the way customers are to be greeted. When developing standards, the firm should use a flowchart of its operations to identify all points of contact between it and its customers. Detailed standards can be written for (1) the way the system should operate, and (2) the behaviour of contact personnel at each point in the system. Hotel front-desk personnel, for example, may be trained to perform to specification in such areas as acknowledging the customer upon arrival, establishing eye contact, smiling, completing the proper paperwork, reviewing with the customer the available amenities and providing the customer with keys to the room.

standards gap
The difference between what management perceives that consumers expect and the quality specifications set for service delivery.

Customer-focused organizations show commitment to the delivery of service quality. They would not set other priorities that interfere with setting standards that lead to good service. For example, a company's orientation towards implementing cost-reduction strategies that maximize short-term profits is often cited as a misguided priority that impedes the firm's progress in delivering quality services. Personal computer companies whose automated service hotlines reduce the number of customer service representatives employed are typical examples. In some instances, customers in need of service have been forced to remain on hold for hours before they could actually speak to a 'real person'. Hotlines were originally named to reflect the speed with which the customer could talk to the manufacturer. Now the name more appropriately reflects the customer's temper by the time he or she talks to someone who can actually help.

Organizations, therefore, that continually bring in automated, non-personal services forget that the interaction between service personnel and the customer aids customer satisfaction. And organizations that keep a customer/staff-centric environment at the heart of its business can provide effective standards by designing and redesigning customer service processes as befits the ever-changing needs of their target audience. By doing this, organizations can close the standards gap.

The delivery gap

The delivery gap occurs between the actual performance of a service and the standards set by management. The existence of the delivery gap depends on

delivery gap
The difference between the quality standards set for service delivery and the actual quality of service delivery.

both the willingness and the ability of employees to provide the service according to specification. For example, do employees wear their name tags, do they establish eye contact and do they thank the customer when the transaction is completed?

One factor that influences the size of the delivery gap is the employee's willingness to perform the service. Obviously, employees' willingness to provide a service can vary greatly from employee to employee and in the same employee over time. Many employees who start off working to their full potential often become less willing to do so over time because of frustration and dissatisfaction with the organization. Furthermore, a considerable range exists between what the employee is actually capable of accomplishing and the minimum the employee must do in order to keep his/her job. Most service managers find it difficult to keep employees working at their full potential all the time.

willingness to perform
An employee's desire to perform to his/her full potential in a service encounter.

Case link
Examine the delivery gap in Case 12: The service is all part of the Craic.

Other employees, no matter how willing, may simply not be able to perform the service to specification. Hence, a second factor that influences the size of the delivery gap is the employee–job fit. Individuals may have been hired for jobs they are not qualified to handle or to which they are temperamentally unsuited, or they may not have been provided with sufficient training for the roles expected of them. Generally, employees who are not capable of performing assigned roles are less willing to keep trying.

employee–job fit The degree to which employees are able to perform a service to specifications.

Another common factor influencing the size of the delivery gap is role conflict. Whether or not the knowledge gap has been closed, service providers may still see an inconsistency between what the service manager expects employees to provide and the service their customers actually want. A waiter who is expected to promote various items on the menu may alienate some customers who prefer to make their own choices undisturbed. For example, how long does it take a McDonald's employee to finally realize that most customers really don't want an apple pie with their meal and are annoyed by the constant prompting? In some instances, customers even finish relaying their order by saying, 'And no, I don't want an apple pie with that.' In more formal settings, persistent waiters may find customers retaliating by not leaving a tip. In other cases, the service provider may be expected to do too many kinds of work, such as simultaneously answering telephones and dealing with customers face-to-face in a busy office. If this kind of conflict continues to occur, employees become frustrated, gradually lose their commitment to providing the best service they can, and/or simply quit altogether.

role conflict An inconsistency in service providers' minds between what the service manager expects them to provide and the service they think their customers actually want.

role ambiguity
Uncertainty of employees' roles in their jobs and poor understanding of the purpose of their jobs.

Another contributor to the delivery gap is role ambiguity. Role ambiguity results when employees, due to poor employee–job fit or inadequate training, do not understand the roles of their jobs or what their jobs are intended to accomplish. Sometimes, too, they are even unfamiliar with the service firm and its goals. Consequently, as role ambiguity increases, the delivery gap widens.

dispersion of control
The situation in which control over the nature of the service being provided is removed from employees' hands.

A further complication for employees is the dispersion of control, the situation in which control over the nature of the service being provided is removed from employees' hands. When employees are not allowed to make independent decisions about individual cases without first conferring with a manager, they may feel alienated from the service and less a part of their job. Furthermore, when control over certain aspects of the service is moved to a different location, such as control over credit being removed from individual bank branches, employee alienation is bound to increase. Employees experience learned helplessness and feel unable to respond to customer requests for help. Consequently, as the dispersion of control increases, the delivery gap becomes wider.

Finally, the delivery gap may also suffer due to inadequate support, such as not receiving personal training and/or technological and other resources necessary for employees to perform their jobs in the best possible manner. Even the best employees can be discouraged if they are forced to work with out-of-date or faulty equipment, especially if the employees of competing firms have superior resources and are able to provide the same or superior levels of service with far less effort. Failure to properly support employees leads to a lot of wasted effort, poor employee productivity, unsatisfied customers and an increase in the size of the delivery gap.

learned helplessness The condition of employees who, through repeated dispersion of control, feel themselves unable to perform a service adequately.

inadequate support A management failure to give employees personal training and/or technological and other resources necessary for them to perform their jobs in the best possible manner.

The internal communications gap

The communications gap is the difference between the service the firm promises it will deliver through its external communications and the service it actually delivers to its customers. Indeed some service organizations guarantee the service and experience that the customer will receive! (See Global Services in Action – Restaurant Promises). If advertising or sales promotions promise one kind of service and the consumer receives a different kind of service, the communications gap becomes wider. Therefore, it is important to ensure that what is communicated is realistic. Again as outlined at the beginning of this chapter, marketing managers need to work with all other departments to ensure that the promises shown in the advertisement can be delivered. External communicators are essentially promises the firm makes to its customers. When the communications gap is wide, the firm has broken its promises, resulting in a lack of future customer trust. A customer who orders a bottle of wine from a menu only to be told it is out of stock may feel that the offer held out on the menu has not been fulfilled. A customer who is promised delivery in three days but who then has to wait a week will perceive service quality to be lower than expected.

The communications gap is influenced primarily by two factors. The first, the propensity of the firm to over-promise, often occurs in highly competitive business environments as firms try to outdo one another in the name of recruiting new customers. The second factor pertains to the flow of horizontal communication within the firm. In other words, 'Does the left hand know what the right hand is doing?' All too often, communications are developed at the firm's headquarters without conferring with service firms in the field. In some instances, new service programmes are announced to the public by corporate headquarters before the local service firms are aware that the new

communications gap The difference between the actual quality of service delivered and the quality of service described in the firm's external communications.

horizontal communication The flow of internal communication between a firm's headquarters and its service firms in the field.

programmes exist. A lack of horizontal communication places an unsuspecting service provider in an awkward position when a customer requests the service promised and the provider has no idea what the customer is talking about. The important thing for marketing managers to do is to seek input from front-line employees and operations personnel before, during and after new programmes are being developed. This will help clear understanding from all sides as everyone will be able to contribute to managing the change effectively.

The perceptions gap

perceptions gap The difference between the service customers perceive they will receive and that which is actually received.

The perceptions gap is the difference between what is, actually, delivered and what customers perceive they received (because they are unable to evaluate service quality accurately). It is important here to ensure that the servicescape and physical evidence have relevant cues to the promises that have been provided. Fine dining restaurants should have exquisitely laid tables and beautifully presented food and wine rather than a cafeteria style layout. Customers should also feel informed about the service delivery and be guided through the dining experience knowledgably by the *Maitre d'* and *Sommelier* so that they can appreciate the quality of service they are receiving.

The perception gap is also noticeable in hospitals. Whitehead, May and Agahi (2007) state that a patient's perception of the treatment that they receive is based in part on the tidiness and cleanliness of the facilities, environment and staff that surround them.

The interpretation gap

interpretation gap This occurs when organizations have communicated their service through promotional activity and it is not interpreted by the customer in the way that was intended.

The interpretation gap is the difference between what a service provider's communication offers (in advance of service delivery) actually promise and what a customer thinks was promised by these communications. Organizations that deliver excellent service quality should certainly pre-test all advertising messages prior to release. This is important for all communications from advertising, brochures, web-pages, telephone scripts and communications materials in and around the servicescape. Target customers' interpretations should be researched to ensure that what is being communicated by the organization is the same as that being interpreted by the target audience. Many organizations have different levels of service – many airlines offer first class and business class. The differences should be clearly communicated so that the customer realizes what additional services they are likely to receive when they pay additional money for a first-class service. At the same time organizations often service guarantees which also need to be clearly documented, with advice on how to get in touch if services have not met those expectations. Donald Porter from British Airways comments that customers do not expect organizations to be perfect 100 per cent of the time. However, 'They do expect you to fix things when they go wrong.' Therefore, when things do go wrong, feedback to customers and service personnel in 'real time' are imperative. Customers whose

SOURCE © JUPITER IMAGES/COMSTOCK PREMIUM/ALAMY

flight is delayed become tense and agitated because they do not know why their flight is delayed and when the flight will be rescheduled. But the interpretation gap can be narrowed if the service provider keeps its customers aware of what has gone wrong and continues with fresh updates as to what will happen next.

The service gap

Organizations that are dedicated to the research and training involved in gaps 1–6 will be able to narrow the service gap experienced between that which is expected and that which is delivered. Some organizations actually apply for accreditation for their successes in service quality – See B2B Services in Action.

B2B services in action
ISO 9000

What is ISO 9000? ISO 9000 consists of five international industrial standards (ISO 9000–9004) that are meant to provide quality assurances for purchasers of international products. Developed by the International Organization for Standardization in Geneva in 1987, ISO 9000 registers and certifies a manufacturer's quality assurance and quality control systems. Ultimately, ISO 9000 is a surrogate measure of a firm's reliability (typically named the most important dimension within SERVQUAL). Interestingly, ISO 9000 does not guarantee that the manufacturer produces quality products, but it does certify that the manufacturer implements quality processes. However, one would hope that a company that follows ISO 9000 quality standards would indeed produce quality products.

The need for ISO 9000 certification is a direct result of increasing global competition. Buyers who purchase from international sources of supply need assurances that suppliers are indeed reputable. This is particularly true in the European Union where the EU Product Liability Directive exerts pressure on all companies within the EU to be ISO 9000 certified. 'The directive holds that a manufacturer, including an exporter, will be liable, regardless of fault or negligence, if a person is harmed by a product that fails because of a faulty component.' Consequently, EU B2B purchasers want to be very careful about selecting sources of supply. For a case in point, manufacturers of component parts in Japan and China are finding ISO 9000 certification to be an absolute necessity to conduct international business.

Recipients of ISO 9000 certification undergo a thorough audit process conducted by a third party that is authorized to conduct the certification process. All aspects of the audited firm are scrutinized including production processes, updating records, maintaining equipment, training employees and handling customer relations. In the end, ISO 9000 lowers potential business-to-business purchasers' perceived risk and provides certified firms with a competitive edge in the marketplace.

Sources: 'ISO 9000 Quality – What is it?' http://www.strategosinc.com, accessed 1 June 2005; 'What is ISO 9000', http://www.qualitymanagmentsurvival.com, accessed 1 June 2005; Philip R. Cateora and John L. Graham, *International Marketing*, 10th ed. (Boston, MA: Irwin McGraw-Hill, 1999), pp. 289–301.

Measuring service quality: SERVQUAL

Although measurements of customer satisfaction and service quality are both obtained by comparing perceptions to expectations, subtle differences between the two concepts are seen in their operational definitions. *Customer satisfaction* compares the consumer perceptions to what consumers would normally expect, *service quality* compares perceptions to what a consumer should expect from a firm that delivers high-quality services. Given these definitions, service quality appears to measure a higher standard of service delivery.

SERVQUAL A 44-item scale that measures customer expectations and perceptions regarding five service quality dimensions.

A frequently used and highly debated measure of service quality is the SERVQUAL scale (Parasuraman, Berry and Zeithaml, 1988). According to its developers, SERVQUAL is a diagnostic tool that uncovers a firm's broad weaknesses and strengths in the area of service quality. The SERVQUAL instrument is based on five service quality dimensions that were obtained through extensive focus group interviews with consumers. The five dimensions include tangibles, reliability, responsiveness, assurance, and empathy, and they provide the basic 'skeleton' underlying service quality.

The SERVQUAL instrument consists of two sections: a 22-item section that records customer expectations of excellent firms in the specific service industry, and a second 22-item section that measures consumer perceptions of a particular company in that service industry (i.e., the firm being evaluated). Results from the two sections are then compared to arrive at 'gap scores' for each of the five dimensions. The larger the gap, the further consumer perceptions are from expectations, and the lower the service quality evaluation. In contrast, the smaller the gap, the higher the service quality evaluation. Customer expectations are measured on a 7-point scale with the anchor labels of 'not at all essential' and 'absolutely essential' (Parasuraman, Berry and Zeithaml, 1991). Similarly, customer perceptions are measured on another 7-point scale with anchor labels of 'strongly agree' and 'strongly disagree'. Hence, SERVQUAL is a 44-item scale that measures customer expectations and perceptions regarding five service quality dimensions. The SERVQUAL model, like the Service Delivery Conceptual Model is also 20 years old that has been debated many times. Carrillat et al. (2007) completed a full analysis of the criticisms and praise and concluded that despite its age it is a very useful diagnostic tool that service managers can still use to identify gaps and shortfalls.

The tangibles dimension

Because of the absence of a physical product, consumers often rely on the tangible evidence that surrounds the service in forming evaluations. The tangibles dimension of SERVQUAL compares consumer expectations and the firm's performance regarding the firm's ability to manage its tangibles. A firm's tangibles consist of a wide variety of objects such as carpeting, desks, lighting, wall colours, brochures, daily correspondence and the appearance of the firm's personnel. Consequently, the tangibles component in SERVQUAL is two-dimensional – one focusing on equipment and facilities, the other focusing on personnel and communications materials.

tangibles dimension The SERVQUAL assessment of a firm's ability to manage its tangibles.

The tangibles component of SERVQUAL is obtained via four expectations questions (E1–E4) and four perception questions (P1–P4). Keep in mind that the expectation questions apply to excellent firms within a particular industry, while the perception questions apply to the specific firm under investigation. Comparing the perception scores to the expectation scores provides a numerical variable that indicates the tangibles gap. The smaller the number, the smaller the gap, and the closer consumer perceptions are to their expectations. The questions that pertain to the tangibles dimension are as follows (Parasuraman, Berry and Zeithaml, 1988):

Tangibles expectations

E1 Excellent companies will have modern-looking equipment.

E2 The physical facilities at excellent companies will be visually appealing.

E3 Employees of excellent companies will be neat in appearance.

E4 Materials associated with the service (such as pamphlets or statements) will be visually appealing in an excellent company.

Tangibles perceptions

P1 XYZ has modern-looking equipment.

P2 XYZ's physical facilities are visually appealing.

P3 XYZ's employees are neat in appearance.

P4 Materials associated with the service (such as pamphlets or statements) are visually appealing at XYZ.

The reliability dimension

In general, the reliability dimension reflects the consistency and dependability of a firm's performance. Does the firm provide the same level of service time after time, or does quality dramatically vary with each encounter? Does the firm keep its promises, bill its customers accurately, keep accurate records and perform the service correctly the first time? Nothing can be more frustrating for customers than unreliable service providers.

A constantly amazing observation is the number of businesses that fail to keep their promises. In many instances, the consumer is ready to spend money if only the service provider will show up and conduct the transaction as promised. As students, you may have experienced the reliability gap while attempting to have the local cable company install its services in your new apartment. Typically, the cable company will approximate the time at which the installer will come to your apartment in four-hour increments (e.g., morning or afternoon). In many cases, you may miss class or work waiting for the cable installer to arrive. All too often, the installer fails to show up during this time period and you must reschedule, missing yet more classes and/or time at work. Further aggravating this process is that you, the customer, must initiate the rescheduling process. Often the cable company offers no apology and provides little explanation other than, 'Our installers are very busy.'

Consumers perceive the reliability dimension to be the most important of the five SERVQUAL dimensions. Consequently, failure to provide reliable

reliability dimension
The SERVQUAL assessment of a firm's consistency and dependability in service performance.

service generally translates into an unsuccessful firm (see B2B Services in Action). The questions used to assess the reliability gap are as follows:

Reliability expectations

E5   When excellent companies promise to do something by a certain time, they will do so.

E6   When customers have a problem, excellent companies will show a sincere interest in resolving it.

E7   Excellent companies will perform the service right the first time.

E8   Excellent companies will provide their services at the time they promise to do so.

E9   Excellent companies will insist on error-free records.

Reliability perceptions

P5   When XYZ promises to do something by a certain time, it does so.

P6   When you have a problem, XYZ shows a sincere interest in solving it.

P7   XYZ performs the service right the first time.

P8   XYZ provides its services at the time it promises to do so.

P9   XYZ insists on error-free records.

The responsiveness dimension

Responsiveness reflects a service firm's commitment to provide its services in a timely manner. As such, the responsiveness dimension of SERVQUAL concerns the willingness and/or readiness of employees to provide a service. Occasionally, customers may encounter a situation in which employees are engaged in their own conversations with one another while ignoring the needs of the customer. Obviously, this is an example of unresponsiveness.

responsiveness dimension The SERVQUAL assessment of a firm's commitment to providing its services in a timely manner.

Responsiveness also reflects the preparedness of the firm to provide the service. Typically, new restaurants do not advertise their 'opening night' so that the service delivery system can be fine-tuned and prepared to handle larger crowds, thereby minimizing service failures and subsequent customer complaints. The SERVQUAL expectation and perception items that address the responsiveness gap are as follows:

Responsiveness expectations

E10 Employees of excellent companies will tell customers exactly when services will be performed.

E11 Employees of excellent companies will give prompt service to customers.

E12 Employees of excellent companies will always be willing to help customers.

E13 Employees of excellent companies will never be too busy to respond to customer requests.

Responsiveness perceptions

> **P10** Employees of XYZ tell you exactly when services will be performed.
>
> **P11** Employees of XYZ give you prompt service.
>
> **P12** Employees of XYZ are always willing to help you.
>
> **P13** Employees of XYZ are never too busy to respond to your requests.

The assurance dimension

SERVQUAL's assurance dimension addresses the competence of the firm, the courtesy it extends its customers and the security of its operations. Competence pertains to the firm's knowledge and skill in performing its service. Does the firm possess the required skills to complete the service on a professional basis? Courtesy refers to how the firm's personnel interact with the customer and the customer's possessions. As such, courtesy reflects politeness, friendliness and consideration for the customer's property (e.g., a mechanic who places paper floor mats in a customer's car so as to not soil the car's carpet).

> **assurance dimension**
> The SERVQUAL assessment of a firm's competence, courtesy to its customers and security of its operations.

Security is also an important component of the assurance dimension. Security reflects a customer's feelings that he or she is free from danger, risk, or doubt. Recent robberies at ATM locations provide ample evidence of the possible harm that may arise at service locations. In addition to physical danger, the security component of the assurance dimension also reflects financial risk issues (e.g., will the bank fail) and confidentiality issues (e.g., are my medical records at the school's health centre kept private). The SERVQUAL items utilized to address the assurance gap are as follows:

Assurance expectations

> **E14** The behaviour of employees of excellent companies will instil confidence in customers.
>
> **E15** Customers of excellent companies will feel safe in their transactions.
>
> **E16** Employees of excellent companies will be consistently courteous with customers.
>
> **E17** Employees of excellent companies will have the knowledge to answer customer questions.

Assurance perceptions

> **P14** The behaviour of employees of XYZ instils confidence in customers.
>
> **P15** You feel safe in your transactions with XYZ.
>
> **P16** Employees of XYZ are consistently courteous with you.
>
> **P17** Employees of XYZ have the knowledge to answer your questions.

The empathy dimension

Empathy is the ability to experience another's feelings as one's own. Empathetic firms have not lost touch with what it is like to be a customer of their own firm. As such, empathetic firms understand their customer needs and

empathy dimension The SERVQUAL assessment of a firm's ability to put itself in its customers' place.

make their services accessible to their customers. In contrast, firms that do not provide their customers individualized attention when requested and that offer operating hours convenient to the firm and not its customers fail to demonstrate empathetic behaviours.

The SERVQUAL empathy dimension addresses the empathy gap as follows:

Empathy expectations

E18 Excellent companies will give customers individual attention.

E19 Excellent companies will have operating hours convenient to all their customers.

E20 The employees of excellent companies give customers personal attention.

E21 Excellent companies will have the customer's best interest at heart.

E22 The employees of excellent companies will understand the specific needs of their customers.

Empathy perceptions

P18 XYZ gives you individual attention.

P19 XYZ has operating hours convenient to all its customers.

P20 XYZ employees give you personal attention.

P21 XYZ has your best interests at heart.

P22 Employees of XYZ understand your specific needs.

Criticisms of SERVQUAL

Since the development of the SERVQUAL instrument, it has received its share of criticism. The major criticisms of the instrument involve the length of the questionnaire, the validity of the five service quality dimensions and the predictive power of the instrument in regard to subsequent consumer purchases. The following discussion focuses on each of these issues and their respective importance to interpreting SERVQUAL results.

The service dimensions described above deal with organizations where encounters are face-to-face. See E-Services in Action – The seven dimensions of E-QUAL for details of how service is measured for e-businesses.

Length of the questionnaire. Combining the expectation and perception items of SERVQUAL results in a 44-item survey instrument. Opponents of the SERVQUAL instrument argue that the 44 items are highly repetitive and unnecessarily increase the questionnaire's length. Opponents further argue that the expectations section of the instrument is of no real value and that the perceptions (actual performance) section should be utilized alone to assess service quality (Conin and Taylor, 1994).

In response, the developers of SERVQUAL effectively argue that including the expectations section enhances the managerial usefulness of the scale as a diagnostic tool due to the gap scores developed for each dimension. Perception scores alone merely rate whether the respondent agrees or disagrees with each question. For example, Table 15.2 provides a set of perception scores and SERVQUAL scores for a hypothetical firm. Utilizing this information for diagnostic purposes, perception scores alone would suggest placing an equal emphasis on improving the reliability and empathy dimensions. Incorporating expectations into the SERVQUAL score indicates that improving the reliability dimension should be the firm's top priority. Given that implementing service quality improvements requires a financial investment from the firm, maintaining the expectation section becomes valuable. Creative suggestions have been made for maintaining the expectations component while at the same time reducing the questionnaire's length by 22 questions. Three approaches have been suggested: (1) on a single scale, ask respondents

---

E-services in action
The seven dimensions of E-QUAL

The importance of service quality in improving customer satisfaction and loyalty in traditional business settings has been established via SERVQUAL. The following recommendations are given for how consumers might evaluate online business via E-QUAL:

1 Accessibility – Is the site easily found? This is measured by the number of search engines where a site is registered and by the number of links to related sites.

2 Navigation – How easy is it to move around the site? A good rule-of-thumb is to be within three clicks of the information that is most desired by customers.

3 Design and presentation – What is the image projected from the site? Design elements include colours, layout, clarity and originality.

4 Content and purpose – The substance (breadth) and richness (depth) of the site.

5 Currency and accuracy are important aspects of the 'content' dimension. The strategic purpose of the site includes sites that are developed for an internet presence (informational purpose) and online store fronts (revenue-producing purpose).

6 Responsiveness – The company's propensity to respond to e-mail messages. The collection of visitor information (e.g., cookies, guest book, contests, chat rooms, clubs, storybooks, auto-e-mail, and options to speak to customer representatives), and what the company does with this information.

7 Interactivity, customization, and personalization – The hi-touch level of service provided. Interactivity, customization and personalization relate to the empathy dimension of service quality. Amazon.com, for example, provides the quality of interaction and personalization that rivals traditional bricks-and-mortar businesses.

8 Reputation and security related to the assurance dimension of service quality – Reputation and security pertain to consumer confidence issues. Consumer confidence is being built via proven encryption technologies.

Sources: Shohreh A. Kaynama (2000) 'A Conceptual Model to Measure Service Quality of Online Companies: E-qual, in Developments in Marketing Science', in Harlan E. Spotts and H. Lee Meadow, eds., *Proceedings of the Academy of Marketing Science*, 22: 46–51.
For more information pertaining to online service quality see A. Parasuraman, Valerie A. Zeithaml and Arvind Malhotra (2005) 'E-S-QUAL: A Multiple-Item Scale for Assessing Electronic Service Quality', *Journal of Service Research*, 7 (3): 213–234.

where they would rate a high-quality company and then where they would rate the firm under investigation; (2) utilize the scale's midpoint as the expected level of service from a high-quality company, and then rate the specific firm in relation to the midpoint above expectation or below; and (3) utilize the end point (e.g., 7 on a 7-point scale) as the expected level of a high-quality company, and rate the specific company relative to the high-quality company on the same scale. All three approaches provide alternatives for assessing customer perceptions and expectations while reducing the questionnaire's length.

The validity of the five dimensions. Another frequent criticism of the SERVQUAL instrument is that the five proposed dimensions of service quality – reliability, responsiveness, assurance, empathy and tangibles – do not hold up under statistical scrutiny. Consequently, opponents of SERVQUAL question the validity of the specific dimensions in the measurement instrument.

SERVQUAL's developers argue that although the five dimensions represent conceptually distinct facets of service quality, they are interrelated. Hence, some overlap may exist (as measured by correlations) among items that measure specific dimensions. In particular, the distinction among the responsiveness, assurance and reliability dimensions tends to blur under statistical scrutiny. However, when respondents are asked to assign importance weights to each dimension, results indicate that consumers do indeed distinguish among the five dimensions, as exhibited in Table 15.3. According to the developers of SERVQUAL, this ranking provides additional evidence of the dimensions' distinctiveness. However, ranking depends upon the type of service offered. For example, the dimensions for services which have a physical element such as manicure or travel by an aeroplane will be different from highly intangible services such as entertainment or education may be will have.

Table 15.2	Dimension	Perception scores	SERVQUAL scores
	Tangibles	5.3	0.0
The diagnostic advantage of SERVQUAL scores	Reliability	4.8	−1.7
	Responsiveness	5.1	−1.0
	Assurance	5.4	−1.5
	Empathy	4.8	−1.1

The diagnostic advantage of SERVQUAL scores

- *Tangibility* is more important for services with more tangible actions. Further, the importance reduces as one shifts from services targeted at people to services targeted at possessions.

- Need for *reliability* is more for services with intangible nature of service act. Services targeted at possessions of the customers will also require more reliability.

- Services targeted at the customer require more *assurance* than those targeted at their possessions. Further, more assurance will be needed for services with intangible acts.

- *Responsiveness* did not allow for any kind of clustering. Customers ranked it last on priority across different service types. Perhaps they are less expectant for this service dimension.

- Information- and people-processing services require more *empathy* as compared to other two types.

- *Prices* were considered relatively more important by consumers of possession and mental-stimuli processing services.

(Chowdhary and Prakash, 2007: 507)

For the statistical enthusiast, a variety of articles offering additional evidence and rationale supporting the viability of the five-dimensional framework is cited in the 'References and Further Reading' section located at the end of this Chapter.

The predictive power of SERVQUAL. The third major criticism of SERVQUAL pertains to the instrument's ability to predict consumer purchase intentions. Research has indicated that the performance (perceptions) section alone of the SERVQUAL scale is a better predictor of purchase intentions than the combined expectations-minus-perception instrument. As such, opponents of the SERVQUAL instrument conclude that satisfaction has a

SERVQUAL	Dimension importance*
Reliability	32%
Responsiveness	22%
Assurance	19%
Empathy	16%
Tangibles	11%

Table 15.3

Relative importance of SERVQUAL dimensions as reported by consumers

Source Leonard L. Berry, A. Parasuraman and Valerie A. Zeithaml, 'Improving Service Quality in America: Lessons Learned', *Academy of Management Executives* 8 (2) (1994): 32–52.

*Consumers were asked to allocate 100 points among the five dimensions. The importance percentage reflects the mean point allocation for each dimension.

more significant effect on purchase intentions than does service quality. Consequently, they assert that managers need to emphasize customer satisfaction programmes over strategies focusing solely on service quality.

The developers of SERVQUAL once again take issue with the preceding objections based on a variety of conceptual, methodological, analytical and practical issues. Consequently, the jury is still out regarding this particular objection. From a managerial standpoint, perhaps the SERVQUAL proponents' most important counterpoint is the diagnostic value of the expectations-minus-perceptions approach. Based on information provided earlier, the developers of SERVQUAL make a convincing argument that incorporating customer expectations provides richer information than does examining the perceptions scores alone.

SERVQUAL: Some final thoughts

The importance of contact personnel. The SERVQUAL instrument highlights several points that service providers should consider when examining service quality. First, customer perceptions of service are heavily dependent on the attitudes and performance of contact personnel. Of the five dimensions measured, responsiveness, empathy and assurance directly reflect the interaction between customers and staff. Even tangibles depend partly on the appearance, dress and hygiene of the service staff.

Process is as important as outcome. The manner in which customers judge a service depends as much on the service process as on the outcome. How the service is delivered is as important as the frequency and nature of the service. Consequently, customer satisfaction depends on the production of services as well as their consumption.

Viewing services as a process raises considerable difficulties for management when trying to write service quality standards. Standards can be examined either from the perspective of the consumer or from that of the operating system. Thus, a specification can be written based on consumers' ratings of the responsiveness of the organization. Unfortunately, although this is a quantitative measure, it does little to guide the behaviour of operations managers and contact personnel.

Consumer perceptions are unpredictable. Ratings of service quality dimensions may be influenced by factors outside the control of the organization that may not be readily apparent to managers. For example, consumer moods and attitudes may influence ratings. Studies have shown that when rating services, consumers use a diverse variety of clues. A recent study shows that, even if a service firm generates a negative disconfirmation for a consumer, it may not be judged as delivering a poor level of satisfaction. Since they are part of the process, consumers may attribute failure to themselves or to factors outside the control of the firm. Such attributions are shown to depend on the physical characteristics of the service firm. For example, a tidy office setting leads negative attributions away from the firm, while a messy office generates attributions of dissatisfaction towards the firm. Untidy and unclean hospitals also make patients feel uncomfortable and dissatisfied with the service they will receive (Whitehead, May and Agahi, 2007).

Assessing the criticisms of SERVQUAL. Finally, the criticisms of SERVQUAL should not be taken lightly. As is the case with most measurement scales, constructive criticism assists in the further development of improved measurement instruments. Moreover, concerns regarding measurement instruments should remind practitioners that firms should not 'live or die' and make drastic decisions based solely on one measurement instrument's results. The value of measurement tools is that they provide management the opportunity to make a more informed decision.

Despite its opponents, SERVQUAL remains a frequently utilized instrument to assess service quality and is currently being modified to address service quality issues in e-business (see E-Services in Action). From the beginning, its developers have claimed that SERVQUAL is a useful starting point for measuring service quality and was never presented as 'the final answer'. The developers of SERVQUAL further contend that when used in conjunction with other forms of measurement, both quantitative and qualitative, SERVQUAL provides a valuable diagnostic tool for evaluating the firm's service quality performance. Overall, as was the case with satisfaction measures, SERVQUAL is most valuable when compared with a firm's own past service quality trends and when compared with measures of competitive service quality performance.

Service quality information systems

A service quality information system is an ongoing research process that provides relevant data on a timely basis to managers, who utilize the data for decision-making purposes (Carrillat, Jaramillo and Mulki, 2007). More specifically, service quality information systems utilize service quality and customer satisfaction measures in conjunction with other measures obtained at various points to assess the firm's overall performance. Components of a service quality information system include the following:

service quality information system An ongoing research process that provides relevant data on a timely basis to managers, who use the data in decision making.

- reports on solicitation of customer complaints;
- after-sales surveys;
- customer focus group interviews;
- mystery shopping results;
- employee surveys; and
- total market service quality surveys.

In general, service quality information systems focus on two types of research: customer research and non-customer research. Customer research examines the customer's perception of a firm's strengths and weaknesses and includes such measures as customer complaints, after-sales surveys, focus

customer research Research that examines the customer's perception of a firm's strengths and weaknesses.

non-customer research
Research that examines how competitors perform on service and how employees view the firm's strengths and weaknesses.

group interviews and service quality surveys. In contrast, non-customer research focuses on employee perceptions of the firm's strengths and weaknesses and employee performance (e.g., employee surveys and mystery shopping). In addition, non-customer research examines how competitors perform on service (via total market service quality surveys) and serves as a basis for comparison.

Solicitation of customer complaints

The primary objectives of soliciting customer complaints are twofold. First, customer complaints identify unhappy customers. The firm's follow-up efforts may enable it to retain many of these customers before they defect to competitors. The second objective of soliciting customer complaints is to identify weaknesses in the firm's service delivery system and take the corrective actions necessary to minimize future occurrences of the same problem. Customer complaints should be solicited on a continuous basis.

The value of continuous customer feedback cannot be understated. Unfortunately, many firms address one complaint at a time and fail to analyse the content of the complaints as a group. Marriott took 15 years to figure out that 66 per cent of the calls to its customer service line concerned requests for an iron or ironing board. As a result of learning this, the hotel designated their maintenance budget that had been earmarked for colour televisions in guest bathrooms, to purchase irons and ironing boards for the hotel. Interestingly, few, if any, customers had ever complained about the black-and-white televisions in the bathrooms. If the colour televisions had been installed, we would have seen a classic example of a firm defining service quality on its own as opposed to listening to the voice of the customer. Chapter 16 takes an in-depth look at analysing customer complaints and developing effective recovery strategies for use when service failures do occur.

After-sales surveys

after-sales surveys A type of satisfaction survey that addresses customer satisfaction while the service encounter is still fresh in the customer's mind.

As part of the service quality information system, after-sales surveys should also be conducted on a continuous basis. Since after-sales surveys pertain to discrete transactions, they are a type of satisfaction survey and, as such, are subject to the advantages and disadvantages of all customer satisfaction surveys discussed in Chapter 12. For example, after-sales surveys address customer satisfaction while the service encounter is still fresh in the customer's mind. Consequently, the information reflects the firm's recent performance but may be biased by the customer's inadvertent attempt to minimize cognitive dissonance.

Although after-sales surveys can also identify areas for improvement, after-sales surveys are a more proactive approach to assessing customer satisfaction than is soliciting customer complaints. Many firms wait for customers to complain and then take action based on those complaints. Given the average customer's reluctance to complain, waiting for customer complaints does not provide the firm with a 'true' picture of its performance. The after-sales survey attempts to contact every customer and take corrective action if a customer is less than satisfied with his or her purchase decision.

Customer focus group interviews

Another important component of the service quality information system involves customer focus group interviews (Reid and Bojanic, 2006). Focus group interviews are informal discussions with eight to twelve customers that are usually guided by a trained moderator. Participants in the group are encouraged to express their views and to comment on the suggestions made by others in the group (Kenyon, 2004). Because of the group interaction, customers tend to feel more comfortable, which motivates them to talk more openly and honestly. Consequently, researchers feel that the information obtained via focus group interviews is richer than data that reflect the opinions of a single individual.

focus group interviews Informal discussions with eight to twelve customers that are usually guided by a trained moderator; used to identify areas of information to be collected in subsequent survey research.

Focus groups are probably the most widely used market research method. However, their primary purpose is to identify areas of information to be collected in subsequent survey research. Although the information provided by the group is considered valuable, other forms of research are generally necessary to confirm that the group's ideas reflect the feelings of the broader segment of customers. Advocates of service quality information systems believe that customer focus groups should be conducted on a monthly basis.

Mystery shopping

Mystery shopping is a form of non-customer research that measures individual employee service behaviour. As the name indicates, mystery shoppers are generally trained personnel who pose as customers and who shop unannounced at the firm. The idea is to evaluate an individual employee during an actual service encounter. Mystery shoppers evaluate employees on a number of characteristics, such as the time it takes for the employee to acknowledge the customer, eye contact, appearance and numerous other specific customer service and sales techniques promoted by the firm. Mystery shopping is a form of observation research and is recommended to be conducted on a quarterly basis. Results obtained from mystery shoppers are used as constructive employee feedback. Consequently, mystery shopping aids the firm in coaching, training, evaluating and formally recognizing its employees.

mystery shopping A form of non-customer research that consists of trained personnel who pose as customers, shop unannounced at the firm and evaluate employees.

Employee surveys

Another vital component of the service quality information system is employee research. When the product is a performance, it is essential that the company listen to the performers. Too often, employees are forgotten in the quest for customer satisfaction. However, the reality is that employee satisfaction with the firm directly corresponds with customer satisfaction. Hence, the lesson to be learned by service firms is that if they want the needs of their customers to come first, they cannot place the needs of their employees last.

employee surveys
Internal measures of service quality concerning employee morale, attitudes and perceived obstacles to the provision of quality services.

Conducted quarterly, employee surveys provide an internal measure of service quality concerning employee morale, attitudes and perceived obstacles to the provision of quality services. Often employees would like to provide a higher level of quality service but feel that their hands are tied by internal regulations and policies. Employee surveys provide the means to uncover these obstacles so that they can be removed when appropriate. Moreover, employees are customers of internal service and assess internal service quality. Because of their direct involvement in providing service delivery, employee complaints serve as an early warning system; that is, employees often see the system breaking down before customers do.

Total market service quality surveys

total market service quality surveys Surveys that measure the service quality of the firm sponsoring the survey and the service quality of the firm's competitors.

Total market service quality surveys not only measure the service quality of the firm sponsoring the survey but also assess the perceived service quality of the firm's competitors. When service quality measures such as SERVQUAL are used in conjunction with other measures, a firm can evaluate its own performance compared with previous time periods and with its competitors. Service quality surveys provide a firm with information about needed improvements in the service delivery system, and measure the progress in making needed improvements that have been previously identified.

Advocates of the service quality information system recommend that total market service quality surveys be conducted three times a year. However, as is the case with all the components of the service quality information system, the recommended frequencies are dependent upon the size of the customer base. Too frequent contact with the same customers can be an annoyance to them. On the other hand, conducting surveys too infrequently may ultimately cost the business its existence.

Overall, the service quality information system provides a comprehensive look at the firm's performance and overcomes many of the shortcomings of individual measures used in isolation. As with all measures, the information system's true value lies in the information it gives managers to help in their decision making. The measures should serve as a support system for decisions but not be the only inputs into the decision process. Managerial expertise and intuition remain critical components of every business decision. Ultimately, the key components that need to be built into every service quality system include the following (Parasuraman, Zeithaml and Berry, 1994):

Figure 15.2

Quality improvements need focus, not just $$$

Source Robert Cooke, 'U.S. Leads in Health-Care Spending, but Not Quality', *Fort Collins Coloradoan*, 21 June 2000, p. B1.

Although adequate resource support is directly related to the successful implementation of service delivery systems, providing support without direction can be a huge waste of resources. For example, the United States leads the world in health care expenditures per capita, yet ranks thirty-seventh in terms of the quality of care provided to its citizens. The United States devotes 10 to 14 per cent of national income to health care, with an average per-capita expenditure of $3,724; meanwhile, England spends 6 per cent and is ranked eighteenth in the world.

- *Listening*: Quality is defined by the customer. Conformance to company specifications is not quality; conformance to customers' specifications is. Spending wisely to improve service comes from continuous learning about expectations and perceptions of customers and manufacturers (see Figure 15.2).

- *Reliability*: Reliability is the core of service quality. Little else matters to a customer when the service is unreliable.

- *Basic service*: Forget the frills if you cannot deliver the basics. Service customers want the basics; they expect fundamentals, not fanciness, and performance, not empty promises.

- *Service design*: Reliably delivering the basic service that customers expect depends, in part, on how well various elements function together in a service system. Design flaws in any part of a service system can reduce the perception of quality.

- *Recovery*: Research shows that companies consistently receive the most unfavourable service quality scores from customers whose problems were not resolved satisfactorily. In effect, companies that do not respond effectively to customer complaints compound the service failure, thereby failing twice.

- *Surprising customers*: Exceeding customers' expectations requires the element of surprise. If service organizations can be not only reliable in output but also surprise the customer in the way the service is delivered, then they are truly excellent.

- *Fair play*: Customers expect service companies to treat them fairly and become resentful and mistrustful when they perceive that they are being treated otherwise.

- *Teamwork*: The presence of 'teammates' is an important dynamic in sustaining a server's motivation to serve. Service team building should not be left to chance.

- *Employee research*: Employee research is as important to service improvement as customer research.

- *Servant leadership*: Delivering excellent service requires a special form of leadership. Leadership must serve the services, inspiring and enabling them to achieve.

Summary

This chapter has focused on defining and measuring service quality. The concepts of service quality and customer satisfaction, discussed in Chapter 12, are intertwined. In general, customer satisfaction can be defined as a short-term, transaction-specific measure. In turn, service quality is a long-term, overall measure. Another difference is that satisfaction compares perceptions to what customers would normally expect. In comparison, service quality compares perceptions to what customers should expect from a high-quality firm. Customer satisfaction and service quality assessments complement each other. Satisfaction evaluations made after each service transaction help revise customers' overall service quality evaluations of the firm's performance. Firms that excel in service quality do so by avoiding potential quality gaps in their delivery systems. Service quality gaps discussed in this chapter include knowledge, standards, delivery and communication. Numerous managerial, marketing and operational factors influence the size of each of these gaps. Ultimately, the goal of every firm is to minimize the service gap – the difference between customer perceptions and expectations. The service gap is a function of the knowledge, standards, delivery and communication gaps and responds accordingly in the combined direction of the four gaps.

One popular method for assessing service quality is the SERVQUAL scale. The original SERVQUAL survey instrument consists of 44 questions that compare consumers' expectations to perceptions along five service quality dimensions – tangibles, responsiveness, reliability, assurance and empathy. Gap scores for each of the five dimensions can be calculated by comparing consumer expectation and perception ratings. The SERVQUAL gaps indicate specific areas in need of improvement and assist the service firm in its continuous improvement efforts. SERVQUAL is only one method to assess a firm's service quality. A service quality information system utilizes a variety of continuous measures to assess the firm's overall performance. The major components of such a system collect information about both customer and non-customer research. Customer research methods include analysing customer complaints, after-sales surveys, focus group interviews and service quality surveys. Non-customer research methods include employee surveys and mystery shopping.

In summary, service quality offers a means of achieving success among competing firms that offer similar products. The benefits associated with service quality include increases in market share and repeat purchases. Ultimately, the keys to delivering service quality are a detailed understanding of the needs of the consumer, service providers who are focused on providing quality and service delivery systems that are designed to support the firm's overall quality mission.

Discussion questions

Case link
See Case 12: The service is all part of the Craic.

1 Consider the seven service delivery gaps – what gaps may Guinness have had prior to the Perfect Pint operation?

2 What are the basic differences between customer satisfaction and service quality?

3 Explain how a manager might use the conceptual model of service quality to improve the quality of his/her own firm.

4 What factors contribute to the size of the knowledge gap?

5 How does the communication gap relate to success in e-business (see Services in Action)?

6 Discuss the basics of the SERVQUAL measurement instrument.

7 Develop specifications for the role of a 'good student'.

8 What are the criticisms of SERVQUAL? What are its developers' responses to these criticisms?

9 You have been hired by a firm to develop the firm's service quality information system. What are the components of this system?

References and further reading

Carrillat, F. A., Jaramillo, F. and Mulki, J. P. (2007) 'The validity of the SERVQUAL and SERVPERF scales – A meta-analytic view of 17 years of research across five continents', *International Journal of Service Industry Management* 18 (5) 472–490.

Chowdhary, N. and Prakash, M (2007) 'Prioritizing service quality dimensions', *Managing Service Quality* 17 (5).

Cooke, R. (2000) 'US leads in health-care spending but not quality', *Fort Collins Coloradoan*, 21 June, p. B1.

Cronin, Jr., J. J. and Taylor, S. A. (1992) 'Measuring service quality: a reexamination and extension', *Journal of Marketing* 56 (July): 55.

Fabien, L. (2005) 'Design and implementation of a service guarantee', *Journal of Services Marketing* 19 (1): 33–38.

Hanks, R. D. (2007) 'Listen and learn', *Restaurant Hospitality* 91 (8): 70–72.

Homburg, C., Hoyer, W. D. and Fassnacht, M. (2002) 'Strategy: dimensions, antecedents, and performance outcomes of a retailer's service orientation', *Business Journal of Marketing* 66 (4): 86–101.

Kenyon, A. J. (2004) 'Exploring Phenomenological Research: pretesting focus group techniques with young people', *International Journal of Market Research* Vol. 46 Quarter 4: 421–441.

Lovelock, C. and Wirtz, J. (2004) *Services Marketing: People, Technology, Strategy*, Pearson Prentice Hall, Upper Saddle River, New Jersey.

Parasuraman, A., Berry, L. L. and Zeithaml, V. A (1988) 'SERVQUAL: a multiple-item scale for measuring customer perceptions of service quality', *Journal of Retailing* 64 (1): 12–40.

Parasuraman, A., Berry, L. L. and Zeithaml, V. A (1991) 'Refinement and reassessment of the SERVQUAL scale', *Journal of Retailing* 67 (Winter): 420–450.

Parasuraman, A., Zeithaml, V. A. and Berry, L. L. (1985) 'A conceptual model of service quality and its implications for future research', *Journal of Marketing* 49 (Fall): 41–50.

Reid, R. D. and Bojanic, D. C. (2006) *Hospitality Marketing Management*, New Jersey: John Wiley & Sons.

Whitehead, H., May, D. and Agahi, H. (2007) 'An exploratory study into the factors that influence patients' perceptions of cleanliness in an acute NHS trust hospital', *Journal of Facilities Management* 5 (4): 275–289.

Wirtz, J. and Kum, D. (2001) 'Designing service guarantees – is full satisfaction the best you can guarantee?', *Journal of Services Marketing* 15 (4): 282–299.

Chapter 16

Service failures and recovery strategies

Don't fight a battle if you don't gain anything by winning.

(General George S. Patton, Jr.)

Chapter objectives

The major objectives of this chapter are to introduce the concepts of service failures, consumer complaint behaviour, service recovery strategies and procedures for tracking and monitoring service failures and employee recovery efforts.

After reading this chapter, you should be able to:

- Discuss the four different categories of service failure types.

- Explain customer complaining behaviour, including the reasons customers do and do not complain and the outcomes associated with customer complaints.

- Describe the issues involved in mastering the art of service recovery.

- Understand the value of tracking and monitoring service failures and employee recovery efforts.

Services in context
Wendy's dilemma

In Part three of this text, we have addressed customer satisfaction and service quality issues as they pertain to assessing and improving service delivery processes. Another key management issue in this area involves tracking and analysing service failures and designing recovery strategies that minimize customer defections. In many instances, excellent service companies utilize service failure analysis as a means to foresee the typical mistakes that are likely to occur and develop recovery strategies to offset their negative consequences. Of course, the primary goal is for service failures never to occur in the first place. However, given the nature of services, service failures do happen and customers do occasionally leave unhappy, never to be seen again.

Although most companies can reasonably predict where service may occasionally fall short, there are some instances that can never be foreseen. One such case involved Wendy's International Inc. and 'the-finger-in-the-chilli-incident'. In the spring of 2005, a Northern California woman claimed to bite into a one-and-a-half-inch-long finger while eating chilli at a local Wendy's restaurant. Wendy's sales plummeted as news of the incident spread worldwide. The woman, while appearing on ABC's 'Good Morning America' reported that: 'knowing a human body part was in her mouth was disgusting'. The woman then filed a lawsuit against Wendy's International Inc. to recover damages.

Wendy's response to the issue never wavered. First, company representatives travelled to the San Jose store where the incident occurred and verified that all of its employees had their fingers intact. They next went to the company's food suppliers for another digit inventory – all were in place. Voice stress analysis tests were given to employees and suppliers to determine their involvement in the incident – all suppliers and employees passed. Suspecting foul play, the company then publicly offered a $100,000 reward for information that would lead authorities to the source of the finger. In addition, a free 'Junior Frosty' give-away to any customer who asked for one was planned as a way to get customers back in the stores. The give-away involved approximately 6,600 corporate and franchised Wendy's that served an estimated 14 million ice cream treats in this 'thank-you-for-your-understanding' gesture.

As a result of Wendy's investigation of its own people and further findings that the woman and her family had previously sued at least a dozen other companies, increased scrutiny was directed towards the accuser who responded: 'Lies, lies, lies, that's all I am hearing. They should look at Wendy's. What are they hiding? Why are we being victimized again and again?' The woman eventually dropped her lawsuit, claiming the pressure associated with the whole incident had become too much to bear.

Over the next several weeks, Wendy's $100,000 reward offer paid off as a tipster came forward to provide information leading to the source of the finger. As it turned out, the finger belonged to a co-worker of the accuser's husband who had severed the digit in the tailgate of his truck months earlier. The husband acquired the finger from the co-worker in return for a relinquished $50 debt. The accuser now faces charges of attempted grand theft in San Jose and further charges are being considered against the husband related to the Wendy's incident.

Despite Wendy's vindication, it came with a hefty price. The company estimates that it lost $2.5 million in sales over the incident. In addition, the company's promise to pay $100,000 to the tipster adds to the cost. However, Wendy's had few alternative approaches available. Paying the woman off early to buy her silence would have been viewed as an admission of guilt. Advertising to the public

▶

that processes were in place to keep fingers out of Wendy's food was not a viable marketing strategy. Relying on the public to believe the whole incident might be a hoax and giving the company the benefit of the doubt was unreliable. The only sound strategy was to defend the brand and hope the truth would eventually be made public and customers would return. Wendy's sales are currently rebounding, but slowly. Time should help.

Sources: Alan J. Liddle, 'Tipster fingers hoax suspect as Wendy's awaits sales comeback', *Nation's Restaurant News* (23 May 2005), 39 (21): 3, 208; Paul Winston, 'Pointing the finger at the real culprit', *Business Insurance* (23 May 2005), 39 (21): 6.

Introduction

service failures
Breakdowns in the delivery of service; service that does not meet customer expectations.

Despite the service firm's best efforts, service failures are inevitable. Planes are late, employees are rude or inattentive and the maintenance of the tangibles surrounding the service is not always perfect. Don't give up! Developing an indifferent attitude or accepting service failures as a part of everyday business can be 'the kiss of death'. The secrets to success are to take a proactive stance to reduce the occurrence of service failures and to equip employees with a set of effective recovery tools to repair the service experience when failures do occur.

The reason failures are inherent events in the service encounter are directly related to the unique characteristics that distinguish services from goods. Due to intangibility, customer comparison of perceptions to expectations is a highly subjective evaluation; consequently, not all customers are going to be satisfied! Due to heterogeneity, variations in the service delivery process are going to occur, and not every service encounter is going to be identical. Due to perishability, supply and demand may match each other only by accident. Hence, service customers will experience delays from time to time, and service workers will occasionally lose their patience while attempting to appease an influx of anxious customers. Finally, inseparability places the service provider face-to-face with the customer, which provides a Pandora's Box of failure possibilities.

Types of service failures

critical incident A specific interaction between a customer and a service provider.

Service failures occur at critical incidents in the service encounter. Each service encounter is made up of numerous critical incidents, or 'moments of truth', which represent the numerous interactions between the customer and the providing service firm. Critical incidents can range from human interactions, such as how quickly a customer service representative at a call centre answers the telephone, to human/servicescape interactions including the comfort of a hotel bed or the ease of use of a self-service technology such as a bank's ATM or an airline's electronic check-in process. Critical incidents may positively or negatively impact the customer's service experience.

Negative critical incidents result in service failures that require the service firm's attention to correct. If done correctly, a service organization can change a dissatisfied customer into a satisfied one, which may in turn lead to positive behaviour, repeat custom and loyalty (Lewis and Spyrakopoulos, 2001; Johnston and Michel, 2008).

Although a firm may receive hundreds of customer complaints pertaining to perceived service failures throughout a year, ultimately these complaints (service failures) can be categorized into one of four main groups: (1) service delivery system failures; (2) failures relating to customer needs and requests; (3) failures relating to unprompted and unsolicited employee actions; and (4) failures relating to problematic customers (see Table 16.1).

Service delivery system failures

Service delivery system failures are failures that relate directly to the core service offering of the firm. For example, airlines that do not depart on time,

system failures Failures in the core service offering of the firm.

Primary failure type	Failure subgroups
Service delivery system failures	Unavailable service
	Unreasonably slow service
	Other core service failures
Customer needs and requests	'Special needs' customers
	Customer preferences
	Admitted customer error
	Disruptive others
Unprompted/unsolicited employee actions	Level of attention
	Unusual action
	Cultural norms
	Gestalt
Problematic customers	Drunkenness
	Verbal and physical abuse
	Breaking company policies
	Uncooperative customers

Table 16.1

Service failure types

Sources Adapted from Mary Jo Bitner, Bernard H. Booms and Mary Stanfield Tetreault, 'The Service Encounter: Diagnosing Favourable and Unfavourable Incidents', *Journal of Marketing* (January 1990): 71–84; Mary Jo Bitner, Bernard H. Booms and Lois A. Mohr, 'Critical service encounters: the employee's viewpoint', *Journal of Marketing* 58 (October 1994): 95–106.

hotels that do not adequately clean their rooms, or insurance firms that do not process their claims are all guilty of service delivery system failures. Understanding and responding to delivery failures are not only important to the customer as they receive redress to their complaint, but are also a learning tool for organizations. Organizations should monitor where, when and how their service delivery fails in order to drive improvements forward and develop the customer/staff interface. By following these guidelines, organizations will remove ineffective delivery processes and reduce costs by having fewer complaints from their customers (Johnston and Michel, 2008; Dutta and et al., 2007). In general, service delivery system failures consist of employee responses to several types of failure. Service system failures occur when the core service delivered to the customer includes tangible defects. For example, the food order is cold or staff appearance is untidy/unkempt. It also includes unavailable service or unreasonably slow service such as long queues at job centres or accident and emergency departments at hospitals. System failures also include facility problems where sauna facilities smell damp through lack of thorough cleaning or no baby-changing facilities in fast-food outlets that clearly appeal to people with young families.

These services failures are very apparent in the service experience. Many services, however, are now delivered through flourishing online service organizations. The apparent failures outlined so far for bricks-and-mortar service transactions are less apparent for online e-tailers. The reason for the differences is due to the lack of personal contact between customers and personnel during the service delivery process. Therefore, e-tailers have to consider failures in their website design, payment procedures and security assurances. See E-Services in Action, Chapter 17 for details of auditing the online experience.

Customer needs and requests

The second type of service failure are failures in implicit or explicit customer requests. This failure occurs when the customer's individual needs are not met, such as seating problems for a party of ten diners who are unable to sit together. The ten diners would clearly have expected to sit together; therefore, this situation is an example of an implicit failure. Therefore, customer needs and requests pertains to employee responses to individual consumer needs and special requests. Consumer needs can be implicit or explicit. Unfortunately implicit needs are not requested. For example, a disabled customer seated in a wheelchair should not be lead to an elevated booth in a restaurant. In contrast, explicit requests are overtly requested. A customer who asks for her steak to be cooked medium-rare and who would like to substitute mash potatoes for the baked potato listed on the menu is making explicit requests.

In general, customer needs and requests consist of employee responses to four types of possible failures: (1) special needs, (2) customer preferences, (3) customer errors, and (4) disruptive others. Employee responses to special needs involve complying with requests based on a customer's special medical,

unavailable service Services normally available that are lacking or absent.

unreasonably slow service Services or employees perceived by customers as being extraordinarily slow in fulfilling their function.

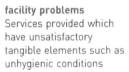

Case link

For system failures see Case 13: Ray's Farm.

facility problems Services provided which have unsatisfactory tangible elements such as unhygienic conditions

customer needs and requests The individual needs and special requests of customers.

implicit needs Customer needs that are not requested but that should be obvious to service providers.

explicit requests Customer needs that are overtly requested.

special needs Requests based on a customer's special medical, psychological, language, or sociological difficulties.

dietary, psychological, language, or sociological difficulties. Preparing a meal for a vegetarian would fulfil a 'special request'. Employee responses to customer preferences require the employee to modify the service delivery system in some way that meets the preferred needs of the customer. A customer request for a substitution at a restaurant is an example of a customer preference. An employee response to a customer error involves a scenario in which the failure is initiated by an admitted customer mistake (e.g., lost festival tickets, lost hotel key). Finally, employee responses to disruptive others require employees to settle disputes between customers, such as requesting patrons to be quiet in movie theatres (Chung and Hoffman, 1998; Bitner et al., 1990).

Unprompted/unsolicited employee actions

The third type of service failure, unprompted and unsolicited employee actions. These failures occur when the employees' behaviour is unacceptable in the eyes of the customer. For example, employees who give the wrong change, a missing reservation items appearing on a bill for valleting a car that did not take place or incorrect delivery day of flowers (Dutta et al., 2007). Often these actions are not initiated explicitly by a change in the customer's needs nor are they part of the core delivery system. Subcategories in this group include (1) level of attention, (2) unusual action, (3) cultural norms, (4) gestalt, and (5) adverse condition.

Within the failure group of unprompted or unsolicited employee action, the subcategory of level of attention refers to both positive and negative events. Positive levels of attention would occur when an employee goes out of his or her way to pamper a customer and anticipate the customer's needs such as providing books and magazines for children at solicitor's offices. Negative levels of attention pertain to employees who have poor attitudes, employees who ignore a customer, and employees who exhibit behaviours consistent with an indifferent attitude.

The unusual action subcategory can also reflect positive and negative events. For example, a Domino's employee happened to see a family searching through the burnt-out remains of their house while making a delivery to another customer in the area. The employee reported the event to the manager, and the two immediately prepared and delivered pizzas for the family free of charge. The family was stunned by the action and never forgot the kindness that was extended towards them during their time of need. Unfortunately, an unusual action can also be a negative event. Employee actions such as rudeness, abusiveness and inappropriate touching would qualify equally as unusual actions.

The cultural norms subcategory refers to actions that either positively reinforce cultural norms such as equality, fairness and honesty, or violate the cultural norms of society. Violations would include discriminatory behaviour, acts of dishonesty such as lying, cheating and stealing, and other activities considered unfair by customers.

The gestalt subcategory refers to customer evaluations that are made holistically; that is, the customer does not describe the service encounter as

customer preferences The needs of a customer that are not due to medical, dietary, psychological, language, or sociological difficulties.

customer errors Service failures caused by admitted customer mistakes.

disruptive others Customers who negatively influence the service experience of other customers.

unprompted/unsolicited employee actions Events and employee behaviours, both good and bad, totally unexpected by the customer.

level of attention Positive and/or negative regard given to a customer by an employee.

unusual action Both positive and negative events in which an employee responds with something out of the ordinary.

cultural norms Service personnel actions that either positively reinforce or violate the cultural norms of society.

gestalt Customer evaluations that are made holistically and given in overall terms rather than in descriptions of discrete events.

discrete events but uses overall terms such as 'pleasant' or 'terrible'. In our airline example, if the customer had not specified the individual failure events but had commented only, 'It is almost unbelievable how poorly we were treated by the employees of your airline, almost a perfect negative case study in customer service', the complaint would be categorized as a gestalt evaluation.

Finally, the adverse conditions subcategory covers positive and negative employee actions under stressful conditions. If an employee takes effective control of a situation when all others around him/her are 'losing their heads', customers are impressed by the employee's performance under those adverse conditions. In contrast, if the captain and crew of a sinking ship board the lifeboats before the passengers, this would obviously be remembered as a negative action under adverse conditions.

adverse conditions Positive and negative employee actions under stressful conditions.

Problematic customers

The final service failure type involves instances where neither the employee nor the service firm is at fault for the service failure. In these situations, the cause of the service failure lies with the customer's own misbehaviour. Service failures involving problematic customers include (1) drunkenness, (2) verbal and physical abuse, (3) breaking company policies, and (4) uncooperative customers. Problematic customer behaviour involving drunkenness occurs when the intoxicated customer's behaviour adversely affects other customers, service employees, or the service environment in general. Verbal and physical abuse refers to the customer verbally or physically abusing either the employee or other customers. For example, if a lover's quarrel breaks out in the middle of a restaurant and the couple begins screaming and/or hitting one another, this situation would qualify as verbal and physical abuse.

A customer who breaks company policies refuses to comply with policies employees are attempting to enforce. For example, a queuing policy or a no substitution policy that is ignored by a customer would create a problematic situation. Finally, an uncooperative customer is one who is generally rude, uncooperative and unreasonably demanding. Regardless of how the service employee attempts to appease this customer, the effort is typically futile. The customer simply will not be pleased.

drunkenness An intoxicated customer's behaviour adversely affects other customers, service employees, or the service environment in general.

verbal and physical abuse When a customer verbally or physically abuses either the employee or other customers.

breaks company policies When a customer refuses to comply with policies that employees are attempting to enforce.

uncooperative customer A customer who is generally rude, uncooperative and unreasonably demanding.

SOURCE © ISTOCK/CARMEN MARTINEZ BANÜS

A couple arguing in a restaurant spoils the dining experience of other customers.

Customer complaining behaviour

In a striking example of the impact of service failures is the high intensity of anger and dissatisfaction that customers feel. Many people can easily remember a time when they had received poor service. Survey respondents were no exception when they were encouraged to 're-experience' a negative service encounter. The respondents stated that they wanted to 'explode' or thought of 'violent acts' and the 'unfairness' of the situation. These intense feelings of anger drove respondents to want to complain or 'hurt' the service provider in some way. Angry and dissatisfied customers, therefore, 'get back' at the organization (Bougie, Pieters and Zeelenberg, 2003). Customers 'get back' at organizations in three specific ways: (1) take public action, (2) take private action, and (3) take no action. Figure 16.1 shows the variety of courses of action available to customers of encounter service failure.

Customers who wish to take public action can do so by taking their complaint to a third party such as an industry watchdog for delayed train services or consumer advocacy groups. Another type of third party that angry customer may feel inclined to report service failures in healthcare, transportation, hospitality, banking or insurance are local or national newspapers. Customers may also seek monetary redress by taking legal action against the service provider for personal injury claims. Consumers can also take public action by complaining immediately through letters or telephone calls to the service provider's head of customer services. Often customers simply take their business elsewhere by defecting from the offending service provider to one of their competitors. These customers may do this by spreading negative word or mouth about this organization. More about customer exit strategies is shown in Complaining Outcomes and Global Services in Action – Call Australia.

Most companies cringe at the thought of customers who complain, while other companies look at complaints as a way organizations can learn from their mistakes (Vos, Huitema and de Lange-Ros, 2008). The truth of the matter is that every company should encourage its customers to complain. Complainers are telling the firm that it has some operational or managerial problems that need to be corrected. Hence, complainers are offering the company a free gift, that is, they act as consultants and diagnose the firm's problems – at no fee. Moreover, complainers provide the firm with the chance to re-establish a customer's satisfaction. Complainers are more likely to do business with the firm again than are non-complainers that have had a bad experience. Consequently, successful firms view complaints as an opportunity to satisfy unhappy customers and prevent defections and unfavourable word-of-mouth communications. Indeed organizations that are really serious about complaints distinguish between complaint handling and complaint management. Complaint handling is an encounter between front-line staff and customers that is in place to resolve the situation in 'real time', whereas complaint management is a multilayered function of the organization incorporating customer retention by understanding the complaints, resolving them and considering changes throughout the organization to reduce complaints over the longer term (Stauss and Seidel, 2005).

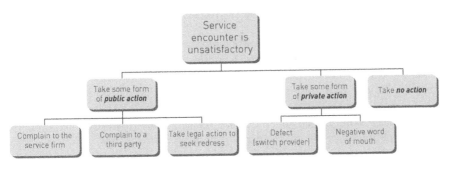

Figure 16.1

Customer response categories to service failures

Source Adapted from Lovelock and Wirtz, 2007: 391.

It's not the complainers the company should worry about; it's the non-complainers. Customers who do not express their complaints are already gone or ready to leave for the competition at any moment. In fact, only 4 per cent of customers ever complain! And out of the 96 per cent of those who do not complain 91 per cent just walk away. Clearly they are a silent majority (Downton, 2002) Having said that, France's hotel and restaurant industry watchdog has admitted that their staff are rude, surly and off-hand and many hotels facilities are in disrepair. The number of complaints to the Committee for Modernisation of the French Hotel Trade state that 24 per cent of hotels guests and up to 38 per cent of restaurant guests complain (Allen, 2007)

Types of complaints

instrumental complaints Complaints expressed for the purpose of altering an undesirable state of affairs.

Based on past research in consumer psychology, complaints can be instrumental or non-instrumental (Alicke et al., 1992). Instrumental complaints are expressed for the purpose of altering an undesirable state of affairs. For example, complaining to a waiter about an undercooked steak is an instrumental complaint. In such a case, the complainer fully expects the waiter to correct the situation. Interestingly, research indicates that instrumental complaints make up only a small number of the complaints that are voiced every day.

non-instrumental complaints Complaints expressed without expectation that an undesirable state will be altered.

In contrast, non-instrumental complaints are voiced without any expectation that the undesirable state will be altered. These kinds of complaints are voiced much more often than are instrumental complaints. For example, complaints about the weather such as 'It's too hot!' are voiced without any real expectation that conditions will change. Another type of non-instrumental complaint is an instrumental complaint that is voiced to a second party and not to the offending source. For example, complaining to a friend about your roommate being a 'slob' is a non-instrumental complaint.

ostensive complaints Complaints directed at someone or something outside the realm of the complainer.

reflexive complaints Complaints directed at some inner aspect of the complainer.

Complaints are also categorized as ostensive or reflexive. Ostensive complaints are directed at someone or something outside the realm of the complainer. In contrast, reflexive complaints are directed at some inner aspect of the complainer. Typically, complaints tend to be more ostensive than reflexive for two reasons. First, people generally avoid making negative comments about themselves so as not to reinforce negative self-esteem. Second, people seldom want to convey negative attributes about themselves to others.

Why do customers complain?

In the case of the instrumental complaint, the reason a customer complains is pretty clear. The complainer wants the undesirable state to be corrected. However, the reason is not so clear when it comes to non-instrumental complaints. Experts believe that non-instrumental complaints occur for several reasons. First, complaining serves a function much like the release of a pressure valve – it provides the complainer an emotional release from frustration. Complaints provide people with the mechanism for venting their feelings.

Complaining also serves as a mechanism for the complainer's desire to regain some measure of control. Control is re-established if the complainer is able to influence other people's evaluations of the source of the complaint. For example, negative word of mouth spread by the complainer for the purpose of taking revenge on an offending business gives the complainer some measure of control through indirect retribution.

A third reason people complain to others is to solicit sympathy and test for consensus of the complaint, thereby validating the complainer's subjective evaluation of the events that led to the complaint. In other words, the complainer wants to know whether others would feel the same way under similar circumstances. If they would, the complainer then feels justified in having voiced the complaint.

Finally, complainers may complain simply to create an impression. As strange as it may seem, complainers are often considered to be more intelligent and discerning than those who do not complain. The implication is that the complainer's standards and expectations are higher than those of non-complainers.

So why don't customers complain?

Compared to problems with goods, a greater percentage of problems with services are not voiced 'because potential complainers do not know what to do or think that it wouldn't do any good' (Gilly, Stevenson and Yale, 1991: 297). This situation is directly attributable to the intangibility and inseparability inherent in the provision of services (see Chapter 2).

Due to intangibility, evaluation of the service delivery process is primarily subjective. Consequently, consumers often lack the security of making an objective observation and may doubt their own evaluations. Just because some customers do not complain does not mean they have no emotional feelings for the service failure. Chebat, Davidow and Codjovi (2005) discovered that non-complainers also feel angry – and to no lesser degree than complainers. However, consumers who complain have different coping methods (as outlined above) than non-complainers. Non-complainers are often resigned and sad that failures have occurred and feel that complaining will be a waste of time and effort (Downton, 2002).

Due to inseparability, customers often provide inputs into the process. Hence, given an undesirable outcome, customers may place much of the blame upon themselves for failing to convey to the service provider a satisfactory description of the level and type of service desired. In addition, inseparability encompasses the often face-to-face interaction between the customer and the service provider, and the customer may feel uncomfortable about complaining because of the physical presence of the provider.

Too much volume? Many of us avoid telling our hairdressers what we really think.

SOURCE © ISTOCK.COM/ANDREA GINGERICH

Finally, many services are technical and specialized. Customers may not feel adequately qualified to voice a complaint for fear that they lack the expertise to evaluate the quality of the service. For example, do customers really know when their auto mechanic has completed everything they were billed for?

Complaining outcomes

In general, complaining behaviour results in four outcomes: voiced complaints, exit, third party complaints and private complaints (Blythe, 2008; Hunt, 1991).

voice A complaining outcome in which the consumer verbally communicates dissatisfaction with the store or the product.

Voice refers to an outcome in which the consumer verbally communicates dissatisfaction with the store or the product. High voice means that the communication is expressed to the manager or someone higher in the organizational hierarchy than the actual provider. Medium voice occurs when the consumer communicates the problem to the person providing the service. Low voice occurs when the consumer does not communicate the problem to anyone associated with the store or product but may be relaying the problem to others outside the store. Consumers also have a 'cyber-voice' by complaining or complimenting service via personal blogs, company blogs and online feedback forums – see E-Services in Action – Cyber Voice.

exit A complaining outcome in which the consumer stops patronizing the store or using the product.

Exit, the second type of complaining outcome, describes the situation in which a consumer stops patronizing the store or using the product. High exit occurs when the consumer makes a conscious decision never to purchase from the firm or buy the product again. Medium exit reflects a consumer's conscious decision to try not to use the store or product again if at all possible. Low exit means that the consumer does not change his or her purchasing behaviour and continues to shop as usual.

retaliation A complaining outcome in which the consumer takes action deliberately designed to damage the physical operation or hurt future business.

The third type of complaint outcome is retaliation, the situation in which a consumer takes action deliberately designed to either damage the physical operation or hurt future business. High retaliation involves the situation where the consumer physically damages the store or goes out of his or her way to communicate to others negative aspects about the business. In medium retaliation, the consumer creates minor inconveniences for the store or perhaps tells only a few people about the incident. Low retaliation involves no retaliation at all against the store, perhaps consisting of only minor negative word of mouth.

Interestingly, the three complaining outcomes are not mutually exclusive and can be considered as three aspects of one type of behaviour that may occur simultaneously. Experiencing high levels of all three outcomes simultaneously can result in explosive behaviour. For example, 'In one example, the customer shouted his dissatisfaction at the clerk and the store manager, vowed never to buy at the store again, went out of the store, got in his car, and drove it in the front doors of the store through the

A car crashing into a shop window might get a few complaints!

checkout counter and between two lines of shelving, destroying everything in its path' (Hunt, 1991). In contrast, a consumer who displays high-voice, low-exit and low-retaliation behaviour would typify a perpetual complainer who nevertheless continues to shop at the store as usual. See B2B Services in Action to discover the frustrations that consumers face when using self-service technology from 'remote' locations and have no immediate chance to complain.

E-services in action
Cyber voice

Consumer online spending was at $54 billion in 2001; three years later it tripled to $3133 billion. In short, although all the hype surrounding the e-commerce revolution has subsided, the numbers are in and the e-commerce retail sector is booming and here to stay.

The phenomenal growth of the e-tail sector has not been without its unique troubles in service delivery, product defects or website failure. Therefore, e-tail customers want to know which products, services and e-tail providers are going to best serve their needs. Epinions.com is a website that has thousands of products and services reviewed online. The reviewers are other customers – not advertisers, not sponsors, and not suppliers. Therefore, the reviews are honest, fair and can be trusted! Reviewers can voice their complaints about any products or service. This gives the opportunity for customers who feel truly aggrieved by an experience they have had with a bank, insurance company, golf resort or ski-guide – they can offload their grievance on epinions.com. At the same time, however, customers who have really had a good holiday, enjoyed a fantastic honeymoon or found an excellent online retailer can also advise fellow customers about their experiences by epinions.com.

Epinions.com is not the only community site; there are thousands of blog sites and consumer forums that give consumers the opportunity to voice their opinions on the poor service they have received. And consumers can say what they like as the websites are not policed by the organization they are complaining about or indeed any governing body. A question, therefore, that has to be raised is who is putting up the complaints? Could it be a former employee who was sacked for misconduct or could it be a rival organization? No-one knows! However, the reviews being put up on the web need to be monitored by organizations, as one upset consumer can ruin the reputation of an organization by 'word of mouse'!

Some reviewers seem to be making a name for themselves as trusted consultants. Reviewers such as Penguinlady offer regular reviews on Hotels and Travel. And consumers who wish to let off steam about who their team has been drawn against for the UEFA cup final can visit the Fanzone Forum at www.uefa.com/fanzone/forums .

Other sites where complaints are voiced, compliments are shared and discussion groups of like-minded people can be found at

http://groups.google.com

www.consumerreview.com

www.slashdot.org

www.extremetech.com.

Sources: G. R. (2000) 'Web Wonderings Consumers' Revenge: Online Product Reviews and Ratings', *EContent*, April.
N. Thompson (2003) 'More Companies Pay Heed to Their 'Word of Mouse' Reputation', *New York Times*, 23 June 2003.

The art of service recovery

service recovery A firm's reaction to a complaint that results in customer satisfaction and goodwill.

Complainers provide the firm with an opportunity to recover from the service failure. When the service is provided incorrectly the first time, an important but often forgotten management tool is the art of service recovery (Reid and Bojanic, 2006). While some companies are great at delivering service until something goes wrong, other companies thrive on recovering from service failures and impressing customers in the process. Customers of service organizations often allow the firm one mistake. Consequently, when a failure occurs, the customer generally provides the business with an opportunity to make

---

B2B services in action
Service recovery strategies for self-service technology

Businesses throughout the world are beginning to understand the importance of self-service technology (SST) in their call centre operations. Gartner Group, with offices in Japan, Australia, Brazil, UK and USA, supply solutions to thousands of businesses from banks and insurance operations to governments and from retail to healthcare. Gartner Group provides self-service technologies to businesses that enables them to cut down on expensive, labour-intensive manual procedures and move towards much cheaper automated self-service operations. Tracey Schelmetic, the Editorial Director for *Customer Inter@ction Solutions* magazine, says call centre

companies get really excited when they talk about the benefits that self-service technology brings. The technology enables 'remote' customers to 'route themselves' to the appropriate department by using their telephone keypad. Similarly remote consumers can order bank statements, book cinema tickets or provide readings from their gas meter. The use of self-service technology (SST) enables call centre staff to deal with more complicated higher-stakes enquiries. Figure 16.2, The Consumer Link to Self-Service Technology shows a framework of the consumer's encounter with an organization's technology.

Figure 16.2

The consumer link to self-service technology (SST) supplier

Source Adapted from Pujari, (2004), 'Self-service with a smile? Self-service technology (SST) encounters among Canadian business-to-business', *International Journal of Service Industry Management*, Vol. 15, No. 2, p. 204.

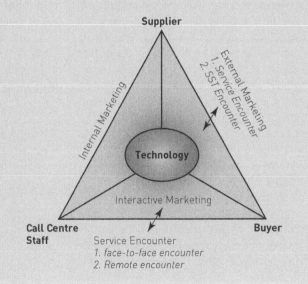

B2B suppliers to self-service technology such as Wes Hayden, CEO of Genesys, stated that customers are now getting used to and often preferring the self-service technologies. But ... what happens when there are service failures in a remote service encounter – how does the customer get redress as there is no-one 'there' to talk to?

For five categories of dissatisfaction see Table 16.2.

It is important to note that service recovery issues for organizations that use self-service technology (SST) are currently letting their business customers, clients and personal customers down as they do not have systems and manual operations in place. Additionally, service providers of the self-service technology often state that the systems fail because it is the call center IT staff that have not installed the technology correctly. Whoever is to blame, the personal customer will seek redress from the call centre and will not accept that the fault lies with the third-party supplier.

Sources: Hayden Wes, CEO Genesys (2005) 'The Call Centre's Love Affair with Self-Service', www.tmcnet.com/usubmit/2005/jul/1165286.htm, accessed 14 January 2008.
D. Pujari (2004) 'Self-service with a smile? Self-service technology (SST) encounters among Canadian business-to-business', *International Journal of Service Industry Management* 15 (2); 200–219.
Schelmetic Tracey, Editorial Director Customer Inter@ctions Solutions (2005) 'The Call Centre's Love Affair with Self-Service', www.tmcnet.com/usubmit/2005/jul/1165286.htm, accessed 14 January 2008.

Source of dissatisfaction	Per cent	Representative quotations
Technology failure	41%	'Could not use the system as the company server was down. We missed [because we missed] the deadline'
Transaction process problems	15%	'Even though it was rectified, it gave us a lot of headache as data on the system was corrupted, we thought that the security was breached'
Post-transaction process problems	13%	It showed us incorrect transactions order, paid more than we should have'
Customer service problems	13%	'Due to extremely busy time of the year, system was painfully slow'
● Waited online for a long time	9%	'Difficult to navigate' 'Useless FAQ' 'No email alert was sent even though it was a significant change in the process'
● User-unfriendly		
● Changed instructions without notice	4%	
Own fault	3%	'We made the mistake of entering a wrong number and got the delivery 4 times over'

Table 16.2

Categories of dissatisfaction

Source Pujari, (2004), 'Self-service with a smile? Self-service technology (SST) encounters among Canadian business-to-business', *International Journal of Management*, Vol. 15, No. 2, p. 210.

amends. Unfortunately, many companies still drop the ball and further aggravate the customer by failing to take the opportunity to recover.

When the service delivery system fails, it is the responsibility of contact personnel to react to the complaint. The content and form of the contact personnel's response determines the customer's perceived satisfaction or dissatisfaction with the service encounter (Sheth and Mittal, 2004).

Ironically, customers will remember a service encounter favourably if the contact personnel respond in a positive manner to the service failure. Hence, even though the service encounter included a service failure, the customer recalls the encounter as a positive event. In fact, a customer will rate performance higher if a failure occurs and the contact personnel successfully recover from the failure than if the service had been delivered correctly the first time. This phenomenon has been termed the service recovery paradox.

service recovery paradox
Situation in which the customer rates performance higher if a failure occurs and the contact personnel successfully recover from it than if the service had been delivered correctly in the first place.

Experts in the area of service recovery recommend that in establishing service recovery as a priority and developing recovery skills, firms should consider the following issues.

Measure the costs

The costs of losing and the benefits of keeping existing customers as opposed to chasing new customers are substantial. In short, the costs of obtaining new customers are three to five times greater than those of keeping existing customers. Current customers are more receptive to the firm's marketing efforts and are, therefore, an important source of profit for the firm. In addition, existing customers ask fewer questions, are more familiar with the firm's procedures and employees and are willing to pay more for services.

Actively encourage complaints

Experts assert that actively encouraging complaints is a good way to 'break the silence'. Remember that complainers who actually voice their complaints to the source of the problem are the exception – most customers don't speak up. In fact, research indicates that the average company does not hear from between 70 to 95 per cent of its unhappy customers (Harari, 1992) This doesn't mean that customers don't complain, only that they complain to friends and family rather than to the company. The average unhappy customer voices displeasure with a firm to 11 other people. If these 11 tell 5 other people, the firm has potentially lost 67 customers (Partow, 1993). Strategies to encourage complaints include customer surveys, focus groups and active monitoring of the service delivery process to ensure customer satisfaction throughout the encounter, before a customer leaves the premises.

Anticipate needs for recovery

Every service encounter is made up of a series of critical incidents, the points in the system where the customer and the firm interact. Firms that are effective in service recovery anticipate in advance the areas in their service delivery process where failures are most likely to occur. Of course, these firms take every step possible to minimize the occurrence of the failure in the first place, but they are prepared for recovery if delivery goes awry. Experts believe that firms should pay special attention to areas in which employee turnover is high. Many high-turnover positions are low-paying customer contact positions, and employees often lack motivation and/or are inexperienced in effective recovery techniques.

A good example of failing to anticipate a need for recovery might involve an airline that changed its flight schedule without notifying passengers. The airline should anticipate that this change will cause passengers problems with connecting flights.

Respond quickly

When a service failure does occur, the faster the company responds, the more likely that the recovery effort will result in a successful outcome. In fact, past studies have indicated that if the complaint is handled promptly, the company will retain 70 to 95 per cent of its unhappy customers. In contrast, if the complaint is resolved in a less timely manner, the firm retains only 64 per cent of unhappy customers (Albrecht and Zemke, 1985). Time is of the essence. The faster the firm responds to the problem, the better the message the firm sends to customers about the value it places on pleasing its customers. Why not give customers what they want, when they want it? Is it really worth it to the firm for employees to actively argue with customers? Additionally, staff should learn rapport techniques – such as making the customer feel important, showing empathy to the situation and 'mirroring the customer's pace of speech' (DeWitt and Brady, 2003: 203). Therefore, training employees to deal with complaints and how to 'recover' the situation is just as important as training service staff to do their job 'right' in the first instance.

Train employees

Expecting employees to be naturals at service recovery is unrealistic. Most employees don't know what to do when a failure occurs, and many others find making on-the-spot decisions a difficult task. Employee training in service recovery should take place on two levels. First, the firm must work at creating in the employee an awareness of customer concerns. Placing an employee in the shoes of the customer is often enlightening for an employee who has forgotten what it's like to be a customer of his or her own firm. For example, hospitals have made interns and staff dress in hospital gowns and had them rolled around on trolleys to experience some of the processes firsthand.

The second level of employee training, beyond developing an appreciation for customer needs, is defining management's expectation towards recovery efforts. What are acceptable recovery strategies from management's perspective? Effective recovery often means that management has to let go and allow employees to take risks, a transition that often leads to the empowerment of front-line employees.

Empower the front line

Effective recovery often means that the employee has to bend the firm's rules and regulations – the exact type of activity that employees are trained not to do at any cost. Often the rules and regulations of the firm tie the hands of employees when it comes to effective recovery efforts, particularly in the area of prompt response. In many instances, firms require managerial approval before any effort to compensate a customer is undertaken. However, the manager is often engaged in other duties, which delays the response and adds to the frustration for both customer and employee. Front-line staff should have a mechanism with which to handle and deal with complainants as soon as possible. Figure 16.3, Is the Complaint Justified? provides a mechanism to help empower front-line staff to move forward when customers complain.

Close the loop

One of the most important activities in service recovery is providing feedback to the customer about how that customer's complaint made a difference. Customer-oriented firms that have a sound recovery strategy solve the customer's problem. However, firms that excel at recovery go the extra mile and re-establish contact with the customer for the purpose of informing the customer how their complaint will make a difference in the way operations are handled in the future. Incorporating the customer's complaint during a training session or developing new procedures to minimize future occurrences of the failure and communicating the impact of the complaint on the company to the customer closes the loop and wins customers for life.

Figure 16.3

Is the complaint justified?

Source Adapted from Blythe, (2008), *Consumer Behaviour*, South-Western, a part of Cengage Learning, p. 327.

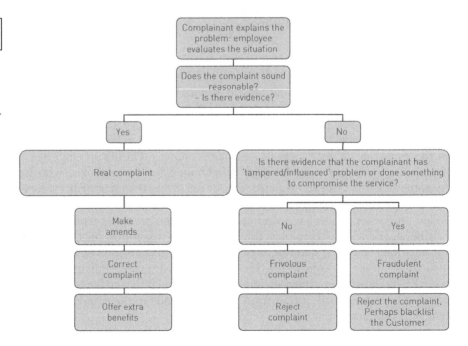

Evaluating recovery efforts: Perceived justice

Throughout the service recovery process, customers weigh their inputs against their outputs when forming recovery evaluations (Hoffman and Kelley, 2000). Inputs could be described as the costs associated with the service failure, including economic, time, energy, and psychic (cognitive) costs. The sum of the inputs is compared to the sum of the outputs, which include the specific recovery tactic (e.g., cash refund, apology, or replacement), the manner of personnel, the service policies developed to handle such situations and the image associated with responsive organizations.

The customer's perception of whether the recovery strategy is acceptable includes evaluations of the recovery process itself, the outcomes connected to the recovery strategy; and the interpersonal behaviours enacted during the recovery process. Accordingly, perceived justice consists of three components: distributive justice, procedural justice and interactional justice.

Distributive justice focuses on the specific outcome of the firm's recovery effort. In other words, what specifically did the offending firm offer the customer to recover from the service failure, and did this outcome (output) offset the costs (inputs) of the service failure? Typical distributive outcomes include compensation (e.g., gratis, discounts, coupons, free upgrades and free ancillary services); offers to mend or totally replace/re-perform; and apologies.

The second component of perceived justice, procedural justice, examines the process that is undertaken to arrive at the final outcome. Hence, even though a customer may be satisfied with the type of recovery strategy offered, recovery evaluation may be poor due to the process endured to obtain the recovery outcome. For example, research has indicated that when implementing identical recovery strategies, those that are implemented 'promptly' are much more likely to be associated with higher consumer effectiveness ratings and retention rates than their 'delayed' counterparts.

Interactional justice refers to the manner in which the service recovery process is implemented and how recovery outcomes are presented. In other

perceived justice The process whereby customers weigh their inputs against their outputs when forming recovery evaluations.

distributive justice A component of perceived justice that refers to the outcomes (e.g., compensation) associated with the service recovery process.

procedural justice A component of perceived justice that refers to the process (e.g., time) the customer endures during the service recovery process.

interactional justice A component of perceived justice that refers to human content (e.g., empathy, friendliness) that is demonstrated by service personnel during the service recovery process.

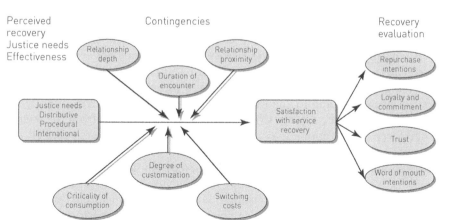

Figure 16.4

A contingency framework for evaluating recovery efforts

Source Hoffman and Kelley, (2000) 'Perceived justice needs and recovery evaluation: a contingency approach', *European Journal of Marketing*, Vol. 34, No.3, pp. 418–432.

words, interactional justice involves the courtesy and politeness exhibited by personnel, empathy, effort observed in resolving the situation and the firm's willingness to explain why the situation occurred.

A limited volume of research exists that specifically examines the influence of perceived justice on recovery strategy effectiveness. However, the bottom line is that the three components of perceived justice must be taken into consideration when formulating effective service recovery strategies. Deploying recovery efforts that satisfy distributive justice without consideration of customer procedural and interactional justice needs may still result in customer defections. If service firms are truly committed to the recovery process and retaining customers for life, all three aspects of perceived justice must be integrated into the service recovery process. Figure 16.4 provides a useful working model of how to evaluate service recovery efforts.

Service failure and recovery analysis: A restaurant industry example

The obvious benefit of service failure and recovery analysis is that management can identify common failure situations, minimize their occurrence and train employees to recover from failures when they do occur (see Global Services in Action for the reasons why services failed in remote locations). The example that follows is an actual study of service failures and recovery strategies in the restaurant industry.

The value of tracking service failures

As is the case in most service industries today, restaurant managers and service personnel are facing intensive customer service pressures now more than ever. When a service failure does occur, the service provider's reaction can either reinforce a strong customer bond or change a seemingly minor distraction into a major incident. For example, an employee's indifferent reaction to a customer's complaint about cold French fries can cost a restaurant several years' worth of business from that particular customer and an abundance of negative word-of-mouth publicity. Consequently, it is imperative that managers have an established service recovery plan to overcome possible service failures.

Analysing service failures and service recovery strategies is an extremely useful management tool. Akao and Mazur (2003) go further and say that analysing service failures and complaints is *priceless*; in fact they give it a special phrase, 'going to the *gamba*' (p. 23). Gamba is a term used by the Japanese to describe a place where learning comes directly from the source. Therefore, organizations that review the types of complaints received and where service delivery has failed these occurrences can be turned into *knowledge* about the customer and the employees. In general, service failure analysis provides the type, frequency and magnitude of various failures. By systematically categorizing consumer complaints, a hierarchy of criteria evolve that reflect the consumer's perspective of effective performance. This is a very important point. Analysing them is not an end in itself. Figure 16.5, Implementing a Customer Complaint Management System clearly shows that analysing the complaints is merely the beginning of gaining knowledge of customer complaints and service failures. Steps 1 to 4 are general procedures when service fails or customers voice their complaints. However, Step 5 clearly suggests that changes need to be made to training manuals, customer service competencies or call centre mandatory texts. So not only does the analysis take place, but the findings are implemented so that the same service failure does not reoccur. Step 6 suggests that the solution is shared with the customer. Therefore, the customer receives information that their complaint has helped improve future service delivery. Receiving an apology letter or a free bottle of wine is one thing – but receiving information from an organization stating that their service delivery has been improved because of the customer's bad experience will certainly make them feel respected and valued. Step 7 suggests that performance measurements would need to be updated. Organizations that change their procedures (Step 5) and share their solutions (Step 6) should monitor the successes. Organizations may be able to cut down the number of complaints, have fewer service failures because of new training and procedures and be able to deal with recovery strategies that respect the customer's needs and provide guidance for staff.

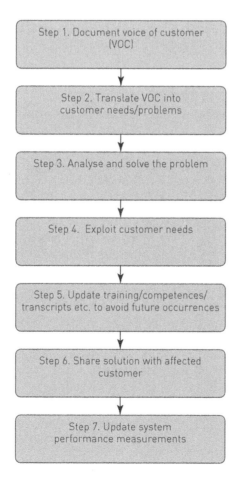

Figure 16.5

Implementing a customer complaint management system

Source Adapted from Gonzalez Bosch and Enriquez, (2005), 'TQM and QFD: Exploiting a customer complaint management system', *International Journal of Quality and Reliability Management* 22(1): pp. 30–37.

However performance is measured, it should be based on what the customer, not upper management, perceives as important. See Global Services in Action – Call Australia – No Worries for details of how their customer complaint management strategy follows the same procedures as in Figure 16.4. Call Australia also clearly state in their Responsibilities that they update and review their complaints and improve their customer service accordingly. This shows that Call Australia continue with Steps 5–7, a process that shows they have service quality at the heart of their operations.

The value of analysing service recovery strategies

In addition to tracking service failures, analysing service recovery strategies is equally enlightening. Service recovery analysis provides a sometimes alarming insight into:

- how personnel react to service failures,
- how consumers rate the effectiveness of the employee's recovery efforts, and
- the relationship between recovery strategies and customer retention rates.

Global services in action
Call Australia – No worries

Call Australia, a telecommunications company that provides excellent rates on their local, national and international calls, takes their customer service very seriously. They have an excellent support network to enable customers or potential customers to ask questions, request appointments and complain. Call Australia is clear about its corporate and social responsibilities in terms of complaint handling and these are shown below:

Our Responsibilities

- Call Australia will provide an efficient, fair and structured mechanism for handling complaints.
- We will provide our customers with access to the complaints handling process, including those customers with disabilities and special needs.
- Call Australia will keep customers informed as to the progress of their

complaint and the expected timeframe for resolution.

- We will regularly review our complaints so that we can improve our standard of customer service.

Call Australia has a Complaints Policy in place. It has been set up so that there is a set procedure should service failures occur. Call Australia Complaints Policy is useful for a number of reasons:

1 It clearly communicates internally and externally what their policy is.

2 It ensures Call Australia staff are trained so that they can live up to the promises laid down in the Complaints Policy.

3 It provides clear guidance to their customers about the service and delivery timescales they can expect, should they have to make a complaint.

4 And finally it reassures customers that their feedback and/or complaints will be dealt with fairly and sincerely.

Handling the complaint

Call Australia follow the procedure outlined below. The procedure is similar to that recommended in Figure 16.5:

- Upon receiving a verbal or written complaint, we will acknowledge your matter via telephone or in writing within 5 business days.
- We will keep you informed of the progress of your complaint, proposed actions and the expected timeframe for resolution.
- Our aim is to resolve complaints in a timely manner and we will generally resolve a matter within 30 calendar days.
- Complex complaints may take longer than 30 calendar days to resolve. In these cases, we will regularly update you on the progress and likely timeframe for resolution.
- We will advise you of the outcome of your complaint. Where you have requested us to do so, we will advise you in writing.
- We may impose a charge for handling your complaint in special circumstances. For example, we may charge you a fee where your complaint requires us to retrieve archived records.
- If we think your complaint requires a charge, we will not impose one without discussion with you.
- If your complaint is upheld in your favour, and we have charged you complaint handling fees, we will refund you the full amount of the fees charged within 30 days.

Sources: Call Australia Complaints Policy 2008.

Recent studies suggest that nearly half the responses to customer complaints actually reinforce a customer's negative feeling towards a firm. Effective recovery strategies often require contact personnel to make decisions and to occasionally break company rules – the types of behaviours that many firms prohibit their employees from initiating. Contact personnel are often frustrated by rules and regulations that tie their hands and often prevent them from assisting a customer when needed. Furthermore, due to the lack of training in recovery efforts exhibited by most firms, many employees simply do not know how to recover from service failures. The result is a poor response or no response to customer complaints.

The restaurant study

This study was conducted by services marketing students and is a great example of the valuable managerial information that can be obtained by monitoring and tracking service failures. The example is presented in a series of steps that can be easily duplicated. We highly recommend this exercise to services marketing classes as a group project. Different groups may investigate different industries or specific businesses.

Step 1: Developing the questionnaire. An example of the questionnaire used to collect the data for this study is provided in the appendix to this chapter. The main objective of the questionnaire is to:

- identify and classify failures in the restaurant industry,
- assess customer perceptions of the magnitude of each failure,
- identify and classify recovery strategies utilized by restaurants to correct failures,
- assess customer perceptions of the effectiveness of each type of recovery,
- assess subsequent patronage behaviours that reflect restaurants' customer retention rates, and
- provide demographic information about respondents.

critical incident technique A method of studying service failures by analysing critical incidents described in story form by respondents.

Step 2: Data collection. The study utilized a data collection method referred to as the critical incident technique (CIT). The purpose of CIT in this study is to examine the sources of customer satisfaction and dissatisfaction regarding restaurant services. In essence, CIT is a qualitative approach to analysing and categorizing critical incidents. The CIT analyses the content of the critical incidents described by respondents in story form.

The actual critical incidents (or stories) for this study were recorded by students. Respondents were asked to report a restaurant service failure that was associated with a positive service recovery, as well as a service failure that was associated with a negative service recovery. Both scenarios were requested in order to identify recovery strategies that were effective as well as responses that were inadequate. Incidents associated with positive recovery strategies accounted for 49.6 per cent of the sample, while 50.4 per cent of the sample was associated with poor recoveries.

In addition, respondents were asked to do the following:

- rate the magnitude of the failure on a scale from 1 through 10, which ranges from trivial to serious;
- rate the effectiveness of the recovery strategy on a scale from 1 through 10, which ranges from poor to good;
- report changes in shopping behaviour subsequent to the service failure attributed to the encounter; and
- provide demographic information on gender, education, and age.

The data collection efforts resulted in the accumulation of 373 critical incidents.

Step 3: Data analysis. The critical incident technique is a qualitative approach to analysing and categorizing critical incidents. More specifically, the CIT utilized in this study involved three steps:

1 *Identify the failure incident.* Initially, each of the 373 critical incidents was systematically categorized through a deductive sorting process into one of the three major failure groups discussed earlier in this chapter: (1) employee responses to service delivery system failures, (2) employee responses to implicit/explicit customer requests and (3) unprompted and unsolicited employee actions.

2 *Identify failure subgroups within the three major groups.* This step involved classifying failures into subgroups within each of the three major failure groups noted earlier. This process resulted in the

identification of 11 unique failure subgroups (five in Group 1, two in Group 2, and four in Group 3).

3 *Classify recovery strategies.* This step involved classifying the service recovery strategies within each failure subgroup. This process resulted in eight final service recovery strategies that are applicable to a variety of food service operations.

Step 4: Establishing the reliability of the categories. An important procedure when categorizing data is to determine the reliability of the categories. Reliability simply refers to the issue of whether other researchers, given the same set of data, would assign each of the critical incidents to the same set of categories. To assess the reliability of the 11 failure subgroups and 8 recovery strategies established through the sorting process in the study, an independent judge (such as a group member not involved in the original categorization) categorized each of the incidents included in the sample.

As a starting point to test for reliability, the critical incidents were pre-sorted into the three main failure categories: (1) employee responses to service delivery system failures, (2) employee responses to implicit/explicit customer requests and (3) unprompted and unsolicited employee actions. The independent judge was then presented with the 11 previously identified failure subgroups and asked to independently sort each failure incident into one of the 11 categories. In this example, the task resulted in agreement rates of 92 per cent, 90 per cent and 90 per cent. Typically, agreement rates of 70 per cent or higher are regarded as acceptable for establishing reliability.

After establishing the reliability of the service failure categories, the independent judge's next task was to verify the reliability of the service recovery categories. Following a procedure similar to the one described earlier, the independent judge was given the stack of recovery strategies and the names of the eight categories of recovery strategies previously identified. The independent judge then compared his/her categorization efforts with the original results. For this study, the recovery agreement rate was 93 per cent, and reliability was established for the recovery categories as well as for the failure categories.

Step 5: Presenting the results. *Demographic results.* Sample demographics revealed 42.5 per cent of the respondents were male while 57.5 per cent of the respondents were female. Regarding education, 68.2 per cent of the respondents did not have college degrees; 21.7 per cent had undergraduate degrees; and 10.1 per cent had 'some' or had completed graduate school. Results concerning the age of respondents revealed that 67.5 per cent were 25 years old or younger; 14.1 per cent were from 26 to 35; and 18.4 per cent were 36 years of age or older.

Statistical tests were used in examining the relationships between demographics and restaurant type, failure type, recovery strategies, failure ratings, recovery ratings, and retention rates. Results revealed no statistically significant findings. These tests provide evidence that the findings, reported across different types of customers and across restaurant types, can be safely generalized.

The failure categories: frequency and definition. After carefully sorting the 373 critical incidents, the following restaurant service failure categories were developed and their reliability established. As described earlier in step 3, the incidents were first sorted into three main failure groups and then into subclass failures within each main failure group.

Group 1, 'Employee Responses to Core Service Failures', accounted for 44.4 per cent of all critical incidents. Core service failures included the following subclass categories (the frequency of occurrence expressed as a percentage of the total critical incidents is reported in parentheses):

- *Product defects* (20.9 per cent): Food that was described as cold, soggy, raw, burnt, spoiled, or containing inanimate objects such as hair, glass, bandages, bag ties, or cardboard.
- *Slow/unavailable service* (17.9 per cent): Waiting an excessive amount of time and/or not being able to find assistance.
- *Facility problems* (3.2 per cent): Cleanliness issues such as bad smells, dirty utensils and animate objects found in food or crawling across the table (e.g., insects).
- *Unclear policies* (1.6 per cent): Restaurant policies that were perceived as unfair by the customer (e.g., coupon redemption, form of payment).
- *Out of stock conditions* (0.8 per cent): An inadequate supply of menu items.

Group 2, 'Employee Responses to Implicit/Explicit Customer Requests', accounted for 18.4 per cent of the critical incidents. Implicit/explicit customer requests included the following subclass categories (the frequency of occurrence expressed as a percentage of the total critical incidents is reported in parentheses):

- *Food not cooked to order* (15.0 per cent): The scenario in which the customer explicitly asks for the food to be prepared in a specific manner (e.g., medium-rare, no mustard) and the request is not honoured.
- *Seating problems* (3.4 per cent): Involved seating smokers in non-smoking sections and vice versa, lost or disregarded reservations, denial of request for special tables and seating among unruly customers.

Group 3, 'Unprompted/Unsolicited Employee Actions', accounted for 37.2 per cent of the total critical incidents. Unprompted/unsolicited employee actions included the following subclass categories (the frequency of occurrence expressed as a percentage of the total critical incidents is reported in parentheses):

- *Inappropriate employee behaviour* (15.2 per cent): Rudeness, inappropriate verbal exchanges, and poor attitudes that were associated with unpleasant behaviours.
- *Wrong orders* (12.6 per cent): The delivery of an incorrect food item to the table, or in the case of fast food, packaging an incorrect food item that was not discovered until the customer was no longer on the restaurant premises.
- *Lost orders* (7.5 per cent): Situations in which the customer's order was apparently misplaced and never fulfilled.
- *Mischarged* (1.9 per cent): Being charged for items that were never ordered, charging incorrect prices for items that were ordered and providing incorrect change.

The failure categories: Magnitude and recovery. In addition to developing the failure categories, we also recorded each respondent's perception of the magnitude of the failure. Respondents rated the magnitude of the failure on a scale from 1 (minor mistake) through 10 (major mistake). In addition, the average effectiveness of recovery for each failure was calculated on a scale from 1 (poor recovery) through 10 (good recovery). Magnitude and recovery rankings presented according to the failures' perceived severity are reported in Table 16.3.

The recovery categories: Frequency and definition. In addition to categorizing the primary service failures in the restaurant industry, a second objective of this study was to utilize the critical incident technique to categorize employee response (recovery strategies) to the various service failures. The service recovery strategies resulting from the CIT approach are defined as follows (the frequency of occurrence expressed as a percentage of the total critical incidents are reported in parentheses):

- *Replacement* (33.4 per cent): Replacing the defective order with a new order.
- *Free food* (23.5 per cent): Providing the meal, desserts, and/or drinks on a complimentary basis.

Failure category	Magnitude	Recovery
1 Seating problems	8.00	5.61
2 Out of stock	7.33	6.00
3 Facility problems	7.25	3.92
4 Inappropriate employee behaviour	7.12	3.71
5 Slow/unavailable service	7.05	5.38
6 Lost orders	6.71	5.82
7 Product defects	6.69	6.21
8 Wrong orders	6.25	6.44
9 Unclear policy	6.16	6.33
10 Food not cooked to order	6.02	5.80
11 Mischarged	5.86	7.71

Table 16.3

Magnitude of service failure

- *Nothing* (21.3 per cent): No action was taken to correct the failure.
- *Apology* (7.8 per cent): The employee apologized for the failure.
- *Correction* (5.7 per cent): Fixing the existing defective order as opposed to replacing the order with a new one.
- *Discount* (4.3 per cent): Discounts were provided to customers for food items at the time of the incident.
- *Managerial intervention* (2.7 per cent): Management in some way became involved and helped resolve the problem.
- *Coupon* (1.3 per cent): Discounts for food items purchased at the restaurant were provided to customers for use on their next visit.

The recovery categories: perceived effectiveness and corresponding customer retention rates. Respondents rated the effectiveness of each recovery on a scale from 1 (very poor) through 10 (very good). Recoveries ranked in declining order of effectiveness and their corresponding customer retention rates are reported in Table 16.4.

The customer retention rates revealed in this study suggest that it is possible to recover from failures, regardless of the type. Overall, customer retention for the incidents considered was above 75 per cent. Even customers experiencing less-than-acceptable recoveries were still retained at a rate approaching 60 per cent. However, in general, the statistical relationship between failure rating and recovery rating does indicate that as the magnitude of the seriousness of the failure increases, so does the difficulty in executing an effective recovery.

Table 16.4	Recovery strategy	Effectiveness	Per cent retention rate
Service failure recoveries	1 Free food	8.05	89.0
	2 Discount	7.75	87.5
	3 Coupon	7.00	80.0
	4 Managerial intervention	7.00	88.8
	5 Replacement	6.35	80.2
	6 Correction	5.14	80.0
	7 Apology	3.72	71.4
	8 Nothing	1.71	51.3

Step 6: Developing managerial implications based on results. This research provides restaurant managers and employees with a list of service failures that are likely to occur in the restaurant industry as well as methods for effectively (and ineffectively) recovering from these failures when they occur. Managers should use this type of information when designing service delivery systems and procedures, establishing policies regarding service recovery and selecting and training service personnel. Remarkably, approximately one out of every four service failures (23.5 per cent) was met with no response by the offending firm. Unfortunately, other research has indicated that this 'no response' rate is typical.

The findings also suggest that it is difficult to recover from two failure types in particular. On a 10-point scale, failures associated with facility problems (failure 3) and employee behaviour (failure 8) had mean recovery ratings of only 3.92 and 3.71 respectively. This amplifies the importance of providing the basics of service delivery well, as recovery from facility problems are particularly difficult. In addition, these findings provide evidence indicating the importance of employee training in the restaurant industry, as employee failures were difficult to effectively recover from as well. The mean recovery rating of all other failure types exceeded the midpoint on the 10-point scale.

The recovery findings provide information concerning the desirability of specific recovery strategies. For example, recoveries involving some form of compensation were rated most favourably. Compensation took the form of free food (recovery 1), discounts (recovery 2), and coupons (recovery 3). On a 10-point scale, these three recovery strategies had mean recovery ratings of 8.05, 7.75, and 7.00, respectively.

Several less effective recovery strategies were also identified. Based on recovery ratings, simply correcting a failure (recovery 6), apologizing (recovery 7), or doing nothing (recovery 8) seem to be less effective, as these recovery strategies had ratings of 5.14, 3.72, and 1.71 respectively.

As a result of this study and others like it that track service failure and recovery strategies, the categorization process reveals enlightening information about the particular industry's 'hierarchy of horrors' and its sometimes feeble, sometimes admirable, attempts to recover from its failures. Managing service firms is a highly complex task. Exercises like this make this point abundantly clear. (Adapted from Hoffman, Kelley and Rotalsky, 1995.)

Summary

The benefit of service failure and recovery analysis is that service managers can identify common failure situations, minimize their occurrence and train employees to recover from them when they do occur. The value associated with developing effective service recovery skills is clear. Two-thirds of lost customers do not defect to competitors due to poor product quality but due to the poor customer service they received when problems occurred.

Many of today's service firms are great as long as the service delivery system is operating smoothly. However, once kinks develop in the system, many firms are unprepared to face unhappy customers who are looking for solutions to their problems. As evidence, nearly half the responses to customer complaints reinforce customers' negative feelings towards a firm. Consequently, firms that truly excel in customer service equip employees with a set of recovery tools to repair the service encounter when failures occur and customer complaints are voiced.

Customer complaints should be viewed as opportunities to improve the service delivery system and to ensure that the customer is satisfied before the service encounter ends. Customers voice a complaint for a number of reasons, including the following: to have the problem resolved, to gain an emotional release from frustration, to regain some measure of control by influencing other people's evaluation of the source of the complaint, to solicit sympathy or test the consensus of the complaint, or to create an impression.

However, it's not the complainers who service firms should worry about, it's the people who leave without saying a word, who never intend on returning and who inform others, thereby generating negative word-of-mouth information. A number of reasons explain why many consumers do not complain. Most simply, customers of services often do not know whom to complain to and/or do not think complaining will do any good. Other reasons consumers fail to complain are that (1) consumer evaluation of services is highly subjective; (2) consumers tend to shift some of the blame to themselves for not clearly specifying to the service provider their exact needs; (3) since many services are technical and special-

ized, many consumers do not feel qualified to voice their complaints; and (4) due to the inseparability of services, consumers may feel that a complaint is too confrontational.

Service failures generally fall into one of four main categories: (1) employee responses to core service failures such as slow service, unavailable service and other core service failures; (2) employee responses to implicit/explicit customer requests such as special needs, customer preferences, customer error and disruptive others; (3) unprompted/unsolicited employee actions, which include level of attention, unusual actions, cultural norms, gestalt evaluations and employee actions under adverse conditions; and (4) problematic customers including drunkenness, verbal and physical abuse, breaking company policies and uncooperative customers.

Service recovery strategies are often industry-specific, such as the restaurant example provided in the chapter. However, in general, responses to service failures can be categorized as two types: (1) responses to service failures that are attributed to the firm, and (2) responses to service failures that are attributed to customer error. Successful tactics for recovery from failures attributed to the firm include acknowledging the problem, making the customer feel unique or special, apologizing when appropriate, explaining what happened and offering to compensate the customer. Successful responses to service failures attributed to customer error include acknowledging the problem, taking responsibility for the problem and assisting in solving the problem without embarrassing the customer. Successful service recovery efforts such as these play an important role in customer retention.

Discussion questions

1 Define and discuss the subclass failures associated with the implicit/explicit request failure category.

2 Discuss the following types of complaints: instrumental, non-instrumental, ostensive and reflexive.

3 What is the service recovery paradox? Provide an example based on your own personal experience.

4 Discuss the following types of failure outcomes: voice, exit and retaliation.

5 What are the pros and cons of complaining customers?

6 Give an overview of the steps, described in this chapter, necessary to track and monitor employee service failures and recovery efforts.

7 Discuss the problems and recovery strategies for e-services and face-to-face and compare the differences.

8 Consider an organization like Ray's Farm – a small organization that has no mechanisms for understanding customer complaints or handling difficult customers – and suggest how a small business should encourage feedback from their visitors.

Case link

See Case 13: Ray's Farm.

References and further reading

Akao, Y and Mazur, G. (2003) 'The leading edge in QFD: past, present and future', *International Journal of Quality and Reliability Management* 20 (1): 20–35.

Albrecht, K. and Zemke, R. (1985) *Service America*, Homewood, IL: Dow Jones-Irwin.

Alicke, M. D, Braun, J. C, Glor, J. E., Klotz, M. L., Magee, J., Sederhoim, H. and Siegel, R. (1992) 'Complaining behaviour in social interaction', *Personality and Social Psychology Bulletin* (June): 286.

Allen, P. (2007) 'Byline Our hotel staff are surly, the French admit', *Daily Telegraph* (London), 6 December.

Bitner, M. J, Zeithmal, V. and Parasuraman, A. (1990) 'Five imperatives for improving service quality', *Sloan Management Review* 31 (4): 236–245.

Blythe, J. (2008) *Consumer Behaviour*, London: Cengage Learning.

Bougie, R., Pieters, R. and Zeelenberg, M. (2003) 'Angry customers don't come back, they get back: the experience and behavioural implications of anger and dissatisfaction in services', *Journal of the Academy of Marketing Science*, 31 (4): 377–393.

Chebat, J.-C., Davidow, M. and Codjovi, I. (2005) 'Silent voices: why some dissatisfied conumers fail to complain', *Journal of Service Research* 6 (4) (May): 328–342.

Chung, B. and Hoffman, D. K (1998) 'Critical incidents', *Cornell Hotel and Restaruant Administration Quarterly* 39 (3): 66–71.

DeWitt, T. and Brady, M. K (2003) 'Rethinking service recovery strategies', *Journal of Service Research* 6 (2) (November): 193–207.

Downton, S. (2002) 'Measurements to Achieve Customer Focus', http://www.downtonconsulting.com/measurements_to_achieve_customer_focus.php, accessed 8 February 2008.

Dutta, K., Venkatesh, U. and Parsa, H. G (2007) 'Service failure and recovery strategies in the restaurant sector. An Indo-US comparative study', *International Journal of Contemporary Hospitality Management* 19 (5): 351–363.

Gilly, M. C, Stevenson, W. B and Yale, L. J (1991) 'Dynamics of complaint management in the service organization', *Journal of Consumer Affairs* 25 (2): 296.

Gonzalez Bosch, V. and Enriquez, F. T (2005) 'TQM and QFD: exploiting a customer complaint management system', *International Journal of Quality and Reliability Management* 22 (1): 30–37.

Harari, O. (1992) 'Thank heaven for complainers', *Management Review* 81 (1): 59–60.

Hayden, Wes, CEO Genesys (2005) 'The Call Center's Love Affair with Self-Service', www.tmcnet.com/usubmit/2005/jul/1165286.htm, accessed 14 January 2008.

Hoffman, K. D and Kelley, S. W. (2000) 'Perceived justice needs and recovery evaluation: a contingency approach', *European Journal of Marketing* 34: 418–432.

Hoffman, K. D, Kelley, S. W and Rotalsky, H. M (1995) 'Tracking serivice failures and employee recovery efforts', *Journal of Services Marketing* 9 (2): 49–61.

Hunt, H. K (1991) 'Consumer satisfaction, dissatisfaction and complaining behaviour', *Journal of Social Issues* 47 (1): 116.

Johnston, R. and Michel, S. (2008) 'Three outcomes of service recovery. Customer recovery, process recovery and employee recovery', *International Journal of Operations and Production Management* 28 (1): 79–99.

Lewis, B. R and Spyrakopoulos, S. (2001) 'Service failures and recovery in retail banking: national quality award', *International Journal of Bank Marketing* 19 (1): 37–47.

Lovelock, C. and Wirtz, J. (2004) *Services Marketing: People, Technology, Strategy*, 6th ed., Englewood Cliffs, NJ: Prentice Hall.

Parasuraman, A., Zeithaml, V. A and Berry, L. L (1994) 'Reassessment of expectations as a comparison standard in measuring service qualityi: implications for further research', *Journal of Marketing* 58 (1): 111–124.

Partow, D. (1993) 'Turn gripes into gold', *Home Office Computing* (September): 24.

Pujari, D. (2004) 'Self-service with a smile? Self-service technology (SST) encounters among Canadian business-to-business', *International Journal of Service Industry Management* 15 (2): 200–219.

Reid, R. D and Bojanic, D. C (2006) *Hospitality Marketing Management*, 4t ed., New Jersey: John Wiley & Sons.

Schelmetic, Tracey, Editorial Director CUSTOMER INTER@CTIONS Solutions (2005) 'The Call Center's Love Affair with Self-Service', www.tmcnet.com/usubmit/2005/jul/1165286.htm, accessed 14 January 2008.

Sheth, J. N and Mittal, B. (2004) *Consumer Behaviour: A Managerial Perspective*, 2nd ed., Thomson South Western: .

Stauss, B., Schmidt, M. and Schoeler, A. (2005) 'Customer frustration in loyalty programs', *International Journal of Service Industry Management* 16 (3): 229–252.

Vos, J. F. J., Huitema, G. B and de Lange-Ros, E. (2008) 'How organizations can learn from complaints', *TQM Journal* 20 (1): 8–1.

APPENDIX

Sample of Critical Incident Form

I. **Introduction/Purpose of Study**

Have you ever been at a restaurant and received poor service?

We are conducting a study on service mistakes or failures made by restaurants and how restaurants recover when a service failure occurs. Would you be willing to participate in this study?

II. **Think of a time when you had an experience at a restaurant where a mistake was made and the restaurant tried to correct that mistake but did a POOR job of recovering. Please describe the nature of this service failure.**

Where? _____

When? _____

What happened? _____

_____

_____

_____

What did the restaurant do to correct the failure?

_____

_____

_____

_____

On a scale of 1 to 10, 1 being a MINOR MISTAKE and 10 being a MAJOR MISTAKE, how would you rate the severity of the mistake?

Minor Mistake   Major Mistake

1   2   3   4   5   6   7   8   9   10

On a scale of 1 to 10, 1 being VERY POOR and 10 being a VERY GOOD, how would you rate the efforts of the restaurant regarding the correction of the mistake?

Very Poor   Very Good

1   2   3   4   5   6   7   8   9   10

Do you still patronize this restaurant?

_____ No, due to the service failure

_____ No, due to other reasons

_____ Yes

III. **Think of a time when you had an experience at a restaurant where a mistake was made and the restaurant tried to correct that mistake but did a GOOD job of recovering. Please describe the nature of this service failure.**

Where? _____

When? _____

What happened? _____

_____

_____

_____

What did the restaurant do to correct the failure?

_____

_____

_____

_____

On a scale of 1 to 10, 1 being a MINOR MISTAKE and 10 being a MAJOR MISTAKE, how would you rate the severity of the mistake?

Minor Mistake   Major Mistake

1	2	3	4	5	6	7	8	9	10

On a scale of 1 to 10, 1 being VERY POOR and 10 being VERY GOOD, how would you rate the efforts of the restaurant regarding the correction of the mistake?

Very Poor   Very Good

1	2	3	4	5	6	7	8	9	10

Do you still patronize this restaurant?

_____ No, due to the service failure

_____ No, due to other reasons

_____ Yes

IV. Demographics

Sex (Categorical choices)

Education (Categorical choices)

Age (Categorical choices)

Chapter 17

Putting the pieces together: Creating the seamless service firm

What is needed now is to surround these individuals with the system – a logically and tightly connected seamless set of interrelated parts that allows people to perform their jobs well.

(Benjamin Schneider and David E. Bowen, 1995)

Chapter objectives

The purpose of this chapter is to tie together the information presented in this book. In order to provide service excellence, the individual components of the firm must act in unison to create a 'seamless' organization. The firm will not act as one if the current culture of the organization is based on departmentalization and functionalism. Consequently, creating and supporting a customer-focused organizational culture is critical. Finally, by conducting a service audit, a seamless service culture is fostered, as personnel throughout the organization come to appreciate the challenges faced and the contributions made by everyone involved in the firm's final service delivery effort.

After reading this chapter, you should be able to:

- Compare and contrast the concept of seamlessness to departmentalization and functionalism.
- Appreciate the historical weakness of marketing in service firms.
- Explain the basic concepts of the three-tiered model of service firms.
- Explain what is meant by the firm's culture and discuss the four methods that facilitate cultural change.
- Discuss the basic components of a service audit.

Services in context
An extraordinary hospitality experience: The Katitche Point Great House

Tired of the same old vacations in the same old hotels? The Katitche Point Great House, strategically located on the island of Virgin Gorda in the British Virgin Islands (BVI), will put a definitive end to your vacation blues. In fact, as you stand on the panoramic horizon pool deck, the word 'blue' takes on an entirely new meaning. Go to http://www.katitchepoint.com and you'll see what we mean as the blue shades of pool water, the Caribbean and the skyline provide a servicescape beyond compare.

The British Virgin Islands are a paradise in and of themselves. Part of the Lesser Antilles, which boasts the most beautiful sailing waters in the world, the BVI is the world's playground for water recreation. The island of Virgin Gorda (Fat Virgin) is best known for the BVI's most stellar natural attraction, called 'The Baths'. The Baths, located on the southern side of Virgin Gorda, are the result of volcanic activity that took place thousands of years ago where huge granite boulders were strewn along Virgin Gorda's southern coastline. The boulders, which often lie upon one another, formed grottos and pools that are now a major tourist attraction for hikers, snorkellers and scuba divers. In contrast to the sandy beaches of the southern section, the northern half of Virgin Gorda is mountainous with peaks reaching nearly 1,400 feet above sea level. Located on a narrow strip of land between the best of what Virgin Gorda has to offer is the Katitche Point Great House.

The Katitche Point Great House is a compound of sorts, or more pleasantly described as a 'small holiday village'. The 'village' comfortably sleeps 8 to 10 people; it consists of a three-level, pyramid-shaped main house; four large bedroom suites, each complete with their own bathroom suite and private verandahs; and a large separate master bedroom suite complete with sitting room and a deep soaking tub that is built into the rocks next to a Koi pond. In all, the Katitche Point Great House is comprised of 22,000 square feet of spacious living space that offers unobstructed panoramic views of the Caribbean in all directions.

Built in 2000, Katitche Point has received many accolades. *Elle* magazine ranked the Katitche Point Great House as the 8th best 'deluxe holiday home around the globe'. *Vogue* magazine included Katitche Point in a special section of its magazine called 'Destination Dreamland' and referred to the property as 'a private paradise'. The United Kingdom's version of The Travel Channel featured Katitche Point in a 10-minute segment on its 'Cool Caribbean' series and called the Great House 'the most stunning villa they've ever seen'. *Barefoot Traveller* featured the Great House's Viking Kitchen and called Katitche Point 'the best that life has to offer'. These comments and many more like them serve as Katitche Point's primary promotional strategy, which is backed up by the website and reinforced by positive word-of-mouth testimonials from fortunate guests.

So, what is the price of this level of luxury? Given the villa's limited capacity and tremendous accommodations, a week's stay at the Katitche Point Great House is not inexpensive. Rates start at $17,500 per week for the full facility during the off-season and peak over the Christmas and New Year's season at $26,000 a week. For those who do not require the separate master bedroom suite, prices are reduced by $5,000 per week. A special honeymoon package is also offered for $6,600 per week based on availability. All rates include full maid service from 8 a.m. to 4 p.m., pool maintenance, laundry service and a gardener! Gourmet chef and masseuse services are also available upon request for additional fees. Although expensive, the Katitche Point Great House offers a once-in-a-lifetime experience for its guests who will never forget this unimaginable holiday destination.

Source: http://www.katitchepoint.com and http://www.b-v-i.com/baths.htm, accessed 11 June 2005 and the good fortune of personal experience.

Introduction

Creating a seamless service organization means providing services without interruption, confusion, or hassle to the customer (Keating and Harrington, 2003; Schneider and Bowen, 1995). Seamless service firms manage to simultaneously provide reliable, responsive, competent and empathetic services and have the facilities and resources necessary to get the job done. Seamlessness applies not only to the provision of services but also to service recovery efforts pertaining to core system failures, implicit/explicit customer requests and employee behaviour.

Seamlessness thrives on tightly connected interrelated parts within the service delivery system. Fictionalization and departmentalization kill seamlessness. For example, consider the following three memos sent to a young manager of a branch bank on the same day (Bateson, 1995):

From the marketing department:
We shortly will be launching a new advertising campaign based on the friendliness of our staff. This is in direct response to the increasingly competitive marketplace we face. Please ensure that your staff members deliver the promises we are making.

From the operations department:
As you are aware, we are facing an increasingly competitive marketplace and, as a result, our profits have come under pressure. It is crucial, therefore, that we minimize waste to keep our costs under control. From today, therefore, no recruitment whatsoever will be allowed.

From the human resources department:
Our staff members are becoming increasingly militant. This is due, in large part, to the availability of alternative employment with our new competitors. We currently are involved in a particularly delicate set of negotiations and would be grateful if you could minimize any disruptions at the local level.

These instructions from the three different departments obviously conflict with one another. To obey the operations department means no recruitment and, therefore, an increase in the workload of contact personnel. The increased workload will most likely be a hot topic during labour negotiations and could be disastrous for the human resources department. Finally, the increased workload, in all probability, will have a negative effect on staff morale. Given the inseparability of the service, the staff's low morale will be visible to customers and will negatively affect customer satisfaction levels.

If this particular branch bank is marketing-oriented, the manager will attempt to trade off the three sets of instructions, giving added weight to the marketing department's instructions. It should be stressed that, in service firms, it is nearly impossible to be totally marketing-oriented. Customers cannot be given everything they want because of the constraints imposed by the firm's service delivery system. For example, in a restaurant setting, every customer cannot be seated and served immediately upon arrival due to seating and available service (personnel) constraints.

If this branch is operations-oriented, added weight will be given to the operations department's set of instructions. The manager may relay marketing's request to the vice-president of operations and ask for clarification. The operations vice-president, in turn, may fire off an abusive memo to her counterpart in marketing. The memo may ask why marketing was sending memos directly to the branches at all and suggest that in the future, all other requests made by marketing should be cleared by operations.

Firms that continue to cling to functional and departmental mindsets are often besieged by internal conflict as departments compete against one another for resources instead of pulling together to provide exceptional service. Consider the marketing department. The marketing department has internal and external relationships that need to work together. For example, the marketing department needs to form good working relationships with the new product development department to ensure they are up to date on the new products and services that will be launched in the future. The marketing department also has to form a relationship with the finance department as they will not be able to communicate details of new service delivery mechanisms to the sales force without the money to pay for the international communications. Similarly the marketing department has external relations. These include the creative agency who will design the advertisements and the media buyers who will buy airtime on the television. Both are required so that the marketing department can promote the new service delivery programmes that the organization is going to launch. All these relationships need to be formed, co-ordinated, implemented across departments within the organization and across companies outside the organization (Mentzer et al., 2001). Therefore, the primary efforts of the service firm should focus on the service delivery functions both internal and external to the organizations and on the personnel providing customer services.

Different cultures within different functional departments sometimes cause tension. However, service orientated organizations will have goals, objectives, planning horizons, departmental structure, people-management systems that are specific to the single department but ones that fit into the organization as a whole. For example, marketing tends to have a longer planning horizon, is less rigidly and hierarchically organized and tends to reward innovation and creativity compared with its operations counterparts. Nevertheless, objectives for the marketing department, or the finance department, are born out of the corporate objectives. Cross-functional co-operation, therefore, should take place as all departments are striving to achieve the same corporate objectives.

In comparison with goods-producing firms, turf wars among departments are more prevalent in service firms due to lack of inventories. Inventories, which provide a buffer between marketing and operations in goods-producing firms, are for the most part nonexistent in service firms. In a service firm, production and consumption often occur simultaneously in a real-time experience and it is the inseparability that encourages harmony across departments.

The historical weakness of marketing in service firms

Service firms often find themselves in a three-cornered fight among marketing, operations and human resources (see Figure 17.1.) Somehow, marketing always seems to lose this fight since marketers tend to have less influence in service companies than in goods companies (Bateson, 1995).

At this point, it is necessary to understand the differences among marketing orientation, the marketing function and the marketing department. Marketing orientation means that a firm or organization plans its operations according to market needs. See Global Services in Action which considers the growing need to include ethnic groups and minorities within advertisement to accommodate the changing needs of the consumer. The objectives of the firm are to satisfy customer needs rather than merely to use production facilities or raw materials (Lovelock and Wirtz, 2007). Marketing orientation is clearly an attitude that puts the customer's needs first in any trade-off. Firms do not necessarily have a formal marketing department in order to have a marketing orientation.

Marketing functions in a firm include tasks such as the design of the product, pricing and promotion. Decisions in these areas are made in order for the organization to operate, but they need not necessarily be made by people with marketing titles nor by individuals in a formal marketing department – the department that traditionally works on marketing functions in the company.

In a typical goods company, the distinctions among marketing orientation, marketing functions and marketing department are not necessary. They are, however, necessary in service firms, where a formal marketing department may not exist. Because the service product is an interactive process, it may be more appropriate to leave the different functional decisions to different departments.

The variety of relationships between marketing and other functions within the organization can be illustrated by the customization/customer contact matrix depicted in Figure 17.2. One axis of the matrix relates directly to the degree of contact the firm has with its customers. The higher the level of customer contact, the higher the level of inefficiency because of the uncertainty introduced by customers. This idea is based largely on the concept of inseparability and the participation of consumers in the service delivery

marketing orientation A firm's view towards planning its operations according to market needs.

marketing functions Tasks such as the design of a product, its pricing and its promotion.

marketing department The formal department in an organization that works on the marketing functions of the company.

customization/customer contact matrix A table that illustrates the variety of relationships between marketing and other functions within the organization.

Figure 17.1

The three-cornered fight for control

Source John E. G. Bateson, *Managing Services Marketing: Text and Readings*, 3rd ed. (Fort Worth, TX: The Dryden Press, 1995).

process. The second axis relates to the amount of customization of the service available to consumers. Once again, we would expect the 'low' state to be preferable for efficiency purposes as it would allow the service delivery system to operate as a production line free from outside influences. A variety of businesses are introduced into the cells to illustrate how the matrix is used.

For example, a travel agency can operate in a number of cells simultaneously. Booking an airline ticket by telephone for a business traveller fits into the low/low cell. But the same travel agency could just as well operate in a different cell if it also maintained a retail operation. From within the retail operation, both high and low customization is possible, depending on whether the customer is a business traveller wanting a ticket or a vacationer planning a multi-stop European trip.

Global services in action
Ethnic marketing – One size *does not* fit all

Advertising plays a significant role in providing exciting lifestyle groups that audiences can join if they wish. And marketers are keen to provide highly targeted lifestyle advertisements aimed at specific cultural segments because all consumers are not homogeneous. Contemporary consumers, however, happily move in and out of many different lifestyle groups on a daily basis. And because consumers 'culture swap' and do not necessarily conform to the behaviours shown in the advertising message (Jamal, 2003) advertising to cultural segments is becoming rather difficult. Cultural segments include nationality, gender, family, social class, ethnic group, religion and so on (Usunier and Lee, 2005). Of all the different cultural segments that advertisers try to target, it is the ethnic group that they are finding the most difficult to connect with.

In the UK 9 per cent of the population are from ethnic groups (Cozens, 2003) and marketers want to appeal to this segment because it represents approximately 5 million people.

There have been some token gestures which include participants from ethic minorities in television advertisements. These include Samuel L. Jackson communicating through the virtues of Barclays Bank or the AA Insurance advertisement which shows a young Asian couple arguing about which insurance company to choose. However, the advertisers are not addressing the true nature of the multicultural environment which exists in the UK.

The following list summarizes these observations.

1 Minority ethnic segments are a significant opportunity for service organizations, brands and manufacturers alike.

2 Some advertising fails as it merely places ethnic actors in advertising roles which could easily have been filled by a white UK-born person.

3 There are few ethnic actors who take the lead role in advertising; however, there has been an increase in ethnic actors in secondary or 'crowd-scene' roles.

4 Using minority actors in advertising places the services brand 'between the devil and the deep blue sea'. Service brands that include minority actors in lead roles have embraced the multicultural diverse community – but there is a fear about the role being scrutinized by both the minority and the majority communities.

5 British culture has positive and negative effects on ethnic cultures. Therefore mainstream advertising may seem

▶

intrusive on the 'cultural values' of minority groups.

6 Many cultures require, even demand, service brands to understand and adapt to their needs and desires.

7 Media in the UK are diverse and many cultures are exposed to mainstream advertisements through Channel 4. However, there are many other TV and radio channels and press that are available for specific ethnic groups. These channels can provide big brands with opportunities to be needs specific.

(Fletcher, 2003; Kenyon, 2008; Class discussion guide, Leeds Metropolitan University)

Advertising for culturally diverse segments is an issue all marketers the world over will need to address. There is a large market out there – but marketers must take care and not offend the balance between the culture of the 'home' country and the culture of the multi-cultural groups.

Sources: D. Fletcher (2003) 'Reaching the Ethnic Consumer', *Admap Magazine*, March, Issue 437, pp. 1–17. C. Cozens (2003) 'Advertisers failing to connect with ethnic groups', *Guardian*, 3 March. A. Jamal (2003) 'Marketing in a multicultural world. The interplay of marketing, ethnicity and consumption', *European Journal of Marketing* 37 (11/12): 1599–1620. J.-C. Usunier and J. Lee (2005) *Marketing Across Cultures*, 4th ed. (London: Prentice Hall).

From an operations perspective, the ideal cell is the low/low cell. In this cell, the degree of customization is minimized so that large parts of the organization can be isolated and run like any other manufacturing plant (Duray, 2002; Chase, 1978). In addition, the level of customization is also minimized so that the operating system is focused on a limited range of output and its efficiency increased. A move into this cell, however, can have major implications for marketing. Customers may be seeking contact and customization and be willing to pay a premium for them.

A top-quality French restaurant might fit into the high/high cell. Compared with McDonald's, this is a different business with a different formula (but, interestingly, the target segment may be the same person on a very different occasion). The loss of efficiency implied by the high/high cell is compensated for by the price that can be charged. It is of course the

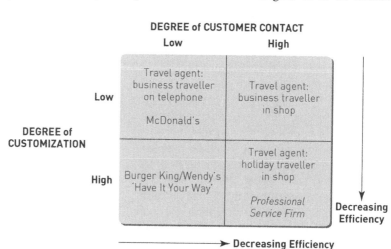

Figure 17.2

The customization/ customer contact matrix

Source Bateson/Hoffman, *Managing Services Marketing*, 4th ed. © 1999 South-Western, a part of Cengage Learning, Inc. Reproduced by permission. www.cengage.com/ permissions.

consumer who will drive how an organization moves between highly customized service orientations to mass/self-service orientation. In the fashion world, mass customization is taking off where the fashion designer and the customer become co-designers. The customer chooses from a range of features on a jacket such as fabrics, buttons and pocket or lapel styles. The fashion designer charges a high premium for the service, but the consumer is willing to pay extra money because they have enjoyed the experience and have a unique garment (Fiore et al., 2004).

The importance of the matrix and this discussion is to show how different cells suggest alternative roles and places for the marketing departments of firms operating within them. Two contrasting examples are the provision of legal services by a traditional law firm and by a franchised firm such as Hyatt Legal Services.

Operationally, the traditional firm will fit into the high/high cell in the matrix. The firm's attorneys will be in intensive contact with clients and will customize each service to meet the needs of each individual client. Except for routine cases, there will be little opportunity for economies of scale in this type of legal firm.

From a marketing point of view, the service product in the high/high cell often is created in the client's offices, away from the home firm of the solicitor. In such situations, it is clear that a central marketing department has little influence over the final product and that most of the marketing needs to be delegated to the field offices, if not to the individual attorneys themselves. The selling function is done by consultants or professionals, so that, too, must be delegated.

The alternative is a firm such as Hyatt Legal Services. This firm represents a clear attempt to move the operating system away from the inefficiency of the high/high cell towards the low/low or, at least, the high contact/low customization cell. By reducing the types of cases handled, operations can be simplified and economies of scale generated. These economies, in turn, can be passed on to the customer through lower fees.

The marketing implications of moving the operation from a high/high cell to a more standardized outcome are relatively straightforward. The service is branded in order to add value for the consumer in a market that traditionally is not heavily branded. The firm depends on systematization and, from an operations point of view, implies centralization. We therefore would expect to find a strong centralized marketing department as well. Clearly, many service firms do not operate in the low/low cell of the matrix, even though they may wish to do so. For many service firms, therefore, the traditional combination of marketing functions in a marketing department breaks down. The result is that there is no strong marketing group to drive a marketing orientation in

Managers working together.

the organization. The weakness of the marketing function is compounded by the strength of the operations group and the linkages between them.

Case link
Examine the customization/ customer contact matrix in Case 14: The Rockwool Group.

Moving beyond departmentalization and functionalization: The three-tiered model of service firms

three-tiered model
A view of service organizations that reconfigures traditional departmental functions into a customer tier, a boundary tier and a coordination tier.

Seamless service is based on a three-tiered model of the service organization (see Figure 17.3) (Schneider and Bowen, 1995). Traditionally, organizations are sliced by functions such as marketing, human resources and operations management. In contrast, the three-tiered model consists of a customer tier, a boundary tier and a coordination tier. Success is based on the effective management and integration of the three tiers.

The customer tier

customer tier The tier in the three-tiered model that focuses on customer expectations, needs and competencies.

As we have discussed throughout this book, attracting and retaining customers is the lifeblood of every service organization. Without customers, the service firm has no reason to exist. The customer tier focuses on customer expectations, needs and competencies. To provide seamless service, management must have a deep understanding of each of these areas from the customer's perspective (see Figure 17.4).

Figure 17.3

The three-tiered services model

Source Benjamin Schneider and David E. Bowen, *Winning the Service Game* (Boston: Harvard Business School Press, 1995), p.244. Copyright © 1990 by the President and Fellows of Harvard College.

Coordination tier
- Cross-functional, service logic
- Management espouses service values
- Service-focused routines and behaviours
- Service coordination team
- Employee involvement

Service Quality Culture
- A passion for service

Boundary tier
- Recruitment/selection
- Training/socialization
- Reward systems
- Servicescapes
- Operations management
- Marketing
- Human resources management

Customer tier
- Customer expectations
- Customer needs
- Customer talents
- Market segment focus
- Measurement systems with feedback

Expectations have been discussed throughout this book and are an integral component in developing customer satisfaction evaluations. As firms have realized the importance of customers, experts believe that businesses now have a fairly good understanding of their customers' expectations but not necessarily of their customers' needs and competencies. At a minimum, service firms must meet customer expectations in order to provide customers with what they want, when they want it and where they want it so that the firms can strategically differentiate themselves from competitors and stay in the service game.

Needs are distinguished from expectations in that customers are generally aware of their expectations but are often unaware of what they need. Chapter 10 provided many examples of products that met with great success such as personal computers and mobile phones, despite early customer research indicating that customers did not feel a need for these products. Mr Yap of Singapore Airlines believes that putting the 'wow factor' into service delivery ensures that customers receive a service over and above what they expected or needed (Wirtz and Johnston, 2003).

The 'wow factors' are created by listening carefully to both their customers (from all around the world) and front-line staff, understanding the ever-changing lifestyles of global customers and monitoring both *compliments* and *complaints*. By constantly researching and analysing these elements, Singapore Airlines can anticipate the needs of their customers. One of their innovative ideas is to enable travellers to use broadband facilities in the air. Business travellers can check their e-mails and tourists can decide which art galleries, exhibitions or restaurants they would like to visit when they touch down.

Examining and understanding customer needs is the foundation for building a competitive strategy that differentiates the firm from its competitors and for providing service excellence.

expectations Consumer expectations pertaining to the service delivery process and final outcome.

needs Security, esteem, and justice; often unrecognized as needs by customers themselves.

---

1 **Bring 'em back alive....** Ask customers what they want and give it to them again and again.

2 **Systems, not smiles....** Saying please and thank you doesn't ensure you'll do the job right the first time, every time. Only systems guarantee that.

3 **Under promise, over deliver....** Customers expect you to keep your word. Exceed it.

4 **When the customer asks, the answer is always yes....**

5 **Fire your inspectors and customer relations department....** Every employee who deals with clients must have the authority to handle complaints.

6 **No complaints, something's wrong....** Encourage your customers to tell you what you're doing wrong.

7 **Measure everything....** Baseball teams do it. Football teams do it. Golfers do it. You should too.

8 **Salaries are unfair....** Pay people like partners.

9 **Your mother was right....** Show people respect. Be polite. It works.

10 **Japanese them....** Learn how the best really do it; make their systems your own. Then improve them.

Figure 17.4

The Ten Commandments of customer service

Source Paul B. Brown and Carl Sewall, *Customers for Life* (New York: Bantam, 1998).

competencies The contributions customers bring to the service production process.

Competencies are the contributions customers bring to the service production process. Service firms that excel look beyond their employees as their only human resources. Throughout much of this book, we have discussed the consumer's involvement in the service delivery process. The customer influences the type and length of demand and often is a major determinant in the success or failure of the final outcome. Consequently, appealing to the 'best customers' can be a source of competitive advantage.

For example, Tesco has a loyalty scheme – just like many service organizations. Tesco do not see their card as a loyalty card – they promote it as the 'biggest customer Thank You card' for their customers (Rowley, 2007). Tesco ClubCard customers can collect points to receive discounted products or lifestyle experiences. Clearly the more the customers spend the more points they get. All customers get the quarterly magazine – the highest lifestyle magazine in circulation across Europe – which contains discounts, vouchers for food, dry cleaning or wines (Rowley, 2007). Additionally, their Tesco Freetime service enables customers to spend their Tesco's points at Alton Towers or Warwick Castle. The Tesco Freetime service is targeted at high-spending customers. And, with their customer database growing all the time, maybe more Tesco's shoppers will save enough points to spend their Freetime courtesy of Tesco.

The boundary tier

boundary tier The tier in the three-tiered model that concerns itself with the individuals who interact with the customers – the boundary spanners.

While the customer tier deals with customer expectations, needs and competencies, the boundary tier concerns itself with the individuals who interact with the customers – the boundary spanners. The boundary tier is where the customer meets the organization and where the critical incidents or 'touch points' occur (see B2B services in Action). Service personnel in the boundary tier must be more flexible, communicative, able to deal with stress and willing to take initiative than their manufacturing counterparts. To the customer, personnel in the boundary tier *are* the organization and occupy a two-way communication role – from the organization to the customer, and from the customer back to the organization.

The key to successfully navigating the boundary tier is to avoid the 'human resources trap'. This trap makes the fatal flaw in judgement of placing the full burden of 'moments of truth' often known as 'touch points' upon boundary-spanning personnel. The firm's non-personnel services, such as the physical facility, the accuracy and timeliness of providing the bill and all the support staff who enable the boundary personnel to perform their jobs, must be in place and working together in order for the firm to provide seamless service. Ultimately, boundary personnel represent the face of the organization and they can deliver exceptional service if they are trained and empowered and the delivery system supports their efforts.

coordination tier The tier in the three-tiered model that coordinates activities that help integrate the customer and boundary tiers.

The coordination tier

The coordination tier is the responsibility of upper management and involves coordinating the activities that help integrate the customer and boundary tiers (see Figure 17.5). Management's most important concerns pertain to

B2B services in action
'Moments of truth' within B2B relationships

IBM are leaders in providing business solutions for governments, banks, insurance companies, hospitals, event organizers – you name it, IBM are probably somewhere in the background. Their business-to-business (B2B) expertise enables organizations to streamline research and development, process applications or project manage labour-intensive tasks. IBM are not just there to provide software for organizations – they seek to build strong relationships with customers such as Deutsche Bank, London's car Congestion Charging scheme and the UK's Ministry of Defence. The relationships that IBM build with their customers enable them to feel proud of their customer service – especially at each 'touch point' or 'moment of truth'. Business-to-business companies like IBM care about service and each time their business customers contact them use the following guidelines:

1 Give their customer's authority.

2 Engage in customer dialog.

3 Share and develop solutions together.

4 Improve their own staff performance.

5 Become a better customer-focused organization.

(Adapted from Heffernan and Lavalle, (2007: 38)

IBM realize that the 'touch points' are very important. 'Touch points', often known as 'Moments of truth', can be with service personnel at a High Street branch, a government officer via the web or IT staff in a hospital call centre. Whoever the business customer is and wherever they may be located is irrelevant because every time a business customer encounters IBM their expertise, prompt behaviour and delivery promises are 'exposed'. The following channels are points where 'touch points' can occur:

- Branch
- Phone
- Web
- SMS devices
- Kiosk/ATM
- Event
- Direct sales force
- Distribution partners.

Just as individual customers rate organizations based on 'wait time', business-to-business customers also rate their relationship with organizations such as IBM on 'wait-time'. 'Touch points' with suppliers are also rated on consistent behaviour, convenience and availability. For example, if the IT staff at the hospital call centre had a malfunction in their online appointment system they would telephone a customer service representative from the organization that installed their computer network. During the telephone call, they would rate the 'moment of truth'. The rating would be based on whether the customer service representative answered the telephone quickly enough, whether a solution to the computer system was established and the online appointment system was 'live' within minutes of the initial call. The 'touch points' are just one element of the relationship that business-to-business organizations have with one another. However, because they are so emotional and take place in 'real time' they have a very strong influence over a relationship; therefore, the interactions should be monitored carefully and consistently.

Sources: R. Heffernan and S. LaValle (2007) 'Emotional Interactions: the frontier of the customer-focused enterprise', *Strategy & Leadership* 35 (3): 38–49.
www.ibm.com.

(1) defining a target market and developing a strategy for effectively attracting this market; (2) ensuring that the boundary tier has the support necessary to meet the expectations and needs of the customer tier; and (3) ensuring that the expectations and needs of boundary-tier personnel are also being met.

The primary challenge of the coordination tier is to get the various departments within the organization to work with one common goal in mind – serving the customer. Before attempting to integrate the various departments of the firm, it is important to understand that each department is driven by its own internal logic – implicit and explicit principles that drive organizational performance (Kingman-Burndage, George and Bowen, 1995). Each department's logic is internally focused on departmental needs and creates seams in the service delivery process. For example, consider the logic behind the following functions: operations management, marketing, and human resources.

Operations logic is driven by the goal of reducing or containing costs through mass production or the use of advanced technologies. Operations and marketing are often in conflict with each other, which creates seams in service delivery. While marketing is concerned with identifying and understanding customer needs and providing goods and services that meet those needs, operations is concerned with how these products and services will be produced and delivered. In essence, marketing is concerned with the management of demand, while operations are concerned with the management of supply. Marketing attempts to focus on meeting demand in the most effective manner in terms of product form, location, price and promotions, while operations is primarily concerned with

internal logic Implicit and explicit principles of individual departments that drive organizational performance.

operations logic The reasoning that stresses cost containment/ reduction through mass production.

Figure 17.5

Southwest Airlines' eleven primary attitudes

Source Kevin Freiberg and Jackie Freiberg, *Nuts! Southwest Airlines' Crazy Recipe for Business and Personal Success* (Austin, TX: Bard Press, 1996).

We are not an airline with great customer service. We are a great customer service organization that happens to be in the airline business.

Colleen Barrett, Southwest
Airlines executive

1   Employees are number one. The way you treat your employees is the way they will treat your customer.

2   Think small to grow big.

3   Manage in the good times for the bad times.

4   Irreverence is okay.

5   It's okay to be yourself.

6   Have fun at work.

7   Take the competition seriously, but not yourself.

8   It's difficult to change someone's attitude, so hire for attitude and train for skill.

9   Think of the company as a service organization that happens to be in the airline business.

10   Do whatever it takes.

11   Always practice the Golden Rule, internally and externally.

meeting demand in the most cost-effective manner. Typical goals of operations management and marketing concerns regarding these goals are displayed in Table 17.1.

The major challenge for operations in a service setting is the involvement of customers in the production process. Compared with raw materials in a pure manufacturing setting, customers are unpredictable and decrease the efficiency of the delivery system. Operations would like to remove the customer from the production process as much as possible, while marketing promotes the importance of the customer in the production process. Consequently, operations and marketing must establish a point of equilibrium between the variety and depth

Operational issues	Typical operation goals	Common marketing concerns
Productivity improvement	Reduce unit cost of production	Strategies may cause decline in service quality
Make-versus-buy decisions	Trade off control against comparative advantage and cost savings	'Make' decisions may result in lower quality and lack of market coverage; 'buy' decisions may transfer control to unresponsive suppliers and hurt the firm's image
Facilities location	Reduce costs; provide convenient access for suppliers and employees	Customers may find location unattractive and inaccessible
Standardization	Keep costs low and quality consistent; simplify operations tasks; recruit low-cost employees	Consumers may seek variety, prefer customization to match segmented needs
Batch-versus-unit processing	Seek economies of scale, consistency, efficient use of capacity	Customers may be forced to wait, feel 'one of crowd', be turned off by other customers
Facilities layout and design	Control costs; improve efficiency by ensuring proximity of operationally related tasks; enhance safety and security	Customers may be confused, shunted around unnecessarily, find facility unattractive and inconvenient
Job design	Minimize error, waste, and fraud; make efficient use of technology; simplify tasks for standardization	Operationally oriented employees with narrow roles may be unresponsive to customer needs

Table 17.1

Operations and marketing perspectives on operational issues

Source © 1989 by Christopher H. Lovelock. Reprinted with permission from Christopher H. Lovelock. Christopher H. Lovelock, 'Managing Interaction Between Operations and Marketing and Their Impact on Customers', in Bowen et al. (eds) *Service Management Effectiveness* (San Francisco: Jossey Bass, 1990), p. 362.

▶

Learning curves	Apply experience to reduce time and costs per unit of output	Faster service is not necessarily better service; cost saving may not be passed on as lower prices
Management of capacity	Keep costs down by avoiding wasteful under-utilization of resources	Service may be unavailable when needed; quality may be compromised during high-demand periods
Quality control	Ensure that service execution conforms to predefined standards	Operational definitions of quality may not reflect customer needs, preferences
Management of queues	Optimize use of available capacity by planning for average throughput; maintain customer order, discipline	Customers may be bored and frustrated during wait, see firm as unresponsive

of products that marketing would like to offer and the cost effectiveness of meeting that demand through efficient operations.

While operations management is internally focused, marketing is externally focused on meeting the expectations and needs of consumers. Ideally, the marketing logic is to provide customers with options that better enable the service offering to meet individual consumer needs. Although ideal for customers, providing numerous options leads to serious cost inefficiencies in a firm's operations.

In addition to often being in conflict with operations, marketing may also find itself in conflict with human resources, creating additional seams in service delivery. For example, marketing would like to staff all personnel positions with individuals who, in addition to being technically competent, possess strong interpersonal skills that enable the organization to better communicate with its customers. The marketing department would argue that hiring personnel who have well developed interpersonal skills in addition to being technically competent is a bonus. In turn, human resources would argue that obtaining and keeping highly trained and personable personnel is much more expensive than hiring people who simply adequately perform their roles in the organization. Furthermore, human resources will point out that certain market segments can be served by personnel who are simply civil with customers and who perform their duties adequately. This point is valid as the customers may not want a Subway's worker to engage them in lengthy conversations about the weather, community happenings, family matters, and so on, and would prefer a civil employee simply to take the order and deliver the food in a speedy manner. Additionally, the food is likely to be less expensive when provided by adequate, as opposed to superior, personnel because of the savings in labour

marketing logic The reasoning that stresses providing customers with options that better enable the service offering to meet individual needs.

costs. The important element here is to ensure that the type of service delivered is right for the circumstances in which the customer and service personnel meet.

Human resources logic is to recruit personnel and to develop training that enhances the performance of existing personnel. In the service encounter, operations, marketing and human resources are inextricably linked. Figure 17.6 depicts the link between operations and human resources. This figure, which compares the degree of customer contact with production efficiency, reveals that the perfect service employee does not exist. Characteristics of the 'right employee' depend on the characteristics of the particular job in question. Some employees will need to be people-oriented, while others will need to be more task-oriented to process 'things' instead of 'people.'

human resources logic
The reasoning that stresses recruiting personnel and developing training to enhance the performance of existing personnel.

The importance of service firm personnel as they interact with customers throughout the service delivery process highlights the link between human resources and marketing. In services, human resources are the only source of quality control. Consequently, the hiring, training and reward structures developed by human resources will ultimately play a major role in how employees interact with the firm's customers.

Despite the opportunity to make major contributions to the firm's overall service effort, human resources departments are often stuck in their own production orientation and have difficulty getting their own acts together, let alone helping the organization provide superior service. Human resources production-oriented activities include mistakes such as using the same employee evaluation forms for everyone in the firm even though the jobs may be very different, conducting canned employee training programmes that never change from year to year, and using generic employee selection

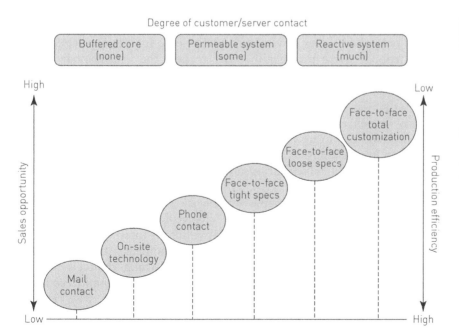

Figure 17.6

Link between operations and human resources

Source R. B. Chase and W. E. Youngdahl, 'Service by Design', *Design Management Journal* 9 (Winter 1992): 12. Adapted from R. B. Chase and N. J. Aquilano, *Production and Operations Management: A Lifecycle Approach* (Homewood, IL: Irwin, 1991).

procedures for a variety of jobs that actually require different skill sets. In contrast, service-oriented human resources programmes would be co-designed and co-taught with relevant managers, and evaluation forms would be thought of as coaching and evaluating devices rather than as rating forms used solely for compensation decisions. Overall, the service-oriented human resources department would work much more closely with its customers – the firm's employees – and form an ongoing, interactive, long-term relationship in pursuit of supporting those who serve the firm's final consumers.

Building the service logic through cultural change

The culture of a brand needs to be managed throughout the organization – particularly where service personnel are involved. Not only are they the 'face of the organization', they represent the brand in a physical form. Prêt a Manger enable their staff to adapt to the many different service encounters that they experience each and every day. The meeting, greeting and servicing process, enacted by personnel, is one of the scenarios that join the organization, its brand image and its culture together. Many organizations have a very prescriptive operating manual that advises staff when to look at a customer, how to greet them and even how close to stand to the customer. But CEO Andrew Rolfe is clear what he wants from his staff by stating 'greet the customers when they arrive; look them in the eye when you put the money in their hand; make sure you say something when they leave; but more than anything else, *be yourself*' (Smith and Wheeler, 2002: 84). This shows that Prêt a Manger trust their staff to 'belong' to the brand culture which they convey through staff training.

This type of customer service and service logic stitches the departmental and functional seams together in order to help the firm provide flawless service. However, before this can happen, the firm's organizational culture must be customer-focused (see B2B Services in Action). The firm's culture reflects the shared values and beliefs that drive the organization – the formally written, the unwritten, and the actual occurrences that help employees understand the norms for behaviour in the organization. In short, organizational culture establishes the 'dos and don'ts' of employee behaviour and provides the basis on which various employee behaviours can coalesce (Mosley, 2007).

Figure 17.7 presents a simple framework for considering the options available when implementing cultural change in the service organization (Bateson, 1995). The figure suggests that culture is internally linked to and partly an outcome of three organizational components: structure, systems and people. Structure relates to the formal reporting channels normally represented in an organizational chart (such as front-line employees reporting to middle managers, who report to regional managers, who report to national managers, who report to the chief executive officer).

culture The shared values and beliefs that drive an organization.

structure The formal reporting hierarchy normally represented in an organizational chart.

The systems component of the framework refers to the people-management systems utilized for control, evaluation, promotion and recognition. Evaluation and promotion systems include both formal and informal components. For example, management by objectives would be a formal component, while 'What do I really have to do around here to get noticed?' would be an informal part of the system. Recognition systems focus on formal and informal rewards as well, ranging from formal rewards such as company trips, to informal 'pats on the back' such as lunch with the boss.

The other two major components of the culture framework are the people who work in the organization and the firm's current culture. Creating a more customer-focused organization can be accomplished by altering any one of the four components: structure, systems, people and culture, individually or together. Even online organizations need to be customer-focused and work together within the overall brand. Remote services are often located far away from the hub of the Head Office and the words of wisdom of the Chief Executive may not be heard. However, organizations must realize the importance of all additional services and personnel working together to provide a seamless service despite being in different buildings or different countries. E-Services in Action provides an outline of online retailers who also audit the performance of their service and compare it to the service provided through their bricks and mortar outlets. It is, therefore, important to compare the service delivered to customers and suppliers, through all channels, whether face-to-face, via telephone or internet to ensure that all elements of the service encounter are adhering to the brand's values.

systems People-management systems of control, evaluation, promotion and recognition.

Changing culture through structure

The organization's culture is a function of its structure. Changing culture through structure, however, is a slow process because in many instances, it takes years to successfully implement anorganizational change in structure. In the effort to create a more customer-focused organization, two approaches to changing the culture through structure have been tried: (1) utilizing the marketing department as a change agent; and (2) restructuring the firm around the servuction system model.

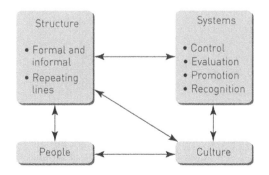

Figure 17.7

Cultural framework

Source John E. G. Bateson, *Managing Services Marketing: Text and Readings* (Fort Worth, TX: The Dryden Press, 1995).

Marketing department as change agents. Marketing departments can be created in order to simply change the current orientation of the firm by creating a customer advocate within the organization. There is a real danger

---

E-services in action
Auditing the online retailer

Sixty-two online retailers were audited by Talisma in the UK Online Retail Customer Service Audit. The retailers included Amazon, Early Learning Centre, Games Station, Harrods JJB Sports and Top Shop. Talisman's findings showed that:

- Although 92% of the online retailers surveyed responded to phone queries within 30 seconds, only 2% were able to communicate with personalized content – by referring to caller ID and customer profile.
- Only 42% of the online retailers answered e-mails within 24 hours.
- There is a lack of self-help tools for visitors.
- Only one online retailer provided the option of an online chat.
- The majority of online retailers audited did not have a unified customer interaction history.

The report containing these findings does not provide pleasant reading for the online retailers, especially as there are over 37 million internet users in the UK. Since the first book was sold by WH Smiths in 1995, via a secure online connection, online retailing has increased at an unbelievable rate. The problem with this, as online retailers will admit, is that it is almost impossible to keep pace with new technology, fraud and the demand. Therefore, online retailers are not able to provide quality customer service at all points of contact. Following the customer service audit, Talisma gave the following recommendations:

- Significantly reduce the time for an agent to execute a customer's service or support request.
- Improve agents' ability to be effective and provide a satisfying customer experience.
- Allow continuous system modifications to accommodate new products without disrupting operations.
- Support the multi-channel delivery of customer service functions – phone, e-mail, online chat and SMS.
- Take advantage of existing investments in contact centre and customer relationship management (CRM) infrastructure.

Online retailers are not able to provide quality customer service at all points of contact.

in this approach, however. Once the marketing department has been created, other departments may quickly transfer the complete responsibility for customer satisfaction to the marketing department, which in turn can cause upset and conflict (Lovelock et al., 1981). However, customer-focused, market-led organizations realize that staff from different departments within the organization should work together to make profitable and collaborative teams (Migliarese and Verteramo, 2005). When all staff understand their organization's mission statement and objectives they realize that all staff are working towards the same goals.

Whilst this seems simple, organizations often find it difficult to understand how each department functions on a day-to-day basis. Consider again the logic of the operations and the marketing departments. Operations departments, by their very nature, tend to be cost-driven. Their focus is on evaluating the operation to find costs to save and procedures to simplify. This outlook tends to have a short-term horizon. Marketing, by comparison, is looking for product enhancements in order to create a competitive advantage. The creation of such an advantage is not something that firms can expect to achieve in the short term.

The coordination of conflicting departments such as marketing and operations often requires the use of unconventional management techniques. To mesh the logic of the different groups and to allow them to understand one another, a number of strategies have been suggested by organizational behaviour theory. Inter-functional task forces are a classic way of forcing individuals with diverse viewpoints to work together and to develop a better understanding of one another's perspectives. In the same way, Inter-functional transfers can create informal networks of individuals from different departments who understand and trust one another.

> **Inter-functional task force** Problem-solving group in which individuals with diverse viewpoints work together and develop a better understanding of one another's perspectives.

For example, operations managers who are promoted to run a marketing department will face initial problems. Their orientation is towards operations, but their new roles require a marketing perspective. If such a transfer can be achieved successfully, the result is usually a general manager who makes rational and clear trade-offs between operations and marketing. Moreover, it also creates a marketing person who has direct contacts in the operations group and who can overcome many of the traditional barriers to change.

> **Inter-functional transfers** Moving, via promotion or transfer, an employee from one organizational department to another to foster informal networks among departments.

Once the organization has achieved a strong customer orientation, the marketing department can shrink. For example, in the early 1980s, many professional service firms created marketing departments in this way. The departments focused on advertising but also on research and customer-satisfaction surveys. The result was a shift in the culture of the firm and a recognition of the importance of the customer's needs and expectations.

Restructuring around the servuction model. A number of service firms have explicitly or implicitly restructured around the servuction model. For example, one major airline has all departments that have direct customer contact report to the head of marketing. Only engineering and the flight crew (pilots) report to the head of operations. Combining all customer-contact departments with the marketing group has reversed the arguments from 'It will cost too much; it is inefficient', to 'The customer needs this; how can we make it happen?'

Changing culture through systems

The firm's culture is also a function of the systems put into place that control, evaluate, promote and recognize the firm's personnel. A number of approaches have been used to change culture through these systems. Some firms, for example, have started to give bonuses to managers at all levels based upon the firm's customer satisfaction scores. The firm's overall research effort can be tailored to measure satisfaction down to the branch level, and managers can be rewarded for improved scores. Unfortunately, the problem with this approach is that only part of the customer's satisfaction is under the control of management. The customer's expectations can be raised by competitive offerings, and satisfaction scores can drop as a consequence.

Another approach has been to introduce revenue into branch manager targets. A major New York bank wanted to change the retail branch manager orientation from one of considering only costs and security to one of considering customers first. The bank introduced a revenue-based performance evaluation system. For the first time, managers had to worry about where the customers came from and had to stop thinking of them as 'people who made a mess of my branch'. Early successes by a few managers produced interesting results. Up to 20 per cent of managers left the company, claiming that this was not what they were hired to do. The balance of the managers woke up the bank's sleeping central marketing department to demand help in getting more customers. The long-term result of the change in the system was an increase in customers as well as in bad debt. The managers had discovered that money is an easy product to sell, and the bank had discovered it needed to revamp its credit control function.

Planning systems can also be used to change the orientation of companies. Formal marketing planning can drive organizations through the logic of marketing and can force them to develop an understanding of consumers' needs. Such planning exercises can eventually become 'mind-numbing', but for the first two or three cycles, the process can be educational for all personnel involved. This approach is all the more powerful if combined with training and/or direct attacks on culture.

Changing culture through people

Outsiders increasingly are being brought into the marketing departments of service firms to try to change the orientation. Such an approach must be supplemented with the development of training programmes inside the firm. Operations people need to be trained in marketing, and marketing people need to understand all the areas discussed in this book.

Changing culture directly

Culture-change programmes are becoming increasingly popular. These programmes range from broad-scale educational activities to highly empowering personnel in order to re-engineer the firm's entire service delivery process around the customer. Figure 17.8 provides a simple way to categorize such activities. Along one axis is the nature of the groups used. Mixed groups are cross-sectional or interdepartmental; family groups can be a department or a naturally occurring group based on process, such as all the individuals involved in loading a particular flight with passengers. The second axis deals with the level of empowerment given to employees. Low levels of empowerment imply that individuals will change their behaviour but that the group will have no authority to change the processes and systems of the organization. High-level empowerment implies an ability to change the organization during the event or series of events. The slogans in the cells represent the hypothetical titles of such change programs, which often involve one or more meetings.

The top left cell refers to putting the customer first programmes that take place in mixed groups within the organization. Seated together in sessions, personnel are lectured to and motivated to put the customer first. Through role playing, they are encouraged to recognize the importance of customers and change their behaviour accordingly.

These types of programmes can be very successful. To be successful, however, the new behaviour needs to be reinforced on the job. If management and front-line personnel do not share the same level of enthusiasm and dedication towards the goal of creating a customer-oriented organization, the value of the lessons learned can be wiped out within hours. Without commitment to change, the new behaviours learned will be trivialized by colleagues, the old behaviours will be reinstated quickly and the value of the programme will be a total loss.

The top right cell, orientation change, overcomes these problems by processing personnel by family groups whose members can reinforce one another on the job. Both cells, however, focus on changing attitudes and individual behaviours. Changing organizational processes and systems are not part of these programmes. This potentially produces role conflict as desired individual behaviours are inhibited by organizational constraints, such as the physical environment or the current operating system.

Change the way you work, in the lower-left cell, draws on the empowerment ideas described in detail in Chapter 10. It implies active empowerment of the personnel attending the programme. Personnel are allowed to break the rules in the context of serving their customers. Because of the mixed group, however, this type of initiative is focused on the individual rather than on process-level empowerment.

> **putting the customer first** The element of the culture change initiative that teaches personnel to put the customer first.

> **orientation change** The element of the culture change initiative that teaches 'families' of personnel to reinforce one another on the job.

> **change the way you work** The element of the culture change initiative that allows personnel to break the rules in the context of serving their customers.

| | Group | |
Empowerment	Mixed	Family
Low	'Putting the customer first'	'Orientation change'
High	'Change the way you work'	'Change the way we work'

Figure 17.8

Categorizing culture change initiatives

Source Bateson/Hoffman, *Managing Services Marketing*, 4th ed. © 1999 South-Western, a part of Cengage Learning, Inc. Reproduced by permission. www.cengage.com/permissions.

change the way we work
The element of the culture change initiative that teaches personnel to flowchart their activities and to re-engineer the process to better serve their customers.

The lower-right cell, change the way we work, refers to initiatives that draw on many of the ideas in this book. Groups are in families and can be asked to flowchart their activities. They can then be asked to re-engineer the process to better serve their customers. The level of excitement in such groups is matched only by the anxiety of their bosses. Empowerment at this level really does place the boss in the role of coach and facilitator, and that is exactly what the boss's role should be. In creating a seamless organization, it is not management's job to force or dictate to employees to deliver service excellence. As Denton (2006:4) stated 'The whole is greater than the parts'. Therefore, management must continually invest in innovative service delivery mechanisms, train their staff and allow 360-degree feedback on new and existing service delivery mechanisms. And at the end of the day if all members of staff from the Chief Executive to the front-line personnel to the back office staff understand that the goal is to better serve the customer, staff are more likely to 'buy into' the new service delivery initiatives.

Tactical questions relating to seamlessness: Conducting a service audit

service audit A series of questions that forces the firm to think about what drives its profits and suggests strategies for competitive differentiation and long-term profitability.

One helpful approach in creating a seamless organization involves conducting a service audit that addresses a number of questions. The service audit directs the firm to think about the forces that drive its current profits and suggests strategies that have been discussed throughout this book that lead to competitive differentiation and long-term profitability. Moreover, the active involvement of front-line and top management personnel in conducting the audit facilitates the change in culture necessary to make the transition from the traditional industrial management approach to an employee- and customer-focused, service-oriented approach.

The service audit: The profit and growth component

How does the firm define customer loyalty? Traditional measures of customer loyalty involve repeat sales, purchase frequency, and increases in amounts purchased. The firm also needs to consider the depth of the relationship. For example, the depth of a customer's banking relationship would be defined by types of transactions and accounts such as savings, checking, certificates of deposit, car loans, home mortgages, savings bond programmes, safety deposit box rentals, and so on.

Does the firm measure profits from referrals? Customer loyalty and satisfaction should also be measured in terms of the customers' willingness to refer the firm to friends, family, and colleagues. Given the importance consumers place upon personal sources of information when selecting from among competing services, encouraging referrals or at least creating an atmosphere where customers freely inform others of the firm's services is crucial.

What proportion of the firm's development funds are spent on retaining customers as opposed to attracting new ones? As discussed in Chapter 15, the benefits of customer retention are clear. Current customers generate referrals, are less expensive to market to, purchase more services more frequently, are knowledgeable about the firm's operating system and, therefore, are more efficient users of the system, and are a great source of information about how the firm can better serve its targeted markets. Unfortunately, under traditional models of management, firms spend the majority of their resources on obtaining new customers while neglecting their existing customers.

When customers do not return, do we know why? Service firms that excel pursue the bad news as well as the good. Traditionally, customer satisfaction assessments are obtained from current customers, who tend to rate the firm towards the more positive end of the scale. Uncovering the reasons customers defect reveals potentially fatal flaws in the firm's service delivery system that other customers have yet to discover and of which the firm may have been unaware. Consequently, contacting customers who have defected provides the firm with the opportunity to make improvements. Moreover, contacting customers who defect makes a positive impression that the firm cares about its customers and may actually lead to recapturing some lost customers.

The service audit: The customer satisfaction component

Is customer satisfaction data collected in a systematic manner? In Chapter 12 and 13, we discussed a number of methods for assessing customer satisfaction and service quality. The key to successful measurement is consistency so that current assessments can be compared with past benchmarks. Satisfaction measurement should also occur on a regular basis and not only when problems arise. Catching minor problems early through periodic customer satisfaction surveys enables the firm to adjust the service delivery system before major gaps in service occur.

What methods are utilized to obtain customer feedback? The service quality information system discussed in Chapter 13 reveals a number of important methods of obtaining customer feedback on a variety of issues. The active solicitation of customer complaints, after-sale surveys, customer focus-group interviews, mystery shopping and total market service quality surveys should be used in conjunction with employee surveys. Too often, employees are left out of traditional customer feedback loops even though they are exposed to vast amounts of information about customers' daily interactions with the firm.

How is customer satisfaction data used? Is the information used at all, or is it stuffed in the bottom drawer of a manager's desk? Customer satisfaction data need to be shared with employees who provide the service. Front-line employees should feel they are an active part of the firm's overall goals and take pride in improvements in customer satisfaction scores. The data should reveal company strengths that can be used for promotional purposes and weaknesses that can be corrected through training programmes or by redesigning the service system itself.

The service audit: The external service value component

How does the firm measure value? One key to providing superior customer service is to define service value from the customer's perspective. Traditional approaches define value internally and frequently miss what is really important to customers. Remember, buyers' perceptions of value represent a trade-off between the perceived benefits of the service to be purchased and the perceived sacrifice in terms of the total costs to be paid.

How is information on customer perceptions of the firm's value shared within the company? Keeping customer information in the hands of top management does little to improve the service effort on the front line. By sharing information about customer perceptions with the front line, the employees become sensitized to the behaviours and outcomes that are really important to customers. Improvements made in these specific areas should increase customer satisfaction scores. Similarly, sharing the information with operations, marketing and human resources personnel should assist each area in understanding the customer's perception of the entire service delivery process.

Does the firm actively measure the gap between customer expectations and perceptions of services delivered? Once customer perceptions are obtained, a comparison with customer expectations is vital in assessing customer satisfaction. Customer perceptions alone do not tell the full story. This point was made particularly clear in Chapter 13 regarding the SERVQUAL scale. Perception scores alone merely reflect whether customers agree with the statement, not whether what they are evaluating is really important to them. Including expectation measures increases the managerial usefulness of the information. Given that making improvements often involves a financial investment, comparing expectations to perceptions assists the firm in allocating resources to the most appropriate areas.

Is service recovery an active strategy discussed among management and employees? Although many firms will spend vast amounts of time and effort to deliver the service right the first time, little discussion centres on appropriate courses of action for employees to take when things do not go according to plan. Consequently, employees are left to fend for themselves while dealing with unhappy customers, and it is apparent that employees often do a poor job in service recovery efforts. Chapter 16 stresses the benefits of both service failure and service recovery analysis. Actively tracking failures and recoveries identifies failure points in the system and allows the firm to minimize their occurrence by training employees in service recovery techniques.

The service audit: The employee productivity component

How does the firm measure employee productivity? If the firm does not measure what it really believes is important, employees will never pay attention to it. In addition, if productivity is measured simply in terms of output and outcomes and not by the behaviours used to achieve these outcomes, the firm may actually be rewarding employees for anti-customer-oriented activities. For example, the employee may be very curt with one customer so that a quick sale can be transacted with another customer who already knows what he or she wants. Service productivity measures such as timeliness, accuracy and responsiveness need to be developed to reinforce these types of customer-oriented behaviours.

The service audit: The employee loyalty component

Does the firm actively pursue strategies to promote employee loyalty? Employee loyalty to the organization is often visible to customers and directly influences customer evaluations of the firm. When employees feel more positive about the firm, customers feel more positive about the services the firm delivers. Preaching that employees are the firm's most important asset and then laying off employees in large numbers during periods of downsizing sends a hypocritical message to both employees and customers.

Does the firm set employee retention goals? Although rarely is 100 per cent the correct level, employee retention saves the firm funds in terms of recruiting and training costs. Additionally, customers prefer the continuity of interacting with the same personnel over time so much that the firm's personnel may be its key differential advantage over competitors. When service personnel do leave, their regular customers often seek them out at their new places of employment.

The service audit: The employee satisfaction component

Are employee satisfaction measures linked to customer satisfaction measures? Employee satisfaction is linked to increases in productivity and external service value. External service value is linked to customer satisfaction and the additional benefit of customer loyalty. The net effects of customer loyalty are increased revenues and profitability for the firm. The outcomes associated with employee satisfaction – external service values, customer satisfaction, customer loyalty, revenue growth and increased profitability – provide feedback and reinforce the company's internal service quality and employee satisfaction.

Are customer and organizational needs considered when hiring? Southwest Airlines invites panels of customers to help select flight attendants. Customers are so sold on the idea that some take time off from their own work schedules to be on the selection team. Hiring people with good job skills is important in manufacturing. Hiring people with good job skills and good interpersonal skills is vital in services.

Are employee reward programmes tied to customer satisfaction, customer loyalty and quality of employee performance? Service firms wishing to enhance the customer focus of their employees must implement behaviour-based reward systems that monitor employee activities and evaluate employees on aspects of their job over which they have control. Traditional, outcome-based reward systems often discourage the development of long-term relationships with the firm's customers in pursuit of short-term profitability.

The service audit: The internal service quality component

Are employees aware of internal and external customers? The ideal service firm should work seamlessly as a team. Each member of the team should understand fully how individual performance affects the performance of other team members as they provide superior service to external customers. Consequently, employees need to understand that the firm's external customers are not the only ones who are depending on their efforts.

Do employees have the support necessary to do their jobs? Does the firm just talk about providing superior service, or does it talk about it and back up it with the support necessary to get the job done right? Over the past few years, Pret, a fast food franchise, has emerged as a firm with some fairly progressive service strategies. Personnel are supported by the latest advances in information technology, self-managing team training, effective food service equipment and work scheduling that enhances employee performance.

The service audit: The firm's leadership component

Does the firm's leadership help or hinder the service delivery process? Service personnel frequently find that even though they want to provide good service, their hands are tied by overbearing, conservative, upper-management types. Frequently, upper management is far removed from the front line of the operation and has lost touch with the realities associated with daily service interactions. The leaders of successful firms act as enablers, coaches and facilitators and they are participatory managers who listen to employees and encourage creative approaches to solving old problems.

Is the firm's leadership creating a corporate culture that helps employees as they interact with customers? Top management sets the tone and provides the resources that support personnel who interact with customers. The links in the service–profit chain discussed in Chapter 10 reveal that employee satisfaction and customer satisfaction are directly related. Top management's job, therefore, is to create an organization culture in which employees thrive.

The service audit: The measurement relationship component

How do the preceding measures of service performance in the service audit relate to the firm's overall profitability? The preceding components of the audit provide strategic measures that aid the provision of superior service. Ideally, the contribution of each measure should berelated to the firm's bottom line. Relating these measures to the firm's overall profitability provides a resounding message throughout the company that service and quality pay!

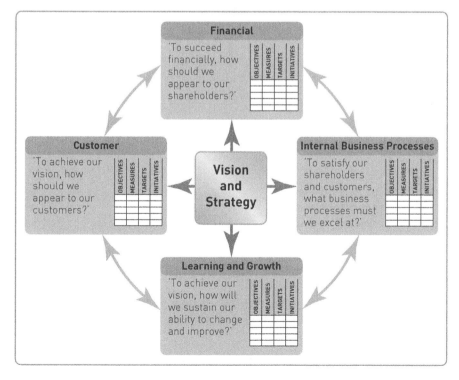

Figure 17.9

The balanced scorecard provides feedback on both internal business processes and external outcomes in order to improve both strategic performance and results.

Source © 2007 Balanced Scorecard Institute, a Strategy Management Group Company.

Summary

In pursuit of service excellence, the individual departments and functions of the firm must act in unison to create a seamless organization. The firm will not act as one if the current focus of the organization is on departmental and functional needs. The three-tiered model of service firms offers an alternative view of how the organization should focus its efforts by segmenting the operation into a customer tier, a boundary tier and a coordination tier. The goal is to have those in the coordination tier work in harmony with personnel in the boundary tier so that customers experience seamless service.

Creating and supporting a customer-focused organizational culture is critical when developing a seamless operation. The firm's culture drives employee behaviour and directly influences the quality of the firm's service delivery system and subsequent consumer evaluations of the firm's service effort. Firms can change the existing culture of the organization by changing the firm's structure, people-management systems, and/or key personnel, or they can change the culture directly through broad-based educational activities or re-engineering the firm's entire service delivery process.

Finally, by conducting a service audit, a seamless service culture is fostered as organizational personnel throughout the organization come to appreciate the challenges faced and the contributions made by everyone involved in the firm's final service delivery effort. The service audit deals directly with such issues as profit and growth, customer satisfaction, external service value, employee productivity, employee loyalty, employee satisfaction, internal service quality, leadership and measures that assess the impact of each of these issues on the firm's bottom line.

The service audit also provides a framework for combining the materials that are discussed throughout this book. In closing, we hope that this book has helped develop your understanding of the special challenges involved in the marketing and management of service operations. With challenge comes opportunity, and as you well know, there are plenty of opportunities in the business community to make the service encounter a more productive and pleasant experience for everyone involved – customers and employees alike. The time has come to make a difference and we look forward to writing about the difference you made in future editions of this book.

Discussion questions

1 Discuss seamlessness as it relates to 'tooth-to-tail' performance. Consider the issues that Rockwool face as they try to produce a seamless service across their different departments.

Case link
See Case 14: The Rockwool Group.

2 Discuss the fight for control among marketing, operations and human resources personnel.

3 Define the following terms: marketing orientation, marketing functions and marketing department. Why is it necessary to distinguish among these terms when discussing service firms? Relate your answer to the customization/customer contact matrix.

4 Discuss each tier of the three-tiered model of service firms separately and then as a combined unit.

5 What is the importance of organizational culture?

6 Explain the relevance of inter-functional task forces and inter-functional transfers as they relate to corporate culture.

7 Discuss the four approaches to directly changing culture as presented in the text.

8 What are the key components of a service audit?

References and further reading

Albrecht, K. and Zemke, R. (1985) *Service America*, Homewood, IL: Dow Jones-Irwin.

Bateson, John E. G. (1995) *Managing Services Marketing*, 3rd ed., Fort Worth, TX: Dryden Press, 1995.

Brown, P. B. and Sewall, C. (1998) *Customers for Life*, New York: Bantam.

Burton, D. (2002) 'Incorporating ethnicity into marketing intelligence and planning', *Marketing Intelligence & Planning* 20 (7): 442–451.

Chase, R. B. and Aquilano, N. J. (1991) *Production and Operations Management: A Lifecycle Approach*, Homewood, IL: Irwin.

Chase, R. B. and Youngdahl, W. E. (1992) 'Service by design', *Design Management Journal* 9 (Winter).

Cozens, C. (2003) 'Advertisers failing to connect with ethnic groups', *Guardian*, 3 March.

Denton, K. (2006) 'High performance work systems: the sum really is greater than its parts', *Measuring Business Excellence* 10 (4): 4–7.

Duray, R. (2002) 'Mass customization origins: mass or custom manufacturing?', *International Journal of Operations & Production Management* 22 (3): 314–328.

Fiore, A. M., Lee, S.-E. and Kunz, G. (2004) 'Individual differences, motivations, and willingness to use a mass customization option for fashion products', *European Journal of Marketing* 38 (7): 835–849.

Fletcher, D. (2003) 'Reaching the ethnic consumer', *Admap Magazine*, 437 (March): 1–17.

Heffernan, R. and LaValle, S. (2007) 'Emotional interactions: the frontier of the customer-focused enterprise', *Strategy & Leadership* 35 (3): 38–49.

Jamal, A. (2003) 'Marketing in a multicultural world. The interplay of marketing, ethnicity and consumption', *European Journal of Marketing* 37 (11/12): 1599–1620.

Keating, M. and Harrington, D. (2003) 'The challenges of implementing quality in the Irish hotel industry', *Journal of Industrial European Training* 27 (9): 441–453.

Kingman-Brundage, Jane, George, William R. and Bowen, David E. (1995) 'Service logic – achieving essential service system integration', *International Journal of Service Industry Management* 6 (4): 2–40.

Lovelock, C. H. (1989) 'Managing interaction between operations and marketing and their impact on customers', reprinted in Bowen et al., eds, *Service Management Effectiveness*, San Francisco: Jossey Bass, 1990.

Lovelock, C. H. and Wirtz, J. (2007) *Services Marketing People, Technology, Strategy*, 6th ed., Englewood Cliffs, NJ: Prentice Hall.

Lovelock, C. H., Langeard, E., Bateson, J. E. G. and Eiglier, P. (1981) 'Some organizational problems facing marketing in the service sector', in J. Donnelly and W. George, eds, *Marketing of Services*, Chicago: American Marketing Association, pp. 148–153.

Loveman, W., Sasser, Jr., Earl and Schlesinger, Leonard A. (1994) 'Putting the service-profit chain to work', *Harvard Business Review* (March–April): 165–174.

Mentzer, J. T., DeWitt, W., Keebler, J. S., Min, S., Nix, N. W., Smith, C. D. and Zacharia, Z. G. (2001) 'Defining supply chain management', *Journal of Business Logistics* 22 (2).

Migliarese, P. and Verteramo, S. (2005) 'Knowledge creation and sharing in a project team: an organizational analysis based on the concept of organizational relation', *Electronic Journal of Knowledge Management* 3 (2): 97–106.

Mosley, R. W. (2007) 'Customer experience, organizational culture and the employer brand', *Journal of Brand Management* 15 (2): 123–134.

Rowley, J. (2007) 'Reconceptualising the strategic role of loyalty schemes', *Journal of Consumer Marketing* 24 (6): 366–374.

Schneider, Benjamin and Bowen, David E. (1995) *Winning the Service Game*, Boston: Harvard Business School Press, pp. 1–17.

Smith, S. and Wheeler, J. (2002) 'The age of experience', in *Managing the Customer Experience*, Harlow: FT Prentice Hall.

Usunier, J.-C. and Lee, J. (2005) *Marketing Across Cultures*, 4 ed., London: Prentice Hall.

Wirtz, J. and Johnston, R. (2003) 'Singapore Airlines: what it takes to sustain service excellence – a senior management perspective', *Managing Service Quality* 13 (1): 10–19.

Chapter 18
Future trends

... future orientation is naturally related to the view that people can master nature, and that the future can in some way be predicted or at least significantly influenced. In societies where future orientation is strong, it is backed by the educational system and by an 'imagination of the future' supported by scientific breakthroughs and technological developments.

(Usunier and Lee, 2005)

Chapter objectives

In this chapter we discuss trends as they relate to the service indlustry.
After reading this chapter, you should be able to:

- Understand how demographic and social trends shape the service industry.

- Appreciate future service characteristics, specifically the characteristic of non-ownership.

- Understand how e-services will develop in the future.

- Be able to describe how and why service organizations include corporate social responsibilities as a benefit for consumers, staff, investors and suppliers.

Services in context
Trends shaping the future of the services industry

There are many trends that will affect the service industry over the long-term. Service organizations need to be aware of these trends so that they can adapt and support their core business in line with the ever-changing needs of the marketplace. Some of the major trends and their implications to the service industry are discussed below.

The world's population

The world's population will increase to 9.2 billion by 2050. However, not all countries will increase their populations at the same rate. For example, populations will fall in Germany and Japan by 2050. In the UK, populations will rise and then fall by 2050. Austria will see a small rise in its population by 2050 and the Congo and Niger will have an increase in their populations by 198 per cent and 274 per cent respectively. These figures are shown in Table 18.1.

There are many reasons why populations increase or decrease. These include economic development, education, the environment, epidemics and other health threats. Additionally, populations change as the status of women changes, together with the opportunity to access family planning information and services. Service organizations need to consider these changes; if, for example, populations change, the type of workforce available will change. Service organizations, therefore, could consider outsourcing some of their services, such as distribution networks, call centres or administration to countries where the population is growing or encourage immigration to fill vacancies in the home country. An example of encouraging immigration has happened through the UK's National Health Service which has advertised jobs for immigrant workers to fill vacancies for nursing staff.

Country	2007	2050	% increase/ decrease
United Kingdom*	60.59 m	63.67 m	
Germany	83.00 m	71.40 m	−13%
Japan	127.70 m	95.20 m	−26%
Austria	8.30 m	9.00 m	+8%
Palestinian Territory	4.00 m	8.80 m	+120%
Democratic Republic of Congo	62.20 m	186.80 m	+198%
Niger	14.20 m	53.2 m	+274%

Table 18.1

World populations

* UK population increases from 2006 to 2050 – however it is predicted that from 2041 the population will decrease.

Populations are living longer

In the developed world the population is living longer. Taking the countries shown in Table 18.1, the life expectancy in those countries at present is:

United Kingdom	77 (Male)	81 (Female)
Germany	76 (Male)	82 (Female)
Japan	79 (Male)	86 (Female)
Austria	77 (Male)	83 (Female)
Palestinian Territory	71 (Male)	74 (Female)
Niger	57 (Male)	55 (Female)
Dem. Rep. of Congo	44 (Male)	46 (Female)

Service organizations need to consider their workforce and of course their target audience. In Japan, for example, the statutory retirement age is 60, moving to 65 by 2013; the UK retirement age is 65. In the UK and Japan employees often continue working after the statutory retirement age, sometimes at the discretion of their employer. Service organizations, therefore, need to consider pension provision and extended working opportunities. At the same time, service organizations need to reconsider their core service offer and make it appealing to the older generation. For example, by 2050 1 in 3 Italians will be over the age of 65; service organizations that deal in health care or are geriatric specialists are likely to have an extended target market. This example is not just applicable to Italy as many developed countries will have a large proportion of their population over the age of 65.

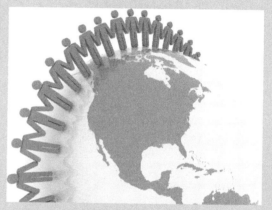

Populations are living longer and service organizations will need to consider their workforce and target audience more carefully.

SOURCE © ISTOCK.COM/ALEX SLOBODKIN

Introduction

This book has demonstrated the need for the service sector to look after their internal affairs by understanding their customers' needs, ensuring that service personnel are trained and rewarded and that suppliers need to be managed and respected. Service organizations must not only look at their internal affairs but also consider the external environment in which they operate. The opening scenario, 'Trends shaping the future of the services industry', highlighted some important information about the growth in world populations and the shift to an ageing population. Monitoring and evaluating the external environment are important to the service organizations that want to survive over the long term. Businesses the world over will need to appraise future population trends, for example, and craft strategies that anticipate change or respond to global market forces. This final chapter identifies some of the external forces that service organizations need to consider in their medium- to long-term marketing plans. The trends identified will follow the themes shown in the different chapters of this book.

The first section of this chapter will follow the themes identified in Part 1, An Overview of Services Marketing by considering the marketing mix and the service characteristics for the twenty-first century. The second section will follow the themes shown in Chapters 4 to 6 of this book by identifying changing customers and changing needs. This will be followed by the third section which will extend thoughts highlighted in Part 2 of this book with regard to global e-services. And finally, the fourth section of this chapter will deal with corporate social responsibility as a strategy for creating a relationship with the customers, employees and suppliers.

Marketing mix and the service characteristics: The twenty-first century marketing mix

The 7 P's of the service marketing mix – Product, Place, Price, Promotion, Physical Evidence, People and Process – have been described, discussed and critiqued in this book. However, to keep abreast of future trends there may be a need to extend the services marketing mix still further. Additional elements to the services marketing mix paradigm would aid the future marketer to plan for tomorrow's customer (Constantinides, 2006; English, 2000). Numerous academics and theorists agree that there is a need to increase or change the elements within the services marketing mix and a short summary of these are shown in Table 18.2.

The authors listed in Table 18.2 are just some who feel there is a need for a change to the services marketing mix. We suggest that the 7 Ps of the services marketing mix be increased to 10, based on murmurings from marketers and academics alike. The additional elements to the mix should be Packaging, Performance and Personalization. The additional elements have been labelled

Author (s)	The need for change
Gummerson (2007)	Consumers buy brands for their symbolic value; they do not buy goods or services, they buy a whole **package** of goods and services. They buy the experience and dream that are symbolized by their perception of the brand's image made up from price, advertising, who uses it and so on.
Constantinides (2006)	The human factor is critical in many service encounters. Staff deliver the service, they process the service and the customer's perception of the quality of the service will be affected by the staff member's **performance**.

Table 18.2

Need to change the services marketing mix

▶

John et al. (2006)	Employees do not just work, they perform. The performance creates the service experience that the customers enjoy. The employee's **performance** occurs *with* customers and other employees within the physical environment. Therefore, service performances evolve and adapt as different customers and different environments change.
English (2000)	The marketing mix should include elements involving relevance, response and relationships.

as such to fit into the P paradigm, as Jobber (2001:48) advised: 'The strength of the 4 Ps approach is that it represents a memorable and practical framework for marketing decision-making'. We wish our services mix to be memorable for future students and scholars and Table 18.3 provides an outline of the Additional Elements of Service Marketing Mix.

The additional services marketing mix elements will enable marketers to focus clearly on some aspects that could make them unique in the future competitive environment.

Service characteristics: Adding non-ownership as the fifth characteristic

Chapter 1 and 2 of this book introduced the characteristics of services marketing and compared them with product marketing. The four service characteristics included intangibility, inseparability, heterogeneity and perishability. The services industry continues to be a dominant force in many developed countries as manufacturing and agricultural industries continue to decline. These service characteristics should still be observed, however, as service operations have increased and diversified and additional service characteristic should be included. The fifth service characteristic, therefore, should be *non-ownership*.

Non-ownership as a service characteristic was introduced by Judd in 1964 and Rathmell in 1974. However, it was mainly excluded from future textbooks and papers that discussed the four main characteristics of services marketing as outlined earlier in this book. The characteristic of non-ownership introduces the idea that during many marketing transactions no ownership of a physical/tangible element occurs. If that is the case, what does the customer buy? The answer is: customers buy 'the right to use'. That is, customers buy the 'right to use' a physical object – such as a marquee for a wedding, the 'right to use' labour to maintain their garden, or the 'right to use' a toll road. In the future, sharing, renting, hiring and so on will become the norm as service organizations find new ways to supply customers with new experiences or new ways to satisfy their needs. Table 18.4, The Service Characteristic of Non-ownership shows several categories that could be included in the proposed new paradigm.

Many services combine all four service characteristics, but can also include the non-ownership element. One of the main reasons that non-ownership should be included as a key characteristic in services marketing is because many customers in the developed world are *time poor*. 'Time poor' is an expression used when describing the concept that consumers have a good

Additional elements	Definition
Packaging	Packaging is a crucial aspect of the service mix. All services are recognized through their brand/logo or name. The consumer recognizes these. Therefore, marketers need to 'package together' the entire service encounter. This 'package' includes what the customer has experienced before, what the advertising shows them, how the price is perceived, how the staff behave towards the customer and so on. Clearly, the consumer will not break down each part of the service. They will, however, perceive the whole 'package' and make a judgement. Therefore, service organizations need to consider that all elements of the services mix create a coherent package. Naturally, different packages can be created for different consumer types.
Performance	Currently people are an element of the services marketing mix and this represents both staff and customers. However, the role that staff play in the service experience should be considered separately. Both Constantinides (2006) and John et al. (2007) note the performances that staff play within the service experience. Staff deliver the service, they have to deal with different types of customers and they are the 'face' of the organization. Therefore, the performance they deliver is not only very important in terms of the smooth running of the organization but is likely to influence *how* the customer experiences their encounter with the organization. Staff also need to adapt their performances due to the many unpredictable, uncontrollable events that can occur in the service environment. Performance, therefore, should be added to the service marketing mix paradigm so that deeper understanding and knowledge can be gained regarding this important element.
Personali-zation	Following on from performance, service personnel often customize their behaviour with different customers. Additionally, service organizations, due to advances in technology and database management, can also personalize the experience and communication that customers receive. The existing services marketing mix considers these two instances through promotional techniques to the masses. However, personalization should be added to the mix to ensure that the customer feels valued and understood.

Table 18.3

The additional elements of services marketing mix

income but little time to spend on leisure activities; hence they are 'money rich, time poor'. Therefore, non-ownership services that reduce the time spent on general household chores or duties such as cleaning, decorating, ironing and grocery shopping are growing. Also in a finite world where the population will increase but resources become scarce or expensive, renting and sharing will increase. For example, car-sharing is a 'rental' concept which is developing in major cities in the developed world, where customers have the 'right to use' a car for a period of time during a day. See E-Services in Action for an example of car-sharing. The concept of temporary possession and access is already working in the services industry.

Table 18.4	Category	Example
The service characteristic of non-ownership	The service operators who rent or hire goods	Customers rent goods from service operators. The customer has the temporary right to use certain physical goods. The goods include renting morning suites for a wedding, hiring a skip during a house renovation, renting a speedboat for fun on holiday. Customers rent or hire these goods because they cannot or do not want to own these items because they do not have enough money or space to keep them.
Source: Categories adapted from Lovelock and Gummesson, 2004: 34.	Place, room and space rental	Customers often rent a room or space. For example, many small businesses rent office spaces as they do not have the capital to buy. Similarly, there is a whole society of allotment keepers where people grow their own vegetable and flowers. The spaces available for them to rent appeal to customers who live in urban areas and do not have gardens of their own.
	Labour and expertise hire	Customers who hire labour and expertise do so because they do not have the necessary skills or time. For example, there are many ironing and domestic cleanings services available for professional people who have no desire or 'time' to iron their clothes or clean their homes. Similarly, image consultants, financial advisers and mortgage brokers are hired for their expertise and knowledge
	Physical facility usage and access	Leisure pursuits such as swimming, climbing and squash require facilities. Customers pay for the 'right to use' these facilities.
	Network access and usage	Due to the many functions available via the internet, customers rent or hire 'space' on the internet. Some small and large businesses use 'data storage' services by placing their data online.

Changing customers and changing needs

The opening scenario "Trends shaping the future of the services industry" highlights changing population trends. Figures 18.1 and 18.2 show the percentage total of the population, in each country, that is over the age of 60.

The fact that there will be a higher proportion of older people in the world clearly affects which service organizations are going to have a bigger target market. This has clear implications for consumer spending. Many UK citizens, over the age of 60, are asset rich, cash rich and have lots of free time. Service organizations will be able to encourage the expanding over-60s market to spend more on healthcare, pension provision and savings (Mintel, 2007). Similarly, business-to-business markets that supply medical and

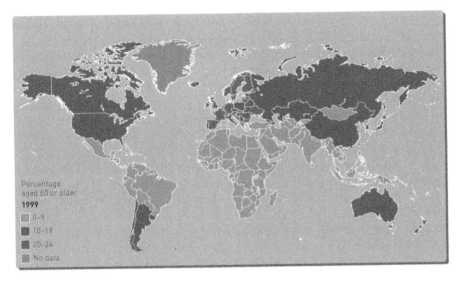

Figure 18.1

Percentage of total population aged 60 years or older in 1999

Source United Nations publication © (ST/ESA/SER.A/179), Sales No. E.99.XIII.11, Copyright © United Nations 1999.

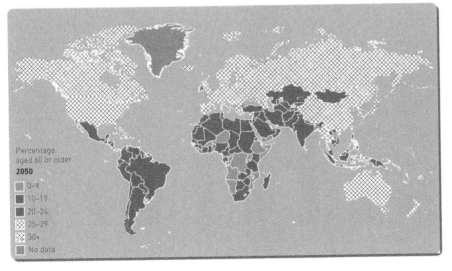

Figure 18.2

Percentage of total population aged 60 years or older in 2050

Source United Nations publication © (ST/ESA/SER.A/179), Sales No. E.99.XIII.11, Copyright © United Nations 1999.

surgical equipment will see a change in the type of equipment ordered as more people will need hip or knee replacements. Consumers today who are getting older and living longer often want to 'stay younger, longer'; therefore, despite the increases in the medical market, there are also opportunities in skincare, laser eye treatments, microscopic hearing devices, holidays and clothes to enable the over-50s to look and feel young. There are a number of other changes in behaviour in the UK market that service organizations need to consider when making future plans. One factor which stands out in developed countries is the number of people living on their own. Figure 18.3 shows the percentage of people who live in single households in regions around the world.

There are three main reasons why people live on their own. One of the reasons for single occupancy in homes across developed countries is because young people stay in education longer, delay marriage and focus on career goals. The second reason accounting for the high number of single households is due to increasing levels of divorce and breakdowns in the traditional family structures. This means that the second category of people living on their own are single-parent households. At the older end of the age range elderly widows or widowers often continue to live on their own in the family home and this makes the third category of one-person households. As Figure 18.3 shows, in Western Europe, nearly 30 per cent of people live on their own and this is predicted to increase. Worldwide, in 1996 the number of single-person households was 153.6 million; by 2006 it had grown to 202.6 million which accounts for 11.8 per cent of total households. The housing market is already aware of this and is building extra homes with the single person in mind. The service sector also needs to consider the entertainment and leisure needs of the single person. Already companies such as Solo and Saga (for the over-50s) offer exciting holidays specifically for single people. There has also been an increase in specialist dating agencies for specific target groups such as professional business people, over-50s, opera lovers, or for people who are sports fanatics!

The population, therefore, is changing. This brings new consumers with new needs. The service sector needs to be aware of these external factors and pre-empt them by offering new services to meet the new demands. Global

Figure 18.3

Proportion of single households by regional area

Source Euromonitor (2008).

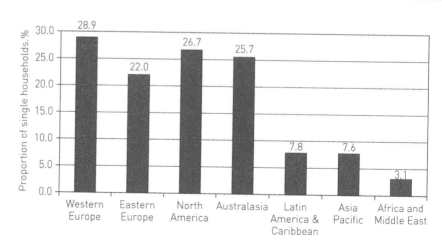

Services in Action shows how Wizzair.com added additional flight services to its portfolio to accommodate the increased migration from Poland to the UK.

Global e-services: The internet services industry

Since the birth of the internet numerous multimedia industries have evolved through a dynamic industry that as yet does not seem to be slowing down. Whilst e-services move ahead at an unbelievably fast pace, there have been some casualties in the traditional services industries. Service organizations that have 'gone out of business' or reduced the number of 'shop fronts' in their portfolio include travel agents, independent retailers and banks. Figure 18.4 shows 'online activities clusters' from internet users across Europe. As can be seen, travel, shopping and bank transactions are some of the most popular activities that occur online.

The internet provides a plethora of goods, services and social communities. There is so much that consumers do not need to leave the house for, to get educated, buy clothes, food or electrical items and socialize via webcam with their friends who live thousands of miles away.

Online retailing is particularly appealing, especially to the younger cash-rich, time-poor generation. These consumers can satisfy their shopping needs at the click of a button. Clearly the attraction is the fact that consumers can shop 24 hours a day, 7 days a week. They can also browse at their leisure and there are

---

Global Services in action
Cultural diversity and integration

Migration has existed for many years and continues to grow. Disparate peoples move in and out of different countries, coexisting to make a culturally diverse community that works together productively. Service organizations attract consumers from different backgrounds, lifestyles and attitudes and due to diverse communities the differences are becoming blurred. Migration, therefore, harmonizes the differences. Harmony also occurs through intermarriage, mixing cultures geographically but also ethnically and socially. Mass media such as films, TV and advertisements also bring together people from many different backgrounds and give the consumer the opportunity to witness integration through comedy, romance and drama. Service industries in addition to the film and TV producers and advertising agencies also need to embrace the growing acceptance of a culturally diverse target audience. For example, Wizzair is a travel company that added flights to Krakow and Warsaw to their portfolio. The availability of these flights was introduced due to the growing number of Polish workers coming to the UK. Polish workers and their families can move in and out of Poland and the UK much easier now that Wizzair introduced the regular flights.

Sources: National Institute of Population and Social Security Research (2008), Population Parsons (2008), Population Reference Bureau (2008), Statistics Austria (2008), www.wizzair.com; Cetron, Micco and Davies (2006).

'no crowds'. However, e-commerce will soon become a thing of the past and v-commerce will take its place. V-commerce, or virtual-commerce, will provide online users with a virtual interactive three dimensional online space that will enhance the shopping experience and drive up sales (www.rackspace.co.uk).

In addition, consumers will choose different types of services for extra convenience and to save money – see E-Services in Action.

Winning trust through corporate social responsibilities

Introducing corporate social responsibilities (CRS) as a strategy

All service organizations are competing for loyal, profitable customers. Therefore, the previous chapters of this book have highlighted different ways services can market themselves as 'better' than their competitors. Service organizations compete on price, accessibility, location and empowered personnel who provide exceptional service. Currently, due to legislative require-

Case link

See Case 15 for an example of one company's approach to their Corporate Social Responsibilities.

ments, organizations are promoting good citizenship as a way of showing customers that their organization has something special to offer. Good citizenship is a concept that has been in action for over 50 years. It began as organizations realized that their interdependence on and between governments, corporations and society at large was an essential way to move forward. Due to rising populations, limited resources, climate change and the

Figure 18.4

Online activities clusters

Source Raban (2004).

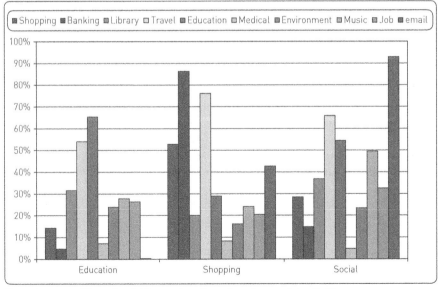

Users focus on different activities – education, shopping, social activities.

welfare of staff and customers, businesses worldwide are becoming more aware of the necessity to act responsibly and promote good citizenship. Indeed service organizations that are customer-focused realize that acting responsibly as one of the ways to increase competitive advantage, protect and raise brand awareness and build trust with customers and employees. Indeed, the Business Impact Taskforce (2000:5) points out that:

> Over 25,000 citizens across 23 countries on six continents were interviewed revealing that impressions of individual companies are more shaped by corporate citizenship (56%) than either brand quality/reputation (40%) or business fundamentals (34%).

E-services in action
City Car Club – Book, jump in and drive away

City Car Club is a membership scheme that allows its members the right to drive a new, often environmentally friendly, car that's just round the corner from businesses and homes within major cities. Members pre-book a car via the internet or phone. Bookings can be made directly from the car also – if the car hasn't been reserved by another member that is! Members go to 'their' cars at the allotted time, jump in and drive away. This is a convenient way of getting around without the expense and hassle of owning a car. City Car Club has hundreds of cars, many of them in London. Each car has its own 'parking space' which is something members do not have to pay for. Members pay £75 to join (this includes £25 drive time). After that they become 'pay-as-you-go members'. 'Pay-as-you-go' enables members to make a payment of £3.96 an hour to 'borrow' a small car such as Vauxhall Corsa or Ford Fiesta, or £4.76 to 'borrow' a bigger car such as Honda Civic Hybrid or Vauxhall Astra.

Car sharing is a relatively new concept in the UK but in Switzerland it has been acceptable for over 20 years. For the past two decades, a growing number of Swiss drivers have preferred to share cars with complete strangers rather than actually own a vehicle themselves.

The Mobility cooperative is the most successful car-sharing group with over 70,000 members; in 2007 it celebrated its tenth birthday. The organization considers itself to be an 'ecological' collective and is the biggest car-sharing business in Europe. Mobility has 1,800 cars to choose from and they also state that their members do not have to wash the car, worry about insurance, take the car to the garage for a service or even change a flat tyre. Just like City Car Club, Mobility members pay an annual flat fee and pre-book their car by phone or via the internet.

The idea of car sharing often saves customers the initial outlay of buying a car. And as more people move to urban areas, parking costs, fuel prices and congestion charges may persuade potential customers to try car sharing rather than car ownership.

Source: Swissinfo.ch, www.citycarclub.co.uk.

City Car Club – book, jump in and drive away.

Corporate and socially responsible behaviour, therefore, is a philosophy that is mutually beneficial to the services brand and their many stakeholders. See B2B services in Action where Fujitsu commit to the Waste Electrical and Electronic Equipment (WEEE) Directive implemented by the European Union.

B2B services in action
Caring for the environment the Fujitsu way

Fujitsu's corporate philosophy clearly demonstrates that they are a good corporate citizen and adhere to the philosophy that corporate social responsibilities (CRS) are at the heart of their brand. One of the elements that they stress in their corporate vision is the pursuit of innovation. However, from the point of view of corporate social responsibilities, they state that they will provide 'secure' services. This is demonstrated in their values for society and environment, employees and customers.

Figure 18.5

Fujitsu's corporate philosophy

➲ Corporate Vision

Through our constant pursuit of innovation, the Fujitsu Group aims to contribute to the creation of a networked society that is rewarding and secure, bringing about a prosperous future that fulfills the dreams of people throughout the world.

➲ Corporate Values

What we strive for:

Society and Environment	In all our actions, we protect the environment and contribute to society.
Profit and Growth	We strive to meet the expectations of customers, employees and Shareholder.
Shareholders and Investors	We seek to continuously increase our corporate value.
Global Perspective	We think and act from a global perspective.

What we value:

Employees	We respect diversity and support individual growth.
Customers	
Business partners	We seek to be their valued and trusted partner.
Technology	We build mutually beneficial relationships.
Quality	We seek to create new value through innovation. We enhance the reputation of our customers and the reliability of social infrastructure.

One of the ways that Fujitsu demonstrates corporate social responsibilities is through their re-cycling programme. In 2003 the European Union introduced a Waste Electrical and Electronics Equipment (WEEE) Directive to ensure that equipment of this nature is re-cycled.

Fujitsu committed itself to the WEEE directive through their 'take back' initiative. The 'take back' initiative enables business customers of Fujitsu to return products that have reached the end of their lives. The service does not end there. Fujitsu takes back the end-of-life products, breaks them down and recycles as much as it can. As Fujitsu has many B2B customers worldwide it has set up a global recycling network so that products from all its customers' products can be recycled efficiently. Business customers may consider Fujitsu as their company of choice when deciding who to install and supply their electrical and electronic equipment, based on the fact that it has been such a good citizen and has displayed admirable corporate social responsibilities.

One of the ways Fujitsu demonstrates corporate social responsibilities is through its re-cycling programme.

Demystifying corporate social responsibilities

So what are corporate social responsibilities and why do organizations use them to form relationships with customers, employees and suppliers? There are many ways to interpret corporate social responsibilities. However, around the world there are benchmarks available to guide service organizations such as those provided by the Department of Trade and Industry (BERR, 2008) for the UK, France and the Netherlands whilst US use GAAP (Generally Acceptable Accounting Principles). These examples have financial reporting as the main focus; however, Table 18.5, 'Demystifying Corporate Social Responsibilities (CSR)' provides a summary of some of the main facets that organizations use to communicate their contribution to the environment and the community at large as an asset.

The table provides information about a selection of service organizations that include corporate social responsibilities as part of their strategies to communicate to the customers, their employees and their suppliers that they are serious about good citizenship. Service organizations need to consider these issues when writing their marketing plans and developing strategies. The reason this is advised is because customers, staff and suppliers are changing and want organizations they are dealing with to help maintain and protect their surroundings and environment. E-services in Action, 'City Car Club', also suggests that organizations are offering services to customers that will save them money, but also help the environment.

Source: Adapted from Business Impact Review Group (2003), Capriotti and Moreno (2007), Capron and Gray (2000), GRI (2002), Ingenhoff (2004), Maignan and Ralston (2002), World Council for Corporate Governance (2008), Kenyon (2008).

Table 18.5	Facet	Explanation and example
Demystifying corporate social responsibilities (CSR)	Corporate profile	Explanation of a company's values, beliefs, corporate strategy and how and where it will operate. The Body Shop is known as a provider of ethical products from natural ingredients. Its Corporate Profile states 'Our business runs on passion, and our five values; Protect the Planet, Support Community Trade, Against Animal Testing, Defend Human Rights, Activate Self Esteem, govern all that we do, from reducing our carbon footprint to ordering our envelopes. To us, there is no other way to work. After all, when you believe in what you do, you do it better.' www.bodyshop.co.uk
	Products and services	Tescos has 140 Fair-Trade lines (45 are Tesco own-label products). This demonstrates that Tesco provides products from suppliers that have an affinity with the ethos of Fair-Trade. They go even further by showing their customers through regular in-store and TV promotions that they are committed to the Fair-Trade movement. They even allow Fair-Trade products to be displayed in strategic places such as highly sought after and expensive 'end of aisle' spaces. (www.tesco.co.uk)
	Employment and human resources	Clear information is provided as to the types of contracts, training provided, promotion opportunities, evaluation/ appraisal and dismissal. Details are shown as to the commitment to be fair in terms of human rights – e.g. anti-discrimination, child labour (including the supply chain).
	Economic action	Details showing how the organization's earnings/profits contribute to the impact upon the local, regional, national and international economy through donations, charity work or grants. John Lewis Partnership is a good example of a service organization that takes economic action by supporting local projects. One of their charitable donations was a £10,000 donation to the Nuffield Theatre in Southampton.
	Social action	Harrods' jewellery buyers severed trade with Myanmar (formally known as Burma) following EU trade sanctions. They performed this social action in 2007 as the Trade Union Congress had identified that Myanmar is a country that has poor human rights issues.

Environmental action	Environmental action is an increasingly topical issue. An organization's carbon footprint is a topic that is discussed regularly. Boots the leading health and beauty chemist across Europe has signalled its commitment to reduce their carbon footprint by managing the 'product journey' through the supply chain. (Delay, 2007)
Corporate governance	BT was very proud when it received the highly prestigious Golden Peacock Global Award in 2007 for their Corporate Social Responsibilities (CSR) but also their holistic Corporate Governance. To receive this award, corporate social responsibilities and its communication to its customers, staff and suppliers, lies at the centre of their business. (World Council for Corporate Governance, 2008)
Corporate ethics	Body Shop, Ben and Jerry's and The Co-operative Bank are known to have corporate ethics as key to their businesses philosophy. These service organizations communicate regularly that they have an ethical stance. They get involved in many human rights issues, go head to head with big businesses and governments in terms of their environmental policies and have been leaders in researching and developing ethical products and services.
Relationship with public	Unipart clearly has a CSR philosophy to understand what makes organizations a cut above the rest. Unipart states up front that its stakeholders are: 'Our Customers, Our Employees, Our Investors, Our Suppliers, The Communities in which we do business'. This shows that CRS *is* their strategy and they are not shy in relating it to their publics. (www.unipart.co.uk)
External criteria	Links to external forces and legislation (e.g. own government and governance with common goals – e.g. G7/G8) thus linking with the national and international criteria on aspects of CSR. Sainsbury's has joined the UK's Ethical Trading Initiative to provide benchmarks for ethical initiatives. Geoff Spriegel, Director, Technical Division, Sainsbury's states 'ETI membership has provided Sainsbury's with the opportunity to benchmark its activities against those of other companies. It has also provided the means to help translate genuine customer concerns into a practical action plan for improved ethical trading across our worldwide supplier base.' (Business in the Community, 2000: 4)

Summary

This chapter has outlined how future trends will affect the service industry. The number of people that live on our planet is going to increase dramatically by 2050. A person's life expectancy will also change as people will generally live longer. Both of these trends will affect businesses who will need to adapt their services to cater for a growing population that may live well into their 80s. All service industries will need to think creatively to tap into this market, particularly businesses in travel, health and leisure. Whilst the population will grow, consumers will still want a highly personalized service that can be adaptable 'in real time'. This chapter suggested that Marketers include Packaging, Performance and Personalization in their plans to focus their operations. Similarly, we recommend that organizations consider non-ownership as the fifth service characteristic. Non-ownership, or sharing ownership for a short length of time, is growing in popularity as consumers wish to explore new leisure activities, be more flexible with their time and aid the environment. This chapter concluded with a suggestion that organizations can win trust with customers based on their Corporate Social Responsibilities. Service organizations have always been competing against each other for the consumer's hard-earned money. Organizations, be they B2B or business to consumer, realize that their social, community and/or environmental policies encourage consumers to view them favourably. Favourable perception develops into trust and in highly competitive markets a trusted relationship between the organization and their consumer is paramount.

The future is always changeable, with new priorities and demands occurring all the time. Changes in the population, technology, consumer needs and globalization are happening now and creating new challenges for the services industry. Consumers may want plastic surgery in their lunch break, while ordering clothes or watching the latest chick flick on their PDA. Alternatively, they may be having a football training session with David Beckham on their Wii. The technology is already here, and service organizations should continue to be creative and innovative to help us satisfy the needs we did not even know existed – yet.

Discussion questions

1 What will service organizations have to consider in their marketing plans to deal with the ageing population?

2 Consider a service organization of your choice, what services should they include in their portfolio to deal with the growth in single-person households?

3 Why will consumers look for organizations that care for the environment?

4 Which service organizations have had to change in light of increased online activities?

5 In addition to retailing online, how should service organizations use v-commerce to drive up sales?

6 How will service organizations use online services in the future?

7 Discuss the different ways organizations could promote their corporate and social activities.

References and further reading

BERR (2008) 'The Department for Business', http://www.berr.gov.uk/, accessed 13 May 2008.

Bodyshop (2008) 'About Us', http://www.thebodyshop.com/bodyshop/company/index.jsp;jsessionid = wDUz1BeHps888Qzt1PLz3Q**.bsprd-app-101-bssfolapp03?cm_ re = default-_-Footer-_-About_Us, accessed 14 February 2008.

Business Impact Review Group (2003) 'Corporate impact reporting initiative', www.bitc.org.uk, accessed 1 March 2008.

Business Impact Taskforce (2000) 'Winning with integrity: A guide to social responsibility', *Business in the Community* (November): 5.

Business in the Community (2000) 'Winning with Integrity – Human Rights', http://www.bitc.org.uk, accessed 10 December 2007.

Capriotti, P. and Moreno, A. (2007) 'Communicating corporate responsibility through corporate web sites in Spain', *Corporate Communications: An Internationall Journal* 12 (3): 221-237.

Capron, M. and Gray, R. (2000) 'Accounting in Europe: experimenting with assessing corporate social responsibility in France: an exploratory note on an initiative by social economy firm', *European Accounting Review* 9 (2): 99-109.

Cetron, M., De Micco, F. and Davies, O. (2006) *Hospitality 2010 The Future of Hospitality and Travel*, Englewood Cliffs, NJ: Prentice Hall.

Constantinides, E. (2006) 'The marketing mix revisited: towards the 21st century marketing', *Journal of Marketing Management* 22: 407–438.

Delay, T. (2007) 'Carbon Footprints in the Supply Chain: The Next Step for Business', http://www.climateactionprogramme.org/features/article/carbon_footprints_in_the_supply_chain_the_next_step_for_business/, accessed 13 May 2008.

English, J. (2000) 'The four 'p's of marketing are dead', *Marketing Health Services* 20 (2): 21-2.

Euromoniter (2008) 'One person households: Opportunities for consumer goods companies', http://www.euromonitor.com/One_person_households_ Opportunities_for_consumer_goods_companies, accessed 10 June 2008.

European Union (2002) 'EU Directive for Recyling Waste Electrical and Electronic Equipment', http://ec.europa.eu/environment/waste/weee/index_en.htm, accessed 13 May 2008.

GRI (2002) 'Sustainability Reporting Guidelines, Global Reporting Inittiative, Amsterdam', www.globalreporting.org/guidelines/2002/gri_2002_guidelines.pdf, accessed 14 February 2008.

Gummesson, E. (2007) 'Exit services marketing – enter service marketing', *Journal of Customer Behaviour* 6 (2): 113-141.

Igenhoff, D. (2004) 'Assessing corporate citizenship communication among 30 German Stock Index companies', paper presented at International Agenda Setting Conference, Bonn.

Jobber, J. D. (2001) *Principles and Practice of Marketing*, Maidenhead: McGraw-Hill.

John, J., Grove, S. J. and Fisk, R. P. (2006) 'Improvisation in service performances: lessons from jazz', *Managing Service Quality* 16 (3): 247-268.

Kanzawa, O. and Takahashi, M. (2005) 'Establishment of global recycle network', *Fujitsu Scientific and Technical Journal* 41 (2): 242-250.

Kenyon, A.J. (2008) 'Exploring Corporate and Social Responsibilities: A Retailer's Challenge' CIRCLE 5th International Conference on Consumer Behaviour, Cyprus.

Lovelock, C. and Gummesson, E. (2004) 'Whither services marketing? In search of a new paradigm and fresh perspectives', *Journal of Service Research* 7 (1): 20-41.

Maignan, I. and Ralston, D. (2002) 'Corporate social responsibility in Europe and the US', *Journal of International Business Studies* 33 (3): 497-514.

Mintel (2007) 'British Lifestyles March 2007', http://academic.mintel.com/sinatra/oxygen_academic/search_results/showand/display/id = 191183/display/id = 269252#hit1, accessed 10 June 2008.

National Institute of Population and Social Security Research (2008) 'Summary of Japanese Population Projections', http://www.ipss.go.jp/pp-newest/e/ppfj02/t_2_e.html, accessed 1 June 2008.

Population Parsons (2008) 'Population figures ('000's) for the territories now comprising the UK and Ireland AD to the year 2050', http://www.populationparsons.com/UK_Population_data%20_sheet.htm, accessed 1 June 2008.

Population Reference Bureau (2008) 'Germany', http://www.prb.org/Countries/Germany.aspx, accessed 1 June 2008.

Raban, Y. (2004) 'Trends in ICTs and future forecasts', http://www.eurescom.de/e-living, accessed 13 May 2008.

Rackspace (2007) 'Shops to survive as virtual stores replace e-commerce', http://www.rackspace.co.uk/default.asp?docId = 15806, accessed 10 June 2008.

World Council for Corporate Governance (2008) 'Golden Peacock Global Award for Corporate Social Responsibility', http://www.wcfcg.net, accessed 21 January 2008.

Statistics Austria (2008) 'Population Forecasts', http://www.statistik.at/web_en/statistics/population/demographic_forecasts/population_forecasts/index.html, accessed 1 June 2008.

Swiss Info.ch (2007) 'Swiss Car sharing continues its expansion', http://www.swissinfo.org/eng/feature/detail/Swiss_car_ sharing_continues_its_expansion.html?siteSect = 108andsid = 7783400andcKey = 1178550082000, accessed 13 May 2008.

Tesco (2008) 'Fair-trade', http://www.tescocorporate.com/page.aspx?pointerid = 245BE78B1CE5459FA4F138C81DA2A3E0, accessed 15 February 2008.

Unipart Group (2008) 'Philosophy and Goals' http://www.unipart.co.uk/Home/AboutUnipart Group/Philosophy Goals/tabid/57/language/ en-GB/Default.aspx, accessed 14 February 2008.

United Nations (1999) 'Population Aging 1999', http://www. un.org/esa/population/publications/aging99/a99cht1.htm, accessed 10 June 2008.

Usunier, J.-C. and Lee, J. A. (2005) *Marketing Across Cultures*, 4th ed., London: Prentice Hall.

Part four
Cases

Case 1

Pass the parcel – Who cares wins

The competitive environment in parcel delivery and courier services is hotting up with firms striving to offer the highest level of customer care, delivery efficiency and least impact on the environment.

This comprehensive case overviews the industry as a whole and then focuses on a key player in the European market, TNT. The final section of the case study explores the radical changes made to TNT's customer care policy and procedures.

The market and the competition

Industry leaders

UPS. With sales of US$36.5 billion and roughly 384,000 employees worldwide, United Parcel Service (UPS) was the largest package shipper in the world in 2004. That year, this Atlanta, Georgia-based company moved 3.6 billion packages to more than 200 countries and territories. The company does not separate out the revenue earned from trucking verses that earned from other forms of transport, including air, as much of its courier services involves a variety of transport forms for each delivery.

In 2003, the company introduced plans to spend US$600 million to improve its pickup and delivery processes. Considered the most technologically savvy of the world's largest shipping firms, UPS uses systems such as UPSnet, with more than 500,000 miles of communications lines, as well as a satellite that tracks hundreds of thousands of packages each day and connects roughly 1,300 UPS distribution plants in 46 different nations.

FedEx. Federal Express specializes in overnight delivery of packages, documents and heavy freight, and is a top express transportation company worldwide. With 2004 sales of US$24.7 billion, the company's 196,000 employees handle 6 million ship-ments each day to more than 220 countries and territories, using more than 71,000 ground delivery vehicles. Its delivery divisions include FedEx Express, FedEx Ground, FedEx Freight and FedEx Custom. This company does not differentiate between revenue earned by truck transport and that earned through air or other means.

In early 2000, FDX diversified into customs brokerage with the purchase of Tower Group International, a unit that eventually formed the core of a new subsidiary, FedEx Trade Networks Inc. The trading unit also provided trade consulting and international transportation and logistics services. In April, FDX changed its name to FedEx Corp., and the core express delivery business took on the moniker FedEx Express. Ground delivery operations were renamed FedEx Ground. To expand its less-than-truckload freight operations, the firm paid US$1.2 billion for American Freightways Corporation in December 2000. FedEx merged American Freightways with former Caliber unit Viking Freight into its FedEx Freight arm. As part of the deal, FedEx assumed US$250 million of American Freightways' debt, a fact which concerned some analysts as FedEx was already spending billions of dollars each year maintaining its costly infrastructure.

DHL Worldwide Network. Belgian based, yet owned by the German Deutsche Post, DHL Worldwide is a global leader in international express shipping. Begun in 1969 as an air shipper of paper from California to Hawaii, the company was soon expanding globally. By the end of 2002, Deutsche Post owned the company, and in 2003 the parent merged its other acquisitions into DHL. By 2003, the company's 160,000 employees used 75,000 vehicles to move more than 1 billion shipments to more than 220 countries and territories. DHL's revenues that year were more than US$28 billion.

Yamato. Yamato Transport Co. Ltd. was the forerunner of private parcel delivery service in Japan, and in 2004, it had been the market leader in that country for two decades. A strong domestic service includes home moving, delivery of refrigerated goods, and facsimile transmission. Links with UPS in the United States allow Yamato to make deliveries in 200 countries outside Japan. Founded in 1919 by young entrepreneur Koshin Kogura, Yamato was the first courier service in Tokyo. By its fiscal year end in March 2004, Yamato employed nearly 132,000 workers and brought in approximately US$9.4 billion per year.

Market Trends

Partly as a result of heightened expectations on the part of business users (which represent over 95 per cent of the market at present), there is a clear demand for a speedier delivery, and the same or next-day sector now accounts for an estimated 55 per cent of volume and 66 per cent of value in the domestic market. A majority of companies are placing increasing emphasis on this aspect of their businesses, not least because an element of premium can be charged for a faster service. The problem is that, as these faster services become the norm rather than the exception, premium prices are less likely to be acceptable to users. Whatever the speed, all clients expect accuracy and timed delivery together with some ability to track their packages.

The market for courier and despatch services heavily favours the domestic sector, with 94 per cent of packages originating and being delivered within the UK. However, this is the less profitable sector in that it only produces 68 per cent of revenue. For this reason, most companies of a reasonable size are seeking to increase their involvement in international despatches.

The UK market is serviced by at least 5,000 businesses, some extremely small, and this has created a highly fragmented supply structure. There will always be a place for small companies serving the needs of local businesses, but the more successful are invariably larger with national coverage a pre-requisite if they wish to tender for important contracts. The market is currently led by the former Post Office subsidiary Parcelforce Worldwide, with other leading players including Securicor/Omega, TNT Express, Parceline, ANC, Lynx and United Carriers. Only the top three players have value shares of 10 per cent or higher.

The international sector is much less fragmented because of the complex infrastructure required. This sector is led by DHL International followed by TNT, UPS and Federal Express.

Adspend is low in relation to sales at less than 0.5 per cent in any of the years 1995–1999. Indeed it fell dramatically in the last of those years as DHL and TNT both reduced their budgets substantially. DHL, however, had previously been the most prominent advertiser, along with UPS. There are two reasons why main media adspend is so low. Firstly, this is essentially a business-to-business market; and secondly, the majority of smaller players tend to rely heavily on directories such as Yellow Pages and Thomsons.

The results of the trade research interviews conducted for the Mintel report indicate a high level of uncertainty about the future of their market. Most were concerned about rising costs which could not be offset by price increases because of the competitive nature of the marketplace. All accepted that the use of e-mail for simple document transfer was forcing a re-think of future plans and a majority foresaw a great deal of consolidation within the supply structure. The need to be bigger in the light of changing demands and the need to invest in new technologies is expected to prompt mergers, acquisitions, alliance and other means of expansion.

Mintel believes that growth in the future will be generated by the increase in use of mail order by consumers, particularly ordering over the internet. This increase in parcel delivery services to households will help compensate for any business-to-business deliveries lost to use of e-mail. Liberalization of the Post Office and a reduction in the monopoly of the Royal Mail would also offer opportunities to dispatch service providers, as has been seen in the rest of the EU.

Several trends are seen to be among the most important facing the industry. First, mergers and acquisitions would continue as companies worked to establish intermodal forms of transport for packages in order to remain competitive. In addition, postal services around the world would continue to partner with courier companies to increase their services in the face of declines in the volume of letter mail.

Increases in sales via the internet were also having an impact on courier services, as they continued to be the distributor of choice for many sales companies. Also, more international shipping was being seen as trade liberalized around the world and the economies of developing countries improved.

TNT

TNT have become a major player in the European and World parcel delivery market through steadily developing competitive advantage in a number of key areas. This case study provides a history to the company, outlines their recent successes in the UK and focuses on their award-winning customer care strategy as a way to gaining sustainable competitive advantage.

TNT UK background

TNT Express Services UK and Ireland is the country's leading business-to-business express delivery company. Established in the UK in 1978, the company has developed its leading position in the time-sensitive express delivery market through organic growth and, with an annual turnover in excess of £750 million, it employs 10,600 people in the UK and Ireland and operates more than 3,500 vehicles from over 70 locations. TNT Express Services UK and Ireland delivers hundreds of thousands of consignments every week – in excess of 50 million items per year. The company has an annual turnover in excess of £750 million and has achieved this success through organic growth rather than acquisition.

TNT's mission is 'to exceed customers' expectations in the transfer of their goods and documents around the world':

> We deliver value to our customers by providing the most reliable and efficient solutions in distribution and logistics. We lead the industry by:
>
> - Instilling pride in our people
> - Creating value for our shareholders
> - Sharing responsibility for our world.

Innovation

In the past twenty-five years TNT has:

- created the first guaranteed nationwide door-to-door, business-to-business next-day delivery service;
- developed a first-to-market range of time-sensitive early morning delivery options; and
- launched the first nationwide door-to-door same-day delivery service – TNT Sameday.

This continuous innovation earned TNT The Queen's Award for Enterprise (Innovation category) in 2000. Committed to the highest standards of service and customer care, the company's achievements have been widely recognized with a series of prestigious industry awards. The company also boasts the coveted UK Quality Award and the prestigious European Quality Award, achieved in 1998, among its portfolio of accreditations for business excellence.

Company culture

The company encourages a 'home grown timber' policy of promoting from within wherever possible. The Managing Directors of the three largest TNT businesses all started on the 'shop floor' – in fact TNT Express Services UK and Ireland Managing Director Tom Bell started working in operations with TNT in Maidstone depot in 1977. He now heads up the multi-million pound UK and Ireland business.

As Tom Bell says: 'You can invest and invest and invest again in leading-edge technology, but our biggest achievement of all is the way we have continuously found innovative ways to bring the best out of our people. At TNT we have created a climate of enthusiasm and success where we constantly strive to beat our previous best and where employees are incredibly loyal to the company.'

Customer Interface Technology and satisfaction

TNT Customer Interface Technology (CIT) embraces the most innovative range of dispatch, tracking and tracing systems available, designed to make TNT even faster and more accessible to customers. The state of the art track and trace system developed by TNT Express uses data from consignment barcodes so that individual packages can be tracked at any point during transit. The system allows the company to advise customers on the status of consignments at any time in the process from collection to delivery. Customers can track shipments via the internet, SMS, WAP-enabled mobile phones, PDA devices and through an e-mail tracking service.

The track and trace initiative was instrumental in helping TNT win the category of 'Best use of Internet/e-commerce' at the Motor Transport Awards 2003 – the transport industry equivalent of the 'Oscars'. The success was the company's 23rd Motor Transport Award in the past 20 years – an unprecedented achievement.

TNT Express has developed a proactive approach to customer care that has resulted in year-on-year revenue and profit growth and culminated in a total of six Motor Transport Awards for Customer Care in the past 20 years.

Corporate sustainability

TNT Express Services has contributed to the success of TNT N.V., the Dutch-based express, mail and logistics giant in its second year of appearing in the Dow Jones Sustainability Index (DJSI) in 2006.

TNT recorded an overall rating of 84 out of a possible 100, the highest recorded score in the transport and express delivery category. In six out of the 18 DJSI criteria TNT recorded the highest score possible in its sector – Industrial Transportation.

The prestigious DJSI tracks the financial performance of the leading sustainability-driven companies worldwide, organizations that combine business success with an ethical, caring and responsible approach across a variety of areas including economic, environmental and social criteria.

Strong evidence exists to show that organizations that adopt a more 'sustainable' approach to business enjoy positive benefits. Financial organizations such as Dow Jones have found that companies with a strong commitment and performance on corporate sustainability have enjoyed greater levels of profitability than similar companies who lack such a commitment.

TNT promotes energy efficiency throughout the operation and has been a signatory to the Department of Environment/Energy Efficiency Office Declaration of Commitment to responsible energy management since 1993. The company is committed to preserving and improving the world in which we live and work.

The company recognizes the importance of developing and sustaining positive relationships with local authorities and communities and consults with them on a range of environmental considerations, in particular on issues relating to new depots such as road access and the impact on residential areas. In 2005 TNT achieved the coveted International Standard for Environmental Management ISO14001.

The very nature of the express delivery market means that the night-time movement of consignments via road and air is imperative. As a consequence, TNT is committed to minimising the effects of noise pollution and has invested in a range of BAe 146 aircraft, that emit engine noise at one-eighth of the levels of Boeing 727 aircraft that they have replaced.

TNT is active in a number of environmental initiatives including a joint venture with Imperial College, London, to develop alternative fuels, a drive to reduce waste reduction at its network of depots and a commitment to buy 10 per cent of its energy requirements from 'green energy sources' in 2004.

In December 2006, TNT launched the world's first zero emission 7.5 tonne vehicle, with a view to taking on similar vehicles if its trial in London in early 2007 – Courier/Parcel Industry – Global Industry Outlook 2006: Courier and Trucking Services – is successful.

The results of the most recent TNT Community Survey stated that the vast majority of businesses and householders consulted had either a 'High' or 'Good' overall perception of the company.

TNT vision

The essence of what TNT strives for: Delivering more:

- Delivering more is about always going the extra mile, about always raising the bar, about always going beyond standard compliance, about always changing the paradigms, about our ambition to always lead.

- Delivering more encompasses a can-do attitude, competitiveness, forward thinking, responsibility, care and ambition.

- Delivering more is optimistic. We are confident that we can overcome obstacles and achieve our ambitious goals.

- Delivering more makes us stand out from the average.

TNT standards

1 Aim to satisfy customers every time.
2 Challenge and improve all we do.
3 Be passionate about our people.
4 Act as a team.
5 Be honest, always.
6 Measure success through sustainable profit.
7 Work for the world.

TNT's quality journey

Operational review

An in-depth appraisal of existing operations was carried out in 1989 to identify opportunities for improvement which could be built upon to achieve demanding quality objectives. Strengths included:

- experienced and capable managers in all depots
- an excellent and competitive service
- very strong financial controls with accurate depot profit and loss accounts prepared every week
- useful management information circulated often in the form of weekly league tables to report service performance, costs and other essential data
- regular management meetings to review costs and service.

The requirement was quite simply to make the company more efficient by achieving a better service at lower unit costs. In communicating the aims to people employed in the company, great emphasis was placed on rejecting from the very start the concept of a cost versus quality trade-off.

Financial savings were expected but these arose as a result of introducing improved working methods and not through quick fixes or by cutting corners. The approach is that time wasted in current processes should be removed and experience shows that implementation of this philosophy produces better service quality as well as improved productivity.

Instilled throughout the company is a belief that cost reductions and service benefits are not incompatible but are both the result of improvements introduced by well managed quality-driven teams.

Performance improvement

Quality is not treated as a separate issue within the company and the continuous improvement philosophy has become an integral part of the business strategy. The aim is for the quality ethic to be thoroughly assimilated into TNT culture and to this end the company has deliberately avoided the use of acronyms such as TQM, QlTs and QATs and so on.

The top team agreed upon a wide-ranging programme of self-assessment against the business excellence model which was very well received by all employees. The initial self-assessment work started to help identify gaps in their performance which were then addressed to produce real business improvements.

Focus on the goal initially of winning the UK Quality Award and after that the European Quality Award helped create the present climate of improvement which exists throughout the company where all TNT people continuously seek to beat previous best individual and team performances.

Customer focus

Feedback from customers caused us to revise the attitude of the company to performance standards. Traditionally the key performance indicator was the level of TNT culpable service failures and success was measured by the extent to which errors were minimised.

Customers told TNT that the question of fault or blame was not an issue and their concern is that the service promised and paid for should always be delivered in full.

As a result TNT made deliveries on time the new prime standard of performance. Weekly reports for each location showing actual results for all of the following outcomes were introduced and this ongoing measurement discipline continues to help refine quality of service:

- deliveries on time
- misrouted and missorted consignments
- copy consignment notes raised and not matched with original documents
- late linehaul services arriving at our hubs
- failures to deliver on time analysed by reason.

Gradually TNT introduced and developed further performance targets for key support processes to encompass their administration and selling functions. They now gather and feedback every week hard information on customer query handling, credit notes, client contacts, complaints received and other key outcomes which provide measures of their ability to satisfy customers.

Frequent and unrelenting reporting disciplines continue to help quickly introduce improvements whenever standards are not achieved. A named individual at each depot is responsible for each key performance outcome and staff are empowered to call on additional resources to achieve required results.

Communications

TNT have developed company-wide poster campaigns to emphasize the need for quality and to underline the fact that everybody is involved in improvement activities. Customer-visible frontline improvement activities were seen as the ones to go for first and these include:

- vehicle loading
- telephone manner
- correct routing and labelling
- drivers delivering on time.

In conjunction with the posters, a 'Driving For Quality' campaign was introduced. New uniforms were designed not only to project the corporate image of the company but also to make a further statement to employees that each and every person has an important role to play in its commitment to quality.

All employee survey responses are reviewed in one-on-one meetings with the individuals concerned and also collectively for each location to ensure that opportunities for improvement are actioned.

Information is disseminated through videos, house magazines and frequent meetings, all of which are supported by constructive briefings and conferences. Channels have been set up to receive employee feedback and to ensure that the views of employees are reflected in decisions affecting company goals, policy and strategy.

Technology

Central to the provision of time-sensitive services offered by the company are leading-edge information technology and communications support systems.

A prime example of the use of technology to increase efficiency and service quality is the TNT Universe System which provides improved customer service and better communications for all staff employed within the company.

More recently the installation of data terminals in TNT express delivery vehicles helps the company to provide up-to-the-minute information for customers about the status of urgent consignments. In addition the in-cab data terminals are enabling TNT to respond immediately to on-demand collection requests placed by customers.

Everyone employed in the company now has a computer screen which provides access to reliable real-time data thus enabling any employee to instantly address external and internal customer requests.

Training

TNT recognized at an early stage the paramount need to continuously improve the performance and skills of staff. As a result, in 1989 the company developed an integrated plan for training all employees with the goal of developing the most effective workforce within the industry.

The aim was and still is to provide a work environment that is conducive to multi-skilling, thus enabling people throughout the business to use practical techniques and skills acquired through company training schemes.

The following cornerstones of best practice people management were adopted:

- Commitment – to train and develop everyone in the company.
- Planning – to provide a framework for identifying and addressing skill gaps.
- Action – to equip employees with the skills needed to satisfy customers through high-quality training.
- Evaluation – to continuously improve the training programmes, appraisal systems and all other people-management processes employed within the business

Expressing excellence

The award-winning TNT Expressing Excellence customer care training initiative arose from a comprehensive review in 1992 of company-wide customer service performance.

Expressing Excellence customer care objectives agreed at that time and still in force today are to:

- improve service quality and provide outstanding customer satisfaction
- operate clear customer care policies soundly based on market research
- continuously communicate and implement improved customer care techniques.

The effectiveness of the Expressing Excellence training initiatives is measured by the degree to which the company meets the following customer satisfaction outcomes:

- Retain clients and increase the number of customers trading every week.
- Improve the percentage of deliveries made on time.

- Reduce the number of linehaul vehicles arriving after scheduled arrival times at the hub depots.
- Decrease the value and number of credit notes issued.
- Reduce customer claims in number and as a percentage of revenue.
- Decrease the number of outstanding invoice queries at the end of each week.
- Increase the frequency of contacts with existing and prospective customers.
- Improve telephone response times. Their success in this area was reported by the *Which* consumer magazine where the following comment appeared: 'If you want to know how to answer the telephone ring TNT.'

Recognition

TNT place great store by the improved motivation which can result from simply recognizing good performances.

The results for all outcomes key to performance are now published every week in league tables and are displayed on result boards at all sites operated by the company.

The publication *Celebrate* magazine was introduced several years ago and this publication which is distributed at regular intervals to all staff gives details of the excellent performances regularly achieved by TNT UK Limited people.

Halls of Fame which celebrate the achievements of the most outstanding people have been introduced at all major locations and annual TNT UK Limited excellence awards continue to motivate.

Recognition of outstanding performances where TNT people have beaten their previous best records is also provided in weekly newsletters and quarterly awards are made to successful teams and individuals.

I Made it Happen awards and many other recognition schemes are now operated to ensure that TNT people are thanked for the exceptional efforts which are made every day and every night in their extremely competitive business.

Results

In the period since the advent of Project 2000 TNT have:

- strengthened leadership of the time-sensitive express parcels market;
- expanded the number of customers trading with the company by 300 per cent;
- gained nearly 80 per cent of the national newspaper primary transport market;
- become the market leader in nationwide shared user garment distribution;
- continuously improved service quality which has resulted in failures being reduced to almost negligible levels;
- lowered unit costs per consignment by more than 20 per cent;
- decreased lost time accidents by 30 per cent;
- improved employee satisfaction levels from 58 per cent to 85 per cent of all staff employed in the company; and
- secured excellent community satisfaction levels which in their local areas of highest employment show 99 per cent positive outcomes.

The impact on financial results has been dramatic:

- Turnover has increased and TNT UK have outperformed the market year after year.
- Profits have increased every year since 1988 and margins have been dramatically improved.

TNT and customer care

The company created a customer care strategy based on four principles that would be readily accepted by people in all parts of the company, whether they are delivery drivers or office workers. These were to ask customers what they want; to ask TNT staff what they need to do the job; to create enthusiasm and success; and to strive to beat the company's previous best performance.

Chris Atkinson, the company's director of customer experience, says: 'In transport you get all sorts of people working for you and it was important that the whole company understood what we were doing. We believe that if you manage people in the right way ultimately you will end up getting the right response from your customers.'

TNT used an independent survey from MORI which identified 14 key areas of customer/supplier interaction that dictate repurchase behaviour. Six of these relate to customer care issues and account for 55 per cent of the reasons why customers decide to buy a product or service – all six have been addressed by TNT.

The most important is how staff treat a customer, accounting for 17 per cent of purchases, followed by how staff handle an enquiry or complaint (12%) and staff enthusiasm for products and services (8%). Also important were after-sales service (7%), staff knowledge of products and services (6%) and how staff represent their company (5%).

Rather than bringing in initiatives and hoping they have a beneficial impact, TNT measures performance in minute detail. Twice a year the company conducts a Customer Loyalty Survey and, from this, each of the 70 depots in the network receives a loyalty report. This is based on 39 customer satisfaction attributes and compares the depot's performance against previous results and against the company as a whole.

'Depots are benchmarked against each other within the UK and the UK is then measured against other countries to see how we're performing. If we're happy with the results from a depot we can congratulate them but if we're not we can isolate the weak areas and assist the depot to improve', Atkinson explains.

Satisfaction

Local depots select a customer satisfaction steering group comprising a driver, loading bank operative, salesperson, administration clerk and traffic office operator. The group is chaired by a supervisor or manager and prepares an action plan to improve the worst five attributes reported in the survey. Regional directors then review the progress of the action plan in monthly meetings.

In order to test performance further, TNT has come up with a concept it calls the Perfect Transaction. This measures all the elements of a delivery such as whether the consignment was collected on time, what condition it arrived in, whether the proof-of-delivery was correctly provided and whether an accurate invoice was produced. 'We take 10 per cent of consignments and measure them at random. We believe that this gives us a good view of what is going on in the business', Atkinson says.

TNT Express Services employs more than 10,000 people in the UK and has 3,500 vehicles which deliver 50 million items a year. Major customers are the responsibility of local depot managers but Atkinson says its aim is to provide a good experience whatever the size of the customer. 'We believe it is important to offer the same level of service for someone sending 50,000 items as someone who gets on the phone from the Yellow Pages and sends one,' he comments.

The company has a customer care charter it gives to customers which states that they will be contacted on a regular basis. This involves a telephone call and a visit at least once every eight weeks, with the frequency determined by the customer's trading patterns. The process identifies customer needs but is also useful in detecting potential areas of customer dissatisfaction at an early stage.

In addition, customers are encouraged to contact their local TNT manager if they have any query or complaint. No calls to managers are screened and customers are put through without being first asked their name or the reason for the call.

TNT has also acted on research by customer service survey company TARP which found that loyalty levels are even higher among those who have had a query or problem successfully resolved than those who have not had them in the first place. 'I would never say nothing will go wrong with delivering a parcel but what is important is how you react to a situation', Atkinson says.

Automated

The company runs three national contact centres to deal with customer enquiries. The most recent of these opened in Gateshead last year to support existing facilities in Atherstone and Lount, Leicestershire. Callers are answered within three rings and go straight through to a customer service agent rather than being processed by an automated system. They are then dealt with either by a response team which takes simple collection requests and provides proof-of-delivery information or by a support function, responsible for in-depth queries.

TNT believes that its customer care policies have played a key part in its recent performance. Its average number of trading customers has grown in each of the past five years to more than 48,000 and its revenue and profit have also increased to £727 million and £69 million respectively in 2005. Over the past three years it has achieved a customer retention rate of 97 per cent among its top 100 daily trading customers.

Atkinson believes that small companies as well as those the size of TNT can benefit from good customer service. 'The basic principle is to take care of your people who will take care of your customers. If that happens everything else falls into place', he says. But it is something that needs constant work and TNT is planning further customer care improvements next year. 'We are setting the bar higher and higher all the time', Atkinson explains.

Staff

Training, staff motivation and internal communications have played a key part in improving TNT's customer service performance.

Enthusiasm, friendliness, commitment and an ability to work with people are taken into account when taking on new staff, alongside academic record and previous experience. Once in place, all employees are given customer care training as part of their induction, with refresher courses every 12–18 months.

In addition, Atkinson believes that the overall level of training – which helped the company win this year's Training category at the MT Awards – boosts morale and creates pride in the TNT brand.

The company recognizes customer care achievements through personal congratulatory letters and a national newsletter. Employees can also receive £100 worth of vouchers under a scheme known as Delivering More.

Employees are encouraged to take part in quizzes, known as the X-Press Factor, covering products, competitors and general market information. Local depots enter a team of six which plays a minimum of three rounds, followed by quarter and semi-finals and a grand final where the winning team wins £3,000 in cash and a silver trophy.

TNT believes the effectiveness of these policies has helped create enthusiasm among the workforce and is shown in good feedback in the People Survey it conducts among staff each year. The results of the survey are made known to staff through a special bulletin.

'There has to be a culture of customer care which is generated throughout the company. If you haven't got the right attitude you'll never get the job done successfully', Atkinson says.

Discussion questions

1 What are the key customer benefits being offered by the courier and parcel service companies? Who are the main customer groups and how do they differ?

2 Discuss the challenges to TNT created by the specific characteristics of services.

3 Explain why customer care is a vital part of TNT's strategy in this competitive industry.

4 What do you see as the main areas of competitive advantage in the future. Explain how TNT can use these to remain a market leader.

5 Critique the methods use to measure customer satisfaction and levels of customer care.

References

Global Industry Overview (2006) 'Trucking and courier services' http://www.warc.com/LandingPages/Generic/Results.asp?Ref = 14271, accessed 20 August 2008.

Management Today (2003) 'Who Cares Wins', 13 January, http://64.233.169.104/search?q = cache:X0rW16zQ2ooJ:www.unep.org/cpi/briefs/Brief14Jan.doc + %22 + Management + Today%

22 + %22who + cares + wins%22 + 2006&hl = en&ct = clnk&cd = 4, accessed 20 August 2008.

Mintel (2000) 'Courier and Despatch Services UK – March 2000', http://academic.mintel.com/sinatra/oxygen_academic/search_results/show&/display/id = 1083, accessed 20 August 2008.

www.tnt.co.uk.

Case 2

Relax and take it easy at The Spa

The Spa in Hampshire

Voted 'The UK's Favourite Spa Retreat' (Conde Nast Traveller Magazine Reader Spa Awards 2007) The Spa at Chewton Glen Hotel and Country Club is a haven that takes guests away from the high-speed hustle and bustle of daily life. Not only is The Spa at Chewton Glen revered as a sumptuous place to visit by British reviewers such as Vincent Crump for *The Sunday Times* (2006), Elisabeth King for the Australian Gourmet Traveller also declares it to be one of the top ten best spa retreats. Indeed there is a long list of accolades and awards attached to Chewton Glen ranging from Laurent Perrier Spa Award – (Joint winner) to 'England's Leading Spa Resort' by World Travel Awards 2006.

Chewton Glen did not begin its life as a hotel. It began as a country house owned by George Marryat between 1837 and 1855. Legend has it that smugglers brought their contraband through the grounds of Chewton Glen before disappearing into the New Forest and beyond. Today there is still a Smugglers Trail that guests can take if they wish to make their way to the seafront. George's brother Capt. Frederick Marryat stayed at the house for extensive periods and must have found inspiration from the magical countryside and seafront to pen his famous novel *'The Children of the New Forest'*. In fact, Chewton Glen was a beautiful, inspiring country house until the 1950s when the Duval family converted it into a hotel. These tales contribute to the hotel's charm and legacy, but Chewton Glen exudes its very own 'Englishness' with a capital E. Staff at Chewton Glen are consummately conservative but can also acknowledge a guest's every need in a quirky and perfectly sympathetic manner. The décor is made up of traditional colours such as claret, olive, gold and creams but then includes the latest Bang and Olufsen sound system in the bedrooms. In 1990 a health club was built onto the side wing of the Chewton Glen Hotel and Country Club. At the time a health club seemed a revolutionary addition to facilities at a hotel, unlike today when most hotels place health and the well-being of guests on their agenda. Following the turn of the twenty-first century, Chewton Glen began a major overhaul of their spa facilities and in 2005 opened a state-of-the-art 'treatment and therapy spa' in partnership with another luxurious brand, Moulton and Brown. The Spa, as it was aptly christened, prides itself on its highly trained therapists and fitness instructors who use ancient and modern techniques to relax or invigorate the mind and body as the guest so wishes. The Spa also has high-tech facilities for guests who wish to exercise using the Life Fitness CV equipment and also holistic therapy rooms for guests who need to gently rebalance their energy flows. Facilities at The Spa are extensive and include:

- 17-metre ozone treated swimming pool
- Hydrotherapy spa pool with hi-tech therapy options
- Aromatherapy saunas and crystal steam rooms
- Relaxation room
- Outdoor whirlpool
- Cold drench showers
- Ten treatment rooms
- Linda Meredith skin care
- Spa Grooming Lounge for Jessana Manicures and Pedicures
- Molton Brown Body Treatments
- Pool bar and lounge with a specially formulated menu to provide great tasting food with healthy benefits
- State-of-the-art gymnasium with personal training available
- Dance studio with daily programme of exercise and relaxation classes.

The Spa, at Chewton Glen Hotel, Spa and Country Club, is just one of the services that is continually improving and developing. And because of the continued investment in the fitness facilities, beauty treatments and availability of therapeutic healing, the number of guests wishing to take advantage of the range of services available at The Spa is increasing year on year.

It is not just the services available at The Spa that pulls guests to Chewton Glen. Many news headlines from around the world include stories about preventative treatments, stress reduction and the benefits of exercise. Therefore, the consumer is being encouraged to seek a change in their lifestyle to avoid ill heath and/or obesity. The hospitality, travel and tourism industry, therefore, have placed spas, health and wellness in their future business plans to provide for the psychological and physical lifestyle changes that consumers are in search of.

Spa tourism

It seems strange that the introduction of a health club and relaxing spa facilities at Chewton Glen was considered to be a revolutionary addition to hotel facilities, when throughout history travel in pursuit of health and spiritual improvement has been the bedrock of the tourism industry. Indeed the Romans and Greeks were great advocates of travel to enhance their own well-being and it was they who brought spas and treatment centres to Britain hundreds years ago. The often quoted definition of wellness – 'a way of life orientated towards optimal health and wellbeing in which the body, mind and spirit are integrated by the individual to live more fully within the human and natural community' (Myers, Sweeney and Witmers, 2005: 1) – demonstrates how wellness affects all of the important factors that when pursued will build upon a person's strength and character. And it is this pursuit of well-being that has sparked the unprecedented growth of wellness centres, holistic retreats and spas (House of Lords Report, 2000).

The word 'spa' is a Latin acronym derived from *Salut per Aqua* meaning 'health or relaxation through water'. The spa became the physical facility that could satisfy the psychological needs of the body, mind and spirit. The term 'spa' grew in popularity during the seventeenth century as health reports became popular. Whilst wellness and spa treatments were once laundered as travel for the European élite particularly during the eighteenth and nineteenth centuries many consumers, from all walks of life, now actively engage in enhancing their personal health and well-being. In addition to the increase in daily news items encouraging changing lifestyles, the aging population of today is very active and demanding and spends more time travelling than their forefathers (Smith and Kelly, 2006). Therefore, the increasing need to stay fit and healthy and the long life expectancy does mean that hydro-treatments and massage may be required more often or in addition to beautification treatment.

Market trends and competitor offerings

Spa tourism is entering a new growth phrase as more and more consumers consider spa therapies and treatments as more than a one-off indulgence. Mintel – Spa Tourism International (2007) states that the worldwide spa industry has grown into a US$40 billion business and between 2003 to 2005 spa visits have increased by 20.2 per cent to 131 million. The UK's spa industry is approximately US$3 billion at the moment which is a major increase from where the spa industry was five years ago (Mintel – Spa Tourism International, 2007).

There are just over 1,400 spas in Europe, with the majority in Germany for guests requiring medicinal purposes or merely as a place of sanctuary. However, European countries are now setting themselves up to encourage travellers to their shores offering a range of spa facilities. For example, Glenbervie House Hotel, near Stirlingshire in Scotland are about to invest £80 million in a luxury state-of-the-art spa village (Daily Record, 2007) Glenbervie House Hotel wishes to become one of the top spa destinations worldwide. Just around the corner, The Apex City Quay Hotel & Spa in Dundee has now positioned itself with the public as the first 'green hotel spa'. This hotel spa's USP is to provide spa facilities whilst keeping both eyes on their impact on the environment. (Travel Trade, 2007).

In Cyprus the destination for Japanese-style Sheiseido Spa treatments is the five-star Four Seasons Hotel. Here guests will receive shiatsu massages, treatments to increase the Qi energy flow and Zen influences to calm the soul. The Four Seasons Hotel is also a destination retreat for the rich and famous and a favourite haunt of Peter Andre and Jorden. For guests who do not have that budget or for those who want the natural elements to improve their skin tone or muscle pains and to 'remove' cellulite, then the Cryotherapy Centre in Poprad, Slovakia is the place to visit. Guests expose their bodies to temperatures as low at minus 120°C and then plunge into mineral water pools or relax in a sauna (Clements, 2007). The medical experience is thrilling and is belived to enliven the mind and body.

Returning to the UK, Urban Retreat is a day spa whose strap-line is 'Time, Space, Comfort'. Urban Retreats are found in Harrods, Knightsbridge, Harvey Nichols, Manchester and Terminal 1 Heathrow Airport. The delights they offer include services such as beauty treatments and gentle massages and they have recently launched Task Men's Treatments at their Harvey Nichols outlet in Manchester. The UK's first public day spa recently opened at London's Bethnal Green with the intention to make spa visiting, and the highly social aspects that it brings, popular with a larger audience. The prices are also much more affordable than those charged at Chewton Glen or Urban Retreats.

With all these different spa hotels and resorts available consumers need to consider their primary purpose and goal for visiting and then choose the appropriate spa to satisfy their needs. Table C2.1 categorizes the main spa types.

The eight spa types are the foundation, but it is clear that within each category there are many varieties. For example, The Spa at Chewton Glen would be categorized as a Resort/hotel spa but as outlined above, The Spa is not an 'add-on' but an integral element to the overall experience that guests can enjoy.

The future

The number of UK and European spa-goers is way behind their American counterparts. Within Europe the gender split and the reasons for visit itself are quite marked; Table C2.2 illustrates the differences.

Different consumers need different things when they try to relax and unwind at a spa. But the range of spas is ever increasing; therefore, the choice of what is available may make more consumers try different treatments that they had never tried before. Indeed spas are becoming very specialist and are segmenting

Spa type	Description	Eight spa types
Club spa	Primary purpose is fitness. Offers a variety of professionally administered spa services on a day-use basis. Guests often join the club close to work place or home for monthly/yearly subscriptions.	
Cruise ship spa	A spa aboard a cruise ship. Provides professionally administered spa services such as fitness and wellness components and spa cuisine menu choices. Caters for wide variety of abilities/ages.	
Day spa	Primarily pampering and beauty treatments (e.g. nail bars, facials, etc.). Offering a variety of professionally administered spa services to clients on a day-use basis.	
Destination spa	Main purpose of visit is to learn and develop healthy habits. Historically a seven-day stay. The lifestyle transformation is part of an intensive programme that encourages guests to maintain a particular regime throughout their stay. Regime are detox and weight loss where learning takes place regarding lifestyle, fitness and healthy eating or comprehensive taught programmes regarding stress management, wellness education, healthy lifestyle, fitness and diet.	
Medical spa	A facility that operates under the full-time, on-site supervision of a licensed health care professional whose primary purpose is to provide comprehensive medical and wellness care in an environment that integrates spa services, as well as traditional, complementary and/or alternative therapies and treatments. The facility operates within the scope of practice of its staff, which can include both aesthetic and preventative procedures and services.	
Cosmetic beauty spa	A spa whose primary service is cosmetic and beauty orientated. Services include cosmetic surgery and dentistry. Provides professionally trained surgeons and nursing staff. After-care is provided in a relaxing non-clinical environment – often a former country house or hotel.	
Mineral spring spa	A spa offering an on-site source of natural mineral, thermal or seawater used in hydrotherapy treatments.	
Resort/hotel spa	A spa owned by and located within a resort or hotel providing professionally administered spa services, fitness and wellness components and spa cuisine menu choices.	

the total spa-going market into ever more distinct groups. Trends to watch for in the future are hotels with spas dedicated to luxury detox, with more slippers than 'boot camp' weight-control facilities where guests are not 'punished' for their gluttonous behaviour but treated with kindness and feeling. Sanoviv in Mexico offers a week-long detoxification programme. Getting a good night's sleep has been something our grandmothers have told us to do and hoteliers worldwide have been trying to offer to their guests for years. Many spas including day spas in London and destination/resort spas offer 'sleep rooms'. The ability to unwind and recognize the healthy benefits of sleep will see more 'sleep rooms' popping up in cities and holiday destinations worldwide in the future.

The key trends in the UK include brand names such as Champney's bringing their spas to towns and cities instead of expanding their portfolio in country retreats. Additionally Champney's now offer their spa range of creams and lotions through High Street stores such as Sainsbury's. This enables existing Champney's spa guests to 're-live' their visit in their own home as well as attracting new customers to Champney's exclusive range of creams and lotions.

Male grooming sales have increased at a phenomenal rate over the past few years and spas 'just for men' have begun to open. In addition to Urban Retreat, there are three other 'men only' spas in the UK. Gentleman's Tonic in Mayfair provides services such as facials, electrolysis, traditional wet-shave, lifestyle advice and a limited but exclusive product range. Wholeman, Bond Street, London offers a wide range of products, such as hair, skin and body creams and lotions as well as treatments.

	UK	Spain	Germany	France	Italy	**Table C2.2**
Gender						Gender and reason for visit
Male %	22	46	47	32	36	**Source** Adapted from ISPA (2007).
Female %	78	58	53	68	64	
Reason for visit						
1st choice	Facials	Sauna or steam bath	Sauna or steam bath	Sauna or steam bath	Sauna or steam bath	
2nd choice	Pedicures	Scotch hose	Hill body massage	Body scrub or wrap	Facials	
3rd choice	Manicures	Hydrotherapy	Facials	Scotch hose third	Pedicures	

Nickel Spa in Convent Garden is different in design than Gentleman's Tonic and Wholeman, which favour a gentleman's club feel. Nickel Spa has a clinical but somehow contemporary look. The treatment rooms, whilst spacious and no doubt expensive, give an air of an operating theatre. Nickel Spa also has a wide range of products on sale in their store beneath the treatment rooms. All of the 'men only' spas are exclusive and charge high prices.

The Apex City Quay Hotel and Spa in Dundee has been heralded as the first 'green' spa. It will be interesting to see if other spas will follow in their contribution to the environment. Many hotels and resorts certainly make claims to being eco-friendly or sustainable, therefore there could be more spas that will calm the body, soul and mind without consumers having the nagging feeling that the experience is costing the earth.

Discussion questions

1 Discuss how you would classify the industry sector that The Spa at Chewton Glen Hotel and Country Club operate in.

2 What are key strengths of Chewton Glen Hotel, Spa and Country Club? What types of service compete with them?

3 What brand extensions would Chewton Glen Hotel, Spa and Country Club consider in their portfolio?

4 Which of Maslow's hierarchy of needs does Chewton Glen Hotel, Spa and Country Club satisfy? How does Chewton Glen Hotel, Spa and Country Club satisfy those needs and to whom?

5 Segmentation, targeting and planning are key elements for all businesses. Which segments do you think Chewton Glen Hotel, Spa and Country Club are targeting and why?

References

Clements, P. (2007) 'A luxury spa needn't cost a fortune. Indulge on a budget', *Daily Mail* (London), 10 September.

Crump, V. for *The Sunday Times* (2006) 'Bolt Hole: Chewton Glen, New Forest, Hampshire Countryhouse posh meets spa chic in deepest New Forestshire spiffing', http://travel.timesonline.co.uk/tol/life_and_style/travel/where_to_stay/south_east_england/article721510.ece, accessed 16 December 2007.

Daily Record (Glasgow, Scotland) (2007) Business '1000 Job at SPA', 4 December.

House of Lords Report (2000) 'Complementary and Alternative Medicine', http://www.parliament.the-stationeryoffice.co.uk/pa/ld199900/ldselect/ldsctech/123/12301.htm, accessed 17 November 2007.

ISPA (2007) Global Consumer Report, http://www.experienceispa.com/ISPA/Education.

King, E. for the Australian Gourmet Traveller (2007) 'The World's Ten Best Spa Retreats', http://gourmettraveller.com.au/the_worlds_ten_best_sp_retreats.htm, accessed 27 December 2007.

Mintel (2007) 'Spa Tourism – International – June 2007', http://academic.mintel.com/sinatra/oxygen_academic/search_results/show&/display/id = 237182/display/id = 282434, accessed 17 November 2007.

Myers, J. E., Sweeney, T. J. and Witmer, M. (2005) 'A Holistic Model of Wellness', http://www.mindgarden. com/products/wells.htm#web, accessed 28 December 2007.

Smith, M. and Kelly, C. (2006) 'Wellness Tourism', Editorial, *Tourism Recreation Research* 31 (1): 1–4.

Travel Trade (2007) 'Scotch Corner: Dundee unveils the "first eco spa"', *Gazette UK & Ireland*, 14 December.

Case 3

Center Parcs – Something for everyone

Remember when you were a child the long summer break from school was fantastic. But for parents it can seem like a nightmare. How do parents provide weeks of fun and entertainment for their children? Well, there are many things parents can do, such as take the children to Blackpool Pleasure Beach, or pack up their bikes and go cycling through France, or for quick bursts of excitement visit the local cinema. However, why not take the whole family to a holiday destination where there are many activities from canoeing, nature trails, cycling, archery or fishing. Or, relax, 'be with nature' and admire the resident birds and animals. Center Parcs is just one of those places that cater for people, with different wants but with a basic need for a fun environment that is away from the hurly burley of twenty-first-century living. From the first time this type of holiday village opened its doors to the public in 1968, its founder offered a unique experience. Firstly, the villas were designed to blend in with the environment and secondly the luxury villas, of which there were 30, had colour TV and central heating. The 'villas in the forest' also had huge windows and were built with natural materials. After 40 years the design principles, the calm, peaceful environments and the ability to harmonize a whole village with nature are guidelines that Center Parcs still adhere to. These aspects were very different from the standard holiday camps that had been built in other European countries.

The birth of holiday villages

'Holiday camps' started to become popular in the UK in the 1920s and grew as the holiday destination of choice by working-class people and honeymooners. Large-scale tourist operators such as Butlins and Pontins joined in this ever-growing holiday phenomenon by offering one-week holiday packages. Accommodation, food and mass entertainment organized by the tour operator's staff were included in the package services. Billy Butlin opened his first camp in Skegness and introduced the UK guests to the Redcoats. Redcoats were, and still are, friendly staff that create a fun atmosphere for children, families and party goers. Butlins currently has three holiday centres. An interesting concept adopted by Butlins is to invite well known brands, such as Pizza Hut and Burger King, into their holiday centres. They believe there is strong synergy between the philosophies of the brand and of course it is appealing to many of their guests. Butlins is now owned by Bourne Leisure Group which also own Haven Holiday Parks and British Holidays. Haven and British Holidays operate 34 holiday parks within the UK. Their parks are mainly located at the seaside which may be the reason they attract 1.5 million customers annually.

Fred Pontin opened his first site in 1946 at Brean Sands in Somerset. Pontins currently has eight holiday centres. Family holiday camps such as these were popular up until the 1970s. Towards the end of the 1970s 'holiday camps' were becoming no longer fashionable. Indeed journalists in the popular press poked fun at 'holiday camps' for offering entertainment such as the 'knobbly knee' and 'glamorous Grandmother' competitions. At the same time, UK tourists wanted to extend their horizons and package tours to Spain and France became the fashionable holiday designations. Pontins offered package holidays to their newly acquired hotels in Sardinia (1963) and Ibiza and Majorca (1964). 'Holiday camps' were becoming passé, so existing operators like Butlins and Pontins began spending millions of pounds to offer their guests additional facilities such as ski slopes, amusement parks and horse riding. Following the high investment and re-branding, 'holiday camps' changed their name and become known as holiday 'centres', 'parks', 'resorts' and 'villages' and their popularity and availability just kept growing. Other operators saw the appeal of offering a resort that included activities, accommodation and food for guests. And in 1967 Piet Derksen introduced a holiday village like no other, to the Dutch market. The philosophy of Piet Derken's holiday village was to create a relaxing space. Center Parcs, known as Sporthuis Centrum Recreatie until 1986, gave people the opportunity to leave their demanding and hectic lives behind and enjoy a peaceful holiday in natural surroundings.

Center Parcs, like Butlins and Pontins, continued to grow and the number of villages increased quickly from its beginnings in the late 1960s with four more opening in the Netherlands by 1975. A spectacular subtropical swimming paradise was launched at the grand opening of the 6th village in De Eemhof in 1980. The Subtropical Swimming Paradise was hailed as an amazing, innovative indoor feature at the holiday village because it was housed within a huge climate-controlled canvas dome – where swimmers could see pine trees as they splashed around to their heart's content. The Subtropical Swimming Paradise, known as Aqua Mundos at European villages, is one of the main attractions at Center Parcs because there is something for everyone. Guests can relax in sun spots under the palm trees, trek along cobblestone paths and rope bridges to exotic café's, take toddlers on miniature slides, fly down wild water flumes, and for those guests who dare swim along with sharks and barracudas! (With a glass partition between them of course).

During 1981 Center Parcs took a bold move and began to expand their network internationally. In the first instance they opened a new village resort at Erperheide on the Dutch border. Further expansion took place in other European countries with the Sherwood Forest village in the UK in 1987, Les Bois-Francs, France in 1988 and Bispinger Heide, Germany in 1995. Expansion continues, with the fourth village in France, Domaine du Bois de Harcholins, near Strasbourg, due in 2010.

The Center Parcs brand we know today is now owned by Center Parcs UK and Center Parcs Europe. Center Parcs UK has four villages in England and Center Parcs Europe has 16 villages: France (2), Germany (4), Belgium (2) and Netherlands (8). All of the Center Parcs villages, no matter where they are located, are designed to embrace their natural surroundings, share an environment with nature and remain a place for relaxation, fun and outdoor activities that all the family can enjoy. These are very different from the Butlins and Pontins in terms of design and layout – but in terms of getting all the family involved, each holiday village has something for everyone.

It is clear that holiday villages, parks or resorts – whatever they may be called – are here to stay and are part of the spectrum of holiday destinations available to consumers. The number of holiday villages has grown and continues to do so. However, with the vast number of operators in this market it is important to sustain these multimillion pound investments. The real leaders in this market will do this by ensuring that the market positioning of the village is clear to the consumer through its philosophy, physical evidence, service delivery and communication.

What's green about Center Parcs?

Ecology, biodiversity and forest management are issues key to the philosophy of Center Parcs. The services offered, be they guest activities, laundry, or heating and lighting, are managed with conservation, energy efficiency and recycling in mind. The starting point for Center Parcs is finding a site that has the least impact on the landscape and vegetation. The Countryside Commission and English Nature are among the many interested parties that offer their services to Center Parcs to ensure that a sustainable environment ensues. Center Parcs continues to adhere to this philosophy by setting targets such as recycling 40 per cent of its total waste by 2008 and using the services of local suppliers to contribute to a healthy local economy.

Is there a green market?

There seem to be regular new editions to environmentally friendly holidays, hotels, restaurants and cafés. Family holidays at Beeson Farm in South Devon, UK offers a green holiday that includes organic meat, fruit, veg., cheese and wine delivered to the holiday cottages via an online local supermarket (Armstrong, 2007). Holidays in active farms is a growing phenomenon and are readily available to guests who like to visit the countryside. People who like to explore cities but also wish to keep their carbon footprint low could stay at Oekotel in Hamberg (www.oekotel.de). At this hotel, rainwater is collected, solar panels are used, bed linen is made from organic cotton and they use biodegradable clearning products. There are many places who believe that it is important to offer something for eco-conscious holiday makers. Organizations such as earthwatch. org also offer guests the opportunity to join research expeditions that will help scientists understand climate change or the ocean's ecosystem around Portugal. Therfore, there are many organizations that include or fully incorporate environmental and sustainable issues as part of their business strategy as they feel it adds appeal.

Center Parcs' belief in being green

The most important element to any service industry is to get the philosophy of the organization right, as this defines its purpose to their stakeholders. The philosophy of Center Parcs UK begins with its mission statement.

> *Mission Statement – 'Everyday, the perfect break, naturally.'*

The statement provides a clear message as to what the organization is going to deliver to its stakeholders. The guest, as an external stakeholder, is promised a 'perfect break, naturally'. As part of Center Parcs' business plan, this promise is supported by the Values and Culture statements specific to their guests. These include:

> *'We give guests a unique and positively memorable experience.'*

Center Parcs understand that guests are not homogeneous and purport to treat each guest individually. Center Parcs also provides the environment in which guests can transport themselves into a safe, natural environment in which to unwind and spend quality time with their friends and family. At the same time, however, Center Parcs still wish to exhilarate and facilitate experiences that are outside the day-to-day living of their guests. They do this by providing a range of sporting activities to excite and invigorate such as 'Pedal Power' for all the family or Tots Tennis for 5-year-olds. A more relaxing experience could be 'A Walk With Trees', an educational meander in the forest, or the 'Creepy Crawlies' mini-safari, which looks at the tiniest beasts through a microscope. Both of these adventures would surely be a memorable, out of the ordinary, encounter. These activities provide an enjoyable break for families who like Center Parcs have a strong commitment to the environment.

Center Parcs' staff are an internal stakeholder and one of the most applicable Value and Culture statements is:

> 'We value high quality staff and the contribution they make in achieving guest satisfaction and value, recognising employee commitment drives business success.'

This statement is very applicable as it gives a clear message to staff that their interaction is vital to the guest's experience. Staff are introduced to the philosophy of Center Parcs during their induction programme. Center Parcs state they are world leaders on ecological and environmental issues. These issues are embedded in the training and culture of working at Center Parcs. Additionally all staff received training on health and safety, guest care and cash handling. Other forms of training take place applicable to the role given to the member of staff. For example, basic food hygiene training is given where appropriate. As staff progress they can continue their career through management development or gain sponsorship to gain a further off-site qualification. This training programme shows Center Parcs' commitment to their staff which in turn should provide the quality service which they believe in.

Another internal stakeholder is the investor. Clearly investors want a return for their money. However, based on Center Parcs' commitment to the environment, the extensive range of

memorable experiences for their guests and the pledge to ensure that staff are trained to the highest quality, it does make you wonder if Center Parcs can satisfy their investors' desire for monetary payback. Center Parcs have a Value and Culture statement specific for their investors:

> 'We are commercial, but not to the extent that we alienate valuable guests or compromise service and safety standards.'

This is a clear statement to investors. Center Parcs state they will be a commercially viable operation, but they state categorically that their Mission Statement and promise to guests will not be compromised. This is a bold statement as it may put off potential investors. However, Center Parcs are 'best in class' at yield management, which should make investors less nervous. Similarly Center Parcs have many restaurants, cafés, merchandising stores and a vast array of activities that make it easy for the guest topart with their money whilst at the holiday village. At the same time Center Parcs assure investors that their call centres sell assertively, which also contributes to the overall yield. Also, Center Parcs' commitment to their ISO 14001 certificate cuts down energy consumption using low-energy light bulbs and recycling heated air – both examples that will please investors.

Center Parcs – Communication of their philosophy

Center Parcs have a superb offer to communicate. The communication messages need to appeal to the main target markets, which are affluent families with children, young professionals and 'empty nesters'. Their philosophy is key, but other elements that will appeal to the target market are the fact that accommodation is of the highest standard, leisure activities and outdoor sports are themed so as to fit with the local surroundings – using key resources such as water, forest, streams and nature trails – and the service provided by staff is of the highest quality. Such premium offers mean premium prices.

Communication should establish three vital goals in the minds of the consumer: (1) to create awareness of what is on offer, (2) to establish a positive image and (3) to promote repeat purchases and hopefully loyalty. Center Parcs have a range of communications including their annual brochure, television advertising and their website. Each type of communication can be used to establish the three vital goals.

Television advertising is used as part of their communication strategy. Television campaigns take place in September and January each year. This is the prime time for communications of this nature to take place, as consumers are considering their holiday plans. Centre Parcs use this communication tool to appeal to a variety of market segments.

Center Parcs advocate that direct marketing is also an essential communications tool. One element of direct marketing is the initial mailing received when a consumer requests information, following a television advertisement or from a visit to the company's website. The mailing that arrives has a CD which gives the potential guest a flavour of things to come. The CD shows many of the activities, whether energetic or relaxing, that can be experienced whilst at Center Parcs. Additionally, 60 per cent of guests are repeat customers; therefore, Center Parcs have a dedicated team of data miners. The data miners use the information stored on Center Parcs' database as a decision-support system. The information can be used for future mailings and more importantly provide guest history information. Center Parcs use direct marketing to advise consumers of special offers and additional services or activities being added to the villages.

Internet bookings are becoming a key distribution tool and Center Parcs have a strong internet presence. Bookings online are growing and holiday parks have taken between 20 per cent and 30 per cent of their bookings via the internet. Center Parcs have a very interactive website, which shows many fun activities, provides details of their ethical policies and enables consumers to book their holiday break on line.

Competitors

The main competitors for Center Parcs are Butlins and Haven Holiday Parks. Over the past two years 26 per cent of the UK population visited a holiday centre 'Mintel Commissioned BMRB – findings based on a nationally representative sample'. This has remained a constant penetration level over the past two years. The top three brands Haven Holiday Parks, Butlins and Center Parcs all had 6 per cent of UK population visiting their holiday villages. Haven Holidays' share has fluctuated with a shift downwards by 2 per cent. Center Parcs, however, enjoyed a shift upwards by 1 per cent. It is interesting to note that some customers enjoy the holiday centre experience and visit 'other' holiday parks, showing that 100 per cent loyalty does not exist in the holiday centre market (see Table C3.1). For example 16 per cent of Butlins' customers also visit Haven Holidays. Center Parcs has the least percentage of customers 'straying' to another holiday park.

In terms of demographic segmentation there is a clear difference, in terms of customer choice, at the lower end of the socio-economic scale (see Table C3.2).

Consumers in socio-economic group C1 are the main visitors to holiday villages. This has changed since 2003 when the C2 group was the socio-economic group that visited holiday parks. Both Center Parcs and Butlins are the main competitors for the AB socio-economic group. To entice this group Butlins has introduced a spa complex and joined forces with Exmoor National Park to offer a wider range of activities that may appeal to the AB customer. Center Parcs has invested over £10,000 on luxury suites which include personal sauna, jacuzzi and outdoor tubs – again appealing to the more discerning guest.

Cleary Haven Holiday Parks appeal to the family far more that Butlins and Center Parcs. Indeed Haven Holidays is particularly dominant in visitors with children under the age of 10 years. They have specific activities for the Under 10s headed by Rory and Bradley, Havens' mascots.

Twenty-first-century guests do not seem to take their 'annual two week break' at holiday centres. This is a clear difference between holiday makers now and holiday makers in the 1960s. Currently, guests visit holiday centres and villages for either a long weekend or one week. This suggests that holiday centres are the place for 'second holidays' rather than being the places that consumers choose as their main holiday. This is particularly noticeable for Center Parcs where only 1 per cent of visitors stay for two weeks. However, Butlins still accounts for 10 per cent of

Table C3.1		Haven Holiday Park %	Butlins %	Center Parcs %
Holiday parks visited during the past two years	All	6	6	6
	Haven Holiday Park	100	16	11
	Butlins	16	100	12
	Centre Parcs	10	11	100

Base: 1,548 adults 15+ October 2005.

Table C3.2	Socio-economic group	Haven Holiday Park %	Butlins %	Center Parcs %
Holiday parks visited during the past two years by socio-economic group	AB	18	23	27
	C1	30	27	44
	C2	26	20	19
	D	18	19	8
	E	9	11	2

Base: 1,548 adults 15+ October 2005.

	Haven Holiday Park %	Butlins %	Center Parcs %
Families	61	39	39

Base: 1,548 adults 15+ October 2005

Table C3.3

Family visitors to holiday parks in the past two years

	Haven Holiday Park %	Butlins %	Center Parcs %
2 week holiday	5	10	1
1 week holiday	43	34	38
Weekend/long weekend	31	35	35
Midweek break (between Mon–Fri)	15	13	20
Day trip	5	8	6

Base: 1,548 adults 15+ October 2005.

Table C3.4

Preferred length of visit to holiday park in past two years by centre visited

guests staying for two weeks, perhaps indicative of its long-standing presence as the 'main holiday destination' for some families. Table C3.4 shows the preferred length of stay at each of the main competitors within the holiday centre market.

Discussion questions

1 How would you use publicity to sustain Center Parcs' profile?

2 Consumers make decisions using the Decision-Making Process Model. Discuss each part of the decision-making process for a family who need to socialize together on holiday.

3 Discuss the risks that consumers need to consider when purchasing a holiday at Center Parcs.

4 What benefits do Center Parcs bring to their local area and to guests?

5 How can market research be used to improve the service environment?

6 What does the consumer information tell you about Center Parcs and its competitors?

7 What would you recommend Center Parcs do to encourage guests to stay longer?

Further reading and references

Armstrong, J. (2007) 'Travel: Green and Pleasant; Devon now offers the cream of Eco-holidays', *The Mirror*, 15 September.
Mintel (2006) Holiday Centres.
http://academic.mintel.com/sinatra/oxygen_academic/ search_results/, accessed 2 September 2007.

www.centreparcs.co.uk.
www.butlinsonline.co.uk.
www.butlinsmemories.com/.
www.oekotel.de.
www.pontins.com.

Case 4

House concerts: Service demands under your own roof

Developed by Stephen Henderson, Leeds Metropolitan University

Premise

Looks at house concerts that are run by music enthusiasts. In the UK, enthusiasts who also have local music venues available run these. In the US, enthusiasts fill the gaps between appearances in distant major cities. In New Zealand, enthusiasts provide musical entertainment for a country often missed by major artists. In all cases, there are strategic and operational service issues to be considered.

Case

In the 1990s, it was generally accepted that touring musicians made little money from ticket sales but were happy to roll out spectacular shows on the basis that merchandise would sell (T-shirts, etc.) and, more importantly, the live concerts would promote the sales of their recorded music. As the world moved into the next century and download sales, mail order music and the supermarket retailers pushed down the price of recorded music, it was not only music retailers who felt the pressure. All of sudden, record companies found that profit margins were just not as good as in the past and that's without considering the burgeoning piracy business reducing their sales in various parts of the world. The artists began to question the role of the record company but, mostly, realized

that playing live was now going to be an important source of income and not just a tool to increase sales of their music.

So, artists became more eager to tour and saw private parties as another source of income. For example, in 2008, *The Sunday Times* suggested that Hannah Sandling, a celebrity stylist, had seen everyone from Tom Jones, Diana Ross and Dionne Warwick to Justin Timberlake at functions limited to a few hundred guests. Clearly, booking artists of such stature needed someone who possessed a large budget for a special event where VIP guests may even get the chance to 'meet and greet' the artist. However, these concerts are not only for those with lots of money in the bank as lesser-known, but good-quality artists like singer-songwriter Boo Hewerdine, make themselves available on eBay. Other websites like www.owngig.com offer the chance for fans to get together and bid for their favourite band. So, the potential for relatively intimate performances with opportunities to meet the artist have become commonplace for some.

Though this makes it sound like a new and exciting phenomenon, actually, these smaller intimate performances have existed for many years in the form of house concerts. Depending on the local structure for public performance, these will occur for varying reasons in different countries around the world. For example, in the US, there can be large distances between major cities and the artist finds it quite handy to play a house concert en route between performances at clubs or theatres in the bigger cities. It basically means that the artist has another 'pay day' rather than a day of travelling, as well as a bed for the night without hotel costs. On the other hand, in a country like New Zealand, there are few cities to play and touring only makes sense for a smaller act if most of the performances are at house concerts. In this way, the fees from a number of performances can help balance the cost of travel to this country. Even in a country like England where public venues are well scattered throughout the land, smaller acts can find house concerts organized by music enthusiasts such as those in York seen at the website www.houseconcertsyork.co.uk.

Of course, not everyone makes their evenings as publicly visible as the group in York because these are often invitations to private homes where the owner has, say, a large conservatory or outside barn that can accommodate between 20 and 50 people to comfortably watch the act. Invitation may be by a discrete e-mail or phone call from the organizer aiming to make sure that only friends or 'friends of friends' are invited. In this way, the chaos and damage that has occasionally resulted from young people publicizing private parties via social networks such as Facebook are carefully avoided.

Financially, house concerts are finely balanced in terms of paying the act from ticket sales. To achieve an acceptable outcome, which may be a minimal 'loss' for some organizers, the ticket price is made more appealing by including some food and drink often prepared by the organizer or some friends. Thankfully for the organizer, the small scale of a house concert means that sound systems are not usually needed though this is not always the case. Again, it is often friends who provide and help set up a stage area and any equipment required though, interestingly, these supportive friends may well pay for tickets in order that they can see the continuation of these intimate evenings. Though the actual format of these performances varies, they give artists the chance to try out new songs in front of a small audience and such spontaneity may even lead to local musicians joining the visiting act for a song or two. In locations without much live local entertainment, the artist is often cheered by good CD sales and, naturally, mingling with the audience can help build a loyal fan base for future appearances. All in all, music fans and artists will often indicate that these intimate evenings are far superior to spending an evening in a large venue holding an audience of thousands.

Discussion questions

1 How does customer participation work in this special type of service?

2 What operational issues occur with a house concert?

3 How might you market this service without inviting trouble at your home?

4 Is primary or secondary research likely to be more useful in a small market like house concerts?

5 What MKIS (Marketing Information System) tools will be most useful in the organizing of house concerts?

6 How does the local nature of house concerts in, say, the US affect market research of customers and suppliers?

References

'Amy Winehouse Fulfils "1 Million Pound Contract" For Roman Abramovich', http://www.gigwise.com/news/43837/amy-winehouse-fulfils-1-million-pound-contract-for-roman-abramovich.

'Bid for acts', http://www.owngig.com.

'Boo Hewerdine on eBay', http://cgi.ebay.co.uk/Boo-Hewerdine-house-concert_W0QQitemZ1202686 22922QQihZ002QQcategoryZ618QQcmdZViewItem.

'Cover story: Goodbye yellow brick road: The day the music industry died', http://www.timesonline.co.uk/tol/life_ and_style/article1070751.ece.

'House Concerts – York', http://www.houseconcertsyork.co.uk/.

'Why music stars are playing private parties', http://entertainment.timesonline.co.uk/tol/arts_and_entertainment/music/article4025186.ece.

Case 5

Fine dining in the sky

The airline dining experience has been with us for nearly 100 years. The early Zeppelin airships included food and champagne in the air fare! And KLM, the providers of the first commercial flights, served a pre-packaged meal for travellers on the 1919 London to Paris route. The meal on the outward journey from London was a cream tea!

'Meals in the air' during the early days of international flights were considered to be as good meals 'on the ground'. Airlines were equipped with full catering facilities and chefs. In the main, those that travelled by air in the early part of the twentieth century were rich, as air travel was an expensive service. However, during the 1960s many customers around the world were getting the 'travel bug'. Airlines and travel agencies recognized the needs of the consumer and offered a package holiday which included air travel, onboard meal and accommodation to the masses. To keep costs low but still provide an onboard meal, kitchens were removed and outside caterers were called in. Catering drastically moved downmarket as pre-packaged, pre-cooked, re-heated meals were served. Since that period many comedians or comedy films have included sketches that ridicule the food supplied by airlines.

During the 1990s new competitors came to the airline industry. The new competitors were low-cost airlines such as easyJet and Ryanair. These airlines do not offer in-flight catering, or a hot ready-made meal. Their strategy is to reduce costs further and indeed make a profit from the in-flight sales of sandwiches and drinks, which are no longer included in the cost of the flight. Many customers taking a short journey from London to Barcelona or Australia to Bali are quite happy to sit in a confined space enjoying quick, efficient in-flight services. But some customers are not happy with this. Therefore, a number of airlines have turned their backs on pre-packaged meals to offer a fine dining experience in the sky. To offer the fine dining experience, full catering kitchens and chefs are now back on board and several airlines are adding to the experience by asking celebrity chefs to set the menu. Guy Martin, the Michelin 3-Star Chef of Paris' Le Grand Vefour is creating dishes for Air France such as Lobster with a light pineapple curry sauce and tarragon gelette. Pistachio-crusted shrimp with a sweet pea tarragon flan was created by Gordon Maybury for the Fives restaurant in Peninsula Hotel in New York. The same dish was replicated on Lufthansa's America to Germany flights in November and December 2005. Neil Perry, Chef at Rockpool in Sydney, tests recipes which are then introduced on Qantas first-class flights. The celebrity marque provides airlines with a point of differentiation to market segments who want luxury wherever they are.

Hermann Friedanck, food and beverage manager for Singapore Airlines, says 'We're in the transportation business; we're all using the same tube, so this is one of the aspects of service that makes us different.... We also have mostly long distance flights, so you don't want someone stewing for a long time over a lousy steak or a piece of bad fish. These are business people, achievers, and they know good food.' Singapore Airlines has had more celebrity chefs than any other airline. The international line-up includes France's Georges Blanc, London's Gordon Ramsay and New York's Alfred Protale. Between them they formulate and suggest 40 to 50 recipes. Whilst the fabulous meals are not made fully from scratch, particular preparations need to be considered when the customer is 30,000 feet in the air. For example, taste buds change at that altitude; therefore more seasoning is required for dishes. Michelle Bernstein, owner of Michy's in Miami, signed with Delta's Business Elite and was amazed when she reported that 'People have actually come into the restaurant after trying the food on the plane!' How's that for customer satisfaction and loyalty!

Discussion questions

1 Survey three fellow students and three businesspeople and ask them to list and rank the top five criteria they consider when booking with an airline. Is quality food a consideration?

2 Airlines innovate regularly to ensure they do not move into the decline stage of the product life cycle. Choose a service organization and apply the product life cycle to it. How has your chosen organization innovated to ensure that they do not move into the decline stage?

3 Consider the many differentiation points available to airlines.

4 Discuss the different segmentation techniques used by airlines.

5 Discuss the different PR opportunities for Singapore Airlines, Lufthansa and easyJet.

References

Jones, P. and Lumbers, M. (2003) 'Appetite and In-flight Catering', Chapter 16 in Bor, R. (2003) *Passenger Behaviour*, London: Ashgate Publishing.

Werner, L. (2006) 'First Class Chefs Take Flight', www.forbes.com, accessed 1 April 2008.
Alexandra J. Kenyon, personal experience.

Case 6

Westin Hotels in Asia: Global distribution

By Jochen Wirtz and Jeannette Ho Pheng Theng

The Westin Stamford & Plaza Hotel is a five-star business, and an incentives, conventions and meetings (ICM) hotel in the heart of Singapore. It opened in 1986 with over 2,000 rooms and 70,000 square feet of meeting and banquet space. The hotel had been enjoying high occupancy rates of above 80 per cent until mid-1997, benefiting from Singapore's position as an Asian business and ICM hub. Its sister hotels, The Westin Banyan Tree in Bangkok and The Westin Philippine Plaza in Manila, were similarly blessed with high occupancies and buoyant markets just prior to June 1997. The economic crisis that hit Asia in mid-1997, however, took the wind out of the Asian markets. Business and ICM arrivals into the three countries declined by some 10 to 25 per cent in 1998. The three Westin hotels saw their occupancies fall by 10 to 20 per cent, as well as a sharp decline in average room rates. To compound things, the pre-crisis economic boom had seen a proliferation of five-star hotel developments in the three cities. Travel management trends in Asia were also undergoing rapid changes. Many of the hotels' corporate clients were not local companies but multi-national corporations (MNCs), which were increasingly centralizing their purchases of travel-related services at overseas corporate headquarters, giving them more bargaining power.

In view of the shrinking market conditions, intense competition and changing travel management trends, the three Westin hotels in Asia had to critically reassess their own marketing and distribution strategies. A new opportunity presented itself in late 1997, when Westin's parent company, Starwood Hotels & Resorts Worldwide Inc., acquired ITT Corporation, which owned the Sheraton Hotels & Resorts, St. Regis Luxury Collection, Four Points Hotels, and Caesars World brands of hotels and casino. This acquisition made Starwood the largest hotel and gaming company in the world, with over 650 hotels in 73 countries employing more than 150,000 employees. Uppermost in the mind of Vice President Operations for the three Westin Hotels, David Shackleton, was the need to leverage on the size and global marketing strength of Starwood, to develop new business for his hotels and gain market share from the competitors. Further information on Westin and Starwood can be found at www.westin.com and www.starwood.com.

Traditional marketing and distribution strategies

Up until the past five years, local companies, local MNC offices, and local travel agents in Asia were the key decision makers, negotiating rates with the local hotels and selecting venues for corporate meetings, company incentives, company social functions, and making hotel reservations for their overseas guests. The marketing and distribution strategies of the three Westin hotels in Asia were thus predominantly focused on the local markets, and sales team efforts were concentrated on servicing and cultivating local decision makers. Well-staffed reservation departments were also important, as direct bookings with the hotels via fax and phone were the preferred method of making reservations.

Advertising and promotional (A&P) activities, to build brand awareness and reach the end customer for the three Westin hotels, were also highly decentralized at individual properties and rarely coordinated across sister hotels. As A&P expenses can be prohibitive, individual hotels tended to target their campaigns at the local market and allocated only a limited proportion of their budgets to overseas advertising.

Moreover, since each individual property was responsible for its own cost and revenue figures, each hotel would focus its sales and marketing efforts on selling its own rooms and facilities. There was minimal cross-selling of other Westin hotels worldwide. In other words, there was no cost-effective and concerted effort by all Westin hotels in reaching out to the travellers.

Travel management trends

However, as travel decisions are being made increasingly closer to the travel dates, decisions about hotel choice and the actual reservations are made closer to the customer. The traditional approach of relying on one's local offices or travel agents takes too long. Hence, hotels that can provide their global customers easier and faster access will have a competitive edge.

Local secretaries' and the individual business traveller's power to select hotels have also been diluted. The three Westin hotels in Asia

saw an increasing trend of their multinational corporate clients centralizing their global hotel room rate negotiations at corporate head office, in order to reduce cost through global volume purchasing and to increase bargaining power. Corporate travellers can only select a hotel that is on the approved listing. The change in corporate travel policies and practices is a result of management's concern with their rising travel and entertainment (T&E) costs. *The 1991 American Express Survey of Business Travel Management* reported that 60 per cent of the 1,564 companies surveyed agreed that rising T&E costs is one of management's top concerns.

Corporate clients were also increasingly turning to travel management companies (TMCs) for a total travel solution. The TMCs, such as American Express and Carlson Wagon Lit, are able to handle all airline, hotel and other travel arrangements. They use mainly global distribution systems (GDSs, global reservation systems containing extensive information on airfares, hotel rates, etc.) such as Galileo, Sabre and Amadeus, for hotel reservations. The Westin Stamford & Plaza in particular had seen an increase in the number of reservations coming in via the GDSs. This reservation channel brings in about 27 per cent of the hotel's transient (non-group) revenue. Even wholesale travel agents, who had traditionally booked directly via fax and phone, were increasingly turning to the use of GDS to improve efficiency and obtain instant confirmation.

On this issue, Mr Shackleton said,

'This trend of centralizing travel management is not new in the United States, Europe, nor Australia, but we in Asia are just beginning to feel the impact. Many MNCs have now organized their home grounds and are extending their centralized management and purchase of travel services to their Asian offices. With the Asian economic crisis dampening demand from large traditional markets like Japan, Indonesia, Malaysia and Hong Kong, we certainly need to grow our markets out of the United States, Europe, and Australia. We need to reassess our marketing and distribution strategies in order to align ourselves with these changes and to be effective in reaching out to these decision makers overseas. Competition among the international hotel chains is very keen. Once we have been selected onto a corporate listing, the battle is far from over. We still have to incentivize the travel managers overseas to select our hotels in Asia over Hyatt, Marriot, and the Shangri-Las, who are also listed. The individual business travellers can still choose among hotels on the approved list. Another development is that meeting and conference planners increasingly need a quick turnaround in exploring possible destinations, checking meeting space and room availability, and finally negotiating the piece of business. Our current process takes days or weeks and is becoming unacceptable to demanding clients.'

Starwood's global marketing and distribution strategies

Since Starwood's acquisition of the ITT corporation in late 1997, a key issue had become to examine how Starwood and its individual properties, such as the Westin, could leverage on Starwood's size, geographic coverage, and brand diversity.

Global selling and cross selling

Roberta Rinker-Ludloff, Vice President of Starwood Global Sales, quoted Henry Ford, 'Coming together is the beginning. Keeping together is the progress. Working together is success.' Starwood's strategy had comprised global selling, cross-selling and improving customer service.

Starwood had formed over 30 global sales offices (GSOs) around the world to manage customer relationships with key global accounts. These GSOs provided a one-stop solution to corporate travel planners, wholesalers, meet-ing planners, incentive houses and mega travel organizations by addressing all accommodation issues including global room rate negotiations, corporate meetings and events planning at any of Starwood's 650 hotels worldwide.

Besides the GSOs, each hotel had its own sales team. With over 2,000 sales managers from individual properties making sales calls and meeting clients daily, how could Starwood produce synergy and leverage on these activities? Team Hot was the answer – a new programme to harness the tremendous power of cross-selling across its 650 hotels in an efficient and automated way. Team Hot provided incentives for hotel sales and catering managers to cross-sell other resorts and hotels under the Starwood umbrella. Programme participants needed to anticipate their clients' accommodation and catering needs outside of their own hotel, and then send the lead to the relevant property(s) via the internet. For leads that resulted in confirmed business, participants received points redeemable for airline tickets, room nights and other rewards. Starwood aimed to generate an additional US$225 million in revenue in 1999 through Team Hot.

Overseas guests no longer wanted to make long-distance calls to hotels for reservations, preferring to call a local toll-free telephone number instead. Starwood had set up nine central reservation offices (CROs) worldwide to provide one-stop total customer service for the guests, including hotel reservations worldwide, enrollment and redemption of Starwood's loyalty programme, and general customer service. With the toll-free numbers, guests only needed to remember one number to book any Starwood hotel.

Technology and automation

Whether it's the individual customer, the travel agent or corporate travel planner, all prefer and are likely to stay with hotels that are easy and quick to book, provide immediate response to customer queries and have rates that are reasonably competitive and up-to-date. Traditional booking methods via direct faxes and phone calls to the hotel were on the decline, as they were cumbersome and required customers to remember multiple phone and fax numbers. Meeting and conference planners increasingly needed quick turnaround and prompt servicing. Starwood used technology and automation to improve the quality of customer service and efficiency. The emphasis was on automating reservations and information provision to the customer.

Starwood's internet capabilities were continuously upgraded, and cutting-edge concepts such as electronic brochures were being pioneered and tested. Individual and corporate clients could gain instant access to information on the facilities and amenities provided by any of the 650 Starwood hotels, and could make online reservations and payment, all at a click of the mouse. Corporate clients could even book their own confidential negotiated rates through the internet. The internet has had great potential in creating value to both travellers and hotels. The revenue from bookings through Starwood's websites had increased 280 per cent in 1998 and over US $48 million worth of meeting leads had already been received through the websites in the first nine months of 1998.

Starwood had also developed its own internal central reservation system called Starlink. Starlink contained up-to-date property information and data on rates and availability for each of the 650 hotels, and fed the information interactively to all the major global distribution systems (GDSs). Seamless interface between Starlink and the GDSs ensured that all Starwood hotel services were instantly available and up-to-date at over 400,000 travel agents worldwide.

Starwood had also enlisted the help of technology to make their mobile global sales force more responsive to corporate clients. Its corporate travel information system soft-ware enabled the global sales manager to negotiate worldwide corporate rates with clients and print/sign the contracts all in one visit. The global sales force automation software would soon allow the notebook-armed global sales managers to negotiate and close group deals all in a single day. GSOs could check hotel availability, propose pricing, explore alternative dates, negotiate the contracts, close the business deal and immediately book guest and meeting rooms. It is a system designed to put all necessary information at a manager's fingertips and certainly to impress the client.

Concerted marketing effort

Individual properties also needed to create more awareness in overseas markets. To share the burden of high advertising and marketing costs, Starwood hotels clustered together and shared advertising space. Certain rates and promotions were also branded across all hotels within a chain in order to facilitate global advertising. All Westin hotels in Asia Pacific, for example, offered advance purchase discounts that have been branded as the Westin Valuestays Promotions.

Aligning individual hotels to Starwood

How can the three individual hotels in Asia leverage on the marketing muscles of Starwood to help them address the trend of centralized corporate purchasing for hotel services and to grow their markets from the United States, Europe and Australia?

With over 650 properties to sell, and Asia being in recession, it would not be surprising if very little of the global sales efforts was being spent to promote hotels in Asia to Americans and Europeans. To compound things, many of the global sales managers and central reservation agents were heritage Sheraton, and were thus not well acquainted with the Westin hotels. David Shackleton believed that the first priority would be to restructure the sales and marketing teams at his hotels to align them with the global Starwood marketing structure. Hence, besides traditional relationship marketing to the local companies and corporate secretaries, the hotel sales and marketing teams were now tasked to also 'market' their individual properties to the GSOs and CROs. Each hotel sales manager was responsible for cultivating close working relationships with specific global sales managers. Hotel sales managers needed to prioritize and discuss their global sales objectives with the GSOs, and ensure that all leads provided by them were followed up promptly. The hotel reservation and distribution marketing managers needed to ensure that property information, rates and availability were constantly kept up-to-date in all the various distribution systems such as Starlink, the internet and the GDSs. Monthly reports on local sales and marketing activities were provided to the GSOs via electronic media. Hotel promotional collaterals were regularly distributed to the GSOs and CROs to heighten their awareness of the three Westin properties. Familiarization trips were also being planned for the GSO and CRO managers to acquaint them with the hotel service experience and enable them to sell the hotels more effectively.

Discussion questions

1 Apart from the preferential rates and good service, what other strategies can Starwood hotels employ to encourage selection and loyalty from corporate travel managers and event planners?

2 Even after corporate travel managers have selected and negotiated with individual hotel chains, the individual corporate traveller can still choose among the various chains listed in his company's directory. How can Westin and the other Starwood brands differentiate themselves from other hotel chains and make themselves the top choice of the corporate traveller?

3 In the long term, would it be more effective for the three Westin hotels in Asia to focus their distribution strategy on intermediaries (travel agent or corporate travel managers), or should they employ multi-channel distribution strategies?

4 What are the key challenges facing the three hotels in its move to leverage on Starwood's marketing and distribution programmes?

Acknowledgements

Jochen Wirtz is an Associate Professor with the Department of Marketing, Faculty of Business Administration, National University of Singapore. Jeannette Ho Pheng Theng is an MSc student with the Department of Marketing and Director of Revenue Management at The Westin Stamford & Westin Plaza Hotels in Singapore.

The authors greatly acknowledge the generous support in terms of time, information and feedback provided on earlier drafts of this case by David Shackleton, Vice President Operations, Central Region for Starwood Asia Pacific, and Philip Ho, Managing Director Distribution and Revenue Management Asia Pacific. Furthermore, the authors would like to acknowledge the assistance of Cindy Kai Lin Koh and Sim Liew Lien in writing up the case.

Case 7

Yield management in budget airlines: The case of easyJet

Gerald L. Barlow

Introduction

The budget sector of the airline industry in both the UK and USA dates back to the 1950s and growth in demand for new holiday destinations, and the growth in air transportation. Initial budget airlines concentrated on the holiday market, offering charter flights. In Europe this meant Spain, France, Greece and the Balearic Islands in the summer and European ski resorts in the winter. Although this market still exists with specialist companies in the UK like Britannia Air, the start of low-cost flights began with 'the battle for the transatlantic business' as seen by Freddy Laker, with Laker Airways and The People's Express. The true budget airlines, however, took shape with deregulation in the United States. The most successful budget airline to develop in America was SouthWestern Airlines, while the main player in recent years in the UK has become easyJet. easyJet is probably following the SouthWestern formula in its operations and development of service and routes. The earliest European low-cost or budget airline still operating with significant passenger numbers and routes in the European market is the Irish carrier Ryanair. The basic premise of business in the budget airlines is of course similar to that of the major intercontinental air carriers. There are, however, major differences between the intercontinental carriers and the budget airlines in both the United States and Europe, which have

knock-on effects throughout the budget airline operations. The major differences between the operating processes and cost base of both types of carriers, are outlined in Figure C7.1. To be effective easyJet operates from low-cost airports (Luton and Liverpool) and flies to low-cost airports (the costs charged to the airline operators are lower at airports like Luton than major international centres like Heathrow or Gatwick). Additionally, it operates only one type of plane, the Boeing 737–500, which again helps to reduce operating and running costs. This has benefits for yield management as it mans only one type of capacity, consisting of 159 seats or units.

Yield management within the airline industry may be a prerequisite, but in the budget airline sector it is still developing. Whether it is called yield management, revenue management or revenue maximization its aim or purpose is clear: to achieve the highest possible income from every single flight within an airline's portfolio of flights and routes. To investigate how budget airlines use and gain competitive advantage from this technique, easyJet is used as an example.

easyJet

easyJet began in November 1995, with two aircraft operating a three flights a day programme between Glasgow, Edinburgh and its base at Luton. Business was brisk and turnover rose from £25 million in 1996 to over £50

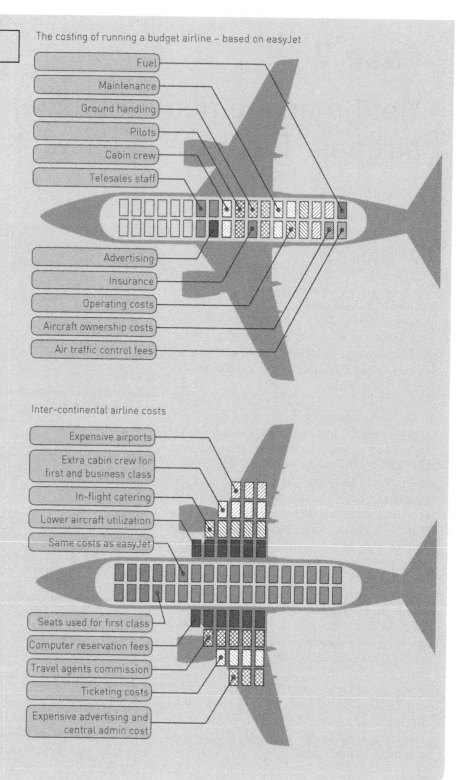

Figure C7.1

Intercontinental airline costs

The costing of running a budget airline – based on easyJet

- Fuel
- Maintenance
- Ground handling
- Pilots
- Cabin crew
- Telesales staff

- Advertising
- Insurance
- Operating costs
- Aircraft ownership costs
- Air traffic control fees

Inter-continental airline costs

- Expensive airports
- Extra cabin crew for first and business class
- In-flight catering
- Lower aircraft utilization
- Same costs as easyJet

- Seats used for first class
- Computer reservation fees
- Travel agents commission
- Ticketing costs
- Expensive advertising and central admin cost

million by the end of 1997. Routes began to expand and by 1998 these included Aberdeen, Edinburgh, Glasgow, Inverness and Belfast, complemented by Holland, Switzerland, Spain, France and Greece on mainland Europe, and adding Liverpool as a second English base. The company was conceived and run by a charismatic chairman, Stelios Haji-Ioannou, then a 31-year-old Greek graduate of the London School of Economics, who admits the idea came as a result of Virgin Airlines' first attempt to operate a franchise on the Athens to London route.

The company operates a no-frills airline, based on short-haul flights, aiming at maintaining a low-cost strategy and providing a quality low-price flight. In the autumn of 1997 Haji-Ioannou signed a $500 million order for a number of brand new Boeing 737–500 planes, due to enter service by the end of 1999, to provide the needed capacity for the company's expansion up to six million passengers. Haji-Ioannou's declared ambition is for easyJet to be the 'McDonalds' of flying, and he is perhaps on course for this aim. The image easyJet is creating is one of simple efficient service, for quick easy use. From the attractively simple but functional black trousers or skirts with orange shirts of the inflight crew, to the very effective and efficient online internet booking system which offers you a simple quick way to book your tickets (thus also providing a good view of a yield management system working minute by minute), easyJet has developed an effective and efficient operation, a single positive brand image and a successful marketing strategy. easyJet and Haji-Ioannou's commitment to Luton has probably done more in its first two years for Luton airport than any other single company or person, including Lorraine Chase and Campari! Future development plans for easyJet, to allow it to achieve its growth potential and fill the capacity created by the new plane acquisitions, include considering additional destinations, such as Munich, Copenhagen, Oslo, Hamburg, Berlin and Stockholm, along with plans to develop further the facilities at Luton airport. Complementary company developments include a chain of internet cafés and a low-cost car hire operation, both of which have implications for the use of yield management. Has easyJet been successful in its aims and objectives to date? By most methods of judgement, the answer must be yes. But perhaps British Airways' attitude is the best measure. In 1996, it described easyJet as the 'peanut airline' at the time of its launch, but just two short years later British Airways had announced the launch of its own low-cost airline, GO. Imitation, it is said, is the greatest of compliments. If you are uncertain of the success of easyJet the best answer is to try it for yourself. easyJet has seen an opportunity to develop direct marketing and sales of short-haul European flights and has used all the operational tools necessary to ensure its success, one of the main tools being the development of its own dedicated yield management programme.

Yield management at easyJet

easyJet uses an automated yield management system based around maximizing the revenue on each flight, every day. The easyJet reservation system is somewhat different from those of most of its competitors in that all its booking must be made directly with the airline reservations staff, via either the phone system or the internet, as no agency bookings are accepted. The yield management system, managed by the revenue manager, is one specifically developed for and by easyJet, and is modified on a regular basis and adjusted as operations mature. easyJet has developed the model to cover each flight route, for every flight and every day. The principal aim is maximization of revenue, while ensuring that the appropriate balance of passengers is met.

easyJet does not segment its customers. However, it does segment its flights into the following categories:

1 destination/route

- business
- leisure

2 flight time

- morning and evening flights
- daytime flights.

easyJet considers that there are, in its sector, two kinds of destination. The first is business destinations, like Glasgow, where the highest percentage of passengers are usually going for a short stay for business reasons. The second destination type is a non-business or leisure destination, like Palma, where the greatest percentage of passengers are going for non-business reasons with a longer stay over. The second segmentation is that of flight time, where the early morning, early evening, weekday flights tend to be regarded as business sector, while the middle day, late evening and weekend flights are non-business or leisure. Each segment/sector has differing booking patterns.

Figures C7.2–C7.7 show different patterns of bookings. Figure C7.2 shows non-business customers, and Figure C7.3 business customers, with Figure C7.4 combining them into a yield booking pattern. The prices can then be established around these expected patterns. The cheapest are available until, say, 25 seats are sold, then the next price bracket until 65, then 80, when the almost full price becomes available. The full price opens approximately ten days from take-off, when the majority of business segment fliers can be expected. Figure C7.5 shows actual bookings received as well as the yield plan.

Figures C7.6 and C7.7 indicate the yield plan for non-business/leisure flights, or weekend flights, together with an actual booking flow.

Figure C7.8 shows a flight yield pattern with the actual bookings received, along with the sales book-out price levels. This indicates that if the bookings received exceed 40 by or before 45 days from take-off, then the rate increases, and if it exceeds 60 seats sold by or before 35 days before take-off, the price increases to the next level, and so on.

Figure C7.9 highlights a similar booking pattern, but with late demand (business sector), and shows the price levels closing later and reopening again as the take-off date comes nearer, in the aim of increasing demand by offering a lower-cost seat.

Why is yield so important to easyJet?

1 Unlike the major airlines, easyJet has a price structure with only a small degree of flexibility: the range in price available for any destination at easyJet is low. For example, Nice starts off at a low of £35 per seat, extending up to £129 depending upon level of bookings and number of days out from take-off. At BA, for a similar flight, the prices ranges from £284 standard fare, to £351 for business class, and the reduction can be very wide nearer take-off, depending upon source, e.g. bucket shop, travel agents' special late offers. This gives the major airlines a larger range of discounting opportunities, and more chance of a contribution to their fixed costs. (Both examples of prices are current at time of writing and one way.)

2 easyJet offers no agency bookings, and passengers can only book or inquire directly via the telephone sales staff and the internet. Therefore it is essential to have an easy and quick reservation system that shuts out and opens the various pricing levels as the take-off

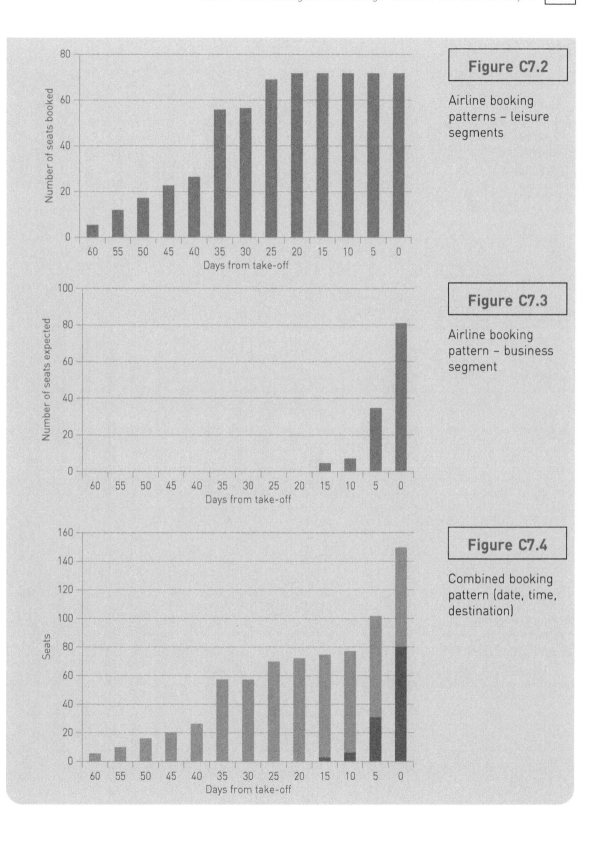

Figure C7.2

Airline booking patterns – leisure segments

Figure C7.3

Airline booking pattern – business segment

Figure C7.4

Combined booking pattern (date, time, destination)

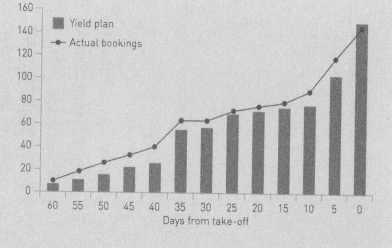

Figure C7.5

Booking plan showing yield forecast and actual (date, time, destination)

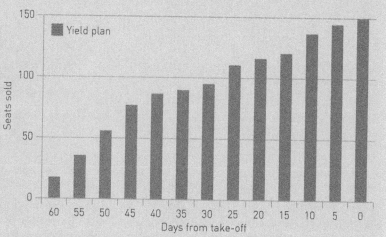

Figure C7.6

Yield plan for non-business destination

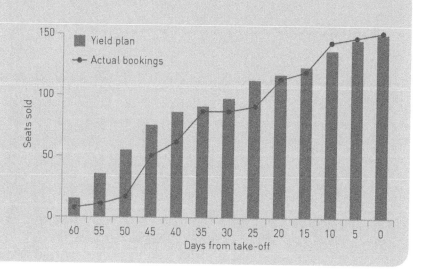

Figure C7.7

Actual booking chart – non-business destination (date, time, destination)

date nears, and the booking pattern becomes clearer. Any problems or delays within the computer yield management booking system could result it:

- staff giving different rates
- lower rates than are necessary being given, and therefore loss of revenue occurring
- staff being able to differentiate prices as a personal choice
- customers receiving unequal treatment, and thus becoming dissatisfied.

3 A system which instils confidence in the operation for management, sales staff and customers.

4 This system permits the staff to achieve a high level of operator efficiency, due to certainty, accuracy and simplicity, which is important to the company, and the operators who are paid on results (bookings achieved).

5 The easyJet internet system is only possible with the use of a real-time yield management system. This system has proved so successful that during November 1999 it set a world record for

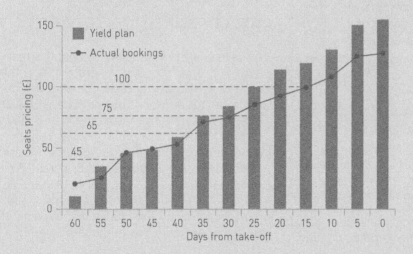

Figure C7.8

Yield pattern of actual bookings received and sales bookout price levels

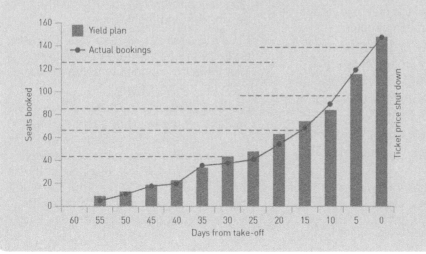

Figure C7.9

Booking pattern for late demand

airline bookings achieved via the net, 60 per cent of all bookings for a specific day.

How does this system vary from the traditional yield system operated by the major carriers?

1 The major carriers have interconnecting flights, which means that yield management can be used to maximize the income over more than one flight. The use of low-cost flights encourages use of other flights, usually more profitable ones. easyJet does not have interconnecting flights or arrangements with other carriers.

2 easyJet does not have cancellations, whereas the major carriers offer this opportunity, with varying complexity.

3 easyJet does not use travel agents, or any form of agency bookings, and this makes the reservations system easier and fully centralized.

4 easyJet does not operate tickets, thus making last-minute bookings easier to operate.

5 easyJet operates from fewer airports, has only one central reservations base and has only a limited number of destinations.

Other major differences between easyJet and the majority of other airlines include:

1 easyJet runs only one type of plane, the Boeing 737–500, which makes operations and reservations much simpler.

2 easyJet offers few onboard services, no duty-free and only limited catering service, which is outsourced.

3 easyJet operates without a ticket and has no actual boarding cards.

4 easyJet runs with very few ground handling crew, and an extremely sales-orientated central head office.

5 New plane purchases have been made and fit into the easyJet model, i.e. Boeing 737–500s.

6 No external sales offices, or airport sales offices, are operated by easyJet. It has no linked or joint sales.

7 Pricing is based strictly upon a revenue maximization process that matches the aims and objectives of yield management.

All these factors help the company to maintain a low variable cost, a key component in any successful yield management system, and provide an opportunity for leverage against its major competitors.

Why do airlines pay so much attention to yield?

Airlines operate in a highly competitive market, and the low-cost operators, by the nature of this, are fiercely competitive. The environment in which they operate is one of high fixed costs, fixed capacity in the short term, a perishable product and seasonal variable demand. According to Arthur Andersen (1997), easyJet fulfils all the established criteria for the effective use of yield management. Dr Scot Hornick of Andersen Consulting has identified five 'functional aspects of yield management', as outlined below:

1 *Market segmentation:* an area that easyJet feels is inappropriate, only segmenting by destination and flight time.

2 *Price management:* systematically offering different prices to different customer segments in response to demand, the main issues for easyJet.

3 *Demand forecasting:* forecasting future demand on the basis of past sales and known future events. Initially easyJet has obvious problems, as past history was short and demand was increasing. It was through good forecasting of future events that yield management was successful. Now easyJet's historic records are

becoming more useful, as it is becoming more established. But, with each new route easyJet opens, problems restart.

4 *Availability and/or capacity management:* limiting or shifting the availability of certain products or services according to customer demand. This is the main backbone of yield management in the airline sector. The capacity in terms of seats at easyJet is fixed, and is managed by good pricing to maximize the use of the limited seat capacity to obtain the maximum sales volume and to satisfy customer demand.

5 *Reservation/negotiation:* in some sectors, management can achieve better yield with the management of price and availability, through the 'up-selling' of specific areas to higher more expensive products or 'cross-selling' to alternative products, so ensuring an even spread of sales. Here easyJet is restricted as it operates a single class product, and the pricing is fixed irrespective of the type or segment of customer. The price offered will be dictated by the yield management system, related to the seat availability and the closeness of take-off date.

Preconditions for yield management are:

1 *Perishable inventory/or seasonal demand:* seats on an aircraft are extremely perishable, for if easyJet fails to sell seats on say the 7.00 a.m. flight to Glasgow, those seats sales are lost for ever.

2 *High fixed costs or sunk costs:* thus resulting in a low or relatively low marginal cost of selling one extra unit. Here the cost of a Boeing 737–500 is a very high fixed cost, while easyJet's marginal cost of selling one extra seat on, for example, the 7.00 a.m. flight to Glasgow is very low.

3 *Fixed capacity either overall or in the short term:* easyJet operates a fixed seat capacity throughout the fleet, on all routes and flights.

4 *Advance purchase of service/product:* easyJet will only accept pre-booked flights.

The use of a yield management system has enabled easyJet to operate its low-price policy successfully from its conception. The main skills needed are developing a good forecasting plan and history to permit the yield system to be successfully developed. The differences between the levels of yield management within the industry are based upon the level of sophistication and actual understanding of the techniques and markets. Lack of systemization, improper use or lack of understanding of the system can lead to erroneous results and decisions. easyJet ensures successful operation through simple systematic operations, and constant modification of the system as the market continues to develop.

Obstacles and success factors

The barriers to the use of yield management in the airline industry are few, but the level of operation and sophistication will depend upon the complexity of the flight programmes and price structures. Table C7.1 summarizes them.

Kimes (1989a) identifies seven key techniques necessary for the success of a yield management system.

1 *Ability to segment:* easyJet has identified two major segments within its operations.

2 *Perishability of inventory:* clearly airline seats, like hotel rooms, are a highly perishable commodity.

3 *Product sold in advance of use:* easyJet, more than most airlines, insists on 100 per cent sales and payment in advance, and offers no in-airport sales desks.

4 *Fluctuation in demand:* clearly with a number of destination and a number of flights at different times per day each day of the week, the demand for the product is subject to considerable variation.

Barriers to yield management

Table C7.1

Source Arthur Andersen (1997).

Business-internal (Features of the business itself which interfere with yield management)		Environmental (Features of the environment in which the business operates)	
Attitudinal (Features of business philosophy, attitudes towards pricing, understanding of yield management)	Operational (Aspects of the way a business operates)	Infrastructural (Factors in the business environment which impede the effectiveness of yield management)	Regulatory (Governmental restrictions on a business's ability to practice yield management)
No awareness of YM.	Cost of technology.	Insufficient supporting infrastructure.	Governmental price restrictions.
Insufficient management skills; incompatible business philosophy.	Dependence on contract business with fixed prices.	Appropriate off-the shelf computer YM technology not readily available.	
Resistance to formalizing information.	Insufficient information.	Rigid seasonality of demand.	
	High staff turnover.		
Negative misperceptions or scepticism towards YM.	Undifferentiated commodity product.		
No clear profit motive. *As applied to easyJet*	Capacity too small.		
Clearly fully aware.	Developed own technology; cost low compared to start-up costs.	New operation real issue.	High risk of governmental restrictions removed, thus opening way for easyJet type operations.
Management skills acquired.		High cost, so developed own model.	
New organization and staff, so no problems.	Lack of information a clear early problem.		
Very clear profit and financial incentives.	Staff new, constant training, ease of operations.		

5 *High fixed costs:* again, the cost of a 737–500 airline is relatively high compared to the ticket price.

6 *Low marginal sales costs:* here easyJet has a competitive advantage over most of its competitors, having very low variable costs.

7 *High marginal production:* here all airlines have a high marginal production cost. If the plane is full, and an extra seat is required for a customer, they are unable simply to produce one more seat and must decline, upgrade, provide an additional plane or compensate. It is here that easyJet, which operates a full-plane policy, with no standby and no interconnecting flights that can cause problems, has a cost advantage.

Kimes (1989b) also identifies five core requirements for the operation of a yield management system.

1 *Booking patterns:* yield management systems require information on how the reservations are made for a specific date. It is from this information that the system tracks and creates a picture of the booking process in the future, and from the past for the future. It is through this process that easyJet is able to: (a) operate is online live reservation system, and (b) create the necessary historic bookings profiles.

2 *Knowledge of the demand patterns by market segments:* as stated above, easyJet has identified, and operates with, two specific flight segments.

3 *An overbooking policy:* most airlines operate an overbooking policy, which when it goes wrong results in upgrades and stand-down discounts. easyJet works with very tight margins, without the back-up of business or first-class upgrades to cover this situation, hence it operates to a pre-booked full-seat capacity.

4 *Knowledge of the effect of price changes:* the team in charge of yield management need to know how changes in price will affect their customers, their occupancy and profitability. The major airlines change prices thousands of times a day, mainly in response to competitive pressure (Kimes 1989b). Clearly this level of yield management system is sophisticated beyond the current needs of easyJet.

5 *A good information system:* to match all the requirements of a successful yield management system, the operator requires a great deal of accurate information. It is in this area that the company has its greatest problem, since it is very young, and therefore lacks the indepth history of a company like British Airways. Additionally, the capturing of such data is very costly, in terms of both the methods used and staff time. This has resulted in easyJet only capturing information on actual bookings. The history on denied bookings is not recorded, an item which most writers (e.g. Orkin 1988; Kimes 1989a, 1989b; Jones and Hamilton 1992; Leiberman 1993) suggest is a prerequisite for successful yield management. However, it is an area in which the company acknowledges information is desirable, and hence this is more a question of the cost of collection and the time involved. The collection would need to be undertaken by sales staff, whose job is designed to be as time efficient as possible to help to maximize both the company's and the employees' income.

How does this system fit in with senior management plans?

Clearly easyJet is focusing on Michael Porter's (1985) low-cost strategy, and its version of yield management helps it along this path. However, without top management commitment the process would fail. To this end, one person, the revenue manager, has full responsibility for the development and management of the system. The system is designed to be user friendly, very simple in operation and adaptable to any changes brought about by internal or external factors.

Conclusion

Theoretically yield management as a management tool in the airline industry has an enormous potential to increase the financial performance of the airline. Sir Colin Marshall (1992) attributed BA's success to cost cutting and sophisticated yield management. However, for a newcomer and a low-price airline, it is not going to be easy. However, easyJet has created a successful system within a short time. It first flew in November 1995, and has seen its market share grow from 0 per cent in June 1996 to 29 per cent by December 1997 on the UK-Nice market (Nice Airport 1997). There are many lessons that companies, not just in the airline sector, can learn from easyJet's dedication and belief in the systems, which were necessary if it was to become truly successful. The findings presented here show how with determination and belief companies operating in a number of sectors could create and use a yield management system, suited to their specific needs to help create more successful operations. The system developed by easyJet perhaps has more in common with some hotel operations than many of its airline competitors, and certainly a number of them could learn from the easyJet experience. As Porter (1985) has pointed out, success comes from innovative products and service, often introduced by a competitor new to the industry.

Source: Ingold, A., Yeoman, I. and Leask, A. (2000) *Yield Management: Strategies for the Service Industries* London: Cengage Learning, pp. 198–210.

Discussion questions

1 With reference to the airline industry discuss the characteristics of services which make pricing strategies challenging in service marketing.

2 Explain how easyJet has developed competitive advantage in the budget travel industry. How can they maintain this?

3 Consider the relationship between supply, demand and pricing for budget airline travel. What pricing strategies and techniques are used to manage supply and demand?

4 Why is the concept of yield management so important to the success of easyJet? Discuss why this might not be the case for all airline operators.

References

Arthur Andersen (1997) *Yield Management in Small and Medium-sized Enterprises in the Tourist Industry.* Brussels: Directorate-General XXIII, European Commission.

Jones, R and Hamilton, D. (1992) 'Yield management: putting people in the big picture' *Cornell Hotel and Restaurant Administration Quarterly* 33 (1): 88–95.

Kimes, S.E. (1989a) 'The basics of yield management' *Cornell Hotel and Restaurant Administration Quarterly* 30(3): 14–19.

Kimes, S.E. (1989b) 'Yield management: a tool for capacity-constrained service firms' *Journal of Operations Management* 11 (4): 348–63.

Leiberman, W.H. (1993) 'Debunking the myths of yield management' *Cornell Hotel and Restaurant Administration Quarterly* 34 (1): 34–41.

Marshall, C. (1992) *BA Company Report* London: British Airways.

Nice Airport (1997) Monthly flight data, January.

Orkin, E.B. (1988) 'Boosting your bottom line with yield management' *Cornell Hotel and Restaurant Administration Quarterly* 28 (4): 52–6.

Porter, M.E. (1985) *Competitive Advantage* New York: Free Press.

Case 8

Activating e-bank users: Exploring the potential impact of e-atmospherics and experiential marketing

Developed by Ronan de Kervenoael, Aston Business School and D. Selcen O. Aykac, Ozyegin University

Secured bank was established as a private commercial bank in the mid 1950s and currently has over $40 billion in assets. It is now the third largest bank in Turkey with over 10.2 million customers, 489 branches and 2,000 ATMs. Since 1999, a call centre and an internet transaction site have been available using state-of-the art technology. *Secured bank* is the leader in foreign trade, financing 25 per cent of Turkey's exports and 19 per cent of its imports, cash management, custody and internet banking and manages the fastest growing credit card loyalty reward programme in Turkey. *Secured bank* has long been renowned for its services' innovation. The culture of innovation that enhances customer expectations is at the centre of both its business and marketing strategies. It was the first to offer multi-currency cash management, internet and telephone banking, Shop & Miles (the first frequent flyer programme credit card), Flexi Card (the first credit card in Europe to allow customers to create their ideal credit card, customized to their specific financial needs) and Minibank (an innovative banking programme for kids).

The rapid advance of internet banking in the past few years has been fuelled by two main factors. On one hand, there is the necessity to reduce costs. Branches are expensive to operate especially regarding simple routine transactions where a trouble-free technological solution is available (bills payment, account checking, money wiring and saving management). Moreover, branch location and numbers are becoming an issue as few banks own their real estate property and prefer renting. The costs of rent in the most prestigious locations have increased to such an extent that profitability levels need to be questioned. On the other hand, while all customers are automatically offered an e-banking access, a combination of factors seems to have been overlooked. Firstly, after a strong growth, on paper at least, in internet banking adoption by consumers, a levelling effect is currently being felt. Secondly, while internet access is available in 80 per cent of Turkish companies, private individual access remains low at around 9 per cent. These figures are mediated by the ongoing changes in technology from dial-up modem to broadband. Thirdly, while the educated young professionals seem to have quickly migrated to e-banking, a large part of the population still lags behind with little hope of skills improvement and regular access. Lastly, an increasing number of users are accessing the services from abroad.

From now on, the key objective is not only to increase the number of e-banking users but also to turn the current users into truly 'active' customers. Profitability of the channel can only be attained by increasing the frequency of usage but above all by cross-selling other services available. While activity-based costing exercises have been conducted, allowing the identification of leaders and potential opportunities for new star products, little is known about the process and sequence of promoting such services. In addition, as a bricks and click business and taking into account the overall population abilities, any strategy needs to accommodate the understanding that customers utilize multiple channels to bank. Still, it has to be remembered that the local branches remain the base for profit calculations and often the favourite point of contact. Local branches should not be perceived in competition with the e-channel. Indeed, the e-banking facilities are a potential source of new services and profits for all branches and complement the current level of service offering. Accessing services such as the central up-to-date databases or personal web analytic allows the branches to deliver a more efficient and tailored service. E-banking has truly enabled *Secured bank* to deliver the promises of its CRM and direct marketing activities.

On the technical side, e-atmospherics have been considered important for delivering the tangible cues of the e-banking services. Similar to branch atmospherics, such as interior design, colours used, flow of movement, illumination level and presence of other customers in the branch, e-atmospherics are relied upon to reduce the level of uncertainty and associated perceived risks tied with the intangibility of the services offered by an e-bank.

Computer-mediated communication (CMC) systems have become a popular feature of advanced websites. Avatars (or digital graphic design characters) which include personal shoppers/helpers, have been in use for many years. Progress has been made in understanding the interplay and combination between text, sound and animation where users can create substantially expressive messages (Poggi, 2000). Usual online written language, as opposed to novels, poetry or jokes for example, lacks sounds and prosodic features such as stress, tone, intonation and rhythm. Prosodic features help to transmit emotions or sometimes disambiguate meaning during reading and speaking actions. In written language, some of these features are substituted with vocabulary and punctuation. New online forms of signs and syntax are appearing such as "☺" and abbreviations often derived from mobile phone SMS (short message services) experiences such as 4U (for you). Other regular e-atmospherics involve audio text picture motions (banners, pop-up), the design of the space ranging from grid, maze to full freedom, the location and abilities of search functions, report on other consumer choices and any specific cultural or lifestyle based cues.

On the experiential side of marketing activities, strategies have moved from 'awareness and convenience', to 'parity and pricing' followed by 'quality and status' and are currently looking at 'technology and globalization'. In the near future, 'human development and community building' seem to be the emerging themes. The latter offers advantages for an experiential one-to-one interaction and the ability for customization. 'Companies need to come down from their Ivory Towers and talk to the people with whom they hope to create relationships' (Lenderman, 2006: 51). Some consumers may not be active users because they have lost control both from a technological and a banking/financial perspective. Hence, they often feel more vulnerable, stressed and even victimized by the current system. Customers will only give up their time (or invest in the bank's proposed activities) for a meaningful experience. The five traditional steps of experiential marketing, 'sense, feel, thinks, act and relate' (Schmitt, 1999), have an important role to play. As social creatures, we humans connect with humans. We don't hug TV screens or radios. If a website can interact with a human being in a live brand experience and form a connection with that person, it greatly increases the meaning and the relevance of that brand.

Discussion questions

1 Why are active users so important for e-banking?

2 How can the company utilize experiential marketing to enhance its strategy?

3 What kind of alternative e-atmospherics exist to develop e-banking user's experience?

4 What are the possible risks involved in using untested technologies claiming to facilitate experiences?

5 What do you know about Turkey as an emerging country applying for EU membership in relation to ICT?

References

Constantinides, E. (2004) 'Influencing the online consumer's behavior: the web experience', *Internet Research* 14 (2): 111–126.

Lenderman, M. (2007) *Experience the Message: How Experiential Marketing Is Changing the Brand World*, London: McClelland & Stewart.

Poggi, I. and C. Pelachaud (2000) 'Performative Facial Expressions in Animated Faces', in *Embodied Conversational Agents*, J. Cassell, J. Sullivan, S. Prevost and E. Churchill, eds, Cambridge: MIT Press.

Sautter, P., Hyman, M.R. et al. (2004) "E-tail atmospherics: a critique of the literature and model extension', *Journal of Electronic Commerce Research* 5 (1): 14–24.

Schmitt, B.H. (1999) *Experiential Marketing: How to Get Customers to Sense, Feel, Think, Act, and Relate to Your Company and Brands*, New York: The Free Press.

http://www.garanti.com.tr.

http://uk.youtube.com/watch?v = JlwcVzUI71o.

http://www.gsb.columbia.edu/execed/open/programs/em.cfm.

https://www.cia.gov/library/publications/the-world-factbook/geos/tu.html.

Case 9

Champions League Final, Moscow 2008: Catering to the masses

Developed by Stephen Henderson, Leeds Metropolitan University

Premise

Looks at the issues created by the management of very large crowds and the requirements of service. Considers the logistical issues and choices made around the recent Champions League Final in Moscow.

Case

In 1999, when Manchester United had at last reached the Champions League Final, Barcelona hosted the game against Bayern Munich. Fans from Germany and England revelled in the idea of a few days in the May sun. Football crazy men appeased their female companions with the idea of a few days on the Spanish beaches with just a 'small' excursion to the Camp Nou stadium for the final. For those fans from Manchester, the match was a fairytale victory as United scored twice in the dying minutes to snatch a 2–1 victory from Bayern Munich. So, when the final whistle blew in Manchester in 2008 to give them, ironically, a semi-final victory over Barcelona, the fans were delirious about the idea of reaching the final in Moscow.

Twenty-four hours later, Chelsea beat Liverpool to gain their place in the final to ensure an all-English final in Russia. With three English teams in the semi-finals, the pundits had already been speculating that the final might well be between English teams. Newspapers in England were asking why this final could not be moved to the newly opened Wembley Stadium in London. UEFA, the European governing body of football was stone-faced about such suggestions. As fans scoured the internet for cheap flights, there was a realization that not only did low-cost airlines tend not to include Moscow in their routings, but the prices of Moscow flights had gone from around £200 to £800 overnight. The need for visas was also a hot topic with something of a 'will they, won't they be needed' as the lead news item for many. The media depressed fans further with the news that Moscow was one of the most expensive capitals in the world, and yet, hotels were already scarce for the days close to the final. Tales emerged of ships heading to Russia ready to drop anchor and make their berths available at so-called cheap rates. As if this wasn't enough, the media were running tales about how tough the local police would be – maybe, after all, cheap accommodation would be available in the cells!

As the exodus of fans from England began, it was suggested that neither club had sold all of their allocation of tickets despite the reduced stadium capacity that had been agreed. However, there were extra flights laid on from London and Manchester with a suggestion that those travelling with match tickets would have visa requirements waived for a 72-hour period. In fact, despite the English media's doom-mongering, the Russian authorities had been busy working out how to deal with the arrival of around 50,000 football fans. After all, Moscow had seen nothing on this scale since the 1980 Olympics. Their plan involved a fleet of buses meeting the arriving fans at the airport and their transport along designated bus lanes to avoid the notorious Moscow traffic jams. On arrival at the Luzhniki Stadium, food, drink and entertainment would be available to get everyone in the mood for the big game. After the match, fans would be transported back to the airport for their charter flights back to England. Of course, some fans made their own way to the Russian capital routed by flights to other European cities and some of these fans were pictured taking a wider look at the capital where a fans' area including karaoke, a small football pitch and a replica of the Champions League trophy itself was positioned in Red Square next to Lenin's tomb. Among the residents of Moscow were fans of the two teams and the owner of Chelsea, Russian oligarch Roman Abramovich, intrigued even those locals with no interest in football. In the end, the worldwide TV audience of millions and a lucky few in the stadium saw Manchester United triumph over Chelsea in a penalty shoot-out after extra time couldn't separate the sides. More importantly for Moscow, all this passed off peacefully with not a hint of trouble reported in the media.

Discussion questions

1 There are eight 'principles of waiting' (see Chapter 12) Choose two principles and discuss their significance when managing football fans.

2 There were many ways in which fans could get a ticket for the Champions' League Final. What would you suggest ticket suppliers do to encourage fans to buy their tickets on-line?

3 What are the main logistical issues around this and how are they resolved?

4 Such large events attract fans without tickets looking to savour the atmosphere – how can this be best managed?

5 Was it fair to ask the fans of the clubs to spend such large sums of money to get to the final?

References

'Champions League build-up photos', http://news.bbc. co.uk/sport1/hi/football/europe/7409559.stm.
'Football fans heading to Moscow', http:// news.bbc.co.uk/1/hi/england/7410520.stm.
'Hefty bill beckons for Champions League trip', http:// news.bbc.co.uk/1/hi/business/7376786.stm.
'Moscow confident of final success', http:// news.bbc.co.uk/1/hi/world/europe/7378139.stm.
'So far, so peaceful in Moscow', http://news.bbc.co.uk/ 1/hi/uk/7412062.stm.

Case 10
BUPA: Ethical relationships

Relationship marketing in a complex and high-contact business can be a challenge. The information provided in this case shows some of the tools used to enhance relationships with a range of diverse stakeholder groups by one of the market leaders in medical insurance and private healthcare.

Background

BUPA began as The British United Provident Association in 1947 to preserve freedom of choice in health care. It believed that with a National Health Service being introduced a year later, there would still be a need for a complementary service enabling people from all walks of life to afford the benefits of choice in where, when and by whom they were treated.

BUPA is now a global health and care organization with bases on three continents and more than seven million customers. The company is formed as a provident association which means that they do not have shareholders and that any profit or surplus made is re-invested in the business.

BUPA's biggest and original business is health insurance in the UK, both for individuals and corporations that want to look after the health of their employees. More than half of the UK's top companies are BUPA customers. As well as health insurance BUPA also provide:

- Care homes
- Health assessments
- Health at work services
- Cash plans
- Childcare
- International services
- Sanitas (Spain)
- Travel services
- Health insurance

BUPA's vision is 'Taking Care of the Lives in Our Hands'. The vision has driven the growth in services offered, growing from funding treatment, to providing treatment and care, to preventing illness and encouraging a healthy lifestyle.

BUPA expands upon its vision in the following statement:

'As we look towards our next half century, our aims remain the same as they did in 1947: to prevent, relieve and cure sickness and ill health, to promote health in any way, and to raise, establish, maintain and administer a fund for defraying medical costs on behalf of our members.'

The organization is committed to being ethical, accountable and respectful. This is reflected in their communications, in which they endeavour to project 'a leading and expert brand that is warm, friendly, open, accessible, caring and empathetic'.

BUPA's business

As membership market leader for private medical insurance, BUPA provides cover to over three million people in the UK including staff in over half of the FTSE 100 companies. Annually, they spend over £800 million on members' healthcare including around £100 million on cancer treatments.

BUPA Hospitals perform a wide range of procedures and continue to attract increasing customer numbers from the NHS. BUPA Wellness offers health assessments and treatment in 47 Wellness Centres across the UK, which assess fitness and detect early signs of disease and illness, as well as private GP, dental and musculoskeletal services. BUPA is also increasingly involved in the provision of residential and nursing care for the elderly. BUPA Care Services is the UK's second largest private provider of care home places, with 299 residential and nursing homes with over 20,000 residents. BUPA has also developed new NHS relationships, opening the first privately run NHS Diagnostic Treatment Centre at Redwood in Surrey and performing thousands of operations every year in its other hospitals on behalf of the NHS

BUPA International is another fast-growing part of the group, caring for over three million customers worldwide in places as diverse as Australia, China, Denmark, Hong Kong, India, Ireland, Malaysia, Saudi Arabia, Singapore, South America, Spain and Thailand. In Spain, BUPA owns Sanitas, a leading private medical insurance company with over one million members which has expanded to provide care homes in addition to its hospitals and clinics. In Australia, they have one million members, representing over 10 per cent of the market.

BUPA established the concept of private medical insurance in the UK, leading the market right up to the 1980s when rapid expansion attracted new competitors. However, it has retained its strong market lead and remains the pre-eminent brand in the sector.

the private sector, which is seeing new entrants and different types of policies. BUPA's marketing challenge is to continually remind people of the benefits of private health and care in a way that positions BUPA as the only and obvious brand to choose, both rationally and emotionally.

BUPA's current advertising strategy conveys the simple and powerful idea that people will 'Feel Better' with BUPA. This promise is being used across BUPA. All its businesses are dedicated to making people feel better, both physically in terms of the standard of treatment and care they receive and emotionally because of the reassurance and peace of mind provided.

With scientific progress, overall public health is improving. Yet, with an ageing population, an expanding range of treatments and a more affluent society, the need for healthcare services is increasing and consumer demand often exceeds what the NHS can offer. Spending on UK health and care cover products, including private medical insurance, health cash plans, dental benefit plans and long-term care insurance reached £4.2 billion in 2004, according to healthcare analysts Laing & Buisson. The number of people covered by private medical insurance policies in the UK, or enrolled in medical schemes self-insured by employers, was 7,576,000 at the end of 2004, up 0.5 per cent on the previous year.

Private healthcare is primarily funded by private medical insurance, the market for which has boomed since the beginning of the 1980s. Of this market, BUPA has a 41 per cent share representing £1.2 billion in revenue.

Marketing and markets

The UK health and care market has changed dramatically recently and further developments are likely due to both NHS structural and attitudinal changes and the expansion of

Stakeholders

The BUPA website identifies clear areas for different stakeholder groups and demonstrates the differing needs of these groups. Visitor interest areas:

- Individuals
- Business
- Intermediaries
- Health professionals
- Bupa members.

A separate area for investors and the press are also clearly signposted.

One part of the communications used to maintain relationships with a large group of intermediaries is a regular newsletter.

A variety of coordinated integrated marketing tools are used to communicate with potential customers. Direct marketing such as a newsletter may be used alongside a direct e-marketing campaign to build relationships with potential customers.

BUPA in the community

As well as these major stakeholders, BUPA also builds relationships with the wider community.

BUPA encourages its employees to take an active role in the communities that are home to the company's offices and care homes. Example of this include BUPA employees helping schoolchildren improve their reading by giving one-to-one attention to those who need a little extra help. The company's employees also renovate facilities such as shelters for the homeless or community theatres. The work has saved voluntary organizations many thousands of pounds and has raised large sums for charities.

One highly successful project involves BUPA's care homes. The residents and their relatives, along with the employees and local volunteers, create 'sensory gardens'. These are designed to stimulate the senses of sight, hearing and smell. Parts of the grounds around the homes are transformed with the use of recycled materials to create pleasant surroundings with wind chimes, flowerbeds and fountains.

These initiatives also reflect BUPA's CSR (Corporate Social Responsibility) policy. For example, each year BUPA awards nearly £1.5 million in grants to the BUPA Foundation, an independent charity that supports projects to advance medical knowledge and improve treatments, and a similar body, the Sanitas Foundation, has helped research and medical education in Spain for eight years.

BUPA-sponsored events

BUPA's sponsorship programme is designed to generate positive publicity and link the company with healthier lifestyles. All types of runners including elite athletes and wheelchair racers take part in the BUPA Great Run Series of events, the centrepiece of which is the BUPA Great North Run in Newcastle, the world's largest half-marathon with 50,000 participants from all over the world. With three further Great Runs, in Edinburgh, Manchester and Portsmouth, the events have raised more than £40 million for good causes.

Ethical relationships

In their relationship with all stakeholders, BUPA have clearly articulated ethical guidelines. Below are some extracts from these guidelines.

ETHICAL BUSINESS PRACTICES IN BUPA

'The best and most successful organizations recognize that they will only prosper in the long term if they satisfy the aspirations of their stakeholders; including customers, suppliers, employees, local communities, investors, governments, public interest and environment groups. To satisfy this intense scrutiny and the demands for greater accountability in society, businesses and other organizations are increasingly recognizing the need to measure, track and report on their social and ethical performance.'

Source: The Institute of Social and Ethical Accountability

Business-to-business ethics

The BUPA Personal Ethics Code for Purchasing Staff is the starting point for business-to-business ethics. This section provides guidelines for purchasing and supply management professionals in dealing with business-to-business ethical issues in their supply chains – to meet compliance criteria, satisfy standards of ethical practice and maintain organizational reputation.

Whenever guidance is required, staff should refer the issue to the Group Purchasing & Property Director.

BUPA encourages purchasing and supply management professionals to consider the long-term implications of their actions and to question objectives that may unintentionally have negative ethical consequences. An example may be an immediate objective to create savings by rationalizing the supply base – but this may then result in smaller suppliers failing to be developed and a monopoly situation beginning to emerge. Purchasing and supply management professionals should seek appropriate guidance, be open about concerns, and engage positively with suppliers and internal customers or peers, however difficult that may be. The resource implications of addressing these issues must be balanced against the potential risk to the reputation of the organization.

Everyone involved in purchasing and supply management in an organization should be aware of the organization's ethical policy and should embrace its principles. Purchasing and supply management professionals have a responsibility for the supply chains from which goods, services and works come into their organization or directly to their customers. Best practice purchasing and supply management includes developing and understanding suppliers' operations and offering guidance and support when improvement is necessary or appropriate. BUPA believes this should include ethical as well as commercial and technical guidance and support.

Where appropriate, encouraging suppliers to comply with BUPA's ethical policy can take place in parallel with the development of monitoring procedures, and may need to take place over a period of time, or be introduced in phases. Purchasing and supply management professionals should consider the effect on suppliers of compliance costs, and seek guidance about existing codes that may be applicable to their business so that new codes are not unnecessarily created. This may well require helping the organization confront long-standing custom and practice which are of dubious ethical standing but which have the appearance of being normal for that business.

Principles

BUPA Purchasing staff shall always seek to uphold and enhance the standing of BUPA and the purchasing and supply profession and will always act professionally and selflessly by:

1 Maintaining the highest possible standard of integrity in all their business relationships both inside and outside the organizations where they work.

2 Rejecting any business practice which might reasonably be deemed improper and never using their authority for personal gain.

3 Enhancing the proficiency and stature of BUPA and the profession by acquiring and maintaining current technical knowledge and the highest standards of ethical behaviour.

4 Fostering the highest possible standards of professional competence amongst those for whom they are responsible.

5 Optimizing the use of resources which they influence and for which they are responsible to provide the maximum benefit to BUPA.

6 Complying both with the letter and the spirit of:

6.1 the law of the country in which they practise

6.2 guidance on professional practice

6.3 contractual obligations.

Members should never allow themselves to be deflected from these principles.

Guidance

In applying these principles, BUPA Purchasing staff should follow the guidance set out below:

1 Declaration of interest – Any personal interest which may affect or be seen by others to affect their impartiality in any matter relevant to his or her duties should be declared.

2 Confidentiality and accuracy of information – The confidentiality of information received in the course of duty should be respected and should never be used for personal gain. Information given in the course of duty should be honest and clear.

3 Competition – The nature and length of contracts and business relationships with suppliers can vary according to circumstances. These should always be constructed to ensure deliverables and benefits. Arrangements which might in the long term prevent the effective operation of fair competition should be avoided.

4 Business gifts – Business gifts, other than items of very small intrinsic value such as business diaries or calendars, should not be accepted. Any accepted items must be recorded in a departmental record available for inspection.

5 Hospitality – The recipient should not allow him or herself to be influenced or be perceived by others to have been influenced in making a business decision as a consequence of accepting hospitality. The frequency and scale of hospitality accepted should be managed openly and with care and should not be greater than the member's employer is able to reciprocate.

Outlook

Future plans for BUPA include increased investment in care home development in the UK and Spain, in hospitals and medical centres in Spain, and systems in UK Membership. The UK Insurance business is expected to maintain its strong position in the health insurance market with continuing customer growth.

The International Insurance business will focus on organic growth in revenues and customers and will also assess potential new geographic markets with a view to further international expansion.

In Care Homes, the business will continue to focus on maintaining occupancy levels and controlling costs, while delivering a high-quality service. Care Homes will continue to expand in the UK and overseas.

The Group benefits from the strength and breadth of its diversified UK and international businesses, its health and care expertise, its continuing focus on improving efficiency and its strong cash generation. BUPA appears to have an attractive range of market opportunities to grow strongly in the future.

(Adapted from Val Gooding CBE, Chief Executive, 18 September 2007, Interim results report 2007)

Discussion questions

1 With reference to the case discuss whether it is possible or even desirable to maintain close relationships with all stakeholder groups.

2 Outline some of the methods that could be used to build relationships with key customers.

3 Consider how the ethical guidance on business-to-business practices would affect your relationship with BUPA if you were a supplier to them.

References

BUPA Interim results report 2007.
BUPA Superbrands UK, Brand profile, 2006, available from www.warc.com.
www.bupa.co.uk.

Case 11

Ticketing: From street corner scalping to corporate touts

Developed by Stephen Henderson, Leeds Metropolitan University

Premise

Looks at the effect of changing demand and technology on the distribution of tickets for large events. Tickets at inflated prices no longer change hands only on street corners but are available on the internet via auction sites such as eBay and even ticket agencies who now have auctions. Is this really offering a customer service?

Case

Organizers of live music or sport are always keen to sell some tangible reminder of the day with programmes, T-shirts, etc. being high up the list of potential souvenirs. Outside of this, those in attendance are mainly in receipt of a service with a number of elements that are difficult for the organizer to control. For example, outside events can be subject to poor weather that has the potential to spoil the enjoyment of those in attendance. Favourite sports teams may get beaten and top musicians may have 'an off night'. With this in mind, a good organizer should be eager to control as many elements of the service as possible.

Normally, as consumers of entertainment, our first experience of the process is that of purchasing a ticket for the event. However, if the event is a popular one, this process can be fraught with difficulty. In days gone by, people wanting tickets for very popular events would queue all night waiting for the ticket office to open whereas, now, they hover over a PC waiting to submit an electronic application when the appointed time for the sale to start arrives. Though using the PC is a more comfortable way to apply for tickets, the outcome is still unpredictable as you have no idea of what is happening in the background and success is often down to luck. Needless to say, this leads to many frustrations for those seeking tickets for popular events.

So, where does the fan left looking for a ticket go? Traditionally, they would have asked other fans for help or resorted to purchasing from touts who buy and sell tickets in a practice commonly known as 'scalping'. Now, the internet is their main refuge where ticket agencies and auction sites form the main sources of tickets. In other words, organizations that add a mark-up to the ticket or sell to the highest bidder.

At a glance, this looks quite straightforward but it hides a number of complexities. Firstly, there are official and unofficial agencies with the former engaged by the organizer who, hopefully, has agreed any booking fee to be charged to the buyer. The latter advertise available tickets and charge anything they like for their service whether they have tickets or not for the event. Artists like U2 have warned fans about using such companies due to the problems experienced by fans though, in truth, you have to ask how easy is it to recognize the official from the unofficial when looking at a website. The booking fees charged by some official sources also frustrate buyers of already expensive tickets, especially when tickets arrive late or are not posted with a secure delivery method underwriting any loss. Secondly, auction sites such as eBay are littered with tickets being auctioned by anyone from the young student who says it is easier than having to work on a newspaper round to a mother who states it is a way to earn money while looking after her children at home. Thirdly, some recognized ticket agencies such as Ticketmaster are not only selling tickets with an added booking fee but offering the option for others to auction tickets on their site. For some, this has been seen as fighting the touts whilst others claim that the venues and promoters are keeping back the best seats to be able to auction them and achieve better prices for hot tickets such as Leonard Cohen's return to the stage in 2008.

Many criticize the overtly unofficial sources as profiteering at the expense of fans but opposing views suggest they are offering a valuable alternative service for them. Reflecting this, the Scottish parliament has introduced laws ahead of the Commonwealth Games in 2014 that will outlaw ticket touts advertising and operating in and around the venues. However, it remains to be seen how this works out and, for example, how the internet will be, or even can be, policed. On the other hand, English politicians have suggested that there is no need for a legal framework and that a voluntary code amongst organizers is required including some better means for the genuine exchange of tickets coming available due to unforeseen circumstances. Companies like Viagogo have emerged to offer this service for sports teams like Manchester United and artists like Madonna where fans can buy spare tickets for a small charge that covers the transaction between the two parties. On the other hand, for some, the simple answer to all this is based on the basic rules of supply and demand. They suggest that ticket prices for popular events should just increase to reduce demand and, as a result, aim to eliminate the secondary market for tickets. Meanwhile, as the debate continues, the customers of ticket sellers are seemingly suffering a poor service that often leaves them with a feeling that official sources are no better than the unofficial ones.

Discussion questions

1 How might ticket agencies measure customer service?

2 How might ticket agencies reflect value for money in the service that they offer?

3 How does the distribution of tickets reflect on the event organizers and other stakeholders such as artists?

References

'Artists "must benefit from touts"', http://news.bbc.co.uk/1/hi/entertainment/7179834.stm.

'Auction sites bite back on touts', http://news.bbc.co.uk/1/hi/entertainment/6523563.stm.

'Confessions of a teen ticket tout', http://news.bbc.co.uk/1/hi/entertainment/6474181.stm.

'Eavis has "easy solution" to touting', http://news.bbc.co.uk/1/hi/entertainment/7179954.stm.

'The economics of ticket touting', http://news. bbc.co.uk/1/hi/entertainment/6477325.stm.

'"Golden age" for live music scene', http://news. bbc.co.uk/1/hi/entertainment/6542871.stm.

'Madonna Endorses Secondary Ticket Market Ahead Of World Tour', http://www.gigwise.com/news/43038/ madonna-endorses-secondary-ticket-market- ahead-of-world-tour.

'MPs Reject Tout Ban', http://www.bbc.co.uk/6music/ news/20071223_notoutban.shtml.

'MSPs approve 2014 Games tout law', http://news.bbc. co.uk/1/hi/scotland/glasgow_and_west/7374302. stm.

'Should ticket touting be illegal?', http://news. bbc.co.uk/1/hi/entertainment/6499721.stm.

'Ticketmaster auctions Leonard Cohen tickets', http:// www. leonardcohenforum.com/viewtopic.php?f = 26&t = 11049&p = 119731.

'Ticket touts face the music', http://news.bbc.co.uk/1/ hi/entertainment/6500877.stm.

Case 12

The service is all part of the Craic

Consumers understand brands and know what to expect in themed bars, restaurants, café's and adventure playgrounds. They do this by looking at the name and conjuring up the images and associations that the name implies. Similarly the retail outlet's physical evidence or store front can also give clues as to the type of experience the consumer will receive when they step inside. Themed pubs and bars have been in the marketplace for many years and the name, logo and tangible elements clearly let customers know what they can expect. The pub chain 'Walkabout' gives the impression of a laid-back Australian culture. The furnishings are bare and 'sun-bleached' and there are crocodiles hanging from the ceiling and posters alerting us to 'kangaroos crossing' – all the light-hearted fun of an Australian themed bar.

Irish bars are another theme that can be seen in over 53 countries worldwide (Irish Pub Concept 2008). Kitty O'Shea's Paris is France's oldest and most treasured Irish bar. It has a good location at 10 rue des Capucines in the second Arrondissement, which is in the centre of Paris. They say their success is because of their authentic Irish décor and friendly Irish bar staff (http://kittyosheas.com/kitty_paris.asp). If you are in Tenerife you could visit the Irish Fiddler and enjoy music 'live' every night of the week. Or call into Murphy's in Japan for Guinness Beef Stew with Bread (winter only!) (http://en.misawairishpub.com/sb.cgi?cid = 7).

The reason they are the most popular of branded themed bars is not because of the décor or Irish stew – it is because of the Craic. Craic is fun, happiness, laughter, drinking, singing, enjoyment or a combination of some or all of them. And the Irish know how to throw a good party. So the Craic is the intangible experience that many people want from a night out in an Irish bar.

O'Neills is a chain of Irish-themed bars owned by Mitchell and Butlers. They are described as the 'largest Irish bar brand in the world'. And they claim to be the 'heart and soul of the high street' (Mitchell and Butlers, 2008). It is also known that the Irish are friendly, warm-hearted and work hard. Therefore, the service provided in Irish-themed bars must match that of a 'true' Irish bartender who will know your name and choice of drink by the end of your visit.

Many Irish bars also have the support of two of the major Irish stout brands – Guinness and Murphy's – which has certainly helped promote and sustain Irish theme bars. In fact, the Guinness heritage began with Arthur Guinness brewing dark English beer, porter, as far back as the 1770s. Arthur Guinness's grandson Benjamin took over the family business and introduced the first trademark label for Guinness stout. Guinness, the brand, therefore came into force in 1862 and by the end of the nineteenth century it was being sold across the world. In fact by the end of the twentieth century Guinness was *brewed* in 40 countries such as Nigeria (1962), Cameroon (1970) and Ghana (1971). And whilst Guinness always sells well in Irish bars such as Kitty O'Sheas, it is actually sold in over 150 countries across the globe (www.Guinness-storehouse.com).

Naturally Guinness is very proud of their stout and they put their heart and soul into each of the 10 million glasses of Guinness that are sold every day throughout the world. They care so much for the brand's reputation, its production quality and how it is delivered to the customer that they set up a team of people to ensure that each pint of Guinness is delivered perfectly every time – in every country! Managing the service delivery of Guinness may not seem such a difficult thing to do – but if you were tasked to ensure that every pub, restaurant or hotel worldwide served a perfect pint consistently, I am sure you would agree this is not an easy task.

The 'Perfect Pint Team' was formed to try to ensure that Guinness reached the lips of its consumers perfectly every time they had a drink, wherever they were drinking it. The Perfect Pint Team were a cross-functional team of people who carefully studied the many different 'touch points' of Guinness to ensure that each intermediary that served Guinness understood their role in pouring the perfect pint. One of the main groups of intermediaries were landlords of pubs and bars – be they Irish bars, traditional English pubs or up-scale concept bars. Landlords of pubs and bars were advised that the service quality they provided was vital in serving the perfect pint using a method known as the 'two-part pour'. Landlords were given recognition, therefore, for their important role through training and promotional material. Training materials came via booklets, leaflets and in some cases on-site training. Steve Kenyon and his staff at O'Niells Irish Bar in Huddersfield, West Yorkshire were filmed for a training video of the 'two part pour', how to put an Irish Shamrock in the head of the pint of Guinness, why it takes 117 seconds to pour a pint of Guinness and how to present the 'perfect pint' to the customer. The training video was sent to pubs and bars in Europe that served Guinness. This type of investment in service quality ensured that landlords felt proud of the drink that they were serving to their customers. Within the trade Guinness became sought after and 'famous' because of the investment made in the 'two-part pour system'. However, it was important that customers were advised of the two-part pour system. To advise the customer, extensive above- and below-the-line advertising campaigns were launched to advise customers to be patient whilst waiting for their perfect pint. An advertising slogan created was 'Good things come to those who wait'. The slogan suggests that the waiting time creates anticipation which in turn will make the customer enjoy the product even more once they receive it. The waiting, anticipation and celebration of receiving the 'perfect pint' was and still is shown in TV advertising campaigns. For example, at the end of the 1990s a TV advertising campaign included a man dancing crazily whilst waiting for his perfect pint. The same theme of patience and anticipation is used in the current TV advertisement – The Andean Domino Race. The current advertisement shows a fantastic community spirit where a whole town has collected household items to create a domino race which culminates in the 'perfect pint', made out of 10,000 books. The advertisement suggests that consumers can become emotionally involved in the creation of their perfect pint. Frow and Payne (2007) discovered in their research regarding the 'perfect customer experience' that Guinness's success was all down to the commitment from their intermediaries, i.e. landlords. Londlords the worldover committed themselves to the two-part pour method. So next time you see a Guinness being served, check for the quality of service provided by the intermediaries wherever you are in the world!

Discussion questions

1 How and why are intermediary landlords important to Guinness's' success?

2 What marketing techniques were used to ensure that landlords were consistent in the service quality they provided to the customer?

3 How was the customer involved in understanding the new service delivery of their pint of Guinness?

4 Consider you are the Marketing Manager for Guinness and you were tasked with ensuring that service quality is upheld at a very large sporting event where Guinness is sponsoring the event. How would you ensure that temporary staff would uphold the quality of the brand?

5 Refer to the section titled Internal Communication Gap in Chapter 15. Choose a service organization of your choice and discuss whether the internal communications that Guinness provided for its intermediaries would be sufficient to provide marketing initiatives to service personnel.

References

Frow, P. and Payne, A. (2007) 'Towards the 'perfect' customer experience', *Brand Management* 15 (2): 80–101.

Mitchell & Butlers (2008) 'Business Navigator' http://www.mbplc.com/managed_content/components/navigator/business_nonflash.cfm?section = pubs &pagetype = about&company = oneills, accessed 20 August 2008.

www.Guinness-stroehouse.com.

http://kittyosheas.com/kitty_paris.asp.

http://en.misawairishpub.com/sb.cgi?cid = 7.

Case 13

Ray's Farm: Operations management at a tourist attraction

Anthony Ingold, Ian Yeoman and Anna Leask

Introduction

'Ray's Farm Country Matters' is a very unusual heritage tourism attraction. The farm is thought to originate in Saxon times and parts of the current farm are thought to date back to the fourteenth century. Until 25 years ago, the farm was of average size (350 acres) and comprised mainly beef, pigs and dairy. Parts of the land were sold piecemeal and when purchased by the current owners in 1982, the farm had only ten acres of land left attached to the farmhouse.

The farm as it remains today is in Shropshire, about ten miles west of Bridgnorth. It incorporates the final western spur of the Wyre Forest; it has a brook, 'Ray's Brook' and is at the start of Shropshire's longest footpath, the Jack Mytton Way. In addition to the woodland walk, along the banks of the brook, the farm is home to a number of rare breeds of animal, many of indigenous species, together with a large collection of owls.

This case will examine the operations management of this attraction in terms of the mission of the owners and in the context of Schmenner's (1995) service operations functions and processes. Schmenner outlines the well-known characteristics of services, e.g. intangibility, service product and consumption usually occur together both temporally and spatially, etc. However, he then goes on to produce a matrix that he calls the Service Process Mix (Schmenner 1995) which defines four major groups. These are Service Factory, Service Shop, Mass Service and Professional Service.

They are characterized by Schmenner on the basis of their degree of interactions and customization on the one hand, then by the degree of labour intensity on the other.

Background

The present owner of Ray's Farm, Frank Cartwright, has an engineering background. On retiring from his engineering business, Mr Cartwright decided to change his focus and invested in the purchase of Ray's Farm. Following a variety of ventures which were only partially successful, Mr Cartwright and his wife decided upon setting up Ray's Farm as a heritage visitor attraction. The emphasis on the attraction has always been upon the quality of provision for the visitor rather than upon maximizing revenue generation. In fact, the Cartwright's are unusual for entrepreneurs in that they wish to keep visitor levels relatively low, in order that the attraction maintains its distinctive natural appeal. Their mission could be described as running a natural resource attraction in such a way as to minimize impact upon the plants and animals, both natural (e.g. kingfishers along Ray's Brook) and farmed (the rare breed species which are maintained in enclosures) whilst providing a memorable visitor experience. Visitors are welcomed at the farmhouse entrance and given a map showing the location of the footpaths around the farm, suggested routeways, and where and how to view the highlights of the attraction.

The collection of owls was started serendipitously by Mrs Cartwright, when she took in an injured owl for care and recuperation. Under her care, the owl was nursed back to good health and Mrs Cartwright began to find a small stream of injured or unwanted owls being bequeathed to her. Originally the intention of the Cartwrights was to care for the owls, then release them or return them to their owners. However, this soon became impossible in many cases, and so began the owl collection, with a considerable diversity of species, and now over 50 in number.

The Cartwrights are now well known for their good animal husbandry, developed from an initial base of interest and dedication. They now have an excellent collection of both wild and domestic animals, many of which are rare British breeds, including pigs and goats. The following sections will examine this heritage attraction from an operational perspective.

Management perspectives

A review of Ray's Farm, even superficially as above, will demonstrate that it does not fit neatly into any of Schmenner's categories in the Service Process Mix. Reviewing the challenges for managers which are outlined by Schmenner, it can be advanced that the management of Ray's Farm borrows attributes from each of the proposed areas.

Low labour intensity (Service Factory/Service Shop)

As will be shown later, Ray's Farm is a low labour intensity operation, not due to mechanization, but by the nature of the operation. Capital expenditure decisions that are made are rela-

tively low key and rather than being based on expansion of the operation are based on quality of provision. However, the owners have obtained grants for capital improvement of the farm from the European Union. Because the operation is heritage based rather than profit driven, much of the work is carried out by traditional methods and little use is made of new technology for the farm operations. The farm also is seen very much to have an educational role, but again, the educational methods are traditional, developing students' interpretative and observational skills. Demand management is limited and promotion is carefully controlled to avoid mass market inflows of visitors. There is no promotion of off-peak visits, but the farm is open to visitors every day of the year, except Christmas Day and weekdays in January and February.

High interaction and customization (Service Shop/Professional Service)

At Ray's Farm, there is considerable scope for economies of scale. Mr Cartwright is vice-chairman of the Marches Countryside Attractions Group, and the group are able to negotiate contracts which provide such economies. For example, Ray's Farm have 150 000 leaflets printed and distributed at a reduced cost because of this membership. Much of the cost control relies upon the family orientation of the operation, with family members providing most of the labour in both human resources and administrative functions. However, the administrative functions are kept to a minimum. With regard to maintaining quality, the main focus of the operation is continual quality improvement; this is the main thrust of any capital outlay. Reacting to consumer intervention in the service delivery process is quite low key in the Ray's Farm operation. There can be little immediate interaction on a daily basis, since the owners are involved in the farm operation and the visitors are allowed to wander along the pathways etc. at will. However, the owners do interact with visitors on an *ad hoc* basis, for example when the visitors are welcomed and when they leave. Thus the owners do gain better-quality visitor information than, for example, an hotel operation does of its customers. Additionally, the owners get feedback from visiting schoolteachers which provides information which can be used to improve the educational value of visits.

The management of the advancement of the people who deliver the service is an interesting area, and one in which Ray's Farm is involved. At present there is very little provision for development of managers or operatives who work in farm tourism/farm heritage operations. This shortfall of provision is currently being addressed (Alexander, Ingold and McKenna 1997) in a European Union project which is assessing the availability and requirement for education and training in four European countries. It is an issue to which the owners of Ray's Farm had given little consideration until the issue was raised by the researchers, but one which the Cartwrights now consider to be of importance. Management of hierarchies of managers and operatives is definitely not an issue at Ray's Farm, as the personnel consist of Mr Cartwright, his wife and his daughter plus two casual workers. Likewise, gaining employee loyalty is not an issue.

High labour intensity (Mass Service/Professional Service)

It is quite clear that Ray's Farm cannot be related to any of Schmenner's criteria – hiring, training, methods development and control, employee welfare, scheduling workforces, control of far-flung locations, startups, managing growth – except in the most limited and parochial of interpretations. Thus it can at least exclude these from being relevant to this operation.

Low interaction/low customization (Service Factory/Mass Service)

In this category there is a re-emergence of some important issues for Ray's Farm. Marketing is one area of importance. Although, as has been stated earlier, the operators of Ray's Farm wish to maintain a high quality product with restricted visitor numbers, they do undertake certain marketing functions. One of these could be said to derive from a modern engineering focus, that of competitive benchmarking for product improvement and quality enhancement. Instead of taking normal vacations to sunny climes, the owners spend their holidays visiting other tourism/heritage attractions to learn and to gather ideas for their own operation. It is during this period that family loyalty is sought, and their daughter looks after the operation while they are away. It could be proposed that there is only limited scope for giving a 'warmth' to the service (particularly in a typical British summer); however, the owners do greet and make visitors feel welcome without stifling any sense of adventure or experiment.

It could be stated that the one key issue for Ray's Farm is the ambience of the physical surroundings and their perception by the visitor. The owners understand this very well and all the management and planning decisions that are taken, are on the basis of providing the visitor with a stimulating yet relaxing environment, which is at the same time tranquil yet encourages a spirit of enquiry. The owners have carried out some limited but detailed market research. This has provided them with a profile of their visitor and their needs and wants. They are thus able to plan the operation to meet these expectations, whilst at the same time attracting the type of visitor that they wish to attract and exclude those visitors they do not wish to encourage.

Finally, whilst there is no hierarchy in the operation other than operates within any family there is undoubtedly a need for standard operating systems on any farm-type activity. It is possibly in these areas that the previous

Table C13.1

Service characteristics
of Ray's Farm

Source after Schmenner (1995).

Schmenner typology	Ray's Farm	
Service features		
Mix of services	Limited	Service Factory/Mass Service
Basis of competition	Wide choice	Service Shop
Introduction of new services	Limited experimentation	Mass Service
Process features		
Capital intensity	Moderate	None
Pattern of process	Rigid	Service Factory/Mass Service
Ties to equipment	Integral	Service Factory
Importance of balance of tasks	Critical	Service Factory
Tolerance for excess capacity	Unwanted	Service Factory/Professional Service
Ease of scheduling	Not done	None
Economies of scale	Not possible	None
Notion of capacity	Unclear	Professional Service
Layout	Line flow	Service Factory
Additions to capacity	Limited and unwanted	None
Bottlenecks	Unlikely to occur	None
Nature of process change	Seldom occurs	Mass Service
Importance of material flow to provision	Incidental	Professional Service
Customer-orientated features		
Importance of attractive physical surrounding	Essential	Similar Mass Services
Customer-process interaction	Great and essential	Professional Service
Customization	Little	Service Factory/Mass Service
Ease of demand management	Not done	None
Process quality control	Informal	Mass Service/Professional Service
Labour-related features		
Pay	Not relevant	None
Skill levels	High	Service Shop
Job content	Very large and high variety	Professional Service
Advancement	Not relevant	None
Management features		
Staff-line needs	No line	None
Means of control	Variable	None

industrial/engineering background of Mr Cartwright will have had most influence. One good example of this is the flow process which has been arranged for the visitor. This takes the visitor right around the farm, with good views of all of the attractions, whilst maintaining security for the visitors, reasonably respecting the environment for the animals, and protecting the natural environments.

Challenges to management summarized

It is perhaps interesting that Ray's Farm, an unusual heritage attraction and definitely a service operation, does not fit easily into any of Schmenner's management challenge categories. In addition, as can be seen from Table C13.1, Ray's Farm does not compare clearly with any of Schmenner's four groupings.

In terms of the challenges provided, Ray's Farm draws heavily upon two of the proposed groupings, but has little to draw from the other two. Schmenner provides a useful framework for analysing service operations, but his categorizations now perhaps require some readjustment since his framework is rather too rigid. It could be argued that this is particularly important for service operations in Europe, where farm tourism and similar service operations are becoming increasingly important.

Source: Leask, A. and Yeoman, I. (1999) *Heritage Visitor Attractions*. London: Cengage Learning, pp. 245–50.

Discussion questions

1 Discuss the advantages and disadvantages of using Schmenner's Service Process Mix to assist Frank Cartwright decide the style of appropriate service.

2 What changes would you recommend to Frank Cartwright for the visitor attraction to be classified as professional service?

3 What changes would you recommend to Frank Cartwright for the visitor attraction to be classified as mass service?

References

Alexander, N., Ingold, A. and McKenna, A. (1997) Unpublished data.

Schmenner, R.W. (1995) *Service Operations Management*, Englewood Cliffs, NJ: Prentice-Hall.

Case 14

The Rockwool Group: Fire extinguisher or wallflower?

Developed by Prof. Paul Houman Andersen, Aarhus School of Business

Introduction

The setting is the autumn of 2001. Mr Stig Damgaard Pedersen rushes out of the door before the morning traffic sets in and makes the drive to the Rockwool Group's headquarters in Hedehusene very long. He is thinking about today's important meeting with the strategy team. As a superior in charge of the Rockwool Group's marketing activities, he is deeply involved in every strategic initiative made by the company, and a wide group of participants will be present at the meeting – from the financial department, the technological department and, not least, from the top management. The main question that is absorbing Mr Pedersen's attention is: What should the Rockwool Group do about the current market development, which has lead to a reduction of the company's profit margin by 50 per cent in 2000 as well as a far worse financial performance than Saint Gobain, which is the biggest international competitor in the market for insulation material.

Company profile

The Rockwool Group is a globally leading company within the production and marketing of stone wool-based products and components. Stone wool is produced in a capital-intensive production process, by which stone melts at approx 1500°C and is transformed into fibres, to which impregnating oil and binding agent are added. After this, the product is shaped into wool 'bats'.

The company was listed on the stock exchange in 1996, but is still dominated by the Rockwool Fund, which owns 23 per cent of the company and has a voting share of 27 per cent. The Fund is non-profit; however, it is owned by the Kähler family, which is also represented in the company's top management and board (Mr Tom Kähler is the group managing director and member of the board). During the past two years, the share price has been downward-sloping.

The company headquarters is situated in Hedehusene, west of Copenhagen, and the central R&D departments are also domiciled here. The Rockwool Group has a turnover of approx DKK 7.9 billion and employs approx 7,400 people, of which 6,000 are employed abroad. Figure C14.1 below reflects the company's economic development.

The company is organized with two main divisions: the insulation division and the systems division. The organizational structure is market-based, organized in regions in which Rockwool operates, as will appear from Figure C14.2. This organizational structure has replaced the previous organization, by which the company was more organized with actual country market managers.

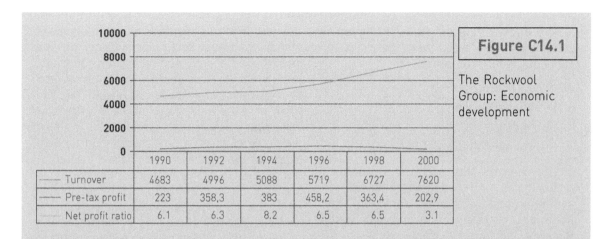

Figure C14.1

The Rockwool Group: Economic development

	1990	1992	1994	1996	1998	2000
Turnover	4683	4996	5088	5719	6727	7620
Pre-tax profit	223	358,3	383	458,2	363,4	202,9
Net profit ratio	6.1	6.3	8.2	6.5	6.5	3.1

Figure C17.2

Organization chart the Rockwool Group (2001)

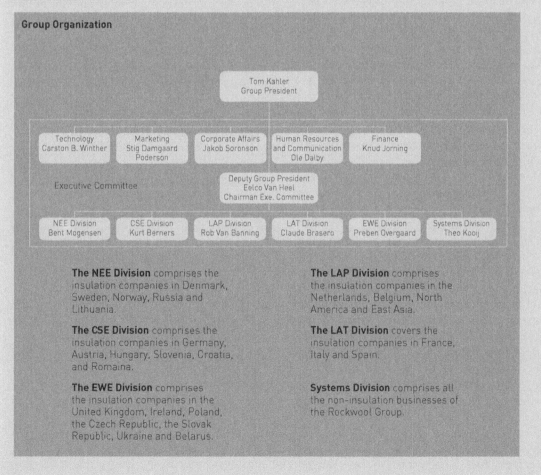

Group Organization

Tom Kahler
Group President

Technology
Carston B. Winther

Marketing
Stig Damgaard
Poderson

Corporate Affairs
Jakob Soronson

Human Resources
and Communication
Ole Dalby

Finance
Knud Jorning

Executive Committee

Deputy Group President
Eelco Van Heel
Chairman Exe. Committee

NEE Division
Bent Mogensen

CSE Division
Kurt Berners

LAP Division
Rob Van Banning

LAT Division
Claude Brasero

EWE Division
Preben Overgaard

Systems Division
Theo Kooij

The NEE Division comprises the insulation companies in Denmark, Sweden, Norway, Russia and Lithuania.

The CSE Division comprises the insulation companies in Germany, Austria, Hungary, Slovenia, Croatia, and Romaina.

The EWE Division comprises the insulation companies in the United Kingdom, Ireland, Poland, the Czech Republic, the Slovak Republic, Ukraine and Belarus.

The LAP Division comprises the insulation companies in the Netherlands, Belgium, North America and East Asia.

The LAT Division covers the insulation companies in France, Italy and Spain.

Systems Division comprises all the non-insulation businesses of the Rockwool Group.

The Rockwool Group is a R&D-intensive company. The development activities are concentrated in four areas:

- Production processes
- Working environment
- Fire safety
- Environmentally sound building.

The company has patented a number of technologies and products, including the actual process of manufacture, on which Rockwool has elevated unique knowledge. Rockwool takes out a great number of patents every year and plays a very important part in benchmarking the industry. Examples on innovative products include: *Flexibats*, which ease the adaptability of the insulation mats during the building process, *Conrock*, which increases the fire resistance considerably in the isolation material, and *Rockwool Silk*, which has a touch-friendly surface that eases the handling of the material and actually won the prize, for which there is much competition, as the product of the year in the Danish weekly magazine *Ingeniøren* (*The Engineer*). The Rockwool Group has also continued working on the original production patent and today has a unique form of production. The company is a typical engineer-intensive one and its core competence is technical product development.

The Rockwool Group has sales and production subsidiaries in all parts of the world as well as a wide agent network. The foreign markets account for a little more than 90 per cent of the turnover, Europe and in particular Germany being the main market areas. Rockwool became international around the same time when they started producing stone wool. In 1935, the company bought the right to produce and market stone wool in Sweden, Norway and Denmark, meaning the company internationalized its production activities very soon concurrently with the export growth and started its first international production activities in Sweden and

Norway in 1938 – one year after the company established itself in Denmark. Later on, the war started and caused restrictions on trade, which cast a damper on the international trade. During the 1940s and the 1950s, further arrangements on knowledge transfer via licence acquisitions were made. The next stone wool factory was established in Germany in 1954 in connection with the rebuilding of the German private housing sector.

The main part of the company's production still took place in Denmark in the succeeding three decades, during which the fuel crisis in particular created considerable growth prospects in the Danish home market and contributed to the creation of Rockwool's considerable fortune. In the mid-1970s, Rockwool really started developing international ambitions, and the company established a group structure that supported its international operations. The internationalization gathered serious speed in the 1980s and the 1990s, when the group spent DKK 4.5 billion on bringing its production plant up to date and establishing or taking over 10 factories, after which the centre of production was moved from Denmark to Europe. In this way, the company achieved transport cost advantages and an increased customer flexibility. In 1988 the Rockwool Group bought a stone wool factory near Toronto, with the intension of supplying the Canadian and North-American market, and continued its expansion in Eastern Europe in the beginning of the 1990s after the fall of the Iron Curtain.

Estimated fixed assets 2002
(million DKK)

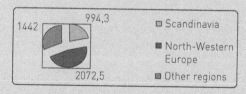

The first factory was established in the former East Germany in 1991, and shortly after, this investment was succeeded by two production plants in Poland. In 1997 and 1998, the

Rockwool Group bought production plants in Hungary and the Czech Republic. In 1999 the company bought the biggest stone wool manufacturer in the Russian Federation. At the same time, Rockwool also bought production plants in Southern Europe, and in 2000 they bought a factory in Malaysia, which is primarily to produce insulating bats for sale for the production of tower blocks with the intension of securing a more energy-efficient utilization of air conditioning facilities. Today (2001), the company has production plants in 14 countries. The outline in Table C14.1 illustrates the geographical distribution of the company's production facilities in order of time.

It is rather expensive to transport Rockwool's stone wool products over a long distance at a competitive price, and consequently there are substantial restrictions on the type of operation. Companies all over the globe frequently offer to buy a licence for Rockwool's patented production technology. However, for strategic reasons, the board has decided for Rockwool to use the technology abroad instead of selling it on licence, partly due to the fact that the Kähler family has spent generations on reaching the current level of knowledge and partly due to bad experiences with previous attempts. As an example, the Finnish competitor Paroc was established on the basis of a licensing agreement with Rockwool, which

Markets	Factories	**Table C14.1**
Skandinavia Western Europe (e.g. Denmark and Scandinavia)	1938 Factories in Denmark, Norway and Sweden 1971 Factory in Wales 1971 Factory in Holland 1980 Factory in France 1954 Factory in Germany 1985 Factory in Germany 1991 Factory in the former East Germany 1998 Factory in the UK 1999 Factory in Italy 2000 Factory in Spain	Establishment of production facilities – chronological outline
Eastern Europe and the Russian Federation	1993–1995 Factories in Poland 1997 Factory in Hungary 1998 Factory in the Czech Republic 1999 Factory in Moscow	
The USA and Canada Asia	1988 Factory in Canada 2000 Factory in Malaysia	

lead to Paroc's take-over of Rockwool's factory in Sweden.

Insulating material for the building industry: Market situation and competitive conditions

The company's main source of income is insulation, and approx 80 per cent of the company's total turnover concerns activities within this area. Three products dominate the insulation market: stone wool, glass wool and oil-based foamed plastics. Stone wool is typically a more expensive product but has a number of advantages compared to the other insulation materials: good insulating power, fire resistance (melts at 1000°C), noise absorption, strength, durability, water resistance and breathability (see Table C14.2 to compare the product characteristics of stone wool with other insulating materials).

The demand for insulation materials is influenced by the construction trends and the authoritative requirements in regard to energy conservation, noise control and fire safety. Stone wool is dominant in Northern Europe, where fire safety is in focus, whereas foamed plastics dominate the southern part of Europe. The US demands primarily stone and glass wool, whereas Eastern European builders primarily use stone wool and foamed plastics. Stone wool has penetrated the northern markets more and more, where energy conservation has supported the sales talks for insulating or reinsulating the building substance with stone wool products. At the moment, price rises for energy, as well as an increasing environmental focus, are also putting the development under pressure. In estimates, approximately 40 per cent of the CO_2 emission in the EU area is related to the heating or cooling of buildings. In 2001, the trading with CO_2-rights was initiated,

Table C14.2 Stone wool compared with other insulation materials	Product characteristic	Stone wool	Glass wool	Foamed plastics
	Insulation	+	+	+
	Fire conditions	Non-combustible Melting point above 1000°C	Non-combustible Melting point above 600°C	Combustible
	Diffusion susceptibility	+	+	-
	Pressure resistance	+	(+)	+
	Compressibility during storage and transportation	(+)	+	-
	Transportation	-	+	+
	Moisture repellence	+	(+)	+

meaning that companies could now trade CO_2 emission rights with each other. Reductions in the consumption of CO_2 (e.g., caused by improved insulation) create the opportunity to sell the consumption rights to others. However, as Figure C14.3 illustrates, the European market is characterized by imbalance.

The new EU fire directives, which are applicable in 2002 and make CE marking obligatory, are also creating expectations among stone wool manufacturers. At the moment, the European market for insulation materials is estimated at approximately DKK 35 billion. With a turnover of approximately DKK 7 billion, Rockwool is the second largest market player. The biggest one is Saint Gobain, which has a turnover of DKK 15 billion. The rest of the market is shared by two medium-sized and a number of small manufacturers. The medium-sized manufacturers are: the Finnish company Paroc which has a turnover of approximately two billion, and Pfleiderer Insulation in Germany which is a lot smaller, but is an aggressive player on Rockwool's most important market (an outline of the largest competitors in the market for insulation materials is given in Table C14.3). The largest competitors outside Europe include Ownes-Corning or Schuller (both from the USA). Furthermore, Rockwool differs from its competitors by focusing one-sidedly on stone wool, whereas the competitors typically produce both stone and glass wool.

Today, Rockwool operates in more than 30 countries, primarily in Europe, and the largest turnover and investments are made in the north-western part of Europe. Most of the sales have typically been centralized on quite few markets. More than half of the company's turnover has been realized in Germany and the Benelux countries. In the 1990s, Germany in particular showed good growth rates (Figure C14.4).

Insulation materials are typically bought by workmen and builders in the construction industry, who typically buy insulation mats through DIY centres and large wholesale companies. Only very little stock orders are made – delivery often takes place at the construction site and usually directly from the factory (especially for large construction projects). This intermediate link makes it hard for Rockwool to differentiate the product characteristics from the competitors' products and materials. As the buyers do not consider insulation material a particularly refined material, price and delivery time are often the most important competitive parameters, which is also why Rockwool has worked on improving reliability of delivery during the past few years (which leads to

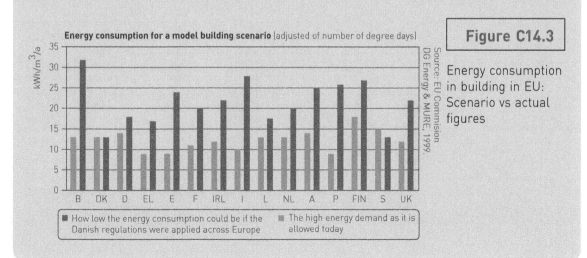

Energy consumption for a model building scenario (adjusted of number of degree days)

Source: EU Commision DG Energy & MURE, 1999.

- How low the energy consumption could be if the Danish regulations were applied across Europe
- The high energy demand as it is allowed today

Figure C14.3

Energy consumption in building in EU: Scenario vs actual figures a marginally improved capacity to supply from 95.6 to 95.9 per cent measured in deliveries on time) and has invested in developing Rockwool as a real brand to increase decision-makers' and end-users' awareness of the choice of insulation materials. A further initiative concerns aiming at e-trade for more effective business relations with DIY centres and timber businesses. In this way the order processing time will be shorter and it will be possible to follow the product flow directly, so that deliveries can always be physically located. This has been very successful – today more than one-third of Rockwool's orders are communicated via e-trading facilities.

Table C14.3		Rockwool	Saint Gobain	Paroc	Pfleiderer
Competitors in the European insulation market 2001: Profile	Turnover (insulation)	DKK 7.6bn (80 % of consolidated turnover)	DKK 15bn (6 % of consolidated turnover)	DKK 2.1bn (55 % of consolidated turnover)	DKK 49bn (13% of consolidated turnover)
	Product types	Stone wool	Stone wool Glass wool Foamed plastics	Stone wool	Stone wool Glass wool
	Market share in Europe	22%	43%	6%	>1%
	Market spread	Largest in Germany	Largest in France (home market)	Largest in Finland and the Baltic states	Germany exclusively
	Production plants	23 production plants in 14 countries	30 production plants in 20 countries	5 production plants in 5 countries	1 production plant (Germany)
	Ansatte	7,400	170,000	1,850	6,000
	Profile	Specialized in stone wool production	conglomerate specialized in glass wool production	Specialized in stone wool production – licence from Rockwool	Conglomerate specialized in technical wood

Market situation for the company's remaining products: systems sale division

The characteristics of stone wool are used in a number of construction-like and industrial connections other than just insulation. Throughout the years, Rockwool has always tried to differentiate its business area by developing a number of new product areas based on stone wool, which are typically more specialized and refined than insulation materials. However, even though the activities during the past three years have seen good business, as for the profit margin, the company has not been able to move its operation focus that much (operating profit/net turnover *100). (see Figure (14.5)

- Rockfon, which is used for acoustic improvements, was introduced in 1962 for outdoor noise control, e.g. from traffic.

- RockDelta, front panels (sandwich), which appeal to architects in particular.
- RockPanel, which are used indoors.
- Grodan, stone wool as a medium for cultivation substrates in market gardens. Introduced in 1969 when Rockwool was the market leader.
- Finally, special fibres from Lapinus Fibres which are used for armouring of braking products, packaging and other special products.

The competitive situation for each of these areas varies a lot and includes a lot of different alternative technologies. The products marketed in the systems sale division are mostly produced by the same production facility as the products from the insulation division; hence by allocating a large part of the production capacity to the systems division, the company has found a way to meet the stagnant demand for insulation mats. However, investments in special production

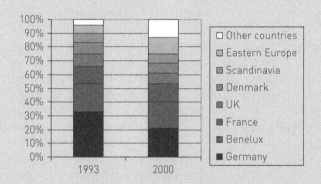

Figure C14.4

Rockwool's markets

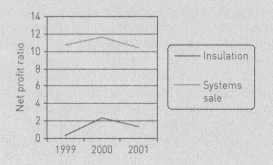

Figure C14.5

Rockwool profit margins

facilities for this division have regarded investments for the industry division. These market areas have developed very differently. Rockfon achieves increased market shares in a declining market, Grodan and Rockpanel show weak growth, whereas RockDelta is growing strongly.

The tasks of the strategy group

The market recession and the poor economic results provide the basis for the tasks of the strategy group. The sale of the Rockwool Group's main product – insulation materials – has been stagnant for a while now. Especially the declining construction trends on the important German market have influenced Rockwool's turnover and earnings.

The first question that comes into Mr Pedersen's mind in the car is the international production structure in the company. The Western European market is very much characterized by over-capacity and, consequently, great competitive and price pressure. Despite having achieved a market share of 20 to 30 per cent in the 1990s by means of an aggressive growth strategy, Rockwool's biggest competitor – the French company Saint Gobain – has also consolidated the overtaking of a number of small companies and now has a market share of more than 40 per cent, including establishments in Rockwool's home market, where the insulation product Isover has a 40 per cent market share against Rockwool's 50 per cent. None of the competitors want to give in to the price competition in the pricing negotiations with the buyers of the European chains in what is called a 'terror balance', where the suppliers constantly bid themselves down to win the order – under close supervision by the competition authorities, who are anxious about cartelization and pricing agreements. Moreover, Saint Gobain's earnings are considerably better than

Rockwool's, which is partly caused by radical rationalizations in the production organization at Saint Gobain, who is capable of supplying great markets for insulation materials, as for example, the Danish market (where the company had a 40 per cent market share), whereas Rockwool is supplying its 50 per cent market share through five factories. Even though it is possible to rationalize the Danish part of the production capacity, the strategy is doubtful. These factories have worked as buffers for the supply of the great German market; a production capacity reduction could cause problems if the market situation in Northern Europe changes and when/if the implementation of the EU fire classification directive will really become recognized in the Southern European markets.

Another question concerns Rockwool's choice of markets. So far North-West Europe has been kept in focus and so has the aim of meeting particular needs for insulation in the market. Perhaps it is time to consider moving on to other markets? Perhaps with other products or with the aim of covering other needs?

Finally, Mr Pedersen is thinking about the product portfolio. Even though the company's largest business area is insulation materials, the profit on the specialized activities has been a lot larger. What would the consequences of this be, if any? Should Rockwool just wait for the market to recover or should they take more radical actions?

Furthermore, Mr Pedersen and the rest of Rockwool are looking at Russia and Eastern Europe, which seemed to be a promising market worth billions of kroner due to a great need for renovation and construction. In comparison the Western European market has a size of approximately DKK 35 billion. During the past few years, Rockwool has increased the production capacity considerably in Eastern Europe. However, the market development is still to come. Construction and the insulation area are under growth, but the tendency is weak for the time being. Rockwool has primarily sold its more refined products to different Russian prestige constructions, but the demand for the bulk sales of 'regular' insulation material is still to come. Mr Pedersen is worried about the heavy investment in Russia. Should they freeze the activity expansion in the east, or should they start all over? Or should they make further expansion?

Discussion questions

1 Discuss the good and bad elements of the seamless service. What issues would Rockwool Group have encountered when trying to achieve their seamless service?

2 Refer to the customization/customer contact matrix shown in Chapter 17. Where would you consider Rockwool Group to be on the axis? Why do you consider them to be in that position?

3 The three-tiered model of service firms should be used by all service organizations. How could Rockwool Group use them to create 'wow' factors? Discuss the four approaches to directly changing culture as presented in the text.

4 How could Rockwool Group use a service audit to improve their organization?

5 What recommendations would you make to Rockwool Group to expand their business in the future?

Case 15

Corporate social responsibility for Mitchells & Butlers plc

Mitchells & Butlers plc is a leading pub, bar and restaurant operator in the UK. They are responsible for the operation of well known pub brands such as All Bar One, Flares and Inn Keepers Lodge. There are over 43,000 employees in the 2,000 business estates and Mitchells & Butlers plc are committed to the well-being of their staff. In addition they care about external factors such as the safety and security of their customers and their impact on the environment, and they have a philosophy of sharing and giving to local and national charities. Their corporate strategy sets the scene for an organization that is honest and fair.

> Mitchells & Butlers has a high quality, well-located estate, focused on long-term growth in the informal, value-for-money, eating and drinking-out markets. Our sales strategy is based on four principal levers, providing our customers with: high-quality amenity; consistently great value; a wide choice of food and drink; and excellent service.
>
> Our proven expertise at every level, combined with a pub estate of exceptional quality in prime locations, continues to deliver on our strategy of driving profitable volume growth and creating shareholder value.

All corporate strategies should give a clear indication as to the organization's responsibilities, accountabilities and framework for the future and Mitchells & Butlers plc clearly show that they wish to be viewed as an organization that provides customers an excellent service, in pleasant surroundings, at an 'honest' price. In addition to the corporate strategy, Mitchells & Butlers plc also provide thorough details of their corporate social responsibilities (CSR), as they are proud of their duty to the internal and external environment.

Their corporate social responsibilities, reported in their annual review, are made of five key elements – see Table 15.1. Each of the key elements has a number of sub-sections and these are also shown.

Each of their corporate social responsibilities are detailed in full in their annual review, which demonstrates to all stakeholders that they are an organization that shows compassion.

With respect to customer and employee safety, Mitchells & Bulters plc present details of how they provide a safe environment for their customers and employees. Naturally they do this by complying with the relevant health and safety regulation; however, they have implemented their own 'BRAG' rating system. BRAG stands for black, red, amber and green and they indicate areas that can be improved over the following year. The coloured rating system is:

Black – imminent, risk emergency action required

Red – critical failure in the management of safety

Amber – legal non-compliance

Green – compliant or minor non-compliance with company policy.

The 'BRAG' rating system goes over and above the risk and compliance assessments that most organizations go through on an annual basis. Mitchells & Butlers plc therefore have implemented a scheme so that they can maintain their excellent health and safety record.

Michells & Butler plc also value the safety of their disabled customers. In 2004 the Disability Discrimination Act came into force in the UK. To comply with the legal regulations Mitchells & Butlers plc spent over £10 million on major and minor building works. To enhance their reputation as an organization that takes their corporate social responsibil-

ities seriously Mitchells & Butlers plc hosted a Disability Awareness Week for all their front-of-house staff and door supervisors. In addition to the legal requirements, which affected the physical elements of the building, staff were trained to successfully deal with disabled customers, be they hard of hearing, wheelchair bound or with sight difficulties. Once again Mitchells & Butlers plc have exceeded the legal requirements of the Disability Discrimination Act by enabling their staff to have empathy with their disabled customers.

Mitchells & Butlers plc also get involved in local and national communities as part of

Marketplace	Responsible retailing Industry issues Retail team training Customer and employee safety Building infrastructure Good food and food safety
Employees	Health and safety Employee policies Employee training Employee benefits and rewards Employee engagement
Community	Community activity Heart of the Community Awards Corporate charity partnership National activity Support in Birmingham
Environment	Minimizing environmental impact Energy efficiency Recycling
Corporate governance	Corporate governance

Table C15.1

Corporate social responsibilities of Michells & Butlers 2007

their corporate social responsibilities. They champion themselves as being 'good neighbours' as their pubs form the community hub in many villages and towns throughout the UK. Employees are encouraged to support charities by hosting events such as sponsored bike rides, sports events for young people or volunteering work. Many worthy causes have received donations from customers and staff of Mitchells & Butlers plc. These include Cancer Research UK, Royal National Lifeboat Institute and the NSPCC. The Anderton Arms, Fulwood, Lancashire and The Bryncoch Inn, Neath, Wales are excellent examples of pubs that have encouraged their customers and staff to be active participants in raising money for worthy causes. In fact Bryncoch Inn has won the Mitchells & Butlers plc 'Heart of the Community Award' on three occasions.

These examples show how Mitchells & Butlers plc corporate social responsibilities form a philosophy that engages all areas of their business both internally and externally.

Source: Mitchells & Butlers plc Corporate Social Responsibility Review 2007.

Discussion questions

1 Why do Mitchells & Butlers plc engage in corporate social responsibilities?

2 Consider you were the Manager for Mitchells & Butlers plc Environment Corporate Social Responsibilities. What recommendations would you make for Mitchells & Butlers plc to minimize their waste, to recycle and to be energy efficient?

3 Employee benefits and rewards are part of Mitchells & Butlers plc corporate social responsibilities. What employee benefits and rewards would you recommend for front-of-house staff?

4 Look back at Table 15.5, Demystifying Corporate Social Responsibilities (CSR). Give examples of how Mitchells & Butlers adhere to those facets.

Case 16

Evolution of an art gallery: Kenny's Bookshop and Art Gallery

Developed by Ann Torres, National University of Ireland

Introduction

Tom Kenny recognizes, among the many legacies his parents instilled, to 'associate with excellence' has a special resonance, as the Kenny family firmly believe 'the work of Irish writers and painters are as good as can be found anywhere.' Moreover, he explains it is worthwhile taking risks and to trust your instincts. Tom illustrates his point by relating the story of:

> 'An American who visited the shop in the late 1960s. He eventually chose P.W. Joyce's History of Ireland, [an out of print book,] but did not have the cash to pay for it, so [I told him I'd] accept a [US dollar] check. [We] struck up a conversation, and I took [him to Naughton's] pub for more stories and laughter with the locals. The customer was William Randolph Hearst, Jr. Not long after, the shop began receiving requests from around the United States for copies of P.W. Joyce's History of Ireland. Hearst, it turned out, had written a syndicated article about how the booksellers had taken a foreigner's check on trust – the article had generated the orders, [and took about two years to fill.]'

The Kenny family has always been entrepreneurial, curious, and keen to take a risk on fresh ideas. Indeed, Desmond Kenny's father, a newspaperman, was one of the founders of the Irish Tourist Board. *Kenny's* is clearly a successful enterprise, experiencing cumulative, but substantial growth over its 63 years. The challenge is to ensure its continued success and prosperity.

The Kenny Gallery is the longest running gallery under the same name and management. Additionally, with over 15 exhibitions a year, *Kenny's* is frequently mentioned in the media. As noted earlier, *Kenny's* pursues its own path and Tom Kenny, Art Gallery Director, has sought to develop a 'different' kind of gallery. Thereby, allowing people to have a relaxed, enjoyable gallery experience, rather than the stuffy, stayed experience typically expected of galleries and museums. Currently, Tom's attention is directed toward the promotion of the gallery and its exhibitions.

Company background

Maureen and Desmond Kenny opened their one-room bookshop, *Kenny's*, in 1940. They had recently graduated from University College Galway (UCG, now NUI, Galway) and wanted to remain in Galway. A friend had suggested a bookshop, which they 'thought was an absolutely wonderful idea, if a bit mad.' Friends and relations donated much of the original stock. 'They emptied their attics for us [and] trunkfuls of books arrived.' However, the economic conditions during the 1940s were difficult and 'in order to survive [during] these tough times there was a need to be innovative and adventurous. This involved using every means possible to promote the bookshop, such as placing display cases in hotels and factories … [and selling] books to the public libraries within Ireland. [Maureen and Desmond] quickly expanded the business beyond just selling books, and in 1944, they published their first book, Walter Macken's *Oidhroacht na Mara*, which is now considered a literary landmark.'

Kenny's has evolved into more than a bookshop, encompassing:

Retail Bookshop specializes in books of Irish interest, but also has an extensive holding of books in other fields including religion, self-help, women's studies, travel, natural history, art, human rights, and world history. The shop provides customers a continuously changing stock over 200,000 volumes. *Kenny's* offers contemporary books, as well as a wide selection of second-hand, out-of-print and antiquarian books, maps and prints.

Book Club is a service offered to *Kenny's* 1,500 book club members in over 44 countries. Every 3 or 4 months, Des Kenny handpicks a selection of books suited to each member's interests and budget. Books are sent to a member's address on approval, and hence, may be returned if not required. Moreover, members may modify their 'plan' as their interests evolve. In addition to the book club, customers may avail of a book hamper as a gift for someone else or themselves.

Book Bindery has the specialized expertise required to 're-cover an old volume, fine bind special editions, or prepare a presentation book.' Highly decorated leather binding 'was first practiced by the Coptic Church in Egypt and became common with the 15th century development of printing. Gerry [Kenny] continues the craft of leather binding books by hand, in tandem with using modern methods for binding paperbacks, thesis and ring binders.'

Book Export Company is *Kenny's* international division and has grown substantially over the last few years, representing a significant portion of *Kenny's* export trade. The export company primarily works with libraries, booksellers, collections, and internet sales in North America, Europe and Asia.

Art Gallery was established in 1968 in the living room of the Kenny's family home located in Salthill. *The Kenny Gallery* was the first architect-built commercial gallery in the West of Ireland. 'Kenny's aim to promote Irish artists by showcasing and exhibiting their work in Ireland and abroad. Over 250 artists are represented and, at any one time, over 1,000 art works are on display.'

Although *Kenny's* incorporates a number of divisions, the focus of this case is *The Kenny Gallery*. Alongside literature, art has always played an important role in *Kenny's*. 'In the 1950's in order to develop the business, Maureen and Desmond turned their attention to Irish crafts and art. [At that time], there were few shops selling craft products such as rugs, sweaters, baskets, ceramics… Artists began to arrive with paintings and sculpture. Soon, the bookshop was hosting art exhibitions. One such exhibition was by Charles Lamb, now a world-renowned Irish painter.' Exhibitions were typically hung on every available space among the book stacks, and sometimes, on the books themselves. In 1968, Maureen and Desmond believed the art deserved an exhibition area of its own.

…continued on the companion website www.cengage.co.uk/hoffman.

Case 17

Kulula.com: Now anyone can fly

Reprinted with the kind permission of De Wits Business School

It was January 2003, 17 months since kulula.com had taken to the skies for the first time. This low-cost airline had survived almost two years in an extremely tough industry and, in addition, claimed to have been profitable since its inaugural flight on 1 August 2001.

Gidon Novick, Comair Limited's executive manager of marketing, was involved in kulula.com's somewhat unusual communication strategy from day one and maintained a close relationship with the advertising agency, morrisjones&co. The brand had been very effectively established and the airline had received two awards: the Marketing Federation of Southern Africa's prestigious 2002 Tusk 'Service Launch of the Year' award; and the Airports Company of South Africa's (ACSA) 'Domestic Airline of the Year' annual customer survey award for 2002.

But despite the hugely successful campaign, which had required only a few minor adjustments over the past 17 months, Novick did not feel comfortable. He realized that the business might soon face a problem – the possibility that the hype in the market had declined to a certain extent or could do so in the near future. He knew that in the fiercely competitive airline industry – an industry that had become even more competitive since the September 11 terrorist attacks – one could never sit back and relax.

It was time to rethink kulula.com's strategy. Novick could not afford to miss a single significant fact in establishing whether the current formula was sustainable or not. Other competitors entering the market – such as national carrier SAA with its own low-cost airline – was a lurking threat. Even the current relationship with kulula.com's advertising agency needed some reconsideration. With this in mind he started studying all the necessary supporting documentation that was lying on his desk.

Background to the low-cost airline industry

Up until 1978 the global airline industry had been controlled mainly by national governments that owned or subsidized the so-called national flag-carriers, which carried the flag of their nation on the tail of the aircraft. Following the deregulation of the domestic airline industry in the US in 1978 and in the UK in 1979, the market was subsequently freed up for the entry of other competitors. The terrorist attacks on the World Trade Centre on 11 September 2001, however, left many of the world's already ailing airlines in a state of crisis, with Swissair, Belgium's Sabena, Australia's Ansett and US Airways going bankrupt. The healthier airlines – British Airways and Lufthansa – experienced a significant drop in passenger numbers.

Excluding Ryanair, the European low-cost segment accumulated losses of almost $300 million between 1996 and 2001, and AB Airlines, ColorAir and Debonair went bankrupt. Compared to the flag carriers, however, the low-cost carriers did very well after the September 11 attacks. Despite the seemingly crowded market in Europe and a 7% market share of the intra-European air travel market, discount airlines such as easyJet, Ryanair, Buzz and Virgin Express had all grown stronger and had placed Europe's traditional flag carriers under severe threat. Between the two of them, Ryanair and easyJet accounted for 88% of the scheduled low-cost market in Europe. A 2002 *McKinsey Quarterly* survey found a pattern that suggested that the first entrants to this market seemed to be the winners. Entrants that came on board later with the same costs and prices had a harder time generating the traffic needed to fill their planes. The survey further predicted that, given the saturated market, consolidation would surely follow.

The operations strategy of the low-cost carriers was simple: secondary airports were used as their lower airport fees kept costs down, and aircraft were of a single type. There were no business class and higher-density class divisions, no free refreshments, no frequent-flyer programmes, no connecting flights, and no possibility of rebooking to other airlines. In addition, direct bookings were predominantly conducted through the internet.

At the time of deregulation in the US, the major airlines had underestimated the potential of the low-cost airlines. Operators such as Southwest Airlines managed to capture domestic market share within a short time but, although many budget operators sprang up after the deregulation, over 80% of them eventually went out of business. Still, the low-cost airline industry in both the US and Europe had shown excellent growth, with Southwest Airlines being the market leader amongst the six largest low-fare carriers. The others included JetBlue Airways (a three-year-old that served 20 cities, claiming to be low-fare, but offering luxuries such as live satellite television), American Trans Air, Air Tran, and Spirit Airlines (privately owned). These airlines together accounted for some 30% of the US domestic air travel market.

In South Africa the Domestic Aviation Policy (accepted in parliament on 1 July 1990), in line with international trends, started the process of deregulation in the South African aviation industry. By December 2002 domestic airline operations in South Africa were primarily divided among four competitors. These were national carrier SAA (60% market share on average across routes) with its partners SA Express (also owned by Transnet) and SA Airlink (10% owned by SAA); British Airways Comair (about 22% market share) with its local BA franchise and its no-frills arm, kulula.com (about 10% market share); and the independent operator, Nationwide Airlines (8% market share). Intensive Air, another low-cost airline, became operational in 2001 but liquidated in 2002. Sun Air was also relaunched in 2001. It offered only business class flights between Johannesburg and Cape Town from Lanseria airport.

Background to kulula.com

Commercial Air Services (Pty) Ltd (Comair) took to the sky for the first time on July 14, 1946, to operate as South Africa's first private airline. Before the 1991 South African deregulation, Comair competed on secondary destinations, such as Margate, a popular holiday resort on the Natal South Coast, and Skukuza in the Kruger National Park. In 1992, however, it entered the main domestic routes.

...continued on the companion website www.cengage.co.uk/hoffman.

Case 18

Nando's International: Taking chicken to the world

Re-printed with the kind permission of De Wits Business School

Late in the day of 27 April 1997, Robert Brozin, chairman and chief executive officer of Nando's International, reflected with satisfaction on the successful listing of Nando's South Africa on the Johannesburg Stock Exchange (JSE). One rationale for the listing had been to insulate Nando's flourishing South African operations from the capital costs and losses that could follow from the restructuring and planned expansion of Nando's international operations. Brozin's international management team was confident that the global infrastructure and the strategic policies that had been developed would allow countries in which Nando's conducted business to reach 'critical mass' by the year 2000. Beyond 2000, international growth and profitability were expected to increase exponentially.

Nando's had been growing rapidly and performing well in its home market. The benefits of reaching critical mass in South Africa were beginning be felt. In February 1997, the turnover of the South African operation had reached R 218 million (In April 1997, US$1 = R 4.44), and the 1995 loss had turned into a net income of almost R 9 million (see **Exhibit 1**). Brozin believed that Nando's success in South Africa was based on their strong culture and the skills developed over the past ten years. He pondered: Will we be able to transfer our corporate culture and high level of skills worldwide, or would we be better off focusing our efforts at home? Have we chosen the right countries to enter? Can we find the right partners and the finance to achieve our global vision?

Origins and expansion in South Africa

Brozin, B.Com (Wits), was the entrepreneur who created the Nando's concept. His staff saw in him a highly creative visionary who enjoyed working with people. His management style and personality reflected a passion and enthusiasm for all aspects of the business. In 1987, Fernando Duarte introduced Brozin to a humble Portuguese restaurant in the Johannesburg suburb of Rosettenville, and to their succulent, spicy, flame-grilled chicken. Duarte, a personal friend, was born in Oporto, Portugal. His family moved to South Africa, where he trained as an audio technician.

Brozin had no background in the food industry, but felt that there was great potential in marketing both the product and the Portuguese dining experience – the warm colours, the lively music, and the friendly and warm ambience. Despite being warned by bankers and analysts that the fast food sector was unprofitable, due to too many players, Brozin was undaunted. As he recalled, 'we had the vision to take this chicken to the world.'

Brozin and Duarte bought the restaurant for about R 80 000, and immediately started planning the expansion of a chain of outlets, first to the Portuguese community in Johannesburg, then to the rest of South Africa, and internationally. The more effort they put in, the more rewards appeared. The fast food industry worldwide looked only for reasonable quality. Brozin wanted to provide both top quality and speed.

Growing from the single restaurant in 1987, Nando's expanded to four outlets in 1990, one in Portugal, and the other three in Johannesburg. In doing so, Nando's redefined service levels for the industry in South Africa. In 1991, to finance rapid expansion, Brozin partnered with the South African-based Hollard group. Each new outlet was operated as a separate company, and the business functioned on a joint venture basis, with the Brozin/Hollard partnership retaining a controlling interest. This structure, however, soon proved to be unwieldy and inefficient. A re-structuring process in 1995 led to the joint venture partners being bought out by Nando's. By this time there were 45 outlets in South Africa and an additional 17 in other southern African countries (Namibia, Botswana, Zimbabwe and Swaziland).

By 1997, Nando's South Africa (including the common monetary area) had grown to encompass 117 stores. The pressure from international competitors, however, began to increase in South Africa after 1995 (see Exhibit 2), raising questions about Nando's future competitive position and growth prospects at home.

Corporate culture

Brozin was aware of the key role that Nando's culture played in all of Nando's activities. This culture was reflected in an easy management style, particular partner selection criteria, and an informal approach to staff in general, and was deeply ingrained in all of their operations. In 1996, Jane Hume was appointed Human Resources Executive. A well-spoken, vibrant, blonde Australian in her mid-thirties, Hume had worked with Nando's on a consulting basis since the early 1990's. She saw her role as 'chief custodian' of Nando's culture, with a vision of Nando's 'to be the best...not the biggest ... the best quick food chain in the world'.

Nando's mission statement and values embodied their culture. The mission was expressed in terms of 'The Nando's Experience' which Nando's strove to give each customer (see Exhibit 3). Underlying this mission was a belief that Nando's was not just about chicken. Nando's five core values, which became an internal mantra, were pride, passion, courage, integrity, and family.

Nando's encouraged an entrepreneurial spirit and the taking of 'ownership'. Head office set the parameters and guidelines, but the Patraos (store managers) ensured that the stores embodied Nando's values. The corporate culture was also disseminated through a 'Covenant', which was distributed to all stores (see Exhibit 4).

The management philosophy at Nando's reflected a view that occasional failures were valuable learning experiences. Brozin summed up the attitude:

> Our nature is one of 'ready, fire, aim'. If we miss the bulls-eye with the first shot, we'll hit it with the next shot. Early on, Brozin saw an opportunity to differentiate Nando's from its competitors by providing superior service. Service delivery was thought to follow from and build upon the strong internal culture at Nando's.

Application of the culture influenced staff selection and training, as well as career and performance management.

...continued on the companion website www.cengage.co.uk/hoffman.

Glossary

activity-based costing Costing method that breaks down the organization into a set of activities, and activities into tasks, which convert materials, labour and technology into outputs.

activity time The time required to perform one activity at one station.

adequate service The level of service quality a customer is willing to accept.

adverse conditions Positive and negative employee actions under stressful conditions.

after-sales surveys A type of satisfaction survey that addresses customer satisfaction while the service encounter is still fresh in the customer's mind.

ambient conditions The distinctive atmosphere of the service setting that includes lighting, air quality, noise and music.

anticipating Mitigating the worst effects of supply and demand fluctuations by planning for them.

apathetic customers Consumers who seek convenience over price and personal attention.

applications-on-tap Computer programs, such as word processing or web design, that can be rented via e-service providers.

approach/avoidance behaviours Consumer responses to the set of environmental stimuli that are characterized by a desire to stay or leave an establishment, explore/interact with the service environment or just ignore it, or feel satisfaction or disappointment with the service experience.

arousal–nonarousal The emotional state that reflects the degree to which consumers and employees feel excited and stimulated.

ASPs Application Service Providers: e-service organizations that rent computer programs such as word processing or web design applications.

assurance dimension The SERVQUAL assessment of a firm's competence, courtesy to its customers and security of its operations.

automation Replacing tasks that required human labour with machines.

basic business strategy A firm's fundamental approach as to whether it produces a standardized, low-cost, high-volume product or a differentiated, customized, personalized product.

beliefs Consumers' opinions about the provider's ability to perform the service.

benchmarking Setting standards against which to compare future data collected.

benefit concept The encapsulation of the benefits of a product in the consumer's mind.

benefit-driven pricing A pricing strategy that charges customers for services actually used as opposed to overall 'membership' fees.

blueprinting The flowcharting of a service operation.

bottlenecks Points in the system at which consumers wait the longest periods of time.

boundary-spanning roles The various parts played by contact personnel who perform dual functions of interacting with the firm's external environment and internal organization.

boundary tier The tier in the three-tiered model that concerns itself with the individuals who interact with the customers – the boundary spanners.

breaks company policies When a customer refuses to comply with policies that employees are attempting to enforce.

buffering Surrounding the technical core with input and output components to buffer environmental influences.

business analysis The way an organization improves its future activities based on past performance and research on how it can innovate its current activities to satisfy the needs of the customer.

business environment The social, technological and financial environment in which a firm operates and markets.

buying centre All the members of the team that play some role in the purchase decision of goods and services for and on behalf of the organization.

capacity sharing Strategy to increase the supply of service by forming a type of co-op among service providers that permits co-op members to expand their supply of service as a whole.

categorization Consumer assessment of the physical evidence and a quick mental assignment of a firm to a known group of styles or types.

central customer information file Main store of information containing data on customer history, characteristics, preferences.

change the way *we* work The element of the culture change initiative that teaches personnel to flowchart their activities and to re-engineer the process to better serve their customers.

change the way *you* work The element of the culture change initiative that allows personnel to break the rules in the context of serving their customers.

climate Employee perceptions of one or more organizational strategic imperatives.

cognitive dissonance Doubt in the consumer's mind regarding the correctness of the purchase decision.

cognitive responses The thought processes of individuals that lead them to form beliefs, categorize and assign symbolic meanings to elements of their physical environment.

commercial cue An event or motivation that provides a stimulus to the consumer and is a promotional effort on the part of the company.

communications gap The difference between the actual quality of service delivered and the quality of service described in the firm's external communications.

communications mix The array of communications tools available to marketers.

competencies The contributions customers bring to the service production process.

competitive advantage A distinctive or unique competence when compared with that offered by competing firms.

competitor intelligence Information gathered on the specific activities of competing organizations.

complementary The result of negative cross-price elasticity in which the increasing price of one service decreases the demand for another service.

complementary services Services provided for consumers to minimize their perceived waiting time, such as driving ranges at golf courses, arcades at movie theatres, or reading materials in doctors' offices.

complexity A measure of the number and intricacy of the steps and sequences that constitute a process.

confirmed expectations Customer expectations that match customer perceptions.

conquest marketing The pursuit of new customers as opposed to the retention of existing ones.

consumer decision process The three-step process consumers use to make purchase decisions; includes the pre-purchase stage, the consumption stage, and the post-purchase evaluation stage.

consumer management A strategy service personnel can implement that minimizes the impact of inseparability, such as separating smokers from nonsmokers in a restaurant.

consumption process The activities of buying, using and disposing of a product.

contact personnel Employees other than the primary service provider who briefly interact with the customer.

continuum of service development A range of service developments from major overhauls to minor style changes.

contrast/clash Visual effects associated with exciting, cheerful and informal business settings.

convergent scripts Employee/consumer scripts that are mutually agreeable and enhance the probability of customer satisfaction.

coordination tier The tier in the three-tiered model that coordinates activities that help integrate the customer and boundary tiers.

co-produce Service produced via a cooperative effort between customers and service providers.

corporate hospitality Entertaining clients in a social atmosphere in order to deepen a relationship.

cost drivers The tasks in activity-based costing that are considered to be the 'users' of overhead.

creative pricing Pricing strategies often used by service firms to help smooth demand fluctuations, such as offering 'matinee' prices or 'earlybird specials' to shift demand from peak to non-peak periods.

critical incident A specific interaction between a customer and a service provider.

critical incident technique A method of studying service failures by analysing critical incidents described in story form by respondents.

CRM system Software that manages customer information and contact.

cross-functional team A group of people who work towards a common goal but are from different departments in the organization.

cross-price elasticity A measure of the responsiveness of demand for a service relative to a change in price for another service.

cross-selling Encouraging a customer to buy an additional service during a transaction.

cultural norms Service personnel actions that either positively reinforce or violate the cultural norms of society.

culture The shared values and beliefs that drive an organization.

customer database Electronic storage of customer information.

customer errors Service failures caused by admitted customer mistakes.

customer involvement Participation and interest in the brand and/or organization.

customer needs and requests The individual needs and special requests of customers.

customer participation A supply strategy that increases the supply of service by having the customer perform part of the service, such as providing a salad bar or dessert bar in a restaurant.

customer preferences The needs of a customer that are not due to medical, dietary, psychological, language, or sociological difficulties.

customer relationship management The process of identifying, attracting, differentiating, and retaining customers where firms focus their efforts disproportionately on their most lucrative clients.

customer relationship marketing Marketing paradigm that focuses on customer retention.

customer research Research that examines the customer's perception of a firm's strengths and weaknesses.

customer retention Focusing the firm's marketing efforts towards the existing customer base.

customer tier The tier in the three-tiered model that focuses on customer expectations, needs and competencies.

customization Taking advantage of the variation inherent in each service encounter by developing services that meet each customer's exact specifications.

customization/customer contact matrix A table that illustrates the variety of relationships between marketing and other functions within the organization.

data collection method The method used to collect information, such as questionnaires, surveys and personal interviews.

data-mining Software used to analyse and interrogate large amounts of customer data.

decline When an organizations services are no longer preferred by customers, sales are low and profits are reducing.

decoupling Disassociating the technical core from the servuction system.

delivery gap The difference between the quality standards set for service delivery and the actual quality of service delivery.

derived expectations Expectations appropriated from and based on the expectations of others.

desired service The level of service quality a customer actually wants from a service encounter.

dichotomization of wealth The rich get richer and the poor get poorer.

direct measures The proactive collection of customer satisfaction data through customer satisfaction surveys.

disconfirmed expectations Customer expectations that do not match customer perceptions.

dispersion of control The situation in which control over the nature of the service being provided is removed from employees' hands.

disruptive others Customers who negatively influence the service experience of other customers.

distributive justice A component of perceived justice that refers to the outcomes (e.g., compensation) associated with the service recovery process.

divergence A measure of the degrees of freedom service personnel are allowed when providing a service.

divergent scripts Employee/consumer scripts that 'mismatch' and point to areas in which consumer expectations are not being met.

dominance–submissiveness The emotional state that reflects the degree to which consumers and employees feel in control and able to act freely within the service environment.

drunkenness An intoxicated customer's behaviour adversely affects other customers, service employees, or the service environment in general.

dual entitlement Cost-driven price increases are perceived as fair, whereas demand-driven price increases are viewed as unfair.

economic customers Consumers who make purchase decisions based primarily on price.

efficiency pricing Pricing strategies that appeal to economically minded consumers by delivering the best and most cost-effective service for the price.

emotional loyalty Attachment due to non-rational reasons.

emotional responses Responses to the firm's physical environment on an emotional level instead of an intellectual or social level.

empathy dimension The SERVQUAL assessment of a firm's ability to put itself in its customers' place.

employee–job fit The degree to which employees are able to perform a service to specifications.

employee surveys Internal measures of service quality concerning employee morale, attitudes and perceived obstacles to the provision of quality services.

empowerment Giving discretion to front-line personnel to meet the needs of consumers creatively.

enduring service intensifiers Personal factors that are stable over time and increase a customer's sensitivity to how a service should best be provided.

energy costs The physical energy spent by the customer to acquire the service.

enfranchisement Empowerment coupled with a performance-based compensation method.

environmental psychology The use of physical evidence to create service environments and its influence on the perceptions and behaviour of individuals.

e-service An electronic service available via the Net and other IT tools that completes tasks, solves problems, or conducts transactions.

ethical customers Consumers who support smaller or local firms as opposed to larger or national service providers.

evaluation of alternatives The phase of the pre-purchase stage in which the consumer places a value or 'rank' on each alternative.

evoked set The limited set of 'brands' that comes to the consumer's mind when thinking about a particular product category from which the purchase choice will be made.

exit A complaining outcome in which the consumer stops patronizing the store or using the product.

expansion preparation Planning for future expansion in advance and taking a long-term orientation to physical facilities and growth.

expectancy disconfirmation model The model in which consumers evaluate services by comparing expectations with perceptions.

expectations Consumer expectations pertaining to the service delivery process and final outcome.

explicit requests Customer needs that are overtly requested.

explicit service promises Obligations to which the firm commits itself via its advertising, personal selling, contracts and other forms of communication.

external data Information gathered outside the operations of the organization.

external search A proactive approach to gathering information in which the consumer collects new information from sources outside the consumer's own experience.

facility exterior The physical exterior of the service facility; includes the exterior design, signage, parking, landscaping and the surrounding environment.

facility interior The physical interior of the service facility; includes the interior design, equipment used to serve customers, signage, layout, air quality and temperature.

facility problems Services provided which have unsatisfactory tangible elements such as unhygienic conditions

factories in the field Another name for multi-site locations.

fail points Points in the system at which the potential for malfunction is high and at which a failure would be visible to the customer and regarded as significant.

financial consequences The perceived monetary consequences of a purchase decision by a consumer.

financial risk The possibility of a monetary loss if the purchase goes wrong or fails to operate correctly.

fixed costs Costs that are planned and accrued during the operating period regardless of the level of production and sales.

flat-rate pricing A pricing strategy in which the customer pays a fixed price and the provider assumes the risk of price increases and cost overruns.

focused factory An operation that concentrates on performing one particular task in one particular part of the plant; used for promoting experience and effectiveness through repetition and concentration on one task necessary for success.

focus group Facilitator-led discussion involving 6–12 participants to gather qualitative data.

focus group interviews Informal discussions with eight to twelve customers that are usually guided by a trained moderator; used to identify areas of information to be collected in subsequent survey research.

forward buying When retailers purchase enough product on deal to carry over until the product is being sold on deal again.

gestalt Customer evaluations that are made holistically and given in overall terms rather than in descriptions of discrete events.

goods Objects, devices, or things.

growth When services and products are introduced to the market sales are slow to begin with but grow as more customers become aware of the new developments.

hard technologies Hardware that facilitates the production of a standardized product.

harmony Visual agreement associated with quieter, plushier and more formal business settings.

heterogeneity A distinguishing characteristic of services that reflects the variation in consistency from one service transaction to the next.

high involvement Allows employees to eventually learn to manage themselves, utilizing extensive training and employee control of the reward allocation decisions.

hire and train personnel During the implementation of major new services and process developments new staff need to be hired and trained.

holistic environment Overall perceptions of the servicescape formed by employees and customers based on the physical environmental dimensions.

horizontal communication The flow of internal communication between a firm's headquarters and its service firms in the field.

human resources logic The reasoning that stresses recruiting personnel and developing training to enhance the performance of existing personnel.

idea generation Ideas are generated through research, new technologies, front-line staff, suppliers and staff.

idea screening Ideas need to be screened for effectiveness, cost and potential.

ideal expectation A customer's expectation of what a 'perfect' service encounter would be.

image value The worth assigned to the image of the service or service provider by the customer.

implicit needs Customer needs that are not requested but that should be obvious to service providers.

implicit service promises Obligations to which the firm commits itself via the tangibles surrounding the service and the price of the service.

inadequate support A management failure to give employees personal training and/or technological and other resources necessary for them to perform their jobs in the best possible manner.

indirect measures Tracking customer satisfaction through changes in sales, profits and number of customer complaints registered.

industrialization Mechanized or automated services that replaced human labour with machines.

industrial management model An approach to organizing a firm that focuses on revenues and operating costs and ignores the role personnel play in generating customer satisfaction and sustainable profits.

inelastic demand The type of market demand when a change in price of service is greater than a change in quantity demanded.

information overload Decision making adversely affected by mismanaged quantity of data.

information search The phase in the pre-purchase stage in which the consumer collects information on possible alternatives.

innovation An all-encompassing term used for major and incremental changes in services, products and processes.

inseparability A distinguishing characteristic of services that reflects the interconnection among the service provider, the customer involved in receiving the service, and other customers sharing the service experience.

instrumental complaints Complaints expressed for the purpose of altering an undesirable state of affairs.

instrumental loyalty Attachment due to rational reasons.

intangibility A distinguishing characteristic of services that makes them unable to be touched or sensed in the same manner as physical goods.

intangible dominant Services that lack the physical properties that can be sensed by consumers prior to the purchase decision.

integrated marketing communications (IMC) Combining a variety of complementary communications methods and media to deliver a consistent message.

interactional justice A component of perceived justice that refers to human content (e.g., empathy, friendliness) that is demonstrated by service personnel during the service recovery process.

inter-client conflicts Disagreements between clients that arise because of the number of clients who influence one another's experience.

inter-functional task force Problem-solving group in which individuals with diverse viewpoints work together and develop a better understanding of one another's perspectives.

inter-functional transfers Moving, via promotion or transfer, an employee from one organizational department to another to foster informal networks among departments.

internal data Information created within the organization through day-to-day operations.

internal logic Implicit and explicit principles of individual departments that drive organizational performance.

internal response moderators The three basic emotional states of the SOR model that mediate the reaction between the perceived servicescape and customers' and employees' responses to the service environment.

internal search A passive approach to gathering information in which the consumer's own memory is the main source of information about a product.

interpersonal services Service environments in which customers and providers interact.

interpretation gap This occurs when organizations have communicated their service through promotional activity and it is not interpreted by the customer in the way that was intended.

interview One-to-one, paired or group posing of structured questions by interviewer.

introduction During this stage of the product life cycle, costs are high due to research and development costs and sales are low as few customers are aware of the new developments.

invisible organization and systems That part of a firm that reflects the rules, regulations and processes upon which the organization is based.

job involvement Allows employees to examine the content of their own jobs and to define their role within the organization.

knowledge gap The difference between what consumers expect of a service and what management perceives that consumers expect.

ladder of loyalty Stages in developing customer relationships.

learned helplessness The condition of employees who, through repeated dispersion of control, feel themselves unable to perform a service adequately.

learning organization A firm which uses information to learn from mistakes and successes and to plan for the future.

level of attention Positive and/or negative regard given to a customer by an employee.

levels of management The complexity of the organizational hierarchy and the number of levels between top management and the customers.

lexicographic approach A systematic model that proposes that the consumer makes a decision by examining each attribute, starting with the most important, to rule out alternatives.

life-time value The worth of a customer from initial purchase to eventual defection to competitor or ceasing to use the service.

linear compensatory approach A systematic model that proposes that the consumer creates a global score for each brand by multiplying the rating of the brand on each attribute by the importance attached to the attribute and adding the scores together.

long-term contracts Offering prospective customers price and non-price incentives for dealing with the same provider over a number of years.

loyalty scheme Rewards for continued business with the organization designed to encourage repeat purchases.

major process innovations Radical introductions of new processes to new markets

major service innovations Radical changes to service delivery mechanisms.

market-focused management model A new organizational model that focuses on the components of the firm that facilitate the firm's service delivery system.

marketing department The formal department in an organization that works on the marketing functions of the company.

marketing functions Tasks such as the design of a product, its pricing and its promotion.

marketing information Any facts, figues or data that can support maketing decision making.

marketing information systems A formal or informal process for managing the information gathered by an organization.

marketing logic The reasoning that stresses providing customers with options that better enable the service offering to meet individual needs.

marketing myopia Condition of firms that define their businesses too narrowly.

marketing orientation A firm's view towards planning its operations according to market needs.

marketing research Information gathered to address a particular marketing problem or requirement.

marketing value chain Each activity in maketing planning adds value to the offering to the customer.

materialismo snobbery Belief that without manufacturing there will be less for people to service and so more people available to do less work.

maturity A period during the product life cycle where sales are at their height.

maximum output per hour The number of people that can be processed at each station in one hour.

media advertising A one-way communications tool that utilizes such media as television and radio to reach a broadly defined audience.

minimum tolerable expectation A customer expectation based on the absolute minimum acceptable outcome.

mistargeted communications Communications methods that affect an inappropriate segment of the market.

mixed bundling Price-bundling technique that allows consumers to either buy Service A and Service B together or purchase one service separately.

molecular model A conceptual model of the relationship between tangible and intangible components of a firm's operations.

monetary price The actual dollar price paid by the consumer for a product.

multi-site locations A way service firms that mass produce combat inseparability, involving multiple locations to limit the distance the consumers have to travel and staffing each location differently to serve a local market.

mystery shopping A form of non-customer research that consists of trained personnel who pose as customers, shop unannounced at the firm and evaluate employees.

needs Security, esteem, and justice; often unrecognized as needs by customers themselves.

negative disconfirmation A nonmatch because customer perceptions are lower than customer expectations.

niche positioning strategy A positioning strategy that increases divergence in an operation to tailor the service experience to each customer.

non-customer research Research that examines how competitors perform on service and how employees view the firm's strengths and weaknesses.

non-instrumental complaints Complaints expressed without expectation that an undesirable state will be altered.

non-peak demand development A strategy in which service providers use their downtime to prepare in advance for peak periods or by marketing to a different segment that has a different demand pattern from the firm's traditional market segment.

nonpersonal sources Sources such as mass advertising that consumers use to gather information about a service.

non-systematic evaluation Choosing among alternatives in a random fashion or by a 'gut-level feeling' approach.

offshoring The migration of domestic jobs to foreign host countries.

one-sided blueprint An unbalanced blueprint based on management's perception of how the sequence of events *should* occur.

operations logic The reasoning that stresses cost containment/reduction through mass production.

opted-in Permission given for contact.

opt-outs Opportunity to withdraw personal information and to cease contact.

organism The recipients of the set of stimuli in the service encounter; includes employees and customers.

organizational image The perception an organization presents to the public; if well known and respected, lowers the perceived risk of potential customers making service provider choices.

organization/client conflicts Disagreements that arise when a customer requests services that violate the rules of the organization.

orientation change The element of the culture change initiative that teaches 'families' of personnel to reinforce one another on the job.

ostensive complaints Complaints directed at someone or something outside the realm of the complainer.

other core service failures All remaining core service breakdowns or actions that do not live up to customer expectations.

outsourcing The purchase and use of labor from a source outside the company.

participant observation The researcher takes on the role of the participants during the activity being researched while observing/recording their behaviour.

part-time employees Employees who typically assist during peak demand periods and who generally work fewer than 40 hours per week.

past experience The previous service encounters a consumer has had with a service provider.

penetration strategy A positioning strategy that increases complexity by adding more services and/or enhancing current services to capture more of a market.

perceived-control perspective A model in which consumers evaluate services by the amount of control they have over the perceived situation.

perceived justice The process whereby customers weigh their inputs against their outputs when forming recovery evaluations.

perceived service adequacy A measure of service quality derived by comparing adequate service and perceived service.

perceived service alternatives Comparable services customers believe they can obtain elsewhere and/or produce themselves.

perceived servicescape A composite of mental images of the service firm's physical facilities.

perceived service superiority A measure of service quality derived by comparing desired service expectations and perceived service received.

perceptions gap The difference between the service customers perceive they will receive and that which is actually received.

perfect-world model J. D. Thompson's model of organizations proposing that operations' 'perfect' efficiency is possible only if inputs, outputs and quality happen at a constant rate and remain known and certain.

performance consequences The perceived consequences of a consumer's purchase decision should the service perform less than 100 per cent effectively.

performance risk The possibility that the item or service purchased will not perform the task for which it was purchased.

perishability A distinguishing characteristic of services in that they cannot be saved, their unused capacity cannot be reserved and they cannot be inventoried.

personalized customers Consumers who desire to be pampered and attended to and who are much less price sensitive.

personal needs A customer's physical, social and psychological needs.

personal selling The two-way element of the communications mix in which the service provider influences a consumer via direct interaction.

personal service philosophies A customer's own internal views of the meaning of service and the manner in which service providers should conduct themselves.

personal sources Sources such as friends, family, and other opinion leaders that consumers use to gather information about a service.

personnel value The worth assigned to the service-providing personnel by the customer.

person/role conflict A bad fit between an individual's self-perception and the specific role the person must play in an organization.

physical evidence/ tangible clues The physical characteristics that surround a service to assist consumers in making service evaluations, such as the quality of furnishings, the appearance of personnel, or the quality of paper stock used to produce the firm's brochure.

physical risk The possibility that if something does go wrong, injury could be inflicted on the purchaser.

physiological responses Responses to the firm's physical environment based on pain or comfort.

pilot run During NSD – new service sevelopment – services and processes are piloted to ensure that adjustments are made before the actual service goes 'live' to the public.

plant within a plant The strategy of breaking up large, unfocused plants into smaller units buffered from one another so that each can be focused separately.

pleasure–displeasure The emotional state that reflects the degree to which consumers and employees feel satisfied with the service experience.

positioning strategy The plan for differentiating the organization from its competitors in consumers' eyes.

positive disconfirmation A nonmatch because customer perceptions exceed customer expectations.

predicted service The level of service quality a consumer believes is likely to occur.

price bundling The practice of marketing two or more products and/or services in a single package at a single price.

price discrimination Charging customers different prices for essentially the same service.

primary research Fist-hand data collected for a specific purpose.

privacy policy Details of how customer data will be used.

probability expectation A customer expectation based on the customer's opinion of what will be most likely when dealing with service personnel.

problem awareness The second phase of the pre-purchase stage, in which the consumer determines whether a need exists for the product.

procedural justice A component of perceived justice that refers to the process (e.g., time) the customer endures during the service recovery process.

process-line extensions Introducing new process delivery mechanisms to existing ones.

process time Calculated by dividing the activity time by the number of locations at which the activity is performed.

product Either a good or a service.

product development A means to enable the introduction of new designs, processes and the marketing of new services.

production-line approach The application of hard and soft technologies to a service operation in order to produce a standardized service product.

product life cycle How a service or product progresses through a sequence of stages from introduction to growth, maturity and decline.

product-line extensions Introducing new products to the existing product mix.

product-line pricing The practice of pricing multiple versions of the same product or grouping similar products together.

product value The worth assigned to the product by the customer.

professional service roles The parts played by personnel who have a status independent of their place in an organization due to their professional qualifications.

psychic costs The mental energy spent by the customer to acquire the service.

psychological risk The possibility that a purchase will affect an individual's self-esteem.

publicity and public relations A one-way communications tool between an organization and its customers, vendors, news media, employees, stockholders, the government and the general public.

putting the customer first The element of the culture change initiative that teaches personnel to put the customer first.

qualitative data 'Wordy' information often gathered on opinions and attitudes in some depth but using smaller samples.

quality circles Empowerment involving small groups of employees from various departments in the firm who use brainstorming sessions to generate additional improvement suggestions.

quantitative measures Numerical information, data in number or coded form usually consisting of large samples.

quantization The breaking down of monolithic services into modular components.

question context The placement and tone of a question relative to the other questions asked.

question form The way a question is phrased, i.e., positively or negatively.

rational mathematician model A model that assumes consumers are rational decision makers using a choice matrix of attributes, brand or company scores, and importance weights.

rationing Direct allocations of inputs and outputs when the demands placed on a system by the environment exceed the system's ability to handle them.

recurrent monitoring data Data gathered form the continuous scanning of the firm's environment.

red-lining The practice of identifying and avoiding unprofitable types of neighborhoods or types of people.

reflexive complaints Complaints directed at some inner aspect of the complainer.

relationship pricing Pricing strategies that encourage the customer to expand his/her dealings with the service provider.

reliability dimension The SERVQUAL assessment of a firm's consistency and dependability in service performance.

remote services Services in which employees are physically present while customer involvement in the service production process is at arm's length.

research orientation A firm's attitude towards conducting consumer research.

reservation price The price a consumer considers to capture the value he or she places on the benefits.

reservation system A strategy to help smooth demand fluctuations in which consumers ultimately request a portion of the firm's services for a particular time slot.

response bias A bias in survey results because of responses being received from only a limited group among the total survey population.

responses (outcomes) Consumers' reactions or behaviours in response to stimuli.

responsiveness dimension The SERVQUAL assessment of a firm's commitment to providing its services in a timely manner.

retaliation A complaining outcome in which the consumer takes action deliberately designed to damage the physical operation or hurt future business.

role ambiguity Uncertainty of employees' roles in their jobs and poor understanding of the purpose of their jobs.

role conflict An inconsistency in service providers' minds between what the service manager expects them to provide and the service they think their customers actually want.

role congruence The property of actual behaviours by customers and staff being consistent with their expected roles.

roll-out During NSD – new service development – this is the final part of the process when the new service goes 'live' to the public.

sales promotion A one-way communications tool that utilizes promotional or informational activities at the point of sale.

satisfaction-based pricing Pricing strategies that are designed to reduce the amount of perceived risk associated with a purchase.

saturation The saturation stage of the product life cycle occurs when there are many competitors seeking the same customers and the marketplace is flooded with similar services and products.

scale of market entities The scale that displays a range of products along a continuum based on their tangibility.

scent appeals Appeals associated with certain scents.

script norms Proposed scripts developed by grouping together events commonly mentioned by both employees and customers and then ordering those events in their sequence of occurrence.

script theory Argues that rules, mostly determined by social and cultural variables, exist to facilitate interactions in daily repetitive events, including a variety of service experiences.

seamless service Services that occur without interruption, confusion, or hassle to the customer.

search The ability and ease at which information can be sought.

secondary data Information that already exists in some form and has been gathered for a previous purpose.

selection and training A strategy that minimizes the impact of inseparability by hiring and educating employees in such a way that the customer's service experience is positive and the employees are properly equipped to handle customers and their needs.

selective agreement A method of dealing with a dissatisfied customer by agreeing on minor issues in order to show that the customer is being heard.

self-perceived service role The input a customer believes he or she is required to present in order to produce a satisfactory service encounter.

self-services Service environments that are dominated by the customer's physical presence, such as ATMs or postal kiosks.

service audit A series of questions that forces the firm to think about what drives its profits and suggests strategies for competitive differentiation and long-term profitability.

service cost per meal The labour costs associated with providing a meal on a per-meal basis (total labour costs/maximum output per hour).

service economy Includes the 'soft parts' of the economy consisting of several sectors.

service failures Breakdowns in the delivery of service; service that does not meet customer expectations.

service gap The distance between a customer's expectations of a service and perception of the service actually delivered.

service imperative Reflects the view that the intangible aspects of products are becoming the key features that differentiate the product in the marketplace.

service improvements The most common type of innovation. They include service improvements which deal with service delivery.

service–profit chain Logical process ensuring that satisfied employees provide excellent customer service which leads to bottom-line profit.

service providers The primary providers of a core service, such as a waiter or waitress, dentist, physician, or college instructor.

service quality An attitude formed by a long-term, overall evaluation of a firm's performance.

service quality information system An ongoing research process that provides relevant data on a timely basis to managers, who use the data in decision making.

service recovery A firm's reaction to a complaint that results in customer satisfaction and goodwill.

service recovery paradox Situation in which the customer rates performance higher if a failure occurs and the contact personnel successfully recover from it than if the service had been delivered correctly in the first place.

services Deeds, efforts, or performances.

servicescape All the non-living features that comprise the service environment.

service value The worth assigned to the service by the customer.

SERVQUAL A 44-item scale that measures customer expectations and perceptions regarding five service quality dimensions.

servuction model A model used to illustrate the factors that influence the service experience, including those that are visible to the consumer and those that are not.

sight appeals Stimuli that result in perceived visual relationships.

signs, symbols and artefacts Environmental physical evidence that includes signage to direct the flow of the service process, personal artefacts to personalize the facility, and the style of decor.

situational factors Circumstances that lower the service quality but that are beyond the control of the service provider.

size/shape/colours The three primary visual stimuli that appeal to consumers on a basic level.

smoothing Managing the environment to reduce fluctuations in supply and/or demand.

social consequences The perceived consequences of a consumer's purchase decision among the consumer's peers or the public in general.

social cue An event or motivation that provides a stimulus to the consumer, obtained from the individual's peer group or from significant others.

social desirability bias A bias in survey results because of respondents' tendencies to provide information they believe is socially appropriate.

socialization The process by which an individual adapts to the values, norms and required behaviour patterns of an organization.

social risk The possibility of a loss in personal social status associated with a particular purchase.

soft technologies Rules, regulations and procedures that facilitate the production of a standardized product.

sound appeals Appeals associated with certain sounds, such as music or announcements.

space/function Environmental dimensions that include the layout of the facility, the equipment and the firm's furnishings.

specialization positioning strategy A positioning strategy that reduces complexity by unbundling the different services offered.

special needs Requests based on a customer's special medical, psychological, language, or sociological difficulties.

standardization To produce a consistent service product from one transaction to the next.

standards gap The difference between what management perceives that consumers expect and the quality specifications set for service delivery.

stations A location at which an activity is performed.

stimuli The various elements of the firm's physical evidence.

stimulus The thought, action, or motivation that incites a person to consider a purchase.

stimulus–response model A model developed by environmental psychologists to help explain the effects of the service environment on consumer behaviour; describes environmental stimuli, emotional states, and responses to those states.

strategic planning A deliberate course of action to move the organization forward into the future.

structure The formal reporting hierarchy normally represented in an organizational chart.

style changes Simple changes to existing styles – such as the introduction of new staff uniforms.

subordinate service roles The parts played by personnel who work in firms where customers' purchase decisions are entirely discretionary, such as waitresses, bellmen and drivers.

substitutes The result of positive cross-price elasticity in which the increasing price of one service increases the demand for another service.

suggestion involvement Low-level empowerment that allows employees to recommend suggestions for improvement of the firm's operations.

supplementary service innovations Add-ons to the existing core service.

survey Used to gather data from a standard set of questions usually from larger samples and often quantitative.

switching costs Costs that accrue when changing vendors.

symbolic meaning Meaning inferred from the firm's use of physical evidence.

systematic evaluation Choosing among alternatives by using a set of formalized steps to arrive at a decision.

system failures Failures in the core service offering of the firm.

systems People-management systems of control, evaluation, promotion and recognition.

tangible dominant Goods that possess physical properties that can be felt, tasted and seen prior to the consumer's purchase decision.

tangibles Items that are part of the firm's physical evidence, such as business cards, stationery, billing statements, reports, employee appearance, uniforms and brochures.

tangibles dimension The SERVQUAL assessment of a firm's ability to manage its tangibles.

target markets The segments of potential customers that become the focus of an organization's marketing efforts.

taste appeals The equivalent of providing the customer with free samples.

technical core The place within an organization where its primary operations are conducted.

technical service quality A level of service quality measured by technology such as speed of transactions per hour at an ATM or consistent temperature within a shopping centre, hence performance is measured mechnically.

technology The level of automation a firm utilizes.

test marketing – During NSD – new service development – services, processes and products are trialled with customers and staff to ensure delivery will run smoothly when it is rolled out to the public.

third parties A supply strategy in which a service firm uses an outside party to service customers and thereby save on costs and personnel.

three-tiered model A view of service organizations that reconfigures traditional departmental functions into a customer tier, a boundary tier and a coordination tier.

tie to the customer The degree of involvement the firm has with its customers.

time costs The time the customer has to spend to acquire the service.

timing of the question The length of time after the date of purchase in which questions are asked.

total market service quality surveys Surveys that measure the service quality of the firm sponsoring the survey and the service quality of the firm's competitors.

touch appeals Appeals associated with being able to touch a tangible product or physical evidence of a service, such as shaking hands with service providers.

traditional/transactional marketing Focus on one-off sales.

transitory service intensifiers Personal, short-term factors that heighten a customer's sensitivity to service.

two-sided blueprint A blueprint that takes into account both employee and customer perceptions of how the sequence of events actually occurs.

type 1 service staff Service staff that are required to deal with customers quickly and effectively in 'once only' situations where large numbers of customers are present.

type 2 service staff Service staff that deal with numerous, often repeat customers in restricted interactions of somewhat longer duration.

type 3 service staff Service staff required to have more highly developed communication skills because of more extended and complex interactions with customers.

unavailable service Services normally available that are lacking or absent.

unbundling Divesting an operation of different services and concentrating on providing only one or a few services in order to pursue a specialization positioning strategy.

uncooperative customer A customer who is generally rude, uncooperative and unreasonably demanding.

unprompted/unsolicited employee actions Events and employee behaviours, both good and bad, totally unexpected by the customer.

unreasonably slow service Services or employees perceived by customers as being extraordinarily slow in fulfilling their function.

unusual action Both positive and negative events in which an employee responds with something out of the ordinary.

upward communication The flow of information from front-line personnel to upper levels of the organization.

variable costs Costs that are directly associated with increases in production and sales.

verbal and physical abuse When a customer verbally or physically abuses either the employee or other customers.

voice A complaining outcome in which the consumer verbally communicates dissatisfaction with the store or the product.

volume-oriented positioning strategy A positioning strategy that reduces divergence to create product uniformity and reduce costs.

willingness to perform An employee's desire to perform to his/her full potential in a service encounter.

woofs 'Well-off older folks', that segment of the population that controls 77 per cent of the nation's assets and 50 per cent of its discretionary income.

word-of-mouth communications Unbiased information from someone who has been through the service experience, such as friends, family, or consultants.

zone of tolerance Level of quality ranging from high to low and reflecting the difference between desired service and adequate service; expands and contracts across customers and within the same customer, depending on the service and the conditions under which it is provided.

Index

r Source UK Ltd.
nes UK
110116

0001B/48/P